THE ENGLISH HYMN

HYMNS
AND
Spiritual Songs.
In Three BOOKS.

I. Collected from the Scriptures.
II. Compos'd on Divine Subjects.
III. Prepared for the Lord's Supper.

With an ESSAY

Towards the Improvement of Chriſtian Pſalmody, by the Uſe of E-vangelical Hymns in Worſhip, as well as the Pſalms of *David*.

By *I. WATTS.*

And they ſung a new Song, ſaying, Thou art worthy, &c. for thou waſt ſlain and haſt redeemed us, &c. Rev. 5. 9.
Soliti eſſent (*i. e. Chriſtiani*) convenire, carmenque Chriſto quaſi Deo dicere. *Plinius in Epiſt.*

LONDON,
Printed by *J. Humfreys,* for *John Lawrence,* at the Angel in the *Poultrey.* 1707.

FACSIMILE OF THE TITLE PAGE OF THE ORIGINAL EDITION
OF DOCTOR WATTS' "HYMNS"

THE ENGLISH HYMN

Its Development and
Use In Worship

By

LOUIS F. BENSON

JOHN KNOX PRESS
RICHMOND, VIRGINIA

"THE ENGLISH HYMN has no rival as a mine of accurate information about the development and use of English and American hymns and hymnbooks. Its range of knowledge and breadth of view marked its author as the pre-eminent hymnologist of his day."

HENRY WILDER FOOTE

From *Three Centuries of American Hymnody*
by permission of Harvard University Press.

Reprinted 1962 from the edition
copyrighted 1915 by George H. Doran Company

Library of Congress Catalog Card Number: 62-13877
Printed in the United States of America
7658

PREFACE

It will be a part of our present task to show how relatively modern a practice the singing of hymns is in the Churches of our English tongue, and with what struggle they won their place. To love hymns in eighteenth century Scotland was to be accused of heresy; in England it was to be convicted of that worse thing, "enthusiasm." "I gave her privately a crown," wrote Dr. Johnson of a girl who came to the sacrament in a bed-gown, "though I saw Hart's hymns in her hand."[1] What seemed memorable to that kind heart was not his act of charity, but his having surmounted on the occasion a churchman's rooted prejudice against hymns. They bore the stamp of a clamorous dissent, and it took the attrition of a protracted circulation to rub off that mark. Not till after the middle of the nineteenth century did the English Hymn win the general esteem which Germany had given to her hymns since the Reformation.

To our literary critics it bears the mark of dissent still, and they find it irksome to give to hymns the attention so cheerfully bestowed on folk-poetry, ballads and lullabies. Remembering that Cowper sometimes "reaches the simplicity of greatness," says Dr. Schelling in his study of the English Lyric,[2] "we may accept . . . even the 'Olney Hymns,' though we need not read them." For Watts, whose noble hymn, "Our God, our Help in ages past," a million Englishmen are singing with voices broken by the strain of war, and for the Wesleys, whose songs might almost be said to have deflected the current of English history, the most that our critic is able to do, as he passes on his singing way, is to accord them "the respect that

[1] *Prayers and Meditations,* Easter day, 1764: *Works of Johnson,* Oxford, 1825, vol. ix, p. 221.

[2] Felix E. Schelling, *The English Lyric,* Boston, 1913, p. 139.

honest devotional effort (even when versified) should
properly.inspire." [3]

We also, as best we may, shall have to consider in its
natural historical connections the question of the relations
to literature of an English Hymnody that has proved so
virile. Indeed, the literature of power, whether a Wesley's
for the upbuilding of a Kingdom or a Kipling's for the
buttressing of an empire, is ever an unchartered libertine.
It will sometimes preach, while it pretends to sing, and
even tread on a critical canon or two as it hews its way to
men's hearts.

Just now we are not defending hymns but alleging the
circumstances making it inevitable that anything in the
line of a serious study of the English Hymn should be so
long deferred, and that our English Hymnology should lag
so far behind the German. Daniel Sedgwick, a self-taught
second-hand bookseller of London (1814-1879), was actually the first collector of the hymn books, and to his little
shop in Sun-street, Bishopsgate, used to resort so many of
the editors as cared enough for the hymns they were handling to inquire into their authorship and text. And yet in
a scientific age the collection and study of old psalm and
hymn books, which are the remains and record of the
spiritual life of contemporaneous Christians, would seem
just as rational as the collection and classification of fossil
shells, which are the remains and record of the animal life
of contemporaneous mollusca. "Really it has awakened,"
wrote a reader of one of the ensuing chapters, "the suspicion that there is no better point of view from which to
study the development and the reactions of Christian belief
than that offered by Hymnody. This is not strange; for
after all beliefs of the first rate in influence receive and, I
have the impression, always have received their best and
final embodiment in poetry and especially lyric poetry."

Once begun the serious study of English Hymns has
proceeded rapidly enough. In the eighth edition of the

[3] *Ibid.*, p. 136.

Encyclopedia Britannica the whole subject of Hymns covered only two pages, which in the ninth edition expanded to eighteen. And by 1892 a considerable company of investigators made possible the publication of Dr. John Julian's *A Dictionary of Hymnology;* since when the sources and history of most of our hymns (though not their text) have been rescued from what in many cases was a very teasing obscurity.

In recognition of the new study, and with a venturous hope of contributing to its advancement, The Faculty of The Theological Seminary at Princeton in 1903 invited the present writer to deliver a course of lectures on the L. P. Stone Foundation upon a subject connected with Hymnology. He decided, with their approval, to go back to the very beginnings of Congregational Song in that branch of the Church with which the Seminary is allied, and to trace the origins, development and decline of the practice of singing metrical Psalm versions which became the characteristic feature of worship in the Reformed Churches of various tongues. The lectures were delivered in February, 1907, under the title, "The Psalmody of the Reformed Churches." [4]

Soon afterward an invitation came for a second course of lectures. And it seemed natural to resume the history of Congregational Song at the point where the former course had left it, and to take up the subsequent or hymn singing period in the Churches that most concern us, those that speak our English tongue. The second course was delivered in February, 1910, under the title, "The Hymnody of the English-speaking Churches." This second course of lectures was reconstructed and rewritten to a larger scale, and printed in *The Princeton Theological Review* in the July number of 1910 and during the years 1912-1914. Once more revised and partly rewritten in the unending struggle

[4]Of these the first, upon the Psalmody of the Calvinistic Reformation, was printed with additions in *The Journal of The Presbyterian Historical Society* for March, June, and September, 1909.

after accuracy, expanded and rounded out in an attempt
to cover the entire field, they form the contents of the
present volume.

The change in the title of the book from that of the
lectures is made for the sake of lucidity. It implies no
change in the theme, the point of view, or the method of
treatment; and it is as well that these should be set forth
as clearly as may be. There are of course more ways than
one of treating the English Hymn historically. The most
obvious is to take up the writers of hymns chronologically,
to group them in periods, and to treat their lives and writings consecutively. This is to deal with Hymnody as a
minor branch of lyrical poetry, and to apply to it the
familiar method of the "Manual of English Literature."
The method is handy and gives us a conspectus of hymn
writing that for some purposes is useful. Nevertheless the
fact that most hymn writers are studiously ignored in the
manuals of English Literature themselves seems to suggest
either that the theme is a very insignificant one or else that
something is wanting in the manner of its presentation.

The truth is that if the methods of the literary historian
are not misapplied to Hymnody, they are at least inadequate. A hymn may or may not happen to be literature;
in any case it is something more. Its sphere, its motive,
its canons and its use are different. It belongs with the
things of the spirit, in the sphere of religious experience
and communion with God. Its special sphere is worship,
and its fundamental relations are not literary but liturgical.
Of all definitions of the Hymn that which claims least
for it best defines it:—it is liturgical verse. In the daily
service book of the old Latin Church the *Hymnus* was the
versified part of the Divine Office, and our democratic ideals
of worship have changed neither its definition[5] nor function.

[5]To apply the word Hymn to some strangely interlaced passages of
rhythmical prose in the service books of the Greek Church, and to
the prose *Te Deum* and canticles of the English Prayer Book, is
convenient but need not be misleading. We speak of the "prose poems"
of a Carlyle without affecting the definition of poetry.

The English Hymn gains its historical significance and its present importance from its inclusion in the hymnal that is put into the hands of the people as the authorized vehicle of their common praise in our Protestant Churches. And the whole body of hymns that have been or are so included constitutes "The Hymnody of the English-speaking Churches."

This point of view is sedulously maintained in the present book, and determines its method. Hymnody is regarded as the later phase of Protestant Church Song. We shall endeavor to show how far the Hymn was from the mind of Churches given over to the custom of psalm singing, and how as that mind was turning toward hymns, they began to shape themselves out of devotional poetry on the one hand and metrical psalms on the other; how one strong will took control of the situation, fixed the definite type of the English Hymn, and engineered a movement to introduce it into public worship. We shall follow the fortunes of this movement and also study the development of the Hymn itself, as with succeeding generations fresh minds came to deal with it and new religious and literary forces and influences successively played upon it.

Our special concern is to follow down the main stream of Hymnody and of hymn singing from its springs to its present fulness. But no by-stream of Hymnody has been consciously neglected. Some of these denominational hymnodies are no more than canals cut to carry the waters of the main stream to a new territory, but others are inlets through which new springs enrich the main current. In any case they are of interest to the dwellers along their shores; and we have set up sign-boards at the various points of junction so that readers intent to follow the main stream need not be diverted.

It will be evident that for the purposes of such a study the hymn books in actual use in the different Churches at various times become our principal sources, and that they, with the proceedings of the authoritative bodies in the several denominations and the lives and works of the hymn writers, constitute the materials which we have to handle. The recovery of these materials, notably of the hymn books, from the litter of the past is no light task; and it is only after twenty-five years of assiduous collecting that the present writer has ventured to bring his studies to so much of a conclusion as is here attained. He can at least aver that he has dealt with his sources at first hand.

With this understanding of the importance attached to hymn books, it will seem natural that the full titles of so many of them should be run into the text as a part of the narrative rather than relegated to a "bibliography." It may be that these, together with an abundance of foot-notes, appear to be so many snags in the course of fluent reading. But to an inquiring mind foot-notes are likely to prove the better part of a book; and even the gentle reader should learn to accept them as a pledge of good faith. Many books would never have been printed had their authors felt obliged to disclose their sources and authorities. It might too be urged that foot-notes, used judiciously, serve to relieve the narrative from an ever impending dulness; and dulness is a fault which author and reader might well conspire to be rid of at any cost save the sacrifice of precision: for inaccuracy is more than a fault, it is a sin.

If the writer were more confident of having pursued a way, in part untrodden, in the spirit of wholesome scholarship, he would have liked to dedicate his book to the reverend and learned Faculty of The Theological Seminary at Princeton, whose sympathy and encouragement helped toward its undertaking and have acted as a spur to its completion.

CONTENTS

CHAPTER I

THE EVOLUTION OF THE ENGLISH HYMN

CHAPTER II

THE LITURGICAL USE OF ENGLISH HYMNS

CHAPTER VII

THE HYMNODY OF THE EVANGELICAL REVIVAL

CHAPTER VIII

THE EVANGELICAL HYMNODY IN AMERICA

CHAPTER IX

THE HYMNODY OF THE ROMANTIC MOVEMENT

CONTENTS

CHAPTER X

THE HYMNODY OF THE OXFORD REVIVAL

CHAPTER XI

TWENTIETH CENTURY HYMNODY

CHAPTER I

THE EVOLUTION OF THE ENGLISH HYMN

I

INTRODUCTORY: PSALMODY AND HYMNODY

1. EARLY RELIGIOUS LYRICS IN ENGLISH

There were English hymns long before the Reformation. Carol singing was brought over from France at a very early date, and by the XIIIth century the Norman carols began to give way to those in English, often retaining the French refrain, and introducing Latin lines taken mostly from the church service. The Carol was devoted especially to rehearsing the events of the Nativity, but it passed into spiritual lullabies and the Complaint of Mary, or of Christ, on the one hand, and into secular songs of the feasts and sports of Yule-tide on the other. Not carols only but a variety of religious and ethical songs mingled freely with those of an amorous or convivial or humorous sort, sung in the markets, ale-houses and halls, and through the country side, by the wandering minstrels, themselves often in minor orders of the Church. Beside these were the less homely hymns to Christ and the Virgin, and more or less mystical devotional verses, such as were written in the monasteries.

These early effusions must be classed as hymns, in our familiar use of that word to designate religious lyrics. But hymns, in the stricter sense of "church song" or "liturgical verse," they were not in fact or in the minds of the clerks who composed them; to whom a "Hymn" meant the stanzas appointed to be read or sung in the Office for the day, of course in the Latin language. The early religious lyrics

19

have a very real interest of their own, and are doubtless worthy of more attention than they have as yet received.[1] But their connection with the English Hymnody afterwards to be developed as the Church Song of Protestantism is of the slightest. They did not furnish a foundation for that Hymnody or give any promise of its coming. The nearest approach to a bond of connection is found in the Christmas Carol, which before the Reformation was allowed to be sung in parish churches in conjunction with Christmas festivities, and which, rather by revival than survival, is making its way into Protestant Church Hymnody.

But between this modern Church Hymnody and the old religious English lyrics lies the deep chasm of the Reformation, with its breach in church order, and the fresh start on the Protestant side, under democratic ideals of worship, of a people singing songs in their own tongue. The Latin Hymn sung by the choir is the expression of the old order and ideals; the Congregational Hymn sung by the people in the vernacular is equally typical of the new.

2. Congregational Song as a Church Ordinance

The Congregational Hymn is thus distinctively the child of the Reformation, and indeed its paternity is quite commonly ascribed to Luther himself. Such ascription is not in accordance with the facts. The singing of religious songs by the people began to play its part in different localities on the continent of Europe, with the first stirring of the new life in the Western Church that culminated in the Reformation of the XVIth century. With the gathering

---

[1] Prof. F. M. Padelford's chapter on "Transition English Song Collections" in *The Cambridge History of English Literature*, vol. ii, 1908, was something of a novelty in such a connection. The appended bibliography includes many of the printed sources of the songs. For the Carol, see Edmondstoune Duncan, *The Story of the Carol*, London, 1911; and Thos. Helmore in Julian's *Dictionary of Hymnology*, London, 2nd ed., 1907, art. "Carols," and supplement, p. 1619.

of the followers of John Hus in Bohemia into congregations, popular song becomes definitely Congregational Song.
A vernacular Hymnody of considerable proportions was
created by the Hussites, and provided with suitable melodies.
These hymns and tunes were embodied in books designed
for the worshippers' hands rather than for the choir. Thus
the congregational hymn-book of the modern type had its
origin, and congregational singing of hymns took its place
as a recognized part of the new kind of worship.[2]

The foundations of Congregational Song as a church
ordinance were therefore laid before the beginnings of the
Reformation in Germany under Luther and in Switzerland
under Calvin. Congregational Song must be regarded as the
liturgical expression of principles common to Protestantism,
that were embodied in Lutheranism and Calvinism alike.
It is of course true that Congregational Song received a
great impulse and development from Luther's hands, and
that his work in establishing it claims the priority over
Calvin's, upon whom Luther's success doubtless exercised
marked influence. But Congregational Song cannot be
rightly regarded as the distinctive possession of either system, nor can it be fairly claimed that the one reformer
showed more zeal in establishing it than the other.

3. Psalmody and Hymnody as Rival Systems of Congregational Song

We have now to note and to explain the fact that while
congregational singing was as much a feature of the new
Protestantism in England and Scotland as in Germany, it
nevertheless happened that German Protestantism proceeded
at once to develop a rich German Hymnody, whereas there
was no English Hymnody in any effective sense until the

[2]The earliest recorded hymn book of the Bohemian Brethren bears
the date 1505. For their Hymnody see Edmund de Schweinitz, *The
History of the Church known as The Unitas Fratrum*, 2nd ed., Bethlehem, Pa., 1901; and J. T. Mueller in Julian's *Dictionary of Hymnology*, art. "Bohemian Hymnody."

XVIIIth century. It happened so in brief because the
Churches in England and Scotland in arranging for the
participation of the people in the service of praise, adopted
the model set up by Calvin in Geneva as over against that
set up by Luther. The practical effect of this was, in a
word, that both the English and Scottish Churches became
psalm singers as distinguished from hymn singers. The
Metrical Psalm was thus the substitute for the Hymn in
England and Scotland, and became the effective obstacle to
the production and use of English hymns.

To understand the ground of this supremacy of the
Psalm, and the suppression of the Hymn involved in it, we
must go back to the minds of the two great leaders of the
Reformation, antagonistic as they were in temperament and
taste and divided in many matters of principle. Their
diverse points of view are nowhere more conspicuous than
in their conceptions of Protestant worship; and among other
issues thus raised was one regarded by each as of great
practical importance,—What shall the people be permitted
and encouraged to sing in public worship?

In reconstructing the musical side of church worship two
proclivities of his own strongly influenced Luther. One
was his love for the old German folk-song, for social singing and for the music of the household and family. The
other was his affectionate regard for the ritual of the old
Church, especially the Latin hymns which for many centuries had made a part of the Daily Office. The utility
of their metrical form was obvious. And the fact that
hymns were free compositions, not confined to Scriptural
paraphrase, constituted no objection to them in Luther's
mind, but on the other hand suggested an opportunity of
filling the Hymn-Form with the doctrines and inspirations of the new evangel. Luther adopted without hesitation the Metrical Hymn of human composition as a
permanent element of his cultus. And he provided German
hymns set to suitable tunes, and put the hymn books into
the hands of the people. From the beginning, therefore,

Lutheran song became Hymnody in the narrower sense of the word. This Lutheran Hymnody was based indiscriminately on Scripture, the Latin and Hussite hymns, popular songs, and the thoughts and feelings of the writer. And from Luther's time to the present the composition of German hymns has proceeded without a break, and their congregational use has continued to be a characteristic feature of Lutheran worship.

Calvin on the other hand was impressed with the frivolity of current French song, and impatient of any melody in any wise associated with it. To the music of the old Church and its elaborate ritual he was possibly indifferent by temperament, but certainly hostile through a conscientious conviction that it was a purely human contrivance and the scaffolding of a merely formal religion. In arranging a worship for the Reformed Church he proposed to ignore the historical development of worship in the Latin Church, and to reinstate the simpler conditions of the primitive Church. He would have nothing in the cultus which could not claim the express authority of Scripture. He found Scriptural precedent for the ordinance of Congregational Song, and saw the advantage of the metrical hymn-form. But the Church's imprimatur on the "Hymn of human composure" gave it no sanctity in his mind. And the *Breviary* itself showed how readily the Hymn served as the embodiment of false doctrine. And so, without denying the breadth of St. Paul's allowance of "Psalms and hymns and spiritual songs," and without denying the Church's right to make its own hymns, he rested upon the proposition that there could be no better songs than the inspired songs of Scripture. He established the precedent of Church Song taken from the word of God itself, and practically confined to the canonical Psalms. The authority of Calvin's opinion and example was such that the usage of singing metrical psalms as instituted at Geneva followed the spread of Calvinistic doctrine through the world as a recognized feature of church order. It became as characteristic of the Reformed cultus as hymn singing was of the Lutheran cultus.

The new Protestant Church Song was thus from the first divided into two separate streams, having Luther and Calvin as their respective sources, and differing in their actual contents. If we attempt to put this new Protestant song in relation to the service of praise in the historic cultus of the Latin Church which it replaced, it appears that the Lutheran Hymnody and the Reformed Psalmody agree in taking the service of praise out of the hands of the choir and restoring it to the congregation, and, with that end in view, in rendering it in the vernacular tongue. But the Lutheran Hymn must be regarded as the lineal successor of the Latin hymns of the *Breviary,* and as carrying forward the usage of hymn singing without a break. The Calvinistic psalm, on the other hand, would have to be regarded as the lineal successor of the old church Psalmody,—that rendering of the Latin prose Psalter in stated portions which constituted the main feature of the Daily Office. It is true that the Calvinistic psalm was run into the mould of the metrical hymn, and being a metrical formula of congregational praise, it may be called a hymn, in the larger sense of that word. But in reality it marked a breach with the extra-Biblical Hymnody of the Western Church, and of the Hussites and Lutherans. It represented a popularization of the old church Psalmody that offered itself as a substitute for Hymnody, whether old or new. Henceforward, for two centuries and a half at least, the Hymn and the Metrical Psalm stand side by side as representing clearly differentiated and even opposing systems of congregational Church Song.[3]

[3]The necessity of marking this distinction is the justification of the word "Hymnody," even though objected to by purists as lacking the highest sanction. Philologically "Hymnody" would seem to be the analogue of "Psalmody," and practically would seem to be a necessity to express the practice of singing hymns, and also the body of the hymns thus sung. The current employment of "Psalmody" to express these things simply ignores the history of two centuries, and obscures

4. The English-speaking Peoples Become Psalm Singers

Which of these contrasting types of Church Song was to establish itself among English-speaking peoples was at first by no means clear.   Both in England and Scotland the impulse behind the early Reformation movement was Lutheran, and in each country the leaders endeavored to forward the movement by means of religious songs of Lutheran type, and in part derived from Lutheran sources.

In England this effort was ineffective.   Some years later than 1531 Myles Coverdale issued the first English hymn-book, his *Goostly Psalmes and Spirituall Songes drawen out of the holy Scripture,* based on the Wittenberg hymn books.   These dull songs made little appeal to the people, and at the same time they were in advance of the limits of the scheme of reform then proposed by Henry VIII.   In 1546 the King put the *Goostly Psalmes* among the prohibited books, and brought its ineffectual career to an end.

the facts: and when, as by some recent writers, the word "Psalmody" is actually applied to the body of the tunes to which hymns are sung, we seem to reach a point at which the article exhibited and the label attached to it have no obvious connection. English writers in general, dealing specifically with hymns, have used the word "Hymnology" to describe the collective body of them or some part of it. Thus James King gathers the body of hymns in widest use in the Church of England under the title *Anglican Hymnology* (London, 1885); and, as if to prove that we have not misunderstood him, entitles his first chapter "History of Ancient and Mediaeval Hymnology." When Mr. Courthope tells us (*A History of English Poetry,* vol. v, London, 1905, pp. 328, 336), that "Hymnology had its rise among the Nonconformists," and that "the style of English Hymnology reaches its highest level" in certain hymns of Dr. Watts, we may not question the lawfulness of his use of the terms but we must affirm its inexpediency. When we have gathered our specimens from the quarry or mine, we have not gathered its "mineralogy" but its minerals, from which the brain and not the hand must construct their mineralogy. Just so, dealing at present with the English Hymn and its liturgical use, it would appear that the word "Hymnody" describes the materials for our study; and that the word "Hymnology" expresses rather that ordered knowledge of hymns to which a study such as ours may be expected to contribute.

In Scotland, on the other hand, Coverdale's contemporaries, the Wedderburns, successfully introduced among the people hymns and songs based on Lutheran models. These played a great part in the development of the Reformation, down to and beyond the formal organization of the Reformed Church of Scotland.[4]

But in both countries the influence of Calvin prevailed over that of Luther, and determined among other things the form of Church Song. The Scottish Church, under Knox's influence, discarded the Wedderburn Hymnody and adopted the Genevan system of Metrical Psalmody into its constitution. The English Church adopted Metrical Psalmody just as effectively, but less formally, as something not provided for in the Prayer Book system, but yet "allowed" to adhere to the margin of that system. Practically both English-speaking Churches entered upon an era of psalm singing which was to be little disturbed through two centuries.

II

THE HYMNS APPENDED TO THE METRICAL PSALTERS (1561-1635) NOT THE NUCLEUS OF AN ENGLISH HYMNODY

And yet neither in England nor Scotland was the psalm book which was put into the hands of the people confined exclusively to canonical Psalms. In both countries the authorized Psalter included not only a complete metrical

'We have regarded the Coverdale episode in England and that of the Wedderburns in Scotland as belonging logically and chronologically to the earlier movement to establish Psalmody rather than to the later movement to establish Hymnody. Their fuller treatment falls therefore within the scope of the history of Metrical Psalmody. There is an accessible reprint of Coverdale's book (without the music) in the Parker Society's edition of his *Remains* (Cambridge, 1846). Of the Wedderburn book there is David Laing's annotated reprint (Edinburgh, 1868), and Dr. A. F. Mitchell's more elaborate edition of *The gude and godlie Ballatis* for the Scottish Text Society (1897). See also his *The Wedderburns and their work* (Edinburgh and London, 1867).

version of the Psalms but also an appended group, relatively small, of hymns and metrical paraphrases of other Scriptural passages and Prayer Book materials.

This common feature, as also the identity of much of the contents of the two Psalters, is explained by the fact that they had a common origin. Both Psalters represent the carrying forward in their respective countries, on somewhat differing lines, of the work begun by the Marian exiles at Geneva. Knox, Whittingham and others of the Puritan party of exiles who were deeply under Calvin's influence, were particularly impressed by the psalm singing he had set up in his little French congregation. In preparing a service book for their own people to take the place of the Prayer Book,[5] they determined to introduce psalm singing, and began the preparation of an English psalm book, of which Calvin's French Psalter was inevitably the model. But even at Geneva, the fountain head of Metrical Psalmody, the addiction to psalms was not absolutely exclusive. The first edition of Calvin's *Genevan Psalter* (1542) included metrical versions of the Song of Simeon, the Commandments, the Lord's Prayer and the Creed; in the complete and final form of the Psalter (1562) the outside material consisted of the Song of Simeon and Commandments versified and two metrical graces at meals. There was thus no departure from Genevan precedent made by including hymns in the English and Scottish Psalters; but in each case the appended hymns were more numerous and more diverse, and demand examination especially as to the actual significance of their appearance there.

1. The Hymns Appended to the English Psalter

The nucleus of the English Psalter, the earliest psalm book of the exiles at Geneva, was annexed to their *Forme*

[5] *The forme of prayers and ministration of the sacraments, &c., vsed in the Englishe Congregation at Geneua: and approued by the famous and godly learned man, John Caluyn. Imprinted at Geneua by John Crespin, M.D.LVI.*

of prayers of 1556 already referred to as *One and fiftie Psalmes of Dauid in Englishe metre,* and beyond the psalms contained only the Commandments versified by Whittingham. Not only the progress of the Psalter itself but also a gradual increase in the number of appended pieces is traced through the earliest surviving English-printed edition of 1560, and in English and Genevan editions both of 1561.

The English Psalter (commonly called *Sternhold and Hopkins,* or the *Old Version*) appeared in its completed form from the press of John Day at London, with a title not without significance for our inquiry: *The whole Booke of Psalmes, collected into Englysh metre by T. Starnhold, I. Hopkins & others: conferred with the Ebrue, with apt Notes to sing them withal, Faithfully perused and alowed according to thordre appointed in the Quenes maiesties Iniunctions. Very mete to be vsed of all sortes of people priuately for their solace & comfort: laying apart all vngodly Songes and Ballades, which tende only to the norishing of vyce, and corrupting of youth.* [Followed by two texts and imprint]. *An. 1562.*

Included in this Psalter, sharing such authorization as it had, are two groups of metrical hymns, one immediately preceding and one following the "PSALMS OF DAVID." In the preliminary edition of 1561 they had numbered seventeen, in the completed edition of 1562 they number nineteen, and in editions immediately succeeding they attain a total of twenty-three pieces. In the edition of 1562 the hymns are as follows:

Before the Psalms—

1. *Veni Creator.* "Come Holy Ghost eternal God."

[*Venite.* In 1562 there is only a reference to Ps. 95 as serving for the *Venite* of 1561.]

2. *Te Deum.* "We praise thee God."

3. *Benedicite.* "O all ye works of God the lord."

4. *Benedictus.* "The only lorde of Israel."

5. *Magnificat.* "My soule doth magnifye the Lord."

6. *Nunc dimittis.* "O Lord be cause my harts desire."

7. *Creed of Athanasius.* "What man soeuer he be that."

8. *Lamentation of a Sinner.* "O Lord turn not away thy face."
9. *Humble Sute of the Sinner.* "O Lorde of whom I do depend."
10. *Lord's Prayer* (D. C. M.). "Our father which in heauen art."
11. *Commandments* (D. C. M.). "Hark Israel, and what I say."
After the Psalms—
1. *Commandments* (L. M.). "Attend my people and geue eare": followed by "A Prayer."
2. *Lord's Prayer* (8. 8. 8. 8. 8. 8.). "Our father which in heauen art."
3. *XII Articles of the Faith.* "All my belief, and confidence."
4. *A Prayer before Sermon.* "Come holie spirit the God of might."
5. *Da pacem.* "Giue peace in these our daies O Lord."
6. *The Lamentation.* "O Lord in thee is all my trust."
7. *Thanksgiving after receiving the Lord's Supper.* "The Lord be thanked for his gifts."
8. "Preserue vs Lord by thy deare word."

In succeeding editions the *Venite* of 1561 ("O come and let vs now reioyce") was restored and the following additional hymns appeared:

1. *Before Morning Prayer.* "Prayse the Lord O ye Gentiles all."
2. *Before Evening Prayer.* "Behold now geue heede suche as be."
3. *Complaint of a Sinner.* "Where rightuousnesse doth say."

All but two of the hymns of 1562 have their "proper tunes" provided: in the remaining cases suitable tunes are indicated. We have thus before us what seems at first sight a not inconsiderable provision for congregational use in the Church of England of hymns as distinguished from psalms. But there are some considerations tending to modify this impression. It was, in the first place, a familiar device at the time to cast in metrical form, and set to music, doctrinal or other material for use by the people. This was partly with a view to furnish religious songs and partly to assist the memory to retain things regarded as desirable for the people to know, and was independent of the question of what should be sung in church. There was, in the second place, no hesitation on the part of the compilers of the early Psalters in joining to the Psalm versions matter intended for such private use. Witness the graces for the family meal in the *Genevan Psalter,* the treatise on music and "A Forme of Prayer to bee vsed in

priuate houses euery Morning and Euening" in the English Psalter of 1562. And, in the third place, it appears
from the title pages of the English Psalter that it was intended for use outside of church. The title of the editions
of 1561-1562 contained the words: "Very mete to be vsed
of all sorts of people priuately." It was not until 1566
that the title page of the Psalter claimed authorization for
its use in church.[6]

It is then obvious that the presence of these hymns in
the English Psalter does not of itself imply, either in intention or in fact, their use in the church services. As to the
actual significance of their inclusion one must form his
own conclusions.

Turning first to the prefixed hymns, the Prayer Book
complexion of the whole group is at once apparent. If
we regard the "Lamentation" and "Humble Sute" as representing the elements of Confession of Sin and Prayer
for Pardon and Peace incorporated in the Order for Daily
Prayer in 1552, then the entire group represents *The Book
of Common Prayer* in the same way that the paraphrases
of Psalms represent the canonical Book of Psalms. We
judge it to be the work of the mediating party who wished
to remove the Genevan taint from the transplanted
Psalmody by mingling Prayer Book materials with the
Scriptural songs of the people. They may have found their
precedent in the Latin Psalters of the old Church, in which
canticles and the creed and Lord's Prayer were added to
the Psalter proper. That these paraphrases of Prayer Book

[6]In 1566 the title reads:—*Newlye set foorth and allowed to bee soong
of the people together, in Churches, before and after Morning and
Euening prayer: as also before and after the Sermon, and moreouer
in private houses.* . . . But in this matter the opinion of many since
was voiced by George Wither in his pamphlet, *The Scholar's Purgatory*
(1624) : "that those metrical Psalms were never commanded to be used
in divine service, or in our public congregations, by any canon or ecclesiastical constitution, though many of the vulgar be of that opinion.
But whatsoever the Stationers do in their title page pretend to that
purpose, they being first allowed for private devotion only, crept into
public use by toleration rather than by command."

materials were intended for use in church services seems
unlikely from the point of view here suggested.   There
is no evidence that they were so used except in so far as the
Puritans of that or a later period ventured to substitute
these metrical versions for the corresponding prose passages
in the required Prayer Book service; their aim being to
avoid the necessity of chanting them.

Turning to the affixed hymns the atmosphere is notably
different, and is plainly that of Strassburg, with its Lutheran hymnody.   The version of the Lord's Prayer (by
Dr. Cox) is a rendering of Luther's metrical version and
is set to his tune.   The "Da Pacem" is a close translation
of Wolfgang Capito's German hymn ("Gieb Fried zu unser
Zeit, O Herr"), made by Edmund Grindal, a Marian exile
at Strassburg.   The last hymn of 1562 is a rendering by
Wisdom of Luther's famous prayer for aid against Turk and
infidel, and is set to his tune.   We judge therefore that the
later group of hymns reflects the influence of a party which
in exile abroad had become familiar with Lutheran hymnody and who favored some recognition of hymns at home;
and moreover that a place in the Psalter was gained for
these few hymns in expectation or at least hope of getting
them sung in the church services.   In favor of this view
we note the rubrics of No. 4, "to bee sung before the sermon," and of two of the added hymns, "to bee sung before
Morning prayer," "to bee sung before Evening prayer."
All three correspond precisely with the church uses designated on the title-page of the 1566 edition already quoted.

As regards the expectation of church use for these hymns
we can say that it was realized in the case of the Communion Thanksgiving.   George Wither, writing in 1623,
says:[7] "We haue a custome among us, that, during the time
of administring the blessed Sacrament of the Lord's Supper, there is some Psalme or hymne sung, the better to keepe
the thoughts of the Communicants from wandring after

[7] *The Hymnes and Songs of the Church,* ed. 1623, p. 63: Farr's
reprint, p. 271.

vaine objects." This was the hymn that shared such employment with psalms. It was sung while seated by the portion of the congregation which had already communicated or which awaited their turn to communicate, and its great length (124 lines) suggests that such use was foreseen. But such use was disassociated from the actual administration of the Sacrament and in a sense semi-private; and it may well be that some parishes made such use of this particular hymn which otherwise admitted psalms alone to the church services.

On the whole these hymns present no more than an insignificant exception to the statement that the Church of England became a psalm singing church. At the first they proved no impediment to the advancing tide of Psalmody. There was no time when their voice could be distinguished from the volume of Psalmody that filled the land. A movement to make use of them developed on the Puritan side; but they were not destined to form the nucleus of an ultimate Hymnal nor to point the way toward it. As time passed there appeared a tendency to reduce their number. In a London edition of 1713, bound up with the Prayer Book, they number only sixteen: in a Cambridge University Press edition of 1737, only thirteen. From the Baskerville edition of 1762 they have disappeared altogether. In later movements to introduce hymns into church worship the hymns of the early Psalter played but an insignificant part.

2. THE HYMNS APPENDED TO THE SCOTTISH PSALTER

The first edition of the psalm book for the Scottish Church appeared in 1564 and 1565 as a constituent part (without separate title-page) of *The forme of prayers and ministration of the sacraments &c vsed in the English Church at Geneua, approued and receiued by the Churche of Scotland, whereunto besydes that was in the former bokes, are also added sondrie other prayers, with the whole Psalmes of Dauid in English meter* . . . (Edinburgh:

Robert Lekprevick).[8] Unlike the "former bokes" at Geneva, and the English Psalter of two years before, the psalms were unaccompanied by paraphrases or hymns.

Oddly enough the song first appended to the Scottish Psalter was a mere love song, appearing in an unlicensed edition of 1568; an impertinent intrusion by its printer, Thomas Bassandyne, which invoked the intervention of the General Assembly, who ordered him to call in the copies sold, and to "delete the said baudie song out of the end of the psalm books." [9]

At the same time Bassandyne was ordered to abstain from printing anything "without licence of the Supreme Magistrate, and revising of sick things as pertain to religion be some of the Kirk appointed for that purpose." But in 1575 Bassandyne again printed the Psalter as *The CL. Psalms of David in English metre. With the forme of prayers* &c.[10] In this (apparently without objection from the Assembly) four hymns were appended to the Psalms: The Commandments (with the "Prayer" following), the Lord's Prayer (Cox), the Lamentation ("O Lord, in Thee is all my trust") and *Veni Creator*. And thereafter the inclusion of some hymns was the rule rather than the exception in the Scottish Psalter. In the edition of 1595 there

[8] Several copies are extant. For facsimile of title-page see Neil Livingston, *The Scottish Metrical Psalter of A. D. 1635. Reprinted . . . and illustrated by dissertations,* &c., folio, Glasgow, 1864, p. 72; and, for description of contents, pp. 13, 27 ff., and appendix. For a collation, see Dickson and Edmond, *Annals of Scottish Printing,* Cambridge, 1890, pp. 220 ff.

[9] No copy has survived. For the action of the Assembly see the Maitland Club ed. of *The Booke of the Universall Kirk of Scotland,* part i, pp. 125, 126. For the text of the "Baudie Song" ("Welcume Fortoun, welcum againe,") see Charles G. M'Crie, *The Public Worship of Presbyterian Scotland,* Edinburgh, 1892, appendix H. It had already appeared in the 1567 edition of the Wedderburn *The gude and godlie Ballatis.*

[10] No complete copy survives, but the late D. Laing's copy and one at the Bodleian, Oxford, contain the Psalms. For a collation of the latter, see Dickson and Edmond, *op. cit.,* pp. 309 ff., and for description of contents see Livingston, *ut supra.*

were ten, all evidently copied from the English Psalter. In 1615 appeared "The Song of Moses," a Scottish paraphrase of Deuteronomy xxxii in forty-three D. C. M. stanzas, divided into six parts for singing "to the tune of the Third Psalme." It was placed before the title page of the Psalms, with a note by the printer (Andro Hart), explaining why he had inserted it and recommending it to the church.[11] In the edition of 1635 the hymns attained a maximum of thirteen; eleven selected from the English Psalter, two of Scottish origin;—the Song of Moses, and "A Spiritual Song," beginning "What greater wealth than a contented minde?"

The whole list thus appearing is as follows:—

1. *Commandments* (L. M.). "Attend my people": with the "Prayer."
2. *Lord's Prayer* (Cox's).
3. *Veni Creator.*
4. *Nunc dimittis.*
5. *XII Articles.*
6. *The Humble Sute.* "O Lord, on whom I do depend."
7. *The Lamentation.* "O Lord, turn not."
8. *The Complaint.* "Where righteousnesse doth say."
9. *Magnificat.*
10. *The Lamentation.* "O Lord, in thee."
11. *The Song of Moses.*
12. *Thanksgiving after the Lord's Supper.*
13. *A Spirituall Song.*

The questions that concern us are whether these appended hymns were authorized, and, if so, for use in church worship, and whether by making use of them the Church of Scotland was at first, and to that extent, a hymn singing church.

No express authorization of them has been shown. On the other hand their appearance was known to the Assemblies, and not rebuked as the appearance of "Welcome

---

[11]A godly brother, to whom he announced his intention of reprinting the Psalter, expressed surprise that the Song of Moses had never found place in earlier editions. Hart thereupon requested him to prepare a metrical version for insertion in the forthcoming edition. The song is signed "I. M.," and its author has been identified as James Melville, nephew of Andrew and minister of Kilrenny.

Fortoun" had been. We must then say that the hymns were tacitly allowed. Such careful students as Dr. Horatius Bonar and Dr. Sprott have assumed as a matter of course that this action or lack of action on the part of the Assembly was with a view to the church use of the hymns in public worship.[12] This assumption involves the position that miscellaneous hymn singing was so much a matter of common consent among Scottish reformers that the appearing of a group of hymns for church worship along with the psalms was not a thing requiring action or even notice by the church authorities. For this there is no evidence in their writings or recorded practice or in the rubrics of the *Common Order*. The probabilities seem to point in a direction precisely opposite. They suggest that the addition of hymns was made so easily simply because their use in church worship was not proposed, and because the singing of spiritual songs by the people or their use as means for instructing the young was acceptable to all. That no one of these hymns was ever used in any Scottish church cannot be affirmed, but if so there is no known record of it. But that the appendix of hymns did not constitute a church hymn book, and that the hymns were not used continuously or generally can be affirmed with confidence, and proved by reference to successive editions of the Psalter itself. No hymns are known to have been appended till 1575, when they number four. In the editions of 1587, 1594 and 1595, they number ten. In 1599 there is but one (the "Lamentation"). In 1602 there are again ten: in one edition of 1611 three, and in another, a small and cheap edition for general

---

[12]Dr. Bonar in *Catechisms of the Scottish Reformation* (London, 1866), p. 302: Dr. Sprott in *The Worship and Offices of the Church of Scotland* (Edinburgh, 1882), p. 33. They are answered with warmth by D. Hay Fleming in *The Hymnology of the Scottish Reformation* (Reprinted from "Original Secession Magazine"), 1884. It seems to be the rule in Scotland that those favoring the use of hymns see clearly that the church has always allowed them, while those opposing hymns are concerned to maintain what was until lately the church's unvarying practice.

use, there are none at all. In 1615 there are ten affixed, and one prefixed on the printer's own motion. In 1629 there is only one hymn. In 1635 there are thirteen, and the "Song" prefixed by the printer in 1615 appears in the appendage with the earlier hymns. The editions of the Scottish Psalter were numerous, in order that the people might have their own copies; the days of "lining out the Psalm" were not yet;[13] and plainly the Psalters in their hands did not furnish the materials for the congregational singing of the hymns.

We do not know under what auspices the hymns were added to the Scottish Psalters. It has already become evident that the printers exercised some liberty in this connection, and that the appendage to the English Psalter furnished a motive and also the materials. We can only surmise the reasons that guided the selection of English material. The apocryphal *Benedicite,* the *Te Deum* and Creed of Athanasius, would be regarded as inexpedient; the alternative Commandments and Lord's Prayer, and the *Venite* ("see Psalm 95") as surplusage; the other omitted hymns as perhaps unnecessary or unattractive.

In Scotland as in England the hymns appended to the Psalter failed to furnish the nucleus of a future hymn book. The increase of their number in 1635 did not imply a movement to make larger use of them in worship, and when the *Psalms of David in meeter* were prepared in 1649-50 there seems to have been no thought given to reprinting the earlier hymns but rather to the question of adding Scriptural paraphrases in the strict sense.

As the result of our examination we are compelled to conclude that in spite of appearances the hymns appended to the English and Scottish Psalters must be regarded as an episode, and one of no great significance, in the history of Psalmody rather than as a link in the continutiy of the development of the English Hymn. Their relation to church worship is indeterminate. They did not become the nucleus of a hymnal. They were hardly even prophetic of the lines

[13]*Cf.* Livingston, *op. cit.,* p. 3.

on which the Hymn developed; for the demand for hymns grew out of long experience in singing metrical psalms, and not out of any satisfaction in the use of appended hymns.

III

THE PROMISE OF AN ENGLISH HYMNODY BY TRANSLATING THE OLD LATIN CHURCH HYMNS (1538-1559) FAILS

The most striking feature of the hymns appended to the English and Scottish Psalters is the appearance in each of a translation of the old Latin church hymn, *Veni Creator Spiritus,* which was in the *Breviary* and had also a place of special honor in the *Pontifical.* It suggests at first sight a purpose of giving the old church Hymnody some recognition along with the new Psalmody, but it had in reality no such significance. In the case of Scotland the appearance of this hymn had probably no significance one way or the other. Under Knox's influence the Genevan model had been transported to Scotland bodily, and there was no question among the reformers of continuing the Latin Hymnody or any other features of the old church services. Whoever chose the hymns for the Scottish Psalter found this one in the English Psalter, chose it and inserted it for reasons we do not know and for uses we can only surmise. But in England the situation was different. The course taken by the Reformation there left ample opportunities for the introduction of an English Hymnody on the lines of the old Latin Hymnody so familiar and so dear to many; of which opportunities the occasion of adding an appendix of hymns to the metrical Psalter may be regarded as the last. What the appearance of the *Veni Creator* alone in this appendix really signifies is not a purpose to embrace this final opportunity, but rather an acquiescence in a situation in which, with the single exception of *Veni Creator,* the whole area of the Latin Hymnody had been excluded from the worship

of the Reformed Church of England. And, before taking
up the lines upon which an English Hymnody did develop,
its failure to develop on the line that seems most natural
and inviting demands some consideration.

There had been from the very first the promise of such
development through the simple process of turning the Latin
hymns into English; a process happening to be consistent
with the scope and direction of the plans of Henry VIII.
Apart from the efforts of reformers the Church had already shown some purpose of meeting the desire of the laity
for a more intelligent part in worship. This showed itself
first in the *Horae* or *Primer,* the layman's book of private
devotion, whether at home or in church; containing offices
for the hours, commandments, creed, litany, the penitential
and other Psalms, with various prayers and materials for
devotion and sometimes for instruction; and including in
the offices the hymns proper to the time. The Ms. *Sarum
Primer* of the beginning of the 15th century, is already
wholly in English and the hymns are translated into prose.[14]
In printed editions of Sarum Primers from 1538, the hymns
are versified in a rude way, not apparently for singing and
certainly not for singing in church. From the Sarum
Primers grew a modified and unauthorized type, of which
Marshall's Primer of c. 1534 is the earliest survivor.[15] The
hand of reform is disclosed by the omission of hymns to
the Virgin; the Latin hymns of the *Sarum Primer* are rejected, and new hymns are furnished on the Latin model:
another effort by an unknown hand toward supplying a
Reformed Hymnody, and paralleling in a small way that of
Coverdale.

By 1539 Henry VIII takes the Primer in hand, and
through Bishop Hilsey issues one based on the *Sarum.*[16] In
1545 appeared the first of many editions of *The Primer set*

[14]Reprinted in Maskell's *Monumenta ritualia Ecclesiae Anglicanae,*
vol. iii.

[15]E. Hoskins, *Sarum and York Primers, with kindred books,* London, 1901, No. 115, and see pp. 193 ff.

[16]Hoskins, No. 142 and see pp. 225 ff.

fvrth by the kinge's maiestie & his clergie, to be taught lerned, and red; & none other to be vsed thorowout all his Dominions." [17] By royal injunction prefixed, this book became the sole authorized primer; the selling, use or teaching of any of the earlier ones being prohibited.

The hymns of this *King's Primer* are a fresh selection, taken with one exception from the *Sarum Breviary*. They mark a great advance over their predecessors in the primers and in Coverdale: the sweetness of their spiritual tone and the excellence of their verse are still appealing. In this book our Long Metre takes its place as the English equivalent of the Iambic Dimeter of the Ambrosian Hymns; and the Trochaic 7s is also successfully introduced.

Before the publication of this *Primer* for private use, the first step had already been taken toward introducing the vernacular into the public worship of the church. The Convocation of 1542 ordered that twice on every Sunday and holy day a chapter of the Bible in English should be read to the people; and in 1544 was set forth a "Litany with suffrages" in English, to be used in processions.[18] Cranmer had also made a beginning in providing English versions of the hymns used in the public services. A letter he sent to the King a few months after the publication of the English Litany, encloses, with other translations and music, a draft of a version of the hymn *Salve festa dies* set to the Gregorian melody. "I have travailed," Cranmer says, "to make the verses in English. . . . I made them only for a proof to see how English would do in song. But, by cause mine English verses want the grace and facility that I would wish they had, your majesty may cause some other to make them again, that can do the same in more pleasant English and phrase."[19]

There is no evidence that any use was made of Cranmer's hymn or of his suggestion to employ a more cunning

---

[17]The title is from a reprint of the edition of 1546 (xvii August).
[18]*Private prayers of Queen Elizabeth*. Parker Society ed: appendix.
[19]*Misc. Writings and Letters of Cranmer*. Parker Soc. ed., p. 412.

hand. In fact during the remainder of Henry's reign no further steps were taken toward vernacular services.

But when under Edward VI the way was opened to introduce English service books, neither the First Prayer Book of 1549 nor the Second of 1552, contained any of the hymns which were an essential part of the offices from which the Prayer Book Services were framed, except a rendering of the *Veni Creator Spiritus* in the ordinal of 1550. The little that is known of the genesis of the First Prayer Book throws scanty light on this omission. The recently printed Ms. of Cranmer's two drafts of his successive schemes of liturgical revision bears no dates.[20] The first is the scheme of a revised Breviary, containing offices for all the canonical hours, in the Latin language throughout, and based on the Reformed Breviary of Cardinal Quignon.[21] The second draft seems to belong to the early years of Edward VI's reign, and marks the transition from the "Divine Office" of the ancient Church to the "Morning and Evening Prayer" of the Church of England. The "Hours" are reduced to two, Matins and Vespers, and the Lord's Prayer and Lessons are in English. Of the Latin hymns of the Breviaries, twenty-six are retained, fourteen being assigned to the days of the week, twelve to the seasons of the Church year.[22] For some reason Cranmer did not use the Breviaries as the sources of his hymns, but took them from the *Elucidatorium Ecclesiasticum* of Clichtoveus, one of the earliest collectors of hymns, following his text.[23] Four of the hymns had never appeared in an English office book, and of these one is by Clichtoveus himself.[24] In the preface of his draft Cranmer says: "We have left only a few hymns which appeared to be more ancient and more beautiful than the rest." [25] In thus dealing with the hymns Cranmer was

[20] First printed in Gasquet and Bishop, *Edward VI and the Book of Common Prayer*, London, 1890.
[21] *Ibid.*, p. 37.   [22] *Ibid.*, p. 32.
[23] *Ibid.*, pp. 353 ff. and 334.
[24] *Ibid.*, p. 354 and note.
[25] *Ibid.*, p. 37.

following the example of Quignon, and to some extent his
preface here follows the words of Quignon's.   The preface
to the First Prayer Book of Edward VI is little more than
a translation of the preface to this second of Cranmer's
drafts; but as there are no Office Hymns in the Prayer Book
the reference to them just quoted of course drops out.[26]

Cranmer's draft shows a purpose of reducing the number of the hymns in use, and a preference for the ancient
hymns as against those more recently added to the Breviaries.   But it does not explain why in turning his services
into English he should have omitted metrical hymns altogether from his Prayer Book.   And no adequate explanation of this singular omission has ever yet been offered.
Mr. Frere, in his *New History of the Book of Common
Prayer,* says that Cranmer omitted the hymns because he
had "failed in his attempts to reproduce them in English
dress, as he had planned to do." [27]   The two difficulties in
the way of accepting this explanation are: *1st* that some
English versions were already at hand in the *King's Primer,*
which were themselves available and whose existence argues
that a capacity to translate other hymns was not lacking.[28]
2nd that English hymns not only failed to appear in the

[26]See the two prefaces in parallel columns in Gasquet and Bishop,
appendix iii.

[27]London, 1901, pp. 309 f.

[28]The following may serve as a specimen of these hymns.   It is from
the edition of August 17, 1546, as "Reprinted without any Alteration"
(n. d.).

> "Felowe of thy fathers lyght,
> Lyght of light and day most bryght,
> Christ that chaseth awaye nyghte,
> Ayde vs for to pray aright.
>
> Driue out darknes, from our mindes.
> Driue away the flocke of fendes,
> Drousynes, take from our eyes,
> That from slouth we may aryse.
>
> Christ vouchsafe mercy to geue,
> To vs all that do beleue,
> Let it profit vs that pray
> All that we do syng or say. Amen."

Prayer Book, but they actually disappeared from the new *Primer* of 1553, which is based on *The Book of Common Prayer,* and contains no metrical hymns, unless rhymed graces be so called.[29] This exclusion of hymns in themselves so good from the place already gained in the Primer seems to imply that the omission of hymns from the Prayer Book arose from a change of sentiment or judgment in regard to them, with which even the new *Primer* had to accord. In the vacillation of Cranmer's mind between Lutheranism and Calvinism, his omission of the hymns from the Prayer Book is *a priori* explicable as due to either influence. He might have argued that the true place of the Hymn was not in the structure of the Offices, where it would be rendered by the choir, but in a hymn-book, where it could be sung by the people, according to the Lutheran precedent. But the absence of hymns from the *Primer* tells against this explanation. He might, on the other hand, have been sufficiently under the influence of his Calvinistic advisers to feel that hymns of human composition had but a doubtful place in public worship. There are indications in the *Zurich Letters* confirming such a supposition; and of the two explanations of Cranmer's change of sentiment it is the more probable.

Whatever Cranmer's motives were, his action, together with the growing predilection of the people for metrical Psalms, proved decisive in excluding the old church hymns from the worship of the Church of England. Hymns appeared again in Elizabeth's *Primer* of 1559; and in the 49th of her Injunctions of that year it was permitted "that in the beginning or in the end of the Common Prayers, either at morning or evening, there may be sung an hymn or such like song to the praise of Almighty God, in the best sort of melody and music that may be conveniently devised, having respect that the sentence of the hymn may be understanded and perceived." It has been suggested[30] that this

[29]*Liturgies of Edward VI.* Parker. Soc. ed., pp. 357-384.
[30]By H. L. Bennett in Julian's *Dictionary of Hymnology,* p. 344².

Injunction contemplated the introduction, among other things, of naturalized Latin hymns. Doubtless the Injunction was broad enough to accomplish such an end if the desire for it existed, but its own declaration of purpose ("for the comforting of such that delight in music") and its language throughout make clear its intention to permit anthems by the choir of florid music in addition to the plain-song which it prescribes for general use. It became in fact the recognized authorization at once of the anthem by the choir and of the Genevan Psalm by the people.

And when the completed Psalter of 1562 was prepared no advantage was taken of the opportunity to provide versions of Latin hymns. It is likely that the interests represented in the prefixed group of "churchly" hymns were not solicitous for the introduction of hymns of any sort into public worship. They found the *Veni Creator* in the Ordinal, and it fell in with their purpose of giving a Prayer Book tone to their appendage of hymns. There is at least no evidence of any desire to modify Cranmer's rejection of the old church Hymnody.

Nor did any such proposal follow. The Metrical Psalm had prevailed. The Latin Hymn remained in the possession of the Roman Catholic Church, and successive editions of the Roman Primer witness its efforts that its people should know the hymns in their own tongue. In the *Primer of* 1604 (Antwerp) appeared an English version of the Vesper hymns from the *Breviary*. This was replaced in that of 1615 (Mechlin) by another version of the same. Twenty of the translations in this Primer have been claimed for Drummond of Hawthornden, a Scottish Protestant of the prelatic type, and printed as his by the editor of the 1711 Edinburgh edition of his works.[31] The *Primer* of

---

[31]They are printed in W. C. Ward's "Muses' Library" ed. of Drummond, London, 1894, but the editor follows Orby Shipley (*Annus Sanctus,* London, 1884, vol. i, preface pp. 12 ff.) in doubting Drummond's authorship. For the opposite view, see Wm. T. Brooke in Julian, *Dictionary of Hymnology,* pp. 312, 313.

1685 has still another version of the hymns; and in that of 1706[32] the whole circle of the Breviary hymns is represented by English versions which are regarded[33] as owing their origin to the distinguished poet Dryden and as being in large part his own work.

This body of vernacular hymns for the use of Catholic laymen had of course no bearing upon the services of their Church, and no influence on those of the Church of England.[34] It gradually passed, with the *Primer* itself, out of use and largely out of recollection until freshly studied in our own time by the Rev. Orby Shipley, an Anglican clergyman who passed into the Roman Church in 1877. But side by side with the Roman Primers appeared numerous editions of Primers of the Henry VIII type, from which devout Anglicans with Roman leanings could use versions of old church hymns in their private devotions. One of them, John Cosin, afterwards Bishop of Norwich, aimed at a general introduction of offices in Primer fashion in his *A Collection of private devotions in the practice of the ancient Church called the Houres of Prayer* (1627), renamed, the year following, by William Prynne, "Mr. Cozens His Couzening Devotions." It contained numerous versions of hymns for the canonical hours, and from it Cosin's own version of *Veni Creator* passed into *The Book of Common Prayer* of 1662, of which he was one of the revisers. There are other evidences that there still lingered in the English Church a feeling for and a feeling after the old Office Hymns which the Church had rejected. But it was confined within a narrow circle and it gradually waned.

[32]*The Primer, or Office of the B. Virgin Mary, revis'd: with a new and approv'd version of the Church-Hymns throughout the Year: to which are added the remaining Hymns of the Roman Breviary. Printed in the Year 1706.*

[33]By Orby Shipley, who prints a full selection in his *Annus Sanctus.* For Dryden's claims of authorship, see preface, pp. 9-12.

[34]Dryden's version of *Veni Creator* in the 1706 *Primer* has become familiar in Protestant use. It had, however, appeared in part iii of his *Miscellanies,* 1693, and in Tonson's folio edition of Dryden's Poems in 1701.

It was not without its influence in turning the minds of devotional poets toward the hymn-form. But by the XVIIIth century the whole area of Latin Hymnody had become, to the Church of England clergy, a remote and unknown country, vaguely indicated as "Popish." It was destined to remain so until the Oxford Revival of the XIXth century, whose leaders encountered much reproach in their efforts to explore it.

And indeed the causes of this neglect lay deeper than even Protestant prejudice. Not till Romanticism, whose spiritual child the Oxford Movement was, loosed the fetters of Classicism were men's minds free to appreciate the old Hymnody and many other things that interest us.

IV

THE EVOLUTION OF THE ENGLISH HYMN FROM THE METRICAL PSALM

The modern practice of singing hymns in English-speaking Churches grew, as has been intimated already, out of the Psalmody actually practised in those Churches. It found its occasion in the dissatisfaction with which the body of metrical psalms, substantially alike in England and Scotland, came to be regarded by many of those who were expected to sing them. It found its opportunity in growing indifference toward Psalmody as a church ordinance, and the consequent degradation into which the practice of Psalmody as a musical performance was allowed to fall. This indifference and neglect was occasioned partly at least by the fact that the strict principle of an exclusive use of psalms in worship had lost something of the earlier force of its appeal to the conscience, and psalms had failed to express fully the thoughts and emotions of the Christian heart.

The new Hymn itself was partly an outspreading of the Metrical Psalm from its original basis of being a strict translation, to embrace a freer method of paraphrase, to include other parts of Scripture, to become an "imitation" or exposition of Scripture, and finally a hymn more or less suggested by Scripture. It was partly also a development of the impulse to write devotional poetry, to which a hymnic turn was given by the felt need of hymns at first for private and then for public use. In the moulding of its form the precedent of the Metrical Psalm no doubt predominated, but at the same time the older Latin ideal of the Hymn, kept alive by Roman Catholic books of devotion, was not without influence, by way of suggestion especially, upon the English Hymn.

The evolution of the Hymn from the Metrical Psalm may perhaps be distinguished as proceeding along three lines, more or less synchronous.

(1) *By way of an effort to improve the literary character of the authorized Psalters.*

Our ineradicable conviction that one choosing the medium of verse should justify his choice by the artistic character of his work gives us a poor point of view from which to regard Metrical Psalmody. It was a utilitarian device, based on devotion to the letter of God's word, aiming merely to cast it into measured and rhyming lines which plain people could sing to simple melodies, as they sang their ballads. The Swiss and French Calvinists, it is true, were able to make large use of the work of Clement Marot, the outstanding poet of France, and secured a version of one third of the Psalter which satisfied Calvin for its accuracy and the whole of France for its beauty. In England and Scotland it was otherwise. The men who made their Psalters were not poets nor even good craftsmen. The poor and prosaic character of their work was an unconscious testimony that English prose was the natural medium of a literal translation of the Hebrew Psalms, and that resort to verse had secured singableness at the expense of literal fidelity; and, on the other hand, that the desire to be as literal as the English metre allowed, had joined with the authors' meagre poetic gifts, to produce a metrical version devoid of the grace or charm of poetry.

Therefore the English and Scottish Psalters were, from the beginning of the XVIIth century, subject to two influences. One was the Puritan demand for greater *literalness*. This culminated in the New England version, the famous *Bay Psalm Book* of 1640, and in the Scottish recension of the Psalter recommended by the Westminster Assembly, commonly called *Rous's Version*, 1650. These represented the Puritan movement to maintain Psalmody in its purity. It was an effectual movement in Scotland. But with the exclusion of the Puritans from the Church of England the movement did little permanently, except to remain as unsettlement and a desire for revision.

The other influence upon the Psalters was that of literary culture, which regarded them with growing dissatisfaction. The earlier private versions following the publication of *Sternhold and Hopkins,*—those, for example, of Archbishop Parker, Sir Philip Sidney and his sister, Sir John Harrington, and Sir John Davies, in England, and of Alexander Montgomerie in Scotland,—were literary efforts or intended for private use, and some remained in Ms. They were no doubt in their way protests against the current Psalters. But in 1619 George Wither in his *A Preparation to the Psalter* laboriously cleared the ground for the introduction of a better version than that employed since the Reformation. And his *The Psalms of David translated into lyrick verse* (1632), and also *The Psalms of King David translated by King James* (1631), were deliberate attempts to impose upon the people of England and Scotland respectively new versions of the Psalms, of which they had no appreciation. The one was ordered to be bound up with every copy of the Bible issued in England, the other was bound up with Laud's Prayer Book for the Scottish Church: and both were futile enough.

Such desire and ability to improve the Psalter as there was in Scotland found its final expression in *The Psalms of*

David in meeter, 1650, in which painstaking work the preponderance of the Puritan motive did not prevent an advance in expression and in smoothness. In England the desire to improve the Psalter was confined to the educated minority. It was expressed, for a long time ineffectually, in criticisms and protests and in private versions of the Book of Psalms offered more or less frankly in the place of the current one. Of these George Sandys' *A paraphrase upon the Psalms of David* attained real literary distinction and was set to music in 1638 by Henry Lawes. It failed, however, to attain any wide use, for which it was indeed poorly adapted.

But in 1695 appeared specimen sheets of a new Psalter by two Irishmen,—Nahum Tate, whom William III had made Poet Laureate, and Dr. Nicholas Brady, who had been zealous for the Prince of Orange in the Revolution, and was then a Royal Chaplain, and the holder also of a London living. Their joint work was completed and published at London in 1696 as *A new Version*[35] *of the Psalms of David, fitted to the tunes used in Churches. By N. Tate and N. Brady.* Both writers were in royal favor, and on December 3 of the year of its publication, their version was by the King in Council "Allowed and Permitted to be used in all Churches, Chappels, and Congregations, as shall think fit to receive the same." In May, 1698, the Bishop of London "persuaded it may take off that unhappy Objection, which has hitherto lain against the Singing Psalms," "heartily recommended the Use of this Version to all his Brethren within his Diocess."

What at present concerns us is to determine the nature of the influence this book was fitted to exert on a psalm singing church. The impression it makes upon ourselves, accustomed to the use of hymns, is not difficult to define. Our opinions might differ as to details, but we are likely to agree

---

[35]The designation of *New Version* thus given has ever since clung to it as distinguishing it from the *Old Version* of Sternhold and Hopkins.

that these new Psalm versions—fluent and rhythmical and eminently singable as they are, following closely the Scripture and yet yielding to the devices of rhetoric as they do,— often make upon us the impression of being hymns rather than psalms in the stricter sense. We feel, at times certainly, as though we had a hymn book in hand, and indeed recognize a number of pieces long familiar to us as hymns.[36] What we wish, however, is to know the impression made by the *New Version* at the time upon one who was accustomed and attached to singing psalms of the *Old Version* in church worship.

Fortunately we have the testimony of one who regarded the attachment of the plain people to *Sternhold and Hopkins* as a sheet-anchor of English religion, and who has given us the impression made upon him by an examination of Tate and Brady. It occurs in *A Defence of the Book of Psalms, collected into English metre, by Thomas Sternhold, John Hopkins, and others. With critical observations on the late New Version, compar'd with the Old. By William Beveridge, D.D., late Lord Bishop of St. Asaph.* (London, 1710). He says:—

"I do not hear, that this [*New Version*] was ever conferred with the *Hebrew,* as the other was.; nor so much as that any of our Bishops, or other learned in that Language, were appointed or authorized to do it. And there is too much cause to suspect, that it was never done. For, if we may take our Measures of its agreeing or disagreeing with the *Hebrew* Text, from its agreeing or not agreeing with the Psalms in the New Translation of the Bible, made out of the *Hebrew,* we may thence conclude, that there was not the Care taken about this, as there was about the Old Version. So far, at least, as I am able to judge, Who having got a Sight of this New Translation of the Psalms in Verse, could not satisfy my own Mind about it, without comparing it with the New Translation in Prose. Which I had no sooner begun, but I found so many Variations, that I thought to have gather'd together all that I judged to be so, throughout the whole Book, without any other Design, but for my own Satisfaction. But

---

[36]Among such: the 34th, "Thro' all the changing Scenes of life"; the 42nd, "As pants the Hart for cooling Streams"; the 51st, "Have Mercy, Lord, on me"; the 84th, "O God of Hosts, the mighty Lord"; and the 93rd, "With Glory clad, with Strength array'd."

when I had gone a little way, I found them multiply so fast upon me,
that I could see no end, and, therefore, was forced to give it over,
and to content myself with observing the reason of it; which, to me,
seem'd to be this: That, whereas the Composers and Reviewers of the
Old Translation had nothing else in their Eye, but to give us the true
Sense of each place in as few Words as could be in Verse, and, therefore, keep close to the Text, without deviating from it, upon any
account: In this New Translation, there is so much regard had to
the Poetry, the Style, the Running of the Verse, and such-like inconsiderable Circumstances, that it was almost impossible to avoid
going from the Text, and altering the true Sense and Meaning of it.
For, hence it came to pass, that although the Authors, doubtless,
designed a true Translation, yet other things crowding into their
Heads at the same time, justled that Design so, that it could not
always take effect." [37]

We conclude that the impression made by the *New Version* upon the lovers of the old Psalter was not very different from that it makes upon ourselves. They recognized
in it the proposal of a new standard in Church of England
Psalmody, a proposed exchange of the Reformation principle of a close translation of the letter of Scripture for that
of a rhetorical paraphrase.

And this perception on their part determined and limited
the career of the *New Version* within the Church of England. It never became the Psalter of the whole Church.
It never dispossessed the *Old Version* in many a village and
country side parish, where, partly from conviction, partly
owing to the force of use and wont, successive generations
of the congregations went on singing the *Old Version* until
well toward the middle of the nineteenth century. But it
worked its way, often against resistance, into one and another parish church of London and its neighborhood, until
it became preëminently the London Psalter, and into widening circles beyond, as those concerned for the improvement
of Psalmody were able to have their way.

On the whole, the influence of the *New Version* was
very considerable. It set up in the Church of England a
new standard of Psalmody, with the same authorization as

[37]Pp. 39-41.

the older one,—that of a Paraphrase which had something of the freer lyrical spirit of the Hymn as against the restrictions of the Metrical Psalm.   It is not unfair to say that the spirit and tendency of the *New Version* appears in the fact that it proved most acceptable to those least bent on maintaining the older type of Psalmody and whose minds were turning toward hymns; that a movement toward introducing them was connected with it, apparently from the beginning, and that by means of its "Supplement" it became the actual medium by which hymns were introduced into many churches in and beyond London.

(2) The second line of the development of the Hymn from the Metrical Psalm was *by way of an effort to accommodate the Scriptural text to the circumstances of present day worshippers.*

In the first enthusiasm at being in the possession of God's word in the vernacular, there was no desire to choose among Psalms equally inspired; and the custom was to sing the Psalter through in course.   But after some experience the Reformed clergy in all the Churches exercised the right of selection.   Even so there remained the inconvenience of singing certain statements in the selected Psalms inapplicable to the congregation.   This became more conspicuous when each statement was put into the congregation's mouth separately and distinctly in the process of "lining out" before singing.   In England both the selection and the lining of the psalm fell into the hands of the parish clerk.   And to him fell consequently the opportunity of omitting or even altering any lines he regarded as inopportune.   While freely exercised, the remedy was irregular, inconvenient to those who could read, and dependent at best upon the discretion and readiness of a class of officials not characteristically gifted with either.   The difficulty was in fact inherent in the strict conception of Psalmody itself, and hardly capable of remedy within its own limits.

A much more serious inconvenience in confining the congregational praise to the Psalter made itself felt in England as it was felt in every country where the Reformed cultus had been introduced. It arose from the fact that the canonical Psalms represented one dispensation and the worshippers another; and the difficulty was that of satisfying Christian devotion with the songs of an earlier stage of revelation. In all Reformed Churches the congregations had been duly trained in the evangelical interpretation of the Psalms; and its expression was a commonplace of preaching and public prayer. The individual believer was of course expected to have in mind the evangelical implications of what he sang; but nevertheless it remained true that the Psalmody was his peculiar opportunity for expression in the church service, and that in Psalmody he could not name his Saviour's name. There was no real solution of this difficulty short of the inauguration of a Christian Hymnody; and toward this solution the Psalmody of all countries inevitably tended.

In England toward the end of the XVIIth century the mass of the people were not ready for so radical a change, and the expedient suggested itself of accommodating the Psalmody to the circumstances of the Christian dispensation by introducing the familiar evangelical interpretations of the Psalms into their actual text. In this way it seemed possible to attain the desired end, while leaving the accustomed form and manner of Psalmody entirely unimpaired and with changes in the words of inspiration only in the sense of interpreting them.

The name of Dr. Watts became, from the second decade of the XVIIIth century, so inevitably associated with this method of accommodating the Psalms, and his influence told so overwhelmingly in favor of its adoption and spread, that it becomes difficult to realize that he was not the inventor of it. He had, however, an English predecessor in John Patrick, "Preacher to the Charter-House, London."

Patrick was one of the divines who hoped to remedy the low estate of Psalmody in the Church of England after the Restoration by producing a version of the Psalms more

acceptable than *Sternhold and Hopkins*. He published in
1679 *A Century of select Psalms and portions of the Psalms
of David, especially those of praise*. His work had less influence in the Church of England than with Nonconformists. Richard Baxter in 1681[38] contrasts the work of the
brothers Patrick. One by his *Friendly Debate* has done all
in his power to destroy concord, the other by his *Psalms*
"hath so far reconciled the nonconformists that divers of
them use his Psalms in their congregations, though they
have their old ones, Rouses . . . the New Englands . . .
the Scots (agreed on by two nations)" and others, "in
competition with it."

Dr. Watts[39] attributed the welcome given to Patrick's
version by Nonconformists to the fact "that he hath made
use of the present language of *Christianity* in several
Psalms, and left out many of the Judaisms."

> "This," he says, "is the Thing that hath introduced him into the
> Favour of so many religious Assemblies. Even those very Persons that
> have an Aversion to sing any thing in Worship but *David's* Psalms
> have been led insensibly to fall in with Dr. *Patrick's* Performance by
> a Relish of pious Pleasure; never considering that his Work is by no
> means a just Translation, but a Paraphrase; and there are scarce any
> that have departed farther from the inspired *Words of Scripture* than
> he hath often done, in order to suit his Thoughts to the State and
> Worship of Christianity. This I esteem his peculiar Excellency in
> those Psalms wherein he has practis'd it."

In this spirit of accommodation to Christian feeling Patrick did not hesitate to introduce the name of Christ, and
to address to Him specifically passages inviting such interpretation.[40]

Patrick also, as his title-page indicates, exercised freely
the right of selection, the same privilege, he asserts in his

[38]Preface to his *Poetical Fragments*.
[39]Preface to *The Psalms of David imitated*, 1719; p. vi.
[40]E. g., Psalm cxviii, part 2, verse 26:—

> "Blest Saviour! that from God to us
>   On this kind errand came,
> We welcome thee; and bless all those
>   That spread thy Glorious Fame."

preface, as every parish clerk practises; and he frankly
avows that there is much in the Psalter unsuited, in his
opinion, to Christian use. In the preface to *A Century of
Psalms,* he says:

> "I considered and pitched upon, those Psalms or portions of them
> which were most proper and of most general use to us Chris-
> tians. . . . But I balked those whose whole aspect was upon David's
> personal troubles, or Israel's particular condition, or related to the
> Jewish and legal Oeconomy, . . . or where they express a temper
> not so suitable to the mild and gentle spirit of the Gospel, such as our
> Saviour repressed in his Disciples, not allowing imprecations of
> vengeance against our Enemies, but rather praying for them; espe-
> cially when that prophetick spirit do's not now rest upon us, that did
> upon David. . . ."

The popularity of Patrick's version made these principles of evangelical interpretation and of selection familiar in
Nonconformist circles, and did something to undermine the
supremacy of the *Old Version* within the Church of England, into some of whose parishes Patrick's version gradually worked its way. By 1691 his *Century* had reached its
fifth edition, and in that year he rounded it out to a full
version of the Psalter, which continued to be reprinted till
the middle of the XVIIIth century as *The Psalms of David
in metre: fitted to the tunes used in parish-churches.*

But Patrick's special importance is as the forerunner and
exemplar of Dr. Watts, who in his work of turning the
Psalms into Christian hymns frankly announced himself as
following out more fully the lines instituted by Patrick. The
full extent of Watts' obligations to his predecessor is indeed
somewhat surprising. They cover not only the rhetorical
style and rhythmical treatment, but extend to the language
itself. Many lines in the two versions are identical; many
more are reproduced by Watts with some alteration; and
there are even whole stanzas which he has borrowed substantially unchanged. Dr. Watts announced his purpose to
be to "exceed" Dr. Patrick by applying his method to every
Psalm and by improving upon his verse.[41]

[41] Preface to *The Psalms of David imitated.*

It was Patrick, therefore, who first occupied successfully this middle ground between the Metrical Psalm and the English Hymn. Actual priority in the device of giving an evangelical turn to the Metrical Psalm belongs neither to Patrick nor Watts. Both were anticipated by Luther, and by the authors of Psalters in Switzerland and Holland. But in England the priority rests with Patrick.

✗(3) The third line of the development of the Hymn from the Metrical Psalm was *by extension of the principle of Scripture paraphrase to cover the evangelical hymns and other parts of the Bible.*

Such extension was implicitly recognized in the original Calvinistic settlement of Church Song. No divine prescription was claimed for the Psalter. Calvin's *Genevan Psalter* included as a matter of fact such materials as the Commandments and *Nunc Dimittis.* From the first days of psalm singing in England, a series of efforts began to provide paraphrases of other parts of Scripture for singing. The Song of Solomon was especially favored, and before the completion of the metrical Psalter, the first fourteen chapters of *The Actes of the Apostles, translated into Englyshe metre, and dedicated to the Kynges most excellent Maiestye, by Christofer Tye, Doctor in Musyke. . . . wyth notes to eche chapter, to synge and also to play upon the Lute* (1553),[42] were actually sung in Edward VIth's chapel. But both in England and Scotland the zeal of the people was for Psalmody, and the other paraphrases took no hold.

Versions of the evangelical canticles and other Prayer Book materials, were prefixed, as has already appeared, to the Psalter of 1562, without it may be any intention of church use. If we are to believe Warton, William Whyttingham introduced their use at once into his church at Durham, "to accommodate every part of the service to the psalmodic tone." [43] However this may be, there was a

---

[42] There is a facsimile in Robt. Steele, *The earliest English Music Printing,* London, 1903, figure 13.
[43] *History of English Poetry,* Hazlitt's ed., 1871, vol. iv, p. 130.

movement in the XVIIth century to sing these paraphrases in place of the corresponding prose passages in the Prayer Book. One notes that in 1621, apparently for the first time, the hymns appended to *Sternhold and Hopkins* are displayed in the title, in *The whole Booke of Psalmes: with the Hymnes evangelicall, and songs spirituall. Composed into 4 parts by sundry authors, . . . newly corrected and enlarged by Tho: Rauenscroft.* This was a private venture, but became a standard in Psalmody, and may have influenced or merely recorded a changing fashion. The movement to utilize the paraphrases was not to enlarge the Psalmody so much as to get the canticles out of the hands of the choir and into those of the people. In effect it made paraphrases, of the canticles especially, a part of Psalmody in numerous Puritan churches. It is surprising to find that this practice survived the Restoration, and left traces in XVIIIth century worship.[44]

Apart from this there was a movement toward Scriptural paraphrases in both England and Scotland with a view of supplementing the felt deficiencies of Psalmody.

In Scotland this showed itself in the proceedings resulting in the new Psalter of 1649-50. The hymns of the old *Scottish Psalter* seem to have been ignored, and attention was fixed upon the work of a small number of writers who were claimants for recognition.

Foremost among them was the influential but eccentric Zachary Boyd, three times Rector and twice Vice-Chancellor of the University of Glasgow, in whose library a mass of his work in paraphrasing Scripture remains in Ms. Boyd published in 1644 *The Garden of Zion,* containing in the first volume metrical histories of Scripture

[44] "It ought to be noted, that both the sixty-seventh and hundredth Psalms, being inserted in the Common Prayer-Books in the ordinary version, ought so to be used, and not to be sung in Sternhold and Hopkins, or any other metre; as is now the custom in too many churches." Chas. Wheatly, *A rational Illustration of the Book of Common Prayer,* cap. 3, Sect. 13.

characters, and in the second, metrical versions of Job, Ecclesiastes, Proverbs and Solomon's Song. Under a separate title, but with continuous paging was appended *The Holy Songs of the Old and New Testament*. In or about 1646 he published *The Psalmes of David in meeter*. The earliest copy known is of the 3rd edition of 1648, and copies of this were sent to most of the Presbyteries with a preface reading like a challenge to attention. To this edition "The Songs of the Old and New Testament," numbering 16, were appended.

The same act of the General Assembly of 1647 which ordered the revision of *Rous's Psalms* had also recommended "That Mr. Zachary Boyd be at the paines to translate the other Scriptural Songs in meeter, and to report his travels also to the Commission of Assembly, that after their examination thereof, they may send the same to Presbyteries to be there considered until the next Generall Assembly." [45] The Assembly of 1648, in sending down the amended *Rous,* also appointed "Master John Adamson and Mr. Thomas Crafurd to revise the Labours of Mr. Zachary Boyd upon the other Scripturall Songs," with a view to reporting them to the next Assembly.[46] There is no record of such a report upon Boyd's songs having reached the Assembly. David Leitch, minister of Ellon, had also presented some hymns of his own to the Commission of the Assembly in 1648, who took steps to further his labors, but do not seem to have brought them before the Assembly itself.[47] In February, 1650, the Commission called upon the Rev. Robert Lowrie, then of Edinburgh, to exhibit his work in versifying the Scripture songs.

With this request the effort to introduce Scripture songs ceased, and the new Psalter appeared without them. This result has been attributed somewhat vaguely to the "troub-

---

[45] *Acts of the General Assemblies,* 1638-1649; ed. 1691, p. 354.
[46] *Ibid.,* p. 428.
[47] See D. J. Maclagan, *The Scottish Paraphrases,* Edinburgh, 1889, pp. 2, 3.

lous times." [48] The record itself suggests a sufficient explanation in the evident fact that the songs offered as available did not commend themselves to the Assembly or its Commission; a situation readily accounted for by an examination of Boyd's crude work. We may agree with Maclagan[49] that those who had the improvement of the Psalmody in hand thought it prudent to have the new Psalter established as soon as possible without waiting for Scriptural songs, which they expected would follow as soon as a collection could be agreed on. With this expectation the "troublous times" no doubt interfered.

In the years preceding the Revolution Patrick Symson, an "outed" minister, deprived of his benefice at Renfrew, occupied his compelled leisure by paraphrasing Scripture. He published in 1685 a little book of *Spiritual Songs or holy Poems. A garden of true delight, containing all the Scripture-Songs that are not in the Book of Psalms, together with several sweet prophetical and evangelical Scriptures, meet to be composed into songs. Translated into English meeter, and fitted to be sung with any of the common tunes of the Psalms* (Edinburgh: Anderson).

Symson's preface assumes that the Church's purpose to add the other Scriptural songs to the Psalms still holds good; and in this he was plainly justified, as after-proceedings showed. But his preface recognizes also that in "putting many more Scriptures into song than were intended for such by the Spirit," he is merely trying experiments, the success of which the Church must judge.

The General Assembly resumed its sessions after the Revolution of 1689; and in December, 1695, Symson became its moderator. In the month following, there was a reference of his *Spiritual Songs* to the Commission for revision.[50] Owing to the loss of the records further proceedings cannot be followed, till in April, 1705, the Commission

[48]Rev. Jas. Mearns in Julian's *Dictionary of Hymnology,* p. 1023.
[49]*The Scottish Paraphrases,* p. 2.
[50]See Maclagan, *op. cit.,* p. 6.

was directed to revise Symson's book for public use, and report to the next Assembly. The work was put into the hands of two committees, one for the East, and one for the West. The committees agreed to exclude Symson's experiments in versifying passages of Scripture that were not songs, so far as their public use was concerned, "seeing if other places of Holy Scripture should be turned into meeter, there would be no end." But they reported 26 versions of Scripture songs as available after revision by a hand skilled in "poecie." These the Assembly of 1706 sent down to the Presbyteries for examination and report.[51] So slight was the response that the Assembly of 1707 continued the reference.[52] That of 1708 ordered the Commission to examine the songs in the light of amendments suggested by Presbyteries, and then to establish and issue them for public use, as was formerly done with the Psalms in 1649.[53] The Commission appealed to the Synods for help in the matter, and failed to elicit any of consequence. It became plain that the Church felt no interest in the songs offered it, and the Commission allowed the whole project to drop.[54]

This whole movement toward paraphrases in Scotland presents some curious features. We see, on the one hand, a stirring within the church of dissatisfaction with the current Psalmody and of sympathy with the movement of the time to modify it. We see the ideal of the Hymn evolving itself in men's minds, and gradually seeking expression in their work. We see, on the other hand, practical hindrances preventing any realization of the ideal in Scotland. There was, to begin with, the prejudice of the plain people in favor of the familiar Psalms. There was also the hindrance from leadership which did not see its way clearly, and was misled by the ambitious influences of authorship. But the greatest hindrance of all was the paraphrasers themselves,

[51]*Acts of the General Assembly,* Edinburgh, 1843, p. 392.
[52]*Ibid.,* p. 419.
[53]*Ibid.,* p. 430.
[54]See Maclagan, *op. cit.,* p. 9.

whose work seemed to be the only available embodiment of the new movement. Their work was of a quality so poor, so far below even the standard of the Metrical Psalms, that it gave even those most zealous for enlarging the Psalmody a feeling of helplessness and indecision, soon merging into hopelessness.

In Scotland, then, we have first to note the work of Boyd and Symson as marking the beginning of the development of the Hymn from the Psalm, and then to note that their work became practically a bar to the introduction of paraphrases into Scotland. The attempt to introduce their work into public use reacted in favor of pure Psalmody. The desire for other Scripture songs never perhaps died out, but when those of Symson were consigned to oblivion in 1709 the whole movement followed them, not to emerge again until the general Assembly of 1741.

In England the contemporaneous movement to supplement the Psalms with other Scripture songs found its fullest expression in the work of William Barton. Barton has been well described as a "conforming Puritan," and was probably vicar of St. Martin's, Leicester, at his death. During the whole of the Civil War period and long after the Restoration he pursued two projects for the betterment of Church Song with unflagging zeal. He stands at and, it must be said, he crosses the dividing line between the old Psalmody and the new Hymnody, and his work faces both ways.

His earlier project was in line with the Puritan demand for a "purer" version of the Psalter. He published in 1644 *The Book of Psalms in metre close and proper to the Hebrew*. It was favorably received, and its third edition (1646) was recommended by the Lords to the Westminster Assembly as their preferred version. The contest between the partisans of Rous and Barton prevented any version from receiving the imprimatur of Parliament. It was a great sorrow to Barton that his version failed to displace the old Psalter, but the substance of it entered to some extent into the Scottish *Psalms of David in meeter* of 1650.

In the preface to his Psalter Barton gave preëminence to the Psalms, and emphasized their appropriateness to present day use. But in 1659 he took an opposite direction, and published *A Century of select Hymns,* increased in 1670 to *Two Centuries,*[55] and, after his death, published complete by his son as *Six Centuries of select Hymns and Spiritual Songs collected out of the Holy Bible* (London, 1688).

In the preface to the *Centuries,* Barton came out boldly for hymns, with the proviso that they be founded on Scripture. He cited the example of the Apostles and early Church and of the Bohemian Brethren. The hymns of the Latin Church, on the other hand, proved how "horrid blasphemy" creeps into hymns forsaking the Scripture basis. He condemns the "Complaint of a Sinner" and "Humble Sute" in the *Old Version* as nonsensical or erroneous. But in applying his principle to his own work, he allowed himself great liberties. It was enough that his hymns were "collected out of the Bible." He selects passages and individual texts from one Testament or both, turns them into verses, and weaves them into the unity of a mosaic hymn: each hymn and often each stanza being preceded by the "proof texts." Three of his *Six Centuries* are "Psalm Hymns," in which he deals in the same way with the Psalms, omitting what he regards as unsuitable, and expounding "dark passages."

Are these productions translations or paraphrases or hymns? In relation to the individual texts dealt with they

[55]Some malign influences were working against Barton. He complains that the appearance of his *Two Centuries* was obstructed for three years by fraud and injuriousness; that *Four Centuries* appeared in 1668 without his knowledge and through deceit; that the adoption of his Psalter was thwarted by enemies; and that an edition of 1500 was printed by stealth to supply Scottish churches that much preferred it to the officially adopted *Psalms in meeter.* Barton's protest that he had no aim but that of promoting godliness perhaps furnishes a key. Some may have thought so much zeal had an eye for personal glory and profit, and have set about to diminish or share them.

are translations, adhering closely to the English prose version. In their freedom in handling and combining unrelated texts, they suggest the paraphrase. In motive and intention and in their general effect they are clearly hymns. Their author so named them: they were so regarded by his contemporaries[56] and by the hymn writers who followed him.[57]

Barton's work thus occupies the very point of transition between the Metrical Psalm and the Hymn, and its influence was very marked upon English Hymnody. In his own Church his immediate influence was barred by the Restoration, when the singing of *Sternhold and Hopkins* was resumed just where it had left off at the Puritan Revolution, and without spirit enough to seek improvement. But among the Independents Barton's hymns as well as his psalms were

[56]In a copy of the 1688 ed. of the *Centuries* a contemporary Ms. index is bound in, showing "In what page of the *Hymn Book* Composed by Mr. Wm. Barton to find any Scripture Therein translated."

[57] "These hymns of Mr. Barton": Simon Browne, *Hymns,* 1720, preface. The following (from Century I) will illustrate Barton's method and manner:—

HYMN 151. *Mediator.*

All People, &c.

I Tim. 2. 5.

ONE God there is, and one alone,
  and Mediator none but one;
The man whom we Christ Jesus call,
  who gave himself full price for all.

I Joh. 2. 1, 3.

If any sin, we have on high
  an Advocate to qualifie,
Jesus the Just, whose blood was spilt
  to expiate our hanious guilt.

Rev. 5. 13.

Blessing and glory and renown
  to him that on the Throne sits down,
And to the Lamb of God therefore
  be praise and honour evermore.

widely introduced and used in some places for a long time.[58]
They accustomed the people to New Testament song and
to a freer handling of Scripture than obtained under Psalmody.   It was among the Independents that the new school
of hymn writers was to arise and conquer the churches.
And it was on them that Barton's influence told most, and
through them that he helped to fix the type and character of
the English Hymn as based upon Scripture and saturated
with it.   There was no essential difference between Barton's
hymns collected out of Scripture and the succeeding hymns
based upon Scripture.   Dr. Watts in the preface to his
Hymns and Spiritual Songs of 1707, has his eye on Barton
when he says: "I might have brought some Text or other,
and applied it to the Margin of every Verse if this method
had been as Useful as it was easy." [59]

V

THE EVOLUTION OF THE ENGLISH HYMN
FROM DEVOTIONAL POETRY

1. Lack of the Hymnic Motive in Pre-Restoration Poets, Except Wither

The Reformation settlement of Congregational Song on
the basis of the Metrical Psalm was a turning away from the
historic source of Hymnody in the Latin Church.   It involved also an indefinite postponement of any enterprise toward producing an original English Hymnody.   The few
original hymns appended to the Psalters were not so much
a promise and beginning of such a Hymnody as a closing of
the account.   In Churches given over to the singing of
metrical versions of Scripture the motive toward producing
hymns was largely lacking.   Verse writing suggested by
ideals of worship took the current form of paraphrasing

[58]The last ed. of the *Centuries* was in 1768.
[59]P. xi.

the Psalms. Devotional verse felt free to clothe itself in elaborated metres and to express itself in ways alien to the unpoetic mind. To Spenser in Elizabeth's time and to Milton in the Puritan period the "Hymn" meant the same thing. It was a religious ode.

Ben Jonson, on the other hand, kept within the stricter limits in the three hymns appearing in his *Underwoods,* with the result that his "Hymn on the Nativity of my Saviour" is still sung.[60] It is not however in the great poets of any time that we seek the origins and development of Hymnody. Their genius shrinks from liturgical restraints, and their pride from what Tennyson called the commonplaceness of hymns.

Of the first group of religious poets under Elizabeth and James, Southwell was a Roman Catholic priest; and some of his carols and devotional pieces are now regarded as contributions to the Hymnody of his Church. Sir John Davies translated Psalms, but his "Hymnes" were addressed to Queen Elizabeth. The Fletchers aimed at no contribution to Hymnody, though the "Drop, drop, slow tears" of Phineas has been recently adopted.[61] Donne was a convert from Catholicism, and wrote generally in an esoteric style, but his touching lyric "Wilt Thou forgive" was frequently sung in his presence as an anthem by the choristers of St. Paul's Cathedral.[62] Some minor poets of these reigns, such as George Gascoigne, William Hunnis, Sir Nicholas Breton, Humfry Gifford, Francis Kinwelmersh, Timothy Kendall and John Norden, furnish here and there among the more numerous Psalm versions a few simple devotional strains, generally personal and meditative and not intended for music, which may nevertheless be regarded as hymns.[63]

Elizabeth's reign and the years following were noted for

[60] "I sing the birth was born to-night"; no. 63 in *The Oxford Hymn Book,* Clarendon Press, 1908.
[61] No. 98 in *The English Hymnal,* Oxford, 1906.
[62] Walton, *Lives,* 1670.
[63] Most of them may be found in the three volumes of *Select Poetry, chiefly devotional,* published by the Parker Society.

an abundance of lyrical poetry adapted to music for solo
or part singing in the home and friendly circle to the accompaniment of lute or viol. Among the song writers and
musicians, so often amorous or frankly pagan, Dr. Thomas
Campion, who was unquestionably a poet and musician,
deserves also to be ranked as a hymn writer. In his *Two
Bookes of Ayres* (c. 1613), "Pure Hymns, such as the
Seventh Day loves, do lead," the first book being given
over to "Diuine and Morall Songs." In these true spiritual
feeling is combined with lyrical beauty to a very unusual
degree, and a number are indeed hymns even in the practical
sense. His "Never weather-beaten sail more willing beat
to shore" is among the loveliest of the lyrics expressing
the heavenly-home sickness, and was included by Josiah
Conder in his *Congregational Hymn Book* of 1836. His
effective "View me, Lord, a work of Thine" is in *The
Oxford Hymn Book,* and other lyrics are equally available.
Campion in his treatise on Counterpoint showed himself observant of the current Psalmody, but he found
his way to the Hymn through the avenue of the song
book.[64]

Quite apart from the song books, and indeed a marked
exception to the general trend of its time was *The Hymnes
and Songs of the Church* (1623) of George Wither. It is
in two parts, the first of Scriptural paraphrases, the second
of hymns for the festivals, holy days and special occasions
of the church. The hymns show a remarkable appreciation
of the office and character of the Hymn, in their tone of
simple piety, their method and structure. Many of them
were repeated, many added, in Wither's *Halelviah or,
Britans Second Remembrancer* (1641), a personal and
household handbook of praise.

[64]For the song books see *Shorter Elizabethan Poems* in Arber's "English Garner," especially A. H. Bullen's introduction. Campion, long
neglected, is now accessible in Bullen's charming volume, *Thomas
Campion: songs and masques,* London and New York, 1903, in "The
Muses' Library."

But the thing really remarkable is the appearance, so unrelated to its time and surroundings, of this fully formed hymn book for the Church of England. What its effect might have been upon the church worship and upon the development of a Church Hymnody, can only be surmised. Wither, in his ambition and his sore need of money, obtained from James I a patent that his *Hymnes and Songs* should be bound up with every copy issued of the metrical Psalter. The effect of this extraordinary proceeding was disastrous. It aroused the animosity of the Company of Stationers, who resorted to every expedient to make the patent a dead letter until they secured its revocation.[65] They were responsible for preventing the circulation of Wither's hymns; as a result of which the hymns soon passed into oblivion and left singularly little influence behind them.[66]

In the group of sacred poets who flourished in the second quarter of the XVIIth century, Quarles, Herbert, Crashaw, Traherne and Vaughan, and even in Herrick and other of the court group, it is not difficult to find materials more or less available for the hymn book, even though no such use occurred to the writers. Quarles had the ear of the plain people, and contributed six Psalm versions to the famous *Bay Psalm Book* of 1640, but he had little lyrical feeling. It has been thought[67] that some of his *Emblems* might be adapted as hymns. But Traherne's "An Hymn upon St. Bartholomew's Day" is merely meditative verse. Herbert delighted in sacred song, often singing his own pieces to the viol. His actual connection with Hymnody came through the appearance in 1697 of *Select Hymns from Mr.*

[65]See E. Farr's preface to his reprint of *The Hymnes and Songs* in the "Library of Old Authors": and *cf. Notes and Queries* for week ending January 13, 1912.

[66]Two have been rescued, and have found a modest place in modern use:—"Come, O come, with pious lays," and "Behold the Sun that seemed but now." These are perhaps Wither's best.

[67]By Dr. Grosart, who yields Quarles considerable unearned space in Julian's *Dictionary of Hymnology*.

Herbert's Temple, in which a C. M. recension of some of
his verses was attempted, and through his later influence
upon the Wesleys.   In Donne's poetry English devotional
verse had recovered something of the churchly and Catholic
spirit which had been repressed in the Church of England,
and this Herbert inherited from Donne.   But neither sought
or found the plane on which the Congregational Hymn
moves.   Crashaw learned to worship in Herbert's *Temple,*
and published his own religious verses as *Steps to the
Temple* in 1646.   He had gone over to the Church of
Rome, and, apart even from their structure, the mystical
contents of his hymns befit the ascetic retreat rather than
the church.   He turned some of the Latin hymns into
English, and his notable version of *Dies Irae* is among the
earliest English versions.   No doubt Vaughan, who also
learned his spirituality from Herbert, came the nearest of
the group to the spirit and form of the Hymn.   His *Silex
scintillans: or sacred poems and private eiaculations* appeared in 1650 (2nd ed., 1655) ; and from it a considerable
number of hymns have passed into the hymn books.   Of
these the best known are "My soul, there is a countrie" and
"Up to those bright and glorious hills."

The work of this company of devotional poets of the
time of Charles I constitutes no doubt an epoch in the
history of English Sacred Poetry, but it did not either in
intent or in result mark the beginning of an English Hymnody.   It is easy to discern in the poets a common purpose
to set apart their gifts to devotional use, but it is idle to ask
if they might not have dedicated them to the use of public
devotions, to have laid in other words the foundation of an
English Hymnody that should be lyrical.   The public use
of hymns rather than psalms in worship was not as yet in
the air.   Of all the company, Wither alone had it in mind,
and in his conception the Hymn was not lyrical but didactic
and wooden, and as much like current Psalm versions as
might be; as his own proposed *Hymnes,* in such strong contrast with his poetry, so amply prove.

2. The New Hymn Writing (1664-1693): the Predecessors of Watts

But after the Restoration, with the palpable decadence of the newly restored Psalmody in the Church of England, as also among Nonconformists, and with the feeling after hymns that was in both English and Scottish air, there came a decided change in the aim and character of devotional verse. The Metrical Psalm, though it was to linger, had played its part: the paraphrase gave little satisfaction to the conscious or unconscious feeling after hymns; and, with the new demand, devotional feeling and homiletic intent expressed themselves in English hymns. It is likely that the revival of the "Catholic" element in Anglicanism, exhibited in Donne's and Herbert's poetry, played some part in this change by turning the attention of many back to the old church Hymnody of the office books and to the English versions of it always kept extant in England by Roman Catholic poets and in current books of private devotions. This influence appears in the "Psalms" for Sunday and season in the *Sermons and devotions* (1659) of Thomas Pestell, a former chaplain of Charles I; and of which some use as hymns has been made recently. Jeremy Taylor's *The Golden Grove, or a Manual of daily Prayers and Letanies fitted to the days of the week,* (1655) is itself Primerwise, and its hymns are "Festival Hymns according to the manner of the Ancient Church."[68]   Taylor, it is true, did not succeed in finding the plane of the Congregational Hymn, but it will appear that the same influences were not wanting upon some of the earliest of his successors who did.

With Crossman (1664) and Ken (c. 1674) in the English Church, and Austin (1668) who had left it for the

---

[68]Bishop Heber adapted two hymns from *The Golden Grove:* "Lord, come away, why dost Thou stay?" and "Full of mercy, full of love" (*Hymns,* 1827). The former was improved by Lord Nelson for *The Sarum Hymnal* 1868, and passed into *Church Hymns* ("Draw nigh to Thy Jerusalem, O Lord").

Roman, we may begin that succession of modern English hymn writers which has never failed up to the present time.

Samuel Crossman was one of the ejected ministers of 1662, but soon afterward he conformed, and became Dean of Bristol. In 1664 he published *The Young Man's Monitor*, to which was appended (with separate pagination) *The Young Man's Meditation, or some few sacred Poems upon select subjects and Scriptures*. These are in the psalm metres, and are clearly hymns. That they were thought more likely to be read than sung we may infer from the motto used: "A Verse may find him whom a Sermon flies." Two of these hymns were brought to modern notice by Lord Selborne, and are found in current hymnbooks.[69] Crossman's work suggests Puritan rather than Catholic influences.

A striking group of thirty-nine hymns[70] appeared in John Austin's *Devotions, in the ancient way of Offices: with Psalms, Hymns and Prayers; for every day in the week, and every holiday in the year* (Paris, 1668). It was a most influential book, of which four editions preserved its Roman form; and which, modified twice for Anglican use, was reprinted as late as 1856. Except for two or three from Crashaw the hymns are original,[71] and give Austin a distinguished place among the earliest English hymn writers. There is ample evidence that these fervid hymns found immediate acceptance beyond the bounds of Austin's own Church. As we shall see, they were at once appropriated by those endeavoring to introduce Hymnody into the Church of England.

Thomas Ken had been educated at Winchester College under the Puritan regime, and returned to it in some capacity in 1665. In 1674 he published *A Manual of Prayers for the use of the scholars of Winchester College,* which contained the injunction: "Be sure to sing the Morn-

---

[69] "My Song is love unknown," and "My Life's a Shade, my daies."
[70] 43 in 3rd ed.: the additions perhaps by the editor.
[71] The best may be found in Lord Selborne's *Book of Praise*.

ing and Evening Hymn in your chamber devoutly." Though Ken's Morning and Evening hymns, now so well known, were not included in the *Manual* till after 1694, we may conclude that they were thus in use within a few years of the Restoration. In these we can hardly fail to recognize an independent beginning of modern hymn writing and singing; not developed out of Puritan precedents, but suggested by the models of the *Breviary*. The Latin hymns had been sung in the daily services of Winchester College up to the Reformation, and not improbably until Ken's own school days.[72] But in any case a *Breviary, Missal* and several works on the Liturgy were among Ken's cherished books.[73] He was evidently attracted by the old church ritual, and his hymns have caught the tone of the Breviary Hymns.[74]

Bishop Ken's hymns have had a marked influence upon English Hymnody in the direction of simplicity, but it must not be assumed that they had immediate influence upon the situation of their time. The *Manual* was a popular little book, often reprinted, but it is to be remembered that the hymns were not in it till the close of the XVIIth century. They were apparently sung in the school from Ms. or printed sheets, and only in 1692 were published in a pamphlet without Ken's knowledge or approval.[75] Until then at least they could not have been widely known.

Richard Baxter, an ejected minister of 1662, has left on record[76] his enthusiasm for psalm singing, and left also an unpublished version of the Psalms. But his *Poetical Fragments* of 1681 contained several original hymns.[77]

[72]See E. H. Plumptre, *Life of Thomas Ken,* n. d., vol. i, p. 34.

[73]*Ibid.,* vol. ii, appendix ii, p. 297.

[74]Ken plainly knew also Sir Thomas Browne's bedside hymn in *Religio Medici,* "The night is come, like to the day."

[75]See Dr. Julian in his *Dictionary of Hymnology,* 2nd ed., p. 1650.

[76]Epistle to the Reader in *Poetical Fragments,* 1681.

[77]The hymn "Now [Lord] it belongs not to my care," taken from his "My whole, though broken heart, O Lord," is still widely used. His *Paraphrase on the Psalms* was printed in 1692.

They were intended for singing, with the stanzas numbered, and a reference of each hymn to the appropriate psalm-tune. While his contribution to modern Hymnody is but small, his figure seems to have stood for something like a centre of the Restoration Hymn Movement, as the close friend of Mason and apparently the begetter of Barton, who traces his work to Baxter's request that he versify the *Te Deum*.[78]

The work of John Mason, rector of Water-Stratford, was at the time far more influential than Ken's. He published in 1683 *Spiritual Songs, or Songs of Praise to Almighty God upon several occasions. Together with the Song of Songs. . . . paraphrased in English verse.* To this, in 1693, the inferior *Penitential Cries* of his friend Thomas Shepherd were added.

Mason's preface is a call to sing God's praises, and the songs are in the C. M. of the psalm book, and numbered as in a hymn book.[79] They are not paraphrases, but free hymns, and it is curious to note the effort to connect them at least mechanically with the strict paraphrases of Solomon's Song.

Mason worked within the limits of the Church of England, but his close friendship with Baxter and the association of his work with that of the nonconformist Shepherd, indicate no doubt his real position and sympathies. The great circulation and influence of his hymns was among Nonconformists. His book was in its 8th edition at the date of the appearance of Watts' *Hymns*. Mason's work had a great influence on Watts, and must be credited with a considerable share both in moulding and in popularizing the English Hymn.

It thus appears that between the dates of the Restoration and the Revolution there arose a not inconsiderable group of original hymn writers, whose work in volume, in character, and in influence, counted for something in the history

[78] See "Epistle" in his *Two Centuries.*
[79] "My Lord, my Love, was crucified," and "Now from the altar of my heart," are the most familiar.

of the English Hymn. It is clear that these earlier writers deprive Dr. Watts of that extreme originality often ascribed to him as "The father of the English Hymn." And yet we shall not be far out of the way if we regard this earlier group as the Predecessors of Dr. Watts. Their work was necessarily somewhat tentative, because it was not until the appearance of Watts' *Hymns and Spiritual Songs* in 1707 that the type of the English Hymn was definitely determined.

CHAPTER II

THE LITURGICAL USE OF ENGLISH HYMNS

I

THE DENOMINATIONAL DIVISIONS OF CHURCH SONG AT THE RESTORATION (1660)

We have considered the development of the English Hymn from the Metrical Psalm. As the Metrical Psalm had been originally cast into the mould of the Congregational Hymn, the change was in the subject matter rather than in the form. This change we have followed through its several phases, from a close translation of canonical Scripture, to a freer paraphrase first of Psalms then of other Scriptural songs, and up to the point where the purpose of turning Scriptural materials into metre met the impulse to give hymnic form to devotional poetry, and coincided in the production of hymns, freely composed and yet more or less based upon Scripture.

The movement toward hymns was always a liturgical one. It had for its motive the enrichment of English worship rather than of English literature. The same thing was true of the Hymn Movement in the period following the Restoration. But what gave it special significance was the weakened hold of the old Psalmody upon the people, the number of men who concerned themselves with the new movement, and the acceptable character of the new hymns themselves. Under such conditions hymn singing began to be practicable, and there followed almost at once a series of experiments in that direction, out of which has developed the now general practice of singing hymns in English-speaking Churches.

We have now, therefore, to trace these early efforts to introduce the new hymns into public worship. They lie within the same period as the tentative hymn writing with which they were closely related; beginning soon after the Restoration of 1660, and culminating with the publication in 1707 of Watts' *Hymns and Spiritual Songs*, which marked an epoch in the use of hymns as well as in their composition.

During the whole of this period we may exclude Scotland from consideration; for such movement toward hymns as appeared there during these years did not get beyond the "Scripture Songs" stage, and even so far was quite ineffective.

Turning to England, it is to find the ecclesiastical situation such as makes impracticable anything like a concerted movement to introduce hymns into worship. At the Restoration the Church of England regains its established position and reinstates the Prayer Book services. The various communities already formed outside the church, principally Independents, Baptists and Friends, refuse to conform to these services, and become "dissenters." The Presbyterian elements which had maintained Puritan ideals of worship within the Church are by the ejectment of their clergy in 1662 forced to take up a position alongside the dissenters. This whole body of dissent, beyond agreeing in disuse of the Prayer Book, fails to find a common basis for worship; and each of the new sects proceeds to deal with questions of worship in its own way. The breach in the uniformity of English worship thus becomes permanent. The Conventicle Act of 1664 does nothing to heal the breach, and very little in the way of suppressing the novel types of worship.

As with worship in general in the Restoration period, so with Congregational Song in particular. It ceases to be a common stream, but divides into denominational branches. Along these branches severally we have to look for the introduction of hymns into public worship.

II

JOHN PLAYFORD LEADS A MOVEMENT TO INTRODUCE HYMN SINGING IN THE RE-ESTABLISHED CHURCH (1671-1708)

In resuming the Prayer Book services and the old Psalmody at the Restoration, there was much needing to be rehabilitated. The dilapidations of the Commonwealth period told most severely against worship of the cathedral or choral type. The choirs had been scattered, and many of the organs destroyed. But even the reinstatement of Congregational Psalmody in parish churches was effected with some difficulty. The authorities were indifferent, the people unconcerned and irreverent, and the ability to read and sing music was largely lost. John Playford tells us that "almost all the choice tunes are lost, and out of use in our Churches."[1] The practice of lining out the psalm had come in, but even in London there were few parish clerks who could set the tune correctly:—"It having been a custom during the late wars and since to choose men into such places, more for their poverty than skill or ability, whereby this part of God's service hath been so ridiculously performed in most places that it is now brought into scorn and derision by many people."[2]

It was in connection with his efforts to improve these musical conditions that John Playford attempted to introduce the new hymns into parochial worship. He was a music publisher of prominence, with a shop in the Inner Temple, and since 1653 parish clerk of the Temple Church.[3] His *Introduction to the skill of Musick* (London, 1654) was already a standard when in 1671 he issued his *Psalms and Hymns in solemn musick of foure parts on the common*

---

[1] Preface to *Psalms and Hymns,* 1671.
[2] *Ibid.*
[3] The account of this interesting man in *The Dictionary of National Biography* needs to be corrected by that in Grove's *Dictionary of Music;* and the numerous allusions to him in the *Diary* of Mr. Pepys (who often "went to Playford's") add the human touch.

tunes to the Psalms in metre: used in Parish-Churches. Also six Hymns for one voyce to the organ. This book is not a new musical setting of the authorized Psalter with its appendage of hymns, or indeed a Psalter of any sort. It is a selection of "Psalms and Hymns" mingling together for the first time on a common footing. The hymns are not segregated, but interspersed among the psalms; each hymn following the psalm tune to which it is set. The psalms were chosen from various current Psalters, including the authorized *Sternhold and Hopkins.* The hymns number seventeen.[4] Of these, fourteen are taken from John Austin's Roman Catholic *Devotions in the ancient way of Offices,* published three years earlier. The remaining three seem to have been written or acquired for this book, and deserve mention in connection with early hymn writing. One in C.M. (to "Canterbury Tune") begins "O Lord my Saviour and support": one in the metre of the 148th Psalm begins "Praise to our God proclaim"; and both are anonymous. The third, entitled "A Hymn for Good Friday," begins "See, sinful soul, thy Saviour's suffering see," and is signed "W. Stroud, D.D."

None of these hymns was introduced into church use by means of Playford's book, which was not kindly received. He attributed its failure to its folio size and its not containing all the Psalms in their order, which "made it not so useful to carry to Church."[5] To which considerations must be added the fact that the tunes, partly from Ravenscroft and partly new, were arranged for male voices, and were beyond the reach of the skill of the period. Apart from such inconveniences of detail, Playford's general proposal of substituting a selection of "Psalms and Hymns" for the accepted system of Psalmody was too precipitate.

Having thus made his first venture with a musician's independence and failed, Playford turned a publisher's eye

[4] The six "Divine Songs for One Voyce" at the end of the book may be excluded as not being hymns in the usual sense of the word.
[5] Preface of 1677.

toward the actual market. He made up his mind that what was practicable was an edition of the *Old Version* in portable size to take the place of Ravenscroft's, with some infelicities of the ancient text corrected, and with the tunes set in plain counterpoint for mixed voices. In 1677 he published: *The whole Book of Psalms: with the usual Hymns and Spiritual Songs; together with all the ancient and proper tunes sung in churches, with some of later use. Compos'd in three parts, cantus, medius, & bassus: in a more plain and useful method than hath been formerly published.*

The phrase "with the usual Hymns" creates the impression that in profiting by his experience of 1671 Playford gave over his attempt to introduce new hymns, and was now simply reprinting the hymns that had always been appended to the *Old Version.* He did, in fact, drop all but one of the hymns offered in 1671; and we may infer that they had not proved acceptable. But in his preface he still maintains the parity of psalms and hymns, and cites the precedents of "The usual Hymns" and of Barton's *Two Centuries of select Hymns.* In the body of his book he preserves the form of the original appendages of hymns, one before and one following the psalms, but he deals very freely with the contents. In the group before the psalms he retains the *Veni Creator, Te Deum, Benedictus, Magnificat* and *Nunc Dimittis* of the *Old Version,* adds Cosin's *Veni Creator,* and provides new metrical versions of the Lord's Prayer, Creed and Commandments. The group following the psalms, entitled "The Rest of the Solemn Hymns," begins with the *Benedicite,* followed by four of the *Old Version* hymns (the Humble Suit, the Lamentation, "O Lord in Thee," and the Prayer after the Commandments). Then follow:

Hymn after Communion, "All glory be to God on high" (a version of *Gloria in Excelsis*).

Hymn for Sunday, "Behold we come dear Lord to thee" (by John Austin).

Morning Hymn, "Now that the Day-star doth arise" (Cosin's version of *Jam lucis orto sidere*).

Hymn on Divine Use of Musick, "We sing to thee whos wisdom form'd" (it had appeared in Dr. Natl. Ingelo's *Bentivoglio and Urania*, London, 1660).

Remembering that Playford was adapting himself to current taste, both his freedom in dealing with the old hymns of the Psalter and his restraint in introducing new hymns show how slight a hold hymns of any sort had upon the people. The actual influence of Playford's book was by way of prolonging the period of psalm singing. It became the standard setting of the *Old Version*. During the rest of the XVIIth and for much of the XVIIIth century it was the dependence of these who clung to the old ways, reaching its twentieth edition in 1757. During this long period Playford's appendages of hymns kept their place in his Psalter, and his Psalter was carried to church by great numbers of people. But it cannot be affirmed that they made much more use of the new hymns than their fathers had made of the hymns originally printed in the Psalters. An addiction to the continued use of the *Old Version* became, in fact, the particular form in which indifference or opposition to hymns expressed itself.

But at the opening of the XVIIIth century two books appeared that aimed at the introduction of hymns into parochial worship; in the one case as supplementing the use of the *Old Version*, in the other that of the *New*. The more ambitious of these two books was the private venture of Henry Playford, who had succeeded to the business of his father, John Playford, and was ambitious to carry forward his father's work. He published in 1701 *The Divine Companion; or, David's Harp new tun'd. Being a choice collection of new and easy Psalms, Hymns, and Anthems. The words of the Psalms being collected from the newest versions. Compos'd by the best Masters and fitted for the use of those, who already understand Mr. John Playford's Psalms in three parts. To be used in churches or private families, for their greater advancement of divine music.* This book was designed as a supplement to the *Old Version* used in the churches, with a view to its being bound up with John Playford's musical edition first published in 1677. Its plan and purpose, however, were taken from the earlier Playford book of 1671. It opened with six Psalm versions set to tunes by Dr. Blow. These were followed by twelve hymns set by various composers, to which in later editions more hymns were added. At the end was a group of anthems. In the hymns John Austin predominates, as he did in 1671; but Crashaw, Herbert and Drummond are also represented.

The Divine Companion had a temporary success; that is to say, its reprinting was several times called for. This success is to be attributed mainly to its tunes rather than to the richness of its hymnody, but the words of the hymns set to the new tunes cannot have been altogether overlooked. To what extent or in what quarters they may have been introduced into parochial worship does not appear. Such use was readily accomplished in parishes where lining was practised. Not one of them played any part in the future hymnody of the Church of England. It may be, on the other hand, that Playford's book exercised a certain influence in keeping the idea of hymn singing before the mind of the Church of England.

The other of the books referred to as appearing at the opening of the XVIIIth century was much more modest in form, but it had a more substantial backing, and was to prove much more influential. It was directly connected with the current movement to improve Psalmody represented by the *New Version* of Tate and Brady published in 1696.[6] Even the party of progress in Psalmody was no doubt more immediately concerned to get a more literary version of the Psalms than to introduce hymns. The *New Version* first appeared without music and without even "the usual hymns," but in all probability a provision of suitable tunes and a small appendage of hymns was a part of the original scheme. At the end of the second edition of

[6]See chapter i, part iv.

1698 there is an announcement of "A Supplement to the New Version," to contain "The Usual Hymns," "Select Psalms done in particular Measures," with "A Collection of the most usual Church-Tunes." It contains also a promise of "Additional Hymns for the Holy Sacrament, Festivals, &c."

The *Supplement to the New Version of Psalms by Dr. Brady and Mr. Tate* appeared in 1700 (London, printed by J. Heptinstall), in sheets with a view to binding up with the *New Version*. In respect of hymns, the standpoint of the *Supplement* differs little from that of Playford's *Whole Book*. It has sixteen hymns in all. Ten are simply fresh paraphrases (in the fluent style of the *New Version* itself) of "the usual hymns." The "Additional Hymns" promised in the advertisement are six:

1. *Song of the Angels at the Nativity.* "While Shepherds watch'd their Flocks by Night."
2. *For Easter-Day* [*First Hymn*]. "Since Christ, our Passover, is slain."
3. [*Second Hymn*]. "Christ from the Dead is rais'd, and made."
Three Hymns for Holy Communion.
4. Hymn I. "Thou God, all Glory, Honour, Pow'r."
5. Hymn II. "All ye, who faithful Servants are."
6. Hymn III. *The Thanksgiving in the Church Communion-Service.* "To God be Glory, Peace on Earth."

These also are paraphrases, five of Scriptural passages, one of the *Gloria in Excelsis;* and the Scripture texts are noted here as carefully as by William Barton himself. This little group of hymns, marking no advance in principle over Playford's, was yet of much more significance in the history of the Hymn; owing to its association with the *New Version* which looked toward the future rather than with the *Old Version* which was a survival from the past. These hymns were thus sown on comparatively good ground, and if they did not spring up immediately and if they did not multiply, they, at all events, were not trodden under the feet of the psalm singers.

The *Supplement to the New Version* was authorized for

use in churches by the Queen and Council on July 30, 1703. It became a very popular little book, often reprinted, but not a constituent part of the Psalter, as the appendages of the *Old Version* had been. It is the exception rather than the rule to find the *Supplement* even bound in with the XVIIIth century copies of *Tate and Brady,* which have survived in great numbers. It follows that the hymns of the *Supplement* could not have been sung as freely as the psalms in churches using *Tate and Brady,* unless they were lined out. But they evoked a limited interest, which it was attempted to quicken by adding three hymns to the sixth edition of 1708.[7]

This group of hymns in the *Supplement* marks the limit of anything in the nature of an authorized provision for hymn singing in the Church of England during the period under review. It was sufficient to establish the principle that hymns were allowable as supplementary to the psalms. The actual practice of parochial hymn singing which it represents must seem small, when we remember that *Tate and Brady* was only then making headway into London churches, and for long afterward was hardly known beyond the bounds of that diocese. These hymns served for a beginning in a time of apathy and musical decadence, and were destined under happier conditions to be taken up and enlarged in number, and even to be embodied within the sacred covers of the Prayer Book itself as a recognized feature of Church of England worship.

The *Supplement* does not, of course, stand for the whole body of hymn singing within the Church of England at the time. There was no likelihood of interference with the general or occasional use of other hymns from the various books that were, as we have seen, available; and it is altogether likely that they found such use by some of progressive spirit. And we have also to take account of the ad-

---

[7]They were the *Benedicite* and a recast of "O Lord, turn not thy Face away," from the *Old Version* appendage, and the "Hymn on the Divine Use of Musick" from Playford's Psalter of 1677.

vances toward hymn singing on that Puritan side of the
Church which had least regard for the Prayer Book system,
under the leadership of such men as Barton, Baxter, and
Mason, and the Puritan recurrence to the hymns appended
to the *Old Version.*

III

RICHARD BAXTER LEADS A MOVEMENT TO INTRODUCE HYMNS AMONG THE EJECTED PRESBYTERIANS (1661-1708)

The subject-matter of Congregational Song was one of
the very numerous issues raised by the Presbyterian divines
in the Church of England before the Savoy Conference of
1661 called by Charles II "to advise upon and review the
said Book of Common prayer."[8]   They took the Puritan
attitude of seeking for "a purer version" than the accepted
Sternhold and Hopkins. The XIIth of their exceptions
against the liturgy was as follows:

"XII. Because singing of Psalms is a considerable part of Publick
Worship, we desire that the Version set forth and allowed to be
sung in Churches may be mended, or 'that we may have leave to
make use of a purer Version."

In Baxter's "Reformed Liturgy," which seems to have
been presented at the same time,[9] there is something like a
bill of particulars:

"Concerning the Psalms for Publick use. We desire that, instead of
the imperfect version of the Psalms in Meeter now in use, Mr. William
Bartons Version, and that perused and approved by the Church of

[8]For the King's warrant for the Conference, see *The Grand Debate
between the most Reverend the Bishops, and the Presbyterian Divines,
appointed by His Sacred Majesty, as Commissioners for the review
and alteration of the Book of Common Prayer, &c. London, Printed
1661,* p. (iv.): more fully in E. Cardwell's *Conferences . . . connected with the revision of the Book of Common Prayer,* Oxford, 2nd
ed, 1841, pp. 298 ff.

[9]*Cf.* Cardwell, *op. cit.,* p. 260.

Scotland there in use (being the best that we have seen) may be received and corrected by some skilful men, and both allowed (for grateful variety) to be Printed together on several Columes or Pages, and publickly used; At least until a better than either of them shall be made." [10]

In view of the actual status of Psalmody in the Church of England, and of the terms of the King's warrant, it is not surprising that the bishops should have answered the Presbyterian exception and desire by saying, "Singing of Psalms in metre is no part of the Liturgy, and so no part of our commission." [11] But the Presbyterians chose to regard this as quibbling, and replied:

"If the word *Liturgy* signifie the publick Worship, God forbid we should exclude the singing of Psalms: And sure you have no fitter way of singing than in Meeter. . . . We hope you make no question, whether singing Psalms, and Hymns were part of the Primitive Liturgy, and seeing they are set forth, and allowed to be sung in all Churches of all the people together, why should they be denied to be part of the Liturgy? We understand not the reason of this." [12]

In "The Grounds of Nonconformity of the Ministers who were Ejected," afterwards drawn up by Calamy, among "other things . . . by some possibly less regarded" was that in order to subscribe to the Prayer Book "They must consent to the Mistranslation of the Psalter." [13]

' These extracts make it abundantly plain that the Presbyterians had much zeal for psalm singing, and that they demanded authorization for a more correct version of the Scripture Psalms. But they make it equally clear that an insistence that congregational song be confined to canonical Psalms or even to Scriptural songs was no part of the Presbyterian position or demand. They raised no objection

[10] *A Petition for Peace: with the reformation of the Liturgy. As it was presented to the Right Reverend Bishops, by the Divines appointed by His Majesties Commission to treat with them about the alteration of it. London, printed Anno Dom. MDCLXI.,* p. 41.

[11] Cardwell, *op. cit.,* p. 342.

[12] *The Grand Debate,* p. 79.

[13] Edmund Calamy, *An Abridgement of Mr. Baxter's History of his Life and Times,* etc., 2nd ed., London, 1713, vol. i, p. 234.

to the hymns of the *Old Version* bound up with the Prayer Book, whether paraphrases or "of human composure." On the contrary the "Reformed Liturgy" drawn up by Baxter, but laid before the Savoy Conference with the general consent of the Presbyterian divines,[14] as a desired alternative to certain parts of *The Book of Common Prayer*,[15] contains this rubric at the end of "The Order of celebrating the Sacrament of the Body and Blood of Christ": "Next sing some part of the Hymn in meeter, or some other fit Psalm of Praise (as the 23. 116. or 103. or 100, &c.)."[16] The hymn referred to is the Thanksgiving at the end of the *Old Version* ("The Lord be thanked for his gifts") ; and the rubric reflects the accustomed use by these divines not only of this hymn but of others appended to the Psalter, with a special predilection for the metrical paraphrases of Prayer Book canticles.

"Those that published the Old Church-Psalms," Baxter said in the preface to his own posthumous *Paraphrase on the Psalms of David in metre, with other Hymns* (London 1692), "added many useful Hymns, that are still printed with the Psalms in Metre." And he makes clear the actual limits of the Presbyterian position by saying in explanation of the literalness of his own version of the Scripture Psalms, —"I durst not venture on the Paraphrastical great liberty of others; I durst make Hymns of my own, or explain the Apocryphal; but I feared adding to God's Word, and making my own to pass for God's."

Baxter's hymn making has been already referred to; but he was in fact the leader at once of the Presbyterians and of the movement to introduce hymn singing into the churches. He was, as has already been said, "the only begetter" of William Barton's *Centuries of Hymns,* which

[14]Calamy, *op. cit.,* vol. 1, p. 158.

[15]The petition was that "the several particulars" of this liturgy "be inserted into the several respective places" of the Prayer Book, "and left to the Ministers choice to use the one or the other." *A Petition for Peace,* p. 22.

[16]*Ibid.,* p. 58.

began to appear in 1659, but he occupied ground far in advance of Barton's ventures. He held that hymns had been sung from the beginning; that "doubtless Paul meaneth not only David's Psalms, when he bids men sing with grace in their hearts, Psalms, and Hymns, and Spiritual Songs: Yea, it is past doubt, that Hymns more suitable to Gospel-times, may and ought to be now used: And if used, they must be premeditated; how else shall Congregations sing them? And if premeditated, they must be some way imposed; How else shall the Congregations all joyn in the same."[17]

It is not likely that most, or perhaps many, of Baxter's colleagues shared to the full these advanced views of his singularly independent mind and temper: nor did his influence establish a distinctive Presbyterian usage of hymn singing. The years following the Ejectment of 1662 were years of poverty and distress, if not of actual persecution, for many of the ministers who had been driven from their parsonages and livings. The Conventicle Act and the Five Mile Act interfered with the assembling of Presbyterian congregations. The groups of people who still gathered about their ejected pastors for the simple rites of worship, so far as they ventured to sing at all, doubtless satisfied their craving for a purer version of the Psalms by employing some one of the current Psalters of the more literal type.

With the Revolution of 1688 and the Toleration Act of William and Mary in the year following, Presbyterian worship came under the sanction of the law, and in a single generation hundreds of Presbyterian meeting houses were built throughout England. They conformed to a common pattern. Internally the great canopied pulpit dominated: beneath it a desk for the precentor, or, more often, "the table pew," with the communion table in the centre, and around it the seats which were then or later occupied by the singers on non-sacramental occasions.[18] In the failure

---

[17]Preface to *Paraphrase on the Psalms.*
[18]*Cf.* A. H. Drysdale, *History of the Presbyterians in England,* London, 1889, p. 443.

to establish any church organization, no general principle
regulated the congregational song, and no book was provided for common use by the congregations. Psalm singing
prevailed, and the Scottish *Psalms of David in meeter of
1650* seems to have been adopted pretty generally. The
pastors were free to supplement the psalms with hymns,
and, in the prevalence of the practice of "lining," could
accomplish it without providing books for the congregation.
Among the ministers of the later or meeting house era of
Presbyterianism there was much diversity of sentiment and
practice in the matter of hymn singing. Matthew Henry,
who, like Baxter, took great delight in Psalmody, both in
public and private, favored hymn singing but preferred
Scriptural psalms and hymns to those wholly of human
composition as likely to have more of matter and less of
fancy.[19] He prepared and printed in 1695 a little volume
of *Family Hymns,* altered and enlarged in a second edition
of 1702. It was designed to encourage Psalmody in the
home and thus to improve the singing in church, and was
introduced by him into his own services.[20] With the exception of *Te Deum,* the hymns are taken from Scripture,
current translations being freely used. Verses out of several Psalms are gathered together to make up a hymn, in
the manner of Barton, with whose standpoint Henry's book
may be said to agree.

On the other hand James Pierce of Exeter, whose Arian
leanings were not yet suspected, held the strictest views in
the way of confining Church Song to the inspired Psalms,
discontinuing even the use of the doxology. In his *Vindi-
ciae fratrum dissentientium in Anglia*[21] he argued for the

[19] J. B. Williams, *Memoirs of the Rev. Matthew Henry,* London,
1828, p. 110.

[20] *Ibid.,* p. 110.

[21] London, 1710. In English, as *A Vindication of the Dissenters,*
London, 1717. In 1786 Mr. Brand Hollis reprinted from it *A Tractate
on Music* (London), for distribution in the First Church of Boston,
with a view to meeting the movement to procure an organ for that
church.

use of "plain tunes," and, strenuously, against the employment of instrumental music, Pierce's attitude toward hymns
was exceptional rather than characteristic of the Presbyterianism of the time; and it is quite likely that any who
shared in it may have sought an Old Testament Psalmody
as offering an available refuge from rising Christological
perplexities.

The temper and tone of current English Presbyterianism
was better represented in the persons of the Presbyterian
divines of Dublin and the south of Ireland. It had indeed
been carried there by the eminent Joseph Boyse, just as
the Scottish type had been transplanted in the North of
Ireland. By his hymn writing Boyse is entitled to a place
among the predecessors of Dr. Watts, but in view of the
lack of permanence[22] in his contributions to Hymnody,
he is more interesting as one of the early leaders in Presbyterian hymn singing. He published in 1693 *Sacramental
Hymns collected (chiefly) out of such passages of the New
Testament as contain the most suitable matter of Divine
Praises in the celebration of the Lord's Supper. To which
is added one hymn relating to Baptism and another to the
Ministry. By J. Boyse, with some by other hands.* This
appeared at Dublin, and in the same year at London from
the press of Thomas Parkhurst, the printer of Matthew
Henry's *Family Hymns.* It contains forty-one pieces by
Boyse, one by George Herbert, and two by Simon Patrick;
and in the baptismal hymn immersion is the only mode
recognized. In 1701 he published at Dublin *Family Hymns
for morning and evening worship. With some for the
Lord's Days. . . . All taken out of the Psalms of David.*
To each volume is prefixed the recommendation of six
Dublin ministers, a significant testimony as to local sentiment and usage.

Of Boyse's resolute Presbyterianism there can be no
question. But if we take the whole body of Noncon-

[22]Two stanzas by him were included in James Martineau's *Hymns
for the Christian Church and Home,* London, 1840 (No. 42).

formist meeting houses in England at the beginning of the XVIIIth century, it is by no means easy to make partition of them between Presbyterians and Independents, who showed so marked a disposition to affiliate. This uncertainty applies to the sentiments of the congregations, to the affiliations of the ministers who occupied the pulpits, even to the terms of the trust-deeds by which the meeting houses were held. And it applies, of course, to the hymn singing. Presbyterianism was not destined to establish itself in England, and its meeting houses were about to fall into the control of men of Arian theology. The congregational song of these meetings was first to come under the domination of Dr. Watts, and then to develop into a Unitarian Hymnody. Apart from this stream of Church Song, thus diverted from its original channel, the early Presbyterian hymn singing seems to have no part or representation in the great Hymn Movement of the XVIIIth century, which it is customary to trace to its source in Independency. But the actual facts seem to be that behind the early Nonconformist hymn singing there was no Independent leader before Watts so influential and so outspoken as Richard Baxter, and that the Presbyterian divines had an inadequately recognized share in laying the foundations of modern English Hymnody.

Too little notice has been taken, for instance, of the efforts of Samuel Bury, a Presbyterian leader in Suffolk. He made a careful study of all available sources of hymns, and (apparently some years before Watts first printed his hymns), published *A Collection of Psalms, Hymns, and Spiritual Songs, fitted for morning and evening worship in a private family,* but containing also sacramental hymns. He prefixed a long list of his sources, including among others Barton, Baxter, Boyse, Crashaw, Dorrington, Burgess, Herbert, Patrick, Mason and Shepherd, Tate and Brady, and Woodford. His work stands in the shadow of his great contemporary and looms small there; but in view of the fact that Bury's book reached a third edition in 1713 and a fourth in 1724, it could not have been without influence upon the situation.[23]

As pointing apparently in the same direction, mention may be made of a movement to better congregational singing in the last years of the older London Presbyterianism. Moved by the unsatisfactory conditions of public worship and especially of the neglect and unskillful performance of Psalmody in Nonconformist churches, a Society of gentlemen in the (then) Presbyterian Meeting at the King's Weigh House in Little Eastcheap employed a teacher of Psalmody and established a course of Friday lectures. The Psalmody Lectures were published by them in 1708 as *Practical Discourses of Singing in the worship of God: preach'd at the Friday Lecture in Eastcheap. By several Ministers.* Of the six lecturers all but one were Presbyterian ministers.[24]

This movement was not primarily to encourage the introduction of hymn singing, but it tended strongly that way. The opening lecturer declared: "I conceive that whatever Songs are Scriptural, are the proper Object of Singing. . . . For I can by no means be of their mind, who in the public Congregations would confine us to that collection of the *Jewish Psalmody,* which is call'd the *Psalms of David.*"[25] The fourth lecturer approves Mr. Stennett's hymns as

[23]The fullest notice of Bury's book is in J. Conder, *The Poet of the Sanctuary,* London, 1851, p. 35. For Bury himself, see *The Dict. of Nat. Biography,* and the references there, especially Murch's *Hist. of Presb. and Genl. Bapt. Churches in W. of England,* 1835, pp. 107 ff. The date of Bury's book is unknown to the writer. It seems to be referred to in the advt. at end of Henry's *Family Hymns,* 1702.

[24]They were Jabez Earle, William Harris, Thomas Reynolds, John Newman and Benjamin Gravener. That the sixth, Thomas Bradbury, was Independent, aided perhaps to broaden the reach of the movement. He was a singular selection. He knew nothing of music, was without poetical taste, became the great opponent of Dr. Watts' scheme for improving Psalmody, refused to allow Watts' Psalms or Hymns to be sung in his presence, and used Patrick's version to the end of his life. *Cf.* W. Wilson, *History and Antiquities of Dissenting Churches . . . in London,* London, 1808-14, vol. iii, pp. 527, 528.

[25]Mr. Earle: p. 4.

"those excellent Composures wherewith" he "hath oblig'd the Christian Church."[26]   The fifth lecturer commends Mr. Watts' views of a New Testament Hymnody in the essay prefixed to the *Hymns* of 1707, which he has "seen since the Composure of this Discourse."[27]   The last lecture is a review of the part played by psalm singing since the Reformation, and the frequent quotations from *Tate and Brady* suggest that the lecturer[28] was content to sing their *New Version* of the Psalter.

This interesting movement[29] began before the publication of Watts' *Hymns,* and was inspired by the same distress at the conditions of Nonconformist Psalmody.   Originally independent of him, it came to accept his leadership.   W. Lawrence, the teacher of Psalmody at the Weigh House, had made a Ms. collection of tunes for "The Gentlemen of the Society" supporting the Friday Lecture.   Upon the appearance of Watts' *The Psalms of David imitated,* the collection was at once adapted to it, and published the same year as *A Collection of Tunes suited to the various metres in Mr. Watts's Imitation of the Psalms of David or Dr. Patrick's Version, fit to be bound up with either* (London, by W. Pearson for John Clark, 1719).[30]   The Gentlemen of the Friday Lecture continued their good work for congregational singing many years.   But Lawrence's book has already brought us to the period at which Dr. Watts' Psalms and Hymns began to dominate the worship of the old Presbyterian Meetings.

[26]Mr. Reynolds: p. 103.

[27]Mr. Newman: p. 154.

[28]Mr. Gravener.

[29]J. S. Curwen in his *Studies in Worship Music,* 1st Series, London, n. d., p. 88, credits it to the "Independents."

[30]Cf. *Hymns ancient and modern: Historical edition,* London, 1909, pp. lxxxv, lxxxvi. Lawrence's successor, Nathaniel Gawthorn, published *Harmonia Perfecta, a complete Collection of Psalm Tunes in four parts* (London, 1730), chiefly transposed from Ravenscroft, and dedicated "To the Gentlemen who support the Friday Lecture in Eastcheap; and for a course of years have encouraged Psalmody."

IV

THE ATTITUDE OF THE SEPARATISTS

We now turn to consider the situation in those religious bodies which had already formed dissenting communities outside the walls of the Church of England, and entered upon the Restoration period with traditions already acquired. There were marked divergences in their attitude not only toward psalm singing but toward Congregational Praise itself as a Christian ordinance. Two of these bodies, the Arminian Baptists and the Society of Friends, on the one hand, had taken up an attitude of actual hostility toward singing in public worship. The other two, the Calvinistic Baptists and the Independents, had struggled against the spread of the same hostility within their ranks, and during the period now under review emerged from the struggle to become jointly instrumental in introducing the English Hymn into actual liturgical use.

At the left we may group together the General or Arminian Baptists and the Society of Friends, as sharing the opinion that singing by the congregation should have no place in the public worship of God.

1. THE GENERAL BAPTISTS OPPOSE "PROMISCUOUS SINGING"

To explain the origins of the great "Controversie of Singing," and the attitude of the General Baptists in England toward Congregational Song, we must go back to about the year 1606,[31] when John Smyth, pastor of a congregation of Separatists at Gainsborough, led his people in a flight to Amsterdam. Once there he found that his real sympathies were not with the principles and practices of the congregation of English exiles already on the ground, but rather with the Dutch Mennonites. He developed intense antipathy to infant baptism, and, failing to secure believers' baptism

[31]Henry M. Dexter, *The true Story of John Smyth*, Boston, 1881, p. 2.

at the hands of the Mennonites, in 1608 baptized himself, thus becoming "the Se-Baptist of Church history."[32]   He formed a separate congregation with anti-Calvinistic principles, adopting not only the theology of the Mennonites, but many of those peculiar practices of their worship that anticipated the Quaker meeting.

In setting forth *The Differences of the Churches of the Separation* (n. pl., 1608), Smyth held that the New Covenant is spiritual, proceeding out of the heart, and that reading out of a book is no part of spiritual worship, but an invention of the man of sin. "We hold, that seeing singing a psalm is a part of spiritual worship, it is unlawful to have the book before the eye in time of singing a psalm."[33] These principles reduce the possibility of singing in worship to the instance of an individual feeling impelled to compose and utter a spontaneous song.   And Robert Baillie testifies that such was the practice in Smyth's congregation.[34]

After the formation of the denomination of General Baptists in England as the result of the labors of Smyth and his disciples, Thomas Grantham, as their mouthpiece, published his *Christianismus Primitivus* (London 1678). In this he held that the New Testament recognizes no promiscuous singing, and no singing by the rules of art, but only the utterance of psalms and hymns sung by such as God hath fitted thereto by the help of His Spirit for the edification of the listening church.   If all sing, there were none to be edified; if pleasant tunes are used, that would bring music and instruments back; if other men's words are sung, that would open the way to the similar use of forms of prayer also.

At a General Baptist Assembly in 1689 it appeared that

[32]Ed. Arber, *Story of the Pilgrim Fathers*, London, 1897, p. 137.

[33]Quoted from the copy in Bodleian Library by R. Barclay, *The Inner Life of the Religious Societies of the Commonwealth*, 2nd ed., London, 1877, p. 106.

[34]*A Dissvasive from the errours of the times*, London, 1645.

a small minority of congregations had begun "promiscuous" singing of psalms. The Assembly called upon them to show "what psalms they made use of for the matter, and what rules they did settle upon for the manner." In response there was produced

"Not the metres composed by Messrs. Sternhold and Hopkins, but a book of metres composed by one Mr. Barton, and the rules produced to sing these Psalms as set down *secundum artem;* viz., as the musicians do sing according to their gamut,—*Sol, fa, la, my, ray,* &c., &c.; which appeared so strangely foreign to the evangelical worship that it was not conceived anywise safe for the churches to admit such carnal formalities; but to rest satisfied in this, till we can see something more perfect in this case, that as prayer of one in the church is the prayer of the whole, as a church, so the singing of one in the church is the singing of the whole church; and as he that prayeth in the church is to perform the service as of the ability which God giveth, even so, he that singeth praises in the church ought to perform that service as of the ability received of God; that as a mournful voice becomes the duty of prayer, so a joyful voice, with gravity, becomes the duty of praising God with a song in the Church of God." [35]

This judgment, received with "the general approbation of the Assembly," is interesting not only as showing that the great majority had not advanced a step beyond the position of Grantham in 1671, but also for the circumstances that occasioned it, as showing the movement of the time beginning to penetrate the isolation of a peculiar sect. It seems to have got no farther within General Baptist circles during the period under review. There is apparently no record of a change of practice until well toward the middle of the XVIIIth century. In 1733 the General Assembly received a complaint from Northamptonshire that some of its churches "had fallen into the way of singing the Psalms of David, or other men's composures, with tunable notes, and a mixed multitude; which way of singing appears to us wholly unwarrantable from the Word of God." But the mood or judgment of the Assembly had at length changed. It admitted that congregational singing was an innovation, practised by "some very few," yet was not a sufficient

[35] J. J. Goadby, *Bye-Paths in Baptist History,* London, n. d., pp. 347, 348.

ground for excluding them. The Assembly could find no clear statement in Scripture as to the manner of singing. It would that all were of one mind, "but as the weakness of human understanding is such that things appear in different lights to different persons, such a concord is rather to be desired than expected in this world. It expressed on the whole an unwillingness to dispute the question or to impose upon all the general opinion and practice.[36]

It may be inferred that the influence of Dr. Watts had begun to be felt by General Baptists, but their actual associations were closer with the later Wesleyan movement. And it was by means of the fervid influences of the Methodist Revival that General Baptist churches were to be multiplied and to become hymn singing churches.

2. THE SOCIETY OF FRIENDS EXCLUDES "CONJOINT SINGING"

The Society of Friends took up a position that opposed singing as practised in the public worship of the time and led to the exclusion of all song from their own meetings. Whether, with Hodgkin,[37] we regard George Fox as an original thinker, or conclude with R. Barclay[38] that his tenets and practices were to a large extent borrowed from the Mennonites and Arminian Baptists, there can be no doubt of the wide area of opinion and practice held by them in common. There is no appreciable difference between the General Baptist and the Quaker position as regards Church Song. It is to be remembered also that Fox's movement was, like that of the General Baptists, an immediate revolt not from Laudian Episcopacy but from Puritan theology and practice. While he "was to bring people off from all the world's religions, which are vain, . . . and prayings, and singings, which stood in forms without power,"[39] and

---

[36]Goadby, *op. cit.*, p. 348.
[37]Thomas Hodgkin, *George Fox*, London, 1896, p. vi.
[38]*Op. cit.*, chap. v.
[39]Quoted in Hodgkin's *George Fox*, p. 35.

while he held up mass book and common prayer and directory to unpartitioned scorn, it was the *Directory* which immediately confronted him, and the Puritan Psalmody which constituted the "singings" audible by him.

The early Friends were not opposed to all singing in public worship. Among several references thereto in Fox's *Journal* is one of 1655 to the effect that "Tho: Holme & Eliz: Holme: att a meetinge in Underbarrow: were much exercised by ye power of ye Lorde in songes and Hymms & made melody & rejoyced: & ye life was raised thereby & refreshed in many: in y^t meetinge."[40] Three years later Fox wrote: "Those who are moved to sing with understanding, making melody to the Lord in their hearts we own; *if it be in meeter,* we own it."[41] By an official pronouncement of the Yearly Meeting of 1675 "Serious sighing, sencible groaning and reverent singing" are recognized as divers operations of the Spirit and power of God, and not to be quenched or discouraged, unless immoderate.[42] This evidently refers to the utterance of an individual, under the direct motion of the Spirit. As formulated by Barclay in his *Apology*,[43] (11th proposition, § 26) the singing of psalms is a true part of God's worship, but the formal customary way of singing in the congregation has no Scriptural nor even Christian ground. To put expressions of the religious experiences of blessed David into the mouths of the wicked and profane is to make them utter great and horrid lies in the sight of God. Acceptable singing must proceed from the Spirit indwelling in the heart. Artificial music, of organs or vocal, has no New Testament warrant.

[40]*The Journal of George Fox, ed. from the Mss. by Norman Penney,* Cambridge, at the University Press, 1911, vol. ii, p. 326. All the references to singing in worship seem to have been left unprinted until this edition appeared (see vol. i. p. 442) ; a fact not without suggestiveness.

[41]G. Fox and Huggerthorne, *Truth's Defence against the refined subtility of the Serpent,* 1658, p. 21.

[42]See R. Barclay, *op. cit.,* p. 461.

[43]"Printed in the year 1678" (n. p.) ; pp. 288, 289.

The singing thus recognized has been compared to that of the singing evangelist introduced in the Moody and Sankey campaigns,[44] but seems more akin to the inspirational utterances of the early Christian assemblies. Such as it was, it was strongly opposed by some from the first,[45] and soon died out. "Conjoint" singing of psalms or hymns taken from a book or the lips of a precentor, was never at any time tolerated in the Friends' meetings. It ranged in Fox's mind with images and crosses, prescribed prayers and sprinkling of infants, as one of the vain traditions and worldly ceremonials from which it was his peculiar mission to deliver men. So far as the actual practice of the meetings is concerned, the result would have been the same in any case, as the repudiation of the musical art by the early Friends must soon have made congregational song quite impracticable.

With this attitude of opposition to the established Psalmody, the Friends, of course, have had no part in its transition to our modern hymn singing. Members of that body have not hesitated to contribute hymns to the common stock, but only in the last half century or so has a movement begun in England and America to introduce general hymn singing (even the hymnal with musical notes) into the Quaker meeting.

3. Benjamin Keach Introduces Hymns among the Particular Baptists

Among the Particular (or Calvinistic) Baptists there was, to say the least, nothing like unanimity in agreeing with their Arminian brethren concerning Congregational Song.

The very full records of the Broadmead Church of Bristol left by Edward Terrill are silent on this point from 1640 to 1670. But from 1671 to 1685 they show that congregational singing was stately practised, under all the

---

[44] R. Barclay, pp. 461, 462.
[45] R. Barclay, p. 462; Fox's *Journal*, vol. i. p. 442.

menaces of persecution.[46] There was, however, a second Baptist congregation in Bristol; and, when in 1675, a joint meeting was proposed, some of its members "were ready to sing Psalms with others beside the church," but a minority "Scrupled to sing in metre as [the Psalms] were translated," and asked permission to keep their hats on or to retire while this was doing.[47] From this and other facts we may infer that there were considerable differences of sentiment and practice among the Particular Baptists.

It was in one of the congregations which had declined to sing that the use of hymns as distinct from psalms began.[48] The innovator was its pastor, Benjamin Keach, a young man who had originally shared the sentiments of the General Baptists, among whom he was reared.[49] In 1668 he became pastor of a congregation of Particular Baptists of Southwark, which prospered under him and built a meeting house on Horsley-down.

Keach was convinced that Congregational Song was an ordinance of Christ, and undertook to realize his convictions among his own people. He first obtained their consent to sing at the close of the Lord's Supper. In the Epistle Dedicatory to his *Breach repaired,* dated April 3, 1691, he fixes the date as "16 or 18 years" earlier, which gives from 1673 to 1675. After some six years of this practice, his church agreed to sing also on "public Thanksgiving days"; and about 1690 they agreed to sing the praises of God every Lord's day.[50]

The songs thus introduced were not metrical psalms, but hymns suitable to the occasion, in manuscript and mostly or altogether composed by Keach himself.

[46]*The Records of the Church of Christ meeting in Broadmead, Bristol, 1640-1687,* London, 1847, pp. 159, 222, 228, 230, 232, 233, 236, 237, 238, 248, 253, 256, 291, 305, 312, 339, 421, 443, 465.

[47]Broadmead Records, p. 242.

[48]Thos. Crosby, *History of the English Baptists,* London, 1838-40, vol. iv. p. 299.

[49]Crosby, *op. cit.,* vol. iv. p. 270.

[50]p. viii.

A very small minority of Keach's congregation had opposed the movement, and this more frequent use of hymns precipitated a bitter controversy; the dissenters being led by Isaac Marlow, who in 1690 printed *A brief Discourse concerning Singing in the publick worship of God in the Gospel Church* (London, printed for the Author). Hercules Collins in the appendix to his *Orthodox Christian,* published in 1680, had urged the duty of congregational singing, as had Keach himself in his *Tropes and Figures* (1682) and *Treatise on Baptism* (1689). John Bunyan also in his *Solomon's Temple spiritualized* (1688), speaks of it as a divine institution in the public worship of the church, to whose members it should be confined. At the First General Assembly of Particular Baptists in 1689 Keach challenged that body to debate the matter. The debate seems to have been entered upon but not concluded, the Assembly thinking "it not convenient to spend much time that way."[51]

The controversy thus opened continued for several years. Keach responded to Marlow in his *The Breach repaired in God's Worship or, singing of Psalms, Hymns, and Spiritual Songs, proved to be an holy ordinance of Jesus Christ* (London 1691), a treatise of 192 pages with an appendix against Marlow covering 50 more. Marlow replied in *The Truth soberly defended* (1692); and other writers on both sides entered the fray. The points actually at issue were afterwards[52] stated by Marlow as three: (1) Whether the only vocal singing in the Apostolic Church was not the exercise of an extraordinary gift of the Spirit. (2) Whether the use of a set form of words in artificial rhymes is allowable. (3) Whether the minister sang alone, or a promiscuous assembly together, sanctified and profane, men and women (even though the latter were enjoined to keep silence in the churches).

By 1692 the controversy had become so heated and

[51]Goadby, *op. cit.,* p. 332.
[52]In his *Controversie brought to an end,* 1696.

abusive that the General Assembly took it in hand, and appointed a committee of seven to examine the pamphlets. Upon their report the Assembly rebuked the pamphleteers, and urged the people neither "to buy, sell, give or disperse" certain pamphlets, including Marlow's *Truth soberly defended.*

Crosby's statement that "a stop was thus put to the troubles that threatened the baptized churches upon this controversy"[53] is clearly unjustified. Marlow and his followers set up an independent congregation without singing; and in 1696 he published his *Controversie of Singing brought to an end,* and which in fact served only to renew it. The General Assembly had decided nothing except that the peace should be kept, but in omitting to decide against singing they left the churches free. And Crosby is no doubt right in saying that "many of them from that time sung the praises of God in their public assemblies who had not used that practice before."[54]

The deeper issues raised in this "controversie of Singing" tended to relegate the question between psalms and hymns to a position of inferior interest and importance. Many Baptist congregations introducing singing confined themselves to psalms without question. It was so generally at Broadmead, but the records show the singing of a hymn as early as 1678, written and handed up by Edward Terrill.[55] A late comer into the controversy, the famous John Gill, in his *Discourse on Singing of Psalms,* 1734 (2nd Ed. 1751), denies not that hymns may be useful, but care must be taken to conform them to Scripture and the analogy of faith; and on the whole he judges them "in a good measure, unnecessary."[56]

But the foundations of hymn singing in Particular Bap-

---

[53]*History of the Baptists,* vol. iii. p. 270. *Cf.* Joseph Ivimey, *History of the English Baptists,* London, 1811-1814, vol. ii. pp. 374, 375.

[54]Crosby, vol. iii. p. 271.

[55]*Records,* pp. 389, 390.

[56]2nd ed., p. 45.

tist churches had been permanently laid by Keach, and a beginning of Baptist Hymnody made.

Keach printed some of his hymns as early as 1676 in his *War with the powers of darkness* (4th Ed.), and three hundred of them as *Spiritual Melody* in 1691. The *Sacramental Hymns* which Joseph Boyse printed at Dublin in 1693 has sometimes been regarded as the first Baptist hymn book. But the immersionist type of the baptismal hymn contained in that book will not serve to detach Boyse from his dearly beloved and heroically defended Presbytery.

The Lord's Supper furnished a natural occasion for the introduction of evangelical hymns. And Joseph Stennett, who in 1690 became pastor of a Seventh-Day Baptist Church in Devonshire Square, London, began to use there sacramental hymns of his own composition. They circulated without, through Ms. copies made "by some Persons who heard them dictated ["lined"] in Publick." [57] Other congregations expressed a desire to use the hymns, and in 1697 Stennett published them as *Hymns in commemoration of the Sufferings of our Blessed Saviour Jesus Christ, compos'd for the celebration of his Holy Supper.* They reached a second edition in 1705, and a third in 1709. He published also in 1712 a tractate of twelve *Hymns compos'd for the celebration of the holy ordinance of Baptism,* of which there was a second edition in 1722. Stennett had been in contact with the "controversie of Singing," and as a preface to his earlier book printed a justification of congregational singing from the hand of one who had been trained in opposition to it, but had changed his views. Stennett's hymns were admired and used beyond the bounds of the Baptist denomination; some indeed have continued in use to our own day.[58] How they affected the Eastcheap lecturer has already appeared. It is of more moment that they attracted the attention of young Isaac Watts, under

[57]"Advertisement" in the *Hymns . . . for the . . . Holy Supper.*

[58]That most widely familiar, "Another six days' work is done," appeared in neither of the above publications.

whose influence Baptist Hymnody was about to pass. His appropriation of several of Stennett's lines into his own work entitles Stennett to be regarded as one of the models from whom Watts worked out his own conception of the English Hymn.

4. THE INDEPENDENTS JOIN WITH THE PRESBYTERIANS IN INTRODUCING HYMNS

There is no reason to doubt that the early Independents as a class were in substantial accord with the general Puritan position as to the singing of psalms. Such certainly was the case with the church of the exiled Separatists at Amsterdam. When John Smyth of Gainsborough developed there his peculiar views of spiritual worship, they found little sympathy. Ainsworth in his *Defence of the Holy Scriptures, worship and ministerie used in the Christian churches separated from Antichrist: against the challenges, cavils and contradiction of Mr. Smyth,* in 1609, professes himself unable to understand why Smyth should not use psalm singing in the services of his church, and he speaks for the whole body of the earlier exiles in saying, we "do content ourselves with joint harmonious singing of the Psalms of Holy Scripture, to the instruction and comforts of our hearts, and praise of our God."[59] In 1612 Ainsworth prepared a complete metrical Psalter for the use of the exiles, accompanying it with tunes and also with a prose rendering for comparison and with annotations for critical study. Some of these versions in Ms. may have been already in use; the printed Psalter was used both in the Amsterdam church and in Robinson's at Leyden, and was by the Pilgrim Fathers out of the Leyden congregation taken to New England.

It cannot, however, be said that when Smyth and his followers formed themselves into a Baptist congregation, they left behind them no elements of controversy as to the

[59]*Defence,* quoted in B. Hanbury, *Hist. Memorials relating to the Independents,* London, 1839, vol. i. p. 181.

propriety of congregational psalm singing. The extreme
spirit of individualism developed, and the Puritan ingenuity
in raising "cases of conscience" led to much difference of
opinion among the Independents on this as on other questions. The hesitation of the Westminster Assembly in dealing with the subject was doubtless with a view to including
the largest possible Independent support. The prevalent
opinion among them perhaps asked no more than that the
subject be left free, especially as regards the choice of a
specific version. But there were troublesome minorities
that objected to congregational singing *per se*, or like that
represented by Mr. Nye,[60] who took Barrowe's earlier position of protest against translating the Psalms into English
metre,[61] though it is not clear how they proposed to make
the singing of a prose version practicable. Some of these
controversialists were especially active at the time. John
Cotton essayed to cover the whole ground of controversy
in his *Singing of Psalms a Gospel-ordinance,* printed at
London in 1647, and again in 1650. No doubt he includes
Old England and New, Baptist and Independent, describing his view of the general situation, in his opening sentence: "To prevent the godly-minded from making melody
to the Lord in Singing his Praises with one accord, . . .
Satan hath mightily bestirred himself to breed a discord in
the hearts of some by filling their heads with foure heads of
scruples about the Duty." These scruples related to singing
with the voice as against singing in the heart; as to who
may properly be allowed to join in it in public worship
(women, carnal men, &c.); as to the subject matter of
praise; and as to metrical versions and invented tunes.
Cotton's defence adds nothing, and was not intended to
add anything, to the general doctrine of Psalmody held by
the Reformed Churches, which it essays to vindicate on the
usual Scriptural grounds.

[60]*Letters and Journals of Robert Baillie,* Edinburgh, 1841, 1842, vol.
ii. p. 121.
[61]See Hanbury, *Memorials,* vol. i. p. 61.

The "controversie of Singing" had spent its force before the period of the Restoration, and seems to have ended in a general adoption of psalm singing in Independent congregations. Several churches are on record in the preceding years as resolving to maintain or take up the "Singing of Psalms."[62] And in June, 1663, Dr. Goodwin and Mr. Nye, as well as Mr. Caryl, in their interview with Charles II, were able to report that "we have in our churches all parts of worship, as preaching, praying, reading, and singing of psalms, and the sacraments."[63] None the less the controversy had produced the familiar effect of stripping from the controverted practice its earlier delight. A conviction of duty is, after all, an inadequate basis for song.

And then, too, the Independents felt the full stress of the persecutions that followed the Act of Uniformity. The Conventicle Act bore hardly upon established congregations with well known places of meeting, to whom the houses of great Puritan families, which often provided shelter and even places for worship to the Presbyterians, were not open. During the enforcement of these Acts, their services could be held only in secluded places and at unexpected hours, with a guard at the door to give notice of interruption. It is obvious that with the need of avoiding observation by neighbors and passers by, singing would be the first "part of worship" to suffer. Speaking of one of the periods of persecution, Neale says that in the meetings "they never sung Psalms." [64] Equally suggestive is a record under date of April 1, 1682, of a church once meeting at St. Thomas', Southwark: "We met at Mr. Russell's, in Ironmonger Lane, where Mr. Lambert, of Deadman's Place, Southwark, administered to us the ordinance of the Lord's supper, and we sang a psalm in a low voice."[65]

[62]*Cf.* Curwen, *Studies in Worship Music,* 1st Series, pp. 83, 84.
[63]Letter of Wm. Hooke, quoted in J. Waddington, *Congregational History, 1567-1700,* London, 1874, p. 579.
[64]*History of the Puritans,* part v. chap. ii.: ed. 1837, vol. iii. p. 265.
[65]Quoted in *Worship Music,* p. 84.

These conditions of restraint ceased with the Revolution of 1688, which brought freedom of worship and a beginning of a meeting house building era to Independents as to Presbyterians. The lengthy sermon and protracted extemporaneous prayer were the main features of worship in the Independent meeting houses. They left little opportunity for psalm singing, and there is no evidence that the new conditions put new heart into it. The singing was still confined to canonical Psalms. While *Sternhold and Hopkins* had been largely given up, no other version was received in common. Some who craved a "pure" version favored Barton's, and others the *Bay Psalm Book* of the New England divines. Nathaniel Homes, afterwards one of the ejected ministers, had called attention to it as early as 1644 in his *Gospel Musick,* reprinting its preface with approval. Three English editions had already appeared and more were to follow, though not necessarily for exclusively English use. Among those who turned toward a modified Psalter Patrick's version became the favorite.

The singing of hymns in Independent meeting-houses began in the last quarter of the XVIIth century,[66] introduced there as elsewhere by divines who had become restless under the limitations of an Old Testament Psalmody. With the right of each congregation to regulate its own worship and the prevalence of the practice of lining out the words, the use of hymns in manuscript required merely the agreement of pastor and people. With the fraternization of Independents and Presbyterians, and the frequent occupancy of Independent pulpits by Presbyterian divines, it would be difficult to distinguish a separate origin of hymn singing in either body. It would be still more difficult to show that the impulse came from the Independent side.

[66]To the 3rd book of R. Davis' *Hymns,* hereafter referred to, was added a group of hymns with the note: "The following Hymns were found in Mr. Browning's Study, and used by him at the Lord's Table." Browning was Davis' predecessor as pastor at Rothwell, and according to Glass (*Early Hist. of Independent Church at Rothwell,* n. d.) his pastorate ended in 1685.

During the last decade of the century hymn singing reached the stage that called for printed hymn books. The *Family Hymns* of Matthew Henry, has been already referred to as published in 1695, though the New Testament hymns were not added till the second edition of 1702. The publisher's advertisement at the end of the 1702 issue shows quite an array of hymn books available at that date, and gives a clue as to what had been and was then in use. There are Mason's *Spiritual Songs* in its seventh edition, with the *Penitential Cries* of Shepherd, in its fifth edition: the Presbyterian Boyse's *Sacramental Hymns: A Collection of Divine Hymns, upon several occasions, suited to our common tunes, for the use of devout Christians, in singing the praises of God,* published in 1694, and gathered from six authors, including Baxter and Mason: *Select Hymns, taken out of Mr. Herberts Temple:* Bury's *A Collection of Psalms, Hymns and Spiritual Songs, fitted for morning and evening worship in a private family:* Baxter's *Poetical Fragments* in its third edition: and Barton's *Six Centuries of select Hymns and Spiritual Songs* in its fourth edition.

This list is substantially a catalogue of the earliest hymn-books of the Independents, as also of the Presbyterians. Simon Browne, in the preface to his *Hymns and Spiritual Songs,* London, 1720, mentioning the books of Barton, Mason and Shepherd, adds: "Beside some collections from private hands, and an attempt to turn some of Mr. Herbert's poems into common metre, these I have mention'd were all the hymns I know to have been in common use, either in private families, or Christian-assemblies, till within a few years past." [67]

To these must be added Stennett's two little books of sacramental hymns, and also a volume of 168 *Hymns composed on several subjects and on divers occasions* (date unknown) by Richard Davis, the Independent minister of Rothwell, to which some hymns by others were added in a second edition in 1694. These warm but artless hymns,

[67] p. 16 of preface.

possibly not known to Browne, were acceptable in Davis's Rothwell congregation and in his evangelistic work through the midland counties, and went further.[68] They were commended by John Gill,[69] and were reprinted in London as late as 1833.[70]

These books make it evident enough that there was a beginning of Independent hymn singing before Watts. We have indeed his own testimony that some ministers had already commenced to use "evangelical hymns."[71] But such use was exceptional; the books marking the tentative efforts of progressive individuals rather than the general practice. In the great body of the meeting houses the singing of psalms obtained exclusively, though not perhaps very jealously. And this occasioned the remark of Enoch Watts, that "a load of scandal" lay on the Independents "for their imagined aversion to poetry." [72]

In view of the new leaven about to be introduced into this situation, and of the fact that from among the Independents was to arise the principal agent of the effective transition from the old Psalmody to the new Hymnody, it is interesting to get as vivid a view as may be of the actual practice of psalm singing by the Independents at the beginning of the XVIIIth century, which constitutes the background against which the work of Dr. Watts is to be set.

There is no difficulty in reconstructing its salient features. The congregational leadership was in the hands of a precentor, generally of most meagre attainments. The singing was still dominated by the universal practice of lining out the psalm. Very few tunes were used, and in rendering

[68]This early book of Davis was distinctively from the Independent side. He and all his works were repudiated by the Presbyterian members of the London "Meeting of Ministers" and by Presbyterians generally. Cf. R. W. Dale, History of English Congregationalism, London, 1907, pp. 479 ff.

[69]See preface to 7th edition, 1748.

[70]A brief List of Hymn Books for sale by Charles Higham, London, 1893.

[71]Essay prefixed to 1st edition of his Hymns, 1707.

[72]His letter in Th. Milner, Life of Isaac Watts, London, 1834, p. 178.

these all the notes were reduced to "a constant uniformity of time." Each note was dwelt upon so long as "puts the Congregation quite out of breath in singing five or six stanzas."[73] Musical ignorance and incapacity accompanied by indifference seems to have been very general, but the Psalmody as practised hardly related itself to music. The people carried no psalm books to church, had neither text nor note before them, and must often have failed to catch or comprehend the line as the precentor gave it out. Instrumental music was excluded by common consent.[74] Many of the people took no part in the psalmody; most of these failing through apathy, but some consciences even at that date had not come through the "controversie of Singing," and refrained for cause.[75]

The apathy of the people doubtless extended to many of their leaders, who as a class were no longer of the educated type of the pastors furnished by the Ejectment. To some extent the people's apathy was even a reflection of the exclusive interest of the average Independent minister of the period in the sermon and prayer. Dr. Watts' own impressions of the Independent psalmody as set against his ideals of the ordinance of Congregational Song are recorded as follows in the preface to his *Hymns* of 1707:

"While we sing the Praises of our God in his Church, we are employ'd in that part of Worship which of all others is the nearest a-kin to Heaven; and 'tis pity that this of all others should be perform'd the worst upon Earth. . . . To see the dull Indifference, the negligent and the thoughtless Air that sits upon the Faces of a whole Assembly while the Psalm is on their Lips, might tempt even a charitable Observer, to suspect the Fervency of inward Religion, and 'tis much to be fear'd that the Minds of most of the Worshippers are absent or unconcern'd: . . . But of all our Religious Solemnities *Psalmodie* is the most unhappily manag'd. That very Action which should elevate us to the most delightful and divine Sensations doth not only flat our Devotion, but too often awakens our Regret, and touches all the Springs of Uneasiness within us."

[73]Watts, preface to *The Psalms of David imitated*, 1719.
[74]*Practical Discourses of Singing* (already cited), pp. 137, 191.
[75]*Ibid.*, Sermon iv.

CHAPTER III

DR. WATTS' "RENOVATION OF PSALMODY"

I

HIS PROPOSAL OF AN EVANGELICAL "SYSTEM OF PRAISE" (1707)

With the work of Isaac Watts (1674-1748) a new epoch began in English Church Song. Behind it was a great personality, clear of vision, fertile of resource, dominant in leadership. And no small part of his equipment was his youthfulness.[1] He planned and began his work in the ardor of youth, its singleness of conviction, its preference of radical remedies over compromise, its comparative disregard of other people's feelings.

There is no better way of approach to Watts' work than that of comparison with the contemporaneous Eastcheap movement toward bettering Nonconformist Psalmody.[2] Both dealt with the same conditions, and sought to undermine the indifference that had produced them. But they differed both in diagnosis and in the remedy proposed.

The Eastcheap lecturers put the emphasis on "The Duty of Singing in the Worship of God." [3] The failure to comprehend this duty had brought about the current neglect and

---

[1] "Many of Dr. Watts's hymns were not, it is understood, written by Dr. Watts at all, but by young Mr. Watts; not by that venerable man with venerable wig, who figures opposite so many a title-page, but by a young immature Christian, who afterwards became this venerable and truly admirable person." Thomas Toke Lynch, in *Memoir* of him, ed. by Wm. White, London, 1874, p. 95.

[2] See the account of it in chapter ii, part iii.

[3] *Practical Discourses of Singing in the Worship of God,* London, 1708, preface, p. iii.

unskillful performance of Psalmody. As to what should be sung they were not agreed. Three favored, or took for granted, the singing of psalms; three favored supplementing psalms with New Testament songs; the other simply recounted the triumphs of psalm singing in the past. But Watts attributed the great part of current indifference to the use of psalms, and exposed the foundations on which Church Song had been laid at the Calvinistic Reformation as inadequate to support a Christian ordinance of Praise:

"I have been long convinc'd, that one great Occasion of this Evil arises from the Matter and Words to which we confine all our Songs. Some of 'em are almost opposite to the Spirit of the Gospel: Many of them foreign to the State of the New-Testament, and widely different from the present Circumstances of Christians. Hence it comes to pass that when spiritual Affections are excited within us, and our Souls are raised a little above this Earth in the beginning of a Psalm, we are check'd on a sudden in our Ascent toward Heaven by some Expressions that are more suited to the Days of *Carnal Ordinances,* and fit only to be sung in the *Worldly Sanctuary.* When we are just entring into an Evangelic Frame by some of the Glories of the Gospel presented in the brightest Figures of *Judaism,* yet the very next Line perhaps which the Clerk parcels out unto us, hath something in it so extremely *Jewish* and cloudy, that darkens our Sight of God the Saviour: Thus by keeping too close to *David* in the House of God, the Vail of *Moses* is thrown over our Hearts. While we are kindling into divine Love by the Meditations of the *loving kindness of God and the Multitude of his tender Mercies,* within a few Verses some dreadful Curse against Men is propos'd to our Lips. . . . Some Sentences of the *Psalmist* that are expressive of the Temper of our own Hearts and the Circumstances of our Lives may Compose our Spirits to Seriousness, and allure us to a sweet Retirement within our selves; but we meet with a following Line which so peculiarly belongs but to one Action or Hour of the Life of *David* or *Asaph,* that breaks off our Song in the midst; our Consciences are affrighted lest we should speak a Falsehood unto God." [4]

If Watts had been alone in these views, probably he would have failed. He goes on to say that

"Many Ministers and many private Christians have long groan'd under this Inconvenience, and have wish'd rather than attempted a Reformation: At their importunate and repeated Requests I have for some Years past devoted many Hours of leisure to this Service." [5]

[4] Preface to *Hymns,* 1707, pp. iv-vi.
[5] *Ibid.,* p. vi.

In the way of remedying the low state of Psalmody it is
not clear that the Eastcheap lecturers had anything in mind
beyond quickening the sense of duty to sing, and attention
to musical instruction such as the Society of Gentlemen
furnished at the King's Weigh House. Watts, on the
other hand, believing that the cause of trouble lay in the
matter and words commonly sung, proposed a renovation
of Psalmody itself. He set up a new standard of Church
Song, having these criteria:

First, it should be *evangelical:* not in the sense that New
Testament songs be allowed to "supplement" Old Testament
Psalms, but so that the whole body of Church Song be
brought within the light of the gospel.

Second, it should be *freely composed,* as against the
Reformation standard of strict adherence to the letter of
Scripture or the later paraphrasing of Scripture.

Third, it should *express the thoughts and feelings of the
singers,* and not merely recall the circumstances or record
the sentiments of David or Asaph or another.

From this point of view Watts planned a full-rounded
"system" of evangelical Hymnody. This system, in form
rather than contents, was in two separate parts; one being
"imitations" of canonical Psalms, the other being hymns
more or less Scriptural in content.

I. As to Psalms. Watts had no intention of laying them
aside.[6] But he drew a sharp distinction between reading the
Psalms and singing them, and between the right methods
of translating them for the particular use designed. He
held that the Psalms are to be read as God's word to us,
and for that end must be translated as literally as possible.[7]
Such translation must be in English prose, since the exigen-
cies of rhythm and rhyme make a really faithful rendering
of the Hebrew into English verse an impossible thing.[8]
Incidentally therefore he held that those who believed we

[6] *Ibid.,* p. vi.
[7] "A short Essay toward the Improvement of Psalmody," 1707, p. 243.
[8] *Ibid.,* pp. 241-242.

may sing nothing but the pure word of God must resort to
a prose translation, and must learn the Hebrew music or at
least employ the method of chanting practiced in English
cathedrals.[9]

For himself he believed that Congregational Song should
represent not God's word to us, but our word to God, and
that the thoughts and language of the Psalms could be
employed only so far as we could properly make them our
own.[10] Ancient Jewish songs were to be accommodated to
modern Gospel worship.[11] This involved the omission of
several Psalms and numerous other passages "improper for
any person but the Royal Author";[12] also the adaptation of
the remaining material so as to make David always speak
as Watts had reason to believe he would have spoken
if he had been a fully instructed Christian living in the day
and under the circumstances of Watts himself.[13] Such
adaptation was really a two-fold process,—making David
speak like a Christian and making him a contemporary of
Watts.

For the first process, that of "Christianizing" the Psalms,
Watts claimed precedents, especially Dr. Patrick's.[14] But
Watts contemplated from the first, and ultimately himself
carried out, a reconstruction along this line far more systematic and thoroughgoing than any one had hitherto ventured upon. On this subject his feelings were deeply stirred,
and he wrote and acted with a studied aggressiveness that
aimed to conquer, but did nothing to conciliate, those whom
he styled "the Patrons of another Opinion."

The second process, however, that of making David a
contemporary, was surely Watts' own conception, and it
involved some curious transformations of the sacred text.
"Judah and Israel may be called England and Scotland, and

[9]*Ibid.*, p. 243.
[10]*Ibid.*, p. 244.
[11]*Ibid.*, p. 254, and preface to *Psalms,* &c., 1719, p. xvi.
[12]Preface to *Psalms,* &c., p. viii.
[13] "Essay," pp. 252-254.
[14]Preface to *Psalms,* &c., p. vi.

the land of Canaan may be translated into Great Britain." [15]
Historical allusions must be modified accordingly.   David
must be made to play the part of an orthodox and patriotic
English Christian of the early XVIIIth century, and all
royal references must be accommodated to the person of the
reigning sovereign.   Only thus, in Watts' words, can the
Psalms "be converted into Christian Songs in our Nation."[16]
If this seem to us now a doubtful device, and seemed then to
a watchful remnant of psalm singers nothing short of sac-
rilege, it did not offend the general taste of the time, and
proved no impediment to the widespread approval of Watts'
scheme for the improvement of Psalmody.

II. As to Hymns. Watts' plan included also the com-.
posing of "Spiritual Songs of a more evangelic frame for
the Use of Divine Worship under the Gospel." Their use
in worship he supports in his "Essay" by five arguments:[17]—

First. A Psalm properly translated for Christian use ,is
no longer inspired as to form and language: only its materials are borrowed from God's word. It is just as lawful
to use other Scriptural thoughts, and compose them into a
spiritual song.

Second. The very ends and design of Psalmody demand
songs that shall respond to the fullness of God's revelation
of Himself. God's revelation in Christ, and our own devotions responding to it, require Gospel songs.

Third. The Scriptures themselves, especially Eph: v,
19-20, and Col: iii, 16-17, command us to sing and give
thanks in the name of Christ. Why shall we pray and
preach in that name, and sing under terms of the Law?

Fourth. The Book of Psalms does not provide for all
occasions of Christian praise, or express all Christian experiences.

Fifth. The primitive "Gifts of the Spirit" covered alike

[15] "Essay," p. 246.
[16] *Ibid.*, p. 246.
[17] *Ibid.*, pp. 256-266.

preaching, prayer and song. It is admitted by all that, under the present administration of Grace, ministers are by study and diligence to acquire and cultivate gifts of preaching and prayer. Why shall they not also seek to acquire and cultivate the capacity of composing spiritual songs, and exercise it along with the other parts of worship, preaching and prayer?

II

HIS FULFILMENT: "WATTS'S PSALMS AND HYMNS"

With this understanding of Watts' "Scheme for the Renovation of Psalmody," we may go forward to consider his own contributions to it.

Dr. Gibbons made himself responsible for the familiar account of the beginnings of Watts' hymn writing, upon information received from the Rev. John Morgan, who claimed to have obtained it from Watts' colleague, Samuel Price.[18] It is to the effect that young Watts, having expressed to his father his disapproval of the hymns sung at the Southampton meeting house, was invited to improve upon them. The hymns in question were those of Barton, of whom Watts' brother Enoch wrote: "Honest Barton chimes us asleep."[19] Watts furnished a specimen hymn, which was so successful that it was followed by others, until a considerable number were in use by the congregation.

This account rests on hearsay evidence, but is probably substantially true. As early as March, 1700, Watts' brother wrote, reminding him of importunities already made to put the hymns into print for the common good.[20]

[18]*Memoirs of the Rev. Isaac Watts, D.D.* By Thos. Gibbons, London, 1780, p. 254.

[19]*Life, Times and Correspondence of the Rev. Isaac Watts, D.D.* By Thos. Milner, London, 1834, p. 177.

[20]Milner, *op. cit.*, pp. 176 f.

Watts printed his first volume of verse in December 1705,[21] as *Horae Lyricae: Poems, chiefly of the lyric kind. In two books. I. Songs &c. sacred to Devotion. II. Odes, Elegys, &c. to Vertue Loyalty and Friendship. By I. Watts. London, printed by S. and D. Bridge, for John Lawrence, at the Sign of the Angel in the Poultrey. MDCCVI.*

The preface is a protest against the moral decadence of current poetry, and a justification of religious themes as suitable for poetic treatment. Book I contains twenty-five hymns and four Psalm paraphrases in the metres of the *Old Version,* and eleven religious songs or pieces of varying metrical form. In Book II Watts spreads his wings "in the free and unconfin'd Measures of Pindar" (which he regarded as best maintaining the dignity of religious themes, and giving a loose to the devout soul),[22] in blank verse and in other metres.

The book as a whole is addressed to lovers of poetry, and Watts' explanation of the inclusion of the hymns reveals much of his mind and purpose. They "were never written with a design to appear before the Judges of Wit, but only to assist the Meditations and Worship of Vulgar Christians." They are a small part of two hundred hymns of the same kind ready for public use if these are approved by the world. They are divided from their fellows and here printed because "in most of These there are some Expressions which are not suited to the plainest Capacities, and differ too much from the usual Methods of Speech in which Holy Things are propos'd to the general Part of Mankind." [23] This partition of his materials was final. The hymns were augmented in the second edition of the *Horae* (1709), but they always constituted a distinct group apart

---

[21]It bears date 1706. For the actual time of publishing, see the writer's note in *The Journal of The Presbyterian Historical Society* for Sept., 1902, p. 358.

[22]Preface, p. [vii].

[23]Pp. [viii, ix].

from his *Hymns and Spiritual Songs* for congregational
use, within whose covers they never appeared.[24]

It appears then that Watts' admission of some hymns to
a place among his poems was not with a view of showing
that hymns could be made poetic, but was the result of a
winnowing process in which the body of his hymns was
freed from the suspicion of being literary. He accounted
himself a religious poet, with a right to address "the
Judges of Wit." He felt also a real sympathy with plain
people and a call to provide them with hymns on the level
of the unpoetic mind. This note of conscientious condescension in his hymn writing he never failed to sound on
every available occasion. He chose the humbler task, and
thus inadvertently secured a permanent fame to which his
poetical effusions give him a doubtful title.[25] What is
more to the point, he thus freed his hymns from the artificial standards and to a large extent from the perverted
taste of his time. Having demonstrated in the *Horae* that
he could compose pindarics, he expected "to be for ever free
from the Temptation of making or mending Poems
again," [26] and was ready to give his hymns to the churches.

The body of the Hymns appeared in July, 1707,[27] in a
16mo. volume, entitled *Hymns and Spiritual Songs. In
three Books. I. Collected from the Scriptures. II. Compos'd on Divine subjects. III. Prepared for the Lord's*

[24]Some of the hymns from the *Horae* came into use after Watts'
death. The two most familiar are:—"Father, how wide thy Glory
shines!" and "Eternal Power! whose high Abode."

[25]On the strength of his *Horae Lyricae,* Watts found a niche in
Johnson's *Lives of the Poets.* A later historian discerns that Watts'
"real artistic successes" are attained in his best hymns: (Courthope,
History of English Poetry, vol. v., 1905, p. 336). For a favorable
view of his metrical experiments, see George Saintsbury, *History of
English Prosody,* vol. ii, 1908, pp. 508, 509.

[26]Preface to 2nd ed. of *Horae Lyricae* (1709), which is a very different book from the first edition.

[27]See "Autobiographical Table" reproduced in E. P. Hood, *Isaac
Watts; his life and writings, his homes and friends;* London, Rel. Tr.
Soc., n. d., p. 345.

Supper. With an Essay towards the improvement of Christian Psalmody, by the use of evangelical Hymns in worship, as well as the Psalms of David. By I. Watts. London, printed by J. Humfreys, for John Lawrence, at the Angel in the Poultrey, 1707.[28] The hymns numbered 210, followed by a group of doxologies, at least three of which must be accounted as hymns. Their arrangement humored current prejudices. Those willing to sing paraphrases only might find 78 in the first book: those willing to sing hymns at the Communion only might find 22 in the third book: those welcoming "free composures" had 110 more in the second book. The hymns were confined to three metres, Long, Common and Short. An inspection of the original text of the hymns shows that the differences between it and the familiar text of later issues are fewer and less important than might have been expected.[29]

[28]The first edition of the *Hymns* was almost thumbed out of existence. At the publication of Dr. Julian's scholarly *Dictionary of Hymnology* in 1892, every copy was supposed to have perished (see 2nd ed., p. 1724). The announcement of the sale of a copy at Sotheby's, London, in Dec. 1901, attracted wide attention, and it brought £140. There are now at least two copies in this country, one in the New York Public Library and one in the writer's collection. An article in *The Guardian* for January 29, 1902, by Rev. James Mearns, was the first account of this epoch-making book ever published. For collation and bibliographical data of this and subsequent editions, with facsimiles of title pages of eds. 1 and 2, see the writer's paper on "The Early Editions of Doctor Watts's Hymns" in *The Journal of The Presbyterian Historical Society* for June, 1902.

[29]The following are among the more interesting of these:

"Come, we that love the Lord," has for its closing lines:
    "We're marching thro' *Immanuel's* Ground
    To a more joyful Sky."
"Come, Holy Spirit, Heavenly Dove," has in the second verse:
    "Look, how we grovel here below,
    And hug these trifling Toys."
"When I can read my Title clear," closes thus:
    "Nor dares a Wave of Trouble roll
    Across my peaceful Breast."
"When I survey the wondrous Cross," has for its second line:
    "Where the young Prince of Glory dy'd."

In a lengthy preface Watts restated and overstated his sense of condescension in his task as an intent to write down to "the Level of Vulgar Capacities" and to furnish in Book I hymns for the meanest of Christians.[30] This language he modified in the second edition. But the fullest and most characteristic expression of his views on Psalmody is contained in "A Short Essay toward the Improvement of Psalmody," from which quotations have been already made. It covers pages 233-276 in the first edition, and did not appear again in print until the collected *Works* after Watts' death.[31] It was his purpose to prepare a fuller treatise on Psalmody, which he never executed.[32]

The *Hymns* being printed, Watts invited criticisms from his friends, and continued his writing. In April, 1709, "the Second Edition. Corrected and much Enlarged," appeared. Some fifty lines of the original hymns were altered, and

"Why do we mourn departing Friends?" has in the fifth verse:
    "Thence he arose and clim'd the Sky."
"Alas! and did my Saviour bleed?" has at the close of the second verse:
        "While the firm mark of Wrath Divine
        His Soul in Anguish stood?"
"Now to the Lord a noble Song!" has in the fifth verse, "ye Skies" (for "ye heavens"), and at the close of the hymn:
        "And play his Name on Harps of Gold!"
In 1707 Watts was capable of offering this to the churches for congregational use (Bk. I, No. 24, vv. 5.6) :—

        "5. There the dark Earth and gloomy Shades
        Shall clasp their naked Body round,
        And welcome their delicious Limbs
        With the cold Kisses of the Ground.

        "6. Pale Death shall riot on their Souls,
        Their Flesh shall noisom Vermine eat,
        The Just shall in the Morning rise
        And find their Tyrants at their Feet."

[30] Preface, pp. viii, x.
[31] There were no less than seven collective editions of Dr. Watts' Works: the earliest being that of 1753, in 6 vols., 4to., ed. by Drs. Jennings and Doddridge.
[32] "Advertisement" to the 2nd ed. of *Hymns*.

145 additional hymns appeared here, and also in a separate supplement to the first edition, printed at the same time.

With this second edition the department of Hymns in Watts' System of Praise was completed. None of the hymns written later was incorporated in subsequent editions; and although Watts toward the end of his life expressed a desire to make some changes of text to accommodate its expressions to modified theological views, no such changes were ever made.[33] This situation is partly explained by the fact that Watts parted with the copyright of the *Hymns*, apparently in 1709. They thus passed out of his control, although a note in the seventh edition of 1720 shows that he still exercised a certain supervision of their printing.

Turning now to the Psalms:—

Among the hymns of the first part of the *Horae* was a little group of four Psalm versions, with the inscription "An Essay on a few of David's Psalms Translated into Plain Verse, in Language more agreeable to the clearer Revelations of the Gospel;" showing that the System of Praise as just described lay in Watts' mind in its integrity from a very early date. And these versions did in fact prove to be the actual nucleus of his own *The Psalms of David imitated,* as published 13 years later. But it is altogether unlikely that Watts originally proposed to depend altogether upon his own resources for filling out his proposed System of Praise. The work he entered upon as his own was the department of Hymns.

We can readily trace the evolution of his purpose regarding the Psalms. In the first edition of his *Hymns,* 1707, he included in all among the Scripture paraphrases fourteen Psalm versions. Referring to them in his preface, he says:

"After this manner should I rejoice to see a good part of the

---

[33]For a discussion of the evidence concerning Watts' desire to accommodate the text to his later views, see the writer's paper already cited, pp. 276-279.

Book of Psalms fitted for the use of our Churches, and *David* converted into a Christian. In the first, second and third Psalms especially, I have attempted a Specimen of what I desire and hope some more capable Genius will undertake.[34]

In the preface to the 2nd edition of the *Hymns,* two years later (1709), Watts states: "Because I cannot persuade others to attempt this glorious Work, I have suffered myself to be persuaded to begin it, and have, thro' Divine Goodness, already proceeded half way thro'." In the preface to the third edition (1712), he speaks of being daily urged to proceed in the work, of having been hindered by professional duties, and of his expectation "e're long to fulfill my Designs." The long illness beginning in that year debarred Watts from his pulpit, but afforded the opportunity of finishing his work upon the Psalms.

The results appeared in 1719 in a 16mo volume with the title:—*The Psalms of David imitated in the language of the New Testament, and apply'd to the Christian state and worship. By I. Watts.* (London: printed for J. Clark, R. Ford and R. Cruttenden).

The volume presents to the eye a marked contrast with the early editions of the *Hymns,* which were rather cheap and poor. Its fine paper and open page, its engraved headpieces and vignettes, suggest an assured welcome. Numerous copies survive with each page set in a frame of handruling, and bound in richly tooled red morocco, in the style of luxurious Prayer Books of the period.

The book contains versions of 138 Psalms; the remaining 12, and some passages from those retained, being excluded from Watts' System as unsuitable for Christian use. Psalms are divided and passages transposed for considerations of convenience; a note explaining that the custom of singing with excessively prolonged notes makes impracticable the singing of more than six or eight verses at one time.[35] Of many Psalms versions in two or three

[34] Pp. x, xi.
[35] Preface, p. xxiv.

metres are provided, differing at times in the degree of closeness to the original, at times in the Christian interpretation adopted.[36]

A characteristic feature is the notes appended to the Psalms, sometimes critical or hermeneutical; often frankly written in the first person, to tell the reader his reasons for what he did, or of the lines he borrowed from some earlier translator. These notes, and the preface of twenty-nine pages, entitled "An Enquiry into the right Way of fitting the Book of Psalms for Christian Worship," were omitted from the second edition, appearing the same year as the first, but in smaller and cheaper form. At the close of this preface Watts characteristically claimed the "Pleasure of being the First who have brought down the Royal Author into the common Affairs of the Christian Life, and led the Psalmist of *Israel* into the Church of *Christ,* without any thing of a *Jew* about him."

With the publication of *The Psalms of David imitated* in the forty-sixth year of his life, the System of Praise which Watts had begun as a youth, and carried forward through years of ill-health, was complete. He was by no means unaware of the importance of his performance, and anticipated something at least of the success it attained. In a note appended to the 1720 edition of the *Hymns,* he says:

"It is presumed that" [*The Psalms imitated*] "in conjunction with this, may appear to be such a sufficient Provision for Psalmody, as to answer most Occasions of the Christian Life: And, if an Author's own Opinion may be taken, he esteems it the greatest Work that ever he has publish'd, or ever hopes to do, for the use of the Churches."

This judgment has been sometimes quoted as referring only to his work upon the Psalms, but it plainly includes his whole System of Praise.

Some notice must also be taken of Dr. Watts' work in hymn writing outside the limits of this System of Praise. Of this the most important was the *Divine Songs attempted in easy language, for the use of children, with some addi-*

[36] *Ibid.,* p. xxvii.

tional composures, which had already appeared in 1715. This book had its origin in the request of a friend for hymns to be used in connection with his catechetical instructions. Both for its contents and its influence it is worthy to stand beside the *Psalms and Hymns;* for it must be regarded as the fountain-head of the afterwards extensive Children's Hymnody in the English language; though its constant reprinting for a century was as a book of verse or a chap book, and not as a children's hymn book. In the course of time objection came to be made to the appropriateness of its theological teachings. But Watts' original preface makes it abundantly clear that he aimed to avoid anything like theological partisanship, and sought to put into simple verse the beliefs and the tone of thought that were generally held at the time. He claimed that "children of high and low degree, of the Church of England or dissenters, whether baptized in infancy or not, may join together in these songs." [37]

In three volumes of *Sermons,* appearing in 1721, 1723, and 1727, Watts printed hymns suitable to the subjects of discourse. In his *Reliquiae Juveniles: miscellaneous thoughts in prose and verse* (London, 1734), Watts returned to "the Service of the Muse" he had abjured twenty-five years earlier, and the hymnic element is very small. It is even smaller in the volume, *Remnants of Time,* printed from his papers after his death. From these sources numerous hymns ultimately found their way into hymn books and into common use, and in 1806 John Dobell printed *Dr. Watts's Fourth Book of Spiritual Hymns,* which he had gathered together in his zeal that nothing be overlooked. Nevertheless the *Hymns* of 1707-09 and *The Psalms imitated* of 1719, which by the middle of the

---

[37] Preface, in the early editions. "For their epoch, they were not far from perfection, as publishers saw." F. J. Harvey Darton in *The Cambridge History of English Literature,* vol. xi, 1914, p. 413. For Abraham Cheere and other forerunners of Watts in writing hymns for children, see Julian, *Dictionary,* art. "Children's Hymns."

XVIIIth century began to appear bound together in a
single handy volume, contained Watts's System of Praise
in its entirety.[38]

III

HIS SUCCESS: THE ERA OF WATTS

I. IN ENGLAND

1. HE DOMINATES THE WORSHIP OF THE INDEPENDENTS

From their first appearance Watts' *Hymns* proved a
spiritual delight to many, and were introduced into such
congregations as were prepared to receive them. On the
other hand many Independent congregations continued their
psalm singing without regard to the new hymns, so strong
was conservative habit and prejudice against hymns. In
view of the extraordinary success ultimately attained, it is
easy to form an exaggerated idea of the facility of their
actual introduction into public worship.

The English Independent congregations at the time
(1707) probably numbered from 350 to 400, and were much
reduced both in size and zeal.[39] The fact that each congregation was free to sing what it chose and under no obligation to make record of the choice, and the further fact
that one copy in a precentor's hands might serve a whole
congregation, make it difficult to trace or estimate the
process of introducing Watts' *Hymns*. If we are to follow
Walter Wilson, the historian of London Dissenting
Churches, the *Hymns* must have found their earliest welcome in the provinces. Writing in 1810, under the full
sway of the Watts tradition, he says:

[38]The hymns appearing in the so-called *Posthumous Works* (London, 1779, 2 vols.) had either appeared before or else were by another
hand. *Cf.* Gibbons, *Memoirs of Watts,* appendix ii.
[39]*Cf.* R. W. Dale, *History of English Congregationalism,* London,
1907, bk. v, chap. v.

"The poetry of Watts was received but slowly into most of our congregations. It is only of late years that it has acquired so general a patronage, and even in the present day there are many who prefer the rhyming of Brady and Tate, or the bald version of the Scotch. The reason is, mankind are afraid of innovation, and it is only by degrees that their prejudices are loosened."[40]

The actual demand for the *Hymns* can be judged from the editions called for. The first edition of 1707 was exhausted apparently before the end of 1708,[41] but the second did not appear until April, 1709, being delayed in the printing. The third edition appeared in 1712, the fourth in 1714. At the appearance of *The Psalms of David imitated* in 1719, the *Hymns* were in their sixth edition; the seventh following in 1720.

The Psalm Imitations, though rousing intense hostility in a minority, found a double welcome, from those wishing to use psalms and hymns jointly, and from those ready for modified Psalm versions though not as yet for hymns. We have Watts' own testimony that some thousands of copies were sold within a year of publication.[42] Within ten years seven editions were called for. The practical effect of introducing the Imitations was to extend the use of the *Hymns* also. Congregations used to Dr. Patrick's versions seemed to be taking but a short step in passing to Watts' Imitations. But, the step once taken, they found themselves within the area of a free Christian Hymnody, in which the distinction between Psalm and Hymn seemed hardly more than a convenience in classification and a deference to accustomed usage.

The strengthening hold of the *Hymns* appears from the preface of Simon Browne's *Hymns and Spiritual Songs,* published in 1720 at London, where he had come as pastor of "The Old Jewry." Its lengthy justification of hymn singing was doubtless directed to the London congregations

[40]*The History and Antiquities of Dissenting Churches ... in London,* &c., vol. iii, 1810, p. 527.

[41]Milner, *op. cit.,* p. 229.

[42]Note to the 7th ed. of *Hymns.*

to which Wilson referred. But Browne found it wise, even
at that early day, to disclaim any purpose of superseding
Watts' *Hymns:* "The World, I hope, will not do me the
injury to think, that I aim at being his rival. These hymns
are design'd as a supplement to his, not intended to supplant them. 'Twill satisfy my ambition, if they may assist
the devotion of private Christians, or publick assemblies,
upon such subjects as he hath not touched." [43]

Twenty-four years later Doddridge was able to say to
Watts:

"Above all I congratulate you that by your *sacred poetry,* especially
by *your Psalms,* and *your Hymns,* you are leading the worship and I
trust also animating the devotion of myriads in our public assemblies
every Sabbath, and in their families and closets every day. This,
Sir, at least so far as it relates to the service of the sanctuary, is an
unparalleled favour by which God hath been pleased to distinguish
you, I may boldly say it, beyond any of his servants now upon earth." [44]

After forty years more the predilection of Independent
congregations for Watts' hymns had become so jealous
that Dr. Gibbons felt called upon to introduce a volume of
his own compositions in these terms:

"But, though [Watts] has done much and perhaps in a happier
Manner than what any after him may be able to perform, yet he has
by no Means precluded the Endeavours of others in the same Service.
Are there not Subjects untouched by him in the almost infinite Extent
of spiritual Matter that may be very suitably wrought up into sacred
Songs? And is it not a Pleasure to the human Mind not to be perpet-
ually restrained to the same Odes, but to have something new with
which to employ itself, though it should not be equal in Composition
with what it has been entertained already; and why should not new
Hymns as well as new Sermons be sent into the World, or if the last
have proved serviceable, why may not the former?" [45]

The situation revealed by this apology and plea had not
come about by authority or contrivance, but by the deepening love of the people for the hymns of Watts. He had
sought and found the plane of their thought and emotion,

[43]Preface, p. [xv].
[44]Doddridge to Watts, Dec. 13, 1744, in Gibbons, *Memoirs,* p. 306.
[45]Preface to the *Hymns adapted to Divine worship* of 1784, pp.
xii, xiii.

and in the general response of their hearts had found his just reward. An illustration of this is furnished by Dr. Doddridge, in a letter to Dr. Watts, dated April 5, 1731 : [46]

"On Tuesday last, I was preaching to a large assembly of plain country people at a village a few miles off, when, after a sermon from Hebrews, vi. 12, we sang one of your hymns, which, if I remember right, was the 140th of the 2nd book, and in that part of the worship I had the satisfaction to observe tears in the eyes of several of the people; and after the service was over, some of them told me that they were not able to sing, so deeply were their minds affected! and the clerk, in particular, said he could hardly utter the words as he gave them out. They were most of them poor people, who work for their living, yet, on the mention of your name, I found that they had read several of your books with great delight; and that your psalms and hymns were almost their daily entertainment: and when one of the company said, 'What if Dr. Watts should come down to Northampton!' another replied, with remarkable warmth, 'The very sight of him would be as good as an ordinance to me.'"

The feeling for Watts' *Psalms and Hymns* thus grew into an intense personal loyalty. It is well known that as late as the XIXth century there were many older Congregationalists who refused to sing any other hymns, and who kept their seats when such were announced.[47]

The supremacy which Watts gained and for a long time kept in the worship of the Independent churches (as also far beyond them) was indeed a triumph of personal influence and of principles that at first seemed radical enough. If we seek a date at which his domination of Independent worship culminated,—that is to say when the use of his *Psalms and Hymns* came nearest to unanimity, and there was least disposition to look beyond its covers—it would lie probably somewhere between the middle and end of the XVIIIth century. But Watts' *Psalms and Hymns* kept their place in the hearts of his people, and continued to be used, either alone or supplemented, until far into the XIXth. If we include all the religious bodies that used them, their actual circulation and use must have continually increased,

[46] Philip Doddridge's *Correspondence and Diary*, London, 1829-31, vol. iii, pp. 74, 75.
[47] *Cf.* W. G. Horder, *The Hymn Lover*, London, n. d., p. 100.

till past the middle of the XIXth century. It is calculated
that in its first twenty-five years a new edition appeared
every year, and claimed that as late as 1864 60,000 copies
were sold within the year.[48]

Striking as are these facts, some of the claims made for
Watts go beyond them. It is difficult to follow even so
competent a hymnologist as Mr. Garrett Horder, when he
says that "For more than a century Watts remained undis-
puted master of the hymnody of the Independents. No
other hymns than his were heard in any of the assemblies";
and again, that "for more than a century Watts was the
only hymnist of the Independent sanctuaries of our land."[49]

Where is the place of that century in the calendar? And
is such absolute uniformity predicable of any single year
of either the XVIIIth or XIXth centuries? It is hardly
conceivable even under the workings of a Uniformity Act,
and least so among Independents. We have to take account
of the little band of opponents and detractors, led by
Thomas Bradbury within their ranks, and by Romaine[50]
without, who accused Watts of lampooning[51] and "bur-
lesquing"[52] the Psalter, and refused to sing "Watts'
Whims":[53] also of the congregations in which psalm singing long continued,[54] partly for conscience' sake, more often
doggedly.

Moreover the very success of Watts' *Hymns* raised up
a succession of imitators, and their use called forth a succession of "Supplements." These Supplements did not respond to any demand of the people for more hymns, but
arose from the ambition of ministers to get their own hymns

[48]Duncan Campbell, *Hymns and Hymn Makers,* London, 1898, p. 38.

[49]*The Hymn Lover,* p. 100.

[50] "Why should Dr. Watts . . . take the precedence of the Holy
Ghost?" Romaine, *Essay on Psalmody,* 1775, p. 106.

[51]Bradbury to Watts, March 7, 1725-6, in Watts' *Posthumous Works,*
vol. ii, p. 202.

[52]Watts to Bradbury, March 15, 1725-6, *Ibid.,* vol. ii, p. 212.

[53]Wilson's *Dissenting Churches,* vol. iii, p. 527.

[54]*Cf.* Wilson, as already quoted.

into use, or their wish for hymns illustrative of a greater number of sermon topics. It is true that their supplementary form bore the strongest testimony to Watts' ascendency, but they also prevented that ascendency from becoming complete. Some gained a considerable circulation. Even the relatively unsuccessful ones were doubtless used in the compiler's own congregation and more or less in the congregations of his friends.

These Supplements began in 1720 with Simon Browne's *Hymns and Spiritual Songs. In three Books* (London), containing 266 hymns, all by himself. This reached a second edition in 1741, a third in 1760, and a number of the hymns continued in later use.[55] In 1769 Dr. Thomas Gibbons (Watts' biographer) published a collection, partly original, of *Hymns adapted to Divine worship: in two Books* (London); and a second (entirely original) in 1784, under the same title. Their narrow welcome and use appears from the statement in the 1784 preface that some copies of the earlier book remained unsold. Nor was the later book ever reprinted. George Burder, author of the once famous *Village Sermons,* published in 1784 *A Collection of Hymns from various authors, designed as a Supplement to Dr. Watts's Psalms and Hymns.* He aimed to gather up the best hymns published since Watts' death by such writers as Doddridge, Newton and Cowper, the Wesleys, and Toplady. His book met a warm welcome, found continuous use, and by 1840 had reached its thirty-seventh edition. So far was Burder from wishing to dislodge Watts from his supremacy that he published in 1812 an edition of the *Psalms, Hymns, and Spiritual Songs by the Rev. Isaac Watts, D.D.,* with some improvement in their arrangement. William Jay of Bath, a warm admirer of

---

[55]A recast of his "Come, holy spirit, heav'nly dove," is still familiar. Browne aimed at "the improvement of Psalmody." He bound up with his *Hymns* "A Sett of Tunes in 3 Parts (Mostly New)," wrote a "book" of hymns in "uncommon metres," and designated an appropriate tune for each hymn.

Watts, but desiring a greater variety of metres and corresponding tunes, published in 1791 *Selection of Hymns of peculiar metre, intended for the use of the Congregation meeting in Argyle Chapel.* It reached a second edition in 1797, and became the basis of his *Hymns as an Appendix to Dr. Watts* (Bath, 1833). The supplementing of Watts assumed great proportions in *A Collection of above six hundred Hymns: designed as a new Supplement to Dr. Watts's Psalms and Hymns. By the Rev. Edward Williams, D.D., and the Rev. James Boden* (Doncaster, 1801). It reached a second edition in 1803, a third in 1806, and a fifth in 1812. Dr. Williams also printed an improved edition of *The Psalms and Hymns of Dr. Watts,* claiming that "as the current editions are almost innumerable, so by far the greater number of them are shamefully incorrect." John Dobell sought even greater bulk in his *A new Selection of seven hundred evangelical Hymns . . . intended as a Supplement to Dr. Watts's Psalms and Hymns* (London, 1806). After additions the title read *more than eight hundred,* and Dobell arranged for binding in with it his *Dr. Watts's Fourth Book of Spiritual Hymns.* In the *Hymns, partly collected, and partly original, designed as a supplement to Dr. Watts' Psalms and Hymns: by William Bengo Collyer, D.D.* (London, 1812), no less than 979 hymns were provided, 57 of them original. Thomas Russell's *A Collection of Hymns designed as an Appendix,* &c. (London, 1813), was somewhat smaller and was more popular, attaining its twenty-second edition in 1843. Dr. Andrew Reed's *Supplement* of 1817 became the nucleus of his more important *Hymn Book* of 1842. Something in the way of concerted action as to Hymnody began to seem expedient, and in 1822 a committee of ministers in Leeds published *A Selection of Hymns for the use of the Protestant Dissenting Congregations of the Independent Order in Leeds.*

This succession of "Supplements" to Dr. Watts' tells its own story of a progress so natural and inevitable as to require little emphasis were it not for the curious and familiar assumption of the exclusive use of Watts' *Psalms and Hymns,* which even Dr. Conder expressed in 1851 by speaking of "our having been for a long time confined to this one Book." [56]

When the Congregational Union undertook the preparation of an official hymn book for general use, Dr. Conder and others who discerned the signs of the times favored a selection of Watts' best and of hymns by others in a single volume.[57] But the majority were unwilling to give up "Watts Entire"; and in 1836 *The Congregational Hymn Book* appeared as still *A Supplement to Dr. Watts's Psalms and Hymns,* containing a good selection of 620 hymns edited by Dr. Conder. The result was that in the years following many congregations gave up the use both of Watts and *The Congregational Hymn Book* in favor of private collections more compact and convenient.

The striking ascendency of Dr. Watts over Independent worship had at last reached its inevitable end. The reaction, equally inevitable to a popularity so great as to be undiscriminating, soon followed. It was discovered that a considerable percentage of Watts' work was prosaic and mechanical, and sometimes in questionable taste. People began to wonder why the churches had so long allowed a single mind to dominate their song. A winnowing of the familiar *Psalms and Hymns* began, and has steadily proceeded to our own time, with the result that in some recent Congregationalist hymnals Dr. Watts' contributions are outnumbered by the Methodist Wesley and the high church Neale. It is, however, to be said that the adoption of a hymn book by a single author had not seemed strange to congregations accustomed to one version of the Psalms. And we may agree with Conder[58] that the addiction of the Independents to Watts fixed the character of their devo-

[56]Josiah Conder, *The Poet of the Sanctuary,* London, 1851, p. 68.
[57]*Ibid.,* p. 69.
[58]*Ibid.,* p. 68.

tions, and under Providence preserved an evangelical tone of sentiment in their church worship.

2. HIS ASCENDENCY OVER THE PRESBYTERIANS TERMINATES IN A UNITARIAN HYMNODY

The measure of welcome given by Presbyterians to the *Psalms and Hymns* of Watts is hardly to be distinguished from that of the Independents with whom they fraternized. Some congregations, desiring an evangelical Hymnody, were ready to introduce the *Hymns;* some awaited the appearance of the *Psalms;* others were prejudiced in favor of the stricter type of Psalmody.

It was the refusal in 1717 of James Peirce, pastor of a psalm singing congregation at Exeter, to continue the accustomed singing of the doxology after the psalm that marked the beginning of the end of English Presbyterianism.[59] He might, and probably did, allege his objection to sing anything but the words of Psalms.[60] But the doxology was specifically Trinitarian, and the time one of dread lest the Arianism that had affected the Church of England should spread to Dissent. Peirce denied holding Arian views, but refused as tyrranous the demand of a committee exercising Presbyterial charge of the five Exeter meetings that he sign a declaration of belief in the Trinity. In this refusal he had wide sympathy. As a result of the Salters' Hall controversy of 1719,[61] to which it gave rise, the majority of Presbyterian ministers became committed to the attitude of non-subscription to any doctrinal formulas. In the fifty years following, most of the churches that did not die out or seek a refuge in Independency yielded one by one to the influences of the time, and drifted through

[59]McCrie, *Annals of English Presbytery*, London, 1872, p. 301.

[60]*Cf.* Drysdale, *History of Presbyterianism in England*, London, 1889, p. 500.

[61]For an account of it see H. S. Skeats, *A History of the Free Churches of England*, 2nd ed., London, 1869, pp. 302 ff. Watts, like Calamy, refused to attend the meeting at Salters' Hall.

various stages of Arian belief into the developed Unitarianism of the latter part of the XVIIIth century.

During the earlier of these years the propriety of using Watts' *Psalms and Hymns* remained unquestioned. But it was inevitable that certain passages should be confronted by the new opinions, especially the "Song of Praise to the ever-blessed Trinity," as Watts entitled the doxologies at the end of his volume of *Hymns*.

Martin Tomkins, dismissed from a dissenting pulpit as an Arian, and attending the Mare Street Presbyterian Meeting at Hackney, frequently protested against the use of the doxologies there. The pastor, the Rev. John Barker, one of the minority for subscription, declined to discontinue the custom. Tomkins printed in 1738 *A calm Enquiry whether we have any warrant, from Scripture, for addressing ourselves, in a way of prayer or praise, directly to the Holy Spirit*, etc.; prefaced by a letter to Mr. Barker, repeating his protests, and reinforced by quotations from Watts' later works. In a letter to Dr. Watts, dated April 21, 1738, Mr. Tomkins put to him the direct question,—

"Whether you now approve of what you have said concerning the *Gloria Patri*, in your Book of Hymns; and whether, upon your present notion of the Spirit, you can esteem some of those Doxologies you have given us there, I will not say, '*as some of the noblest parts of Christian worship*,' but as proper Christian worship? And if not, whether you may not think it becoming you, as a lover of truth, and as a Christian minister, to declare as much to the world; and not suffer such forms of worship to be recommended by your name and authority, to the use of the Christian Church in the present time and in future generations?"

On the margin of this letter (then in Mr. Palmer's possession) Dr. Watts had endorsed some twenty remarks, and opposite the last paragraph wrote:

"I freely answer, I wish some things were corrected. But the question with me is this: as I wrote them in sincerity at that time, is it not more for the edification of Christians, and the glory of God, to let them stand, than to ruin the usefulness of the whole book, by correcting them now, and perhaps bring further and false suspicions on my present opinions? Besides, I might tell you, that of all the books I have written, that particular copy is not mine. I sold it for a trifle to

Mr. *Lawrence* near thirty years ago, and his posterity make money of it to this day, and I can scarce claim a right to make any alteration in the book which would injure the sale of it." [62]

A perhaps exaggerated impression of the change in Dr. Watts' views served to endear his *Psalms and Hymns* to the Presbyterians. Some congregations, by the simple expedient of omitting certain passages and the doxologies, kept them in use until the end of the XVIIIth century.[63] But long before that various ministers, by modifying or supplementing Watts, had prepared for their congregations praise books more consonant with the new views. In most of them Watts' text was freely "tinkered." The report was industriously circulated that he had planned and even executed a revision of his *Hymns* on Arian lines, all evidence of which was suppressed at his death.[64] The report was plainly unwarranted, but it encouraged the hymn book makers to do for him what they supposed he would have done on his own behalf.

The eminent Michaijah Towgood is thought to be the editor of *A Collection of Psalms and Hymns for Divine worship* (London, 1757; 2nd ed.: 1779). In it Watts was supplemented by Tate and Brady, Addison, Doddridge and Browne. Michael Pope of the Leather Lane Meeting, London, followed with *A Collection of Psalms and Hymns for Divine worship* (London, 1760). Of these more than half were from Watts, freely altered; and there were original contributions from Kippis, Grove and other Presbyterians. Two books, the first partly, the second wholly, edited by Dr. Enfield, had a much longer life:—*A new Collection of Psalms proper for Christian worship* (Liverpool, 1764), and *Hymns for public worship, selected from*

[62]These documents were printed from the originals by the Rev. Samuel Palmer in his notes to Johnson's *Life of Watts* (1791). They were reprinted in the Boston *Memoirs of Watts and Doddridge* (1793), and substantially in Milner.

[63]*Cf.* preface to *A Collection of Hymns and Psalms,* ed. by Kippis et. al. 1795.

[64]See "The Early Editions of Watts's Hymns," already cited.

various authors, and intended as a Supplement to Dr. Watts's Psalms (Warrington, 1772). To the latter the editor's neighbor, Mrs. Barbauld, contributed six hymns, two of which are still sung. *An abridgment of Dr. Watts's Psalms and Hymns, with some alterations,* &c. (cir. 1780), edited by W. Wood and B. Carpenter, is interesting for its reversion to that author and restoration in the main of his text.

The new "Presbyterianism" had already been augmented by recruits from the Church of England, who brought with them a taste for liturgical worship. A series of psalm and hymn collections appended to Forms of Prayer began with *A Form of Prayer and a new Collection of Psalms, for the use of a Congregation of Protestant Dissenters in Liverpool* (Liverpool, 1763).[65] Theophilus Lindsey's *A Collection of Psalms and Hymns for public worship,* which followed in 1774, was appended to Dr. Samuel Clarke's rescension of the Prayer Book. The most interesting of the group is *A Collection of Hymns for public worship: on the general principles of natural and revealed Religion* (Salisbury, 1778). It aimed at the common denominator, shunning spheres of controversy. It reflects also the poetic feeling of one of its editors, Benjamin Williams, last minister of the old Presbyterian congregation in Salisbury: it has metrical variety, and attains a flavor of letters.

By this time the number of available hymn books was considerable in England, and two were about to appear in the North of Ireland, where the Scottish *Psalms in meeter* had so far continued in vogue:—the *Hymns for the use of the Presbyterian Congregation in Lisburn* (Belfast, 1787), and a Londonderry *Collection of Psalms and Hymns proper for Christian worship* (1788). The older Presbyterianism was being completely submerged by Unitarianism of the more aggressive type, as represented by Priestley, leaving

[65]*Cf.* an interesting note by Jas. Martineau in the index to *The University Hymn Book,* Cambridge, Mass., 1895, under "Collet, Samuel."

hardly a vestige of its earlier denominational existence beyond the name "Presbyterian" still applied to Unitarian chapels. Newcome Cappe of York endeavored to keep to common ground by confining himself to Psalms in *A Selection of Psalms for social worship* (1786), and George Walker of Nottingham published *A Collection of Psalms and Hymns for public worship, unmixed with the disputed doctrines of any sect* (Warrington, 1788). But Priestley himself, in his *Psalms and Hymns for the use of the New Meeting in Birmingham* (1790), freely modified Watts "for the sake of rendering the *sentiment* unexceptionable to Unitarian Christians." "It is to *long use* only," he claimed in the preface, "that many of Watts's own verses are indebted for the little offence they now give even to the ear, and much more to the understanding." Unhappily the fire by which the mob destroyed his dwelling and the New Meeting House consumed the new hymn books also to such an extent that his people had to fall back upon Watts' *Psalms and Hymns* in their unexpurgated form, as used at the Old Meeting.

In London and its vicinity "the generality of the Presbyterian Societies [had] contented themselves solely with Dr. Watts's Psalms."[66] To correct this four ministers, headed by the venerable and admirable Andrew Kippis, combined to issue *A Collection of Hymns and Psalms for public and private worship; selected and prepared by Andrew Kippis, D.D., F.R.S., & F.S.A.; Abraham Rees, D.D., F.R.S., F.L.S.; the Rev. Thomas Jervis, and the Rev. Thomas Morgan, LL.D., London, 1795.* Its 690 pieces were selected and pruned "to promote just and rational sentiments of religion." There was a second edition in 1797, and supplements in 1807 and 1852. This collection found a wider acceptance and use than any of its predecessors, which were mostly confined to the localities in which· their several editors ministered. It was probably fairly representative of the Unitarianism of the XVIIIth and early XIXth cen-

[66] Preface to the Kippis *Collection,* 1795.

turies. But the celebration of the Divine nature and works
to which it was mainly devoted does not appear to have
aroused any warmth of feeling in the compilers, and their
avoidance of the area of personal Christian experience
seems to leave the worshipper a spectator at Bethlehem and
Calvary rather than a participant in redemption.[67]

The individualism of the Unitarian movement militated
not only against a standard of doctrine but even against a
common hymn book. English and Irish Unitarian Hymnody has no corporate history, but proceeds by a succession
of individual hymn books; and in their production the
years following the publication of the Kippis *Collection*
were the most active. The earlier period of Unitarian
Hymnody may be regarded as ended when in 1840 Dr.
Martineau published his *Hymns for the Christian Church
and Home*. And it has been estimated that in the forty-five
years intervening between Kippis and Martineau on an
average one Unitarian hymn book, large or small, was
issued every year.[68] Of these the most significant, from the
point of view of circulation and use, were Robert Aspland's
A Selection of Psalms and Hymns for Unitarian worship
(1810),[69] Dr. Lant Carpenter's *A Selection of Psalms and
Hymns for social and private worship* (Exeter, 1812), and
*A Selection of Hymns and Psalms for Christian worship.
By H. E. Howse, jun.* (Bath, 1830). Howse claimed no
"superior assortment of hymns," but offered to the poor
"a good sized Hymn Book at a low price" (in 32mo 1s.),
and seems thus to have met a need.

But a few collections of the period have a special interest
as bearing upon the development of a Unitarian Hymnody.
The need of it, and also the ideal of it as presented to the
minds of the early leaders, are set forth in George Walker's
preface of 1788:—

[67]*Cf.* a Unitarian estimate in Julian, *Dict. Hymn.*, p. 1193.
[68]Valentine D. Davis in Julian, *ut supra.*
[69]In this the term "Unitarian" seems to have first appeared on the
title-page of a hymn book.

"The great change in religious faith which has taken place in this island, since the period in which the different collections of Psalms or Hymns of most general acceptation were first introduced, has rendered it highly improper, if not absolutely criminal, to continue any longer in the use of what the mind at present revolts from. Whatever be the faith of any society, no worship ought to be presented to God, which contradicts that faith. It had indeed been well if the peculiarities of religious faith had never intruded into a part of worship, whose characteristic features are gratitude, and a virtuous conformity to the will of God. As our predecessors however unhappily thought otherwise, it is the principal object of this collection to remove the offence, which their doctrinal zeal has occasioned to their successors."

The ideal thus set forth of a Hymnody doctrinally colorless was that held in common by perhaps all the early leaders; and prior editors of Unitarian hymn books had not only sought to contribute new hymns according with it, but had felt free to "accommodate" to it hymns already in use. But the acrid vigor of Walker's insistence on the pressing duty of modifying existing hymns was occasioned by the persistence of the people's predilection for the one version of the Psalms bearing an "evangelical interpretation" and their doubtless illogical attachment to the evangelical hymns of Watts and Doddridge. Walker applied his principle (especially to Watts) with a strong though unskilled hand; "the alterations bearing no small proportion to the whole work, and in many of the psalms and hymns the retaining the name of the original author must be considered as a mere acknowledgment of the source from which the composition was derived." [70] In this course he was followed by subsequent editors, with the inevitable result that in extracting the color of doctrine from the hymns, much of their vigor and warmth also passed out.

The first generation of Unitarians, who had been familiar with the original text of these hymns, objected to the changes, but in course of time, as the modified texts passed from book to book, only the more curious were aware that Watts, Doddridge, Wesley, Toplady, Newton, and Cowper

[70] Preface, p. vii.

had expressed themselves quite otherwise than in the lines bearing their names in the Unitarian hymn books.[71] But Robert Wallace, a minister at Chesterfield, became dissatisfied with the "altogether unwarranted" liberties editors had taken with the originals, and with the method itself of obtaining a Unitarian Hymnody by a process of expurgating orthodox hymns. He was influenced also[72] by Mrs. Barbauld's plea[73] for more warmth and a freer scope for the language of the affections than was then thought permissible in Unitarian worship. He gave much time to preparing a hymn book in which "no wanton or unadvised deviations" from the originals were admitted and for which new hymns were sought. It appeared as *A Selection of Hymns for public and private worship* (Chesterfield, 1822; 2nd ed., 1826), a notable rather than very influential step in the right direction.

In the debates and contests between Evangelicals and Unitarians little attention had been given to Unitarian hymn books. In the legal proceedings respecting the Lady Hewley Fund, among numerous Unitarian publications introduced into the pleadings to exhibit their tenets, no reference appears to have been made to the hymns used in their chapels. But in 1834 the editor of *The Christian Observer*, the great Evangelical organ, happened to take up a hymn book that for two and a half years had been in

[71] Some of the hymn book editors were no exception. Thus Dr. Lant Carpenter, explaining his references to his sources, says: "A large proportion of the older hymns were in the first instance taken from collections in common use among Unitarians, with which I had long been familiar, and which therefore might appear to me less altered from the originals than they really were." *The Christian Observer*, Oct., 1834, p. 594.

[72] See his preface of 1822.

[73] *Devotional pieces, compiled from the Psalms and the Book of Job; to which are prefixed Thoughts on the devotional taste*, &c. (London, 1775), pp. 14 ff. Both the selection and essay were coldly received by the Priestley circle of Unitarians to whom no doubt it was especially addressed, as also by the public. *Cf.* Grace A. Ellis, *Memoir of A. L. Barbauld*, Boston, 1874, vol. i, p. 74.

his hands for review, and "utterly forgotten,"—*A Collection of Hymns for the use of Unitarian Christians in public worship and in the private culture of the religious affections* (Bristol, 1831). This book, edited by Dr. Lant Carpenter, differed in no respect from numerous predecessors in the extent and freedom of its use of evangelical hymns "accommodated" to Unitarian views. But to the editor the method was plainly a novelty, and in a belated review he subjected both method and results to a scathing condemnation.[74] For "torturing the sacred strains of orthodox lyrists till they uttered sounds utterly discrepant to those intended by their authors" he charged the editor with "heinous crimes against right feeling," "indecent, unfeeling, and pregnant with enormous evils," but in so far as the mutilations were acknowledged and fairly pointed out, not with dishonesty. He found, however, numerous hymns of evangelical writers, whose names were attached to them, seriously altered and without any indication of such changes being given. These alterations he characterized as "secret and disingenuous," misleading, and "in truth the most disgracefully dishonest."

The subsequent debate made it clear that in the omission of indications of alteration Dr. Carpenter was guilty of nothing worse than that ignorance of his materials and carelessness in their handling that obtained generally among the compilers of hymn books. But the larger questions raised in this debate are still of living interest. The practice of signing an author's name to what he did not write is even now common enough, but ought to find no defender. The question of the extent to which an editor is justified in "accommodating" the sentiments of another's hymn to the views of himself or his constituency is larger and more difficult. It involves matters of principle, expediency and good taste; and every editor must decide them for himself. *The Christian Observer* was doubtless unaware that honored

---

[74]The review is in the number for July, 1834; for the subsequent debate see the numbers for October and December of the same year.

editors of its own school had "accommodated" the Wesleys' hymns to Calvinism by expunging such phrases as favored "universal redemption," "the second rest," and the like. To bind an editor of any school by a rigid rule that a hymn must in all cases be taken verbatim or left alone would not promote the best interests of Hymnody. On the other hand, an expurgated Hymnody such as was developed by early Unitarianism is well adapted to promote just such bad feeling as *The Christian Observer* manifested, and at best fails to win one's regard.

This was the view taken of the current Unitarian Hymnody by the accomplished John R. Beard of Manchester, whether or not he was influenced by the unpleasant debate in the pages of *The Christian Observer*. To him "it seemed a sort of reflection on either the talent or the devotional feeling" of Unitarians that they were "necessitated to employ in their psalmody the compositions of Trinitarian and Calvinistic writers" "in an altered if not mutilated shape." The necessary adaptation involved frequently "matters of high doctrinal importance," tending "to create in the minds of Unitarian compilers a certain jealousy which, in pruning away the exuberance of orthodoxy, destroyed sometimes the richness of scriptural truth," and involving changes "alien from the original spirit of the hymn" and "in many cases repugnant to taste and feeling." [75]

"The natural resource," Mr. Beard said, "is to prepare a collection of hymns composed exclusively by Unitarians." [76] His hymn book, so prepared, appeared as *A Collection of Hymns for public and private worship. Compiled by John R. Beard. London and Manchester, 1837.* Of living writers whom he enlisted in his project Dr. Bowring leads with 82 hymns; William Gaskell follows with 79, J. C. Wallace with 64, J. R. Wreford with 55,

---

[75] From his preface of 1837.
[76] In his proposals printed in *The Christian Teacher and Chronicle,* 1836.

J. Johns with 35, Jacob Brettell with 16, Harriet Martineau
and Jane Roscoe with 5 each, Hugh Hutton with 3, William
S. Roscoe with 1. Of the generation that had passed, Mrs.
Barbauld, then regarded as its foremost Unitarian hymn
writer, leads with 14 hymns, John Taylor follows with 12,
Edmund Butcher and William Roscoe with 8 each, Emily
Taylor with 7, Sir J. E. Smith with 6, W. Lamport with 3,
Dr. Estlin and Dr. Drummond with 2 each, William
Drennan and P. Houghton with 1 each. If to these names
we add George Dyer, John J. Taylor and Lant Carpenter
of Beard's contemporaries and Helen Maria Williams
(author of "While Thee I Seek, protecting Power") of
the prior generation, the representation of the later Unitarian hymn writers is practically complete. There are
also no less than 56 hymns by American Unitarians. The
representation of the earlier writers is far less inclusive.
Of the original Arian or semi-Arian group, including Henry
Grove, Thomas Scott, Roger Flexman, and John Breckell,
there are no hymns. Of the writers of developing Unitarianism, there are 6 by Henry Moore, 4 by Thomas
Jervis and 1 by William Enfield, but Benjamin Williams,
Andrew Kippis and George Walker are not represented.

Beard's *Collection* is thus an anthology of the original
hymn writing of a developed Unitarianism, and affords a
basis for estimating it as affecting the ideal of the Hymn
and as contributing to the store of hymns. Unitarian
Hymnody should be set not only against Dr. Watts' System
of Praise which made its background, but also against the
Hymnody of Christian Experience developed, as will duly
appear, by the great XVIIIth century Revival. Its criterion
is doctrinal. It is a protest against and a substitute for
hymns "with sectarian peculiarities" (by which we may
understand what is called evangelical doctrine) and "the
fervors of fanaticism"[77] (by which we may understand
Methodism). This sense of protest accounts for the devotional coldness and aloofness from Christianity of the

[77]Beard's preface.

earlier hymn writing, and this sense of reconstruction accounts for a gradual return to the area of Christian experience and that "warmth of the true Christian life" sought for and expressed in Beard's *Collection*. Apart from the doctrinal feature the Unitarian Hymnody showed no special development of the Hymn in any way. The Arian hymns had affiliated strongly with Metrical Psalmody; the Unitarian hymns to a large extent pertain to the realm of devotional poetry rather than of Hymnody proper; and of both the proportion is small that can be said to rise above the level of the commonplace.[78] Among Beard's contributors time has set the seal of approval on the work of two. Sir John Bowring found a ground where all Christian hearts may meet in such hymns as "God is Love, His mercy brightens," and "In the cross of Christ I glory"; as did also John R. Wreford in his "Lord, I believe; Thy power I own," and "When my love to Christ grows weak." Among Unitarians themselves, Beard's *Collection* was less used as a source book for later compilers in England than in the United States.

As a protest against hymn tinkering and as a novel effort to reconstruct Unitarian Hymnody out of materials exclusively Unitarian Beard's *Collection* is of permanent interest. As a hymn book intended for congregational use it was a complete failure. It involved an entire separation of Unitarian Praise from the main stream of English Hymnody, the renunciation of all the great hymns of the Church, however unexceptionable from the Unitarian standpoint; and for this the ministers and congregations were by no means ready. "The plan strikes us," said *The Christian Examiner,* "as most extraordinary.[79] And in this

[78]This is Henry Ware jr's estimate of Beard's *Collection*—"We are not certain that there exist any better than a few of the best of these. There are many that are only tolerable, and some that are intolerable; many incomplete, many prosaic and commonplace, and some unsuited to use in public worship." *The Christian Examiner* (Boston), March, 1838, p. 94.

[79]November, 1836, p. 271.

judgment most people are likely to concur. As a protest also against the "accommodation" of orthodox hymns, Beard's efforts were to prove equally in vain.

After the rise of this new Unitarian Hymnody there was no further (old) Presbyterian Psalmody or Hymnody in England, beyond that of a faithful remnant in the Northern counties and some scattered congregations of resident Scotchmen, until the formation in 1836 of the Presbyterian Church in England, which began its career by harking back to *The Psalms of David in meeter* of 1650.

3. His Ascendency over the Baptists Leads up to a Homiletical Hymnody

Among the older General Baptist churches the strong prejudice against public singing lingered through much of the XVIIIth century, encasing their worship in a hard shell which even the influence of Watts found it hard to penetrate. And as one by one these churches yielded to the modern spirit, it would be hard to measure his part in the many inducements to the change. There was no notable church extension in the denomination until the Methodist Revival, when numerous congregations of those led to adopt Baptist sentiments were organized in Yorkshire and neighboring counties. These new churches came at once within the influence of Methodist hymn singing. With some seceders from the Old Connexion they formed in 1770 the New Connexion, under whose auspices the first General Baptist hymn book appeared at Halifax in 1772 as *Hymns and Spiritual Songs, mostly collected from various authors; with a few that have not been published before.* In 1785 Samuel Deacon, a village clockmaker and pastor of Barton, published his original hymns as *A new composition of Hymns and Poems chiefly on Divine subjects; designed for the amusement and edification of Christians of all denominations, more particularly those of the General Baptist persuasion* (Leicester, 1785). These homely hymns had much of the revival spirit, and became known by the name of *Barton Hymns,* which was given them in the second edition (1797).

In 1791 the General Baptist Association authorized a new hymn book, which appeared in 1793 as *Hymns and Spiritual Songs, selected from various authors* (London, D. Taylor). But in 1800 John Deacon, who had helped to compile it, issued on his own account *A new and large Collection of Hymns and Psalms* (London, H. D. Symonds); and this, after winning its unauthorized way among the churches, was revised by a Committee of the General Baptist Association, and in 1830 formally adopted as the hymn book of the Connexion,[80] under the title of *The General Baptist Hymn Book.*

Among Particular Baptist churches some were already singing hymns, especially on sacramental occasions, when Watts' *Hymns* first appeared. His *Hymns,* and later his *Psalms,* doctrinally acceptable, fell in with the desire to enlarge the use of hymns, and helped much also to create such a desire. It is significant that after the appearance of Stennett's two little booklets of sacramental hymns no Baptist hymn book was published until 1769. There is little difficulty in filling the apparent gap of half a century. It was the time when Watts' *Psalms and Hymns* were gradually working their way into the churches and into the hearts of the Particular Baptists, and establishing there a place only second to that they held among his own people.

But one effect of the use of Watts' hymns was to encourage the habit of employing the last hymn in the service as an application of the sermon. In the course of time it became apparent that the *Hymns* were not in sufficient variety to cover all the sermon themes. Preachers were led to search other books for hymns pertinent to their sermons, and a number to compose hymns of their own on the Watts model, to be lined out to the people after the ser-

[80]*Cf.* H. S. Burrage, *Baptist Hymn Writers and their Hymns,* Portland, Me., n. d., p. 632.

mon.[81]. With some of these compositions in hand, but especially in view of the publication in 1760 of the hymns of Miss Anne Steele, two pastors, John Ash of Pershore and Caleb Evans of Bristol, felt that the time had come for a Baptist hymn book. They published at Bristol in 1769 *A Collection of Hymns adapted to public worship.* As it was designed to supersede Watts' *Psalms and Hymns,* many of his best hymns were included. Of the new Baptist writers, there were 62 by Miss Steele, and some by Beddome, Daniel Turner, Joseph Stennett, and James Newton. It was well received, and continued in use for more than half a century, reaching a tenth edition in 1827. But it was far indeed from superseding Watts in Baptist use. So many churches remained which were unwilling to give up his *Psalms and Hymns* and yet desired other and especially Baptist hymns, that John Rippon, Gill's successor at Carter Lane, published in 1787 *A Selection of Hymns from the best authors, intended to be an Appendix to Dr. Watts's Psalms and Hymns* (London, T. Wilkins). This book of 588 hymns was conceived in the interest of the "Hymn after Sermon," in the belief that "A too great Variety is a thing scarcely to be conceived of," and full use was made of the Hymnody of the Wesleyan and Evangelical revival.[82] Rippon's judgment and taste, his command of originals, and his editorial discretion, were such as to ensure lasting success, and to secure to himself a permanent place in the history of hymn singing. His *Selection* reached its tenth edition in 1800, enlarged by sixty hymns, and was again enlarged in 1827. After Rippon's death, it appeared in 1844, increased by an addition of 400 hymns, as *The Comprehensive Rippon,* containing 1174 hymns. When we remember that these were an appendix to "Watts entire," we become aware of the lengths to which the homiletical

---

[81]*Cf.* preface to Rippon's *Selection,* 1787. Rippon states that only then was the practice of singing without lining "gaining ground" in some congregations "in London, at Bristol, and elsewhere."

[82]Preface, p. 3.

conception and use of hymns naturally leads. Well had
Rippon feared, in introducing his original 588 hymns, "that
after sermon there will be many Subjects sought for in
vain, both in this Appendix, and in Dr. Watts." [83]

Rippon's *Selection* became, in connection with Watts, a
standard of Baptist Hymnody, which it did so much to
enlarge. It served also as a source book for the makers of
many hymn books in the Church outside, in a period when
hymnal making was largely done with scissors; and by this
means Rippon has permanently impressed himself upon the
Churches as having influenced their choice of hymns. His
book in itself carries forward Particular Baptist Hymnody
to our own time, being used in Spurgeon's Tabernacle till
1866 in connection with Watts.[84] It was also a link of
connection between Baptist Hymnody in England and
America, and was reprinted in New York as early as 1792.

There appeared, however, from one motive or another,
a considerable number of other Baptist collections during
the earlier years of the XIXth century. One line of these
represents the desire of hymn writers to give currency to
their own compositions. Among such, not of sufficient
importance to be grouped with the Baptist "School of
Watts" hereafter to be noticed, were:—Jonathan Franklin's
*Hymns and Spiritual Songs, composed for the use of the
Baptist Church at Croyden, Surrey* (1801; 3rd ed., 1823);
W. Augustus Clarke's eccentric *Hymns doctrinal and experimental for the free-born citizens of Zion* (1801); W.
W. Horne's *Sion's Harmony of Praise* (1823), with 98
originals and the declaration, "I am happy to class with
those whom I have denominated choristers"; and John H.
Hinton's (116) *Hymns by a Minister* (1833).[85]

Another line of hymn books purposed no more than to
supplement Watts or Watts and Rippon on themes over-

[83]Preface, p. 4.
[84]Preface to Spurgeon's *Our own Hymn Book.*
[85]Sketches and specimen hymns of these writers may be found in
Burrage, *op. cit.*

looked by them. Such were James Upton's *A Collection of Hymns designed as a Supplement to Dr. Watts's Psalms and Hymns* (1814; 3rd ed., 1818); George Francis' *A Selection of Hymns* (1824); and the much more successful *A New Selection of Hymns* (1828), compiled by a committee of Particular Baptist ministers, and edited by W. Groser; of which 60,000 copies were sold in ten years.[86] It was enlarged in 1838 as *A Selection of Hymns for the use of Baptist Congregations,* and a supplement was added as late as 1871. More independent of the Watts tradition were John Bailey's *Sion's Melody* (1813) with some originals; James H. Evans' *Psalms and Hymns, selected chiefly for public worship,* and the Scottish *A Selection of Hymns adapted for divine worship* of Christopher Anderson, both of 1818; and John Stenson's *The Baptist's Hymn Book* (1838) with many of his own hymns.

Still a third line of hymn books came from the high Calvinistic element among Particular Baptists, and represented their dissatisfaction on doctrinal grounds with the continued use of Watts' *Psalms and Hymns* and the supplementary *Selection* of Rippon. In turning from Unitarianism to the rigid wing of the Particular Baptists, we have crossed from the extreme left to the extreme right of the theology of dissent; and while the Unitarians were renouncing Watts' *Psalms and Hymns* as "Trinitarian and Calvinistic," the high Calvinist Baptists were turning from them as not sufficiently differentiated from Arminianism. *A new Selection of Hymns* by John Stevens of Meard's Court Chapel, London, appeared in 1809, and as rearranged by J. S. Anderson in 1871 is still in use. William Gadsby, who like Stevens was a writer of hymns, published *A Selection of Hymns for public worship* in 1814. To this nucleus a second part of 157 of his own hymns, a supplement compiled by him, nearly the whole of Hart's *Hymns,* and a further supplement by J. C. Philpot, were successively annexed; and the whole, edited by Gadsby's son John, is still

[86]Preface, ed. 1838, p. i.

in use as *Gadsby's Hymns*.[87]   Some of the Hymns in Watts'
and Rippon's books give, Gadsby said in his original preface,
"as legal a sound as if they had been forged at a certain
foundry," the allusion being of course to Wesley's meeting
house known by that name.   Edward Mote published in
1836 *Hymns of praise. A new Selection of Gospel Hymns,
containing all the excellencies of our spiritual poets, and
many originals. For the use of all spiritual worshippers.*
To Mote spirituality and Calvinism were inseparable, and
his collection, which reached a third edition in 1853, is an
anthology of Calvinistic praise.   The latest of the group,
and probably the one in largest present use, appeared in
1837 as *The Saints' Melody. By David Denham.*   Denham
disparaged neither Watts nor Rippon, but rendered them
superfluous by the very extent of his collection gathered
and arranged to illustrate the Five Points of Calvinism.
By a curious coincidence, hardly undesigned, his book and
its supplement (now known as *Denham's Selection*) and the
rival selection of Gadsby with its supplements, attain to an
identical total of 1138 hymns.   It would seem that all
varying tastes among the high Calvinist element thus found
a provision as ample as it has proved permanent.

II.   In Scotland

1.   His Influence: the "Translations and Paraphrases" (1745, 1781)

In Scotland Watts' *Psalms and Hymns* circulated largely,
and their influence brought about a renewal of the long
shelved movement for what was called "The improvement
of the Psalmody."   In 1741 an overture came before the
General Assembly proposing that some Scripture passages

---

[87]John Gadsby also published *A Companion to Gadsby's Selection of
Hymns* and illustrative *Memoirs of Hymn-writers and compilers* (4th
ed., 1870).   "The work has now reached its 4th Edition.   Had I
written only smooth things, it would probably ere this have reached
its 10th," p. 157.

be turned into metre for use in public worship. This was
the beginning of the movement out of which came the
famous "Scottish Paraphrases." [88]

The proposal had come at the very close of the session,
and was referred to the Assembly's Commission without
discussion. That probably would have been the end, had
not the Presbytery of Dundee interested itself, and secured
from the Assembly of 1742 the appointment of a committee
to make a collection of paraphrases. This committee ac-
complishing nothing, it was enlarged, and in 1745 presented
a collection of forty-five paraphrases. After much debate
the Assembly agreed so far as to order these printed and
sent down to Presbyteries for their "observations" on them
and on the whole project.[89] They appeared in July, 1745,
as *Translations and Paraphrases of several passages of
Sacred Scripture. Collected and prepared by a Committee
appointed by the General Assembly of the Church of Scotland. And by the Act of last Assembly, transmitted to
Presbyteries for their consideration. Edinburgh, printed
by Robert Fleming and Company, Printers to the Church of
Scotland, MDCCXLV.*

This pioneer volume of Scottish Presbyterian Hymnody
reveals the extent to which Dr. Watts' influence was
behind the movement toward hymns. Of the forty-five
pieces, no less than nineteen are by him, five are by his
follower Doddridge, and several others are based upon
hymns of Watts. In the Scottish contributions and compilations which make up the remainder, the manner of Watts
is hardly less evident. In both the title and preface of
the volume care is taken to emphasize the purely Scriptural character of the proposed additions to Psalmody, and
the securing of this end furnishes the only obvious justification of the system of hymn tinkering which the compilers

[88]Extracts from the minutes of General Assembly and of Presbyteries covering the movement are conveniently gathered in Maclagan,
The Scottish Paraphrases, Edinburgh, 1889, pp. 167 ff.
[89]*Acts of General Assembly.* Edinburgh, 1843, p. 681.

carried to a great extreme. The paraphrases so printed had as yet no status, and by refraining from any report upon them the Presbyteries succeeded in blocking their authorization. A determined minority kept the matter alive for ten years. It being alleged in 1749 that the confusions incident to the Jacobite rising had caused the copies of the *Paraphrases* in the hands of numerous Presbyteries to be mislaid, a new edition was printed in 1750, and again sent down. Perhaps to satisfy the minority, these amended paraphrases were authorized for private use, and they obtained some unauthorized public use.[90] But their approval still awaited the action of Presbyteries. In 1755 it appeared that thirty-two Presbyteries had never yet acted on the *Paraphrases*. Such determined opposition seems to have disheartened the progressives, and while the delinquent Presbyteries were formally ordered to report to the next Assembly, the whole project was allowed once more to drop out of sight as still impracticable.

The agitation of the proposal to enlarge the Psalmody acted as a constant stimulus to hymn production, and numerous collections of original hymns were published within the bounds of the Church of Scotland. That of John Forbes, *Some Scriptural Hymns, selected from sundry passages of Holy Writ, intended for the service of the Church in secret or society, as may be thought agreeable* (Aberdeen, 1757), plainly presents his productions as candidates for liturgical use; and hence they are kept within the limits of paraphrase. John Willison, on the other hand, in his *One hundred Gospel Hymns* (Edinburgh, 1747), professedly refrains from paraphrasing Scripture, "seeing this design is under consideration by publick authority, and committed to hands more capable." He offers freely composed gospel hymns as "much adapted to Sacramental Occasions"; presumably for meditative use, as he could hardly have contemplated their liturgical employment at that date. William Cruden, in his *Hymns on a variety of Divine subjects*

[90] Preface to edition of 1781.

(Aberdeen, 1761), takes a middle course, which may be described as a more or less free paraphrasing of Scripture; hardly presuming to suppose he can contribute to the enlargement of church Psalmody he so earnestly desires, but hoping that the use of his hymns in families "may be attended with no impropriety." Cruden's preface is interesting as showing the state of feeling which underlay the movement for the authorization of paraphrases:

"Several attempts have been made of late years to improve our Psalmody: and yet when we consider the vast extent of the subject, its inconceivable importance to mankind, and how delightful a field the plan of redemption spreads to view; 'tis surprizing that more has not been done in that way; especially when many subjects, dry and uninteresting, are every day canvassed, and almost exhausted by the unwearied efforts of genius. Also when so loud a cry has been raised of late, thro' many corners of our national church, for the reformation of our music in the praises of the sanctuary; it might have been expected that frequent attempts would have been made, to enlarge the matter of our Psalmody, by an addition of New Testament Hymns suited to these days of clearer light, and superior advantages vouchsafed to us above former ages."

It may be presumed that such views and feelings were gradually extending, but it was not till twenty years had elapsed from the failure of 1755 that the *Paraphrases* were again brought to the attention of the General Assembly. In 1775 the Presbytery of Glasgow and Ayr sent up an overture alleging that many ministers and congregations desired to employ them in worship, and praying that their use be authorized. This overture resulted in the appointment of a committee who entered systematically upon the compilation of an enlarged collection of paraphrases, and after some disagreements on their part and the customary postponements on the part of the Assembly, were able to present their completed work to the Assembly of 1781, and to solicit definite action upon it. The Assembly passed an "Interim act anent the Psalmody," sending down the *Paraphrases* to the Presbyteries for examination and report, "and in the meantime they allow this collection of Sacred Poems to be used in public worship in congregations where the Minister finds it for edification." [91]   The committee was authorized to correct and publish the collection, and the exclusive right to print it was vested in James Dickson, printer to the Church. This act, however lacking in finality, is the authorization on which the use of the *Paraphrases* has ever since rested. Excepting to extend the printer's patent, the Assembly has at no time taken further action concerning them. It is probable that those who had at heart the enlargement of the Psalmody, thought it prudent to rest satisfied with what they had gained. Most of the Presbyteries also were content to take no action. That of Kirkcaldy, on the other hand, condemned the collection as defective in execution; and expressed their unanimous opinion that it ought to be rejected.[92]

The new collection appeared in 1781 as *Translations and Paraphrases, in verse, of several passages of Sacred Scripture. Collected and prepared by a Committee of the General Assembly of the Church of Scotland, in order to be sung in churches. Edinburgh, printed and sold by J. Dickson, Printer to the Church of Scotland, MDCCLXXXI.*

It included the forty-five paraphrases of the earlier edition, often much revised, and twenty-two that were new; among the later several of the best-known, such as "Few are thy days, and full of woe," "Come, let us to the Lord our God," and "Where high the heavenly temple stands." [93] Apart from their inherent value, the interest of the *Paraphrases* of 1781 lies in their success. They mark no development in the principles of Scottish Psalmody, but they embody the means by which the earlier authorization of paraphrases became actually carried out in public worship.

[91]Extract from "Act of the Assembly," in 1781 ed. of *Paraphrases*.
[92]Maclagan, *op. cit.*, p. 183.
[93]The last of these is one of several regarding which an interminable controversy as to their authorship has been waged between the partisans of Michael Bruce, a young poet, and of the Rev. John Logan, one of the Assembly's committee. For a partial bibliography of the very voluminous controversial literature, see Julian's *Dict. of Hymnology*, p. 189.

In one respect, however, the collection of 1781 registers an advance. At the end appears a little group of "Hymns." The preface offers no explanation, saying merely, "a few Hymns are subjoined." Of these hymns, three are Addison's, first appearing in the *Spectator,* one is Watts' ("Bless'd morning, whose young dawning rays"), and the last is probably of Scottish origin ("The hour of my departure's come"). Most of these are decidedly "hymns of human composure," and constitute an apparently unconsidered intrusion of free Hymnody into the Scriptural Paraphrases of the Scottish Church.

The use of the *Paraphrases* being not of obligation, their introduction into the worship of the parish churches was by no means universal, and was not always accomplished without disturbance. Where minister and people were agreed in wishing the *Paraphrases,* their introduction involved no more than the protest or perhaps secession of one or more irreconcilables. At Leith, in 1782, where the Rev. John Logan, one of the active spirits in the movement, and the alleged author of a number of the *Paraphrases,* gave notice on his own responsibility that the "Additional Psalmody was to be introduced into the public worship, Sabbath next," [94] the session met and protested against the precipitant manner of making the change, but seem to have submitted. There were, however, many among the ministers and people of the Scottish Church, who never received the *Paraphrases,* or took any part in singing them, to the end of their lives. Although they were soon customarily printed along with the Metrical Psalms and bound up with them at the end of the Bibles, from numerous pulpits they were never announced, and from numerous private copies of the Bible containing them they were torn out or pasted down.[95] This opposition was partly that of the advocates of the singing of psalms alone, but by no means altogether. It was a time of bitter feeling, and, in the minds of many

[94]Maclagan, *op. cit.,* p. 40.
[95]*Cf.* J. S. Curwen, *Worship Music,* 1st series, p. 166.

Evangelicals, the movement for enlarging the Psalmody
had been allowed to fall into the hands of the party of
"Moderates." The presence in the Assembly's committee
of Logan, and the Blairs, the Wisharts, Cumming, Robertson and Alexander Carlyle, made such association inevitable in the case of the *Paraphrases* of 1781. Dr. Martin
of Monimail, one of the minority of the committee, claimed
that he had no proper share in the compilation, and that the
results were not what he was led to expect.[96] He may have
been prejudiced by the fact that all but one of his own
compositions, and all those "of a pious lady of his acquaint-
ance" which he fathered, were rejected; but he was one of
many who looked at the *Paraphrases* as unsound in some
particulars and as lacking generally in evangelical tone and
feeling.

The attitude of the Secession in regard to Church Song
does not appear to have differed greatly from that of the
Church of Scotland. Soon after the secession of 1733, the
attitude of the Burgher portion is revealed by the determination of the Associate Synod in 1748 to enlarge its Psalmody.
Ralph Erskine had published his *Gospel Sonnets* in 1726-
1734,[97] and had become a seceder in 1737. The Synod
recommended him to put the songs of Scripture into metre
for its use, basing its action upon the similar recommendation of the General Assembly of the Church of Scotland of
1647 to Zachary Boyd.[98] A committee was afterwards
appointed to examine Mr. Erskine's work, but his death in
1752 stayed the whole project of enlarging the Psalmody.
The subject did not come up again till 1787, and nothing
was actually done till the Synod in 1812 authorized the use
of "the Paraphrases and Hymns of the Church of Scot-

[96]See letter of his grandson in *Free Church Magazine*, August, 1847.
[97]In 1726 as *Gospel Canticles;* in 1734 as *Gospel Sonnets or Spiritual
Songs.* It contains little entitling Erskine to rank as a hymn writer.
The early Moravian editors adapted some material from it, and his
"O send me down a draught of love" (taken from a longer piece)
was in the Scottish *Presbyterian Hymnal* of 1876.
[98]See D. Fraser, *Life of Erskine*, Edinburgh, 1834, p. 508, note.

land." [99]   The anti-Burgher portion of the Secession seems
to have occupied a similar position.   Their *Solemn Warning* of 1758 does not deal with Psalmody, but their original
position was doubtless that of the manifesto of the General
Associate Synod of 1804.   It places the Psalms and New
Testament songs on a common plane of privilege as the
divinely inspired and only authorized Church Song.   Its
only protest is against all allegation of a lack of evangelical
spirit in the Psalms, and against substituting for them
"hymns of human composition containing erroneous doctrine." [100]

While the principles of the Secession favored New Testament songs, it is probable that the *Paraphrases* of the
Church of Scotland, which happened to contain the only
New Testament songs practicable, were not employed in
the services of either branch.   In this way the Seceders
furnished a refuge for many who came from parishes in
which the *Paraphrases* were used; but it was only by
further secessions from their own ranks that the principle
of a restricted Psalmody was ultimately maintained.

2.   Early Scottish Hymn Singing

Another branch of separated Presbyterians carried for-
ward the process of enlarging the Psalmody in advance of
the Church of Scotland itself.   This was the Presbytery of
Relief, formed in 1761, and, until merged in the United
Presbyterian Church in 1847, known as the Relief Church.
Some of these men were not contented to be confined to the
Paraphrases of the mother Church, principally because they
lacked   clear   evangelical   expression. [101]   James Steuart
showed the way to a new Hymnody, and in 1786 printed at
Glasgow *Sacred Songs and Hymns on various passages of*

[99]On this whole subject, see Maclagan, *op. cit.*, pp. 17-19; and also
Mc Crie, *The Public Worship of Presbyterian Scotland*, Edinburgh,
1892, pp. 196-301.

[100]*Narrative and Testimony . . . by the General Associate Synod,*
1804, pp. 163, 169.

[101]*Cf.* Maclagan, *op. cit.*, p. 28; McCrie, *op cit.*, p. 306.

Scripture; selected for the Congregation at Anderstoun, and introduced it into the worship of his church. It offended those of the congregation opposed to "human hymns," some of whom seceded, but the book was retained. Hutchison of Paisley adopted Steuart's book with the addition of new hymns, and still more were added by James Dun of Glasgow. The ground being thus prepared, the Synod in 1793 was overtured on the subject, and, after hearing from the Presbyteries, agreed in 1794 to enlarge the Psalmody not only by paraphrases of Scripture, but by hymns agreeable to its tenor. A committee was appointed to select them, which included Messrs. Steuart, Dun and Hutchison, and they, doubtless as had been arranged, at once reported, recommending the book compiled by Steuart and completed by Dun. The book was approved by Synod, and published at Glasgow in 1794 with a new title as *Sacred Songs and Hymns on various passages of Scripture, approved by the Synod of Relief, and recommended to be sung in the Congregations under their inspection.* The book contains 231 hymns, "collected from several authors," the hymns of Watts leading. The preface is frank in its justification of a New Testament Hymnody, but there is perhaps a certain lack of candor in its statement that the hymns following are, when not paraphrases of passages of Scripture, founded upon individual texts. To justify this statement, each hymn is preceded by a reference to its Scriptural source; that of Addison's "When all Thy mercies, O my God," being Psalm civ, 34,—"My meditation of Him shall be sweet: I will be glad in the Lord": that of Cowper's "O for a closer walk with God" being Genesis v, 24,—"Enoch walked with God." [102] The anticipated opposition, whether or not thus hoodwinked, proved not very serious, and the new hymn book was soon in use throughout the Relief Church.[103] According to the historian of that Church, the

---

[102]*Cf.* McCrie, *op. cit.,* p. 307.

[103]It was revised in 1833, and was a progenitor of the *Hymn Book of the United Presbyterian Church,* 1852.

new book developed a new animation in the service of
praise, and was followed by "a corresponding improvement
in church music." [104]

The Relief Church was not the first religious body in
Scotland to make use of free hymns and to introduce a
hymn book into its services. The Glassites, or Sandemanians, while adhering to psalm singing in their public worship, used in their fellowship meetings the *Christian Songs,*
whose first edition appeared in 1749 at Edinburgh, and
which we shall notice more fully in another connection.[105]
After the Scots Old Independents were founded in 1768
there was an open channel to and fro between their Hymnody and that of the Glassites. Many Glassite hymns were
in *Hymns and Spiritual Songs* (Glasgow, 1781), which
reached a seventh edition in 1798, and in *A Selection of
Hymns adapted to public worship* (Glasgow, 1819), which
with changes and additions is still used by this disappearing
sect. The hymn book of these Independents had been
preceded by a publication of *Psalms . . . or Hymns
founded on some important passages of Holy Scripture*
(Edinburgh, 1777). These were the work of Alexander
Pirie, a man of parts who found a refuge among the Independents after prosecution for heresy in both branches of
the Secession. Eleven of these hymns passed into the
Synod of Relief's book of 1794.[106]

A little booklet, *A Collection of Hymns and Spiritual
Songs* (Glasgow, 1755) and the later *A Collection of
Hymns for Christian worship* (Edinburgh, 1762) and *A
Collection of Hymns and Spiritual Songs, extracted from
various authors, and published for the use of Christians of
all denominations* (Edinburgh, 1778),[107] all suggest the

[104]G. Struthers, *History of the Relief Church,* 1843, p. 376.
[105]Under "The Hymnody of the Evangelical Revival."
[106]One is still remembered:—"With Mary's love without her fear,"
and all are of the Watts type.
[107]These early Scottish hymn books the writer has not come upon,
one) of the Rev. James Mearns. See Julian, *Dictionary,* p. 1026.
and he owes his knowledge of them to the hand (always a careful

introduction of hymns into some Scottish congregations of the independent sort. But Congregationalism there had no hymn book till the appearance at Edinburgh in 1800 of *A Collection of Hymns for the use of the Tabernacles in Scotland,* which continued in use for half a century. It was nevertheless an inadequate, ill-arranged and injudiciously "tinkered" collection. And, with a view to displace it in his "Church in Albion Street Chapel, Glasgow,"[108] the famous Ralph Wardlaw laboriously prepared *A Selection of Hymns for public worship* (Glasgow, 1803). An improvement on the "Tabernacle Collection," and bearing a distinguished name, it attained much popularity, as evidenced by thirteen editions. But here also the hymns were badly arranged and more than badly "tinkered." Wardlaw's *Selection* is still referred to as the source of eleven hymns by himself there appearing, of which "Lift up to God the voice of praise" and "Christ—of all my hopes the ground" are widely used.[109] The only other Congregationalist hymn book of the period was *A Collection of Hymns from the best authors, adapted both for public and family worship. Selected and arranged by Greville Ewing and George Payne* (Glasgow, 1814). This publication was perhaps thought to be expedient after the unpleasantness that had arisen between the respective Glasgow congregations under Wardlaw and Ewing,[110] and it attained to eleven editions, but except in greater fulness it marked little advance over Wardlaw's *Selection.*

Baptist hymn singing also had an early beginning in Scotland. Sir William Sinclair, Bart., composed and printed for the use of the Baptist church he formed in his castle of Keiss in Caithness, and of which he was pastor, *A Collection of Hymns and Spiritual Songs. By Sir William Sinclair, Minister of the Gospel of God, and servant of*

[108]See W. L. Alexander, *Memoirs of Ralph Wardlaw,* Edinburgh, 1856, pp. 69-71.
[109]All of the hymns are in the *Memoirs,* appendix C.
[110]*Memoirs,* pp. 114 f.

Jesus Christ (1751).[111] In the same year as the Relief collection there appeared *A Collection of Christian Songs and Hymns in three Books* (Glasgow, 1786) which by change and supplementing became eventually *Psalms, Hymns and Spiritual Songs in three Books, selected for use in the Scotch Baptist Churches* (new impression, enlarged, Glasgow, 1841). Its very title suggests the continuing influence of Dr. Watts, but the hymns were selected from a variety of sources, including the Glassite *Christian Songs,* and were subjected to free alteration in the interests of orthodoxy. The ninth edition (1827) was made notable by prefixing to each hymn a descriptive epithet, such as "cheerful," "grave," "plaintive," or even "cheerful & plaintive." This was with a view to the selection of a suitable tune. There were also some foot-notes showing how "this hymn may be altered to suit a single person." This collection was the standard of Praise in the limited number of Scottish Baptist churches for two generations.

And no doubt the hymns of John Barclay were sung in the assemblies of the Bereans, who followed him out of the Church of Scotland. Barclay thought the singing of secular songs a great sin, and would confine the singing of spiritual songs to true believers. Them he would have to sing at all times, and, inconsistently denying that there was any distinction between sacred and secular music, composed for them hymns and paraphrases in a great variety of metres adapted to the airs of Scottish songs.[112] The earliest of these appeared as *Rejoice evermore: or Christ all in all. An original publication consisting of spiritual songs, collected from the Holy Scriptures; . . . Glasgow: printed by W. Bell, for the Author. M. DCC. LXXVII.* There followed *A Select Collection of new original spiritual songs, paraphrases, and translations; together with the most useful and agreeable of these formerly published* (Edinburgh, 1776); and (beside his metrical version of

---

[111]It was reprinted in 1870. See Julian's *Dictionary,* p. 1027.

[112]Barclay's views are set forth in the preface to *Rejoice Evermore.*

the Psalms) one other collection, entitled *The Experience and Example of the Lord Jesus Christ illustrated and improved for the consolation of the Church, making a copious variety of subjects for the purpose of Divine praise* (Edinburgh, 1783). The whole number of hymns and paraphrases thus appearing is very large, and must have responded to some welcome from the congregations Barclay founded. Beyond their bounds, these striking hymns did not go, and they are unknown to the hymn books.[113] Barclay must be relegated to the ranks of unsuccessful paraphrasers in Scotland, stirred by Watts' example, but not inspired with like gifts.

But, so far as Presbyterian Scotland is concerned, the Relief Church was the first to carry forward the enlargement of Psalmody to the full freedom of an evangelical Hymnody, officially embodied in a church hymn book, and used by authority in public worship.

In the Church of Scotland no further action followed the *ad interim* allowance of the *Translations and Paraphrases* in 1781. The close of the XVIIIth century was a period of indifference and of that slovenly performance of public worship pictured in the anonymous *A Letter from a Blacksmith to the Ministers and Elders of the Church of Scotland*. The enlargement of the Psalmody came before the Assembly again early in the XIXth century, and specimens of "Additional Psalmody" were submitted in 1811, 1814 and 1820. The latter were printed as *Additional Psalmody; submitted to the General Assembly, 1820; and printed by their order, for the inspection of Presbyteries* (Edinburgh; Peter Hill & Company, 1821). Its thirty-two Psalm versions aim at introducing metrical variety: its seventeen paraphrases of other Scriptures include "Father, whate'er of worldly bliss" (I Tim. vi, 6-8), and "Lo! he comes with clouds descending" (Rev. i, 7). These efforts were quite futile and deservedly so. And nothing was accomplished

---

[113] Two of Barclay's hymns may be found in Odenheimer and Bird, *Songs of the Spirit*, N. Y., 1871.

until after the middle of the XIXth century, when the
Church came under the general influences that play upon
and mould modern Church Song in all denominations, notably the powerful influences emanating from Oxford.
Meanwhile the Church was left to its historic Psalter of
1650, and the paraphrases and five appended hymns of
1781. The *Paraphrases* were not only the first, but remain
the only characteristic Hymnody of the Church of Scotland. They were of the school of Watts, but the new Scottish writers and a deft editorial hand gave them a marked
individuality. The latest historian of Scottish Literature
has not hesitated to say that they "form incomparably the
best collection of sacred lyrics, for its size, which has ever
been made in the English language." [114] There are few who
would deny to them a dignified restraint, a grave devotion
and a somewhat haunting sonorousness of rhythm. But
they owed their origin to the desire for a distinctively
evangelical Hymnody; and it is not difficult to understand
that they should be regarded by many as somewhat lacking
in contents and somewhat cold in tone.

[114] J. H. Millar, *Literary History of Scotland*, New York, 1903, p. 379.

CHAPTER IV

DR. WATTS' "RENOVATION OF PSALMODY"
(Continued)

IV

HIS SUCCESS: THE ERA OF WATTS IN AMERICA

I. The Congregationalists (1735-1834)

1. The Great Awakening Turns the Churches to his Evangelical "System of Praise"

When Watts' *Hymns* of 1707 and his *The Psalms of David imitated* of 1719 appeared, the Puritan sense of the duty of singing psalms prevailed generally in New England, although "cases of conscience" still kept alive the memory of the "controversie of Singing." [1] But the total neglect of music had compelled the suspension of all singing in some congregations, and in others had brought about conditions in Church Praise which the Rev. Mr. Symmes described as "indecent." [2] In the lack of music books and the inability to sing by note, a very few tunes were sung from memory, "tortured and twisted as every unskillful throat saw fit," producing a medley of discordant noises; something, as Mr. Walter reports,[3] like five hundred different tunes roared out at the same time," with the singers often

---

[1] *Cases of conscience about singing of Psalms,* Boston, 1723. It is reprinted in S. H. Emory, *The Ministry of Taunton,* 2 vols., Boston, 1853, vol. i, pp. 269 ff.

[2] *The Reasonableness of Regular Singing,* Boston, 1720.

[3] *The Grounds and Rules of Musick explained,* by Thomas Walter, A.M., Boston, 1721.

one or two words apart, and in a manner so drawling that he himself has "twice in one note paused to take breath."

Inconceivable as it seems, this disorder had acquired the force of a tradition, and the attempt to better it involved the churches in years of bitter controversy between the advocates of "the usual way" and those determined to introduce "regular singing."

Through these confusions the voice of Watts did not reach the people at all. He none the less had his eye on New England. Before *The Psalms of David imitated* was printed, some were submitted in Ms. to Cotton Mather for his examination and approval :[4] the 107th Psalm as printed was entitled "A Psalm for New England": he sent over copies of all his books, and was, through correspondence with Colman and others, kept informed of conditions. Meantime he was content to bide his time, and discouraged his friends from premature efforts to introduce his System of Praise.[5]

The first American reprint of *The Psalms imitated* came from the Philadelphia press of Benjamin Franklin in 1729. It represents his admiration for Watts rather than any actual demand, since Franklin two years afterwards complained of its remaining unsold upon his shelves.[6] Franklin published another reprint in 1741; and in the same year appeared the first Boston edition from the press of Rogers and Fowle.

The first American reprint of the *Hymns* appeared in Boston, 1739 (J. Draper for D. Henchman) :[7] the first

---

[4]See letter in George Hood, *A History of Music in New England,* Boston, 1846, p. 155.

[5]See his correspondence in *Proceedings of the Massachusetts Historical Society,* 2nd series, vol. ix, especially pp. 397, 401, 408.

[6]In his "An Apology for Printers" (June 10, 1731): reprinted in A. H. Smyth's ed. of Franklin's *Writings,* N. Y., 1905, &c., vol. ii, p. 173. *Cf.* Paul L. Ford, *The many-sided Franklin,* N. Y., 1899, p. 195, where is a facsimile of the title page of 1729.

[7]Not in Evans' *American Bibliography.*

Philadelphia edition in 1742 (Franklin): the first New York edition (Hugh Gaine) in 1752.[8]

Throughout New England it was only as one and another parish first reëstablished the old Psalmody on a musical basis, that any need was felt for more singable materials than *The Bay Psalm Book* furnished. Even then there was no generâl turning toward Watts. It was rather in congregations deeply moved by the revival influences of "The Great Awakening" that the desire arose for song more in consonance with the revival preaching and more expressive of the evangelical fervor which the preaching aroused. The coming of Whitefield and his large share in the Great Awakening might be presupposed to favor the introduction of the hymns of the Wesleyan Revival, with which he had some association in England. But he was no singing evangelist, and never a propagandist of the Methodist Hymnody: he preferred a sober strain of song, and greatly admired Watts' *Psalms and Hymns*.

At Northampton itself Jonathan Edwards, returning from a journey, found that the congregation had begun to sing Watts' *Hymns* in his absence; "and sang nothing else, and neglected the Psalms wholly." He "disliked not their making some use of the Hymns; but did not like their setting aside the Psalms," and compromised by arranging that when they sang "three times upon the Sabbath," they should sing "an Hymn, or part of a Hymn of Dr. Watts', the last time, *viz:* at the conclusion of afternoon exercise."[9]

This was in 1742, and shows how with the spread of

[8]The early American reprints of Watts may be grouped as follows:
Psalms alone: Philadelphia, 1729, 1741, 1753, 1757, 1760, 1766, 1773. Boston, 1741, 1743, 1761, 1763, 1766, 1767, 1768, 1770, 1771, 1772 (2), 1773 (2). New York, 1754, 1756, 1760, 1761, 1772. Woodbridge, 1760. Portsmouth, 1762. Norwich, 1773, 1774.
Hymns alone: Boston, 1739, 1743, 1769, 1771, 1772 (2), 1775. Philadelphia, 1742, 1767, 1771, 1772. New York, 1752, 1771. Norwich, 1775.
Psalms and Hymns together (earlier issues were sometimes bound together): New York, 1761. Boston, 1767, 1773. Philadelphia, 1778.
[9]Letter of Edwards in *Proceedings of Mass. Hist. Soc.*, 2nd series, vol. x, p. 429.

the revival the people began to sing from Watts with a certain spontaneity in which sincerity counted for more than precedent. The singing was not confined to the meetings. John White reports[10] that at Gloucester in 1744 the singing of Watts' *Hymns* had taken the place of the usual diversions of the people when met together. A new phenomenon was the "singing through the streets, and in Ferry-Boats" by companies of people coming or going between the meetings. To this Chauncy objected as "ostentatious."[11] Gilbert Tennent, in a letter in *The Pennsylvania Gazette,* refused to defend it :[12] Jonathan Edwards on the other hand failed to find any valid objection against it.[13] Edwards thought "abounding in singing," both in and out of meeting, a natural expression of the feelings awakened.[14] The disorderly singing in meeting, and the careless singing of sacred words at home,[15] he liked no better than Chauncy.[16] To the objection taken by many to the "making use of Hymns of humane Composure," Edwards responded in terms as decided as those of Watts himself.[17]

In parishes which kept to the old Psalmody through the Revival period, the introduction of either the Imitations or *Hymns* of Watts involved difficulties. Apart from the prejudice of many against hymns[18] and their affection for *The Bay Psalm Book,* the free character of Watts' Imitations and his omission of several Psalms[19] told against it. There was also a preference of many others, especially

[10]*The Christian History,* Boston, vol. i, 1743, p. 41.

[11]*Seasonable Thoughts on the state of Religion in New England,* Boston, 1743, p. 126.

[12]Reprinted in his *The Examiner, examined, or Gilbert Tennent harmonious,* Phila., 1743, pp. 64-66.

[13]*Some Thoughts concerning the present Revival of Religion in New-England,* Boston, 1742, pp. 317-323.

[14]*Some Thoughts,* p. 182.

[15]*Ibid.,* p. 316.

[16]*Seasonable Thoughts, p.* 239.

[17]*Some Thoughts,* p. 184.

[18]*Cf. Proc. of Mass. Hist. Soc.,* 2nd series, vol. ix, pp. 401, 408.

[19]*Ibid.,* p. 369.

the "liberal"-minded, for the smooth renderings of Tate and Brady.[20]

The parish of Spencer, Mass., affords an illustration of the actual situation. After making trial for some time of *Tate and Brady,* the church met in June, 1761, and decided to restore *The Bay Psalm Book* for four Sabbaths, then to use Watts' Imitations till September, and finally meet for decision. At the meeting the vote stood, for *The Bay Psalm Book,* 33; for *Watts,* 14; for *Tate and Brady,* 6. It was agreed to refer the matter to three ministers, who recommended a trial of *Tate and Brady* for six months. After eight years adherence to *The Bay Psalm Book,* it was voted in May, 1769, to make the trial of *Tate and Brady* as recommended. There was a dissatisfied minority, and it was agreed to use *The Bay Psalm Book* and *Watts* jointly "till the church and congregation shall come to a better understanding as to what version may be sung." This arrangement continued until October, 1769, when it was agreed to adopt Watts' *Psalms and Hymns,* by a vote of 26 in his favor, and "about 6 votes for the old version."[21] Even so Spencer was years ahead of very many New England parishes.

A number of churches followed the lead of the Brattle Street Church, to which we shall more particularly refer, in adopting *Tate and Brady,* supplemented by a selection of hymns taken mostly from Watts: Worcester in 1761,[22] Newton in 1770,[23] Charlestown in 1772,[24] Westminster in 1773.[25] The Old South of Boston balked at the freedom of Watts' Imitations, and requested Thomas Prince to make a revision of *The Bay Psalm Book,* to which, as published and introduced in 1758, was added an appendix of fifty hymns,

[20]*Ibid.,* p. 369.

[21]Jas. Draper, *History of Spencer, Massachusetts,* Worcester, 2nd ed., n. d., pp. 110, 111.

[22]W. Lincoln, *Hist. of Worcester,* 1837, p. 179.

[23]F. Jackson, *Hist. of Newton,* 1854, p. 136.

[24]*Memorial Hist. of Boston,* vol. ii, p. 319.

[25]W. S. Heywood, *Hist. of Westminster,* 1893, p. 282.

all but eight of which are from Watts.[26]   On the other hand
the Imitations, without the *Hymns,* were adopted by the
South Church at Portsmouth, N. H., as early as 1763;[27]
and in 1769 Byfield voted to "make trial" of both.[28]

The parishes were thus feeling their way and of many
minds.   The use of Watts' *Psalms and Hymns* did not become general throughout New England Congregationalism
until after the Revolution.   They were introduced at the
Old South in Boston in 1786: in 1790 at Worcester[29] and
Newton:[30] in 1791 at Shrewsbury.[31]   To make the Imitations palatable at that epoch to the newly won liberties of
America, some changes were necessary in those passages in
which Watts had made David appear as a patriotic Englishman.   Outside of Connecticut these changes were made
without common action of the churches, under the auspices
of private printers.

Connecticut, which had its distinctive church government,
took also a distinctive attitude toward Watts.   In the first
place its adoption of his System of Praise included only
the Imitations.   In the second place, the Connecticut Association superintended two revisions of their text, with a
view of "accommodating it to America" and also of filling
out the omitted Psalms.   The earlier of these[32] appeared at

[26]*The Psalms, Hymns and Spiritual Songs of the Old and New
Testament,* . . . *being the New England Psalm Book revised and improved* . . . *with an addition of fifty other Hymns* . . . Boston: N.E.,
1758, 2nd ed., *1773.*

[27]C. W. Brewster, *Rambles about Portsmouth,* 2nd series, 1869, p.
338.

[28]Joshua Coffin, *Sketch of Hist. of Newbury,* &c., 1845, p. 235.

[29]Lincoln, p. 179.

[30]Jackson, p. 141.

[31]A. H. Ward, *History of Shrewsbury,* 1847, p. 179.

[32]The history of these various adaptations of Watts' Psalms to
American conditions is an interesting and distinctive episode in the
progress of American Church Song. But in spirit and intent they
were a prolongation of the older Psalmody, to whose history a fuller
account of them may be relegated. The writer has attempted such an
account in "The American Revisions of Watts's Psalms" in *The Journal of The Presbyterian Historical Society,* for June and Sept., 1903.

Hartford in 1785 *as Doctor Watts's Imitation of the Psalms of David, corrected and enlarged by Joel Barlow. To which is added a Collection of Hymns; the whole applied to the state of the Christian Church in general. Hartford: printed by Barlow and Babcock. M, DCC, LXXXV.* The later was made with the concurrence of the Presbyterian General Assembly, and appeared at Hartford in 1801 as *The Psalms of David . . . by I. Watts, D.D. A new edition, in which the Psalms, omitted by Dr. Watts, are versified, local passages are altered, and a number of Psalms are versified anew, in proper metres. By Timothy Dwight, D.D., President of Yale College. At the request of The General Association of Connecticut. To the Psalms is added a Selection of Hymns: Hartford: printed by Hudson and Goodwin. 1801.*[33] In the third place, the Connecticut Association, while proposing to retain *The Psalms imitated* as the main feature of Church Praise, provided at each revision its own collection of hymns (in the stead of Watts' *Hymns*) as an appendix to the Psalms. The hymns appended to Barlow's revision numbered 70, selected from Watts, with a few originals added. Like the revision itself, they were set aside when Barlow's name became discredited in Connecticut. Dwight, between his own preference for a large collection and that of a number of his advisers for a small one,[34] compromised on an appendix of 263 hymns. Of these 168 were from Watts, 95 by other writers, mostly of Watts' school. "Dwight's Watts" was received with great favour and used in Connecticut churches, perhaps without an exception; and in some was retained for over thirty years.[35]

Dwight's book was not interfered with by *The Hartford Selection of Hymns,* 1799, edited by Nathan Strong, Abel

[33] In this appeared the familiar "I love Thy Kingdom, Lord," as a rendering of the 137th Psalm.

[34] See his preface of 1800.

[35] *Cf.* O. E. Daggett, "The Psalms in Worship," *The New Englander,* July, 1846, p. 328.

Flint, and Joseph Steward.   This reached an eighth edition in 1821, but was especially designed for use in connection with revival services.   Some pastors were, however, finding Dwight's selection of hymns too limited.   He had spoken in his preface of the "so great reverence" for Watts in this country at that time.   Of this, Samuel Worcester of Salem, warmly interested in Church Song, was made painfully aware.   He thought room could be made for the new hymns desired and for a selection of tunes in one volume with Watts' *Psalms and Hymns* by the process of dropping some of the less used psalms and hymns and shortening the longer ones.   A volume so made up he published at Boston in 1815 as *Christian Psalmody, in four parts; comprising Dr. Watts's Psalms abridged; Dr. Watts's Hymns abridged; select Hymns from other authors; and select Harmony.* The churches resented this mode of dealing with Watts, and the book was met by charges of "mangling," "amputating," and "robbing" Watts, and by calls for "Watts entire."[36]   In view of this prejudice and demand and the solicitation of his publisher, Worcester abandoned his *Christian Psalmody,* enlarged the selection of hymns it contained, and, against his own taste and judgment, appended them to the complete *Psalms and Hymns* of Watts.   The new collection appeared at Boston in 1819 as *The Psalms, Hymns and Spiritual Songs of the Rev. Isaac Watts, D.D., to which are added select Hymns from other authors; and directions for musical expression.   By Samuel Worcester, D.D.*   It was revised in 1823, and again in 1834 by his son, and came into wide use throughout New England and even beyond it.   Familiarly known as "Watts and Select," it became one of the best recognized channels of Watts' ascendency over Church Song, and so continued as long as the churches were disposed to regard the ever widening area of English Hymnody in the light of an appendage to Watts' *Psalms and Hymns.*

[36]S. M. Worcester, *Life of Rev. Samuel Worcester,* Boston, 1852, vol. ii, p. 267.

2. AN AMERICAN SCHOOL OF CHURCH MUSIC

The transition from the older Psalmody to Watts in New England became associated with a great change in the character of the tunes used in the churches. The formation of singing societies and choirs led to a desire for tunes less simple than the accustomed settings of the older psalm tunes, and in greater variety. Reprints appeared at Boston and Newburyport of recent English tune books by William Tans'ur and Aaron Williams, and became very popular; and a group of native composers began to introduce compositions of their own into the tune books and choirs. The most notable of these and the most influential in effecting the change was an eccentric but gifted tanner's apprentice of Boston, William Billings, who had printed in 1770 his first book of original compositions, as *The New-England Psalm-Singer: or, American Chorister, containing a number of Psalm-tunes, Anthems and Canons. In four or five parts. [Never before published.] Composed by William Billings, a native of Boston, in New England* (Boston, Edes and Gill). The book proved acceptable to New England singing schools. During the war Billings wrote or adapted patriotic psalms, and set them to stirring melodies of his own composition. His original "Let tyrants shake their iron rod," to his tune "Chester," and his "Lamentation over Boston," beginning "By the Rivers of Watertown we sat down and wept," are now best remembered.[37] The words stirred the patriotic heart, and with their striking melodies were sung at home and by the choirs, and especially in the military camps. The New England soldiers learned the words by heart, and every fifer the tunes, and carried them to whatever part of the country duty called them.

In 1778 Billings published at Boston *The Singing Master's Assistant, or Key to practical Music.* Its tunes of lively rhythm and captivating melody, with much inde-

[37]Words and music may be found in his *The Singing Master's Assistant*, 1778; the former as No. 12, the latter as No. 33.

pendence of movement in the various voice-parts and some unexpected harmonic results, proved very popular with singing schools and church choirs, and drove out the slower and more solemn psalm-tunes. Billings established a distinctively American school of church music,[38] carried on by Jacob Kimball, Oliver Holden,[39] Daniel Reed,[40] Timothy Swan,[41] and others, who were his followers; and it dominated Congregational Song in New England for many years.

The new music, while tickling the senses, lacked the reverence and spiritual feeling of the old. But the close of the Revolution was particularly distinguished for the absence of just those qualities; and the swing and virility of the new tunes suited the occasion, while the exciting contests of the voice-parts gave welcome occupation to the singing schools and the new choirs.

The reader of *The Diary of William Bentley, D.D., Pastor of the East Church, Salem, Massachusetts,*[42] covering 1784-1802, can follow the agitated efforts to improve the Psalmody in a parish where the minister was bent on bettering the singing, the visits of successive "professors," the fortunes of a parochial singing-school, thought by some

[38]The personality and work of this one-eyed, illtaught, and enthusiastic natural genius, form an engaging theme, from whatever view-point it be approached. The only adequate materials for studying him are the music, treatises, prefaces, &c., contained in the series of his tune books. The most satisfactory approaches to the musical side of his work are found in Dr. F. R. Ritter's *Music in America,* new. ed., New York, 1890, chap. iii; and Louis C. Elson's *The History of American Music,* New York, 1904, chap. i. Something of the human side appears in George P. Upton's *Musical Pastels,* Chicago, 1902, in a sketch of him, wrongly entitled "The first American Composer." It is now well established that both Hopkinson and Lyon were his predecessors (see O. G. Sonneck, *Francis Hopkinson and James Lyon,* Washington, 1905); though the fact abates nothing of Billings' original force.

[39]Composer of "Coronation."

[40]Composer of "Lisbon" and "Windham."

[41]Composer of "China."

[42]Salem, Mass., 1905, 1907.

to encourage immorality, the introduction of instrumental music;[43] and he will find also a brief outline of the history of New England Psalmody.[44]

The new style of church music did not spread over New England without considerable protest. Andrew Law of Connecticut, one of the most successful "Professors of Psalmody" contemporaneous with Billings, resisted his influence from the first, and in his numerous books of instruction and of tunes aimed to avoid the seductive "fuguing tunes." By the beginning of the XIXth century the protest against the new music became more pronounced. The Middlesex Musical Society voiced the opposition in the preface to its *Middlesex Collection of Church Music: or, Ancient Psalmody revived* (Boston, 1807):

"The spirit and flavor of old wine are always depressed by the commixture of new. . . . The principal design of [this work] is, to form and improve a taste for music, well adapted to promote religion and piety. . . . Patronage and co-operation are earnestly solicited, from all those in the community, who are well disposed to the public institutions of religion, and desirous that the singing in our solemn assemblies may be performed 'with the spirit and with the understanding.' And it is hoped the time is not far distant, when none will have the temerity to advocate or countenance profaning the house of the LORD, by offering a Babel confusion of tongues, as an act of homage in divine worship."

This reads like a retort to the preface of *The First Church Collection of sacred musick* of the previous year:

"In the knowledge and practice of sacred musick, as might justly be expected, the psalmodists of the elder continent are vastly superior to those of America. But is this fact a sufficient reason for the total disuse of American musick? . . . Instead therefore of ridiculing the productions of our age and country, and indiscriminately condemning to oblivion the incipient efforts of the American composer, let us, while we reject his worst, commend his best; and, by using them alternately with the labours of able masters, form him to a riper judgment and a purer taste . . . In the exercise therefore of that charity, which teaches us not to please ourselves merely, but our christian brethren also, with a view to their edification, we humbly commit our endeavours to their use."

[43] "There is now no ground of complaint against the catholics."
[44] Vol. ii, p. 371.

We thus get the atmosphere of the controversy which helped to clear the air, and which, together with the spread of better musical knowledge and taste, eventually prepared the way for the Lowell Mason epoch in American church music.

It is likely that the most voluminous of the composers of this period, Samuel Holyoke of Massachusetts, counted himself a reformer, and that he regarded *The Columbian Repository of sacred harmony* (Exeter, N. H., n. d.), published in the first decade of the XIXth century, as adapted to forward the reaction from the extremes of the Billings school. Whether it was so or not, his book remains as a colossal monument of the ascendency of Watts over the congregational praise of New England. This folio volume of 496 pages contains nothing less than a complete reprint of Watts' *Psalms of David imitated*[45] and his *Hymns and Spiritual Songs,* with every Psalm version and hymn set to its special tune in four parts. As an offering to New England choirs, unable to read at sight or to use so great a variety of music, it was ineffective from the first; but as a New England tribute to Dr. Watts its testimony remains unimpaired.

The closing pages of Holyoke's book are occupied by a "Supplement" of tunes "suited to Metres in *Dr. Belknap's* and *Tate & Brady's* Psalms and Hymns, which are not in Dr. Watts'." This supplement serves to remind us that a dissenting type of Congregationalist Hymnody had already risen in New England, which now demands consideration.

3. THE LIBERALS COMPILE "NON-TRINITARIAN" HYMN
BOOKS (1753-1823)

The church at Brattle Square, Boston, had been the first

---

[45]Holyoke seems to have taken as his text of *The Psalms imitated* an Americanized version first printed by Isaiah Thomas at Worcester in 1786, and characterized by its omission of the C. M. Version of Psalm 21.

to break away from the fixed order of New England Congregationalism. Though regarded as radical, it was organized upon the basis of the Westminster Confession, and in the matter of Church Praise was most conservative. When Thomas Brattle, whose will was probated May 23, 1713, bequeathed his organ to the church, the congregation voted that they did not think it proper to use the same in the public worship of God.[46] To the efforts of its pastor, Benjamin Colman, Watts attributed the introduction of his Imitations into several New England parishes.[47] In 1739 Colman got his church to vote for a collection of hymns to be selected from Watts, but found that even the attempt to use a new version of the Psalms so endangered the peace of the church that he decided to leave things as they were.[48] Nevertheless the Brattle Street Church, after Colman's death, led the way in hymn singing among Boston churches, adopting in 1753 *Tate and Brady* with an appendix of hymns to be selected by a committee.[49] This appeared in 1754 as *Appendix, containing a number of Hymns, taken chiefly from Dr. Watts's Scriptural Collection,* and was enlarged from time to time to include 103 hymns.[50] *Tate and Brady* with this appendix, and sometimes with D. Bayley's *Essex Harmony* or his *Psalm Singer's Assistant,* bound in, appeared often in the next half century, and became the means of introducing hymns of Watts into a number of parishes.

The installation of Jonathan Mayhew over the West Church in 1747 was the first definite recognition of the

[46]S. K. Lothrop, *History of Brattle-Street Church,* Boston, 1851, pp. 61, 62: more fully in "The first Organ in America," *New England Magazine,* Oct., 1902, pp. 212 ff.

[47]*Proc. of Mass. Hist. Soc.,* 2nd series, vol. ix, pp. 365, 397.

[48]*Ibid.,* p. 365.

[49]See preface to "Brattle Square Collection," 1825.

[50]The hymns numbered 77-100 in the *Appendix to Tate and Brady* published by S. Kneeland, Boston, 1760, were an addition to the Brattle Street Appendix made by Mather Byles for the Hollis Street Church.

Arian opinions and tendencies which had crossed over from English Presbyterianism; and by the last quarter of the century nearly all the Congregationalist pulpits in and near Boston were filled by Unitarians.[51]

Mayhew found *Tate and Brady* in use at the West Church, and asked for no change during his life, though a choir took the place of the precentor about 1754.[52] No hymns were sung in the West Church till the appearance in 1783 of *A Collection of Hymns, more particularly designed for the use of the West Society in Boston,* (2nd ed. 1803; 3rd, 1806).[53] Its opening hymns were entitled "Toleration" and "Persecution," but it contained also hymns on "Jesus, worshipped by all the Creation," "The Atonement of Christ," and "Christ's Propitiation improv'd." William Bentley of the East Church, Salem, already an avowed Unitarian,[54] followed with *A Colection of Hymns for publick worship* (Salem, n. d. but 1788),[55] which reached a third edition, and was used in the East Church until 1842.[56] Its only interest lies in the selection, at so early a date, of the Salisbury *Collection* of 1778 as the source of nearly all its hymns. Six years later Jeremy Belknap "performed a very important service for the non-Trinitarian churches"[57] by publishing *Sacred Poetry. Consisting of Psalms and Hymns, adapted to Christian devotion, in public and private. Selected from the best authors, with variations and additions* (Boston, 1795). This important (it has been called

---

[51]*Cf.* A. P. Peabody in *The Memorial History of Boston,* vol. iii, pp. 467 ff.

[52]Chas. Lowell, Discourse in the West Church, Boston, 1820, p. 26.

[53]Bentley says it was edited by Dr. Howard. See his *Diary,* vol. ii, p. 371.

[54]*Ibid.,* vol. i, p. 98.

[55]In the "Bibliography" of the *Diary,* vol. i, p. xxxvii, it is dated 1789, but came from the printer in November, 1788 (vol. i, p. 109). The writer's copy was "The Gift of Rev. Mr. Bentley, 1789." For an interesting defence of the theology of his *Collection,* made to his father, see *Diary,* vol. i, p. 114.

[56]*Diary,* vol. i, p. xiii.

[57]Dr. Peabody in *Memorial History of Boston,* vol. iii, p. 473.

"famous")[58] book has been described by Dr. Peabody[59] "as an index of the religious belief and feeling of the churches that welcomed its advent." If so, it would be easy to show that the churches held all the cardinal doctrines of Calvinism. But Belknap's own curious point of view is thus revealed in his preface:

"In this selection those Christians, who do not scruple to sing praise to their Redeemer and Sanctifier, will find materials for such a sublime enjoyment; whilst others whose tenderness of conscience may oblige them to confine their addresses, to the Father only will find no deficiency of matter suited to their idea of 'the chaste and awful spirit of devotion.'" [60]

Belknap's book won great favor, and continued to satisfy a considerable proportion of the "non-Trinitarian churches" through and beyond the first quarter of the XIXth century.[61] Freeman's *A Collection of Psalms and Hymns for publick worship* (Boston, 1799: 2nd ed., 1813), for King's Chapel, was made from its American predecessors just referred to, the English books from the Liverpool Collection of 1763 to Enfield's of 1795, and *Tate and Brady*.   In 1808, the year of Henry Ware's election as Hollis Professor at Harvard, the Brattle Street Church annexed to its collection *Hymns for public worship. Part ii;* whose exclusion of "most of the capital doctrines of the gospel" was at once challenged by *The Panoplist*.[62]   From the Panoplist's point of view William Emerson's *A Collection of Psalms and Hymns* (Boston, 1808), was even more open to the same charge.   His book was ineffective, but interesting for an attempt to refine and enrich "Columbian musick" by "prefixing to each psalm and hymn the name of a tune, well

[58]By Dr. S. A. Eliot, in *Heralds of a Liberal Faith,* Boston, 1910, vol. i, p. 103.

[59]*ut supra.*

[60]In Watts' familiar line "Save in the death of Christ my God," Belknap's only alteration was the substitution of "But" for "Save."

[61]2nd ed., 1797; 3rd, 1801; 4th, 1804; 5th, 1808; new. ed., 1812, often reprinted.

[62]See the review in the number for Sept. 1808; the reply of "Brattle Street" and editorial comments thereon in the Nov. number.

composed and judicially chosen" as "a valuable auxiliary to musical bands."

To Philadelphia Unitarianism came directly from England with Dr. Priestley; and in 1812 Ralph Eddowes and James Taylor, who had charge of the little congregation Priestley founded, published *A Selection of sacred Poetry, consisting of Psalms and Hymns from Watts, Doddridge, Merrick, Scott, Cowper, Barbauld, Steele, and others.*[63] Eddowes had already published a tract on *The inconsistency of several passages in Doctor Watts's Hymns with Scripture and with each other.*[64] But, the inexpediency of using "Watts entire" being thus demonstrated, Eddowes drew freely from him and other evangelical sources, and in his collection of 606 hymns aimed not unsuccessfully to avoid offence to the orthodox bodies that enveloped his little congregation.

Little account of the Philadelphia book was taken in New England, although the situation there was regarded as unsatisfactory. It was becoming a matter of reproach that numerous churches, though now enrolled on the "liberal" side, persisted in using Watts' *Psalms and Hymns,* to which they had formerly become attached.[65] And not less so that of all the books aiming to supersede Watts or Psalm versions, the "only collection now in common use" was Belknap's with "its unnatural combination of eager Arianism and half-willing Orthodoxy."[66] Two books were prepared with a view of meeting this situation. The earlier was Henry F. Sewall's *A Collection of Psalms and Hymns, for social and private worship* (N. Y. 1820; 2nd ed., 1827). This urbane expression of "a calm and rational faith" was favorably regarded by Boston periodicals,[67] but failed of adoption by New England churches. It retains, however,

---

[63]2nd ed., 1818; 3rd, 1828; 4th, 1846.

[64]Included in *A Coll. of Pieces and Tracts* pub. by the First Unitarian Society, Phila., 1810.

[65]*The Christian Disciple,* vol. iii, 1821, p. 341.

[66]*Ibid.,* pp. 76, 362.

[67]E. g. *The Christian Disciple* for 1821, pp. 76, 360-369.

the distinction of introducing five originals of William Cullen Bryant. The other book had a nearly similar title, *A Selection of Hymns and Psalms, for social and private worship* (Andover, 1821; 2nd ed., Cambridge, 1824; 11th ed., Boston, 1832). It was compiled by J. P. Dabney, with an eye for practical considerations: being smaller, cheaper, better arranged, and with less tinkering of familiar texts, than Sewall's. It came into very considerable, though far from universal, use in the churches. We may perhaps regard these two books, and the new West Church *Collection* of 1823, as closing the earlier series of liberal or Unitarian hymn books; to be followed in turn by the remarkable series of a more "literary" type that distinguished the mid-century.

The books of this early period are characterized by their omissions rather than their inclusions, as being the work of men (except perhaps Freeman), who "had not made up their own minds" "on the subject of the nature and offices of Jesus."[68] Meantime they avoided the area "still controverted among Christians" (Sewall), and "what savors of party spirit and sectarian notions" (Emerson). This meant practically to alter or omit the older hymns of evangelical implication and to multiply hymns confined to "the natural or universal aspects of religion." It resulted, except in the case of Belknap's anomalous book, in a marked coldness of tone as contrasted with Watts'. Belknap, Emerson, Eddowes and Sewall avowedly aim to adapt their books to "Christians in general." Dabney is the only one who recognizes that his "cannot meet with very general acceptance."

II. THE PRESBYTERIANS (1739-1827)

1. "NEW SIDE" CHURCHES VENTURE TO SING WATTS' "IMITATIONS"

The Presbyterian Church of the colonies was by its varied inheritance and its own practice a psalm singing Church.

[68]Ralph Waldo Emerson, in Sprague, *Annals of the American Unitarian Pulpit*, New York, 1865, p. 245.

It cannot, however, be claimed that an exclusively Scriptural Psalmody was made a church principle, since the Adopting Act of 1729 failed to include the Westminster *Directory for Worship* as a part of its written constitution. Neither was there any special psalm book in prescribed or even general use. But the hold of the Scottish type of Psalmody was materially strengthened by the great volume of immigration from the North of Ireland. The Scotch-Irish brought with them *The Psalms of David in meeter* bound in with their Bibles, and to their minds almost a part of it. They had been accustomed to a Scriptural Psalmody as of course: few of them knew any psalm book but their own: and they were not of the temper that is personally concerned with the literary or musical development of Church Song.

Thus reinforced, the whole lump of Presbyterianism became more impervious than some other Churches were to the leaven of Watts' influence. Indeed, the Scotch-Irish gift for colonization tended to remove whole sections of the Church beyond contact with that influence. It carried large numbers away from the established centres of civilization, and segregated them in frontier settlements, where their own ways were unquestioned and their minds became incurious. And so it could happen, that, when in 1763 the reunited Synod of New York and Philadelphia was questioned as to whether churches were at liberty "to sing Dr. Watts's imitation of David's Psalms," the Synod was not prepared to give a full answer, "as a great number of this body have never particularly considered Dr. Watts's imitation."[69]

There was, on the other hand, within the Church an aggressive element, Scotch and Scotch-Irish, well informed as to Watts' work and influence, and fully prepared to resist it. And just beyond the Church's borders a number of small bodies were forming, who represented one or other type of Scottish dissent; unalterably set in principle on the strictest platform of psalm singing, and in practice con-

[69]*Records of the Presbyterian Church,* ed. 1904, p. 331.

fined to "Rous' Version." Neither their principles nor interest called them to quench the embers of strife in the larger body or to refuse a refuge to the disaffected.

Under these circumstances it was inevitable that Presbyterian hymn singing should be deferred, and that its introduction should involve controversy. There was indeed no general desire to sing hymns among Colonial Presbyterians. The progressives asked no more than liberty to choose their own psalm book; and it was not till the beginning of the XIXth century that the Church formally authorized the use of any designated hymn book.

The first influence that modified the uniformity of the old Psalmody, among Presbyterians as among Congregationalists, was the quickened evangelical fervor aroused by the Great Awakening; which revival became indeed the occasion of splitting the Church itself in 1741 into "New Side" and "Old Side" synods.

This influence is nowhere more clearly brought out than in the *apologia* of the Trustees of the Church in New York for the change in their congregational Psalmody:[70]

"That during the times of the Revival of Religion in the years 1739, 1740 and 1741 when God said to this church, arise, shine for thy light is come, &c., there was a vast accession of people to this Light and to the brightness of this churches rising; in that period the poetick writings particularly the Hymns of the sweet singer of our Israel became of excellent service and for the divine relish which in the use of them had affected many minds. During that remarkable season, many of the people became desirous of introducing some one of the New Versions of the Psalms, into the stated publick worship of the congregation; and from their knowledge and experience of their suitableness to animate and raise their own devotion, hoping this might produce the same effect on others. After this matter had been some years under consideration and by the private use of the New Version, the old Version had become every day to the Taste of many more and more flat, dull, insipid and undevotional . . . and it had been judged that no objection could arise against introducing Doctor Watts version but from ignorance of the difference between the old version and that, or from some unreasonable prejudice, the ministers, elders, deacons and trustees with the approbation of the principal part of the

[70]Ms. Journal, quoted in Briggs, *American Presbyterianism*, New York, 1885, pp. 280, 281.

congregation, . . . desired that, that version might be proposed to the congregation to be introduced in a months time unless sufficient reason to the contrary should be signified to Mr. Pemberton in the mean time."

The minority at once organized as a Scotch Presbyterian Society, and complained to Presbytery, which body referred the matter to the (New Side) Synod of New York. Synod in 1752 appointed a committee to adjust the difficulties, with power to authorize the use of Watts' Imitations, and a larger committee in 1753. In 1754 Synod adopted the findings of this committee objecting to certain proceedings, but deciding that "since Dr. Watts's version is introduced in this church, and is well adapted for Christian worship, and received by many Presbyterian congregations, both in America and Great Britain, they cannot but judge it best for the well-being of the congregation under their present circumstances, that they should be continued."[71] The disturbance in New York continuing, the Synod of 1755 directed "that the Scotch version be used equally with the other."[72] This direction was not obeyed. The Synod of 1756 rebuked the majority for their adherence to Watts, but also revoked their order of the previous year; thus leaving Wattts' Imitations in sole possession of the field.[73] The offended minority withdrew from the New York church to form "The Scotch Church," which was taken under the care of the Associate Presbytery, representing one of the secessions from the Church of Scotland.

The introduction of the "new version" into churches newly established involved less difficulty. That at Newburyport, organized by Whitefield's supporters in 1746, used Watts' Imitations from the beginning; and they were recommended by the Presbytery of Boston as "well adapted to the New Testament Church."[74] Newburyport and its

[71] *Records,* p. 260.
[72] *Ibid.,* p. 267.
[73] *Ibid.,* p. 275.
[74] H. C. Hovey, *Origin and Annals of "The Old South" in Newburyport,* Boston, 1896, p. 53.

Presbytery were independent, but the process of church extension under the New Side Synod of New York developed some similar situations. Samuel Davies, whom the Presbytery of New Castle ordained for missionary work in Virginia, introduced there not only *The Psalms imitated* but even the *Hymns* of Watts. Two of the former were sung at the installation of John Todd over a Hanover congregation on November 12, 1752, and printed in full in connection with Davies' Installation sermon.[75] In 1755 he wrote from Hanover that Watts' *Psalms and Hymns* were "the system of psalmody the Dissenters use in these parts," and in the same year made requisition upon the London Society for Promoting Religious Knowledge for "a good number" of the *Psalms and Hymns* for the use of his black people. He had found there are no books they learn so soon or take such pleasure in, as they have "a kind of ecstatic delight in psalmody."[76] Davies' use of the *Hymns* was independent and exceptional at that date; and in connection with the writing and publication of hymns of his own composition, makes him a pioneer of Hymnody in the American Presbyterian Church.

After Davies' departure for Princeton John Todd "was called to wear his mantle"; and when a petition was presented to the recently formed Presbytery of Hanover, "desiring their opinion, whether Dr. Watts's psalmody might with safety be used in the churches," Todd delivered by invitation of that body a trenchant defence of "Gospel Songs" and of the use of Watts' *Psalms and Hymns* as "the best now extant":—*An humble attempt towards the improvement of Psalmody: The propriety, necessity and use, of Evangelical Psalms, in Christian worship. Delivered at a meeting of the Presbytery of Hanover in Virginia,*

[75]*A Sermon preached at the Installation of the Revd. Mr. John Todd,* Glasgow, 1754, pp. 17, 113.
[76]*Letters from the Rev. Mr. Davies,* 2nd ed., London, 1757, p. 12; W. H. Foote, *Sketches of Virginia* [first series], Philada., 1850, pp. 286, 289.

October 6th, 1762 (Philadelphia: Andrew Steuart, 1763).
"I am fully persuaded," he said, "that the churches in these
parts have received very great advantage from [Watts']
excellent compositions, especially his sacramental hymns."
By others in the Presbytery this opinion was not shared.

Even on the New Side the change in the Psalmody was
hesitating and gradual. The Old Side churches furnished
no occasion for the Synod of Philadelphia to adjudicate on
Psalmody during the whole period of the schism. When in
1763 the query already noted as to the status of "Dr. Watts's
imitation" in the reunited Church reached the Synod of
New York and Philadelphia, it is plain that recent investi-
gation had convinced many that the Imitations could not
be regarded as Psalm-versions. In the Synod of 1764 there
was hot debate, and the situation was difficult between
lingering Old Side scruples and the New Side precedent in
the New York case. No conclusion could be reached till the
Synod of 1765 compromised upon a hesitating allowance
of the Imitations in these terms:

"The Synod judged it best, in present circumstances, only to declare
that they look on the inspired Psalms in Scripture, to be proper matter
to be sung in Divine worship, according to their original design and
the practice of the Christian churches, yet will not forbid those to
use the imitation of them whose judgment and inclination lead them
to do so." [77]

In the very year of this query, John Miller, by training
a Congregationalist, was complained of to the Presbytery of
Lewes, Delaware, for introducing Watts' Imitations into
his Duck Creek charge. The Presbytery sustained him, but
his other charge at Dover, continued to sing "Rous' Version" for many years.[78]

At Philadelphia, in the Second Church, initiated by
Whitefield's visit, and shepherded by Gilbert Tennent, no
steps toward changing the Psalmody were ventured on till
1773. At the Whitefield Memorial Service, October 14,

[77] *Records,* p. 345.
[78] S. Miller, *Life of Samuel Miller,* Phila., 1869, vol. i, p. 22.

1770, Watts' hymn, "A Funeral Thought," and Wesley's "Ah! lovely appearance of death," taken from Whitefield's hymn book, were sung by a company of young people,[79] but doubtless regarded as "anthems."[80] On March 15, 1773, the congregation voted to introduce Watts' Imitations. So much protest was made that a second congregational meeting was held on March 22, which ratified the choice by a vote of 38 for Watts, and 8 for Rous.[81] The minority vainly petitioned the session to reinstate "Rous" as the only way to restore order and peace, and appealed to the First Presbytery of Philadelphia, which refused to interfere, "as the aforesaid Psalms are used by a large Number of the Congregations within the Bounds of the Synod, and the Synod have allowed the use of them."[82] An appeal brought the matter once more before the reunited Synod. That body in 1774 declined to decide the case on its merits, on the belated plea that it had no time to consider the versions in question; but in view of earlier permissions to use "Dr. Watts's imitation," refused "to make any order to forbid the congregation to continue the practice now begun."[83]

Thus once more the matter of changing the Psalmody was left to the decision of the congregation concerned, and the way was officially left open both for the forbearance which Synod earnestly enjoined, and for the years of bitter parochial strife which its decision assured. Meantime, in the years preceding the Revolution, the change to Watts was effected in some parishes, and in many more the advocates of such change were steadily increasing in number.

In many minds the wish for improvement in the substance of Praise must have been accompanied also by a longing for

---

[79] J. Sproat, *Discourse occasioned by the death of George Whitefield,* Phila., 1771.

[80] The New Side Synod of N. Y. had recommended the disuse of anthems on the Lord's Day. *Records,* p. 260.

[81] Ms. minutes.

[82] Ms. minutes, May 21, 1773.

[83] *Records,* p. 448.

its better rendering. The Presbyterian Psalmody of the time appears to have been as deplorable as that of New England before "regular" singing was introduced. The adhesion to "Rous" carried with it generally an exclusive regard for the few "common tunes" to which that version had been sung in the old country. The ability to render them with musical correctness had long been lost, and the universal practice was to have the psalms lined out by a precentor, who might or might not know the rudiments of music. John Adams, accustomed to the New England improvements, reports that even in New York in 1774, the Psalmody of the "Old Presbyterian Society" is "in the *old way*, as we call it—all the drawling, quavering, discord in the world."[84] Attending the college chapel at Princeton, seven days later (August 27), he notes that the scholars sing as badly as the Presbyterians at New York."[85] It is altogether unlikely that much better conditions prevailed in towns and settlements less accessible to observant travellers.

There had been, however, at Philadelphia a beginning of "the art of psalmody," in which many Presbyterians were concerned, and as early as 1760 a school in which it was taught.[86] In 1761-2 James Lyon, a Nassau-Hall graduate of 1759 and afterwards a Presbyterian clergyman, published by subscription the most elaborate book of church music that had yet appeared in the colonies:—*Urania, or a choice Collection of Psalm-Tunes, Anthems, and Hymns, from the most approv'd authors, with some entirely new: in two, three, and four parts: the whole peculiarly adapted to the use of churches and private families: to which are prefix'd the plainest, & most necessary rules of psalmody.*

[84]*Works of John Adams,* vol. ii, Boston, 1850, p. 348.
[85]*Ibid.,* p. 356.
[86]O. G. Sonneck, *Francis Hopkinson and James Lyon,* Washington, 1905, p. 127. As early as 1763 there appeared at Philadelphia from the press of Anthony Armbruster, *Tunes in three parts, for the several metres of Dr. Watts's version of the Psalms; some of which tunes are new. Price one shilling & sixpence, stitched.* There was a 2nd ed. in 1764.

By James Lyon, A.B. (Philadelphia). Among the sub-scribers are many connected with Nassau-Hall, and prominent Presbyterian clergy and laymen in Philadelphia and elsewhere. It was followed by *The lawfulness, excellency and advantage of instrumental musick in the public worship of God, urg'd and enforc'd, from Scripture, and the examples of the far greater part of Christians in all ages. Address'd to all (particularly the Presbyterians and Baptists) who have hitherto been taught to look upon the use of instrumental musick in the worship of God as unlawful. By a Presbyterian* (Philadelphia, Wm. Dunlap, 1763). This Presbyterian plea for the organ is with a view of improving the congregational singing in the Philadelphia churches, of which the writer says that "the miserable Manner in which this Part of their Worship is dron'd out, seems rather to imitate the Braying of Asses, than the divine Melody so often recommended in Scripture."[87]

But the list of subscribers prefixed to some early copies of *Urania* shows that "the art of psalmody" had attracted the attention of some influential men in the Second Church. And, from the young people's choir of 1770 already referred to, and the ensuing struggle to introduce Watts, we may infer that some beginning was soon attempted in the way of bettering church music there. But any such attempt there or elsewhere was effectually blocked by the Revolution.

[87]P. 19. There is a copy in The Pennsylvania Historical Society. The pamphlet appeared in April, and was so readily bought that Dunlap advertised a 2nd ed. on June 16. In the same month a burlesque 2nd ed. was advertised as published by Andrew Steuart, viz. *A Cudgell to drive the Devil out of every Christian place of worship: Being a second edition (with necessary improvements, which now render the sense entirely plain) of The lawfulness, excellency and advantage, of instrumental music, in the public worship of God, but chiefly of organs.* (Sonneck, *op. cit.,* pp. 131, 132. Hildeburn, No. 1883). "Presbyterian" states that St. Paul's Church, Philadelphia, was "the only *English* Congregation in the Province" having an organ at that time, though the two other Episcopal churches were then raising organ funds (pp. 28, 30).

In the decimated and impoverished congregations at the close of the war, Psalmody was maintained with difficulty. The complaint[88] that the services had largely "lost even the appearance of devotion" may be explained by the religious apathy and irreverence which the Revolution left behind it. But the fact that "many" did "not join in singing the praises of God" or give their attention to the singing in progress, is partly at least explained by the deplorable conditions to which the singing was reduced. If it was so bad musically before the war, it was certainly no better afterward. Samuel Blair at Neshaminy describes the congregations as "drolling out the tones of ill-measured dullness, or jarring with harsh discord."

2. THE GREAT "PSALMODY CONTROVERSY"

From other points of view than the musical, there was apparent need of some reconstruction of Presbyterian Psalmody. The number of those using or wishing to use Watts' Imitations and even his hymns, was always growing; but, even so, *The Psalms of David imitated* contained many objectionable allusions to the British sovereign and state. On the other hand, in almost every congregation in the Scotch and Irish settlements of the South and West there was at least a determined minority resisting change. Any suggestion, on the part of the more progressive element, of Watts' superiority, was enough to turn a congregation into a debating society. Any effort to introduce Watts into public worship was to disturb and often to convulse a parish, if not indeed a larger area.

It may have been with a hope of uniting the two parties that a proposal was made to the Synod of 1785, with a view of attaining "the nearest uniformity that is practicable," that "the Synod choose out, and order some of their number to take the assistance of all the versions in our power, and

[88]Preface to proposed Directory for Worship, in *A Draught of the Form of the Government and Discipline of the Presbyterian Church in the U. S. A.*, New York, S. & J. Loudon, 1787, p. 53.

compose for us a version more suitable to our circumstances and taste than any we now have."[89]   After some debate, the proposal was carried by a small majority.   The committee reported progress in 1786, and was continued.   No further report from them is recorded.   The minutes of the Synod of 1787 contain the bare statement: "The Synod did allow and do allow, that Dr. Watts's imitation of David's Psalms, as revised by Mr. Barlow, be sung in the churches and families under their care."[90]   There is nothing in the record to connect this with any previous action; but John Black, who was present, stated in a sermon at Marsh-Creek in 1790,[91] that the action was taken upon the report of the committee theretofore appointed, to the effect, that having compared such versions as they could obtain, they did not apprehend any so well calculated for christian worship, as that of Dr. Watts, as amended by Mr. Barlow of New England."   He adds that *Barlow's Watts* "was then laid before Synod for their consideration, who, after mature deliberation, gave it their judicial sanction."

But the unexpected part of Mr. Black's testimony is what follows, to the effect that "the committee had also added a book of hymns to this version; but it was laid aside; not because Synod disapproved of the thing in itself, but because some parts of the collection seemed to them exceptionable." There is no reason to question his testimony as to the proposed book, and his interpretation of the mind of the Synod is confirmed by the fact that its committee to prepare a new *Directory for Worship* embodied hymn singing in their draught of their Directory printed in that same year.   That the Synod in 1787 was already prepared to examine a specific hymn book on its merits goes far to explain why hymn singing slipped into the written constitution of the Church with so little debate or even notice.   Even so, two

[89] *Records*, pp. 513, 514, 522.
[90] *Ibid.*, p. 535.
[91] *The duty of Christians, in singing the praise of God, explained. A Sermon. By John Black.* Carlisle, Kline & Reynolds, 1790, p. 46.

questions remain to puzzle us. First: if any hymns were considered in 1787, why not Watts' *Hymns,* which were not "exceptionable," had become dear to many, and were beginning to find their way into churches, without authorization? Second: what was the "book of hymns" added by the committee? It would seem probable that it was the appendix of seventy hymns (mostly from Watts; a few of his own), which Barlow added to his revision of Watts' Imitations as presented to, and adopted by, the General Association of Connecticut. Nevertheless surviving copies of one of the first issues of *Barlow's Watts* containing the certificate of its authorization by Synod, and printed at Philadelphia in 1787 by Francis Bailey, have, bound in with the psalms and bearing a separate title,[92] a collection of 139 hymns, whose presence in that connection has not been explained. The collection is of unusual excellence and variety for that time, being brightened by lyrics of both the Wesley brothers, Miss Steele and others later than Watts. In view of the fact that such men of culture as Dr. Ewing, Dr. Robert Davidson, and Dr. Alison, were on the committee, it remains as an interesting possibility that this collection is the first tentative hymn book of American Presbyterianism.

The approval of *Barlow's Watts* by the Synod of 1787 involved no change of attitude, except that it gave finality to a position which heretofore might seem to be held tentatively. Synod's action was taken in full view of the controversy then raging in the South and West between the partisans of "Rous" and those of Watts, in the presence indeed of representatives of both sides from the disturbed

[92]*Hymns suited to the Christian worship in the United States of America. Philadelphia: printed by Francis Bailey, at Yorick's Head, in Market Street. MDCCLXXXVII.* The title of the edition of "Barlow's Watts" which it follows reads: *Psalms, carefully suited to the Christian worship in the United States of America. Being an improvement of the Old Version of the Psalms of David. Allowed by the reverend Synod of New York and Philadelphia, to be used in churches and private families* (Same imprint and date).

Presbytery of Abingdon.[93] The pleas of neither side moved Synod from its position:—it would not commit the Church to any type of Psalmody; it had already approved both "Rous" and Watts for use in worship, and approved both still; any question as to which should be preferred in any given case was a parochial issue, to be handled forbearingly no doubt, but not to be brought before Synod.[94]

The issue between "Rous" and Watts was thenceforward, then, merely a parochial issue. But, in the years following, the aggregate of parishes affected by it was so great, and the consequences so serious, as to make these years of controversy something like a distinct era in the history of the Presbyterian Church.

In Virginia the issue was definitely framed in a fruitless appeal to the Presbytery of Hanover to discipline the Rev. Charles Cummings for abetting the use of Watts. But Mr. Cummings was forced out of his charges by the uneasiness of his people; and the atmosphere of party feeling is revealed by the inquiry from some in various congregations to Presbytery in 1784, as to whether they would be endangered by attending upon the Word preached by Mr. Cummings.[95] In Tennessee the Psalmody question played a principal part in the tumultuous disorders in the newly formed Presbytery of Abingdon, which came before the Synod of 1787. In the North Carolina settlements every proposal to introduce Watts bred trouble. At New Providence the use of his Imitations for one Sunday by a pulpit supply (William C. Davis) started the suspicion that the pastor (James Wallis) had connived with him, and permanently disrupted the church, the minority forming a separate congregation.[96] At Poplar Tent, where, about 1785, Mr. Archibald, the pastor, determined to introduce

[93]*Records*, p. 515.
[94]*Ibid.*, p. 537.
[95]*Cf.* W. H. Foote, *Sketches of Virginia, second series*, 2nd ed., Philadelphia, 1856, pp. 124, 125.
[96]W. H. Foote, *Sketches of North Carolina*, New York, 1846, p. 249.

Watts upon his own authority, some of the Rous party left
and some stayed to interrupt the worship.[97]   The result of
the controversy in North Carolina was a permanent schism;
those favoring a strict Psalmody withdrawing to form an
Associate Presbytery.

The fiercest heat attained in the controversy, and the
greatest devastation it left behind, were in the new settlements of Kentucky.   Elsewhere the Rous advocates might
be regarded as acting on the defensive, but in Kentucky
their cause found an aggressive champion in the person of
the Rev. Adam Rankin, who came to Lexington in 1784.
He sincerely thought he heard a divine call to purge the
Church of the taint in its Congregational Song, and his
enthusiasm for the exclusive use of psalms not only possessed his mind but perverted it.   When he found in 1785,
at the Cane Run conference of the young churches, that
his associates were not in sympathy with him nor anxious
to agitate a vexed question, he at once entered upon a campaign of fierce and bitter polemic, in the role of a prophet
hurling epithets upon his opposers.   Censured by Presbytery
for traducing his brethren and barring the singers of Watts
from the Communion, and suspended for contumacy, he
and his supporters withdrew to form what came to be called
"the Rankinite Schism," composed of twelve congregations,
whose fortunes we need not follow.[98]

The Rankin polemics and schism threw a blight upon
Kentucky Presbyterianism from which few if any congregations escaped.   The spirit of dissension was kept alive for
years, and in many places Psalmody became the main issue
and concern of religion.   Internal feuds prevented attention
to the inroads of vice and infidelity, and the high promise
of Presbyterianism lapsed into spiritual and material decline.

[97]*Ibid.*, p. 442.
[98]For the "Rankin Schism" see R. Davidson, *History of the Presbyterian Church in Kentucky*, New York, 1847, chap. 3, and "Origin of
the Rankinites" in *Evangelical Record*, Lexington, vol. ii, Sept., 1813.

In Pennsylvania, East and West, the ground was laid for the fire of controversy, but the change to the new Psalmody was made with less disturbance, because more gradually and with more of the spirit of mutual concession. In Philadelphia the change was effected in the Third Church unanimously in 1788.[99] In the West the Presbytery of Redstone, through its entire career, kept its records clear of any allusion to the Psalmody controversy. Watts' Imitations, and afterwards his *Hymns,* found their way into the churches through the homes, and frequently were used at first in rotation with "Rous."[100] In some churches, even the use of the Imitations was postponed, as in the First Church of Carlisle, until well into the XIXth century.[101]

3. HYMN SINGING UNDER THE NEW (1788) "DIRECTORY FOR WORSHIP"

The real issue in the Rous-Watts controversy was not between a literal or a freer Psalmody, but between an Old Testament Psalmody and an evangelical Hymnody. That issue once decided, it remained for the Church to embody its convictions and practice in the constitution then being framed. This was effected by Synodical adoption of *The Directory for the worship of God, of the Presbyterian Church in the United States of America,* on May 16, 1788. Unlike some other parts of the draught reported by the committee of 1787, its chapter "Of the Singing of Psalms" was adopted intact. The title of the chapter is still that of the corresponding chapter of the *Westminster Directory* of 1644, but where the opening sentence of the original had declared "the duty of Christians to praise God publiquely by singing of Psalms," the new Directory asserts that such duty is to be fulfilled "by singing psalms or hymns." The

[99]J. W. Scott, *An Historical Sketch of the Pine Street, or Third Pres. Church,* Philadelphia, 1837, p. 31.

[100]Jos. Smith, *Old Redstone,* Philadelphia, 1854, p. 290.

[101]C. P. Wing, *History of the First Pres. Ch. of Carlisle,* Carlisle, 1877, p. 167. Watts was not used till 1824.

other changes deal with the propriety of cultivating a knowledge of music, of giving up the practice of lining, and of devoting more time to "this excellent part of divine service" than was usual.

The cultivation of music thus enjoined began at once in some churches, in others had already begun under the numerous "Instructors of Psalmody" raised up under the impulse imparted by Billings, especially Andrew Law of Connecticut. These teachers went from place to place, establishing "Psalmody classes." In the region around Philadelphia, the Presbyterian churches shared in a general[102] movement to improve sacred music, under the leadership of Andrew Adgate. He founded there in 1784 an "Institution for Promoting the Knowledge of Psalmody," afterwards the "Uranian Academy."[103] In 1787 he was preparing to establish "an Institution for Cultivating Church Music free to all."[104] Samuel Blair paid tribute to his benevolence, assiduity and success, and rejoiced in the great improvement he had effected, saying that "Public worship hath assumed, comparatively, a celestial grace; and the temples of religion, . . . now resound with vibrations of well-ordered and commanding melody."[105] Mr. Blair's wish that Adgate's "important services" may continue with the encouragement of all denominations"[106] was thwarted by his falling a victim to the yellow fever epidemic of 1793, while serving on the Committee of Alleviation.[107]

This movement to improve singing was inevitably a move-

---

[102]Saml. Blair, *Discourse* (1789), p. 25, note.

[103]Sonneck, *op. cit., pp.* 183, 184.

[104]Preface to his *Psalms and Hymns.*

[105]*A Discourse on Psalmody. Delivered by the Rev. Samuel Blair, in the Presbyterian Church in Neshaminy, at a public concert, given by Mr. Spicer, Master in sacred music: under the superintendency of Mr. Erwin, Pastor of that Church* (Philadelphia, John McColloch, 1789). This scarce pamphlet is the principal evidence of the Presbyterian participation in the Adgate movement, and was published "to enliven and diffuse the spirit of improvement in Psalmody" (preface).

[106]*Ibid.,* p. 25, note.

[107]*Minutes of the Committee,* Philadelphia, 1848, pp. 45, 200.

ment toward the use of Watts or of other hymns. The monotony of metre and rude rhythms of "Rous' version" would not serve the purpose of the "masters in sacred music." That is why, in so many parish records, the giving up of lining and the adoption of Watts are recorded as a single entry.[108] Copies have survived of *Select Psalms and Hymns for the use of Mr. Adgate's pupils: and proper for all singing-schools. Philadelphia: Printed at the Uranian Press, by Young and M'Culloch, Corner of Chestnut & Second Street. MDCCLXXXVII.* The forty hymns were chosen from Watts, Wesley, Steele and others, aiming at metrical variety. Adgate and his colleague, "Mr. Spicer," had also their own music books: the *Uranian Instructions* of 1787, *Rudiments of Music* (1788), *Selection of Sacred Harmony* (1788), *Philadelphia Harmony* (1788); all originally Adgate's, and sometimes, in later editions, carried forward by Spicer. *The Art of Singing,* and other works of Andrew Law, also played a considerable part in the improvement of Presbyterian singing.

No immediate steps were taken by the General Assembly in providing the hymns to be sung under the new *Directory.* In the minds of many, "Hymns" and "Watts" were synonymous. The use of the *Hymns and Spiritual Songs* was not formally authorized until 1802; but at least as early as 1788 editions of *Barlow's Watts,* bearing the clerk's certificate of Synod's authorization, appeared with the *Hymns* bound in. Evidently some churches did not await their authorization. Watts' *Hymns* may be called the first hymn book of American Presbyterianism, disregarding the proposed book of 1787. The second was an independent local venture, with two title pages: *A Version of the Book of Psalms, selected from the most approved versions. . . . Approved of by the Presbytery of Charleston:* and *A Collection of Hymns for public and private worship. Approved of by the Presbytery of Charleston.* (both) *Charleston, Printed by*

[108]E. g. in the Third Church of Philadelphia, Sept. 29, 1788.

J. McIver, No. 47, Bay, MDCCXCVI. This book was prepared by Dr. George Buist of Charleston with the advice of Dr. Hugh Blair.[109] The hymns are from many sources, including the English Arian hymn books, and with a preference for the Scottish *Paraphrases.* The book was used by the Presbyterian churches in the city and neighborhood of Charleston until at least 1809.[110]

What must be regarded as the third Presbyterian hymn book was the small collection annexed by President Dwight to his revision of Watts' Imitations for the Connecticut Association, to take the place of Barlow's; inasmuch as these hymns were specifically allowed by the General Assembly of 1802, in connection with the revised Psalms, and at the same time as the allowance of Watts' *Hymns.*[111] The Assembly had cooperated in securing Dwight's revision of the Imitations, as it had cooperated with other projects of the Connecticut Association; but apparently without sharing the prejudice aroused by Barlow and without much interest in the results of Dr. Dwight's labors. And in the end it appears to have been satisfied that churches under Connecticut influence, or which preferred Dwight to Barlow, should make use both of his revised Imitations and his collection of hymns.[112]

The great body of the Church had no apparent desire for a hymn book of their own. As early as 1796 the Assembly was overtured to appoint a committee to compile one, but the proposal was allowed to lie on the table.[113] In 1817 the Presbytery of Philadelphia sent up to the Assembly for its approbation "a copy of a collection of Hymns, intended for the use of society meetings; the Presbytery having declined to express their opinion of the book, thinking it

---

[109]Preface.

[110]*Sermons by the Reverend George Buist, D.D.,* New York, 1809, vol. i, pp. 311, 312, note.

[111]*Minutes 1789-1820,* p. 249.

[112]On this subject see the writer's "The American Revisions of Watts's Psalms," already cited, pp. 25-26.

[113]*Minutes, ut supra,* p. 116.

proper that it should be submitted to the Assembly."[114]
This was presumably *Hymns for social worship, collected
from various authors* (Philadelphia: W. W. Woodward,
1817), the work of James P. Wilson, pastor of the First
Church of Philadelphia. It contained 181 hymns, and in
intent and contents ranges with the "Supplements to
Watts." After reference to a committee, the consideration
of the book was indefinitely postponed.[115] No further
attempt was made to prepare a hymn book for the special
use of the Church till the proceedings that culminated in
the *Psalms and Hymns* of 1831.

In recognizing hymn singing in its constitution the
Church was far from the intention of cutting itself off
from psalm singing. It approved, rather, Dr. Watts'
System of Praise as a whole, with its two departments of
Psalms and Hymns. Nor did the desire for an evangelical
Hymnody among the people imply dissatisfaction with
Watts' Imitations. Probably no parish introduced his
Hymns apart from the Psalms: some had them bound up
with Barlow's Revision from the first: many remained
satisfied with the revised Psalms alone. The use of *Barlow's Watts* became so widespread as to make it the
characteristic praise book of Presbyterianism, and the addition to it of the *Hymns* became a more and more common
practice till toward the end of the first quarter of the XIXth
century, when it may be regarded as practically universal.
Hindered as it was by the Scottish predilection for an Old
Testament Psalmody, the Presbyterian Church was slower
than some others in attaining the full measure of Dr. Watts'
System of Praise, but perhaps in no Church did his ascendency become more complete. It was a result so belated that,
when viewed in connection with the progress of English
Hymnody as a whole, it seems like a step backward. A
full century had passed since the first appearance of Watts'
Hymns. The area of Hymnody had been widened perma-

[114]*Ibid.,* p. 641.
[115]*Ibid.,* p. 667.

nently under the Evangelical Revival, and its contents greatly enriched not only by fresh hymns but by new types of hymns. During the first quarter of the XIXth century the only apparent contact of the Presbyterian Church with this newer Hymnody was through the proffer of Dr. Wilson's little book of 1817;[116] its only dealing with it was to "postpone indefinitely."

III. The Baptists (1754-1827)

1. Their Gradual Adoption of Watts' "Psalms and Hymns"

If the earliest New England Baptists practised psalm singing at all, they probably, like their neighbors, lined the psalms out of *The Bay Psalm Book*. But the Baptist immigrants had come out of the heated atmosphere of the "controversie of Singing," and many of them during the years when persecution had favored the habit of not singing, lest attention be attracted to the meetings.

The First Church of Boston introduced singing before 1728, lining the psalms until 1759;[117] the Newport church during the short pastorate of John Cromer, beginning in 1726.[118] In the First Church of Providence there was no singing till the coming of President Manning in 1771. Even then its introduction was only accomplished by allowing the women to vote for it, and caused a division.[119]

In the Middle Colonies and to some extent in the Southern, the introduction of singing into Baptist churches was effected through the influence of a body of Welsh Baptists

---

[116]Even Dr. Wilson did not know that his 176th hymn, "Jesus! lover of my soul," was by one of the Wesleys.

[117]N. E. Wood, *History of the First Baptist Church of Boston,* Philadelphia, 1899, pp. 220, 243.

[118]A. H. Newman, *History of the Baptist Churches in the United States,* ed., Philada., 1898, p. 115.

[119]R. A. Guild, *History of Brown University,* Boston, 1867, pp. 207-210.

settled on the Welsh Tract in Delaware.[120] They adopted in 1716 an English Confession of Faith of 1689, but with the addition of two articles from a confession published by Benjamin Keach and his son Elias in 1697, one being on the duty "Of Singing Psalms, &c."[121] The increase of immigration soon made Philadelphia a Baptist centre, and in 1742 the Philadelphia Association ordered the printing of a new edition of the Confession of 1689 as their own,[122] with the insertion of two articles, one on the singing of Psalms,[123] the other on laying on of hands upon baptized believers. These articles, thus incorporated in their doctrinal statement, prove to be identical with those of Keach as already adopted by the church on the Welsh Tract in 1716.[124]

The Bay Psalm Book was probably in use in and around Philadelphia as well as in New England. In Boston the First Church changed to *Tate and Brady* in 1740, "so long as no objection should be offered against it":[125] the Baldwin Place Church sang *Tate and Brady* till about 1770.[126] And it may be that some Baptist demand in and around Philadelphia helped to encourage Franklin to reprint that version in 1733.

In America as in England Baptists were not greatly concerned to preserve a strict Psalmody, owing partly to the desire for sacramental hymns. When the "controversie of

[120]Morgan Edwards, *Materials toward a history of the Baptists in Delaware State,* in *Pennsylvania Magazine of History,* vol. ix, p. 52.

[121]W. J. McGlothlin, *Baptist Confessions of Faith,* Philadelphia [1911], p. 294.

[122]*Minutes of the Philadelphia. Baptist Association, 1707-1807,* Philada., 1851, p. 46.

[123] "*Singing psalms* met with some opposition, especially at Cohansey": Morgan Edwards, *ut supra.*

[124]*A Confession of Faith . . . Adopted by the Baptist Association met at Philadelphia, Sept. 25, 1742. . . . To which are added, Two Articles, viz. Of Imposition of Hands, and Singing of Psalms, in Publick Worship:* Philadelphia, B. Franklin, 1743; often reprinted.

[125]N. E. Wood, *op. cit.,* p. 220.

[126]D. C. Eddy, *Memorial Sermon,* Boston, 1865, p. 30.

Singing" was disposed of, the introduction of hymns hardly raised an issue.

But the Great Awakening was less immediately effective in modifying the practice of the Baptist churches of New England than of the Congregational. The Baptist churches had largely lapsed into a cold "Arminianism," and held aloof from the earlier stages of the Revival, partly because they regarded it as a Calvinistic movement, and partly from a sense of isolation from their neighbors. The Revival had first to create "New Light" churches, and to modify the theology and the spirit of the old churches before the evangelical *Psalms and Hymns* of Watts could commend themselves to New England Baptists.

In the churches centering at Philadelphia the atmosphere was different, and the way more prepared by the evangelical Calvinism already prevailing in them. Franklin's reprints of *The Psalms imitated* in 1741 and of the *Hymns* in 1742 were probably used in some of them about Philadelphia. In Boston, *Tate and Brady* was not displaced by Watts' *Psalms and Hymns* till after 1770 in the Baldwin Place Church,[127] and in 1771 in the First Church.[128] Their adoption became ultimately very widespread, and they rooted themselves deep in the hearts of a great body of Baptists.

2. Obstacles to Watts' Ascendency

But several considerations tended to impede to some extent the ascendency of Watts in American Baptist Hymnody.

There was, first, *the tendency to establish a denominational Hymnody,* especially to supply hymns suitable to "believers' baptism." Morgan Edwards has preserved the hymn that had been used at the "Baptisterion" on the banks of the Schuylkill, just beyond Philadelphia.[129] The earliest

---

[127]D. C. Eddy, *op. cit.,* p. 30.

[128]N. E. Wood, *op. cit.,* p. 266.

[129]*Materials towards a history of the Baptists in Pennsylvania,* vol. i, Philada., J. Crukshank, 1770, pp. 131, 132.

American Baptist hymn book, *Hymns and Spiritual Songs,
collected from the works of several authors* (Newport,
1766), opens with sixteen hymns on Baptism. And so, in
1808, after the appearance of many books, the anonymous
The Boston Collection of sacred and devotional Hymns
"was compiled principally with a view to accommodate the
Baptist Churches of Boston and its vicinity, who have long
desired such a collection, for the purpose of singing at the
administration of" Baptism.

From the first, however, the desire of many went beyond
baptismal hymns. They wanted Baptist hymn books, that
should make available the new store of hymns, Baptist and
other, written since Watts' time and made current in English collections; and many were moved to contribute hymns
of their own composition. The independent and individualistic spirit combined with denominational insistence, that
has always characterized Baptists, developed and has maintained a striking proclivity toward the multiplication of
hymn books. The great array of these tends to obscure the
actual extent of the use of Watts' *Psalms and Hymns* in
Baptist congregations.

The Newport book was followed by two at Philadelphia:
*A choice Collection of Hymns, in which are some never
before printed. Philadelphia: printed in the year 1782,*[130]
and *A choice Collection of Hymns, from various authors,
adapted to publick worship: designed for the edification of
the pious of all denominations; but more particularly for
the use of the Baptist Church in Philadelphia* (Enoch Story,
1784). Both of these appear to have been prepared for his
following of "Universal Baptists" by Elhanan Winchester,
after his exclusion from the pulpit of the First Baptist
Church. The latter is said to have been used in the Church
of the German Baptist Brethren (Dunkers) already formed
at Germantown.[131] It certainly furnished much of the ma-

[130]Not in Hildeburn's *Issues of the Pennsylvania Press.* The writer's copy is recorded by Evans.

[131]Ms. note in the writer's copy.

terials of the Brethren's first English hymn book, *The Christians Duty*, printed in 1791.[132]

In 1788 the Philadelphia Association determined to have an official book for the associated churches.[133] It appeared as *A Selection of Psalms and Hymns, done under the appointment of the Philadelphian Association. By Samuel Jones, D.D. and Burgis Allison, A.M.* (Philadelphia, R. Aitken & Son, 1790 : 2nd ed., 1801 ; 4th, 1819). The psalms were all from Watts : most of the hymns from Rippon's *Selection* (London, 1786) and one "printed in London, 1774" ; apparently Conyers'. The book was highly regarded within and beyond the Association. *Hymns on different spiritual subjects* (Norwich, 1792) by Benjamin Cleveland,[134] as also the later *Hymns and Spiritual Songs on various subjects. By the Rev. Ebenezer Jayne* (Morristown, 1809), were offerings of original contributions, of which Cleveland's hymn, "Oh, could I find from day to day," alone survived.

John Stanford, lately come from England to New York, prepared *A Collection of evangelical Hymns* (T. and J. Swords, 1792) for the use of the congregation gathered in his school room. It included selections not only from Watts but from the best English hymn writers of the time. And John Asplund, lately come from Sweden, and still remembered by his *Baptist Register,* was responsible for an American reprint of Richard Burnham's *New Hymns* (Thomas Hall, Boston, 1796). The outspoken Calvinism of these hymns was perhaps the reason for their reprinting.

It is likely that many of the Baptist hymn books were not intended to replace Watts in church worship : a number bore on their title-pages the assurance that they were only supplements to his *Psalms and Hymns.* Of these the most popular, here as in England, was Rippon's *Selection.* Two

[132]See chap. viii, II, 2, (2).
[133]*Minutes*, p. 239.
[134]*Cf.* H. S. Burrage, *Baptist Hymn Writers and their Hymns*, Portland, Me., n. d., pp. 223, 641.

reprints of it appeared in 1792, at New York and Elizabeth, and were followed by others, in various places. *A Selection of evangelical Hymns supplementary to Doctor Rippon* (Burlington, N. J.: S. C. Ustic) appeared in 1807: and a further attempt to enrich his *Selection* was made by Dr. William Staughton in an edition to which he added *An Appendix, from the Olney Hymns, with additional Hymns, original*[135] *and selected* (Philadelphia: W. W. Woodward, 1813; rev. and corr., 1827).

In a more independent spirit William Parkinson, of the First Church in New York, published in 1809 *A Selection of Hymns and Spiritual Songs . . . as an Appendix to Dr. Watts's Psalms and Hymns,* which, he says in his preface, "in most congregations of Christians are constantly used." William Collier's *A new Selection of Hymns* (Boston, 1812), was also a supplement to Watts. That such books were actually used in connection with Watts appears from the preface of Daniel Dodge's *A Selection of Hymns and Psalms* (Wilmington, 1808), an effort to combine the best from Watts and Rippon for the convenience of those who found it burdensome to carry both books to church, but could not agree to dispense with either; "some being passionately fond of one and some of the other." A later book, Thomas B. Ripley's *A Selection of Hymns for Conference and Prayer Meetings* (Portland, Me., 1821: 2nd ed., Bangor, 1831) also called itself a Supplement to Watts.

A second consideration tending to impede the ascendency of Watts was *the preference of a considerable proportion of Baptist people for songs of a lower literary grade.* The strength of the Church was among the uncultured; its extension was by means of evangelistic methods. "The mass of the Baptists were indifferent or hostile to ministerial education." They craved highly emotional preaching and songs of the same type in free rhythms that could be sung to popular melodies with choruses.

[135]Staughton had printed a volume of Juvenile Poems, and wrote many hymns in a style no longer in vogue.

This showed itself as early as 1784[136] in the *Divine Hymns, or Spiritual Songs* (Norwich) of Joshua Smith, a New Hampshire layman, and others, which gave currency to the hymn on "Christ the Appletree,"[137] and made odd additions to other hymns. This book in varying forms[138] was very popular. Its 1803 edition was the first hymn book used in the First Church of Portland, Maine.[139] "Spiritual songs" appeared in most Baptist hymn books. John Courtney's *The Christian's Pocket Companion* (Richmond, 1805: rev. ed., 1831) contained "one hundred and seventy-eight pages of" them. They were sung also without book.

"This kind of composition," says Mr. Parkinson in 1809, "has, for several years past been greatly abused—Songs have been circulated, not only in Ms. but also in print, which have been so barbarous in language, so unequal in numbers, and so defective in rhyme, as to excite disgust in all persons even of tolerable understanding in these things; what is infinitely worse, so extremely unsound in doctrine, that no discerning Christian can sing or hear them without pain." Believing that "many of them, notwithstanding, contain valuable ideas," Mr. Parkinson aimed to "lessen the use of several hymn books now in common circulation" by furnishing "those who choose to make use of them with a greater variety and more correct edition of what are called *Spiritual Songs* than they now possess."[140] We may judge existing conditions by the character of some of the 170 songs appended to Parkinson's *Selection* with a view of ameliorating them. In the first Newton's un-

---

[136]Brinley catalogue, lot 6038.

[137]The first stanza of this hymn ran (ed. 1794):—

> "The tree of life, my soul hath seen,
> Laden with fruit, and always green;
> The trees of nature fruitless be,
> Compar'd with Christ the Appletree."

[138]For some of the known editions, see W. DeL. Love, *Samson Occum*, Boston, n. d., p. 180, note.

[139]Burrage, *op. cit.*, p. 643.

[140]Preface to Parkinson's *Selection*, 1809.

fortunate lines are altered to serve as a refrain after each stanza:—

> "Then be entreated now to stop
> For unless you warning take,
> Ere you are aware you'll drop
> Into the burning lake."

The third is "A Dream" of Judgment Day. The fifth is entitled "Miss Hataway's Experience" and includes her conversation with "an uncle from whom she had large expectations." The fifteenth begins, "Ye scarlet-colour'd sinners, come."

Parkinson's *Selection* had reached a third edition in 1817, and Southern Baptists had called for three editions of Jesse Mercer's *The Cluster of Spiritual Songs, Divine Hymns and social Poems: being chiefly a collection* (Augusta, Ga.).

By this time the new zeal for missions was developing a demand for an educated ministry, and drawing a sharp line of cleavage between its advocates and the "anti-effort" Baptists. In the Hymnody the line was not so sharply drawn, but as a rule the less educated congregations, especially in the South, carried forward the use of "Spiritual Songs." An especial favorite was Starke Dupuy's *Hymns and Spiritual Songs, selected and original* (Louisville, c. 1818: 22nd ed., 1841; revised by J. M. Peck, 1843), emotional and often illiterate. Even in New England David Benedict's *The Pawtucket Collection of Conference Hymns* (1817) reached an eighth edition (1843). In Kentucky Absolom Graves' *Hymns, Psalms and Spiritual Songs* (with 111 of the latter), appearing in 1825, reached a second edition in 1829. In Virginia Andrew Broadus published in 1828 his *Dover Selection of Spiritual Songs* by recommendation of the Dover Association, but in his better *Virginia Selection* of 1836 the "spiritual song" element is apologized for as an allowance made for "popular liking." William Dossey's *The Choice; in two parts* (3rd ed., 1830) was largely used in the South, and included over a hundred of his own hymns.

There were, on the other hand, many Baptist churches, especially in the North and East,[141] which had yielded very partially or not at all to "popular liking," and had never given up the use of Watts' *Psalms and Hymns*. But their pastors had required hymns to supplement Watts, and the people complained of the inconvenience of using more than one book and the difficulty of finding the hymns as given out. This led to something like a concerted effort to conserve the better type of Baptist Hymnody. James M. Winchell, who had developed congregational song in his First Church of Boston,[142] published there in 1818 *An arrangement of the Psalms, Hymns, and Spiritual Songs of . . . Watts, to which are added, indexes . . . to facilitate the use of the whole . . . ,* with which was bound up *A Selection of more than three hundred Hymns, from the most approved authors* (1819). "Winchell's Watts" attained, and for many years held, in New England a use so wide that it has been described as "universal."[143] In 1820 the same office was performed for the churches centering at Philadelphia by *The Psalms and Hymns of Dr. Watts, arranged by Dr. Rippon; with Dr. Rippon's Selection in one volume.* An improved edition appeared in 1827, and was commended to the churches by a large number of ministers as the best hymn book "in use among Christians."[144] In the copies of this edition a portrait of Dr. Watts was not unfitly prefixed.

[141]Samuel Holyoke published in 1804 *The Christian Harmonist: containing a set of tunes adapted to all the metres in Mr. Rippon's Selection of Hymns, in the Collection of Hymns by Mr. Joshua Smith, and in Dr. Watts's Psalms and Hymns* (Salem). It was "designed for the use of the Baptist churches in the United States"; and the three books named are plainly those in most general use in the class of churches which Mr. Holyoke regarded as likely to patronize his enterprise.

[142]*Cf.* R. H. Neale, *Address at 200th Anniversary of First Baptist Church,* Boston, 1865, p. 38.

[143]Neale, *ut supra.*

[144]*Cf.* "recommendations" preserved in Sommers and Dagg's ed., Phila., D. Clark, 1838.

V

HIS INFLUENCE UPON THE ENGLISH HYMN

In attempting now to estimate the place of Dr. Watts in the history of the English Hymn, it is convenient to distinguish the bearings of his work and influence upon the development of the Hymn itself, upon the production of hymns, and upon hymn singing.

As to *the Hymn*. Watts undertook to construct Congregational Song *de novo*. He offered his System of Praise to the churches as a substitute for all that they had been accustomed to sing; and as such it came to be received in its full scope and entirety by vast numbers of people to whom the old Psalmody, or the earlier Hymnody, became as though they had never been. Even to historians of English Hymnody the work of Watts has bulked so large as to throw a deep shadow of obscurity over all his predecessors. Thus Montgomery makes the oft-quoted remark that "Watts may almost be called the inventor of hymns in our language"; regarding him as so far departing from all precedent, "that few of his compositions resemble those of his forerunners," and as establishing a precedent to all his successors.[145] Again, Mr. Horder in his *Hymn Lover*,[146] calls Watts "the real founder of English Hymnody," and claims that "what Ambrose was to the Latins; what Clement Marot was to the French; what Luther was to the Germans; that, and perhaps more, was Watts to the English."

It is difficult to regard Watts, as Montgomery does, as altogether or almost the inventor of English hymns; and surely Mr. Horder has put Watts' work somewhat out of perspective. Ambrose stands at the fountain head of all metrical Congregational Song; and Sternhold, not Watts, is the English sponsor of the movement to provide the people with vernacular songs, which Luther and Marot represent. When Watts wrote, great stores of metrical

[145]*The Christian Psalmist,* Glasgow, 1825, Introductory Essay, p. xx.
[146]W. G. Horder, *The Hymn Lover,* London, n. d., p. 96.

Psalm versions had been accumulating for a century and a half. Some passages from these Watts incorporated into his own work: many more, equally available, lay ready to his hand. Even the "Christianized" Psalms of Watts were a development rather than a creation, as has already appeared. Of hymns, in the narrower sense, there were many, and of good hymns not a few. If Watts had lacked his gift of hymn writing but retained his practical sagacity, he could have compiled an English hymn book out of existing materials, whose excellence would not be questioned today. With Marckant, Austin, Wither, Cosin, Herbert, Tate, Mason, Ken, Baxter, Herrick, Crossman and Stennett, still holding a place in our hymn books, it is idle to regard Watts as inventing the English Hymn.

It may even be that Watts could not write a better hymn than Ken's Morning and Evening hymns, a more useful Christmas hymn than Tate's "While shepherds watched," or a Sunday hymn with more of tender charm than Mason's "My Lord, my Love, was crucified." But he could bring to bear upon his hymn writing a discernment, and a combination of resources, spiritual, intellectual, poetic, utilitarian, possessed by none of his predecessors or all of them if put together. He was not alone in perceiving that an acceptable evangelical Church Song was a spiritual need of his time, but he had the ability to foresee, as other men could not, the possibilities and limitations of the Congregational Hymn in filling that need. With great assiduity he dedicated his ample gifts to the embodiment of what he saw. He produced a whole cycle of religious song which his own ardent faith made devotional, which his manly and lucid mind made simple and strong, which his poetic feeling and craftmanship made rhythmical and often lyrical, and which his sympathy with the people made hymnic. Probably the whole body of his work appealed alike to the people of his time, whose spiritual needs he so clearly apprehended. The larger part of his work proved to be an abiding enrichment of Church Song, and to many its only adequate expression.

His best hymns remain permanently, after the winnowing of two centuries, among the classics of devotion.

But Watts' work was more than an extensive reinforcement of the stores of available hymns. By the force of its very fitness it established a definite and permanent type of English Hymn. And this type, rather than any particular hymns, is the real expression of Watts' mind and purpose, and constitutes his special discovery. Purposing to construct Church Song anew, he sought for the true basis of a sympathetic devotion. He found it not in a poet's mind, but in the thoughts and feelings and aspirations held in common by the largest number of Christians. That common ground he selected as the available area of Congregational Song, within which he sank his foundations, and proceeded to erect his System of Praise on lines kept within the same limits by careful measurement. By this criterion Watts' work may be tried, both as to form and substance.

(a) *As to Form.* Watts invented no hymn measures, but fell back upon the rudimentary forms of verse used in psalm singing. In the original edition of his *Hymns,* he confined himself to the three simplest and most often used metres of the current *Sternhold and Hopkins,*—common, long and short. In the second edition, he added the metre of their 148th Psalm,—6. 6. 6. 6. 4. 4. 4. 4. In *The Psalms imitated* he rendered "some few Psalms in Stanza's of six, eight or twelve lines, to the best of the old Tunes." He sought no musical development of Congregational Song, beyond a better rendering of the psalm tunes. He rather accommodated himself to the conditions of musical decadence surrounding him, with a view to immediate usefulness; saying,[147] "I have seldom permitted a Stop in the middle of a Line, and seldom left the end of a Line without one, to comport a little with the unhappy Mixture of Reading and Singing, which cannot presently be reformed."

The Hymn Form thus indicated is even simpler and more restricted than that of the earlier Metrical Psalm. But in

[147]Preface of 1719, p. xxvii.

Watts' own hands the succession of rhythmic periods acquires a dignity of cadence peculiarly satisfying, and, with his pure and nervous English, constitutes a hymn style in pleasing contrast with the halting measures of Sternhold and Hopkins and the rather rippling effects of Tate and Brady. With his eye on the practical requirements of common song, Watts gave to the Hymn Form other features that distinguish it from the formlessness of the Metrical Psalm:—the adaptation of the opening line to make a quick appeal, the singleness of theme that holds the attention undivided, the brevity and compactness of structure and the progression of thought toward a climax, that give the Hymn a unity.

(b) *As to Substance.* The content of the Hymn, as Watts conceived it, was Scriptural, as being a response to Scripture. It was an evangelical interpretation of revealed truths as appropriated by the believer. The adoration of God in nature and providence being expressed in the Psalms, the great theme of the Hymn proper became the Gospel in the full width of its range, including man's deliverance from the terrors of the law. The Hymn thus became primarily an expression of Christian experience.

This raises the question whether Watts stands sponsor for the homiletical ideal of the Hymn, as against the liturgical. He was trained in that conception of worship which the sermon and not the season dominates; and plainly he designed his hymns to meet the demand from the pulpit for hymns that would illustrate and enforce the sermon themes. This demand was undoubtedly one of the moving causes in the change of Nonconformist Praise from Psalmody to Hymnody. Granting that the sermon was Scriptural, Watts' conception of the Hymn as a response to Scripture made such an use of hymns natural; and, granting that the minds and hearts of the people were centred in the sermon, the homiletical use of hymns would not necessarily interfere with the best interests of Congregational Song.

Whether for good or ill, there is no doubt that Watts, both by his example in appending hymns to his own printed sermons, and by supplying so many hymns adapted to being appended to other people's sermons, greatly encouraged the homiletical use of hymns. But his hymns are seldom homilies, and they are made liturgical, in the broad sense of that word, by confinement within the common ground of Christian experience and avoidance of individualism, whether elevated or eccentric. They are filled also with reverence and a deep sense of God's majesty and goodness, that evoke a recurring note of adoration and praise. And, before committing Watts to the homiletical ideal of the Hymn, we must remember that his own hymns were designed to be used in connection with psalms as a single System of Praise.

In doctrine the hymns of Watts were Calvinistic in tone and often in detail. This was not from any polemical intent, but because Calvinism was the form of belief held in common by the writer and the singers. He aimed to avoid "the more obscure and controverted Points of Christianity" and "the Contentious and Distinguishing Words of Sects and Parties . . . that whole Assemblies might assist at the Harmony, and different Churches join in the same Worship without Offence." He held that in "Treatises of Divinity which are to be read in private," precision of statement should be aimed at, but that in hymns expressions should be sought "such as are capable of an extensive Sense, and may be used with a charitable Latitude. . . . that what is provided for publick Worship shou'd give to sincere Consciences as little Vexation and Disturbance as possible."[148] This was no more than to carry into the sphere of belief the same search for the common ground he had already made in the sphere of experience. Watts lived long enough to see the common ground of belief much narrowed by the Arian movement, and to read the polemical Hymnody of the Calvinistic controversy. And in the course of time it has no doubt become impracticable for the Churches to

[148]Preface of 1707, pp. vii, viii.

confine their Hymnody to the things held in common. Nevertheless there are but few today who would question the soundness of the principle announced by Watts, or seek to use the Hymn as a weapon of polemics rather than as a bond of union.

Of Watts' determination to keep the Hymn within the common ground in the sphere of the understanding, nothing needs to be said, beyond noting his success in carrying out that aim. His remarks upon the subject were in fact addressed to literary critics, who he feared would misunderstand the purpose of his work. But in the aim itself there was nothing really novel. It involved nothing more than loyalty to the Protestant principle that every part of public worship should be conducted in a language understood by the people.

VI

HIS INFLUENCE UPON HYMN WRITING: THE SCHOOL OF WATTS

Upon the *production of hymns* also Dr. Watts' work exercised a great influence, not wholly for good. The art that hides art beneath apparent simplicity seems to the observer to be the most imitable of all literary forms: and a success so striking as that of Watts inevitably breeds imitators. Moreover the reiterated assurances of Watts' prefaces that his hymns were not poetry, but only measured verse written down to the level of the meanest capacity, were a distinct encouragement to many who could not write poetry to believe they could write hymns. In this way Watts' hymns became a direct model for the construction of other hymns, and he became unconsciously the founder of a school of hymn writers.

The five familiar hymns of Joseph Addison appeared in *The Spectator* between July and October, 1712, five years after the publication of Watts' *Hymns*. When two had thus appeared, there followed in the number for August 19, an unsigned letter from Watts himself, alleging that the reading of them had encouraged him to try his own hand, and accompanied by a version of Psalm 114, afterwards included in *The Psalms imitated*. Looking behind this pleasantry, we may infer the actual connection between the two writers to be that Watts' example and influence had encouraged the older poet to write hymns. But Addison had his own thoughts and style, and if an actual follower of Watts in hymn writing, was no imitator of him, and was not especially of his school.

The exact measure of Watts' influence upon the Wesleys is not easily appraised. We know that when John Wesley went on his mission to Georgia, he took with him the *Psalms and Hymns,* and that in his first hymn book, printed at Charleston in 1737, a large part of the contents is by Watts. Some of his hymns found permanent place in the Wesleyan books, and both brothers felt high admiration for them. But other influences affected the Wesleys more deeply, and are more evident in their original and translated work. Watts served them by way of suggestion and encouragement rather than as furnishing a model for their own hymns.

With Watts' contemporary and friend, Dr. Doddridge, it is different. His hymn writing was one of several lamps "kindled at Watts' torch."[149] The hymns were homiletical in motive, mostly intended to be sung in his own chapel at the Castle Hill, Northampton, after the particular sermon in the glow of whose composition they were composed. After Doddridge's death 370 of the hymns were published by his friend Job Orton, with quite superfluous notes, as *Hymns founded on various texts in the Holy Scriptures. By the late Reverend Philip Doddridge, D.D.* (Salop, 1755). They reached a second edition in 1759, and a third in 1766, with small additions. Many reprints followed and the *Hymns* gained the place of a standard publication. The book does not range technically with the "Supplements to

[149] His *Rise and Progress* and Catechism in verse were others.

Watts," but already in 1755 a letter of Mrs. Doddridge speaks of numerous ministers intending to introduce it in that capacity,[150] and such it actually became in fact. The effect of it was to augment by so much the available body of hymns of the Watts type, covering some new themes and special occasions with hymns of decided merit and usefulness. Doddridge must be accounted first scholar in the school of Watts. Chronologically he had been preceded by Simon Browne. But Browne's hymns as a whole hardly justified their existence, whereas Doddridge's constituted a worthy extension of Watts', and the best of them attained a position to be described as classical.

Dr. Thomas Gibbons, the next in the succession of Independent hymn writers, took his impulse from Watts, without sharing Watts' gift. Nor could he succeed in getting either of his collections already referred to into the churches. The earlier one has, however, the special interest of containing the hymns of his friend President Davies of Princeton, whose Mss. had come into Gibbons' hands. And President Davies' hymns remain as an interesting testimony of how far Watts' influence had spread. They attained wider liturgical use than those of Gibbons, and at least two of them[151] have proved permanently useful. But in the work of both writers we can detect the beginnings of that process which perpetuates the form and manner of a literary type apart from its original inspiration. Neither Watts nor Doddridge had been free from a tendency to prosaic dullness, and at the weaker hands of their imitators this tendency found a marked development.

The most popular, after Watts, of XVIIIth century Independent hymn-writers, was Joseph Hart, who is usually reckoned a disciple of the school of Watts. He published

---

[150] John Stoughton, *Philip Doddridge,* ed. Boston, 1853, p. 120, note.
[151] These are "Lord, I am thine, entirely thine," and "Great God of Wonders! all thy Ways." For a reprint of Davies' hymns and a study of them by the present writer, see *Journal of The Presbyterian Historical Society* for Sept. and Dec., 1904.

in 1759 (119) *Hymns composed on various subjects, with the Author's experience,* to which later supplements added some hundred more. They were introduced in his own chapel in Jewin Street, London, with immediate acceptance, and gained a wide use among Calvinistic Nonconformists of different connections. Repeated editions were called for, and their reprinting has continued till the present time. An inspection of these hymns makes it evident that Hart was not of Watts' school. His work addresses a lower plane of education and taste than Watts, with his eminently respectable surroundings, had in mind. Moreover a congregation bred to sing only psalms and hymns of the Watts type could not have carried these strange measures, which were fitted to the melodies of the Methodist Revival. These warm and even passionate strains are explained by Hart's associations with the Moravians, in one of whose chapels he was converted, and these new measures he learned in his attendance at the Tabernacle at Moorfields. Hart belongs rather with that evangelistic movement, with which, whether Calvinistic or Arminian, Watts had little sympathy.

On the Baptist side of Independency also, Watts became a controlling influence. We have already traced the beginnings of a Particular Baptist Hymnody down to Stennett's *Hymns for the Holy Ordinance of Baptism* of 1712. Then followed a breach in Baptist hymn making. In the thirty-seven years following, the silence was broken only by two faint voices. In 1734 Mrs. Anne Dutton appended a group of hymns to her poem on *The Wonders of Grace,* and in 1747 Daniel Turner of Reading published *Divine Songs, Hymns and other Poems.*[152]

The year 1750 begins a new period in Baptist hymn writing, but it is a Hymnody of the school of Watts. Benjamin Wallin's *Evangelical Hymns and Songs* of that year counted for something, but two volumes of *Poems on subjects chiefly devotional, by Theodosia* (Bristol, 1760)

---

[152]Turner is best known through his enlargement (pub. 1794) of Jas. Fanch's "Beyond the glittering starry skies."

counted for much. The hymns of Anne Steele appearing thus, and in a posthumous third volume (Bristol, 1780), were framed on the familiar model, but added a new note to the contents of the English Hymn. Exchanging the common ground for the feminine standpoint, she gave us the Hymn of Introspection and of intense devotion to Christ's person, expressed in fervid terms of heightened emotion. Composing under the shadow of affliction and ill-health, she added to English Hymnody the plaintive, sentimental note.

A number of these hymns remain in common use, and Miss Steele is still regarded as the foremost Baptist hymn writer. But the measure of our regard for her hymns reflects but faintly the enthusiasm of their welcome. Those concerned for a Baptist Hymnody soon perceived that a great light had arisen among themselves: it had become practicable to consider the compilation of denominational hymn books to supplement Watts. Through these, already noted, her hymns became known in all English Churches; and through reprints of these and also a Boston reprint of her poems,[153] they became eventually familiar in America. So far reaching and so deep was the impression made by Miss Steele that when Jeremy Belknap published his *Sacred Poetry* at Boston, 1795, he was moved to include her hymns to an extent justifying him in devoting nearly half of his preface to a biographical sketch of her. And when the people of Trinity Church, Boston, grew weary of the authorized Psalmody, and the vestry ventured in 1808 to print a parochial hymn book, 59 of its 152 hymns are Miss Steele's; a tribute, as the preface explains, "to her poetical superiority, and to the ardent spirit of devotion which breathes in her compositions." It is easy to understand that the depth and sincerity of feeling in Miss Steele's hymns made Tate and Brady and even Watts seem cold. But in the course of time it has become plain to many that those

---

[153] *The Works of Mrs. Anne Steele,* Boston, 1808, 2 vols., 16mo. (a reprint of the English ed. of 1780). "Mrs." was a courtesy title.

of her hymns that were most closely patterned on Watts were also those best adapted to congregational use.

There were now practical inducements for hymn writing, and the years from 1760 till towards the close of the XVIIIth century constitute what is still the only very significant era of Baptist Hymnody. Miss Steele was followed in 1768 by John Needham of Bristol, whose *Hymns devotional and moral on various subjects* added 263 to the available store, but added nothing in the way of advance on his great model, Dr. Watts, whom he closely imitated. At the West, Benjamin Beddome was producing a weekly hymn for use after his sermon at Bourton. Some of these appeared in Baptist hymn books during his life, and in 1817 no less than 830 were gathered up by Robert Hall as *Hymns adapted to public worship or family devotion, now first published from the manuscripts of the late Rev. B. Beddome, M.A.* In merit and in actual use Beddome stands beside Miss Steele. During the same period John Ryland of Northampton was contributing hymns to *The Gospel Magazine* and to current hymn books. John Fellows printed his *Hymns on Believers' Baptism* in 1773 and *Hymns in a great variety of metres* in 1776. John Fawcett published in 1782 his *Hymns adapted to the circumstances of public worship and private devotion* (Leeds). Richard Burnham began to publish his *New Hymns* in 1783, and Samuel Medley gathered into several volumes, beginning with 1785, his hymns that had appeared in leaflets and periodicals. The hymns of Samuel Stennett were contributed to Rippon's *Selection* of 1787. And we may close the list with the *Walworth Hymns* of Joseph Swain (London, 1792), who could follow the traditional model as well as any, but had also a distinct gift for a somewhat freer spiritual song. All of these men are still of some interest to the student of English hymns: they contributed to the permanent body of Evangelical Hymnody, and retain a minor place in current hymnals. Such as they were, they, with Miss Steele, represent the golden age of Baptist Hymnody, and serve to show how it shone with a light reflected from the person and work of Dr. Watts.

Beyond the bounds of Independency his influence is just as apparent in the hymn writers of the later Presbyterian and Unitarian group, of whom Joseph Grigg and Mrs. Barbauld are most familiar; and in Scotland in the work of Ralph Erskine and the writers of the *Translations and Paraphrases*. Indeed the whole history of English hymn writing points back to the fact that Watts established once for all a definite type of Hymn. Partly because of its essential fitness, and partly from the accident of its furnishing a mould which is the easiest to fill out, it has happened that from his time till ours the work of hymn writers without special force or inspiration of their own has tended to revert to the original model.

VII

HIS INFLUENCE UPON HYMN SINGING

After all, the Hymn is intended to be sung. The Hymn Form and the writing of hymns have little significance apart from hymn singing. And it is so with the work of Dr. Watts. Whatever importance be attached to his influence upon the ideal of the English Hymn and upon hymn composition, any final estimate of his place in Hymnody must be based upon the record of his success in getting his hymns sung. For that was the sum of his achievement. His greatest influence, that is to say, lay in his undoubted leadership in the establishment and extension of hymn singing as a part of congregational worship in the stead of the ordinance of psalm singing maintained since the Reformation.

We have already said that he may not be regarded as the "Inventor of the English Hymn." It is equally true that he cannot with strict accuracy be called the founder of the ordinance of hymn singing in our English-speaking

Churches. The Restoration Movement toward hymn singing cannot justly be ignored, any more than the early hymn
writers can be overlooked. Hymn singing had begun
before Watts, and hymn books were in use before the
publication of his. Nevertheless it is his figure that stands
out against the deplorable conditions of Psalmody at the
beginning of the XVIIIth century. He does not stand
alone, but his personality commands the situation, his mind
plans the remedy purely from personal resources, and his
strong will overcomes the force of tradition, of conviction,
of sacred associations, of habit, of prejudice, and, not least,
of indifference. The aggressiveness and even bitterness of
tone assumed by Watts in his prefaces and treatise on
Psalmody, standing in contrast to his habitual moderation,
mark his method of a deliberate attack upon the position
of the psalm singers; to whom indeed some things therein
said seemed little short of blasphemous. He raised the issue
squarely of Hymn against Psalm. While *The Psalms
imitated* did actually serve as a bridge over which numerous
psalm singers crossed almost unconsciously into Hymnody,
Watts himself did not offer them as a compromise or half
way measure, but only as a supplement to his *Hymns,* first
published, and followed by the Psalms after an interval of
twelve years.

This assault upon the Metrical Psalm might have counted
for little, might indeed have proved a destructive influence,
if Watts had not been able to replace the overthrown Psalmody with a Hymnody that satisfied the religious sentiment
more completely, and yet retained a sufficiency of the
familiar form and tone of the accustomed psalm. The number of those who read Watts' arguments against Metrical
Psalmody was limited, though his views were widely spread
for at least a century by means of debates and "Psalmody
sermons." But to a multitude of devout hearts the evangelical *Psalms and Hymns* in themselves furnished an incon-
trovertible argument against a longer continuance in the old
Psalmody. It is this wonderful adaptation of Watts'

System of Praise to meet the situation and to change it that gives it some consideration to be regarded as a work of genius.

The full scope of Dr. Watts' personal agency in the movement which has transformed all but a comparatively insignificant minority of English-speaking Churches from psalm singing into hymn singing Churches, it is impossible to estimate. His more immediate influence was confined to the Nonconformist Churches of England and to Churches of corresponding type in America; and even in these operated more slowly than is sometimes imagined. Watts had many friends and admirers in the Church of England, and among them not a few who would gladly have witnessed the introduction of his System of Praise. But as against Anglican tradition his influence was immediately ineffective. Upon the unchurched masses whom the Wesleys reached with their preaching and hymns, Watts had no influence, and for them a quite moderate degree of concern. When we set the Watts movement against the two other XVIIIth century movements, that were to introduce hymn singing among the unchurched and into the Church of England respectively, the two features that stand out are:—*first,* that the priority lay with Watts, and that his influence to an undetermined extent permeated the others: and *second,* that while the two other movements were connected with revivals and dependent upon stimulated emotions, the movement inaugurated by Watts was not in intent revivalistic, but purely liturgical, a sober and deliberate undertaking for the "Renovation of Psalmody" in the ordinary worship of the Church.

CHAPTER V

THE HYMNODY OF THE METHODIST REVIVAL

I

ITS ANTECEDENTS AND BEGINNINGS
(1721-1738)

1. JOHN WESLEY AIMS TO UPLIFT PAROCHIAL PSALMODY

During the early decades of the XVIIIth century the *Hymns* and *The Psalms imitated* of Watts were gradually but surely replacing the older metrical psalms in the Nonconformist churches of England, and establishing themselves there as the norm of Congregational Praise. In the parish churches, on the other hand, the use of hymns of any sort was sporadic and occasional, while the singing of metrical psalms was the universal practice. In the countryside and villages the *Old Version* of Sternhold and Hopkins was still used, but in London and a few towns, the *New Version* of Tate and Brady was beginning to get a hearing. The hymns of Watts had given a new spiritual interest to congregational song in the chapels which the *New Version* failed to impart to that of the city churches introducing it. But in church and chapel alike the clinging to the old custom of lining out the psalm and the dull and drawling rendering of the notes emphasized the continued indifference to the musical side of Psalmody. In London churches a disposition was manifesting itself to relegate the singing altogether to a choir made up of "charity children" or such others as were available.

Such were the conditions of Congregational Song at the beginning of the Methodist Movement within the Church of England toward the middle of the century. In connection with this Movement, the singing of hymns gained not only a great extension but also a quite new power and import. It recovered the emotional fervor of the first singing of vernacular psalms by the Huguenots, and repeated the spiritual triumphs of the Reformation Psalmody. In the same connection the English Hymn itself acquired a new development in several directions, and Hymnody was permanently enriched by a large body of available hymns, many of which remain in present use, and some of which attain the highest rank.

The leader who played the part in Methodist Hymnody which Calvin had taken in Huguenot Psalmody was, contrary perhaps to the general impression, John Wesley and not his brother Charles. He planned it, prepared the ground, introduced and fostered it, moulded and administered it, and also restrained its excesses. But Charles Wesley, by reason of the bulk and quality of his contributions to the new Hymnody, became distinctively the Poet of Methodism; and indeed contests with Watts the first place as a writer of English hymns. In the matter of dates and precedence it is convenient to remember that Charles Wesley was born at the Epworth rectory in 1707,[1] the very year of publication of Watts' *Hymns;* his brother John four and a half years earlier. John Wesley published his first hymn book in 1737, eighteen years after Watts had completed his System of Praise with the publication of *The Psalms of David imitated* in 1719. And two years later Charles printed his first hymns.

There was much in the inheritance and early training of the Wesley brothers which explains their interest in Hymnody, and which prepared them for their great work in it. There was, to begin with, in both a strong inherited bent toward poetry and the poetic expression of feeling. Samuel Wesley, the father, printed a volume of his verses (*Maggots,*

---

[1] December 18th, Old Style. For the discussion as to year see John Telford, *The Life of Charles Wesley,* rev. ed., London, 1900, pp. 19, 20.

1685) before leaving Oxford, and followed it with a series of later poems of which *The Life of our Blessed Lord and Saviour Jesus Christ* (1693) is best known. Careless and too voluminous, these works are yet not wanting in imaginative and forceful expression. In the Psalm versions appended to his *The pious communicant rightly prepared* (1700), and elsewhere, Samuel Wesley showed himself as by no means an incapable hymn writer.[2] It was no accident that five of his children, Samuel, Jr.,[3] John, Charles, Emilia, and Mehetabel, exhibited in varying degrees the poetic gift, and cultivated the art of verse. We find the father in 1706 recommending his son Samuel to make "translations of the Bible into verse" in the effort to reconcile fancy and devotion; and in 1725 approving verses on the 85th Psalm by his son John, who was then contemplating an entrance into holy orders.[4]

It may be added that the children of Epworth rectory were trained to social singing of psalms, and apparently of hymns, in the family circle; a somewhat unusual custom at the time, the neglect of which Samuel Wesley attributed to the general decay of piety and the uninteresting character of the Psalm versions and of their tunes.[5] The attitude of the Epworth household toward current Church of England Psalmody was the same that Watts had taken toward Nonconformist Psalmody. Before Watts' *Hymns* appeared, Samuel Wesley wrote to his son Samuel of the "sorry Sternhold Psalms,"[6] and in a paper in the *Athenian Oracle*

[2] One of his hymns, "Behold the Saviour of Mankind," still has place in the Methodist hymn books of England and America. In the first impressions of the *Dunciad* (1728), Pope pilloried S. Wesley along with Watts; both names being afterwards erased, perhaps owing to protestations from without. *Cf.* Geo. J. Stevenson, *Memorials of the Wesley Family*, London [1876], p. 68.

[3] Two of his hymns are retained in the English *Methodist Hymn Book*.

[4] L. Tyerman, *Life and Times of Samuel Wesley*, London, 1866, pp. 311, 392.

[5] *Ibid.*, p. 311.

[6] *Ibid.*, p. 310.

complains that most of the psalm tunes are so vile that even Orpheus could not make good music of them. He describes the usual rendering of the psalms as "the reading them at such a lame rate, tearing them limb from limb, and leaving sense, cadency, and all at the mercy of the clerk's nose."[7] In his *Advice to a young Clergyman,* referring to efforts to improve the singing at Epworth Church, he attributes the preference of the common people for Sternhold and Hopkins' version over that of Tate and Brady to their "strange genius at understanding nonsense." [8]

John Wesley, in his turn, ridiculed the Psalmody of the town churches as "the miserable, scandalous doggerel of Sternhold and Hopkins"; at first droned out, two staves at a time, by "a poor humdrum wretch," and then "bawled out" "by a handful of wild, unawakened striplings" "who neither feel nor understand" what they "scream," while the congregation is "lolling at ease, or in the indecent posture of sitting, drawling out one word after another."[9]

Our particular concern with these passages is in their exhibition of the young Wesleys as already in the accustomed exercise of social Psalmody, and of John especially as deeply moved by the degraded conditions of parochial Psalmody. For it was their love of social Psalmody that made Methodist Hymnody what it was, and it was the desire to better parochial Psalmody that furnished John Wesley with the original motive of his work in Hymnody.

The social singing of psalms and hymns passed naturally from the Epworth rectory to the meetings of the Holy Club that Charles Wesley founded at Oxford in the spring of 1729, for the cultivation of method in study, devotion and good works,[10] and of which John became the leader on his return to Oxford in November of the same year. John

---

[7] *Ibid.,* pp. 311, 312.

[8] Thos. Jackson, *Life of Charles Wesley,* London, 1841, vol. ii, p. 509.

[9] L. Tyerman, *Life and Times of John Wesley,* 5th ed., London, 1880, vol. ii, pp. 282, 283.

[10] "This gained me the harmless name of Methodist." Chas. Wesley to Chandler (28 April, 1785).

was an admiring reader of Dr. Watts[11] and of course familiar with Watts' work in Hymnody; and, in view of Wesley's later dealings with them, we may infer that Watts' *Psalms and Hymns,* in connection perhaps with Tate and Brady's *New Version,* furnished the materials for the singing of the Holy Club.[12]

2. The Moravians Reveal to Him the Spiritual Potentiality of the Hymn

When John Wesley determined on the missionary life, and on October 14, 1735, embarked for the new colony of Georgia, he was accompanied by his brother Charles[13] and Benjamin Ingham; they being three out of thirteen Oxford "Methodists."   And Wesley's account of their common life on board the "Simmons" reads much like a protracted meeting of the Holy Club.   The minds of both brothers had come under the influence of Tauler, Law, and other mystical divines, but both were Anglican clergymen of the severe high church type.   They aimed at a devotional and church life that was "primitive," and were scrupulous in the observance of rites and ceremonies, the weekly fasts and Eucharist, and Baptism by trine immersion; and were of a spirit too intolerant for missionary success.[14]

[11]*The Journal of the Rev. John Wesley, A.M.,* ed. by *Nehemiah Curnock,* standard ed., London and New York, n. d., vol. i, p. 139, note. This edition of the famous Journal, with its decipherment of the unprinted Diaries, is indispensable to understanding the development of Wesley's mind and work in Hymnody as in other directions.

[12]*Cf. Journal,* vol. i, p. 243, note.

[13]Though Charles went as secretary to Governor Oglethorpe, he was ordained just before starting, that he might officiate in the colonies. *Dict. of Nat. Biography,* art "Chas. Wesley"; Thos. Jackson, *Life of Charles Wesley,* London, 1841, vol. i, p. 44.

[14]The claim of some modern Anglicans that the Wesleys were high churchmen is successful enough as to this early period of their lives (1725-1738), and within those limits freely admitted by Methodist writers. *Cf.* Jas. H. Rigg, *The Churchmanship of John Wesley,* rev. ed., London [1887], "chap. ii, Period of ritualistic high churchmanship." For a more carefully discriminating statement, see *Journal,* vol. i, p. 167, note.

Wesley's kit included a considerable collection of books. Among them were some that became the sources of Wesleyan Hymnody: Tate and Brady's *New Version of the Psalms,* and apparently the *Supplement,* with its tunes; Watts' *Psalms and Hymns;* George Herbert's Poems; Hickes' edition of *Devotions in the ancient way of Offices,* containing John Austin's hymns; the *Divine Dialogues with Divine Hymns* of Henry More; Dean Brevint's *Christian Sacrament and Sacrifice;* and some of the works of Norris of Bemerton. Hymns by others, including his father and brother Samuel, were among his manuscript materials.

The brothers had as fellow-voyagers twenty-six German Moravian colonists, with their new bishop, David Nitschmann. The Moravians made much of hymn singing on board in all weathers, and in the stress of storm it became the characteristic expression of an unruffled faith.[15] On the third day John Wesley began the study of German, "in order to converse with" the Moravians, and soon took part in their daily worship.[16]

This intercourse with the Germans marks the beginning of Moravian influence upon the spiritual life of both Wesleys, and was to have a marked effect on Wesleyan Hymnody. Its immediate effect was to make an indelible impression of the spiritual possibilities of the Hymn and of a fervid type of hymn singing far removed from the dull parochial Psalmody or congregational praise of Nonconformist chapels. The fervor and spontaneity of this Moravian song was ultimately to be reproduced in the hymn singing of Methodist meetings. A secondary effect was to turn John Wesley to the study of the German Moravian Hymnody, and to set him to the making of English translations.[17] The *Journal* for October 27, 1735, has the entry,

[15] *Journal,* vol. i, p. 142.
[16] *Ibid.,* vol. i, pp. 110, 113.
[17] *Cf.* Sermon cxxi in *The Works of John Wesley,* ed. New York, 1831, vol. ii, p. 443.

"Began *Gesang-Buch.*" This has been identified[18] as the first of the hymn books for the congregation at Herrnhut, published that same year by Count Zinzendorf: *Das Gesang-Buch der Gemeine in Herrnhut.* Wesley had also access, either on shipboard or in Georgia, to the pietistic hymn books of Johann Anastasius Freylinghausen, *Geist-reiches Gesang-Buch, den Kern alter und neuer Lieder,* &c. (Halle, 1704), and its second part, *Neues Geist-reiches Gesang-Buch,* &c., appearing in 1714.[19] These became the German sources of the Wesleyan Hymnody, and are of decided import.

3. He makes Hymn Books as a Missionary, and as an Associate of Moravians

One of the disclosures of Wesley's newly deciphered diary is the grip which hymns took upon his mind and heart, when once he had caught the fervor of Moravian Hymnody; the share of his daily life given over to hymn singing; his assiduous study of hymns, sometimes continuing through the working hours of successive days. The English Hymn, that had found so capable a tutor as Watts, had been waiting for so devoted a lover as Wesley. He at once began, and pursued with extraordinary carefulness, the selection, revision, translation and composition of hymns for the varied uses of his American ministrations. He introduced hymn singing into those "companies" formed at Savannah and Frederica, which were the prototype of the Methodist "society,"[20] and even into the Sunday church services. In the list of grievances against Wesley presented by the Grand Jury for Savannah in August, 1737, the first was his alterations of the authorized metrical psalms, and

[18]*Journal,* vol. ii, p. 6.
[19]The two parts, combined into one under the title of the first, by G. A. Francke, appearing at Halle in 1741, remain the best expression of the Hymnody of the Pietistic Revival, from which the Methodist Revival drew not only some of its hymns but also some of its earliest tunes.
[20]*Journal,* vol i, pp. 228, 229.

the second his "introducing into the church and service at
the Altar compositions of psalms and hymns not inspected
or authorized by any proper judicature."[21]

These psalms and hymns were at first a manuscript collection,[22] and Wesley tested them by repeated readings and
discussions with friends, as well as in the sick-room and in
social devotions.[23]   He then arranged with Lewis Timothy
of Charleston to print a selection of them.[24]

This, Wesley's first hymn book, appeared as *Collection
of Psalms and Hymns. Charles-town, 1737*, without his
name; a roughly printed little volume of 74 pages.[25]   Of
its pieces, numbered as 70, one half are from Watts, 7 from
John Austin, 6 adapted from George Herbert, 2 from
Addison; and the Wesleys are represented by 15:—5 of
Samuel, Sr., 5 of Samuel, Jr., and 5 translated from the
German by John himself.   There is none by Charles
Wesley,[26] who had returned to England.   The pieces are
grouped in three divisions, as "Psalms and Hymns for
Sunday" (hymns of general praise); "for Wednesday or
Friday" (suitable for fast days); and "for Saturday"
(hymns especially addressed to God as the Creator of all
things).   Beyond the "primitive usage" recognized in this
grouping, there is little or nothing to suggest high church
views, and no provision for festivals or sacraments.   The
outstanding feature of the collection is indeed the submis-

[21]*Ibid.*, vol. i, p. 385.

[22]*Ibid.*, vol. i, p. 230 n.

[23]*Ibid.*, vol. i, pp. 243, 259, 269 n.

[24]*Ibid.*, vol. i, pp. 257 n., 275, 347.   Wesley was reading the proofs
in April, 1737: p. 349.

[25]Long lost to sight, it was reprinted (though not in facsimile as
stated) by Dr. George Osborn in 1882, from what was supposed to be
the only surviving copy.   For the history of this copy, see Rev. R.
Green, *The Works of John and Charles Wesley: a Bibliography*,
London, 1896, p. 12, and additional note in the 2nd ed., 1906, p. i.
There is another copy in the Lenox Collection of the New York
Public Library.

[26]Probably the explanation is that ". . . his Mss. were not at his
brother's disposal."   A. E. Gregory, *The Hymn-book of the Modern
Church*, London, 1904, p. 156.

sion of Wesley's churchliness to his good judgment in giving the foremost place to Dr. Watts, the dissenter.

Wesley reached England, on his return, on February 1, 1738; bringing from Georgia a sense of spiritual and ministerial defeat. He came into close affiliation with London Moravians, and, under Peter Böhler's advice, he, with his brother Charles and others, formed "our little society" on May 1, 1738, at the home and book-shop of James Hutton. It afterwards removed to Fetter Lane, and, though in connection with the Church of England, became the nucleus both of organized Methodism and of organized English Moravianism.[27]

It was no doubt for the use of this, and like societies at Bristol and Oxford,[28] that John Wesley printed, without editor's or publisher's name, his second hymn book: *A Collection of Psalms and Hymns. London: printed in the year 1738.*[29] The little book is eclectic. The threefold grouping of the hymns, intended to represent the usage of "antiquity," is retained from the 1737 book. Watts still leads, with 36 numbers out of a total of 76. The Church Psalmody is represented by 16 of Tate and Brady's versions; the Prayer Book by the *Veni Creator;* and Bishop Ken's three hymns may be included with these. Mysticism is represented by four selections from Norris of Bemerton, and Moravianism by four translations from the Herrnhut collection; English poetry by Herbert, Dryden, Addison and Roscommon.

With this little book, the earlier and preparatory stages of Wesley's work for Hymnody are brought to a close. Its contents illustrate and embody most of the influences that played upon Methodist Hymnody or became its sources; except indeed that it contained nothing of the work

[27] *Journal,* vol. i, p. 458.

[28] *Ibid.,* vol. i, p. 458.

[29] The only known copies are in the Didsbury College Library and the Archepiscopal Library at Lambeth. There is a full description of its contents in *The Poetical Works of John and Charles Wesley,* ed. by G. Osborn [13 vols.], London, 1868 seq., vol. ii, pp. 35-42.

of Wesley's father and brothers; of Charles, notably, whose great gift waited for the deepening of his spiritual experience and the inspiration he drew from the stirring scenes of the coming revival.

II

THE METHODIST HYMNODY (1739-1904)

1. THE "MOVEMENT," AND CHARLES WESLEY AS ITS POET

While living in London, in close association with Moravians and under their influence, the Wesleys passed through those remarkable spiritual experiences which brought to both the rest and joy of faith, and determined their future careers. Charles dated his evangelical conversion as on Whitsunday (May 21), 1738; John his as on the Wednesday following (May 24).

Charles began at once to proclaim his new hope to such friends as would hear him, and to preach in the churches, as long as they would receive him. In the summer of 1739 he entered that itinerant ministry, in Whitefield's way, that during seventeen years carried him through England and Wales, and twice into Ireland. John first visited the Moravians at Herrnhut. Returning in September, 1738, he found his immediate sphere in the "Religious Societies," more or less Moravian in complexion, which in London and elsewhere supplemented the Church services with less formal devotions. To these meetings he preached his new way of "saving-faith"; teaching them to sing the hymns he had gathered and translated. The first word in his resumed diary, under the date of September 20, 1738, is "Singing."[30] In the spring of 1739 he went to Bristol at Whitefield's entreaty, to carry on the work already begun there, and on May 12 laid the corner-stone of "The New Room," really the first Methodist Chapel. Late in the same year he

[30]*Journal,* vol. ii, p. 75; and see p. 71, note.

founded at London his own "United Society," and on November 11 first preached in the disused King's Foundery in Moorfields, which, purchased and refitted, became the headquarters of Methodism. From this year Wesley ordinarily counted the foundation of the Methodist Societies.

In this memorable year appeared the third of the Wesleyan hymn collections, the first to bear the name of either brother, as *Hymns and sacred Poems. Published by John Wesley, M.A. Fellow of Lincoln College, Oxford; and Charles Wesley, M.A. Student of Christ-Church, Oxford.* [Colossians iii. 16]. *London: printed by William Strahan; and sold by James Hutton, Bookseller, at the Bible and Sun, without Temple-Bar; and at Mr. Bray's, a Brazier in Little-Britain. MDCCXXXIX.* Of this there were three editions within the year, and two subsequently.[31] Its contents are in two parts, containing 64 and 75 pieces, some of them hymns for singing, and some poems for reading. No less than 42 are adaptations from George Herbert, and there are 22 of Wesley's renderings from the German. Some "Verses" were included which "were wrote upon the Scheme of the Mystick Divines," and the preface of eight pages is largely devoted to a renunciation and exposure of their errors.

This book reflects the spiritual experiences of the year, and is itself memorable as the first printing of hymns from Charles Wesley's pen. The second part opens with a hymn beginning, "Where shall my wand'ring Soul begin?" This is probably the hymn he commenced the day after his conversion, broken off "for fear of pride," but finished under the encouragement of Bray the mechanic, and sung with "great joy" when, on the Wednesday evening, John came to announce his own faith in Christ.[32] It was thus the first hymn of the Methodist Revival. Toward the close of the volume appeared the fine group of festival hymns which

[31]Green, *Bibliography,* p. 15.
[32]Chas. Wesley's Diary, May 23, 24, 1738.

afterwards helped to recommend hymns to the Church of England.[33]

Charles Wesley had written hymns already, but with his new experience the fountain of spiritual song opened within, which was never to fail him. Thenceforward he became distinctively the poet of the new Movement, and poured forth psalms and hymns in a stream uninterrupted until his death. But his hymns did not come from the cloisters. In the early years of the Revival, he was as active and ardent an evangelist as John himself. "He loved the stir, the tumult, the triumph of those great out-door gatherings, where testimony must be borne before mobs which might at any time endanger the property and even the lives of preacher and hearers . . . [He] was moved to his highest flights of praise by hard-won victories amongst his wild hearers in Cornwall, or Moorfields, at Kingswood, or Walsall."[34] The composition of the hymns was thus closely related to the progress of the Revival, which they in turn did much to foster; and the long series of books and tracts in which they appeared are an essential part of the Revival records.

The poetical publications of John and Charles Wesley, jointly or separately, cover a period of fifty-three years, and number fifty-six (excluding tune-books); and the contents of not less than thirty-six of these are exclusively original, with much original work appearing in the collective volumes. The majority appeared without name of author or editor; eight under John's name, three under Charles', and six under their joint names.[35]

[33] "Hark how all the Welkin rings" (*Christmas-Day*); "Sons of Men, behold from far" (*Epiphany*); "'Christ the Lord is ris'n to Day'" (*Easter-Day*); "Hail the Day that sees Him rise" (*Ascension-Day*); "Granted is the Saviour's Prayer" (*Whitsunday*).

[34] Gregory, *The Hymn Book of the Modern Church*, p. 160.

[35] Of the numerous short-lists of these publications, none seems to be both accurate and complete. The best bibliography is Green's: and he contributed to Telford's *The Methodist Hymn Book illustrated* (2nd ed. rev., London, n. d. [1909], pp. 497 ff.) a convenient list of the works in which the hymns therein included first appeared.

The custom afterward grew up of ascribing to Charles Wesley's pen not only the hymns published under his name but also all those published under the joint names or anonymously, excepting only the translations and very few originals admittedly written by John. Such a conclusion never rested on solid ground, and is gradually yielding to the conviction that John's share in the hymn writing was greater than had been supposed; a conviction which the recently published notes of his diary tend to strengthen. The editors of the Wesleyan Methodist hymn book of 1875 went so far as to affix merely the letter "W" to "those hymns which first appeared in publications for which the Wesleys were jointly responsible" (including "Jesu, Lover of my Soul" under this category); on the ground that "it cannot be determined with certainty to which of the two brothers a hymn should be ascribed."[36] This course proved very unwelcome to Methodists,[37] and has since been departed from. But the uncertainty remains none the less. There is some evidence that the brothers agreed not to distinguish their several contributions of the hymns published jointly.[38] It is however to be noted that this uncertainty pertains chiefly to the early publications, and that as the Revival progressed, John grew content to leave the hymn writing to his brother, and also that, in giving its permanent form to Methodist Hymnody, he admitted that "but a small part of these hymns is of my own composing."[39]

The brothers cooperated again in a second collection of *Hymns and sacred Poems,* 1740. Its title-page, barring the date, is identical with that of 1739, with whose later editions it was incorporated. It added to English Hym-

---

[36]Note prefixed to "Index to the Hymns."

[37]See Telford, *The Meth. Hy. Bk. illus.,* p. 12.

[38]See David Creamer, *Methodist Hymnology,* New York, 1848, p. 18; Osborn, *The Poetical Works,* vol. viii, p. xv.

[39]John Wesley's preface to the Large Hymn Book of 1780. On the whole subject consult Osborn, *The Poetical Works,* vol. viii, pp. 15, 16; Telford, *Meth. Hy. Bk. illus.,* pp. 8-12; *Journal,* vol. i, p. 477, note.

nody three famous hymns, usually ascribed to Charles
Wesley: "Jesu, Lover of my Soul," "O for a thousand
tongues to sing," and "Christ, whose glory fills the skies."
While not formally a hymn book for the societies, this,
with the 1739 volume, contributed not less than 100 hymns
to the permanent Methodist Hymnody. Its contents are
distinctively Methodist. The preface sets forth Wesley's
doctrine of Christian Perfection. There is a "Hymn for
the Kingswood Colliers," one "To be sung in a Tumult,"
one "On admission of any person into the Society," and a
group on "The Love-Feast." Wesley had taken an impas-
sioned stand against the doctrine of Election in a sermon
published as *Free Grace* in the autumn of 1739, after
Whitefield had gone to America. Appended was a long
hymn on "Universal Redemption." This hymn, with another, on the same theme, were now included in the new
book, adding to the great offense already taken by Whitefield.[40] The sermon and the hymn led to the separation
of the Revival forces into two camps, the Calvinistic under
Whitefield, the Arminian under Wesley, to the organization
of Lady Huntingdon's Connexion and of Calvinistic Methodism in Wales.[41]

In deep depression at the defection from the inmost circle
and the consequent confusions, the Wesleys printed at
Bristol early in 1741, and then in London, a tractate of
eighteen hymns, as *Hymns on God's everlasting love. To
which is added the cry of a reprobate, and the Horrible
Decree,* followed by a second tractate with the same title;
the two being afterwards combined. The hymns mingle
most tender appeals with scathing satire of the doctrines
of the opposition, described as "hellish" and "satanic," and

[40] "My dear, dear Brethren,—Why did you throw out the bone of
contention: Why did you print that sermon against predestination?
Why did you, in particular, my dear brother Charles, affix your hymn,
and join in putting out your late hymn-book?" Letter of Whitefield,
Feb. 1, 1741. Tyerman, *Life of Geo. Whitefield,* New York, 1877, vol.
i, p. 465.

[41] Tyerman, *Life of John Wesley,* vol. i, p. 317.

presented with little fairness. The hymns are on fire with excitement and indignation at what threatened to undo the prospects of the Movement. The Wesleys had the precedent of the Reformers in employing satire and invective in their Hymnody. We may nevertheless count it fortunate that their work, immensely effective as it was at the time, was not of such a character as to establish a new precedent for the Controversial Hymn.

The success of these hymn tracts, scattered broadcast, read and sung in Methodist homes and societies, is probably responsible for the long series of hymn tracts in which further Wesleyan hymns were published. Capable of being printed quickly to meet the occasion, sold for a few pence and readily bought, the hymn tract became a favorite instrument for the inspiration and instruction of the early Methodists, and for cultivating their spirit of devotion. The series of hymn tracts ran for fifty years (1741-1791), numbering not less than thirty.

A small group offered hymns for times of civil disquiet and Methodist persecution:—*Hymns for times of trouble and persecution* (1744); *Hymns for times of trouble* (n. d.), *Hymns written in the time of the tumults* (1780). Another provided for national occasions and passing events—*Hymns for the public Thanksgiving-Day* (1746), *Hymns for New Year's Day* (1750), *Hymns occasioned by the Earthquake, 1750* (2 parts), *Hymns for the year 1756, Hymns on the expected Invasion* (1759), and for *Thanksgiving, Nov. 29, 1759, Hymns for the National Fast, 1782,* and two numbers of *Hymns for the Nation in 1782.* Another provided for the festivals of the old Church Year:—*Hymns for the Nativity* (1745); and *Hymns for our Lord's Resurrection, for Ascension Day, Hymns of Petition and Thanksgiving* (Whitsunday), and *Gloria Patri* (Trinity), all of 1746. With these we may group *A Hymn at the Sacrament* (1744), two numbers of *Funeral Hymns* (1746, 1759), and *Hymns for the Watchnight* (1746). For the household were *Graces before meat* (1746), *Hymns for children* (1746, 1791), and *Preparation for death* (1772). More general in character were a little *Collection of Hymns* (1742) for the poor, *Hymns for those that seek, and those that have, redemption in the Blood of Jesus Christ* (1747, 10 editions), the most important of them all; and *Hymns of Intercession* (1758).

Charles Wesley (for the bulk of the work was his) was thus the poet-laureate of Methodism, with an ode for every occasion. Such a companionship of hymns through passing years was never provided before or since, and was an unique feature in the upbuilding of Methodist character. In the extension also of the Revival, these hymn tracts, widely distributed among the poor and degraded, played a considerable part.

Returning now to the date at which the series of hymn tracts began, we find that the Wesleys again cooperated in publishing a third volume of *Hymns and sacred Poems,* 1742, whose preface and "many of the following verses" dealt with Christian Perfection. This volume contributed a hundred hymns to the permanent Methodist Hymnody. A special interest attaches to the joint publication of *Hymns on the Lord's Supper. With a preface concerning the Christian Sacrament and Sacrifice. Extracted from Doctor Brevint* (Bristol, 1745). Its 166 hymns testify to the deep reverence for the sacramental side of religion that characterized both brothers, and the demand for ten editions shows how much those views influenced the earlier Methodist worship.[42]

Independently of John, Charles Wesley published by subscription in 1749 *Hymns and sacred Poems. In two volumes. By Charles Wesley, M.A., Student of Christ-Church, Oxford* (Bristol). His friends took 1145 copies

[42]In 1871 the whole book (together with John Wesley's earlier *Companion to the Altar*) was reprinted as *The Eucharistic Manuals of John and Charles Wesley.* The aim of the editor (W. E. Dutton) was to make it appear that the Wesleys held sacramental views in accord with those of the modern Catholic party.

of these volumes,[43] which contain many acceptable hymns, and whose profits helped him to set up housekeeping at Bristol. While partly laid aside, Charles Wesley occupied himself with writing versified comments on Scripture texts, often original, sometimes following earlier commentators. These, to the great number of 2030, he published as *Short Hymns on select passages of the Holy Scripture* (2 vols., 1763), from which nearly a hundred were taken into Methodist Hymnody. Four years later he printed *Hymns for the use of families, and on various occasions*, many of which relate to his own household and friendships, and hallow the daily life of the home.

Charles Wesley wrote hymns to the very end, and left behind him in manuscript three small quarto volumes of hymns and sacred poems, an uncompleted metrical version of the Psalms and five quarto volumes of hymns on the Gospels and Acts.[44] The Psalms were printed in *The Arminian Magazine,* and all have been printed with pious care in Dr. Osborn's edition of *The Poetical Works*. It is the great number of the short hymns on Scripture texts that accounts for the vast total of Charles Wesley's work.

2. Hymn Books for "The People Called Methodists"

Most of the books and tracts we have enumerated as those in which the Wesleyan Hymns first appeared were used to sing from in the revival services, societies, bands or classes. A number are to be regarded as hymn books. But from the first establishment of Sunday, as well as weekday, services Wesley felt the necessity of providing hymn books that should be cheap, compact, and sufficiently inclusive. The earliest of these was *A Collection of Psalms and Hymns. Published by John Wesley, M.A.* (London, 1741); sold at one shilling in binding, and containing 152 pieces. This was kept in print during the whole of Wesley's life, remaining in use till superseded by the *Supplement*

[13]Telford, *Life of Charles Wesley,* p. 248.
[44]*Cf.* Jackson, *Life of Charles Wesley,* vol. ii, p. 457.

of 1831. An abridgment of it was bound up with *The Sunday Service* of 1784, and used in congregations employing that service.[45] In 1753 he published *Hymns and Spiritual Songs, intended for the use of real Christians of all denominations,* made up entirely of selections from the *Hymns and sacred Poems* of 1739, 1740 and 1742. This became distinctively the Methodist hymn book, remaining in common use till the appearance of "The Large Hymn Book" of 1780, and in poorer societies long afterward. A volume of *Select Hymns* was also published in 1761 with tunes, and in 1773 printed without the tunes. In Wesley's judgment the societies were thus amply supplied with hymn books; "so that it may be doubted whether any religious community in the world has a greater variety of them." [46]

Yet this very variety was an inconvenience to people who could not afford to buy so many books, but wished for more of the hymns than any one volume contained. An urgent demand arose for a more inclusive collection. Wesley resisted it for years. But after the opening of the City Road Chapel in 1778 he yielded, and began his preparations. The new book was announced on the cover of *The Arminian Magazine* for October, 1779, and appeared in 1780 as *A Collection of Hymns for the use of the People called Methodists. London: printed by J. Paramore, at the Foundery:* with the now famous preface, dated Oct. 20, 1779, and signed by John Wesley. It was published at three shillings, and contained 525 hymns; all taken from the brothers' previous publications, and all but ten written by members of the Wesley family. They were grouped under the heads of Christian experience, and designed to constitute "a little body of experimental and practical divinity." [47]

This collection became at once the book of common song

---

[45]*Cf.* Green, *Bibliography,* nos. 30, 376, 378.
[46]Preface of 1779.
[47]Preface.

in Methodist congregations.[48]   After Wesley's death it was
tampered with by the manager of the Methodist Publishing House, who made a succession of alterations, beginning
with the 1793 edition, and culminating in that of 1797,[49]
which dropped 24 hymns Wesley had chosen, and added 65
(including "Jesu, Lover of my Soul") which he had not
included.   The Conference of 1799 appointed a committee
"to reduce the large Hymn Book to its primitive simplicity
as published in the second edition,"[50] which was attempted,
partly then, and partly later, but never carried out in
strictness.   In 1831 some changes were made, and a "Supplement" added.   This served until 1875, when the book
was revised, and "A new Supplement" added, nearly as
large as the original *Collection*.[51]   It was not until 1900,
one hundred and nine years after Wesley's death, that steps
were taken, even then reluctantly, for a thorough revision
and remodelling of Wesley's *Collection*.   The revision was
made largely in the spirit of catholicity, to which even the
fervor of Wesleyanism has been compelled to bow, and
the new book appeared in 1904 as *The Methodist Hymn
Book*.[52]   For the first time the name of John Wesley dis-
appears from the title of the hymn book, and his arrangement of the hymns is given up; but even so nearly one half
of the contents is ascribed to Charles.   The whole number
of hymns is 981, and some 300 are of the XIXth century.

[48]*The Morning Hymn Book* also continued to be used, in accordance
with Wesley's preference for hymns of thanksgiving and prayer rather
than hymns describing inward states for use in public worship. *Cf.*
"Early Methodist Psalmody" in *A New History of Methodism,* ed. by
J. W. Townsend *et al.,* London, 1909, vol. ii, p. 561.

[49]For the editions, see Green, *Bibliography,* No. 348.

[50]Wesley had, however, made "corrections" for the 3rd ed., 1782.

[51]The edition of 1831 is fully annotated in Geo. J. Stevenson, *The
Methodist Hymn Book and its associations,* London, 1869: that of
1875 in his *The Methodist Hymn Book illustrated,* London, 2nd ed.,
1894.

[52]For an interesting account of the method of revision, see Telford,
The Methodist Hymn Book illustrated, London, n. d., pp. 12-14. Telford does for the new book what Stevenson did for the old.

As Charles Wesley wrote hymns, so John compiled hymn books, to the end of his life. *A Collection of Psalms and Hymns for the Lord's Day* (1784) has been referred to as bound up with *The Sunday Service*. In spite of the fulness of the *Collection* of 1780, it appeared, to Wesley's vexation, that societies were using hymns he had not authorized. This was largely through the agency of Robert Spence, a York bookseller. He published in 1781 *A Collection of Hymns from various authors*, enlarged as *A Pocket Hymn Book, designed as a constant companion for the pious: collected from various authors*. A large proportion of the hymns were taken without authority or acknowledgment from various Wesley publications. Apparently to offset it, and also to include some good hymns omitted from the 1780 *Collection*, but widely called for,[53] Wesley published in 1785 *A Pocket Hymn Book, for the use of Christians of all denominations*. It was not reprinted, but under the advice of Conference Wesley reprinted the Spence book in 1787 (London: printed by J. Paramore; with the same title as that of 1785), expunging 37 hymns as dull and prosaic, or "grievous doggerel." Spence submitted to Wesley's authority,[54] but his little book afterward became a favorite in America.

In extreme old age, Wesley published his last collection, *Hymns for children* (1790), chosen from his brother's *Hymns for children and others of riper years* (1763). These hymns show that the Wesleys were minded to carry on the Children's Hymnody Watts had begun, but many are beyond a child's comprehension. In an interesting little preface Wesley contrasts Watts' method of writing down to the child's level with his brother's efforts to lift up the child to his own:—his brother's hymns are "in such plain and easy language as even children may understand; but when they do understand them they will be children no longer."

[53]Preface.
[54]Tyerman, *John Wesley*, vol. iii, p. 539.

III

THE METHODIST SINGING

1. John Wesley as Music-Master

Wesley gave the same forethought and attention to the musical as to the literary side of Methodist Song, keeping its direction in his own hands. His equipment for this undertaking was his sound musical feeling, a very limited technical knowledge, and an unusual practical sense. Perceiving the importance of the Hymn Tune to the purpose he had in view, he provided a body of "authorized" hymn tunes, and expected that none other should be sung by his followers. His cardinal principle was that the tunes should invite the participation of all the people; and, next, should keep within the limits of sobriety and reverence. The tunes were to express the words, avoiding "vain repetitions" to fill out the music. Florid and fuguing tunes he likened to "Lancashire hornpipes."[55]

Wesley prepared four Methodist tune books, and perhaps consented to the use of two more. As early as 1742 he printed *A Collection of Tunes, set to music, as they are commonly sung at the Foundery.*[56] The hymns set are those of the three volumes of *Hymns and sacred Poems.* Its price of six pence was intended to make it available to the poor; and in printing the melody alone he appealed to the unskillful. The book was so full of musical errors as to defeat its own end, but is interesting as showing the tunes first used at the Foundery. There are only three of the *Old Version* psalm tunes. Very few of these remained in the actual use of parish churches, and these were inevitably associated with the dull, drawling parochial Psalmody. The tunes of the *Supplement to the New Version* were freely drawn upon; six German melodies, which Wesley had

[55]*Minutes of Conference,* 1768.
[56]A reprint was bound up with that of the Charleston collection of 1737.

sung with the Moravians, were taken from Freyling-hausen's *Gesang-Buch;* and some eleven tunes were apparently new.[57]

The conversion in 1746 of Mrs. Rich, wife of the proprietor of Covent Garden Theater, put Charles Wesley in touch with the London musical circle in which J. F. Lampe, Handel and others moved.[58] Handel set three of Charles' hymns to music. Lampe published a musical setting of twenty-four as *Hymns on the great Festivals, and other occasions* (London, 1746; 4to). Handel's tunes were not printed: Lampe's were generally admired, and their use was "allowed" in Methodist services. The store of Methodist tunes was increased by the adaptation of popular melodies and by local tunes which Wesley came upon in his travels.[59]

Some of these tunes, with others, were gathered together by Thomas Butts, a companion of the Wesleys, in his *Harmonia Sacra* (c. 1753). Wesley commended this book, but objected to its more florid tunes, which he thought irreverent, and its old Psalm tunes, which he thought dull. Wesley's own *Sacred Melody,* published in 1761, to bind up with the *Select Hymns* of that year, is little more than an amended reproduction of Butts' book, omitting the objectionable tunes. The 102 tunes of *Sacred Melody* represent all those in use with Wesley's approval.[60] A class of tunes of a more florid type, and characterized by much repetition of the words and breaking up of the lines, came into such wide popularity later that they were known in time as "The Old Methodist Tunes." As a matter of fact these tunes represented the taste of the later eighteenth century in

[57]*Cf.* J. T. Lightwood, *Hymn Tunes and their story,* London, n. d. pp. 121-125.

[58]Telford, *Charles Wesley,* pp. 150-154, 230-234.

[59]Lightwood, *op. cit.,* p. 128.

[60] "All the tunes in *common use* among us." Wesley's preface. For a good characterization of the contents of *Sacred Melody,* see "Early Methodist Psalmody" in *A new History of Methodism,* vol. ii, appendix C, pp. 558-560.

general and not of the Methodists in particular as distinguished either from churchmen or dissenters.[61]

In speaking of the actual Methodist tunes Wesley says in the preface to his *Sacred Melody* of 1761 that he had been engaged for twenty years endeavoring to persuade musicians to follow his directions in setting down the tunes, but in vain. He has at last prevailed, and the tunes are here "pricked *true,* exactly as I desire all our congregations may sing them." In this book appeared Wesley's "Directions for Singing," to be observed carefully in order that "this part of Divine worship may be the more acceptable to God, as well as more profitable" to singer and hearer. These seven rules became canonical, and are, briefly : "Learn *these* tunes before any others ; sing them exactly as printed ; sing all of them ; sing lustily ; sing modestly ; sing in time ; above all sing spiritually, with an eye to God in every word." They exhibit the practical mind and indomitable will of Wesley covering the minutest details of Methodist Song. And both Wesley's Journal and the minutes of the Annual Conferences show how closely the observance of these rules was looked after, and any breach of them in spirit or letter detected.

2. THE NEW TYPE OF CONGREGATIONAL SONG

Behind these regulations there was a marked spontaneity in the early Methodist singing. It was the utterance of simple and unlettered hearts in whom the Wesleyan evangel had awakened a great happiness. They sang because their overcharged feelings could not keep from singing. The new hymns both fed and expressed the new feelings ; and the thrill of spiritual passion leaped from heart to heart of a great concourse singing together "Blow ye the trumpet, blow," "O for a thousand tongues to sing," or "Soldiers of Christ, arise."

This Methodist Song in its spiritual spontaneity, its fervor and its gladness, fulfilled to a remarkable degree the

[61]*Cf.* Lightwood, *op. cit.,* chaps. v and viii.

Apostolic ideal of Christian Song; and the injunctions of
Wesley inevitably recall the figure of St. Paul, striving
not to stimulate so much as to regulate the "tongues," and
dealing prudently with their excesses and infelicities. The
Methodist excesses at the first were simply the noise of too
much physical exuberance and the confusions inevitable to
singers musically ignorant. Wesley instructed his preachers to interrupt the noisy hymn, and interpolate questions
to the congregation:—"Now do you know what you said
last? Did it suit your case? Did you sing it as to God,
with the spirit and understanding also?"[62] The ignorant,
he insisted, should be taught to sing by note and acceptably.[63] On their behalf he himself published two tractates:
A short Introduction to Music, and *The Grounds of vocal
Music.* Refined, scholarly, of Anglican training and with
churchly sympathies, neither of the Wesleys conceived or
abetted congregational song that was vulgar in its literary
contents or flippant in music or indecorous in expression.
They cultivated a Hymnody that should be reverently and
decently ordered without any sacrifice of its heartiness.

As time went on the excesses of exuberance naturally lessened, and were followed by the creeping in of formality.
Wesley thought slow singing in itself tended to formality,
doubtless having in mind the droning of the psalms in parish
churches of the time.[64] But a new danger arose with
the formation of a body of "Singers" to lead the worship of
the chapels. The singing originally had required little
leadership. Until the hymns were familiar or the people
could read, the lines were read out, and the tune started by
the preacher or any one available. As hymn and tune grew
familiar, they sounded forth impulsively. But with church
organization came the choir; and, with the choir, first the
more intricate tune, then the anthem, and finally the organ.
The Minutes of 1768 protest against the florid tunes.
Those of 1787 prohibit the introduction of anthems, as

[62]*Minutes of Conference,* 1746.
[63]*Minutes,* 1765.   [64]*Minutes,* 1768.

not properly joint worship. In 1796 an exception was allowed on special occasions. On such occasions, it appears from the Minutes of 1800, even "theatrical" singers had been introduced into the chapels to sing elaborate solos and choruses. A few years later Richard Watson printed a pamphlet on *Singing Men and Women,* rebuking them as a class for unduly magnifying their office.[65]

The question of instrumental music had little import during Wesley's life. In the open air meetings the great volume of sound would have drowned out any accompaniment, as it often drowned out the voices of those sent to break up the meetings. And in none of the chapels were the circumstances of the people such as to make likely any proposal to install an organ. The bass-viol seems to have been first introduced, as a support to the leader's voice. The clarionet and other instruments followed, as was the custom in the parish churches also. Not more than three chapels introduced the organ while Wesley lived.[66] The Minutes of 1796 prohibit organs until proposed by the Conference. The Minutes of 1808 show that some had already been introduced, but consent is refused to the erection of any more. The introduction of an organ in Brunswick Chapel, Leeds, produced bitter controversy and a secession of "Protestant Methodists," whose protest was against instrumental music. Daniel Isaac's *Vocal Melody, or, Singing the only music sanctioned by divine authority, in the public worship of Christians* (York, 1827), reveals in its title the ground of this protest; although Isaac himself refused to join the seceders. In this, as in much beside, the Church Song of Methodism has since yielded to modern influences. Practically all of the 9,000 churches of Wesleyan Methodism in England to-day have their organ and choir;[67] and in 1910 a monthly periodical, *The Choir,* was established

[65] Curwen, *Worship Music,* 1st series, p. 57.
[66] *A new History of Methodism,* vol. i, p. 515
[67] *The Choir* for January, 1910, p. 1.

in the interests of Methodist church music. The congregational singing of present day Methodism has also exchanged something of its early fervor for the more tempered enthusiasm that comes with years and educational progress. But it still retains a certain characteristic flavor of its own; a certain potentiality also of regaining the old warmth and volume under the stimulus of revival preaching.

IV

THE PART OF THE WESLEYS IN THE DEVELOPMENT OF THE ENGLISH HYMN

It is evident that a place must be given to the Wesleyan Hymnody in the history of religion itself. The Wesleys inaugurated a great spiritual revival; and their hymns did as much as any human agency to kindle and replenish its fervor. They conducted the propaganda of a new theology: we can scan Wesley's sermons to discover its contents, but in the hymns it was sung by multitudes; and of the two media of its dissemination, the song was probably the more effective. John Wesley led an ecclesiastical revolt, and, failing to conquer his own Church, established a new one of phenomenal proportions: the hymns prefigured the constitution of the new Church and formed the manual of its spiritual discipline. The Wesleyan Hymns are thus deeply written into the religious history of English-speaking peoples. We might sum up the Wesleys' work in Hymnody by saying that they perceived the spiritual possibilities of hymns and of hymn singing, and that they realized them, apparently to the full.

With this glimpse toward the wider bearings of their work, it remains nevertheless to estimate more precisely the place and importance of the Wesleys in the history of the English Hymn and the extension of hymn singing. It will be convenient to regard their work as:—

1. *A great enrichment of the stores of English Hymns.—*

The work of Charles Wesley as a hymn writer attained vast proportions, including some 6,500 hymns. In distinguishing major from minor poets, it is customary to regard the mere bulk of an author's production as an evidence of power and an element of impressiveness. The same consideration doubtless applies to hymn writers. But in Charles Wesley's case his inventiveness and facility were coupled with a total inability for self-criticism. The inward impulse to give rhythmical expression to convictions and feelings hardened into a habit. And this, stimulated by the assurance of an eager welcome for anything he might publish, led him to produce a considerable body of material in no way worthy of his own powers.

But for all practical purposes the contribution of Charles Wesley to devotional poetry was confined to the limits of the selection made by his brother John for the Methodist *Collection* of 1780, and its supplements. The pamphlets and volumes in which the hymns originally appeared were allowed to go out of print, and dropped out of sight; and some part of his work remained unpublished. The Methodists were so well satisfied with their hymn book as to be incurious as regards the outlying material. Moreover, Charles Wesley had remained a consistent churchman to the end. He had controverted many of his brother's opinions, and protested against his whole course in establishing an independent Methodist Church. Loyalty to John Wesley's memory left the Methodists indisposed toward any attempt to magnify the name or reputation of Charles. His family deemed it prudent to keep his manuscripts and family papers in careful custody, and it was not till after Miss Wesley's death in 1828 that they passed into the possession of the Wesleyan Conference.[68] No adequate biography of Charles Wesley was written until 1841. No attempt was made to collect the numerous poetical publications, or even to prepare any connected account of them, until 1848, when an American, Joseph Creamer of Baltimore, published his

[68]See Jackson, *Life of Charles Wesley*, preface.

Methodist Hymnology.[69]   The whole body of the Wesleyan Hymns was not collected and printed until in 1868-1872 the London Conference Office published *The Poetical Works of John and Charles Wesley* in thirteen 12mo volumes.

But while in this way the presentation of Charles Wesley's work as a whole was deferred, and his actual contribution to Hymnody narrowed down to the contents of the Methodist *Collection,* even so that contribution was unprecedentedly large.   Even in the first edition the number of hymns counted as his was about as large as in the entire System of Praise of Dr. Watts, and in the revision of 1875 it attained the great total of 724 hymns.   The whole number of these hymns must be regarded as having come into actual use.   If any escaped being sung, it was nevertheless read devotionally.   After a century and a quarter the revisers of 1904 speak of "the delicate task of removing hymns from Wesley's original book,"[70] and their new *Methodist Hymn Book* retains 429 hymns ascribed to Charles Wesley.   His whole contribution to English Hymnody cannot therefore be estimated in figures smaller than these, and the number of his hymns in actual use to-day has been estimated as 500.[71]

Beside such figures the contribution of John Wesley is relatively small.   His share in writing the original hymns cannot now be determined.   In the *Collection* of 1780, twenty-seven numbers are admittedly his, mostly renderings from the German.   These, though few, give him an unique place as a hymn writer at the head of the small band who have transferred foreign hymns so deftly that they breathe naturally under English skies.   A number of them may fairly be included among the classics of English Hymnody.

[69]The *Wesleyan Hymnology* of Rev. Wm. P. Burgess (London, 1845, 2nd ed. 1846), was simply "A Companion to the Wesleyan Hymn Book," with brief remarks on the hymns, intended to promote their profitable use.

[70]Preface to the *Meth Hy. Bk.,* p. iv.

[71]Gregory, *op. cit.,* p. 165.

But John Wesley, in connection with the exercise of the new function of an Administrator of hymn singing, stands related to the whole body of the Wesleyan Hymns as their editor. The editor's function is at all times essential to the well-being of Congregational Praise, and Wesley was the first of note in the long line of English hymnal compilers. He exercised his function autocratically, but on the whole with distinguished success. Charles Wesley's hymns owe much to the strong hand of his brother, not only for the winnowing they so much needed, but for the verbal revision to which he subjected them insistently, before their first appearing and after it. His entire freedom in this respect has been regarded as inconsistent with the protest in the preface of the *Collection* against the alteration of his own or his brother's hymns by other hands. "I desire," he says, "they would not attempt to mend them; for they really are not able. None of them is able to mend either the sense or the verse."[72] There is nothing in the protest inconsistent with the practice. Wesley sincerely believed he could improve other people's hymns, whether Watts' or his brother's, and along with this self-confidence had a total lack of confidence in the ability of other "hymn-tinkerers." The results in his case went far to justify the self-confidence. Unhappily the practice rather than the protest established a precedent for an editorial custom of "tinkering" hymns which afterward went to great lengths, and only too often failed to justify itself.

2. The work of the Wesleys *modified the ideal of the English Hymn itself,* both on its spiritual and literary sides, and *established new types of hymns.*—No one can turn from the earlier hymns to the Wesleyan without being conscious of a change of atmosphere, a heightening of emotion, a novelty of theme, a new manner of expression.

(1). This change reveals itself, first, through a *new evangelistic note in the hymns.* In the quiet of his study Watts

[72]Both Whitefield and Toplady were among those who in their published hymn books had already offended in this direction.

had aimed to improve the character of the Service of Praise. The Wesleys struck a new note,—the proclamation of an unlimited atonement and free gospel, with the yearning cry of the field preacher to "all that pass by." They sounded it in revival hymns, directly addressed to sinners, and glowing with the exhorter's excitement. They aimed to bring the unchurched and unsaved within the sound of the gospel, and to use song as a means of his conversion and upbuilding. And so, when the hymns were gathered into the Methodist *Collection,* the first section of the book bore the title, "Exhorting and Entreating to return to God."

The Wesleys may be said to have introduced the Evangelistic Hymn, as we use that term to-day. Their lead was more or less followed through the whole breadth of the Evangelical Revival, and by the extending line of latter-day revivalists. There will always be some to contend that evangelistic hymns should be confined to revival meetings as distinguished from the Church's stated worship, and that a rhymed appeal to sinners is not a hymn in any true sense. But the quickened sense of responsibility for evangelization which spread from the Methodist Movement into all the Churches has learned to regard such questions as largely academic. The Evangelistic Hymn has a secure place not only in the ordinary church hymnal but even in the collections of the straitest Anglicans. For this the Wesleys are responsible, even though the evangelistic hymns of Charles Wesley have not as a class come into much use beyond Methodism. Each subsequent revival has tended to develop its own Hymnody. But for the character of too much of this later Hymnody the Wesleys cannot justly be regarded as responsible. The Evangelistic Hymn as conceived by them is simple, direct and tender; expressed in rippling measures that would catch the ear of the passer-by and assist his memory. But from triviality and from vulgarity the Wesleyan hymns are characteristically free.

(2). The work of the Wesleys, notably of Charles, greatly affected the *Hymn of Christian Experience.* At his hands this becomes the predominating theme of Hymnody. He felt an impulse to translate every new spiritual experience into song; and the spiritual needs of the converts, as disclosed in the class-meetings, broke through his natural reserve, and called upon him to bare the deepest feelings of his soul, and lay them at the feet of those who needed his sympathy and guidance. The hymns are frankly autobiographical. They portray, without any effort to tone down his own heightened emotions to the average level, his personal spiritual history:—his unrest and even agony under bondage to the law, his instantaneous conversion and the assurance of faith, the period of ecstatic joy, the ups and downs of the pilgrim progress to the "second rest," his delight in the anticipation of death.

In this way the Methodist Hymnody developed into something more than a body of Church Song. As finally gathered into the *Collection* of 1780, it constituted what John Wesley called the fullest account of Scriptural Christianity in existence. The whole area of the operations of the Spirit in the heart is there charted out with firmness and precision. The experiences are primarily the Wesleys' own. But it was a feature of their method to anticipate, and in a remarkable degree to evoke, in their converts a repetition of their own experiences. And the Hymnody did much in developing the type of piety we still describe as Methodist. Methodist though it was, Dr. Martineau, the Unitarian, wrote of it in 1869:[73]—"After the Scriptures, the Wesley Hymn Book appears to me the grandest instrument of popular religious culture that Christendom has ever produced."

This conception of the Hymn, and this turning of the congregational praise book into a manual of spiritual discipline, were not the expression of the Wesleys' theory of worship imposed upon the Revival. They were rather the result of the Revival experiences with the poor and unlettered, the observation of the great educative power that lay

[73] *Life and Letters of James Martineau,* New York, 1902, vol. ii, p. 99.

in the use of hymns which the Revival itself had called forth and shaped. In the fulness and precision of its dealings with the Christian life, the Methodist *Collection* remains unique, but its new emphasis on the Hymn of Experience became a precedent, and was extended through the various channels of Hymnody that more or less directly had their source in the Revival.

The value of the precedent thus established will be variously appraised. From the liturgical point of view the Hymn of Experience seems to violate the traditions, and to create a new standard of Church Praise. Instead of a congregation uttering its corporate praise with a common voice, we have a gathering of individuals conducting their private devotions in audible unison. And when the Hymn of Experience becomes autobiographical, it gives rise to the double question, how far its writer's individual experience is fitted to be a norm of Christian experience in general, and how far putting another's experience into the mouth of a promiscuous congregation lends itself to the promotion of religious insincerity.

In applying these tests to Charles Wesley's autobiographical hymns, there is no occasion to separate the body of them from the Wesleyan Method, of which they became the effective instrument. In the case of a great majority of them, their use has been confined within the limits of Methodism. Of the remainder some, by reason of their emotional intensity and spiritual exaltation, are clearly unfitted for general and indiscriminate use.[74] Others have awakened a response in the common heart of English-speaking Christendom; though even in the case of some of these there is no unanimity of opinion as to the fitness of such intimate strains for general worship.[75]

---

[74] "They are too good for such purposes." Burgess, *op. cit.*, p. 266.

[75] *E. g.*, of "Jesu, Lover of my Soul," Canon Ellerton, the hymn writer, has said "Most clergymen, I suppose, would hesitate before selecting it as the vehicle of the ordinary worship of a mixed congregation." H. Housman, *John Ellerton,* London, 1896, p. 237.

(3). The work of the Wesleys led the way toward *a churchly or Liturgical Hymnody.* The idea of celebrating the Christian festivals in verse had of course been held in common by many devotional poets: even that of a "Christian Year" which should be a poetic illustration of the Prayer Book began with Bishop Ken rather than with Keble. But in the Wesleys' time the thought of a "Hymnal Companion to the Prayer Book" was not in men's minds, and the work of Wither in that direction had been long forgotten.

The Wesleys had planned to carry on their work in the Church of their fathers, and as late as 1750 printed hymns under their names as "Presbyters of the Church of England."[76] The group of hymn tracts for various festivals of the Christian Year contains some of the best hymns of that type in the language, and perhaps indicates the line on which the Wesleyan Hymnody would have developed apart from the revival influences. Even after the Church proved inhospitable to the Wesleys' work and their hymns, the brothers remained in its ministry, churchmen at heart and to a great extent in practice.

The *Hymns on the Lord's Supper* of 1745 would seem a strange intrusion into the body of their experimental Hymnody, if we did not understand how the Church service and the Methodist meeting continued, in the mind of both brothers, to exist side by side, each complementing the other. They regarded the Lord's Supper as the crown of Christian worship, and held it in profoundest reverence. This book of 1745 is the witness of their desire that their followers should share their views. It is a "hymnal companion" to the Prayer Book "Order of the Administration of the Lord's Supper," by no means neglectful of the "Catholic" aspects of that service. John Wesley required of his people frequent communions in their parish churches; and, after the permanent organization of Methodism as a separate church, arranged for it a liturgical and sacramental

[76]*Hymns on the Lord's Supper* (title pages of some editions).

scheme of worship, modified from *The Book of Common Prayer,* with its own Hymnody "for the Lord's Day" services. The churchly and sacramental proclivities of the Wesleys permanently impressed themselves on English Methodism, and, as embodied in its Hymnody, differentiate that Hymnody from the early Nonconformist "System of Praise," and no less from later types of Revival Hymnody, which give scant recognition to church or sacrament. "Never at any time was there a danger of the Methodist Societies cutting themselves off from the Catholic Church by neglect of the Sacraments, or of their becoming an exclusively evangelistic organization on the plan of the Salvation Army."[77]   There was thus nothing anomalous in the fact that the Wesleys should be the first within the bounds of the Church of England to celebrate its festival days in adequate songs and to provide a Sacramental Hymnody.

(4). The work of the Wesleys set up a *new standard in Hymnody on its literary side.* Their hymns are in line with the earlier devotional poets rather than with Watts. They controverted Watts' canon of hymn writing and laid down a new one,—a hymn should be a poem.

John Wesley's taking to Georgia a copy of Herbert's Poems, and his repeated efforts to utilize its verses in his hymn books, are significant. The brothers had been trained in the very atmosphere of sacred poetry. Samuel Wesley's preface to his *An Epistle to a friend concerning Poetry* (1700) was a vigorous, even violent, philippic against the profligacy and "infidel principles" of current letters, especially poetry; and all the poets of the Epworth rectory aimed to rebut the prevailing notion that religion offered no fit themes to poetry. So far the standpoint of Watts and the Wesleys was one, but only so far.

Watts insisted that the Hymn must be kept outside the realm of poetry, stripped of poetic suggestiveness, and be written down to the level of the meanest capacity. Wesley

[77]Gregory, *Hymn Book of the Modern Church,* p. 177.

maintained that the Hymn should be a religious lyric and create the impression of lyrical poetry; that the masses must be lifted up to the level of the Hymn, and made to feel the beauty and inspiration of poetry. By this standard he tried not only the work of Watts, but of his brother Charles, of a group of whose hymns he said, "Some are bad, some mean, some most excellently good."[78] And when his Methodist "System of Praise" was finally complete, he made the proud boast:[79]—

> "May I be permitted to add a few words with regard to the poetry? . . . In these Hymns there is no doggerel, no botches, nothing put in to patch up the rhyme, no feeble expletives. Here is nothing turgid or bombast on the one hand, or low and creeping on the other. . . . Here are (allow me to say) both the purity, the strength and the elegance of the ENGLISH language: and at the same time the utmost simplicity and plainness, suited to every capacity. Lastly, I desire men of taste to judge (these are the only competent judges;) whether there is not in some of the following verses, the true Spirit of Poetry: such as cannot be acquired by art and labour; but must be the gift of nature. By labour a man may become a tolerable imitator of SPENSER, SHAKESPEAR, or MILTON, and may heap together pretty compound epithets, as PALE-EYED, WEAK-EYED, and the like. But unless he is born a Poet, he will never attain the genuine SPIRIT OF POETRY."

In the judgment of a recent historian of English Poetry,[80] Wesley "was fully justified" in making this boast, and his brother Charles was "the most admirable *devotional* lyric poet in the English language."

Incidental to the poetic freedom with which Charles Wesley wrote was the marked metrical development he gave to the English Hymn. Tate and Brady in the new Psalmody,

---

[78] *Journal*, December 15, 1788.

[79] In preface to the *Collection* of 1780.

[80] W. J. Courthope, *A History of English Poetry*, vol. v, London, 1905, p. 343. Prof. Felix E. Schelling, in his more recent *The English Lyric* (Houghton Mifflin Co., 1913) occupies the familiar critical attitude, and has been quoted in our preface. "The critical world is yet but half-persuaded that a hymn can be poetry," the late Frederic M. Bird said in the preface of his *Charles Wesley seen in his finer and less familiar Poems*. New York: Hurd & Houghton, 1867.

and Watts in the new Hymnody, had confined themselves to the simple metres of the old Psalmody. This was with a view of meeting the musical limitations of the congregations, but not without a thought for the quasi-sacredness acquired by these metres as the traditional vehicles of praise, Charles Wesley cast aside all such scruples, and wrote freely in the rhythms and measures most natural or effective; some suggested by German originals, some his own. He wrote hymns in some thirty metres, whose freshness and variety became a marked feature of the Methodist *Collection*. He rather neglected the familiar Iambic metres of the psalm books, purposely no doubt, and excelled in his handling of trochaic metres. Some of his irregular or "peculiar" metres have less reason for being there.

The early Methodists, always under the pressure of John Wesley's schooling, seem to have had little trouble with the novel metres. But their ability to handle the less simple metres gradually lessened. By the XIXth century a considerable part of the *Collection* had, for that reason, become practically obsolete. Toward the middle of the century the matter was taken up, and some of the hymns restored into actual use. On the other hand, a variety of metres introduced by the Wesleys have now become familiar and standard measures in English Hymnody.

Upon the writing of hymns Charles Wesley's influence was less immediate and less clearly marked than that of Watts. He cannot be said to have established a school of hymn writers. His poetic inspiration and even his peculiar style discouraged imitation. Of the associates of the Wesleys who remained Methodists, Thomas Olivers[81] and John Bakewell[82] are each remembered as the author of a single hymn. John Murlin, one of Wesley's preachers who survived him, printed (81) *Sacred Hymns on various subjects,* which reached a second edition (Bristol, 1782), but are not remembered. In the generation immediately following the

[81] Author of "The God of Abraham praise."
[82] Author of "Hail! Thou once-despised Jesus."

Wesleys, there were virtually no Methodist hymn writers at all. No need was felt of adding to the Wesleyan Hymns, and certainly there was no hope in any Methodist mind of improving upon them.[83] Of the Wesleys' associates who became Moravians, those who wrote hymns show the influence of Herrnhut rather than of Charles Wesley. On the Calvinistic side of the Revival there was more opportunity for hymn writers than on the Methodist. And it is one of the humors of the situation that the polemic and indignant Toplady so "evidently kindled his poetic torch at that of his contemporary, Charles Wesley." Montgomery's remark[84] that if Toplady's "Deathless principle, arise" had appeared without name, it might have been confidently set down as the production of Charles Wesley, may be extended to cover a number of Toplady's hymns. Upon hymn writers in general Charles Wesley's influence operated less by way of furnishing models for imitation than by gradually enlarging their conception of the Hymn, in its themes, its methods and its metrical structure.

V

THE WESLEYAN HYMNS IN THE CHURCH AT LARGE

We have yet to consider the part of the Wesleys in the extension of hymn singing. And perhaps it needs to be emphasized that their immediate work in this direction was effected within the ranks of their own followers. It was effected by developing among them a new type of fervid song learned from the Moravians, and by establishing a great denomination of which hymn singing was the characteristic note.

[83] Among later Methodist hymn writers, mention may be made of William M. Bunting, W. Morley Punshon, Benjamin Gough, E. Evans Jenkins, J. Lyth, E. J. Brailsford, A. H. Vine, T. B. Stephenson, and Edw. Boaden.

[84] *The Christian Psalmist,* 1825, preface, p. xxvi.

When we come to "The revolution in Church Psalmody" which the editor of Wesley's Journal foresees in his work in Georgia and his hymn book of 1737,[85] we need to remember that Watts and not Wesley was the leader in that revolution. Even the familiar statement of Green that by the Wesleys "a new musical impulse was aroused in the people which gradually changed the face of public devotion throughout England,"[86] needs to be qualified. The fervor of Methodist song was evoked by Methodist experience. It does not appear to have passed over even to the Calvinistic side of the Revival itself. The influence of the Wesleys in "changing the face of devotion" was somewhat indirect, and to a great extent it was deferred.

When we think of the contagion of Methodist fervor as inoculating the ranks of the psalm singers outside with its love of the Wesleyan Hymns and its passion for hymn-singing, we are far away from real XVIIIth century happenings. The actual relation of the work of the Wesleys in Hymnody to the Churches outside of Methodism involves some very peculiar features. Perhaps there is no readier way of understanding it than that of pointing the contrast in this respect between their work and that of their predecessor, Dr. Watts.

To-day it is a commonplace to couple the names of Watts and Charles Wesley at the head of English Hymnody, with little disposition to ask which name is the greater. But this attitude of the modern Church toward them has been attained very gradually. It involved a complete readjustment of the claim of the two men upon the Church's favor, that became possible only after a gradual enlargement of the Church's heart; in effecting which the Wesleys have been among the chief agents. Historically there was the sharpest contrast between the church's reception of Watts' Psalms and Hymns and of Charles Wesley's. Two features of the original situation sufficiently explain this.

[85] *Journal,* vol. i, p. 229.
[86] *Short History of the English People,* ed. London, 1884, p. 719.

First. The contrast existed already in the actual work of the two men, judged from the point of view of availableness for general use. Watts' felicity lay in his gift for locating the common level and his refusal to soar. He embodied the theology of his surroundings, and kept within the average range of spiritual experience. This self-restraint gave his work something like a universal appeal. When he had once persuaded Nonconformist Churches that they wanted hymns, the Churches felt that his hymns were just what they wanted. His entire System of Praise, without sifting or retrenchment, commended itself alike to Independents, Presbyterians, and Baptists. Thus it could happen that in many quarters what now is called the "Hymnal" was referred to simply as "Watts."

Nothing of this kind could have happened to Charles Wesley. His work did not commend itself to current taste as poetry. To the average worshiper it would hardly suggest itself as adapted for singing; for he had no experience of the use of anything like this as material of praise, and knew no tunes in these strange metres. Its theology was aggressively in the opposition, and heated by the controversial spirit. Its spiritual tone was strange and unreal to the man who had not come under Methodist training. Moreover the high spiritual levels on which Charles Wesley moved were immeasurably above the average experience or even ambition. And, at a time when the churches expected to receive their materials of praise as a unit, if not indeed from a single hand, no one of the successive collections of the Wesleys' hymns could have been a candidate for adoption in any branch of the Church, or by any company of Christians outside of Methodism. The very necessity of selecting the available hymns, imbedded in a mass of material not attractive to general taste or conviction, was tantamount to a postponement of the rightful claims of the Wesleys to a share in the Hymnody of the Church at large.

Second. There was the same contrast in the extent of

the opportunity for the general diffusion of their hymns afforded by the respective circumstances and surroundings of Watts and Charles Wesley.

Watts moved on the social uplands of English Nonconformity. He was universally looked up to by dissenters, and he freely met "bishops and other clergy" on their own level. His position could not have been more favorable for disseminating that System of Church Praise he regarded as his great work. But while Watts advanced by the highways seen and respected of all, the Wesleys worked behind the hedges separating them from both Church and dissent. In so far as either had any real knowledge of the Wesleys and their work, they were regarded by churchmen as schismatics and ranters, and by socially respectable dissent as sentimentalists and sensationalists. They sought to reach the masses neglected by Church and dissent alike, and by methods disapproved of by both. They forsook the conventional order, aroused intellectual contempt, awakened intense theological bitterness and incurred social ostracism, and even personal violence. It is difficult now to reproduce, even to the imagination, "the Reproach of Methodism," and to appreciate the isolation of the Methodist Movement from contemporary religious activity or stagnation.

It would be idle to deny that the Wesleyan Hymns suffered from these associations. The contagion of this fervid Methodist song could not be felt, so long as the Methodists and the churches were not brought into contact. The real charm of the Wesleyan poetry could not be perceived, so long as men regarded it as the mere vehicle of Methodist errors, or failed to regard it at all, as unworthy of attention. There resulted an inevitable postponement of any use of the Wesleyan Hymns by the churches outside. And even more permanently the hymns retained a Methodist taint, from which nothing but the change of feeling that time brings could wholly free them.

Whitefield's use of some of the Wesleyan Hymns at his Tabernacle helped a few of them across the wall separating

Arminianism from Calvinism. But Lady Huntingdon's Connexion and the Moravian Methodists developed their own hymn writers and their own Hymnody. One and another of the choice spirits among the Church of England clergy who caught the glow of the Revival, introduced some of the Wesleyan hymns into their new hymn books, and gave them their first opportunity for a wider use. Some of these hymns passed from one collection into others, and were gradually added to. They made their way on their own merits, as it is evident that many compilers knew nothing of the source of the materials they used. Even so, the Wesleyan hymns thus used in the latter part of the XVIIIth century were few, and their use itself limited. The Independents were under the spell of the Watts tradition. In the first outstanding Baptist collection (Ash and Evans, 1760) the infusion of Wesleyan hymns was very trifling: in that of Dr. Rippon (1787) it was larger. In the early XIXth century the inclusion of some Wesleyan hymns became the general rule, and their number has gradually increased to its present proportions. But in such use, through the first half-century and beyond, there was a very common feature which every student of hymn books has observed; that is to say, that even where compilers have been careful to give the names of other authors, the hymns of the Wesleys were frequently printed as anonymous, or ascribed to some other author. Doddridge, Toplady, De Courcey, Cennick, Cowper and Montgomery, were among the names given as the authors of Wesleyan hymns in English and American collections of note. Of Wesleyan hymns, given without any name, or with a wrong name appended to them, Mr. Burgess[87] found 27 in Rippon's *Selection* (18th ed.), 15 in Willcock's *Collection,* 24 in Montgomery's *Christian Psalmist,* 22 in Bickersteth's *Christian Psalmody,* and 29 in Conder's *Congregational Hymn-Book.* It is not surprising that Burgess saw in this coincidence a furtive use of Wesleyan materials, and something like a conspiracy

[87]W. P. Burgess, *Wesleyan Hymnology,* 2nd ed., London, 1849, p. 9.

to suppress the truth, due to Calvinistic prejudice. And yet, among the compilers Burgess arraigns, James Montgomery was influenced by no such motive, and in the pages of the very book referred to he paid tribute to Charles Wesley's genius, ranking him next to Watts. An explanation of the situation must include Montgomery as well as Rippon.

The explanation of the manner of Charles Wesley's treatment lies largely, if not wholly, in the general ignorance of hymn book compilers concerning their materials. We have already said[88] that Daniel Sedgwick, a shoemaker's apprentice and second-hand book dealer, not born until 1814, was the first to make a collection and systematic study of English hymn books. And only when in middle life he began to put his knowledge at the service of compilers, was there a beginning of the lifting of the dense cloud of ignorance covering the sphere of minor letters now appropriated to what we call Hymnology. This ignorance was well distributed over the whole extent of Hymnody. But it must be admitted that as regards Charles Wesley there was something like a concentration of ignorance. In the 13th number of *Notes and Queries* (Jan. 26, 1850), established as "a medium of inter-communication between literary men," etc., a correspondent asks:

> "Can any of your readers inform me who was the author of the well-known Christmas-Hymn, 'Hark the Herald Angels Sing,' which is so often found (of course without the slightest shadow of authority) at the end of our Prayer Books? In the collection of poems entitled *Christmas-Tyde,* published by Pickering, the initials 'J. C. W.' are appended to it; the same in Bickersteth's *Hymn Book.* In the last number of the *Christian Remembrancer,* it is incorrectly attributed to Doddridge. . . . If the author of the hymn cannot be determined, it would be interesting to know its probable date. . . ."

It may be noted that the writer in *The Christian Remembrancer* who in 1850 attributed the hymn to Doddridge was none other than John Mason Neale, a diligent student of the old Latin and Greek church Hymnody.

[88] In the preface.

Three weeks after the appearance of the inquiry in *Notes and Queries,* came a reply (the only one) from another correspondent:

"I believe [the hymn] to be the composition of the Rev. Charles Wesley, the younger brother of the celebrated John Wesley. He was the author of many of the hymns in his brother's collection, which are distinguished for their elegance and simplicity. I am not able to find out, for certain, whether he had another name; if he had, it was probably the occasion of the initials (J. C. W.) your correspondent mentions."[89]

The need for such an inquiry in such quarters sixty-two years after Charles Wesley's death, and the uncertainty of the only reply, fully explain the failure of the editors of hymn books to give him proper recognition. There was no conspiracy among them to suppress the facts. But there was a common ignorance concerning Charles Wesley and his work. And it may be that in his case there was an element of wilfulness in this ignorance that had its roots in theological or ecclesiastical prejudice. Whatever the motives to disassociate his name from his hymns may have been, the net result was in his favor. A number of these unfathered hymns gained a sure place in the affection of the Churches. And when they came to realize the actual extent of Charles Wesley's contribution to the common stock, the time had come when the fact could be accepted even gladly, as an evidence of the large area of Christian truth and feeling which all the Churches hold in common.

[89]Doubtless the initials were originally intended to represent J. and C. Wesley.

CHAPTER VI

THE HYMNODY OF THE METHODIST REVIVAL
(Continued)

To complete the account of Methodist Hymnody in England it will be necessary to follow its fortunes among those dissenting Methodist bodies which cut themselves off from the main stem of Wesleyanism. But these schisms and their growth into large independent denominations pertain to the period following Wesley's death. And considerations of chronology demand attention to the Hymnody of English Moravianism, whose beginnings were contemporaneous with those of Methodism, and so closely connected with the Revival as to give rise to the name of "Moravian Methodism." We must also follow the Wesleyan Movement across the sea, and study the Hymnody of that great Methodist Church which Wesley himself lived to found in America.

VI

THE MORAVIAN HYMNODY

1. After the Breach with Wesley the Moravians Develop an Eccentric Hymnody (1741-1754)

The "Unitas Fratrum," as renewed at Herrnhut by Count Zinzendorf, claims descent from the Bohemian Brethren, who made the first hymn books of Protestant type.[1] The Moravians inherited this hymn making and hymn singing disposition as well as some of the earlier hymns. But on the Moravian Hymnody Zinzendorf stamped his own ardent and peculiar personality by his hymn writing, his singing

[1]See chap. i, part I, sect. 2.

meetings and his hymn books for both Herrnhut and London congregations.[2]

This was the German Hymnody that so deeply influenced the Wesleys on their voyage to America, and it was brought to England by Brethren from Herrnhut who established the little circle of Moravians at London. When the Wesleys returned to London they entered this circle as guests of James Hutton and spiritual pupils of Peter Böhler; and their association with the Moravians was for a time very close. On May 1, 1738, Böhler and Wesley joined in drawing up regulations for the society at Hutton's house, later at Fetter Lane.[3] How far Wesley's *A Collection of Psalms and Hymns* of 1738 represents this association, and this society (as yet neither Moravian nor Methodist), can only be conjectured. With the breach between Wesley and the Moravians that quickly followed, the development of an English Moravian Hymnody became as inevitable as was the writing of the Wesleyan Hymns.

The Moravians naturally drew their inspiration from Herrnhut, and their first effort was a little book of hymns translated from the German. It was put to press in October, 1741, by James Hutton, and seems to be that submitted to Dr. Doddridge and read by him "with great pleasure."[4] Between 1742 and 1748 followed *A Collection of Hymns with several translations from the Hymn Book of the Moravian Brethren* in three parts.[5] There had been also

[2]For Zinzendorf and German Moravian Hymnody, see E. E. Koch, *Geschichte des Kirchenlieds und Kirchengesangs der christlichen, insbefondere der deutschen evangelischen Kirche*, 3rd ed., vol. 5, Stuttgart, 1868, pp. 283-352. For his hymns, see also Albert Knapp, *Geistliche Gedichte des Grafen von Zinzendorf*, Stuttgart, 1845 (but as to text consult Julian, *Dictionary of Hymnology*, p. 1302[1]).

[3]Wesley's *Journal*, vol. i, pp. 458, 459.

[4]David Benham, *Memoirs of James Hutton*, London, 1856, p. 75: and see Doddridge's letter of Nov. 18, 1741, p. 62.

[5]Part i, 1742 (Hymns 1-187, with 188-239 in appendix of 2nd edn., 1743) : part ii, 1746 (Hymns 240-403, and some unnumbered: part iii, 1748, with 126 numbered, and some unnumbered verses; the hymns increased to 161 in 1749.

in 1742 *A second Collection of Hymns, never before printed, with several new translations from the Hymn-Book of the Moravian Brethren* (London, J. Hutton, 83 hymns); and there followed in 1752 *Some other Hymns and Poems, consisting chiefly of translations from the German.* These hymns by numerous hands represent the common desire of the London Society to express its peculiar views in social song; but up to this point they "were never regularly authorized nor always passably reviewed." [6]

Zinzendorf had planned a hymn book,[7] the details of which he committed to John Gambold,[8] one of the Oxford "Holy Club," and afterwards a leader in London Moravianism. This, the first authorized hymn book, appeared as *A Collection of Hymns of the Children of God in all ages, from the beginning till now. In two parts. Designed chiefly for the use of the congregations in union with the Brethren's Church. London printed; and to be had at all the Brethren's Chapels, MDCCLIV.* The book is a 12mo. of 804 pages, with the hymns set up in double columns. In motive and in contents, as in size, it was quite without precedent. Part i was nothing less than an attempted thesaurus of Christian Hymnody:—Anthems from Scripture (1-110); Scripture Hymns (111-181); Hymns of the Primitive Church (182-245); Hymns of the Ancient Brethren (246-297); German Hymns of the XVIth century (298-336); old Hymns of the English Church (337-431); German Hymns of the XVIIth century (432-481); English Hymns of the same age (482-536); English and German Hymns at the end of the XVIIth and in the XVIIIth century (537-695). Such an eclectic undertaking was certainly remarkable for its time, though probably of greater interest to us than to those for whose use it was intended.

---

[6]Preface of 1754.
[7]Spangenberg, *Life of Nicholas Lewis Count Zinzendorf,* tr. by Saml. Jackson, London, 1838, p. 430: Hutton's *Memoirs,* pp. 302, 303.
[8]L. Tyerman, *The Oxford Methodists,* London, 1873, pp. 192, 193: Hutton, *ut sup.*

The second part may be regarded as the authorized presentation of the "Hymns of the present Congregation of the Brethren" [9] (460 numbered; many without numbers): including so much of the contents of the earlier hymn books as space allowed. The early and exuberant development of Moravian Hymnody here revealed for our inspection was vitally connected with that of Herrnhut, from which much of it was directly translated. It seems at first like a high-colored and repulsive morbid growth that had been grafted from without upon the stem of English Hymnody. In reality it was the new development of a real spiritual life, at first perverted into fantastic shapes, but capable of culture and ultimately flowering into a characteristic and permanent type of English Hymn.

It is desirable that this type be kept in mind while inspecting the vagaries of the early hymns. It is simply the embodiment and expression of Zinzendorf's peculiar type of "heart religion." As in his theology it is enough to know Christ as sacrificed, while the mysteries of the Divine nature are ignored as not practical, so in the hymns, "the Lamb" ever wounded and dying is the chief, almost the only, object of praise and prayer, to the virtual ignoring of the Divine majesty.[10] The atmosphere of the hymns is that of a childlike simplicity, a tender devotion to Christ's person, and a joyful confidence in his passion. Unfortunately Zinzendorf had first to pass through a period when

[9] The preface of 1754: according to that of the 1789 *Collection,* "all such hymns of former Hymn-books used among us, which were thought to merit a place." But this should not be construed to imply that Gambold thought that all the hymns he admitted in 1754 had intrinsic merit. His standard of Hymnody was inconceivably low, but his preface acknowledges the inferiority of some of the hymns, put in because "even these little Hymns have got their lovers, who would be sorry to lose them all at once" (preface, 1754, p. 12).

[10] "Do not wonder that they scarce speak of any Thing else but the Wounds, and Blood, and Death, and Atonement of our Redeemer; for this is the weightiest Matter in Heaven and Earth." Preface to *A second Collection,* 1742.

his thinking assumed a mystical vagueness, his zeal flamed into fanaticism and his affections were perverted by sentimentality: he imposed upon his followers a copious selection of the "fleshly-spiritual" hymns of Johann Scheffler, and from them formed his own early style of hymn writing. Through this valley of humiliation Zinzendorf dragged his English as well as German followers, and to this period the *Collection* of 1754 belongs.

The immediate impression the hymns make upon the eye is that of foreignness, owing to the unusual metres and frequent long-drawn-out stanzas. This was due to the wish of the authorities that the melodies used at Herrnhut should be retained, no matter in what language the hymns were sung; and it has continued to give a characteristic verse-form to Moravian Hymnody in all parts of the world. The sense of foreignness is increased by the foreign English of many of the hymns. This was owing partly to the inherent difficulty of adapting English to German metres, and partly to the unfamiliarity of some of the translators with English grammar and the meanings of the words they used.[11] Whether foreign or native, the English of the hymns is often illiterate, and much of the verse pure doggerel; not unnaturally so since Hutton and Gambold must have been almost the only educated men among these hymn writers.[12] Both the foreignness and illiteracy of

[11]See the correspondence of James Hutton and "the Director of the Psalmody," printed at the end of the third part of the collection of Hymns (2nd ed., 1749), and reprinted in *Memoirs of Hutton,* appendix iv, pp. 592, 593.

[12]Unless we regard Zinzendorf himself as among them. He wrote one English hymn, translated one of Luther's and versified the Articles of the Church of England, for the 1754 *Collection* (see note at end of preface). John Cennick did not become a Moravian till 1745, and his well known hymns enter very slightly into the earlier Moravian hymn books. Of Hutton's hymns there is a selection in the *Memoirs.* A few are still in Moravian use; one ("Teach me yet more of Thy blest ways") is known more widely. It is claimed that Gambold contributed no less than 11 translations and 28 originals to the *Collection* of 1754. A list of these can be found in Tyerman, *The Oxford Methodists,* pp. 192, 193.

Moravian Hymnody were gradually removed by redaction and retranslation, without impairing that German strain that still testifies to its source.

The Brethren's Hymns of 1754 deal principally with the slaughtered Lamb, with the emphasis on the physical side of the passion,—the sweat and blood, the wounds, the opened side which becomes the sphere of the believers' communion, and the "corpse." They abound in whimsical allegories and perverted spiritualizations. The ideas conveyed by their imagery are often shockingly coarse, and again unintelligible.[18] The amatory conception of the mystical union with Christ, and also the Moravian discipline of the sexes, led to some passages which, however innocently intended, are undeniably indecent.[14]

2. WESLEY REPUDIATES IT (1749)

These hymns of a people with whom he had so nearly identified himself shocked and chagrined John Wesley: the more so in view of the earlier influence of the German

---

[18]This (from No. 386) is on a level with much else:—

> "O blest Trinity!
> And Side's cavity
> Of the Son who bore our torment!
> Take now towards your Contentment,
> This our Cross's Church,
> As a glowing torch."

And this (from No. 460):—

> "Ye Cross's—air birds, swell the notes
> Of the sweet Side-hole Song,
> That Fountain's Juice will clear your throats,
> And help to hold it long.
> Each Day and Year shall higher raise
> The Side-hole's glory, love and praise:
> Hallelujah! Hallelujah!
> To the Side *Gloria!*"

[14]On this unpleasant subject it will be sufficient to instance Hymn No. 268, and to refer to Southey's *Life of Wesley and rise and progress of Methodism,* ed. London, 1846, pp. 172-174, & notes xx and xxi.

hymns upon himself and upon his brother's hymn writing. Wesley had been captivated by their fervor and piety, and, with his imperfect knowledge of German, had only partially apprehended their doctrine and imagery. Charles probably knew no German,[15] and must have derived his impressions at second hand. Henry Ward Beecher gave wide currency to the view that the Moravian Hymnody was "the fountain in which Charles Wesley was baptized," and "his hymns are only Moravian hymns re-sung." [16] Grossly exaggerated as is this view, it is true that Charles Wesley caught something of the Moravian tone and manner,—its atmosphere of confiding love and a certain familiarity of intercourse with the Saviour. After he had comprehended the infelicities of Moravian Hymnody, John Wesley maintained a close watch upon his brother's hymns for anything in the amatory way; and this presumably explains the omission of "Jesu, Lover of my Soul" from the Methodist *Collection* of 1780.

But John Wesley went much farther. As early as 1748, at that time the declared enemy of Moravianism, he concluded it to be his "bounden Duty . . . to publish to all the World" a few of the Hymns "as a standing Proof, that there is no folly too gross for those, who are wise above that is written." [17] They appeared, without his name, as *Hymns composed for the use of the Brethren. By the Right Reverend and Most Illustrious C. Z. Published for the benefit of all mankind, in the year 1749*. This was followed by the anonymous *The Contents of a folio History of the Moravians or United Brethren, printed in 1749 . . . with suitable remarks. . . . By a Lover of the Light* (London: J. Roberts, 1750); in which special attention was directed to the hymns embodying the Moravian views of marriage as admittedly "not fit to be read by any that

[15]Jackson, *Life of Charles Wesley*, vol. ii, p. 456.
[16]Introduction to the *Plymouth Collection*, N. Y., 1855, p. v.
[17]*Journal*, Dec. 15, 1758. It is in *Extract* No. vii (1754), p. 110; afterwards suppressed, and restored in the standard ed., vol. iii. p. 389.

attach bad ideas to bad expressions." [18] Zinzendorf declared that "J. Wesley's extract from our hymn-book has done us no injury";[19] but it is to be noted that only two of the hymns selected by Wesley were reprinted in the 1754 book, and that the text of other hymns was somewhat modified.

The publication of this hymn book, so conspicuous from its size, attracted renewed attention to the Moravian Hymns. Their weaknesses were again exposed, by the Rev. John Watson,[20] in *A Letter to the Clergy of the Church of the Unitas Fratrum, concerning a remarkable book of Hymns used in the Congregations, pointing out inconsistencies and absurdities* (London, 1756). It is difficult to estimate the extent to which the *Collection* of 1754 was actually "used in the Congregations." [21] Its size and price were against it, and the eyes of some must have been opened to perceive its offensiveness. There is a report that those in authority endeavored to suppress it: they certainly neither revised it nor provided anything in its place until years after Zinzendorf's death.

The second authorized hymn book, with 257 numbered hymns, appeared in 1769 as *A Collection of Hymns, chiefly extracted from the larger Hymn Book of the Brethren's Congregations* (London: at the Brethren's Chapels); and shows by its very title that the 1754 book was still of authority. The abridgment was nominally made upon complaints of the earlier book as too voluminous, but incidentally much undesirable material was dropped out. It was used for twenty years "in all [Moravian] places of

[18]See Tyerman, *Life of John Wesley,* vol. ii, pp. 99, 100. Tyerman regarded this pamphlet as Wesley's, but there seems to be no evidence of it. *Cf.* Green, *Wesley Bibliography,* p. 71. But Wesley believed and circulated (see *Extract of Journal,* No. ix, published in 1759, pp. 5, 74) the scandalous charges of grossly immoral practices among the Moravians, supported by alleged revelations from within.

[19]*Memoirs of Hutton,* p. 218.

[20]Perpetual curate of Ripponden, in the parish of Halifax.

[21]Preface of 1789.

worship, both at home and abroad, where divine service is performed in the English language." [22] And with it closes the earlier period of English Moravian Hymnody; certainly the most singular episode in the history of the English Hymn.

3. THE NORMAL PERIOD OF MORAVIAN HYMNODY (1789-1901)

The normal period of English Moravian Hymnody began with *A Collection of Hymns, for the use of the Protestant Church of the United Brethren. London printed: and sold at the Brethren's Chapels, MDCCLXXXIX.* Zinzendorf had been dead for twenty-nine years; Moravian experience had been sobered and its educational standard elevated. In this book the early hymns are carefully sifted and the residue reshaped. New material is drawn from the Barby *Gesangbuch* of 1778 and the collections of other Churches; and some from manuscript sources, including unpublished hymns of Cennick, father-in-law of the editor, the Rev. John Swertner. The usual themes of Christian worship are provided for, and a rational classification of the hymns is made. An index of first lines of all the stanzas testifies to the Moravian custom of singing a single stanza in an ejaculatory way and of making up a hymn from scattered stanzas. Such an index became henceforward a feature of Moravian hymn books. With each hymn is given the number of the appropriate tune in the *Choral Buch* (Leipzig, 1784) of the Rev. Christian Gregor (editor of the *Gesangbuch* of 1778), which became the standard in England. Some few new metres were provided for in the Rev. Christian Ignatius La Trobe's *Hymn-Tunes sung in the Church of the United Brethren* (London, n. d.).

A "new and revised edition" of the *Collection* appeared at Manchester in 1801; a *Supplement* in 1808. These were combined and improved in 1826; and after this date the

[22]*Ibid.*

hymn book became *Liturgy and Hymns for the use of the Protestant Church of the United Brethren.* The revisions so far had been in the charge of Bishop Foster.[23] Some years later the hymn book was officially committed to the hands of the poet Montgomery, who had been educated at Fulneck for the Moravian ministry. By him it was subjected to a scrutiny more searching and a rescension more free than were ever before given to a hymn book; and the results were laid before the Provincial Conference of 1847.[24] The new edition, with Montgomery's revisions and additions, appeared in 1849. An appendix followed in 1876, and a further revision in 1886; and the hymn book is once more in the hands of revisers for a new edition.

During his travels in America Count Zinzendorf established at Philadelphia in 1742 a Moravian Church of his English-speaking converts;[25] and there is record of the publication, apparently for their use, of *A choice Collection of Hymns: with several new translations from the Hymn Book of the Moravian Brethren. Philadelphia: Isaiah Warner and Cornelia Bradford, 1743.*[26] Twenty years later appeared *A Hymn Book for the children belonging to the Brethren's congregations. Taken chiefly out of the German little book. In three books . . . Philadelphia: printed in the year MDCCLXIII.*[27] Except for these two publications the needs of the Philadelphia church and of

[23]Holland and Everett, *Memoirs of James Montgomery,* London, 1854-1856, vol. vii, p. 154.

[24]*Memoirs of Montgomery,* vol. vi, pp. 266, 267; vol. vii, pp. 154-157.

[25]Spangenberg, *op. cit.,* p. 315; Abraham Ritter, *History of the Moravian Church in Philadelphia,* Phila., 1857, p. 19. Zinzendorf had already prepared and printed for the Lutheran and German Reformed people to whom he preached at Germantown, a little collection of German hymns new and old,—*Hirten Lieder von Bethlehem* (Germantown, C. Saur, 1742).

[26]Hildeburn's entry of it (*Issues of Penna. Press,* No. 810) is apparently copied from an advertisement: Evans' (*American Bibliography,* No. 5304) is evidently copied from Hildeburn. Neither had seen the book.

[27]There is a copy at Penna. Hist. Soc.

congregations of English-speaking people formed elsewhere were apparently supplied by importing copies of the successive editions of the English hymn book till 1813,[28] when a reprint of the Manchester *Collection* of 1801 issued from the press of Conrad Zentler at Philadelphia. With this the *Supplement* of 1808 was included. A reprint of the edition of 1826 followed and remained in use till 1851. In that year, by resolution of the Provincial Synod of 1849, appeared the first American *Liturgy and Hymns* (Bethlehem), based on Montgomery's rescension of 1849. The name of the author was appended to each hymn, and a reference given to a suitable tune in the Rev. Peter Wolle's *Hymn Tunes, used in the Church of the United Brethren* (Philadelphia, 1836). *The Liturgy and Hymns of the American Province of the Unitas Fratrum* of 1876 (Bethlehem) was the result of a movement, begun in the Synod of 1864, to bring Moravian Hymnody "up to the standard of modern hymnology, without destroying its Moravian character." [29] This movement was carried still further in the third edition of *Offices of Worship and Hymns* (Bethlehem, 1891),[30] intended for church-schools and prayer and praise meetings.

By these successive revisions in England and America the Moravian Hymnody was no doubt relieved of much that was offensive or foolish, its translations were bettered, its versification made more smooth. But it cannot be questioned that in the course of the process, notably at Montgomery's hands, its distinguishing features have become less conspicuous, its characteristic flavor somewhat diluted; and there has been incorporated with it a large body of the hymns common to all the Churches. In the infelicity of their hymns that aimed to emphasize their sectarian tenets, and in the progressive tendency of their Hymnody

[28] "Prior to that time, hymn-books were imported from England." Preface to *Liturgy and Hymns*, Bethlehem, 1876.
[29] Preface, p. 6.
[30] 1st ed., 1866: 2nd ed., 1872.

to conform to a common Christian standard, the experience of the Moravians has been much like that of others who felt themselves to be "a peculiar people."

Moravian hymn singing has been distinguished by its emphasis on the spiritual side, the hearty participation of the whole congregation, its free use of musical instruments, and its devotion to the German choral type of tunes.[31] Incidentally the division of the congregation into "choirs," according to sex, age and condition, brought about special provision for Children's Hymnody; in which field the Moravians have to be credited with more of priority than of excellence. In estimating their influence on Hymnody, it must be remembered that it was the German rather than the English Moravian Hymnody which, through its contact with the Wesleys, put a new warmth into English hymn singing, and something of its tone of familiar and confiding love into the English Hymn. Some of Zinzendorf's German hymns have entered into English Hymnody, through versions of Wesley and others:—notably "Jesus, Thy blood and righteousness"; "O Thou to whose all-searching sight"; "Jesus, still lead on"; and "Christ will gather in His own."

English Moravianism has developed very few hymn writers of distinction. Of its early contributors, hymns and translations by John Gambold, James Hutton, John D. Lilley, John Miller, L. T. Nyberg, John Swertner and some others, are still in Moravian use; hymns of John Cennick and William Hammond are in common use. But Cennick's early hymns were written while he was associated with Wesley, who corrected them for the press; and much of his best work was done while assisting Whitefield, who gave his hymns their circulation. The *Psalms, Hymns, and Spiritual Songs* (London, 1745) of Hammond are of merit, but must have been written before joining the Moravians.

[31]For the singing at Fulneck, see J. S. Curwen, *Studies in Worship Music,* 2nd series, pp. 57 ff; for that in America, see Ritter, *Moravian Church in Philadelphia,* chap. xxv.

Of later Moravian hymn writers C. I. La Trobe and Bishop F. W. Foster are esteemed within the denomination: James Montgomery is the one distinguished name. And he, by reason of the looseness of his affiliations and his catholic-heartedness, must be counted as belonging to the general choir rather than with Moravians.

VII

DEFLEXIONS OF METHODIST SONG AFTER WESLEY'S DEATH

When the lines between Wesleyan Methodism on the one hand and Moravianism and Calvinistic Methodism on the other had been definitely established, Wesley himself became and continued to be the centre of union of the United Societies. By the Deed of Declaration the United Societies became, on Wesley's death in 1791, a "Connexion" but not a separate Church; with provision for a continuance of Wesley's authority in a Conference of ministers. But the great question of the relation of the Connexion to the Established Church remained undetermined, and the people were unwilling that either an autocrat or body of ministers should exercise Wesley's authority. There followed a period of controversy, resistance to authority and schism. Numerous preachers were expelled; and one after another of these became the leader of an independent movement, and with his sympathizers the nucleus of an independent Methodist sect. In the course of time these seceding bodies have grown in numbers to constitute in the aggregate almost one half of British Methodism, and demand therefore some attention to their Hymnody. In the case of each secession its leaders and people took in their hearts their warm love for Methodist Song and in their hands their familiar copies of Wesley's *Collection* of 1780. The *Collection* thus became the nucleus of the independent Methodist Hymnody, and with such changes and supplements as gave expression to denominational proclivities, continued to form the main body of it.

(1) THE METHODIST NEW CONNEXION was formed by the followers of Alexander Kilham, expelled by Conference in 1796 for administering Holy Communion, and stood for the rights of the laity, especially that of receiving the sacraments in their own chapels. Its first Conference authorized an issue of the *Collection,* with a significant supplement of hymns for sacraments and festivals.[32] A few years later a *Supplement* of 276 hymns was issued, which passed through several editions. In 1835 appeared the larger *Hymns for the use of the Methodist New Connexion. Principally from the Collection of the Rev. John Wesley, M.A.* In the preface the argument for Social Praise is traversed *de novo.* The *Collection* is regarded with discriminating admiration, and from it and the *Supplement of* 1831 the editors extracted "all that which, for poetic merit," spiritual fitness, "and for adaptation of metre to the existing taste for psalmody, was suited to the object which they had in view." This served till the demand for some of the newer hymns, led to the issue of *Hymns for Divine worship. Compiled for the use of the Methodist New Connexion* (London, 1863). For this the sources of Hymnody were widely examined, and its editor, the Rev. Henry Piggin, attempted not only to verify the text, but also to give the authorship and date, of each of its 1024 hymns. The Hymnody of the New Connexion was happily amalgamated with that of the Wesleyan Methodists by the official adoption of *The Methodist Hymn Book* of 1904, in whose preparation representatives of the Connexion had cooperated.

(2) THE PRIMITIVE METHODISTS stood for freedom in revival methods, and organized after the expulsion in 1808 of Hugh Bourne, caused by his persistence in holding camp meetings. In this innovation Bourne was much influenced by the reports brought over by Lorenzo Dow of the

[32] *A new History of Methodism,* vol. i, p. 501.

success of the camp meeting experiment in America.[33] In England as in America the camp meeting was felt to demand a new type of hymn, familiar in style, adapted to stirring melodies, and making use of the refrain or "chorus." Bourne had already printed in 1809 *A general Collection of Hymns and Spiritual Songs for camp-meetings, revivals, &c.,* in which he made much use of Dow's hymn book, and included his own characteristic "Camp Meetings with success are crown'd." The book became so popular that its sale often paid the expenses of conducting a mission on new ground;[34] and the rude heartiness of the singing did much to extend the new Church, giving rise to the expression, "You sing like a Primitive." [35]

The Annual Meeting in May, 1821, directed the preparation of a larger collection, "properly suited to the purposes of worship,"[36] which appeared the same year as *A Collection of Hymns, for camp meetings, revivals, &c., for the use of the Primitive Methodists. Edited by Hugh Bourne* (Bemersly near Tunstall). This collection of 154 Hymns, including many from the earlier book, came to be known as *The small Hymn Book,* and to be widely identified by its opening couplet:—

> "Christ he sits on Zion's hill,
> He receives poor Sinners still."

With the demand for more hymns, Bourne issued in 1825 *The large Hymn Book, for the use of the Primitive Methodists.* Of its 536 hymns, there are some twenty new hymns by Bourne, sixteen by William Sanders, a pastor who afterwards came to America, and 146 by "Hugh Bourne

[33]*History of the Primitive Methodists.* By Hugh Bourne, reprinted in Lorenzo Dow's Works. See ed. New York, 1854, vol. ii, p. 267. The American camp meeting and its Hymnody will be duly considered later in this chapter.

[34]*A new History of Methodism,* vol. i, p. 586: "Primitive Methodist Psalmody" in *The Choir,* No. 1, for Jan. 1910, p. 9.

[35]*The Choir, ut supra.*

[36]Preface of Aug. 10, 1821.

and Wm. Sanders, jointly." [37] Bourne was thus one of the founders of English "Camp-meeting Methodism" and for many years the ruling spirit of its Hymnody. He regarded the camp meeting as the development of Wesley's field preaching, and its songs as a needed supplement to Wesleyan Hymnody. It is altogether unlikely that Wesley would have approved the camp meeting, and it is quite certain that he would have said sharp things of the hymns of Dow and Bourne and Sanders.

With the growth of the denomination, some years after the superannuation of Bourne, the Conference put its Hymnody into the hands of John Flesher, Bourne's successor in the Book Room. He prepared, and published in 1854 *The Primitive Methodist Hymn Book. Partly compiled from the large and small Hymn books, prepared by the late Mr. Hugh Bourne, partly from hymns by numerous popular authors, . . . and enriched with original Hymns, and selected ones, altered or re-made.* It was loyally accepted, widely used (9th ed. 1861), and slightly revised in 1864. Flesher's sense of unfitness for the task, his dependence on his wife's scrap books, and his denial that "Providence had stereotyped the production of any poet," are naively set forth in the preface. His habitual mutilation of the texts of the hymns must have been a trial to some "Primitives," and brought some reproach upon the denomination. It is likely that more were annoyed by his omission of so many revival hymns; and this led to a new collection for camp meetings, edited by William Harland.[38]

But the denomination was growing into a great Christian community, and must have been gradually elevating its educational standards, for by its next step in Hymnody it passed, as by a bound, to the foremost place in the newer Methodist Church Song. Its new book, prepared by direc-

---

[37] For Sanders, and for such of these hymns as are retained in the standard *Hymnal* of 1887, see Dorricott and Collins, *Lyric Studies,* hereafter referred to.

[38] *The Choir,* for Jan. 1910, p. 9.

tion of the Conference of 1882, appeared in 1887 as *The Primitive Methodist Hymnal*. Of its 1052 hymns, 500 are Wesleyan: the remainder is a judicious winnowing of the whole body of Hymnody ancient and modern. Much editorial care was given to the texts of the hymns, and an annotated edition appeared as *Lyric Studies: a Hymnal Guide. By Revs. I. Dorricott and T. Collins* (London, n. d.). After twenty-five years, the Hymnody was further enriched by a carefully prepared *Supplement* of 295 hymns, especially aiming to make use of recent hymns.[39] This appeared in September, 1912, and was warmly welcomed by a Church that delights in being "modern." Doubtless some future winnowing will reduce the inconvenient bulk of 1347 authorized hymns.

(3) THE UNITED METHODIST FREE CHURCHES represent a succession of schisms, whose departures from Wesleyan Hymnody are less characteristic. "The Protestant Methodists" went out in 1827 on occasion of erecting an organ by the trustees of Brunswick Wesleyan Chapel, Leeds, in opposition to the majority of the members and the local preachers.[40] They stood against encroachment upon simplicity of worship, which Wesley so much feared, especially against instrumental music, the introduction of which Wesley hedged about with restrictions. Seventy local preachers and a thousand suspended or revolting members became the nucleus of Protestant Methodists. With this body united in 1834 the followers of Dr. Samuel Warren, father of the famous novelist, expelled during the controversy as to the formation of a theological training school. The two bodies united as the "Wesleyan Methodist Association," and adopted Wesley's *Collection,* with a small supplement of their own. Another Supplement[41] was prepared

[39]For an authoritative account of it, see *The British Weekly* for January 25, 1912.

[40]The controversy turned upon technical points. For particulars see A *new History of Methodism,* vol. i, pp. 425, 426, 514, 517.

[41]For an account of it, see G. J. Stevenson in Julian, *Dicty. of Hymnology,* p. 731.

in 1853 for a body of "Wesleyan Reformers," formed at the expulsion of Everett and Dunn[42] for contumacy.

When the Wesleyan Methodist Association and the Reformers united in 1857 as "The United Methodist Free Churches," they appointed James Everett and Matthew Baxter to prepare a new hymn book, which consisted in Wesley's *Collection,* with a Supplement (1861) of 250 hymns.[43] This served until the appearance in 1889 of *Methodist Free Church Hymns,* well prepared, but without special distinction. In 1907 the Methodist Free Churches joined with the Methodist New Connexion and the Bible Christians to form "The United Methodist Church." With the adoption by that body of *The Methodist Hymn Book* of 1904, the Hymnody of the Free Churches rejoined the main stream of Methodist Hymnody, from which it had never widely diverged.

(4) THE BIBLE CHRISTIANS grew out of the expulsion of William O'Bryan for unauthorized missionary work in Devon and Cornwall; and first organized as an independent congregation at Shebbaer in 1815. They were separated from the New Connexion principally for lack of facilities for intercourse; and their Hymnody is not much differentiated from that of the Wesleyan Methodists, from whom O'Bryan was no willing seceder. At the time of their first Conference in 1819, he prepared a denominational hymn book, known later as *A Collection of Hymns for the use of the People called Bible Christians.* It was enlarged in 1838, and again revised in 1862. It is little more than a rearrangement of Wesley's *Collection.* A new hymn book was ordered by the Conference of 1885, and appeared a few years later with a similar title. In 1907 The Bible Christians joined with the New Connexion and the Free Churches to form The United Methodist Church, using *The Methodist Hymn Book* of 1904.

⁴²Samuel Dunn, became a hymn writer, and his *Hymns for pastors and people,* were published by his brother (London, 1862).
⁴³*Ibid.*

The Primitive Methodists are thus left as the only great body of British Methodists who decline to unite in a common Hymnody. The Methodist Church of Australasia has also adopted the English *Hymn Book*. In Canada the various divisions of Methodism used Wesley's *Collection*, or the book in vogue in the same body at home. With the union of the Wesleyan Methodists and Methodist New Connexion in 1874, a new book appeared as *Methodist Hymn Book* (1880).[44] It aimed to preserve all the hymns of 1780 whose use had survived the century, and added some 300 more. At the great reunion of Canadian Methodism in 1883 the book was adopted by the United Church, and republished as *Methodist Hymn Book. Compiled and published by authority of the General Conference of the Methodist Church* (Toronto and Halifax, 1884). The preparation of a new hymn and tune book has been proceeding since 1910; but many still cherish the hope of a common Methodist Hymnal for use throughout the world.

VIII

THE HYMNODY OF AMERICAN METHODISM

1. Wesley's Effort to Control it (1784)

John Wesley's first hymn book had been printed in America in 1737, for his use as a Church of England missionary. As it happened the *Hymns and sacred Poems* of 1739 was reprinted by the Bradfords at Philadelphia in 1740.[45] Whitefield had brought it over, and was at work in Phila-

---

[44]"Music was provided in *Methodist Tune Book* (Toronto and Halifax, 1881). A belated edition of Wesley's *Collection* and Supplement "with accompanying tunes by eminent composers" had appeared in 1874 (Toronto: Methodist Book Room).

[45]*Hymns and sacred Poems. Published by John Wesley, M. A., Fellow of Lincoln College, Oxford; and Charles Wesley, M.A., Student of Christ Church, Oxford.* [Text] *Philadelphia: printed by Andrew and William Bradford, and sold for the benefit of the Poor in Georgia. MDCCXL.*

delphia, but did not reprint the book for use in his meetings, for which indeed it was poorly adapted. It was published by subscription; one of his devices to raise money for Georgia, where he was carrying forward the Wesleys' work.

By 1766 Embury in New York and Strawbridge in Maryland began to form Methodist societies. In their meetings copies of any of the English hymn publications of the Wesleys that were in the hands of Methodist immigrants were presumably made to serve for lining out the hymns. Three of these were reprinted by Melchior Steiner of Philadelphia in 1781, gathered into a single volume of 357 pages, in three parts:—*i. Hymns for those that seek and those that have redemption in the Blood of Jesus Christ* (pp. 4, 65); *ii. Hymns and Spiritual Songs, intended for the use of real Christians of all denominations* (pp. 4, 136); and *iii. A Collection of Psalms and Hymns. Published by John Wesley, M.A., Fellow of Lincoln College, Oxford; and Charles Wesley, M.A., Student of Christ Church, Oxford* (pp. 4, 144). The first of these parts was the hymn book then in general use in English congregations, and the second in class meetings; and in England also it was customary to bind the two together.[46] This reprint was probably for the use of St. George's Church, established in Philadelphia about 1770, and having the largest Methodist house of worship in America.[47]

From time to time Wesley had responded to the appeal of his American followers for more preachers. When at length he thought the time had come to organize them into a church, his provision ranged from his appointment of "Doctor Coke and Mr. Francis Asbury, to be joint Superintendents" to the smallest detail of their worship. He wished the Sunday worship in America as in England to be liturgical, and prepared a modification of *The Book of*

---

[46] See R. Green, *Bibliography*, 2nd ed., 1906, No. 165. In Steiner's reprint, parts ii & iii are so designated in the heading of each page.

[47] Jno. Lednum, *A History of the rise of Methodism in America*, Philadelphia, 1859, chap. v.

Common Prayer, printed at London, 1784, as *The Sunday Service of the Methodists in North America. With other occasional Services. London: printed in the year MDCCLXXXIV.*[48] Having then, as always, a great dread of the intrusion of doggerel or objectionable hymns into Methodist Song, he printed at the same time and for the same use *A Collection of Psalms and Hymns for the Lord's Day. Published by John Wesley, M.A., Late Fellow of Lincoln College, Oxford; and Charles Wesley, M.A., Late Student of Christ Church, Oxford. London: printed in the year MDCCLXXXIV.* It contained 118 numbers, selected from the *Psalms and Hymns* of 1741, one of the most useful hymn books at home. A supply of these two books in sheets he sent over by the hands of Coke and his companions, with a commendatory letter, dated from the wharf at "Bristol, Sept. 10, 1784" where they embarked; advising "all the travelling-preachers to use [the liturgy] on the Lord's day, in all their congregations, reading the litany only on Wednesdays and Fridays, and praying extempore on all other days."

Coke presented this letter, with the printed sheets, at a "General Conference" (the first) held at Baltimore in December, 1784. The Conference "agreed to form a Methodist Episcopal Church, *in which the Liturgy* (as presented by the Rev. John Wesley) *should be read,* and the .sacraments be administered by a superintendent, elders, and deacons, who shall be ordained by a presbytery, using the Episcopal form, as prescribed by the Rev. Mr. Wesley's prayer-book."[49] After the Conference Coke had Wesley's

---

[48]The history of this book is not altogether clear. It appears to have been prepared before deciding on Dr. Coke's mission, and some copies apparently preceded him to America. There were two differing issues of the first edition in 1784. (See sale catalogue of Bishop John F. Hurst's library, items 2403, 2404.) For later editions, see Green's *Bibliography,* appendix to 2nd ed., p. viii.

[49]Whatcoat's notes (the italics are his), quoted in Abel Stevens, *History of the Methodist Episcopal Church in the U. S. A.,* New York, n. d., vol. ii, pp. 183, 184.

letter printed at Philadelphia, as also *Minutes of several conversations between the Rev. Thomas Coke, LL.D., the Rev. Francis Asbury and others, at a Conference begun in Baltimore, in the State of Maryland, on Monday, the 27th of December, in the year 1784. Composing a Form of Discipline for the Ministers, Preachers and other members of the Methodist Episcopal Church in America* (Philadelphia, Chas. Cist, 1785). He then had the whole collection bound up into one volume as the credentials, the Liturgy,• the Discipline and the Hymn Book of the new Church.

Wesley's act in preparing a liturgical constitution for American Methodism, and choosing their psalms and hymns, was quite characteristic, and its ratification by the Conference a matter of course. The American bishops presumably did their best to carry out Wesley's wishes. Authority was given to "our Helpers to read the Morning and Evening Service out of our Liturgy on the Lord's Day," and the Preachers were directed to "sing no hymns of [their] own composing." [50] Such a prohibition seems strange enough, in view of the habits of the Wesleys themselves, to say nothing of Watts and Doddridge. No doubt it was based on Wesley's own observation of revival scenes, and aimed to suppress the doggerel verses given out spontaneously under the excitements of emotional preaching and caught up by the responsive crowd.

A second edition of the prayer book with the *Psalms and Hymns* appeared at London in 1786. In the preface to *A Pocket Hymn Book* of 1790, Bishops Coke and Asbury promised a third edition with "a complete version of the Psalms, selected from the best divine Poets that have written." No such edition is known, and the promise disappeared from later issues of the preface. There was, however, a "fourth edition" (London, 1790) in which prayers for "George, Thy servant, our King and Governor," "and especially Thy servants the Rulers of these United States"

[50]*Minutes of several Conversations*, 1785: Questions 34, 55.

are strangely commingled.[51] This edition also contained the *Psalms and Hymns.*

For a few years *The Sunday Service* with its hymn book was used in the principal congregations,[52] but even there gradually allowed to disappear, with the gowns and bands of the preachers and other refinements dear to Wesley's heart. In John Street Chapel, New York, the plan adopted seems to have been that of so preoccupying the time of worship with Sunday love-feasts and other exercises that no opportunity remained for reading *The Sunday Service.* In many places the book was never introduced,[53] and was indeed too large and expensive to meet the conditions of the time. In the *Discipline* of 1792, there is for the first time no mention of *The Sunday Service.*[54] It had been shelved by common consent.

In fact the Church that was developing on the field in America was a different one from that laid out on paper in England. In his liturgical arrangements Wesley had ignored the fact that liturgical worship did not accord with the taste or habits of the class of people who had embraced Methodism in America. The people were ignorant, the preachers itinerant, the meetings as often as not in the cabins or in the fields, and the singing largely without books, other than the one in the preacher's hand. The tunes must be very familiar or very contagious, the words given out one or two lines at a time if not already known. Under these conditions the development of free ways in worship and of a rude type of popular song, indifferent to anything in the way of an authorized Hymnody, seems to have been inevitable.

[51]Also a "fourth edition" of 1792 with the American allusions omitted.
[52]Stevens, *op. cit.,* vol. ii, p. 198.
[53]*Ibid.*
[54] " "The Sunday Service' appears never to have been popular in the American Societies, and was laid aside the instant they were free from the direct supervision of Mr. Wesley." D. Sherman, *History of the Revision of the Discipline,* New York, 1874, p. 25.

2. The Struggle Between "Mr. Wesley's Hymns" and Popular Songs (1784-1848)

There was much in these conditions that would have appealed to Wesley's heart. But if he had been on the field he would have insisted on the intrusion of educational standards into the revival methods being pursued, and he would have checked at the fountain head, as even in his absence he tried to do, the development of an illiterate and often vulgar Revival Hymnody. Most of all he would have distinguished between the freer method of field work and the established sanctities of God's house.

In his absence the bishops had to deal with a considerable spirit of "American independence," and much unregulated enthusiasm. American Methodism became the fullest embodiment of a condition obtaining in several denominations, viz., that the popular religious songs do not necessarily agree with the authorized Church Song. This no doubt was an incident of the choice of the revival method of church growth. It is of the very nature of revival enthusiasm to develop its own song, and of all religious agencies it is the least amenable to church authority. The entire course of Methodist Episcopal Hymnody may be viewed as a continuous effort to keep the Church on a level sufficiently described as Wesleyan, and a failure to cooperate therein on the part of a considerable section of the people who preferred the plane of the Revival Hymn and the popular Spiritual Song.

That such was the situation from the very first appears from the *Minutes* of a Conference begun in Virginia and ended at Baltimore in April and May of 1784.[55] The 14th query was, "How shall we reform our singing?" and the answer: "Let all our preachers who have any knowledge in the notes, improve it by learning to sing true themselves, and keeping close to Mr. Wesley's tunes and hymns."

[55]*Minutes of the Methodist Conferences annually held in America, from 1773 to 1794, inclusive,* Philadelphia, 1795, p. 71.

We are now at the point where the *Psalms and Hymns* attached to *The Sunday Service* becomes the first authorized hymn book of American Methodism, and is proving unpopular. This suggests the inquiry, What other hymn books had been in use before its organization and were still available? Our only information is supplied by the bishops' preface of 1790, already referred to:—

"The Hymn-Books which have been already published among us are truly excellent. The select Hymns, the double collection of Hymns and Psalms (the latter of which may be supplied by a complete version of the Psalms, selected from the best divine Poets that have written, which we promise to publish with a third and more complete edition of our Prayer-Book) and the Redemption-Hymns, display great spirituality as well as purity of diction. The large Congregational Hymn-Book is admirable indeed, but is too expensive for the poor, who have little time and less money. The Pocket Hymn-Book lately sent abroad in these States, is a most valuable performance for those who are deeply spiritual, but is better suited to the European Methodists, among whom all the before-mentioned books have been thoroughly circulated for many years."

This list is somewhat puzzling. A recent historian of Methodism[56] has assumed that the opening reference to the books "already published among us" implies "us American Methodists"; adding that "these native reprints have utterly perished." Without insisting that both writers of the preface were Englishmen, it must be said to be very improbable that so many "reprints," one of them "large" and "expensive," should have appeared and disappeared without leaving a trace. The "select Hymns" is probably Wesley's *Select Hymns:* [133] *with Tunes* [102] *annext* of 1761, and which (with or without the tunes) reached a tenth edition in 1787. Possibly its tunes are those referred to at the Baltimore Conference. "The double collection of Hymns and Psalms" is presumably the collection of 1741 in two parts, or its abridgment attached to *The Sunday Service;* an enlargement of the Psalms being promised in connection with a new revision of the *Service.* "The

[56]Prof. J. A. Faulkner in *A new History of Methodism,* London, 1909, vol. ii, p. 142.

Redemption Hymns" may refer to either the English edition or Steiner's reprint, or to both. "The large Congregational Hymn-Book" was surely the standard *Collection* of 1780; a book so important that some copies must have been in the hands of American ministers.

The disparaged "Pocket Hymn Book" is more doubtful. We know three books of that name then extant:—(i) The (York) *Pocket Hymn Book* of Robert Spence, the book-seller (1781 and later), unauthorized and disapproved of by Wesley for some "objectionable" Hymns. (ii) *A Pocket Hymn Book for the use of Christians of all denominations* (London, 1785); Wesley's unsuccessful protest against Spence. (iii) Wesley's book, with the same title, of 1787; really an adaptation of Spence's.

There had been apparently a reprint of Spence's book at New York as early as 1786.[57] Two years later appeared *A Pocket Hymn Book: designed as a constant Companion for the pious. Collected from various authors. Ninth Edition.*[58] *Philadelphia: printed by Joseph James, Chesnut-street. M. DCC. LXXXVIII.* This was Spence's book, with "Part II," of 27 hymns, added, probably by Bishop Coke.[59] In 1790 appeared the "tenth" and "eleventh" editions, with the same title, printed at Philadelphia for John Dickins, the Book Steward, and containing the bishops' preface now under discussion.[60] It is a reprint of

[57]Our only knowledge is from the item "Pocket Hymn Book, designed as a Constant Companion of the Pious (Wesley's). New York, 1786," in *A Catalogue of the Liturgies . . . in the Stinnecke Maryland Episcopal Library. Privately printed, 1881.* The book itself cannot at present be found.

[58]This does not mean that eight previous editions had been printed *in this country*, as is assumed in the Report of the Committee to the Bishops on *The Revision of the Hymn Book of the Methodist Episcopal Church*, New York, 1878, p. 5.

[59]In choosing, for reprinting, a book Wesley did not like, Coke was no doubt led by considerations of its handy size and suitableness, but it may be noted that Spence was his intimate friend.

[60]There appeared also a "ninth edition," with the same title and contents, and without the bishops' preface of 1790, at *Baltimore: printed for Rice and Co., Market-Street, 1791.*

the 1788 book, with the hymns of "Part II" numbered consecutively, and with new hymns (258-285) here added by the bishops. Their preface (already quoted in part) announces it as "a choice and complete Pocket Hymn Book," of which they intend "to strike off an impression of twenty or thirty thousand copies," to stop "the general cry of our congregations 'that they cannot procure Hymn-Books.' " "It has received the Approbation of the Conferences, and contains many valuable Hymns which the former Editions did not." As of the former editions so of this, the profits are to be applied to charitable uses. And all respecting the authority of bishops and Conference are urged to purchase no hymn books but those signed by the two bishops.

There is evidently something interesting here, if only we knew what it was. Were the bishops annoyed by surreptitious editions published for private gain (and yet the congregations "cannot procure Hymn-Books")? And what was the disparaged "Pocket Hymn-Book lately sent abroad in these States"? Was it a reprint of Spence's, but without the bishops' appendix? Or had Wesley sent over a supply of his *Pocket Hymn Book* of 1785, unwelcomed at home?

We cannot say. A link has dropped out of the early history of American Methodist Hymnody. The certain thing is that the bishops made up their minds during Wesley's life that the book of Spence which Wesley disliked so much was better adapted to American conditions than any of his own, and took steps to furnish the congregations with an ample supply. They may have argued that a hymn book for the pocket did not interfere with the Sunday *Psalms and Hymns* any more than the permitted extempore prayers during the week interfered with *The Sunday Service.* In fact the extempore prayers and the *Pocket Hymn Book* superseded *The Sunday Service* and its hymn book. The *Pocket Hymn Book,* and not the *Psalms and Hymns* of 1784, or even the famous *Collection* of 1780, is the nucleus of the Hymnody of American Methodism. In the eighteenth edition of 1793 the hymns are increased to 300; and these constituted the authorized Hymnody till the beginning of the XIXth century. It was prevailingly but not exclusively Wesleyan. David Creamer classified its hymns as 223 by Charles and 15 by John Wesley, 26 by Watts; the remainder by Hart, Cowper, Medley and others.[61]

Ezekiel Cooper became book steward in 1800, with authority to publish approved books. The *Pocket Hymn Book* had never been copyrighted and was being reprinted by outside parties. It was perhaps the suggestion of that thrifty man to revise the book and secure its copyright. The revision appeared as *The Methodist Pocket Hymn Book, revised and improved: designed as a constant Companion for the pious of all denominations. Collected from various authors. Philadelphia: printed by Ezekiel Cooper, No. 118 North Fourth Street, near the Methodist Church. 1802.* Opportunity was taken to drop a few, and add a few other hymns, to rearrange the contents, and to smooth some halting lines of the text. The real motive of the revision appears in the notice that "the copy-right is secured." It contained 320 hymns. To meet the demand of a growing Church for more hymns, Daniel Hitt, assistant to Cooper's successor, and Bishop Asbury,[62] laid before the Conference of 1808, the manuscript of a Supplement. This was accepted and appeared as *A Selection of Hymns from various authors, designed as a Supplement to the Methodist Pocket Hymn Book, compiled under the direction of Bishop Asbury and published by order of the General Conference. First edition. New York: published by John Wilson and Daniel Hitt, for the Methodist Connection in the United States. John C. Totten, printer, 1808.* It was published separately for those who had the earlier book. Bound up

[61]See *A new History of Methodism,* vol. ii, p. 143.
[62]See extracts from Asbury's Journal in Carl F. Price, *The Music and Hymnody of the Methodist Hymnal,* N. Y. [1911], p. 20.

with it, the whole became known as "The Double Hymn Book"; an inconvenient arrangement that perhaps explains its short life.

There had never yet been an American edition of the *Collection* of 1780, which Wesley had prepared as a common hymnal for Methodism. In 1814 a cheap reprint appeared at Baltimore as *A Collection of Hymns, for the use of the People called Methodists; in miniature. By the Rev. John Wesley, A.M. First American, from the eighteenth London, edition* (Baltimore: the Diamond Press, 1814). To many American Methodists this brought their first knowledge, and to most their first sight, of what the Wesleyan Hymnody was in its fulness and purity; and in the minds of the curious must have raised many questions both as to the omissions of their own book and its garbled texts.

At all events the Book Agents, with the assistance of the Book Committee,[63] prepared and, by authority of the Conference of 1820, published *A Collection of Hymns for the use of the Methodist Episcopal Church, principally from the Collection of the Rev. John Wesley, M.A., late Fellow of Lincoln College, Oxford. New York: published by N. Bangs and T. Mason for the Methodist Episcopal Church. Abraham Paul, printer, 1821.* This change of title in the authorized hymn book was well adapted to create an impression that the Church had at last changed the basis of its Hymnody, forsaking Spence, and restoring Wesley. But the preface made no such claim, professing nothing more than a revision of "The Double Hymn Book"; omitting some [fifty] of its hymns, adding a few from Wesley's *Collection,* and restoring some injudiciously tinkered texts. To facilitate the use of this book, and to provide for the first time something like an authorized body of tunes, the Book Concern issued *The Methodist Harmonist* (New York, 1821: rev. ed., by order of Conference, 1833). The hymn book itself was slightly revised in 1832, and a sup-

---

[63]Dr. Floy in *The Methodist Quarterly Review,* April, 1844, p. 170.

plement was added by Nathan Bangs in 1836; and so continued in use till 1849.[64]

3. A NEW TYPE: THE CAMP MEETING HYMN (1800)

Having followed so far the authorized Methodist Hymnody, we have now to consider a marked development of its freer side in connection with the Great Revival of 1800. The Revival was not distinctively a Methodist movement, but began in Logan County, Kentucky, under the preaching of a Presbyterian Boanerges, the Rev. James McGready. The unique feature of the Revival was the camp meeting. The first one was held near the Gaspar River Church in July, 1800. The people far and wide had been notified by Mr. McGready to come prepared to encamp on the ground; and a great concourse formed a regular encampment of tents or covered wagons in the form of a hollow square, with a preaching-stand and rows of logs for seats in the centre.[65] The camp meeting idea was received with immense favor, and "spread like wild-fire" through Kentucky, into the Cumberland settlements of what is now Tennessee, into the Northwestern Territory and through the Carolinas.[66]

The Presbyterian clergy of the Kentucky settlements participating in this revival were not more than five,[67] the general body standing aloof. The assistance of the Methodists was thus the more welcome; and once admitted as assistants they soon became leaders, and gained the preponderating influence. This was natural enough in view of their emotional enthusiasm and familiarity with revival methods. But in the judgment of a Presbyterian historian

[64]For a critical examination of the whole contents, see an article [by Dr. J. Floy] in *The Methodist Quarterly Review*, April, 1844, pp. 165-206. All of its hymns are annotated in D. Creamer, *Methodist Hymnology*, New York, 1848.

[65]Robert Davidson, *History of the Presbyterian Church in the State of Kentucky*, New York, 1847, p. 134.

[66]*Ibid.*, pp. 135, 136.

[67]*Ibid.*, p. 135.

of the Revival the Methodist predominance was gained largely by means of their hymns and hearty hymn-singing :—

"They succeeded in introducing their own stirring hymns, familiarly, though incorrectly, entitled 'Wesley's Hymns'; and as books were scarce, the few that were attainable were cut up, and the leaves distributed, so that all in turn might learn them by heart. . . . This will be acknowledged to have been of itself a potent engine to give predominance to the Methodists, and to disseminate their peculiar sentiments." [68]

The book thus referred to was presumably *The Pocket Hymn Book,* of which the "23rd edition" had just appeared,[69] and the hymns those long familiar in Methodist use. But with the tumultuous enthusiasm that soon developed, the old hymns were felt to be too sober to express the overwrought feelings of the preacher and the throng. Spontaneous song became a marked characteristic of the camp meetings. Rough and irregular couplets or stanzas were concocted out of Scripture phrases and every-day speech, with liberal interspersing of Hallelujahs and refrains. Such ejaculatory hymns were frequently started by· an excited auditor during the preaching, and taken up by the throng, until the meeting dissolved into a "singing-ecstasy" culminating in a general hand-shaking. Sometimes they were given forth by a preacher, who had a sense of rhythm, under the excitement of his preaching and the agitation of his audience. Hymns were also composed more deliberately out of meeting, and taught to the people or lined out from the pulpit.

Many of these rude songs perished in the using, some were written down, passing from hand to hand. The camp meeting song books which began to appear in the first decade of the XIXth century doubtless contain such of these as proved effective and popular. The song books represent also a second stage of Camp Meeting Hymnody, the development of a special class of song writers making

[68]*Ibid.,* p. 141.
[69]Philadelphia: H. Tuckness, 1800.

more effort to conform to the rules of rhetoric and versification and with more claim to permanent use.

A distinctive type is thus established, the Camp Meeting Hymn. It is individualistic, and deals with the rescue of a sinner: sometimes in direct appeal to "sinners," "backsliders," or "mourners"; sometimes by reciting the terms of salvation; sometimes as a narrative of personal experience for his warning or encouragement. The Camp Meeting Hymn is not churchly, but the companionships of the rough journey to the camp reappear in songs of a common pilgrimage to Canaan, the meetings and partings on the ground typify the reunion of believers in Heaven, and the military suggestions of the encampment furnish many themes for songs of a militant host, brothers in arms in the battle of the Lord. In Kentucky the martial spirit of the Revolution had been kept alive and developed by Indian wars as nowhere else in the Union;[70] and the military ideal pervades many of these early songs. A longing for the heavenly rest and a vivid portrayal of the pains of hell were both characteristic; and a very special group of hymns was designed for the instruction and encouragement of the "seekers," who at the close of the sermon came forward to the stand or "altar," and occupied the "anxious bench."

The literary form of the Camp Meeting Hymn is that of the popular ballad or song, in plainest every-day language and of careless or incapable technique. The refrain or chorus is perhaps the predominant feature, not always connected with the subject-matter of the stanza, but rather ejaculatory. In some instances such a refrain was merely tacked on to a familiar hymn or an arrangement of one. In its purely emotional aim the Camp Meeting Hymn is not perhaps singular, but the crudity of its methods and effects sometimes makes it very harrowing to refined feelings and seemingly destructive of reverence.

Of the tunes to which the Camp Meeting Hymns were

[70]*Cf.* B. St. James Fry in *The Methodist Quarterly Review,* July, 1859, p. 408.

sung the leaders demanded nothing more than contagious-
ness and effectiveness. Their attitude was expressed in the
query attributed to Wesley,—"Why should the devil have
all the good tunes?" and was embodied in a favorite hymn
called "Wesley's music." [71] Their resources were what
might be expected of men in a situation almost apart from
books: words were adapted to the popular melodies then
current and to remembered songs, or to tunes that had
been used on circuit; and simple melodies were composed
on the spot. These latter were not written down in the
camps or printed in the song books, but through all the
XIXth century the "Social Hymn Books" of various
churches contained tunes, still familiar, whose origin was
more or less correctly ascribed to the "Western Revival."
It is likely also that the negro "spirituals" embody many
reminiscences of the revival melodies of the South.

The camp meeting became and for many years continued to be the distinctive method of Methodist evangelization and church growth in practically all parts of the
country.[72] Many of the song books of the earlier years
have doubtless perished. *Hymns and Spiritual Songs for
the use of Christians: including a number never before
published* was first printed at Philadelphia in 1803 by John
W. Scott (a Presbyterian), and reached a ninth edition by
1812. It was plainly inspired by the Revival, and contains many songs of the sort sung in camps. *Wiatt's im-
partial Selection of Hymns and Spiritual Songs* (Philadelphia: Solomon Wiatt, 1809), with its "Methodists'
Song" and "Shouting Song" was militantly Methodist, and

[71] It began:—

> "Enlisted in the cause of sin,
> Why should a good be evil?
> Music, alas! too long has been,
> Press'd to obey the Devil."

No. cxxxvi in a collection of *Hymns and Spiritual Songs* without title-
page, but bought "the 25 of Sept., 1813."

[72] *Cf.* Stevens, *op. cit.*, vol. iv, pp. 238, 427, 432.

of the proselyting type, as its "The Beauties of Predestination" and "Against the Calvinian Doctrine" sufficiently attest. It contains however but one hymn marked "For a Camp Meeting."

Probably the Hymnody of the Kentucky Revival, so far as preserved, and certainly the hymns most used through immediately following years in Methodist camp meetings throughout the Kentucky and Tennessee circuits, appear in *The Pilgrim Songster; or a choice Collection of Spiritual Songs: with many songs never before in print. By Thomas S. Hinde.* It was published in 1810 and reached a third edition in 1828 (at Cincinnati), and appears to have been printed surreptitiously at Baltimore and Philadelphia. Of its 120 hymns, the authorship of nearly one half was even then unknown to the compiler: but nearly a third of the whole number were written by two members of the Western Conference, John A. Granade and Caleb Jarvis Taylor.[73] These never found their way into the authorized books, but were widely known and loved through the Western settlements.[74]

The Camp Meeting Hymn appears as a recognized type as early as 1811 and as far East as Poughkeepsie in *Hymns on select passages of Scripture: with others usually sung at Camp-meetings, &c.* Of this there was also a Chambersburg imprint of the same year. And very soon the making of song books for use in camp meetings begins to assume the proportions of what looks like an industry.

John J. Harrod's *Social and Camp-Meeting Songs for the pious*[75] appeared at Baltimore in 1817, was a favorite in the South, and reached a fourth edition in 1822. *Songs*

[73]For the book, its hymns and its associations, see the paper by B. St. J. Fry, already referred to.

[74]*Cf.* Stevens, *History of M. E. Church*, vol. iv, p. 116.

[75] "For the pious." This unpleasant phrase was Spence's (see *ante*) and had just figured in the title of a Philadelphia book, *A choice Collection of Hymns and Spiritual Songs. Designed for the use of the pious* (Jonathan Pounder, 1814). The book was not revivalistic, and to it the Presbyterian, E. S. Ely, contributed.

of Zion. Being a Collection of Hymns, for the use of Christians. By a preacher of the Gospel of Christ Jesus (Haverhill, 1818) represents the New Light movement[76] which had an almost simultaneous origin among the Methodists in North Carolina under James O'Kelley, the Baptists of New England under Abner Jones and Elias Smith, and the Presbyterians in the Kentucky Revival under Barton W. Stone.[77] The three parties had united in 1806 as "Christians," and Elias Smith had made for them *A Collection of Hymns, for the use of Christians,* which reached a fourth edition at Portland, Maine, in 1811. Both books are of the camp meeting type and on the camp meeting level, though actually used in field meetings, halls and churches, rather than camps.

The Camp-Meeting Chorister . . . for the pious of all denominations (Philadelphia: J. Clarke, 1827) was plainly a publisher's enterprise, but was well received, and after passing through three printings was enlarged in 1830. Immensely popular was *The Zion Songster* of Peter D. Myers, printed at New York in 1829 and reaching a ninety-fifth edition in 1854. It was a gathering of the songs "generally sung at camp and prayer meetings and in revivals."

The fiery anti-slavery agitator, Orange Scott, printed at Brookfield, 1830, *A new and improved Camp Meeting Hymn Book.* It was intended for New England use, and "suits the Compiler better than any he has ever seen." Also for New England use was *A choice Selection of Hymns and Spiritual Songs, designed to aid in the devotions of prayer, conference, and camp-meetings* (Windsor, Vt., 1836). With these we may group a still later New England book, M. L. Scudder's *Songs of Canaan,* which in the second edition of

[76] "I know not any sect nor part,
But such as are New-Lights in heart." From Hymn 7.

[77] For the movement itself see Stevens, *op. cit.,* vol. iii, pp. 30 ff; *The Life, conversion, etc., of Elias Smith. Written by himself, vol. i,* Portsmouth, N. H., 1816; and Davidson, *op. cit.,* chap. viii, "*The New Light Schism.*"

1842 became *The Wesleyan Psalmist*. It was distinguished by printing the melodies, familiar or new.

Harrod had claimed inclusiveness for his later book, *The new and most complete Collection of camp, social and prayer meeting Hymns* (Baltimore, 1830), with 276 hymns and the "usual choruses." But no less than 478 were included in the next Baltimore book, *Pious Songs. Social, prayer, closet and camp meeting Hymns, and choruses.* (2nd ed., Baltimore, 1836). *The Sweet Singer of Israel* (Pittsburgh, 1837), edited by Alfred Brunson and Charles Pitman, was probably for the Ohio market, where James Quinn had himself "superintended one hundred and thirty or forty camp-meetings." [78]

The camp meeting was not exclusively Methodist. The title of "General Camp Meeting," applied from the first in Kentucky, indicated Presbyterian and Baptist' cooperation. But camp meetings hardly became distinctive of Baptist revivalism, and among Presbyterians were generally regarded as alien and undesirable. The Cumberland Presbytery was accused of irregularities in ordaining preachers to meet the demand of the Kentucky Revival and was dissolved by the Synod of Kentucky. Its "Revival members" organized at first as an independent "Council," then as a new Cumberland Presbytery, and with their followers established "The Cumberland Presbyterian Church" in February, 1810. The new Church may be said to have been born at a camp meeting, and amid such surroundings it continued to feel preeminently at home for some forty years. It was singular, perhaps unique, in that for all but five of these years it had no authorized Hymnody.[79] Methodist, Baptist and other hymn books were in its pulpits, and from them the hymns were lined out. But of these the current camp meeting song books were the favorites, and the Spiritual Song

[78]Stevens, *op. cit.*, vol. iv, p. 349.
[79]*Cf.* B. W. McDonnold, *History of The Cumberland Presbyterian Church*, 4th ed., Nashville, 1899, p. 315.

rather than the Hymn was for many years the standard of its Praise.

The camp meeting was originally justified by the scattered settlements of a new country and its lack of meeting houses. From the beginning it revealed elements of danger, and carried the seeds of inevitable dissolution in the intense excitement under which it was carried on and its wide production of hysteria and other nervous complaints.[80] Among the Cumberland Presbyterians the camp meeting "died a lingering death" in the decade from 1840 to 1850.[81] Among Methodists it stayed longer, though the later Methodist song books are less characteristically "for the camp," and less addicted to the Camp Meeting type of Hymn. As the camp meeting was displaced by the more decorous protracted services of the modern summer settlement, so the Camp Meeting Hymn gave way to the modern type of Spiritual Song associated with the names of Moody and Sankey. For under any circumstances the love of "popular" song abides. The same streak in human nature that delights in the strains of the music hall demands the "spiritual song" of a kindred type. And possibly an element that conscientiously flees the associations of the music hall is the most insistent upon a compensatory light music in the Sunday school and the church.

4. EFFORTS TO REINSTATE AND TO MODERNIZE THE WESLEYAN HYMNODY (1847-1905)

We return to the authorized Methodist Hymnody at a time of discontent with the continued use of the *Collection* of 1821 and its Supplement, and of agitation for a more convenient and adequate hymn book. In the midst of which the Southern conferences separated from the main body on the graver issue of slavery, and in May, 1846, held

---

[80]The "Jerks" "became epidemic from Michigan to Louisiana," Stevens, vol. iv, p. 432.
[81]McDonnold, pp. 370, 371.

the first General Conference of "The Methodist Episcopal Church, South." That body found time, even in the stress of reconstruction, to debate the usefulness of "particular meter hymns" before deciding to appoint a commission to prepare a revised hymn book of its own.[82] It appeared at Nashville in 1847 as *A Collection of Hymns for public, social and domestic worship,* containing 1047 hymns; some 600 of them by the Wesleys and 150 by Dr. Watts.[83] Four years later its principal compiler, Thomas O. Summers, also a hymn writer, put forth through the Book Agency *Songs of Zion: a Supplement to the Hymn Book of the Methodist Episcopal Church, South.* Its 503 hymns are mainly those for which he could not find room in the authorized book, but he consented to admit some "doggerel Hymns" in hope of winning over those persisting in introducing camp meeting song books. The *Supplement* was evidently intended to rank with the "Social Hymn Books" of the North, and after twenty-two years' use, was slightly enlarged (1873).

In May, 1848, the Northern Church also appointed a committee of revision, whose book appeared as *Hymns for the use of the Methodist Episcopal Church. Revised edition* (New York: Lane and Scott, 1849). The revision was largely inspired by Dr. James Floy and, owing to his zeal and care, it gave American Methodism the fullest and most correct presentation of the Wesleyan Poetry it has ever had. For the intensely practical mind of American Methodism had from the first discriminated in its use of the

[82]There is a sufficient account of its proceedings in Carl F. Price, *The Music and Hymnody of The Methodist Hymnal,* New York and Cincinnati, n. d. [1911], pp. 23, 24.

[83]For a detailed review, see "The New Hymn Book" in *The Quarterly Review of the M. E. Church, South* for January, 1848, pp. 69-131. As illustrating the state of hymnological knowledge of the time, we note that of its "anonymous hymns," the reviewer states that "Rock of Ages" has, by Richard Watson and others been confidently claimed for C. Wesley; by others, however, . . . as confidently claimed for Toplady." After carefully weighing the evidence he finds it "impossible to determine . . . which of them is the author" (p. 128).

Wesleys' hymns, and had taken no steps to make the body of the Wesleyan Poetry familiar or even accessible to its people.

The *Hymns* of 1849 was to remain the authorized book for thirty years, and was several times set to music.[84] But it had hardly appeared before complaints began that it served better as a collection of devotional poetry than as a congregational hymn book. The church hymn book became less than ever a bond of unity and means of uniformity in worship, and served many dissatisfied pastors and ambitious compilers as a point of departure.

Their private ventures came from the press in considerable number. Differing in purpose and quality as they did, the Social Hymn Book type may be said to have modified and then succeeded the Camp Meeting Song Book type. Intended for prayer and conference meeting, the Social Hymn Book sought a mean between "the stern and elevated literary taste" of the church hymn books and "the light and irreverent style of singing" of the song books, "tending to dissipate rather than inspire true devotion." "Every Church needs a social hymn book," said Stephen Parks in the preface (from which we have just quoted) of his *Methodist Social Hymn Book* (New York: Carlton and Porter, 1856); to which debatable proposition most denominations would at that time have assented. McDonald and Hubbard's *The Wesleyan Sacred Harp* (Boston, 1855) offered pleasing melodies for social worship, and made large use of the authorized *Hymns*. *The Chorus* of A. S. Jenks and D.

---

[84]*Hymns for the use of the Methodist Episcopal Church. With tunes for congregational worship.* [ed. by Sylvester Main and William C. Brown.] New York: Carlton and Porter [1857].

The Heart and Voice; ... Hymn and Tune Book, designed for congregational singing in the Methodist Episcopal Church, and for congregations generally. [Ed. by A. S. Jenks.] Philadelphia: Perkinpine and Higgins [1865].

New Hymn and Tune Book: an offering of praise for the Methodist Episcopal Church. Edited by Philip Phillips. N. Y.: Carlton and Lanahan [1866].

Gilkey (Philadelphia: 4th ed., 1858) aimed to perpetuate in the class room and prayer meeting the most illiterate and vulgar type of camp meeting chorus and song. H. Mattison's *Sacred Melodies for social worship* (New York, 1859) applied the same aim to the better class of songs, and is still interesting for its hitherto unprinted camp meeting and popular melodies, "written out from the lips of those who knew them," and as actually sung.

The active career of Philip Phillips, "the Singing Pilgrim," lay largely within the period of thirty years now under review. His songs ministered to and increased the appetite for popular religious song, and his very numerous publications serve to mark the transition from the Social Hymn Book type to the modern "Gospel Hymns" type arising with the development of an order of singing evangelists. The new books were introduced into Methodist gatherings and Sunday schools and then boldly into the church services. In many quarters such books as *Devotional Melodies, The Zion Songster, Winnowed Hymns, Hallowed Songs,* and *Chautauqua Carols* rivalled or even displaced the authorized hymn book. In 1879, the *Methodist Quarterly* declared:—

"Lyrically, or hymnically, the Methodist Episcopal Church is demoralized to an extent that would call down the heartiest denunciations of John Wesley, and of St. Paul too, could they enter upon a fresh tour of episcopal supervision. Denominational purity, uniformity, efficiency, and progress, all unite in imperative demand for a revised Hymnal." [85]

The reviewer was pleading for a revision already accomplished and awaiting approval. It had been pressed upon a reluctant General Conference (vainly in 1872, successfully in 1876) by those of the leaders who felt that the authorized Hymnody was suffering because it had been allowed to fall behind the times. A great body of modern hymns

[85]Dr. R. Wheatley, "The revised Methodist Hymnal," in *The Methodist Quarterly Review,* July, 1879, p. 525. The above list of fugitive song books, which might be much enlarged, is confined to those mentioned by the reviewer as then in especial vogue.

had grown up, even a new (Anglican) school of church music, both occupying new ground. The Baptists, Congregationalists, Presbyterians and Episcopalians, had already taken possession of the new ground, and it behooved the Methodists to follow, even to the casting aside of so much of their familiar and characteristic Hymnody as had now lost its appeal.[86] Such counsels prevailing in 1876, the project was put in the hands of a representative committee of fifteen, who worked in geographical sections, and finally presented to the Board of Bishops a new book with tunes, appearing as *Hymnal of the Methodist Episcopal Church* (New York and Cincinnati, 1878).

The problem of adding a new Hymnody to an old already too large was great. 381 numbers of the old book were dropped; but even so 767 remained, to which were added 371 new hymns, making a total of 1138.[87] The size of the new book followed the bad fashion of the time;[88] but the collection was bound to suffer for it, since so great a bulk transcends the limited sphere of the affections and appalls the memory. Much of this material served no good end. The musical settings under the authority of the committee were of very mixed character and not always in the best interests of Congregational Song. But on the whole the new *Hymnal* was fairly abreast with the denominational hymnals of the time and was like them in being less distinctively denominational than of old and more catholic-hearted.[89]

In the Church at the South, the desire for a small hymn book for poorer churches and social meetings was met by the publication of *The new Hymn Book* (Nashville; So.

[86]*Cf.* Report of Committee on Revision to the Bishops, New York, 1878, pp. 6, 8, 14.

[87]Report, p. 22.

[88]*Songs for the Sanctuary* had 1342 hymns.

[89]The contents of the *Hymnal* may be studied in the carefully annotated edition of Dr. Charles S. Nutter, *Hymn Studies,* New York, 1884; 2nd ed. 1888; 3rd ed., 1897. Its appended "History of official hymn books" omits the first.

Meth. Publ. House, 1881), prepared under authority of the Conference of 1878. It was little more than selections from the larger hymn book, with the addition of some "spiritual songs." The new book was inadequate for all church occasions, but the feeling still remained that the Church book was too large. It should be cleared of useless material to an extent permitting selections from the later Hymnody. The Conference of 1886 authorized a new hymnal upon these lines; the whole number of hymns not to exceed 800. The book appeared as *Hymn Book of the Methodist Episcopal Church, South* (Nashville, 1889); and also set to music as *Hymn and Tune Book*. The preface is perhaps more Wesleyan than the book as a whole; the hymns ascribed to Charles Wesley numbering 294 out of a total of 918. The collection, if more than ample, was a good one for its time and constituency.[90]

We have now come to a period of change so rapid that by the beginning of the XXth century even so recently made hymn books as those of the Methodists began to wear an old-fashioned look. It was no doubt a consciousness of change in feeling and in the emphasis of Methodist faith, together with a new desire to magnify the things held in common, that stirred the Methodists in America as in England to revise their Hymnody.

Numerous memorials had come to the Northern Conference of 1900, setting forth that by reason of its size the *Hymnal* of 1878 was not used in many churches, in which song books, "often pernicious," took its place. These furnished sufficient ground for authorizing the preparation of a new hymnal, "of about 600 hymns." Spurred on by its Committee on Federation, the same Conference invited the other branches of Methodism to join in preparing a common catechism, order of worship, and hymn book. Under this conflicting legislation the preparation of a denominational hymnal had proceeded to the point of being

[90]An annotated edition by Prof. Wilbur F. Tillett, appeared at Nashville in 1889 as *Our Hymns and their authors.*

announced for publication in 1902 when it was suspended by the bishops in the interest of the common hymnal project.

In the South the desire for "a pan-Methodistic Hymnal" had been voiced (thus euphoniously) at the Conference of 1886.[91] That of 1902 authorized the bishops to join with those of the North in preparing such a book. The result of the labors of the joint commission was published through the Book Agents, North and South, in 1905 as *The Methodist Hymnal. Official Hymnal of the Methodist Episcopal Church and the Methodist Episcopal Church, South.* It had 717 Hymns against 1138 in the hymnal of the Northern and 918 in that of the Southern Church. More significantly it had 129 of Charles Wesley as against 563 in 1849, 310 in 1878, and 294 in 1889.

The *Hymnal* appeared in an unprecedented edition of 576,000 copies,[92] and received an amount of attention from the press also unprecedented. From the outside it was obvious that in its hymnological and musical standard the new book marked a great advance over its predecessors. The only Methodist hymnal with which it could be compared was the English *Methodist Hymn Book* of 1904. The two were not unlike in spirit and method, but the American was smaller by 264 hymns and carried on the American tradition of a less full representation of the Wesleyan Hymns: its musical standard was more "popular" and less "Anglican" than the English.

From within the *Hymnal* evoked much appreciation, and also much criticism, which, however sincerely deprecating the modernization of Methodist Hymnody, was often ill-informed. It is to be regretted that the characterization of the book by a recent historian of American Methodism

[91] "Report of the Committee on Hymn Book."
[92] Carl F. Price, *The Music and Hymnody of the Methodist Hymnal,* N. Y. [1911], p. 55. This contains a full account of the preparation of the *Hymnal* and description of its contents. There is also an annotated edition of the Hymnal: *The Hymns and Hymn writers of the Church,* ed. by Dr. Charles S. Nutter and Wm. F. Tillett, N. Y. and Nashville, 1911.

as "a scanty product, good as far as it goes," whose lack of bulk "will make the suppression of the 1907 [sic] book a necessity in a short time," should be incorporated as though a part of *A new History of Methodism*,[93] rather than a dissenting opinion. If the history of American Methodist Song makes anything clear, it is the unwisdom of authorizing a Hymnody too large for convenience or familiarity, and so justifying the intrusion of unauthorized song books that are at least handy. The moderate proportions of the *Hymnal* indicate rather one of several directions in which its compilers have sought to bring Methodist Song abreast with the best contemporary standards.

IX

DIVERGING CURRENTS OF AMERICAN METHODIST HYMNODY

American Methodism has suffered many schisms, occasioned by problems of race and slavery or by revolt from what was regarded as tyrannical in Methodist Episcopacy. The hymn books of these dissenting bodies were declarations of independence rather than the embodiment of sectarian doctrine or usages; and it is the measure and manner of this independent spirit as applied to the Hymnody that gives these hymn books such interest as they have.

(1) THE REFORMED METHODIST CHURCH began with the secession of a few farmers and mechanics in two Vermont towns, and in 1814 adopted congregationalist government.[94] *The Reformed Methodist Pocket Hymn Book* soon appeared, and a revised edition in 1828 at Taunton, excluding some hymns "thought to be improper." It had a first book of hymns from the current Methodist Episcopal *Collection,* a second from Watts, and 27 "favourite pieces."

[93]London, 1909, vol. ii, pp. 145, 146.
[94]Wesley Bailey in Rupp, *History of Religious Denominations in U. S.,* Philadelphia, 1844, pp. 466 ff.

The Watts section implies deference to proselytes from Congregationalism. The reference of each hymn to its page in the *Collection* or its number in "Watts" shows that many (no doubt from poverty) brought to the Reformers' services the books to which they had been accustomed.

(2) THE METHODIST SOCIETY was a secession in 1820 from the John Street Church in New York after disputes concerning administration.[95] William M. Stilwell, their first pastor, issued *A Selection of Hymns for worship* (New York, 1821), and the temporary growth of the movement for liberty called for a second edition in 1825. It was a free selection of 426 hymns, classified in Wesley's fashion.

(3) THE AFRICAN METHODIST EPISCOPAL CHURCH printed its own hymn book of 314 hymns and spiritual songs at Philadelphia in 1818; claimed as "the first Book of Song published by the Children of Oppression, the very first to give expression in their own selected language, of the Christian hope of the race."[96] George Hogarth, the Book Steward, made much trouble by copyrighting a new edition of 1836 as his personal property: but the Church regained control and issued reprints up to 1872.

Since 1868 the book had been in the hands of Bishop H. M. Turner for revision, and in 1873 the Publication Department issued at Philadelphia *The Hymn Book of the African Methodist Episcopal Church; being a Collection of Hymns, Sacred Songs and Chants, designed to supersede all others hitherto made use of in that Church. Selected from various authors.* It was a dumpy and independent little book. Some Methodist bodies had been weakening their addiction to the Wesleyan Hymnody, aiming to become eclectic. Bishop Turner reversed the process, reverting to that Hymnody so largely that his book "may be regarded as strictly a Wesleyan hymn book." In other Methodist bodies the authorities were aiming to suppress the camp meeting songs. Bishop Turner on the other

[95] W. M. Stilwell in Rupp, *op. cit.*, p. 424.
[96] Preface: ed. of 1898, p. xi.

hand was confronted with revival outbursts of "negro spirituals," which he thought "devoid of both sense and reason";[97] and to drive them out reintroduced a large number of the "precious old 'Zion' songs," and some of the new "Gospel Hymns." This was the authorized hymn book from 1873 to 1892, and in those years of the Church's upgrowth that began after the civil war its sale was very large. "The old hymns gave way to the new, and the children of freedom sang a new song from their own Church Book."

Under directions of the Conference of 1888 both to revise this and to prepare a new (musical) hymnal "separate and apart from our Church hymn book," there appeared first *Hymnal adapted to the doctrines and usages of the African Methodist Episcopal Church* (Philadelphia, 1893) mainly an abridgment of the 1873 book, but with some originals by bishops and ministers; and later *The African Methodist Hymn and Tune Book* (Philadelphia, 1898), with an increase of some 200 hymns and a musical standard suggesting that of the Methodist Episcopal *Hymnal* of 1878. The book was prepared under difficulties, and its publication was hailed in a letter from the Bishops as "the consummation so devoutly wished for and prayed for by our fathers—a Hymn and Tune Book of our own to be used by our people."

THE AFRICAN METHODIST EPISCOPAL ZION CHURCH, through most of its long career, has had to content itself with the use of current Methodist Episcopal hymn books. In 1888 it adopted Philip Phillips' antiquated setting of the *Hymns* of 1849, originally appearing in 1866,[98] and reprinted it as *New Hymn and Tune Book: an offering of Praise for the use of the African M. E. Zion Church of America.* Only recently has the denomination attained the satisfaction of having a hymn book of its own.

(4) THE METHODIST PROTESTANT CHURCH was organized in 1830 by the reformers who had long contended for

---

[97]His preface, June 2, 1873.
[98]See *ante,* note 84.

the rights of the laity. Among them were John J. Harrod of Baltimore, whom we have met with as an industrious compiler of song books, and Thomas H. Stockton, a contributor of verses to the periodicals who had the editorial instinct. Some use was made of Harrod's books, and Stockton became editor of the *Hymn Book of the Methodist Protestant Church. Compiled by authority of the General Conference* (Baltimore, 1837: 2nd ed., 1838; 4th, 1842). It "was the first Methodist Hymn Book to give the names of authors," [99] and its 829 hymns represent a wide survey of the field. It has also been characterized as "the best Methodist hymn book which had appeared up to that time." [100]

After twenty-two years appeared the *Hymn Book of the Methodist Protestant Church. Compiled by authority of the General Conference of 1858* (Baltimore, 1859). More than half of it was from the earlier book, and 73 spiritual songs were appended, to obviate recourse to revival song books. An unusual step was calling upon David Creamer as a hymnologist "to verify the hymns." [101]

In the meantime the Northern and Western conferences had gone off on the slavery issue, and regarded the new Southern book as tainted. A scheme for joining with the Wesleyan Methodists in preparing a common hymnal tarried, and, in the pressing need of supplying the churches with something, a hymn book for Methodist Protestants alone was put together and hurriedly and imperfectly printed in 1860.[102] Seven years later these conferences organized

[99]See note in T. H. Stockton, *Poems* (Phila., 1862), p. 305. The opening and two other hymns in the *Hymn Book* were his: for others, see *Poems*. Stockton was a prominent figure, but his hymns are forgotten. His "Stand up for Jesus!" appeared in a volume so named (Phila., 1858), and was several times set to music, but yielded to Geo. Duffield's hymn drawn from the same incident, and with a similar opening.

[100]J. Alfred Faulkner in *A new History of Methodism*, vol. ii, p. 146.
[101]Preface.
[102]For the circumstances, see A. H. Bassett, *A concise History of the Methodist Protestant Church*, Pittsburgh, 1877, pp. 185, 189-191.

as "The Methodist Church." For it there appeared *The Voice of Praise: a Collection of Hymns for the use of the Methodist Church* (Pittsburgh, 1872). It was largely the compilation of Alexander Clark,[103] and is notable for the fresh sources from which he drew, including current periodicals and manuscripts.[104]

The Methodist Church reunited with the Methodist Protestant in 1877; the official hymn books of each body being approved for further use.[105] But in view of a strong sentiment for a single book with tunes[106] it was ultimately decided to purchase the copyright and plates of a hymnal compiled by William McDonald and L. F. Snow under the supervision of Eben Tourjée. It had been published in 1874 as *The Tribute of Praise,* and had already finished its course as an independent venture. With some insertions, it appeared in 1882 as *The Tribute of Praise and Methodist Protestant Hymn Book. Edited by Dr. Eben Tourjée.* To give it a denominational flavor original hymns contributed to the earlier books were gathered up and printed in a supplement to this.[107] When *The Tribute of Praise* had been made to serve for nineteen years, it was replaced by *The Methodist Protestant Church Hymnal* (Meth. Prot. Publ. Board, 1901), which attained a circulation of 50,000 copies within a year. This comely and serviceable book was patterned closely upon the new type of hymnals that had appeared in the preceding decade; from which (rather than the sources) the bulk of its contents was transferred. From them it differed in a somewhat larger representation of Charles Wesley (69 out of 531 hymns) on the one hand

[103]Bassett, p. 222.
[104]It included Geo. H. Boker's battle-lyric, "God, to Thee we humbly bow."
[105]Bassett, p. 257.   [106]Preface of 1882.
[107]Thomas H. Stockton (5), Alexander Clark (4), William Rinehart (1), L. J. Cox (1), S. W. Widney (2), J. Varden (1), A. H. Bassett (1), A. E. Dennis (2), J. H. Robinson (1), and D. Trueman (1). These are the hymn writers of Methodist Protestantism. Only five of these hymns were retained in 1901.

and of spiritual songs on the other. It was a great contrast to anything that had preceded it in American Methodism, anticipating *The Methodist Hymnal* by four years.

(5) THE WESLEYAN METHODIST CONNECTION was founded in 1843 during the slavery agitation. The seceders, from Methodist Episcopal and Methodist Protestant Churches, brought with them their hymn books, and these became the first hymn books of the Connection.[108] In 1883 an edition of the Methodist Episcopal *Hymnal* of 1878 was put forth as *The Wesleyan Hymnal with tunes.* Even the *Sacred Hymns and Tunes designed to be used by the Wesleyan Methodist Connection (or Church) in America* (Syracuse, 1895) was little more than an abridgment of the Methodist Episcopal book, with the addition of some spiritual songs.

THE FREE METHODISTS cooperated with the Wesleyans in preparing a joint-book, appearing in 1910 as *The Wesleyan Methodist* (and also *The Free Methodist*) *Hymnal.* More than 200 of its 730 hymns are Charles Wesley's, and Watts has 54, but there are many hymns and songs of a lower grade; and indeed the words, run in between the staves of the music, seem of minor consequence. Lowell Mason, Thoro Harris, I. B. Woodbury and W. B. Bradbury are the largest contributors of tunes. Many others are designated as "with chorus," and secular melodies are utilized, such as "Maryland, my Maryland," "Bonnie Doon" and "Home, Sweet Home." The standard of Church Praise thus indicated, whatever may be thought of it, was no doubt deliberately chosen.

(6) A REVIEW OF AMERICAN METHODIST HYMNODY. We have now reviewed the whole course of American Methodist Hymnody. Its source was naturally Wesleyan, but it is by no means a mere extension of the Wesleyan Hymnody over new territory. At the first American Methodism refused to take its hymn book from Wesley's hand, and was never solicitous for the integrity or purity of that

[108]Preface of 1910.

Hymnody. The Church authorities sought at most to select from its abundance and to maintain its level; while the revival zeal of the people persistently overflowed its banks and fairly flooded the lowlands of Methodism with a revivalistic Hymnody.

The Wesleyan Hymn was thus the inheritance: the Camp Meeting Hymn the most distinctive feature of American Methodist Hymnody, both as to its own practice and as to its influence on other Churches. In one sense a development of the Evangelistic Hymn of the Wesleys, the Camp Meeting Hymn was at best a deterioration and at worst a parody. Camp Meeting Hymnody separates itself from Wesleyan Hymnody just as in England "Camp Meeting Methodists" established a "Primitive Methodist Church" outside of the Wesleyan.

The illiteracy and emotionalism of the Camp Meeting Hymn gradually yielded to changing conditions, the spread of education, and the uplift of the Methodist organization itself, which has never lost sight of the Wesleyan traditions. But whether the great body of the Church will accept the new Hymnody, and accepting it make it a vehicle not only of common praise but of the old revival spirit, remains to be determined. For the new Hymnody is not so much an expression of Methodist individuality as it is an effort to come abreast of the other Churches in catholicity.

The contribution of American Methodists to the store of English hymns has been prolific on the revival side, but rather scant in the sphere of church Hymnody. Two or three of the camp meeting song writers have been named: the great majority remains unknown. Of the contributors to mid-century hymn books, beside the Methodist Protestant writers referred to, Thomas A. Summers is remembered for two children's hymns, and one by Robert A. West in the *Hymns* of 1849 is still used. To the Social Hymn Book era belong William Hunter ("Joyfully, joyfully onward I move"), and William McDonald ("I am coming to the cross"). Mary A. Lathbury's two favorite hymns were

written for Chautauqua services. Mrs. Van Alstyne
("Fanny Crosby") is the most voluminous and probably
most popular of the recent "Gospel Hymns" school. Besides
these, in the new *Methodist Hymnal* Benjamin Copeland,
Emily H. Miller and Frank M. North[109] have two hymns
each, and nine other American Methodist writers are represented by one.[110]

APPENDIX. (7) In the group of Methodist Churches is
sometimes included THE UNITED BRETHREN IN CHRIST,
owing to its Arminian creed and its Methodist affiliations
dating from the associations of Otterbein and Ashbury.
It is however an independent body, less generally known
than some others, probably because its work was confined
for so long among German-speaking people.[111] There were
no English hymn books till James T. Stewart of Ohio published, with the approval of the General Conference, *The
Sacrifice of the Heart; or, a choice Selection of Hymns
from the most approved authors, for the use of the United
Brethren in Christ* (Cincinnati: Emporium office, 1826);
followed by a collection of 332 hymns made by Jacob
Antrim, an Ohio revivalist (Dayton, O., 1829).[112] A third
English hymn book, prepared at the instance of the Virginia
Conference by William R. Rhinehart and Jacob Erb, appeared in 1833 as *A Collection of Hymns, for the use of the
United Brethren in Christ, taken from the most approved
authors, and adapted to public and private worship,* and in
1837 was taken over by the General Conference and reissued
from its office at Circleville. This was the church hymn
book till 1849. It follows the arrangement rather than the

[109]The timely "Where cross the crowded ways of life" is his.

[110]Lewis R. Amis, David H. Ela, Caroline L. Rice, Lovie R. Stratton,
Caleb T. Winchester, William F. Warren, Samuel K. Cox, Elijah E.
Hoss, and John H. Stockton.

[111]*Cf.* H. G. Spayth, *History of the Church of the United Brethren
in Christ,* Circleville, O., 1851, p. 157, and the preface of Hanby's
continuation (in the same vol., p. .204).

[112]See W. A. Shuey, *Manual of U. B. Publ. House,* Dayton, 1892,
p. 7.

contents of John Wesley's *Collection* of 1780, including much of lower literary grade.

The next hymn book was prepared by Henry G. Spayth, appearing as *A Collection of Hymns for the use of the United Brethren in Christ. Prepared by order of the General Conference of 1845* (1849). Spayth is remembered as the earliest historian of his Church, and not for any service in improving its English Hymnody, he having been educated as a German. His book proved "deficient in variety, fulness and richness,"[113] and was superseded by a new one with the same title as that of 1833 and 1837 (Dayton, O., 1858), containing 1070 hymns. The compilers aimed to avoid "on the one hand the spirit of dry formalism, and on the other, that of uncultivated enthusiasm," including within these limits many of the standard hymns and many from the revival song books.

The United Brethren fell in line with the general movement toward a "hymnal with tunes," and published *Hymns of the Sanctuary, and social worship. With tunes. Dayton, O.: U. B. Publ. House, 1874.* As compared with the Methodist *Hymnal* of 1878, it is somewhat larger and considerably less Wesleyan, with a more "popular" tone in hymns and music, and from the stand-point of its constituency a more usable book.

The denomination has been rather prolific in the publication of smaller social and revival hymn books and in those for Sunday school use. Joseph Bever's *The Christian Songster* (Dayton, 1858) ranges with camp meeting song books, and was popular at revivals. *The Otterbein Hymnal* (1890) met the demand of the poorer churches for a small and inexpensive book, and under the name of *The People's Hymnal* sought the undenominational market.[114]

In its transition from a German to an English-speaking Church the United Brethren brought nothing from German Song, and it has made no appreciable contribution to Eng-

[113]Preface of 1858.
[114]*Cf.* Shuey, *Manual,* pp. 101, 102.

lish Hymnody. It has taken from the hymn books of its
neighbors such hymns and songs as it thought adapted to
its worship and evangelistic work. Its use of the Spiritual
Song has been no greater than in some Methodist bodies,
and its Hymnody has little to distinguish it from theirs.

(8) THE EVANGELICAL ASSOCIATION arose in 1800 out
of the evangelistic labors of Jacob Albright among Pennsylvania Germans, owing to the unwillingness of the Methodist
Episcopal Church to use German; and is Methodist in doctrine and discipline. The earliest hymn books were German,
but with the spread of the English language an English
hymn book was prepared in 1834 by J. M. Saylor and J. P.
Leib, under appointment of the Eastern Conference.[115] The
larger and later *The Evangelical Hymn-Book* (Cleveland:
The Evangelical Association, c. 1868) was made up from
current hymn books, including a number of Sunday school
hymn and tune books of the Bradbury type, and owed much
to that of the Methodist Protestants. It contained 1254
hymns. *The Hymn Book of the Evangelical Association*
(Cleveland, 1882), prepared by order of the General Conference, was smaller (875 hymns), made less use of Charles
Wesley, and more of modern writers, and was on the whole
an improved but in no way distinctive collection. In 1891
disciplinary measures resulted in splitting of the denomination. The *Hymnal of the United Evangelical Church* was
ordered by the first conference of the new body, appearing
in 1897. Its literary and musical standard is perhaps the
lowest of any church hymnal of its decade. The hymns for
ordinary church use are set to the old familiar American
tunes, accompanied by a large selection of "Gospel Songs";
and these are followed by a hundred "choruses" for ejaculatory use in revival meetings. The book is to be judged
no doubt from the standpoint "of a Church so preeminently
evangelistic as the United Evangelical." [116]

[115]*Landmarks of The Evangelical Association,* Reading, 1888, pp.
71, 74.
[116]Preface.

CHAPTER VII

THE HYMNODY OF THE EVANGELICAL REVIVAL

I

IN WHITEFIELD'S CIRCLE (1741-1770)

The separation on doctrinal grounds of the Wesleys and
George Whitefield in 1741 proved to be a permanent
division of the XVIIIth century Revival forces into Methodists and Evangelicals. Whitefield, by reason of his flaming
zeal and influence over men, must be regarded as the leader
on the Calvinistic side, but he had nothing of Wesley's
impulse and ability to organize his followers, and indeed
no ambition beyond that of preaching the gospel far and
wide. Contemporary observers and critics saw no distinction between Methodists and Evangelicals, even regarding
Whitefield as the originator and leader of Methodism.[1]
But by the participants themselves the line of theological
demarcation was keenly felt from the beginning; and as the
Revival progressed each party tended to develop its peculiar
methods and even to make a separate sphere of operations.
As the Revival extended into the Church of England, the
Evangelical clergy came to resent the imputation of Meth-
odism and to lament its nonconformity to parochial order.[2]

There was no one on the Evangelical side who shared to
the full John Wesley's deep sense of the importance of the
Hymn, his delight in hymn singing, or his skill in adminis-

[1] So Tindal described Whitefield in his Continuation of Rapin's
History of England.

[2] *Cf.* J. H. Overton, *The Evangelical Revival in the Eighteenth Century,* ed. London, 1900, pp. 45 ff.

tering it as a Christian ordinance; and certainly no one who equalled Charles Wesley in the facility and felicity of his hymn writing. Nevertheless the Evangelical Revival caught and retained something of the glow of Methodist Song, developed its own hymn writers, and established the permanent lines of an Evangelical Hymnody. Most of all, it exercised an influence on the general extension of hymn singing more immediate and effective than that of Methodism itself.

Whitefield had shared in the use of hymn singing by the Wesleys as an aid to evangelism. In his early ministry and preaching tours he made use of the metrical psalms bound up with the Prayer Book, the *Psalms and Hymns* of Dr. Watts, or the Wesleyan hymns, as one or the other type happened to be convenient or acceptable. It is not clear that he was a writer of hymns, but he made some use of manuscript hymns adapted to special themes or occasions.[3] Like Wesley he encouraged also social hymn singing as an act of devotion or even as a witness-bearing in unexpected places.[4] The practical influence of Whitefield's preaching, wherever he went, outside of such parish churches as suffered him, was overwhelmingly in favor of the singing of hymns as distinguished from metrical psalms. This was not only from the force of his personal example in using hymns freely, but because the evangelical fervor he aroused demanded an evangelical response from his auditors. His influence in this respect was widespread; and we have already noted its part in bringing about "The Era of Watts" in American Churches.

A number of the preachers associated with Whitefield became themselves hymn writers. John Cennick, while still assisting him, published his *Sacred Hymns for the Children of God, in the days of their pilgrimage. By J. C.*

---

[3]See the hymn "for her Ladyship" in *The Life and Times of Selina Countess of Huntingdon,* ed. London, 1844, vol. i, p. 117: and that in L. Tyerman, *Life of George Whitefield,* New York, 1877, vol. ii, p. 241.

[4]Tyerman, *op. cit.,* vol. i, p. 241.

(London, 1741-42); and *Sacred Hymns for the use of Religious Societies. Generally composed in dialogues* (Bristol, 1743). Many of these hymns commended themselves to Whitefield, and some are still widely known and sung.[5] To the later collection, Joseph Humphreys, a co-worker, contributed six hymns.[6] Cennick also introduced into some of the societies classes for hymn singing patterned after the "choirs" of the Moravians, to whom his heart already turned.[7] In 1742 Robert Seagrave published his *Hymns for Christian worship: partly composed, and partly collected from various authors* (London: 4th ed., 1748); of which 45 were original. The first ("Now may the Spirit's holy Fire") Whitefield afterwards made the opening hymn of his own collection; but only "The Pilgrim's Song" ("Rise my Soul, and stretch thy Wings") can be said to have survived.[8] Seagrave was in Anglican orders, and in his preface denies the divine prescription of psalm singing. Just at the point of leaving Whitefield for the Moravians William Hammond published his *Psalms, Hymns, and Spiritual Songs* (London, 1745). His hymns are of merit,[9] and numerous versions of Latin hymns anticipated by nearly a century the revival of Protestant interest in Latin Hymnody.

Seagrave's book was prepared for his congregation at Loriner's Hall, where he was Sunday evening lecturer for many years, but it was used more widely. It is likely that all these collections had more or less use in the societies, or at the temporary Tabernacle at Moorfields; but when

---

[5]Among them, "Children of the heav'nly King," "Jesus, my All, to Heav'n is gone," "E'er I sleep, for ev'ry Favour," "We sing to Thee, Thou Son of God" and "Brethren let us join to bless."

[6]Among them, "Blessed are the sons of God."

[7]See Tyerman's *Whitefield*, vol. ii, p. 148.

[8]Seagrave's hymns are highly regarded by Josiah Miller, *Singers and Songs of the Church*, 2nd ed., London, 1869, pp. 152, 153; and have been reprinted by Daniel Sedgwick.

[9]"Awake, and sing the song," and "Lord, we come before Thee now," are arranged from longer hymns in this book.

the new Tabernacle was opened in 1753, Whitefield felt that he should have a hymn book of his own. It appeared as *Hymns for social worship, collected from various authors, and more particularly design'd for the use of the Tabernacle Congregation, in London. By George Whitefield, A.B., late of Pembroke College, Oxford, and Chaplain to the Rt. Hon. the Countess of Huntingdon, London: printed by William Strahan, and to be sold at the Tabernacle, near Moorfields. M DCC LIII.*[10]

The Countess of Huntingdon had "turned Methodist" under the influence of her sister-in-law, Lady Margaret Hastings, who married Benjamin Ingham, one of Wesley's preachers; and became a member of the society meeting in Fetter Lane. She was especially moved by Whitefield's preaching. On his return from America in 1748, she exercised her right as a peeress to appoint him her chaplain, and opened her house in Park Lane that he might preach to semi-weekly gatherings of the aristocracy. She endeavored in vain the next year to reunite the Wesleys and Whitefield, and threw her influence on the side of Whitefield. It was his hope that Lady Huntingdon would assume charge of the societies he had founded, the management of which interfered with his freedom as an evangelist;[11] and it was largely through her encouragement that he undertook to erect the new and larger Tabernacle at Moorfields[12] for whose use his hymn book was prepared.

Whitefield's *Hymns* contained 132 "for public worship"; 38 "for Society and Persons meeting in Christian-Fellowship." It included hymns by all four of his hymn writing

[10]The book is described in *The Athenaeum* for Nov. 14, 1903, as "the excessively rare first edition of Whitefield's 'Hymns,'" and mention made of a copy that "has just changed hands at the price of 200 guineas." But the 1st ed. is far from being "excessively rare." The copy at the 6th McKee sale in May, 1902, brought $4.50: the writer's copy was purchased from an experienced London dealer in 1896 at half a guinea.

[11]*Life and Times of the Countess of Huntingdon*, vol. i, pp. 116, 117.
[12]*Ibid.*, pp. 202, 203.

co-workers; notably of Cennick, the use of whose "Hymns in dialogue" was justified by a reference in the preface to the antiphonal singing of cathedral churches and of the "Celestial Choir."[13] A score of the hymns of the Wesleys were included, but the hymns of Watts predominated. Whitefield aimed at a standard of Praise combining the doctrine and dignity of Watts with the evangelical fervor of Charles Wesley and his own colleagues. He thought congregational hymns "ought to abound much in Thanksgiving," and "be of such a Nature, that all who attend may join in them without being obliged to sing lies, or not sing at all." This was to confine his choice within what we have called Watts' "Common Ground," and to avoid the individualistic Wesleyan hymns. It involved also some textual changes in the Wesleyan hymns used; a freedom which Wesley bitterly resented.[14]

The actual use of Whitefield's hymn book by his own societies, and beyond them, was very large. Daniel Sedgwick has found thirty-six editions between 1753 and 1796.[15] Through it a number of hymns now familiar, were given circulation. Its greatest permanent importance lay in its influence with the early Evangelical clergy of the Church of England, which made it the forerunner and even the model of the earlier group of hymnals in the Church of England.

II

IN LADY HUNTINGDON'S CONNEXION
(1764-1865)

Whitefield did not found a new denomination, nor did Lady Huntingdon assume the leadership of his societies,

---

[13] "Represented in the Book of Revelations, as answering one another in their heavenly Anthems."
[14] See his preface to the Methodist *Collection,* of 1780.
[15] Tyerman's *Whitefield,* vol. ii, p. 294.

which were destined to disintegration. Her aim was rather to improve the Church of England. She claimed the right to build private chapels, and to furnish them with preachers by appointing clergymen as her domestic chaplains; and by so doing built up gradually a "connexion" within the bounds of the Church. But the opening of her chapel in Spa Fields in 1779 was opposed. She was obliged to take shelter under the Toleration Act, to register her ministers as dissenting ministers, and her chapels as dissenting places of worship.[16] The parochial clergy among her chaplains (Romaine, Venn, Beveridge, and others) withdrew, and her work took shape as a new denomination, "Lady Huntingdon's Connexion."[17]

Lady Huntingdon shared the Methodist feeling for hymns; and in the meetings at her different houses she made hymn singing familiar in those aristocratic circles into which Methodism itself made no effort to penetrate. From her social influence, her headship of her many chapels, and her intimate relations with church and dissent, she was especially well situated to aid the extension of hymn singing; and she was an influence behind the movement to introduce hymns into the Church of England. She concerned herself with the development of an evangelical Hymnody, combining evangelical fervor with Calvinistic doctrine, primarily for her own chapels but having wider bearings.

Whether or not Lady Huntingdon contributed hymns of her own composition is uncertain. As early as 1748 Doddridge, writing after preaching at her house, confesses to his wife:[18] "I have stolen a hymn, which I steadfastly believe to be written by good Lady Huntingdon." The opinion that she was a hymn writer was shared by others, until it acquired the force of a tradition. Josiah Miller regarded it "as proved beyond doubt that she was the author of a few hymns of great excellence," and asserted

[16]See her *Life and Times*, vol. ii, pp. 309 ff.
[17]*Ibid.*, p. 490.
[18]*Correspondence and Diary of Philip Doddridge*, vol. v, London, 1831, p. 74.

that a known list of them was lost.[19] But such a claim is
not supported by actual evidence.

Lady Huntingdon's part in the preparation of hymn
books for her chapels is much more certain, though not
wholly defined. It is doubtful if full materials for a history
of the Hymnody of her Connexion now exist. The earliest
hymn book now known is *A Collection of Hymns. London.
Printed for William Lee at Lewes, in Sussex, MDCCLXIV*.
It is compiled from James Allen's *Kendal Hymn Book* of
1754 and other sources, and has a Moravian rather than a
Calvinistic flavor. "Society Hymns" and "Congregational
Hymns" are distinguished; and the preface is an earnest
evangelistic appeal, which, according to Miller,[20] was
written by the Countess herself. It was followed by a series
of local hymn books which plainly had her approval and
probably her supervision. The first was. *The Collection of
Hymns sung in the Countess of Huntingdon's Chapel,
Bristol* (Bath, 1765, 3rd. ed., 1770). The distinction between "Society" and "Congregational" hymns was continued, but large use was here made of Watts, Charles
Wesley, and current Calvinistic hymn writers. Then came
*A Collection of Hymns sung in the Countess of Hunting-
don's Chapels in Sussex* (Edinburgh, n. d.; c. 1771). Then,
next, *A Collection of Hymns sung in the Countess of Huntingdon's Chapels, Bath* (Bristol, c. 1774), in which the
greater festivals are provided for, and there are fifty-
one hymns "for the Sacrament." There followed *The
Collection of Psalms and Hymns, sung in the Countess
of Huntingdon's Chapels, in Lincolnshire* (Gainsborough,
1778).

During these formative years Lady Huntingdon appears
to have encouraged, or perhaps permitted, her ministers to

[19]*Singers and Songs of the Church*, London, 1869, p. 183. The only
hymn he mentions as hers is the well-known "O when my righteous
Judge shall come." For all really known of its history, see Julian,
Dictionary of Hymnology, p. 854.

[20]*Singers and Songs,*.p. 182.

make hymn books for their own use. Thomas Maxfield,[21] one of the first of Wesley's lay preachers, later in Anglican orders, had revolted from Methodism, and brought a considerable following over to the Calvinistic side. He printed *A Collection of Psalms and Hymns: extracted from various authors: with some never published before. London: printed and sold at his chapel in Rope-maker's Alley, Little Moorfields, &c., MDCCLXVI* (2nd. ed., 1768; 3rd ed., 1778). He aimed in this to emphasize his newly adopted Calvinism. Its "Collection of Hymns" (250) and "Collections of Psalms" (150) are followed by a series of independently numbered groups "for the Nativity," for "New Year's Day," &c., evidently in imitation of Wesley's hymn tracts. The Revs. Herbert Jones and William Taylor were the preachers of the new Spa Fields Chapel whose erection occasioned Lady Huntingdon's withdrawal from the Church of England. They published for it in 1777 a *Collection* mostly compiled from the earlier books and from Whitefield's.[22]

But the time had come, in Lady Huntingdon's judgment, for a common hymn book for her now very numerous chapels.[23] It would promote uniformity, and the profits on its sale would help to support the work.[24] She personally undertook the selection of the hymns, relying upon the assistance of her cousin, the Hon. and Rev. Walter Shirley.[25] The new book appeared as *A select Collection of Hymns to be universally sung in all the Countess of Huntingdon's Chapels. Collected by her Ladyship. London MDCCLXXX.* Its 298 hymns represent in the main her choice of the hymns already used in her chapels; and comprise a compact devotional presentation of the Calvinistic

---

[21]For Lady Huntingdon's relations with Maxfield, see her *Life and Times,* vol. i, pp. 33, 34.

[22]*Ibid.,* vol. ii, p. 306.

[23]There were over 80 at the date of her death.

[24]Preface of 1808.

[25]Her *Life and Times,* vol. ii, p. 201, note.

interpretation of the gospel of grace.[26] This collection stood the test of use, and the maintenance of it in its integrity became a matter of loyalty to the Countess. Supplements were added in 1796 and 1808, after her death; and in view of numerous "surreptitious editions," more or less incorrect, the book was copyrighted by her Trustees.[27] Some independent supplements followed: Isaac Nicholson's full *Collection of Hymns . . . for Mulberry Gardens' Chapel* (1807); John Sartain's *Psalms and Hymns* for Brighton (1819); Thomas Young's *The Beauties of Dr. Watts, with popular Hymns* (1819); and the Appendix of "G. H." of Worcester in 1848. In 1854 a new hymn book appeared by order of the Conference as *The Countess of Huntingdon's Connexion Hymn Book,* and this also has been supplemented by the now dwindling denomination (*The Connexion Hymn Book with Supplement,* 1865).

Lady Huntingdon was intimate with the Wesleys, the hostess of Zinzendorf, the friend of Watts and Doddridge, and the center of the group of hymn writers developed on the Calvinistic side of the Revival, whether of Whitefield's following or her own, or remaining, like Toplady, in the established Church. Of her immediate circle, her cousin Walter Shirley contributed several hymns to her *Collection,* and is still remembered for his "Sweet the moments rich in blessing," a recast of a hymn by James Allen, and appearing in the 1770 edition of the *Bristol* collection. A more copious writer was Thomas Haweis, whose hymns appeared as *Carmina Christo; or Hymns to the Saviour* (Bath, 1792). This book of Haweis was regarded by many as a companion to her Ladyship's *Collection,* and was often bound up with

[26]Nos. 62-64, "The Joy of Faith," from Toplady's *Psalms and Hymns* of 1776:

> "How happy are we,
> Our election who see,
> And can venture our souls on Thy gracious decree."

is an anti-Wesleyan presentation of the grounds of evangelical joy, set forth in the Wesleyan rhythm.

[27]Preface of 1808.

it. From it come his familiar hymns: "From the cross uplifted high," "Enthron'd on high, almighty Lord!" and "O Thou, from whom all goodness flows." Lady Huntingdon's concern for the Calvinistic Methodist movement in Wales brought her the friendship of William Williams, its chief hymn writer. Williams had also printed in early life an attempt at hymn writing in English, *Hosannah to the Son of David; or Hymns of Praise to God* (Bristol, 1759). It is claimed[28] that after seeing this book Lady Huntingdon induced him to prepare his *Gloria in Excelsis: or Hymns of Praise to God and the Lamb* (Carmarthen, 1772). It is certain that she included a number of hymns from this book in her *Collection,* including "O'er those gloomy Hills of Darkness," a forerunner of the later Missionary Hymnody. His "Guide me, O Thou Great Jehovah" (first written in Welsh), was printed as a leaflet for use by the students of Lady Huntingdon's college and included in the *Collection* for Sussex (c. 1771); being thus started on its great career.

To develop and maintain an interest in hymn singing demanded attention to its musical interests, if only to conquer the lethargy resulting from the degraded ideals and methods of Church of England psalmody. Whitefield had no special gift for musical leadership, but Lady Huntingdon was interested in music and not satisfied merely to adopt the Wesleyan tune books. She knew most of the prominent musicians, including Handel, and included the words of the choruses of his *Messiah* in her *Collection.* This suggests her ambitions for her chapel services, but the withdrawal of these anthems after her death indicates a conclusion that they were beyond the available musical resources. She engaged Giardini, the great violinist of her day, to compose some tunes for her chapels,[29] and secured others from

[28]E. Morgan in Daniel Sedgwick's reprint of Williams' two publications as above, London, 1859, p. x.

[29] "Is it true that Lady Rockingham is turned Methodist? It will be a great acquisition to the sect to have their hymns set by Giardini." Horace Walpole, June 25, 1768, in Toynbee ed. of his *Letters,* vol. vii, Oxford, 1904, p. 205.

Giordani, another Italian musician in London, with a very similar name. At her request, the younger Charles Wesley, whose musical career she had assisted, composed a tune for her favorite "In Christ my treasure's all contained."[30] Among her chaplains Thomas Haweis was the most musical, and composed tunes published after her death as *Original Music suited to the various metres*. The curious oblong shape assumed by the Connexion hymn books has not been explained, but may have been adopted as convenient for printing tunes to be bound up with them.

III

SOME BY-STREAMS OF THE HYMNODY
(1748-1808)

Several by-streams of Hymnody can be conveniently traced from this point.

Benjamin Ingham, Lady Huntingdon's brother-in-law, had been the Wesleys' fellow-voyager to Georgia, and on his return became an evangelist. He turned over to the Moravians many societies he founded in Yorkshire and adjacent counties, but ultimately organized his followers as a new sect (Inghamites), making a sort of bishop of himself and ordaining his preachers. He published for them *A Collection of Hymns for Societies. Leeds: printed by James Lister, 1748.* Of its 88 hymns 15 are from Watts, 8 from the Wesleys, 5 from Cennick: his own share is undetermined. Later a group of his helpers put forth *A Collection of Hymns for the use of those that seek, and those that have redemption in the Blood of Christ. Kendal: printed by Tho. Ashburner. MDCCLVII* (2nd ed. with appx., 1761). James Allen and Christopher Batty were the largest contributors, and the flavor of the whole is Moravian.

---

[30] Her *Life and Times*, vol. i, p. 230.

Much of its contents is doggerel.[31] A year later Ingham
sent Batty and Allen northward to inquire into a movement
inaugurated by John Glas. They returned as converts to
the Glassite discipline and theology, and in the disputes and
disruption that followed the Inghamite connexion was
almost completely wrecked.

The Rev. John Glas had been deposed from the ministry
of the Church of Scotland in 1728. He formed at Perth
and elsewhere churches aiming to revive primitive discipline,
with such ordinances as feet washing, the love feast and
community of goods. In public worship they were psalm
singers, but for their fellowship meetings were composed
Christian Songs, first appearing at Edinburgh, 1749. Its
38 songs increased in number with each new edition, the
fifth (1775) having 95 songs and 11 "elegies." The eighth
(1794) added a second part of 25 songs, enlarged to 114
in the fourteenth edition of 1872. An edition printed for
the Edinburgh congregation in 1875 was little more than a
reprint of the first part of the 1794 edition. Most of the
songs were on themes already familiar, but many show
more than the usual lyrical feeling and facility, and are
referred to current Scottish and English song-tunes. Beside
its long popularity in Glassite congregations, now become
few and small, the *Christian Songs* is of some interest as
the source of hymns in various collections.[32]

[31]The book is known as *The Kendal Hymn Book.* Allen's "Glory to
God on high" came into wide use: his "While my Jesus I'm possessing"
was the basis of "Sweet the moments rich in blessing." Christopher
and William Batty afterwards printed *A Publication of Hymns, in two
parts* (4th ed., Nottingham, 1803). Christopher's "Captain of thy
enlisted host" had some use.

[32]These can be traced through Julian's *Dict. of Hymnology,* art.
"Scottish Hymnody," pp. 1030 f. Glas' son-in-law Robert Sandeman
came to Boston in 1764, and established churches known as Sande-
manian in several towns. For their history see Williston Walker,
"The Sandemanians in New England" in *Annual Rept. of Amer. Hist.
Assn.* for 1901, vol. i, p. 133. A hymn book for their use appeared as
*Christian Songs; written by Mr. John Glas, and others. The seventh
edition Perth, printed: Providence, reprinted. MDCCLXXXVII.*

James Relly, a convert and afterward a preacher of Whitefield's, broke with him on doctrinal grounds, adopting very comfortable views of the union of the whole race with the Redeemer. His London society was probably the first attempt at organized Universalism, and kept its meeting house open till 1830.[33] He published at London in 1754 *Christian Hymns, Poems, and Spiritual Songs, sacred to the praise of God our Saviour:* the fifty-page poem and first book of hymns by himself, the second by his brother John. It is easier to understand that these rude hymns should support the charge of antinomianism brought against Relly, than that they should prove attractive in reading or worship. But they were reprinted in 1758, 1777, and 1791, and were associated with the Universalist movement in America. It was no doubt natural that each of these XVIIIth century sectarian movements should aim at having its own Hymnody.

As independent in spirit as these founders of sects, but in doctrine straitly Calvinistic, was Rowland Hill. At one in his views with Whitefield and Lady Huntingdon, an imitator of the former's methods and associated with the latter's work, he was as unwilling to become the colleague of either as unable to keep to the lines of the Church of England, of which he was an ordained clergyman. After an itinerant ministry of twelve years, he founded in London the famous Surrey Chapel. During a fifty years' ministry there, with some use of church formularies but without episcopal sanction, he exerted an influence in popularizing hymn singing that was not unfelt in the Church itself. Hill had published at London in 1774 *A Collection of Psalms and Hymns, chiefly intended for the use of the poor;* and on opening Surrey Chapel in 1783 printed for it *A Collection of Psalms and Hymns, chiefly intended for public worship* (M. Pasham, 1783). He believed in the sacred use of popular melodies, and his organist, B. Jacob,

[33]Richard Eddy, "The Universalists" in *American Church History Series,* vol. x, p. 349.

coöperated with him, as appears from a *Collection of Hymn Tunes* (c. 1800). His hymn "When Jesus first, at Heav'n's command," set to "Rule Britannia," with which he stirred the hearts of the Volunteers during the Napoleonic wars, was long remembered.[34] An early Sunday school worker, Hill also popularized the ideal of a Children's Hymnody. Jacob prepared for him a tune book for Watts' *Divine and moral Songs,* and Hill himself published *Divine Hymns attempted in easy language for the use of children* (and revised by Cowper: 1st ed., 1790) ; *A Collection of Hymns for children* (1808) ; and *Hymns for schools* (1832). As a hymn writer, Hill was of Watts' school; and the prefaces of his various collections show that he contributed to them much more material than can now be identified. Of the hymns that were new in one or other edition of the *Collection* of 1783, "Cast thy burden on the Lord," "We sing His love who once was slain," and "With heavenly power, O Lord, defend," are in common use to the present time.

IV

IN THE CHURCH OF ENGLAND (1760-1819)

1. INTRODUCTION OF HYMN SINGING BY THE EVANGELICALS (1760-1776)

Both the Wesleys and Whitefield had proposed an evangelistic movement within the Church of England. It is difficult to conceive the reshaping of the Church that would have resulted, had they been allowed to fulfil their purpose. In fact their gospel, their methods, and most of all their "enthusiasm," aroused general hostility, and closed the parish churches against the "New Light" and the new song it inevitably awakened. There were nevertheless in the ranks of the clergy some minds open to evangelical impres-

---

[34]It is in William James, *Memoir of the Rev. Rowland Hill,* 3rd ed., London, 1845, p. 349.

sions, and the actual effect of the Revival was to develop in the Church of England an Evangelical Party.

The early Evangelicals were Calvinists, in sympathy with Whitefield. They moved in Lady Huntingdon's circle, and were thus in direct contact with the new Hymnody. Some of them, like Beveridge of Everton, and Grimshaw of Haworth, had control of their own churches; but, in London especially, the Evangelicals were dependent upon Lady Huntingdon's house, the chapels she erected, the proprietary chapels others were allowed by the bishops to establish as the only form of church extension then practicable, and the endowed "lectureships" in various parish churches where the nomination of the lecturer was in the hands of the parishioners.[35] By means of these the opportunity was found to preach an evangelical gospel within the Church of England; and also to introduce hymn singing into its services, without having to encounter the opposition inevitable in parish churches with long-established traditions in favor of psalm singing.

The first of the Evangelical leaders was the excellent William Romaine, hustled from place to place in London before he could obtain a hearing. As it happened, he was a conscientious opponent of hymn singing in general and of the Hymnody of the Revival in particular. He held the extreme Calvinistic position as to the exclusive use of inspired words in Praise, and was able to impose his views upon his own congregation. But he could not stay the rising tide of hymn singing or make a breach between the gospel and the hymns of the Revival.

In Martin Madan the new hymn singing found an effective sponsor. He and his friends had built the chapel in connection with the Lock Hospital, near Hyde Park Corner, which introduced Evangelicalism into the West End. For its use he prepared and published *A Collection of Psalms and Hymns, extracted from various authors, and published*

[35]See G. R. Balleine, *A History of the Evangelical Party in the Church of England*, London, 1908, pp. 60-63.

by the Reverend Mr. Madan. London: printed by Henry Cock: and sold at the Lock Hospital, near Hyde Park, MDCCLX. The book was plainly modelled on Whitefield's, and often uses his textual alterations. Its 170 hymns were put together without arrangement, beyond a grouping of "Sacramental Hymns." There was nothing to distinguish it as being of the Church of England. Its choice of hymns and bright and cheerful tone gave immediate satisfaction. For some six years it had the field to itself, reaching a second edition in 1763, a fourth in 1765, and a twelfth in 1787. Madan's knack in reconstructing the work of other hands made his book a permanent influence both for good and evil. A number of familiar hymns still bear the marks of his editorial revision. Madan was a musician, and, to accompany his hymn book, printed *A Collection of Psalm and Hymn Tunes, never published before, 1769. Edited by M. Madan.*[36] It was reprinted both in England and America, and included 33 tunes from his own hand. These florid strains, then new, gained much vogue: "Helmsley" and "Huddersfield" still survive. The contempt expressed for these tunes by the modern Anglican school views them out of perspective. If they tickled the ear, it was with a view of arousing faculties that slept through the droned notes of parish Psalmody and of quickening the pace of the singing. And in this they were successful.

The humorous and sturdy John Berridge was as early on the field as Madan, but less effective. He published *A Collection of Divine Songs, designed chiefly for the Religious Societies of Churchmen in the neighbourhood of Everton, Bedfordshire* (1760). As may be inferred, Berridge was already a "Methodist," a field-preacher, and encourager of societies outside the parish churches. His collection is mostly Wesleyan, with some hymns from Watts and some originals. With a change in doctrinal views Berridge became

"Not wholly satisfied with the collection [he] had published. The

[36] Generally called "The Lock Collection."

bells, indeed, had been chiefly cast in a celebrated Foundery, and in ringing were tunable enough, none more so, but a clear gospel tone was not found in them all. Human wisdom and strength, perfection and merit, give Sion's bells a Levitical twang, and drown the mellow tone of the gospel outright." [37]

With such convictions Berridge attempted to suppress his *Divine Songs,* buying and destroying every copy he could secure. During a six months' illness in the early seventies he composed a large number of hymns. A few of these appeared in *The Gospel Magazine,* or elsewhere: most were laid aside till in 1785 he printed the whole body of them as *Sion's Songs, or Hymns: composed for the use of them that love and follow the Lord Jesus Christ in sincerity. By John Berridge, M.A., Vicar of Everton* (London). There were 342 hymns of a homely type, without classification or even an index of first lines, but numbered as a hymn book. They were sung no doubt through the circuit of Berridge's preaching and societies, but made no marked impression on Evangelical Hymnody. New editions in 1805 and 1820 may have been as much designed for reading as for singing, as was J. C. Philpots' reprint of 1842.[38]

Seven years after Madan's *Collection* and Berridge's earlier hymn book, Richard Conyers, Vicar of Helmsley in Yorkshire, published *A Collection of Psalms and Hymns, from various authors: for the use of serious and devout Christians of every denomination* (London, 1767). This is the third of the Church of England hymnals, revealing by its title how broad was the sympathy of the early Evangelicals. The printing of a fifth edition at York in 1788 shows that it helped to extend and provide for hymn singing at the North. Conyers followed Madan's lead and appropriated fully two thirds of the contents of Madan's *Collection.* He

[37] Preface to *Sion's Songs,* 1785.

[38] There is a good account of Berridge and his hymns in Thos. Wright, *Augustus M. Toplady,* &c., London, 1911, pp. 252-60. Gadsby's *Memoirs of Hymn-Writers and Compilers* is fuller, but inaccurate. Berridge's best remembered hymns are: "Jesus, cast a look on me," "O happy saints, who dwell in light," and "Since Jesus freely did appear" (in altered forms).

was however happy in getting his friend Cowper interested in his book and in securing contributions from that poet. His second edition of 1772 will always have a place as the original source of "There is a fountain fill'd with blood," and "Oh! for a closer walk with God."

The fourth of the Evangelical series appeared in 1775. That was also the year of Romaine's philippic against the new Hymnody, in which he reveals the situation as he saw it:

"The hymn-makers . . . have supplied us with a vast variety, collection upon collection, and in use too, new hymns starting up daily— appendix added to appendix—sung in many congregations, yea admired by very high professors to such a degree, that the psalms are become quite obsolete, and the singing of them is now almost as despicable among the modern religious, as it was some time ago among the prophane." [39]

Romaine, no doubt, is speaking not of the Church at large, but of the small group of churches affected by the movement which he represented at London, and De Courcy (whose recent appointment by Lord Dartmouth as Vicar of St. Alkmund's, Shrewsbury, caused a great stir) represented at the West. The latter's *A Collection of Psalms and Hymns, extracted from different authors . . . with a preface by the Reverend Mr. De Courcy* (Shrewsbury, 1775: 2nd ed., 1782), might seem a defiance of Romaine; for its distinction lay in the increased number of authors from whom it drew, adding for their accommodation "appendix to appendix" in its later editions.

But in the project of widening the area of the Evangelical Hymnody these later editions had been preceded, and probably influenced, by another hymn book of greater importance: *Psalms and Hymns for public and private worship. Collected (for the most part), and published, by Augustus Toplady, A.B., Vicar of Broad Hembury. London: printed for E. and C. Dilly, 1776.* "It *ought*," Toplady said, "to be the *best* that has yet appeared, considering the great number of volumes (no fewer than between forty and

[39] *An Essay on Psalmody,* London, 1775, pp. 104, 105.

fifty), which have, more or less, contributed to this Compilation."[40] In its 418 hymns many Nonconformists, beside Watts, were represented, some of them new to Church of England hymn books. The book was occasioned by Toplady's removal to London, and was made for the evening congregation he had gathered in the Huguenot Chapel in Orange Street. Toplady regarded hymn singing as an ordinance of God, "which He designs eminently to bless at this present day," and dismissed Romaine's protest against hymns, of the year before, with contempt.[41]

Toplady's book was more pronouncedly Calvinistic than its predecessors. Such titles as "Original Sin," "Election Unchangeable," "Electing Grace," "Efficacious Grace," "Imputed Righteousness," "Preserving Grace," and "Assurance of Faith," show that the "Five Points" were carefully illustrated. In 1770, and the years following, the Calvinistic Controversy had reached its crisis, and none had contributed more to its heat and bitterness than Toplady. The separation of the two parties was final, and his hymn book expressed his conviction[42] that the Church of England belonged on the Calvinistic side. In view of the extreme virulence of his attacks upon Wesley, Toplady's inclusion of a number of Wesleyan hymns is noteworthy. Unlike most of his contemporaries, Toplady must have identified the authorship of these hymns:[43] and it is to be added that

[40]Preface.

[41]"What absurdity is there, for which some well-meaning people have not contended?" *Ibid.*

[42]*Historic Proof of the doctrinal Calvinism of the Church of England* (1774).

[43]It is quite certain that the editor of Toplady's *Works* could not distinguish even Toplady's hymns from those of the Wesleys. He prints "Christ whose glory fills the skies" and "Father, I want a thankful heart," as Toplady's (vol. vi [1794], pp. 420, 428). This act of Row's is the sole basis for the charge that Toplady appropriated as his own some of Charles Wesley's hymns (David Creamer, *Methodist Hymnology*, N. Y., 1848, pp. 45-47). Row in his turn is accused of printing some of Toplady's hymns as his own (Gadsby, *Hymn Writers*, 4th ed., 1870, p. 157).

he carefully altered the text of such as he used.[44] And here, for the first time in a hymn book, "Rock of Ages" and "Jesu, Lover of my Soul," stand side by side.

Even more unexpected, in view of the history of the Evangelical Party, is the aesthetic motive in Toplady's book. "God," so the preface opens, "is the God of *Truth*, of *Holiness*, and of *Elegance*. Whoever, therefore, has the honor to compose, or to compile, anything that may constitute a part of his worship, should keep those three particulars, constantly, in view." If only these quaint words could have been taken to heart by the Evangelical Party, Toplady's hymn book would not only have put into circulation the greatest English hymn, but would have prevented that perverse ignoring of the aesthetic side of human nature which proved so serious a barrier to the spread of evangelical religion, and palliated the excesses of the Oxford Revival in the century following.

Toplady did not live to reprint his hymn book. A second edition, somewhat modified, appeared in 1787, edited by his friend Walter Row. For this there continued a demand sufficient to keep it in print during the first quarter of the XIXth century.

Toplady included only six of his own hymns[45] in his *Psalms and Hymns,* though he had been a hymn writer from his youth.[46] The larger number of his hymns appeared at Dublin in 1759 as *Poems on sacred subjects,* and portray the stress of thought and feeling that accompanied his transition to Calvinistic views. Long afterward he printed 26 hymns in *The Gospel Magazine,*[47] and five

[44]E. g. in "Blow ye the trumpet, blow," the Wesleyan "The all-atoning Lamb" becomes "The sin-atoning Lamb."

[45]They were "Holy Ghost, dispel our sadness"; "A debtor to Mercy alone"; "Thou fountain of bliss"; "Rock of Ages"; "What tho' my frail eye-lids refuse"; and "How happy are we."

[46]See Wright, *Augustus M. Toplady,* p. 23.

[47]In 1771, 1772, 1774, 1776. "Rock of Ages" appeared in March, 1776. There is a complete list in Wright, p. 100. *The Gospel Magazine,* the source of so many evangelical hymns, ran from 1766 to 1772, and was revived in 1774. Toplady became its editor at the end of 1775.

others are traceable. Toplady's hymns have been widely appreciated and largely used. In *Denham's Selection* (Baptist), a considerable body of them is still available, but on the whole the number in actual use is constantly diminishing. His polemic hymns have died a natural death: his deep and sincere hymns of Christian experience invite a sympathetic reading rather than a congregational employment: and the conviction can hardly be resisted that his poetic inspiration and even metrical method were borrowed from Charles Wesley. His "Rock of Ages" isolates itself from the body of his work in its impressiveness and usefulness, and maintains its place at the head of English hymns.

Mention must also be made of the *Select Psalms and Hymns* of David Simpson (Macclesfield, 1776; 2nd ed., 1780; new ed. 1795). It was made for the great congregation in the church built for him at Macclesfield after the rector of the parish church had thrown him bodily out of his pulpit; and is chiefly notable for the new hymns it introduced and for the inclusion of anthems.

We thus have before us the first group of Church of England hymn books. Their dates of publication cover only seventeen years, and they have much in common. Generally entitled *Psalms and Hymns* they show no concern with the old metrical Psalmody. They are collections of hymns, gradually expanding from the 170 of Madan to the 600 and over of Simpson. The hymns are thrown together without arrangement and without indications of their authorship, and there are no musical notes or suggestions. From the prefaces we may infer that Madan stood alone among the editors in giving attention to the musical side. In the body of hymns also, there was much that was common to the books. Watts, and to a less degree the Wesleys and Joseph Hart, furnished a nucleus and a considerable share of their contents. Watts' followers, especially Doddridge and the new Baptist hymn writers, were drawn upon; and also the group more or less affiliated with Whitefield or using *The Gospel Magazine* as their medium of publication. Of the editors themselves, only Toplady and Berridge contributed hymns of note, but Newton and Cowper offered their first-fruits.

The group of hymn books shows a very determined purpose to introduce hymn singing and great activity in providing materials for it. They do not of course represent the Church but a small party within it. The new movement was an intrusion of the outside Revival forces. The Hymnody showed its revival origin and character in the evangelistic note, in its concern with experimental religion, and its warmth amid chilling surroundings; and once within the dikes, revealed it yet further by its obliviousness of principles and practices distinguishing church from dissent, and its subordination of the sacramental side of religion. Inspired as it was by a Calvinistic movement the Hymnody was inevitably consistent with Calvinism. This showed itself negatively in its omissions or alterations of Methodist hymns. Positively it was in general content to express a deep sense of sin, an entire dependence on God for deliverance and the discovery of his method in Scripture. With Toplady came more of the terminology and specific statements of Calvinism. It is from this adhesion to the principles of the Revival rather than of the Church of England that these early hymn books derive their larger import; for they helped to establish the foundations of an Evangelical Hymnody not only within but beyond the Church of England.

2. "OLNEY HYMNS" (1779) FILLS OUT THE TYPE OF THE EVANGELICAL HYMN

In line with the earlier Evangelical hymn books, but an event important enough to stand alone, came the publication in 1779 by John Newton, then curate of Olney, of 280 of his own hymns and 68 of his friend William Cowper, under the title of *Olney Hymns in three Books. Book I. On select texts of Scripture. Book II. On occasional subjects. Book III. On the progress and changes of the spiritual life* (London: W. Oliver, 1779). Both men had contributed hymns to *The Gospel Magazine,* and to one or other of the Evangelical hymn books. Newton had appended eighteen pages of "Hymns, &c." to his *Twenty-six Letters on religious subjects* of 1774.[48] As early as 1771 Newton proposed to Cowper that they jointly compose a volume of hymns, partly from "a desire of promoting the faith and comfort of sincere Christians," partly "as a monument to perpetuate the remembrance of an intimate and endeared friendship."[49] Before the work had proceeded far, Cowper was prostrated by brain trouble, and Newton ultimately completed it alone.

The hymns were conceived in the very spirit of their time and surroundings. From them we could reconstruct the actual working of the Revival in an English parish under Evangelical leadership; and they may be regarded as bringing the Hymnody of the Evangelical Revival to a close. In them the offices of the Prayer Book yield to the sermon, the church year is superseded by the civil, the sacraments are subordinated, and the Revival method expresses itself in the evangelical theology, the strenuous activity in the sphere of individual emotion, the didactic element employed to instruct and edify the simple believer, and the expository dealings with Scripture. Many of the hymns had been actually a part of the revival services at Olney, being written for special occasions, or to be sung after some special appeal from the pulpit, or to be made the theme of an exposition by Newton in the prayer meetings held at the Great House.[50]

In the making of these hymns Cowper, as long as he was able, wrought with the feeling and craftmanship of a true poet, and clothed them with the tender charm of his own spirit. Newton poured into them the pulsing life of an

---

[48]Including Cowper's "God moves in a mysterious way," and his own "While with ceaseless course" and "I asked the Lord."

[49]Preface, p. vi.

[50]E. g. (Diary, Dec. 6, 1772) "Expounded my new hymn at the Great House on the subject of a burdened sinner." Josiah Bull, *John Newton,* London, n. d., p. 183.

intense and commanding personality, and proved himself capable at his best of producing great hymns. When his inspiration failed it was like him to have "done his best" to fill the spaces left by his friend's silence. And even when most prosaic and homiletical Newton's work has the quality of being alive and the gift of appealing to other minds. Indeed the *Olney Hymns* are to be taken as a whole,[51] and measured by the unity of the impression they created. Their appeal was immediate, and to an unusual degree permanent. Even in our own day, Faber, the Roman Catholic hymn writer, speaks of their "acting like a spell upon him for years, strong enough to be for long a counter-influence to very grave convictions, and even now to come back from time to time unbidden into the mind."[52]

This influence of *Olney Hymns,* securing for it so many reprintings[53] and so wide a circulation, was much more than that of a hymn book. In form the book was available for congregational use (being arranged precisely as Watts' *Hymns* had been), though some of its materials were not suitable. To what extent it was so employed is not now discoverable. But it furnished many with their favorite songs and devotional reading. It played a part among Evangelicals akin to that of Wesley's *Collection* of the following year among Methodists. It became a people's manual of evangelical doctrine and an instrument of spiritual discipline.

But the place of its hymns in Hymnody itself is a very considerable one. They were inevitably recognized as a very notable accession to the store available for Evangelical

[51]The best study of the *Olney Hymns* is Montgomery's "Introductory Essay," written for Collins' Glasgow ed., and often reprinted. In his contentment with Cowper's poetic grace, Montgomery perhaps overlooks something of Newton's bluff virility.

[52]Frederick Wm. Faber, *Hymns,* preface to ed. of 1861.

[53]3rd ed., 1783; 9th, 1810. It was kept in print during most, if not all, of the XIXth century. The numerous American reprints seem to have begun in New York in 1787 (Evans' *American Bibliography,* vol. vii, item 20588).

use. They began at once to furnish materials for the hymn books. The proportion of them that became familiar and endeared to various denominations is surprisingly large. In the Church of England a number won a place from which even the reconstructions of the Oxford Revival have been unable to dislodge them.[54] At the lowest estimate six must be accorded a classical position: three of Cowper's —"Hark my soul! it is the Lord," "Oh! for a closer walk with God," "God moves in a mysterious way," and three of Newton's—"Come, my soul, thy suit prepare," "Glorious things of thee are spoken," "How sweet the name of Jesus sounds."

Olney Hymns exercised also a decided influence upon the evangelical ideal of the Hymn, not so much in the way of modifying as in the way of confirming and deepening it. Like Charles Wesley's it was an influence favoring the use of hymns as an expression of the most private experience, and like his again, Newton's method was autobiographical. If indeed he intended all his hymns for public use, he was careless of Whitefield's dictum that congregational hymns should confine themselves to sentiments common to the singers. This inward-looking of "the old blasphemer" begat intense remorse and measureless self-contempt, and made the Hymn of Experience an instrument of self-reproach. In the same way Cowper's dreadful depression, and Newton's sympathy with him, tinged *Olney Hymns* at times with the shadow of the cloud hiding the divine Presence. It can hardly be denied that the indiscriminate use of such materials by congregations introduced an element of unreality and morbidness into Evangelical Hymnody, from which it was slow to recover. On the other hand, Newton's perfect faith in the salvation offered, his glorying in its efficacy, his wonder at its grace, the tender note of his love for the Saviour, the exultation of his triumphant faith;—all these things entered into the warp

[54] In the latest edition of *Hymns ancient and modern* there are six by Newton and seven by Cowper.

and woof of the Evangelical Hymnody, and Newton's close relating of personal experience with the truths and narratives of Scripture became preëminently the accepted method of that Hymnody. Any who were brought up in some one of the evangelical churches, in the period after Watts' domination had passed, are likely to recall a number of Newton's hymns, a few of Cowper's also, as inevitably associated with the gospel there proclaimed and the type of religion there practised.

3. Movements to Introduce Hymns in the Main Body of the Church (1724-1816)

Olney Hymns marks a point of transition in Church of England Hymnody. It was the last of a group of books bringing the Evangelical Hymnody into the Church without remoulding or even rearranging it into accommodation with the Prayer Book system of parochial worship. It was to be followed by a group of books, still Evangelical, that aimed to adapt the new Hymnody to the methods and manners of the Church.

The point is thus a convenient one at which to turn from the small Evangelical Party to the main body of the Church where Psalm singing prevailed and the Prayer Book system was unimpaired by revival influences outside, in order to discover what progress had been made there in introducing the singing of hymns.

In this main body there was no unity of feeling or purpose in regard to the use of hymns in public worship.

(1) There were first the stand-fasts, who through the entire XVIIIth century maintained the position Bishop Beveridge had taken at its beginning, that the good estate of the Church was bound up with the continued use of the Sternhold and Hopkins version of the Psalms, and that the traditional method of singing them need not be disturbed. Outside of the Church Watts had successfully attacked the divine prescription of the Psalms, and the hymns of himself and his school had largely displaced them in Non-

conformist use. At the borders of the Church the Wesleys had disregarded Psalmody and instituted a popular Hymnody of feeling and experience. All these changes tended to strengthen the position of the Metrical Psalm in the minds of the conservative and stiff churchmen, and led them to constitute themselves special guardians of that Metrical Psalm, originally the creation and the badge of Geneva. Psalmody had come to seem to them a characteristic part of the Prayer Book system and the hymns a menace. The more widely Watts' hymns spread, and the more fervid the Methodist Song grew, the more obvious it became that the Hymn was stamped with the hall-mark of dissent and, even worse, of "enthusiasm." The prejudice against hymns in churchly circles grew very strong. Dr. Samuel Johnson plumed himself for having let it yield to a charitable impulse.[55]

(2) There were the less extreme conservatives, just as anxious to maintain the old Psalmody, but who lamented the prevailing apathy fallen on the ordinance, and saw the force of the demand for hymns suitable for holy days and occasions. Bishop Gibson had suggested the remedy in his *Directions given to the clergy* (1724) on his translation to London. He urged the great need of a better and heartier musical performance and laid out a "Course of Singing Psalms" covering the Sundays, Christmas, Easter, Whitsunday, and some church occasions. The expedient was a good one and somewhat widely adopted; but it was also quickly appropriated by the advocates of hymns. In 1734 "R. W." printed at Nottingham *The excellent use of Psalmody, with a course of Singing Psalms for half a year,* adding an appendix of twenty-eight hymns for the festivals, the Communion, morning and evening, midnight, and funerals. Still later the Rivingtons reissued *The excellent use,* bound up with their tractate of (12) *Divine Hymns* and *Hymns taken from the Supplement to Tate and Brady's Psalms.*

[55]See preface.

In this group of conservatives Romaine belonged, as has appeared, and although foremost in adopting the theology of the Revival, was more strenuous than most in resisting its Hymnody. His *A Collection out of the Book of Psalms, suited to every Sunday in the year* (London, 1775), shows by its title that he followed Bishop Gibson's lead, but he went a step farther by adding notes on the evangelical interpretation of various Psalms. To us who look back it seems very plain that the addition of evangelical annotations to the "Singing Psalms" could not stay the intrusion of a pronouncedly evangelical Hymnody, any more than the appropriation of Psalms to Christian festivals could illustrate their full significance.

(3) There were those, and perhaps Romaine had no quarrel with them, who were fully persuaded that hymns had a real function in the Christian life, and favored their use provided only they were not introduced into the stated church services. As early as 1727 there appeared *A Collection of Psalms, and Divine Hymns, suited to the great festivals of the Church, for morning and evening, and other occasions* (London; J. Downing, 1727). It was in all respects a hymn book, with the hymns numbered for use, and included "a Table of Psalms on practical subjects, which may be of use to Parish-Clarks."[56] Notwithstanding this suggestive reference (on the title-page) to parish clerks, the preface opens with the declaration: "I have no thought of proposing the Use of any Part of this *Collection* in the Publick Service." Of hymn books, however, as of greater ventures, it is true that man proposes and Providence disposes. And it is not unlikely that some parish clerks who consulted the Table were tempted to line out the Hymns. The few psalms in this book were from Denham and Patrick. The hymns constituting the majority of its forty-

[56]This apparently unnoticed book preceded by ten years John Wesley's Charleston *Collection*, which Dr. Julian calls "the first hymnbook compiled for use in the Church of England." *Dictionary of Hymnology*, p. 332.

nine pieces "were collected from several Books, some of which are not easy to be met with." The little book was published cheaply for general distribution and for binding up with others of like size in a series printed by Downing "for promoting Christian knowledge and Practice." The practical effect of this book and others like it was undoubtedly to familiarize hymn singing.

In this group we may include also the "Religious Societies," whose origin dates back to the last quarter of the XVIIth century and which survived to play a part in the Revival under Wesley and Whitefield. That formed at Romney, Kent, in 1690, had its own hymn book as early as 1724: *The Christian Sacrifice of Praises, consisting of select Psalms and Hymns, with doxologies and proper tunes. For the use of the Religious Society of Romney. Collected by the author of the Christian's Daily Manual. London: printed by William Pearson, for John Wyat, at the Rose in St. Paul's Church-Yard, 1724.* This recently recovered volume has 41 Psalm versions, with 27 hymns selected from Austin, Playford, Patrick, and the *Supplement to the New Version.* It was no doubt prepared for use apart from the church service, but the custom of attending Preparation Sermons and Communion in churches[57] suggests another possible avenue through which hymn singing entered the parish churches.

(4) There was also in the main body of the Church a constantly growing party of progress in Psalmody, whose plans for its improvement included some use of hymns,[58] and whose efforts it will be convenient to distinguish as two parallel movements.

One of these was plainly suggested by the new and hearty hymn singing of the Revival, and took shape in the cultivation of music in several of the charitable institutions of London. To furnish suitable tunes especially, a series of

[57]G. V. Portus, *Caritas Anglicana* (an inquiry into Religious Societies) London, 1912, p. 17.

[58]But not particularly the hymns of the Evangelical movement.

books was published in which "Psalms, Hymns and Anthems" were printed with equal freedom. Such an use of hymns is partly explained by the "Charity Hymns" and those written to grace special occasions in these institutions. In the case of the Lock Hospital, the musical movement coincided with the Evangelical. Its chapel was used not only by its inmates, but by a strongly contrasting West End Evangelical congregation who rented sittings.[59] The hymn book and tune book prepared for their common use by Martin Madan have already been noted.

At the "Asylum or House of Refuge for Female Orphans" at Westminster Bridge, the improvement of its music under William Riley took the form of antagonism to the tunes made popular by the Revival. His *Parochial Music corrected* (1762) dwelt especially on the light fuguing tunes of the "Methodists," which were creeping into the Church through the "Lectureships" in parish churches that gave Evangelicals their opportunity. Nevertheless here as elsewhere the use of hymns followed musical improvement. Riley's *Psalms, and Hymns for the Chapel of the Asylum or House of Refuge for Female Orphans* (n. d.; after 1762) included the words of the hymns.[60] For the Foundling Hospital a series of books was published, beginning with *Psalms, Hymns and Anthems used in the Chapel of the Hospital for the Maintenance and Education of Exposed and Deserted Young Children* (1774). It contained sixteen hymns, including some of Addison's and which by 1796 had increased to twenty-two. One of the Foundling

[59]Balleine, *The Evangelical Party*, p. 61.

[60]Rev. Jacob Duché, the refugee rector of Christ Church, Philadelphia, became chaplain of the Asylum in 1782 (C. Higham in *New Church Magazine*, London, Sept. 1896, p. 461). He is said to have edited the editions of 1785 and 1789 (W. T. Brooke in *Morning Light*, Nov. 16, 1895); and is credited with the authorship of three of the Asylum hymns (*New Ch. Maga. ut supra*, pp. 464, 465). Duché preached Swedenborgian views, and one of these hymns appears in New Church hymnals up to the present day (*Hymns for use of the New Church*, London, 1881, No. 575: "Come, love Divine! thy power impart.")

hymns, often appearing as a leaflet pasted in at the end of the 1796 edition, was our familiar "Praise the Lord! ye heavens adore Him." For the Magdalen Hospital five separate collections were printed, beginning with *The Hymns Anthems and Tunes with the Ode used at the Magdalen Chapel* (n. d.). This contains twenty-seven hymns by Ken, Addison, Doddridge and others, including a version of *Dies Irae*. This was followed by *A second Collection of Psalms and Hymns;*[61] *A third,* and *A fourth Collection of Hymns for the use of the Magdalen Chapel.* These were afterward rearranged as a single volume.

The singing of the inmates became a marked feature of the life of these institutions and something like a feature of London life itself; drawing the general public to the chapel services and to the united service held annually in one of the churches and later in St. Paul's. "Charity children" were, moreover, commonly distributed among the parish churches, to act as a choir, taking their hymns with them. In this way they did much toward making hymn singing familiar and popular; just as in our own day the Sunday schools, coming into the churches with their liturgical services, have so widely affected the ordinary worship of non-liturgical churches.

(5) The other section of the progressive element was less free in its ways. It was more or less interested in musical improvement: the desired improvement in the subject matter of Psalmody it had found by introducing Tate and Brady's *New Version* (1696) into its parish churches. It was not interested in the Revival Hymnody nor in the hymn books of the Evangelicals, but favored supplementing the psalms with a few hymns for festivals and other church occasions. We have already described[62] the early embodiment of such desire in the *Supplement to the New Version,* first printed

---

[61] There is suggestiveness in the advertisement it carries of its publisher's shop: "Where also may be had, Six favourite Hymns used at the Tabernacles of the Rev. Mess. *Whitefield* and *Wesley.*"

[62] See chap. ii.

in 1700, with its paraphrases of canticles and six other hymns increased to nine in 1708.

In 1741 John Arnold of Great Warley, Essex, printed a setting of the psalms, in the Playford fashion, as *The Compleat Psalmodist*. *In four books:* the fourth being "A Select Number of Divine Hymns on various occasions," mostly the festivals and Good Friday. He included one each from Ken and Watts and two from the Tate and Brady *Supplement,* and sixteen less familiar. Most of the hymns were *de trop,* and were dropped out of later editions, but one, "Jesus Christ is ris'n to-day," ultimately attached itself to the *New Version.* It was partly taken (like its stirring tune) from the earlier *Lyra Davidica: a Collection of Divine songs and Hymns* (London, 1708): a book from an unknown hand, notable as an early attempt to interest English people in the "divine songs" and "pleasant tunes" of the Germans.

The *Supplement* itself was kept in print, and copies of Tate and Brady bearing dates up to the middle of the century occur with the *Supplement* bound in. Its hymns were not therefore lost to sight; but the usual surviving copies of like dates have no hymns. We may infer that many parishes using Tate and Brady grew disposed to rest satisfied with the good qualities of the psalms themselves.

During the last quarter of the century there came some change in the situation. A disposition showed itself in what we may call Tate and Brady circles to make more use of the hymns in the *Supplement,* and to facilitate such use by attaching them to the printed Psalters. The Rivingtons issued in 1779 a small tractate entitled *Hymns taken from the Supplement to Tate and Brady's Psalter,* and an undated copy of the same has turned up which is thought to be earlier.[63] This tractate was intended to be inserted or bound in current copies of Tate and Brady. In a London trade edition of Tate and Brady of 1780, four hymns selected

[63]Catalogue of Charles Higham & Son, London, No. 503, October, 1911, item 1950.

from the *Supplement* appear printed at the end of the psalms, following the Gloria Patri, with separate pagination, and headed simply as HYMNS. They are:

Come, Holy Ghost, Creator, come.
While Shepherds watch'd their flocks by Night.
Since Christ, our Passover, is slain.
Christ from the Dead is rais'd, and made.

In a Cambridge Press edition of 1782 a new selection of hymns is printed at the end of the psalms, reflecting something of the current Hymnody, and including only one hymn from the *Supplement*. They are:

High let us swell our tuneful notes (Doddridge).
Hark! the herald angels sing (Wesley).
Christ from the dead is rais'd, and made (Tate and Brady).
My God, and is thy table spread (Doddridge).
Awake, my soul, and with the sun (Ken).

In London trade editions of 1790 and 1792 all the above hymns are printed, except "While Shepherds watch'd." In another London trade edition of 1790 are the four hymns of 1780, with Ken's Morning and Evening Hymns on printed slips pasted in. The latter, and the Easter Hymn, "Jesus Christ is ris'n to-day," also appear on printed slips pasted in University Press editions. Thenceforward it became the rule to print a group of hymns after the psalms as though a constituent part of the Psalter, and this continued so long as the *New Version* was kept in print. By the beginning of the XIXth century the Clarendon Press had its distinctive selection consisting of fifteen of the sixteen hymns[64] and metrical canticles of the *Supplement* of 1700, with "O Lord, turn not Thy face away" from the Appendix to the *Old Version,* and the four hymns from the Cambridge edition of 1782. The Cambridge Press selection differed by including all sixteen of the *Supplement* hymns, and by adding (from about 1816) "Jesus Christ is ris'n to-day" and Ken's Evening Hymn; but some copies from the Cambridge Press had a smaller selection.

These facts and dates are fitted to correct some current

[64]The Commandments, "God spake these words," being omitted.

impressions of the hymns appended to Tate and Brady's
New Version. It has been a sort of fashion to regard them
as something negligible in the history of Church of England Hymnody. It is assumed that they owe their place to
the mere whim of the printer, and that their consequent
introduction into worship was quite fortuitous and even
humorous. This familiar assumption appears to find its
only support in a surmise of Charles B. Pearson, who, in
an essay on "Hymns and Hymn-writers," says:

"The introduction of hymns for Christian seasons in particular services is due, probably, to 'the stationers' before the Revolution, and to
the University printers in modern times, more particularly to one of the
latter about half a century back, who, being a Dissenter, thought fit to
fill up the blank leaves at the end of the Prayer-book with hymns suggested by himself,—a liberty to which, apparently, no objection was
raised by the authorities of the Church at that day, and thus 'factum
valet.'"[65]

What the actual evidence seems to show is that the
hymns were added neither by dissenters nor by Evangelicals, but by the Prayer Book party itself, and that they
were printed in the Psalters because they were already being
used in the services, and with a view of avoiding the necessity of inserting the little booklets and printed slips containing them. Indeed their significance seems to lie in their
direct connection with the original *Supplement* of 1700, as
showing how the continuous demand of the churchly yet
progressive element for a few liturgical hymns to supplement the psalms kept open a channel of its own digging
for the introduction of hymn singing into the Church of
England.

It thus appears that in its own way and within its defined
limits the Prayer Book party co-operated with the freer
movements that were making a hymn singing Church. Its
special contribution was in getting its hymns printed in the
Psalters as though a part of the authorized Psalmody.
From this position they were never dislodged. And as the
Psalters were ordinarily bound up with the Prayer Books,

[65]*Oxford Essays,* 1858.

the hymns became for all practical purposes a part of the Prayer Books themselves, even those distributed by the "S. P. C. K." Whatever the legal niceties as to authorization may have been, henceforward the opponents of hymn singing—and they were many and bitter—were handicapped by the presence of the hymns within the sacred covers of the Prayer Book itself.

4. THE PERIOD OF COMPROMISE: "PSALMS AND HYMNS" IN PARISH CHURCHES (1785-1819)

We now take up the Hymnody and hymn book making of the Evangelical Party from the date of *Olney Hymns* (1779). It was, as has been said, the last of the earlier series that had little to distinguish them from the hymn books of dissent; and the conservatives were justified if they regarded it as a somewhat extreme example of that type. Just how the Evangelical leaders regarded it is difficult to estimate. Most of them probably welcomed it for its hymns; none certainly as the model for a church hymn book.[66] The series of hymn books immediately following might seem to indicate a reaction from the unchurchly tendencies of *Olney Hymns*. But their altered complexion in reality reflected the change passing over the Evangelical movement itself. Like Methodism it had begun within the Church but apart from the parochial order and worship. Its beginnings had been extra-parochial, and even to the end of the XVIIIth century its strength lay in proprietary chapels, endowed lectureships and other centres of influence that had a measure of freedom. But with the waning of the century the movement began to draw established parishes within its control and to influence parishes not to be accounted Evangelical. The Evangelicals themselves moderated their views, sought a closer conformity to

[66]Its publication probably seems more notable to us who look back than it did to the Evangelical leaders of the time. Richard Cecil, in his authorized *Memoir of the Rev. John Newton* (ed. H. T. Warren, Finsbury, n. d., p. 26), makes only incidental mention of it.

the order and manners of their Church, and became disposed to affiliate more with the moderate element of the
Prayer Book party.

These changes favored first of all the extension of hymn
singing into the regular services of parish churches, and
consequently a compromise with the accustomed order of
psalm singing in those churches, by which both psalms and
hymns should have equal recognition and use in parochial
"Psalmody." To provide for this the new series of Evangelical hymn books became not only in name but in reality
collections of "Psalms and Hymns."

From *Olney Hymns* we pass at once to *Psalms and
Hymns, collected by William Bromley Cadogan* (1st ed.,
1785: 4th, 1803), rector at Chelsea and also at Reading.
It contains a complete metrical Psalter, with 150 hymns
chosen and arranged in the earlier manner. There is a
similar provision of psalms in the *Psalms and Hymns* of
John Venn (London, 1785) and in Basil Woodd's book of
1794, hereafter to be described. And, it may be added,
Church of England hymn books continued to be "Psalms
and Hymns" down to the Oxford Revival. These Evangelical leaders took as much pains as Romaine himself to
provide Psalm versions that should maintain or revive an
interest in psalm singing. One of them indeed, Richard
Cecil, followed Romaine for a while. His *Psalms of David*
(1785) is confined to canonical Psalms, the versions drawn
from the best available sources, including Addison and
Milton. Not until 1806 did he add *Hymns for the principal
festivals of the Church of England.* His collection had
reached a thirty-second edition by 1840. Thomas Robinson,
in the hymn book made for his church at Leicester (before
1790) included nothing from either the *Old* or *New Versions* of the Psalms. He may have been moved by associations of them with his unwelcomed coming to Leicester,
"when the choir bellowed the most unsuitable psalms instead
of those which he instructed the clerk to announce."[67]

[67]Balleine, *The Evangelical Party,* p. 121.

The conjunction of Psalms and Hymns in parish worship did something to bring more closely together the two main agencies of hymn singing—the Evangelicals, who cared most for hymns, and the moderate Prayer Book element, which wished to retain Psalmody supplemented by hymns for holy days and occasions. It remained for Basil Woodd, an Evangelical leader of the second generation,—not a rector but preacher and indeed proprietor of Bentinck Chapel, Marylebone,—to take a further step, and bring the two parties to something very like the unity of a common ground in Hymnody. His project was to adapt Hymnody to the Prayer Book system itself. He conceived the ideal of a hymn book that should be "the companion to the Book of Common Prayer."

The book in which Woodd embodied his ideal appeared at London in 1794 as *The Psalms of David, and other portions of the Sacred Scriptures, arranged according to the order of the Church of England, for every Sunday in the year; also for the Saints' Days, Holy Communion, and other services.* The promise of the title was scrupulously fulfilled. Under the heading of each Sunday and holy day of the Christian Year a metrical psalm was designated to serve as the Introit provided for in the rubrics of the first Prayer Book of Edward VI. Then followed one or more hymns, adapted to the Epistle or Gospel or subject of the day. The whole was followed by selections of hymns for Communion, Baptism and other church offices and occasions, and a few for general use in public worship. The selection of hymns, from all the materials then available, was good, and in later editions some originals were added.

In a word this interesting book stamped Hymnody with the mark of the Church rather than of a party. It pointed the way of making hymns a constituent part of the liturgical order rather than a formless body of song intruded from without under the Revival impulse. It was Woodd in 1794, and not Heber in 1809-22, who first worked out the ideal of "A Hymnal Companion to the Prayer Book," and thus anticipated the form in which ultimately Hymnody came to be accepted by the straitest school of churchmanship as an enrichment of the service.

This is not to say that Woodd set up a model at once followed by succeeding editors. On the contrary the editor next succeeding was that uncompromising Evangelical, Charles Simeon of Cambridge, who trained so many evangelical preachers and by deed of trust constituted Evangelicalism as a distinct denomination within the bounds of the Church. Simeon sought every occasion to vindicate his "regard for the Liturgy and Services of our Church."[68] His real concern was for the sermon and for a Hymnody that would illustrate its doctrine and enforce its appeals. He published in 1795 *A Collection of Psalms and Hymns.* It contained a much abridged selection of psalms. Otherwise the book affiliates in contents and manner with the earlier Evangelical group. Its hymns follow the subject of discourse, its "Time and seasons" are Morning, Evening, Spring, Summer, Harvest, and so forth. Even Easter and Christmas appear only in the table of contents and in this way—,"*Christmas-Day,* See *Incarnation.*" As more than a hundred scattered parishes came to be included in "The Simeon Trust," the use of his *Collection* was widespread and long continued.[69] It thus kept alive in these and doubtless other parishes a distinctly Evangelical Hymnody, in no way differing from that of dissenting bodies holding similar convictions.

The general trend was, however, otherwise. The influence of Woodd's more churchly conception, even in his own party appears, for example, in Biddulph's *Selection of Hymns accommodated to the service of the Church of England* (2nd ed., 1804); in Cecil's similar *Appendix* of 1806, already referred to; and in John Venn's *Appendix* of the same year *Containing Hymns for the principal festivals of*

---

[68]*Cf.* Wm. Carus, *Memoirs of the Life of the Rev. Charles Simeon,* chap. xii, 3rd ed., London, 1848, pp. 210 ff.

[69]The 13th edition appeared in 1837.

the Church of England; and for family and private use. Venn's book was decidedly evangelical under its churchly frame work and its expedient of "private" hymns. He represented the "Clapham sect," the new missionary society and *The Christian Observer;* and his little book introduced hymns into many "country congregations," for whom it was designed. In extending hymn singing beyond the Evangelical pale, Woodd played a greater part.

But, in general, those concerned for the integrity of the Prayer Book system were not yet converted to the latter day Hymnody. They saw with dismay hymn singing spreading from parish to parish, and new hymn books appearing on every side. Of these, during the first two decades of the XIXth century there were not less than fifty.[70] A number of them were designed for use in a single parish. Of those of more general type, the most important, not already mentioned, were: J. Fawcett's *A Collection of Psalms and Hymns from various authors* (Carlisle, 1802; 4th ed., 1811); J. Kempthorne's *Select portions of Psalms and Hymns from various authors* (London, 1810); Thos. Cotterill's *A Selection of Psalms and Hymns for public and private use* (Newcastle, 1810; 8th ed., Sheffield, 1819); and G. T. Noel's *A Selection of Psalms and Hymns from the New Version . . . and others* (London, c. 1811).[71]

[70] The fullest, though incomplete, list is in Julian's *Dictionary,* pp. 333, 334.

[71] The hymn books of this period introduced a few new hymn writers. To Fawcett's book Joseph Dacre Carlyle contributed his hymns including "Lord, when we bend before Thy throne." Cotterill wrote many for the various editions of his *Selection,* and they attained considerable use. To its 9th edition, John Cawood contributed, among others, "Hark! what mean those holy voices?" and "Almighty God, Thy word is cast." The most voluminous writer was William Hurn, who, while vicar of Debenham, published *Psalms and Hymns, the greater part original* (Ipswich, 1813), containing more than 250 of his own. Their number was greatly increased in his *Hymns and Spiritual Songs* (Woodbridge, 1824), after he had seceded from the church. During this period also Sir Robert Grant was publishing hymns in *The Christian Observer* (1806-1815) and Reginald Heber printed his in the same periodical (1811-1816).

It seemed to the conservatives that a purely voluntary system of worship was intruding into, if not threatening to supplant, the Prayer Book system. "The importance which, in many places, attaches to the Hymn Book," said Bishop Marsh, "is equal, if not superior, to the importance ascribed to the Prayer Book.[72] The objections urged against the Hymn Book were mainly two: It may tend to introduce false doctrines or to undermine Church doctrine in the minds of those using it; or it may (as in some instances already) offend against reverence in worship by the "flippancy and vulgarity" of its contents.

There were, doubtless, elements of disorder, and even of danger, in this unchecked zeal for hymnal making. But the opposition took deeper ground and aimed at the total suppression of hymn singing itself as introduced and practised without even the shadow of authority. Woodd, in his preface, had cited the uniformity statute of Edward VI, authorizing the use of "any Psalm or Prayer taken out of the Bible at any due time," and Queen Elizabeth's Injunctions of 1559, permitting "an hymn or such-like song" "in the beginning or in the end of common prayer." He claimed also that the prose hymns and *Veni Creator* in the Prayer Book involved an authorization of the singing of Hymns. Some of his successors endeavored to strengthen their cause by securing permission to dedicate their collections to some friendly prelate.[73]

Some bishops, on the other hand, were so confident that nothing but the *Old* or *New Version* of the Psalms was authorized for use that they warmly protested against, or even prohibited, the employment of hymns within their

[72]*A Charge delivered at the primary visitation of Herbert, Lord Bishop of Peterborough, in July, 1820; with an appendix, containing some remarks on the modern custom of singing in our churches unauthorized Psalms and Hymns.* London, 1820.

[73]The editors of *Psalms and Hymns, selected for the Churches of Buckden* (1815) dedicate it by permission to Bishop Tomline (of Lincoln); and in the 2nd ed. (1820) state it to be "sanctioned by the authority of that distinguished prelate."

dioceses. We find Simeon in 1814 writing to an Evangelical friend to "put aside Hymns" rather than to continue his unseemly contest with his bishop.[74] The Bishop of Exeter is said to have prohibited the use of Ken's Morning and Evening Hymns within his diocese.[75]

The opposition was brought to a head by the publication in 1819 of an eighth and enlarged edition of Thomas Cotterill's *A Selection of Psalms and Hymns for public and private use, adapted to the services of the Church of England. Sheffield: printed for the editor, by J. Montgomery at the Iris-office, 1819:* and his attempt to enforce its use upon his congregation at St. Paul's, Sheffield. This caused much disturbance in the congregation, of which some outside opponents of hymns took advantage; and suit was brought against Cotterill in the Consistory Court of the Archbishop of York. The Chancellor decided that hymn singing was an irregularity without due authority, but he assumed that none could wish to attack a practice that had become so general and was so edifying. He refused costs and postponed sentence upon Cotterill for his irregularity, virtually reducing the issue before him to a question of the merits of Cotterill's book, which "certainly contained a great many excellent Psalms and Hymns to which there could be no reasonable objection."[76] He intimated that the interests of religion required a compromise of the suit, and offered the services of the Archbishop as mediator. In the end the compromise was effected. Cotterill's book was withdrawn, and a new one,[77] smaller and less markedly evangelical, was prepared under the eye of Archbishop Harcourt and at his expense, and the Sheffield church was supplied with a sufficiency of copies, each bearing the in-

---

[74]*Memoirs,* ed. cited, p. 272.

[75]*The Christian Observer,* July, 1822, p. 435, n.

[76]For the legal proceedings, see *An Inquiry into historical facts relative to parochial Psalmody* [by J. Gray], York, 1821, pp. 46 ff.

[77]*A Selection of Psalms and Hymns for public worship,* London, T. Cadell, 1820 (29th ed., 1840).

scription: "The gift of his Grace the Lord Archbishop of York."[78]

These curious proceedings, from which no appeal was taken, did not change the irregular status of Hymnody, but they certainly discouraged further legal contests. In 1822 H. J. Todd, of the York diocese, published a pamphlet,[79] urging the sole authority of the old Psalmody; in 1820 the Bishop of Peterborough charged against the liberty exercised by parishes in introducing hymn books,[80] in which he was followed by the Bishop of Killaloe, Ireland, in 1821.[81] But in general the ground was regarded as cleared of practical obstructions, and the making of new hymn books proceeded apace in the years following the York settlement.

In these books the influence of Cotterill's, in spite of its suppression, is very marked. Though somewhat on earlier lines, it was a fresh selection, at which the poet Montgomery assisted. And it had the distinction of introducing into church use some fifty of his hymns, thus contributing to the permanent enrichment of Hymnody. In the interests, real or supposed, of the "good taste" at which Cotterill aimed, Montgomery also altered freely the texts of his predecessors. As Cotterill's *Selection* served as a source book for numerous succeeding compilers, it happened that these tinkered texts frequently remained the standard till very recent times, in some cases to the present day.

We may now regard hymn singing in the Church of England as having passed the stage of intrusion and even of toleration, and to have reached that of substantial recognition. It had not superseded the singing of metrical Psalms but had reduced the Psalter to a selection of psalms, with which hymns were incorporated on equal footing. As to its prevalence we have the testimony of the editors of the

---

[78]*An Inquiry*, &c., pp. 74, 75.

[79]*Observations upon the metrical version of the Psalms*, London, F. C. & J. Rivington, 1822.

[80]See note no. 72.

[81]Fully quoted in Todd, *op. cit.*, pp. 22 ff.

Buckden *Selection:* "There are, perhaps, not many large congregations in our national Church, where some Psalms, different from the old and new versions, and some Hymns, founded upon the history and doctrines of the Gospel, have not been admitted." More authoritative was the assumption of the Chancellor at York that no one having the interests of religion at heart would wish to disturb "the prevalent usage," "so edifying and acceptable to congregations."

This change had found its opportunity here, as elsewhere, in the decadence and indifference into which the old Psalmody had fallen. It had been brought about, first by the desire of musical improvement and for the recognition of church festivals and fasts, but mainly by the "enthusiasm" of the Evangelical Revival, and the persistence of the Evangelical Party within the Church.[82] The practice of hymn singing had passed beyond the limits of party, but had not as yet brought itself into close relation with the Prayer Book system. The supply of hymn books was copious, and their very diversity had already suggested the need (not yet filled) of a collection of hymns compiled and issued under competent authority.[83] The Hymnody itself bore the marks (never yet obliterated) of its Evangelical origin in its general non-sectarian character, its dealings with individual experience, and its mingling together of the work of churchman and dissenter.

[82]The valuable introduction to *Hymns ancient and modern, Historical edition,* 1909, appears to the present writer to ignore the main agency of the Evangelicals within the Church in introducing Hymnody, and to transfer it to the musical development of London Charities.

[83]See Todd, *op. cit.,* pp. 28, 29.

CHAPTER VIII
THE EVANGELICAL HYMNODY IN AMERICA

I

ITS ADOPTION DELAYED BY VARIOUS CAUSES

The Evangelical Revival may be said to have come to America bodily in the person of Whitefield. He embarked for his second visit in August, 1739, fresh from the revival scenes that had accompanied his preaching in England. His connection with the Wesleys was still close, and his reprint of their *Hymns and sacred Poems* at Philadelphia in 1740 has been already noticed.[1] But it was during this visit that John Wesley's publication of Arminian views called forth Whitefield's vigorous protest, and no doubt emphasized the Calvinism of his own preaching in the American tours that fanned the revival flame first kindled at Northampton into the widespread Great Awakening.

When Whitefield came, the American Churches were still under the sway of the Metrical Psalmody tradition. The Church of England congregations closed their doors upon him, and the Great Awakening had no effect upon their dull parochial psalm singing. The Baptists, especially in New England, were at first indifferent, and the Revival had to create an Evangelical party before it could arouse an interest in an Evangelical Hymnody. Among Congregationalist and Presbyterian psalm singers the effects of the Revival on Church Song were immediate and final. It started an irrepressible demand for a Hymnody corresponding to the evangelical preaching. At that time Whitefield had taken no steps toward developing a characteristic Hymnody of

[1]Chapter vi, part VIII, section I.

his own, and seems to have made little use of the Wesleyan Hymns. He was, however, then and always, in spite of Dr. Watts' coldness toward his revival methods, a great admirer of that divine's "System of Praise." A friend, going to Whitefield's bedroom on the last night of his life, "found him reading in the Bible, and with Dr. *Watts's* Psalms lying open before him."[2] We may hence presume Whitefield's entire acquiescence in the fact that the actual effect of the Great Awakening was to start the "Era of Watts" in American Hymnody.[3]

In 1753 the Hymnody of the Evangelical Revival found an English embodiment in Whitefield's own *Hymns for social worship,* prepared for his Tabernacle; copies of which he no doubt brought with him on subsequent visits to America. While in Philadelphia, during his sixth visit, he wrote to his friend Robert Keen, on September 21, 1764,— "I received the hymn-books,"[4] referring apparently to a consignment of his own, the twelfth edition of which had just appeared. During the following year, while he was still in America, or after he had sailed for home on June 9, the first American reprint of the hymn book appeared, from the press of William Bradford, Philadelphia, 1765.[5] In the following year, while he was in England, the Bradfords printed *A Collection of Hymns for social worship. Extracted from various authors, and published by the Revd. Mr. Madan, and the Revd. Mr. Whitefield. Philadelphia: W. & T. Bradford, 1766:*[6] a book whose identity is not obvious.

In the year 1768, there were two American reprints of

---

[2]Jno. Gillies, *Memoirs of George Whitefield,* London, 1772; p. 271.

[3]*Cf.* Chapter iv, part IV, sections I, 1; II, 1.

[4]This clause does not appear in the letter as printed in Whitefield's *Works,* London, 1771 (vol. iii, pp. 314, 315); but may be found in L. Tyerman, *Life of George Whitefield,* ed. N. Y., 1877, vol. ii, p. 477.

[5]Hildeburn, *Issues of the Pennsylvania Press,* item 2181.

[6]*Ibid.,* item 2204. No surviving copy of either of these issues was known to Hildeburn. Evans, in his *American Bibliography,* has merely copied Hildeburn's entries.

Whitefield's *Hymns for social worship,* one by James Parker at New York, and one "Re-printed for, and sold by John Mein, in Boston"; both described on the title as "The Thirteenth Edition." In London new editions continued to appear for many years. There is no record of further American reprints, and Whitefield's death at Newburyport in 1770 does not seem to have suggested a republication.[7] He had made no effort to create a new American denomination, and the actual use of the known reprints of his hymn book is far from clear. At a time of struggle to escape from the bonds of a literal Psalmody, the warm and free Hymnody of Whitefield's collection must have seemed to most established congregations a novelty indeed.

On the whole the introduction of the Evangelical Hymnody in the larger sense was considerably delayed by various causes. There was first of all the addiction to Metrical Psalmody which held fast the Episcopal and many Presbyterian churches till the XIXth century. There was the barrier of language which set apart the Dutch and German Reformed and the Lutheran peoples from participation in English Hymnody of any sort. There was again the enormous popularity of Watts in the Presbyterian and Congregational and in many Baptist Churches, as they became emancipated from the Psalmody tradition. And yet it was not till after the Revolutionary War that the use even of Watts' *Psalms and Hymns* became universal in Congregational churches, and it was not till 1802 that the use of the *Hymns* of Watts was formally authorized by the Presbyterian General Assembly.

It thus appears not only that the introduction of the Evangelical Hymnody was delayed, but that it was not synchronous in the various denominations. While Congregationalists and Presbyterians were still in the Era of

---

[7] In the case of hymn books particularly, the lack of any record of publication is far from conclusive. For instance the Boston reprint of 1768 of Whitefield's collection is not mentioned in any bibliography known to the writer.

Watts, the Baptists had introduced the Evangelical Hymnody; the Methodists had brought over the Wesleyan Hymnody, the Episcopalians were still confined to metrical psalms, the German Reformed had not even begun to use English.

These differences in date are not however so great that it matters much in what order we take up the period of the Evangelical Hymnody in the various denominations. It seems natural to begin with those whose Church Song we have traced from the decline of Metrical Psalmody through the Era of Watts:—the Baptist, Congregationalist and Presbyterian. Then may follow the Churches which crossed at once from the singing of psalms into the use of the Evangelical Hymnody without passing through the intermediate stage of any era of Watts' supremacy:—the Protestant Episcopal and Reformed Dutch. Then come the foreign-speaking Churches that brought here a Hymnody in their own tongues; which, on adopting the English, they supplemented by the Evangelical Hymnody of their neighbors:—the German Reformed and Lutherans. The denominations born on American soil may be considered chronologically or in connection with the Churches out of which they came, as the interests of lucidity suggest. American Methodism kept in the main to the Hymnody of the Methodist side of the Revival, and to that home-made Revival Hymnody so often seeming like a parody of the Wesleyan; and during the period now under review requires no further consideration.

II

ITS USE BY THE BAPTISTS

1. Its Early Welcome among Regular Baptists
(1790-1850)

The Baptist Churches, when once their XVIIth century scruples against singing had been left behind, had found less difficulty in the way of introducing hymns than other Churches where the Psalmody tradition prevailed. And when their XVIIIth century tendency to "Arminianism" had been turned into strenuous Calvinism by the "New Light" of the Great Awakening and the conflict with Methodism in the new evangelization, the Baptists were in as favorable a position as any to receive the new Evangelical Hymnody.

Their churches had been among the earliest in America to adopt Watts' *Psalms and Hymns.* Their first denominational hymn book (Newport, 1766) had for its special motive the desire for Baptismal Hymns, and did not go beyond Watts in the evangelical direction. But the 1790 *Selection* of the Philadelphian Association was largely based on the 1767 *Collection* of N. Conyers, one of the Church of England Evangelicals, and the 1792 reprint of Rippon's *Selection* put American Baptists in early possession of much of the Evangelical Hymnody.

Here, as in England, Rippon's *Selection* was not used as a substitute for Watts' *Psalms and Hymns,* but as supplementing them on "Subjects of discourse" left unprovided for; and the same thing was true of the *Selection* added to Watts by Winchell in 1819. These supplements did not, however, greatly appeal to the less educated type of preacher, and were regarded as especially insufficient to meet the needs of evangelistic work. So that Watts and the Evangelical Hymnody and Revival Songs held a contemporaneous place in Baptist Church Song, and in studying its history during the Era of Watts[8] we have therefore covered also so much of the period of the Evangelical Hymnody as lay within the dates of our study.

We left off at the point where the hold of "Watts entire" upon educated congregations was strengthened by the use in New England of Winchell's *Watts' and select* and in the Middle States of *Watts and Rippon,* while to the West and South there was a wide preference for "Spiritual

[8] *Ante,* chap. iv, part IV, section III.

Songs." In the West the situation was probably bettered by H. Miller's *A new Selection of Psalms, Hymns, and Spiritual Songs, from the best authors* (Cincinnati). It was strong in Watts and the Baptist writers of his school, used some of the later Evangelical Hymnody and included a large collection of "Spiritual Songs," often of the better type. It was a book of the sort that influences thousands of plain people without gaining much notice beyond its constituency; it reached a fifteenth edition in 1833, and a twenty-first in 1839.

In New England the situation was little affected by the publication of *Manual of Christian Psalmody* (Boston and Philadelphia, 1832), which was merely a variation of Lowell Mason's *Church Psalmody* made by Rufus Babcock Jr., of Salem, and designed to supersede Winchell; nor by Linsley and Davis' *Select Hymns, adapted to the devotional services of the Baptist Denomination* (Hartford, 1836: 2nd ed., 1837), designed only to supplement Winchell. To the latter Mrs. Sigourney contributed some hymns, of which "Laborers of Christ, arise" became widely used.

Many congregations in the Middle States, as well as the South and West, introduced *The Baptist Hymn Book; original and selected. In two parts. By W. C. Buck, pastor of the East Baptist Church, Louisville, Ky.* (Louisville, 1842). Ten thousand copies were sold within two years, and the revised edition of 1844 long continued to be reprinted. Buck was an educated man, a famous platform speaker, and in his old age a Confederate chaplain. But his collection of 868 "Hymns" and 211 "Songs" did not much further the best interests of Baptist Hymnody.

In many sections the demand grew for a hymn book more modern than Winchell's or Rippon's Watts and better than Miller's or Buck's, on which it was hoped the churches might unite. In 1841 the Publication Society began preparations to meet the demand, only to learn that a Boston publishing house was about to issue a hymn book with similar aims. To this, though only a publisher's enterprise, the Society decided to lend its name in order to avoid a multiplication of hymn books.[9] It appeared as *The Psalmist: a new Collection of Hymns for the use of the Baptist Churches. By Baron Stow and S. F. Smith. Boston: Gould, Kendall, and Lincoln. 1843.* Stow was a successful Boston pastor, and Smith was becoming known as a writer of hymns and the patriotic song "America."

Judged from a modern standpoint *The Psalmist* had many faults. Its size (1180 hymns) was due to the demand for a hymn on every important sermon topic.[10] The editors' ignorance of the sources of the hymns and too free dealings with the texts were also of the time, however regrettable; their entire ignorance of the Wesleyan Hymns and their handling of them surely inexcusable at so late a day.[11] Again the book was of its time rather than in advance of it in its use of 303 numbers from Watts, 57 from Doddridge, 52 from Miss Steele, and 41 from Beddome, and in having 700 hymns in long and common metre. The attempt throughout to curtail the hymns to a mechanical standard of four stanzas or less, seems intended to gratify preachers who wished full sermons and short hymns, and is described by a reviewer as "convenient."[12]

And yet on the whole *The Psalmist* marked a decided advance. It gave the Baptists precedence over other denominations in leaving behind the "Psalms and Hymns" era of compromise with the Psalmody tradition. It delivered them from the weight of "Watts entire" and rose superior to the Baptist predilection for "Spiritual Songs." It added to the Evangelical Hymnody, already familiar, much from Montgomery and other newer writers, and was the best selection of hymns the Baptists had ever had; "the best

[9] Note prefixed to *The Psalmist.*
[10] Preface, p. 6.
[11] For this they were properly brought to book in *The Methodist Review*, July, 1849, p. 448.
[12] *The Christian Review*, Sept., 1843, p. 452.

collection," said *The Christian Review* (of which Smith was editor), "ever published in the English language."[13]

Hymn writing by American Baptists up to that date is represented in *The Psalmist* by eleven writers. Twenty-six hymns by Smith outnumber those of all the others. His "The morning light is breaking" and "Softly fades the twilight ray," are widely sung, "While through the land the strains resound"[14] of his "My country, 'tis of thee." Of other writers are two by Adoniram Judson, two by Sewall S. Cutting who edited a book of his own, *Hymns for the vestry and fireside* (1841), and one by Henry S. Washburn who in old age gathered his *Vacant Chair and other poems.*

The Psalmist fulfilled expectations in the North, becoming a bond of unity between the churches. It was set to music in 1860, and supplemented by *The Baptist Harp* (Philadelphia, 1849) for social services. In the South it failed through its omission of many hymns of local popularity, and Drs. Richard Fuller and J. B. Jeter were engaged to embody these in *A Supplement* (1850). But the Southern Publication Society made its own book, *The Baptist Psalmody; a Selection of Hymns for the worship of God* (Charleston, 1851); and this, with Sidney Dyer's *The Southwestern Psalmist,* later *Dyer's Psalmist* (Louisville), shared in the South the position taken by *The Psalmist* in the North. Dyer contributed sixteen hymns to his collection, and published two volumes of his verse. These books, with revival song books, such as Elder (Jacob) Knapp's *The Evangelical Harp* (Utica, 1845), and John Dowling's popular *Conference Hymns* (New York, 1849), bring Baptist Hymnody down to the time when Beecher's *Plymouth Collection* and the Andover *Sabbath Hymn and Tune Book* began to change the face of Congregational Song.

[13]September, 1843, p. 450.
[14]O. W. Holmes to S. F. Smith, Octo. 21, 1888. For the history of the hymn see the writer's *Studies of Familiar Hymns,* Phila., 1903, chap. ix: for Smith's collected hymns and verse, see his *Poems of Home and Country,* New York, 1895.

2. DIVERGING CURRENTS OF BAPTIST HYMNODY

There arose, however, during the period under review, a number of denominations holding Baptist views but separate from the main body; and whose Hymnody in some cases demands separate consideration.

(1) THE FREEWILL BAPTISTS. Henry Alline, born at Newport in 1748, became a fiery evangelist in Nova Scotia and a great disturber of church relationships.[15] Among his numerous publications was a collection of no less than 487 original *Hymns and Spiritual Songs,* somewhat in Doddridge's manner, but without his distinction. The Freewill Baptists of Nova Scotia and New England may be regarded as Alline's disciples. In New Hampshire, during a visit to which Alline died in 1784, the first Freewill Baptist church had been founded in 1871 by Benjamin Randall,[16] who dated his conversion to impressions produced by Whitefield's death, but who became an aggressively anti-Calvinistic Baptist. A third edition of Alline's *Hymns* "with some enlargements" under Randall's auspices,[17] appeared at Dover in 1797; another at "Stonington-port, (Con.)" in 1802.[18]

With the growth of the denomination the demand arose for a denominational hymn book, and the General Confer-

---

[15]There is an account of Alline and his work in *The Christian Instructor,* Pictou, Nova Scotia, vol. iv, 1859, for February and the months following. See also D. Benedict, *Genl. Hist. of Bapt. Denomination,* Boston, 1813, vol. i, pp. 282 ff.

[16]See Benedict, vol. ii, pp. 410 ff.

[17]The enlargements consisted of a Farewell Hymn by Alline, an added hymn by Benjamin Randall, and an account by David McClure of Alline's death. Alline's hymn, addressed "to the Christians," confirms Benedict's statement that some of his followers preferred that name.

[18]Some of Alline's hymns are in Elias Smith's *Hymns for the use of Christians* (1805). His best hymn, "Amazing sight, the Saviour stands," was included in Nettleton's *Village Hymns,* and taken thence into Dr. Hatfield's Presbyterian *The Church Hymn Book* (New York, 1872). There, and even in the Freewill Baptist collection of 1832, it is marked "Anon."

ence arranged for the publication of *Hymns for Christian Melody. Selected from various authors. Boston: published by David Marks, for the Free-will Baptist Connection* (1832). It gathered its 1000 hymns from practically all available sources, and is distinguished by its large use of the "Methodist Selection," and an avoidance of "Hymns of the lower grade." The statement of the preface that "Experience has proved no composition of an inferior character can long be used to edification," may refer back to the outgrown hymns of Alline, or to later attempts to introduce current revival songs. This book was superseded in 1853 by an even larger and carefully prepared collection of 1232 hymns, *The Psalmody: a Collection of Hymns for public and social worship. Compiled by order of the Freewill Baptist General Conference* (Dover, N. H.). In this there is less of the Wesleys, but it is notable for a section of "Anti-slavery" Hymns, a cause to which the denomination committed itself as early as 1835 to the detriment of its own growth.

(2) THE DUNKERS (Tunkers, German Baptist Brethren, The Brethren) who organized at Germantown, near Philadelphia, in 1723, found need for an English hymn book as early as 1791:—*The Christians Duty, exhibited, in a series of Hymns: collected from various authors, designed for the worship of God, and for the edification of Christians, recommended to the serious, of all denominations. By the Fraternity of Baptist's. The first edition. Germantown, printed by Peter Leibert, 1791.* (2nd edition, 1801; 3rd, 1813). The collections prepared by Elhanan Winchester for the "Universal Baptists" of Philadelphia[19] must have been among "The several sorts of Hymn Books" referred to in the preface as "in Meeting at once," and served as a source book for much of the materials of this. Many of the hymns of Watts and of the Evangelical Revival were included, with one "For washing of Feet." This collection of 352 hymns was enlarged rather than modified by *A*

[19]Chapter iv, part iv, section III, 2, (1).

Selection of Hymns, from various authors, supplementary for the use of Christians. First edition. Germantown: published by John Leibert, June 2, 1816: the original book reaching a fourth edition in 1825.

Many Dunkers took part in the settlement of the Middle West; and the West had its own hymn book in *A choice Selection of Hymns, from various authors recommended for the worship of God* (stereotype edition, Henry Kurtz, Poland, O., 1852). It had many of the hymns from *The Christian's Duty,* and a new one "At washing feet," around which ordinance a controversy arose in the West.

After the unavoidable separations of the Civil War, in which they took no part, this quaint and good people united (as though nothing had happened) in General Meeting, which published *A Collection of Psalms, Hymns and Spiritual Songs . . . adapted to the Fraternity of the Brethren* (Covington, O., 1867). Tunes were provided in a musical edition, *The Brethren's Hymn and Tune Book* (1872; revised edition, 1879). Of the 818 hymns at least 125 deal with death and heaven, but neither in that proportion nor in other features is there much to differentiate the Brethren's Hymnody from the current evangelical hymn books of the more solid type from which it was compiled with some pains. After the unfortunate split of 1882 the Progressive Brethren published a much inferior book, *The Brethren Hymnody with tunes* (Wilmington, O., 1884), about equally divided between hymns of the standard type and "many favorites of the later variety" popular in Sunday schools and evangelistic services. The conservatives followed in *The Brethren Hymnal: a Collection of Psalms, Hymns, and Spiritual Songs . . . Compiled under direction of the General Conference of the German Baptist Brethren Church* (Elgin, Ill., 1901), which also, it must be confessed, creates an impression of a lowered educational standard.

(3) THE MENNONITES began coming to America at a very early period, and may be grouped under the Baptists

in the sense that they practice believers' baptism only, though ordinarily by affusion. Small in number, they are yet divided into twelve independent sects, several of which speak German exclusively. Even in the parent body singing in English was long deferred, beginning with *A Collection of Psalms, Hymns, and Spiritual Songs. Suited to the various occasions . . . of the Church of Christ. By a committee of the Mennonites* (Mountain Valley, Va.: 4th ed. with an appendage of German hymns, 1859). It also has its hymns "For feet washing," but is otherwise compiled from the hymn books of the time with little distinctiveness and less distinction. *Hymns and Tunes for public and private worship and Sunday schools. Compiled by a committee* (Elkhart, Ind.: Mennonite Publ. Co., 1890) is a fresh selection, with original contributions both of hymns and music. *A choice Collection of spiritual Hymns . . . designed for the use of the Evangelical United Mennonites and all lovers of Zion* (Goshen, Ind.: E. U. Mennonite Pub. Soc., 1881) has no less than six hymns "For feet washing," and exhibits an educational standard somewhat below the average.

(4) THE CHURCH OF GOD. John Winebrenner, while pastor of the German Reformed church at Harrisburg, Pa., conducted a revival whose methods were criticized, and he left that denomination in 1825 to continue revival work in the neighborhood. Several congregations were formed, and in 1831 a new denomination, "The Church of God in North America," which, while avoiding the name, is a Baptist Church. For its hymn book it naturally adopted its founder's *A Prayer Meeting and Revival Hymn Book; or a Selection of the best "Psalms and Hymns and Spiritual Songs," from various authors, for the use of social prayer meetings and revivals of religion. By John Winebrenner, V.D.M.* (Harrisburg, 1825). It is a compilation of 501 hymns, afterward increased by 72, including some of a standard character, but prevailingly of the revival and camp-meeting order. With the spread of the Church it reached

a tenth edition in 1851. Its style of Church Hymnody, however unconventional, is natural enough in view of the denominational origin and conditions.

(5) THE DISCIPLES OF CHRIST (Campbellite Baptists; Christians), though left to the last, represent the most important schism of the Baptist body, and are now one of the largest American Churches. They trace their origin on the one side to the Kentucky Revival; Barton W. Stone, one of its Presbyterian leaders, organizing in 1804 a body without a creed, called "Christians": on the other to Alexander Campbell, organizing "non-sectarian" congregations, joining the Redstone and then the Mahoning Baptist Associations; diverting many Baptist congregations from the speculative Calvinism then prevailing and from their denominational allegiance; uniting in 1827 with the followers of Stone to form a church with no creed but the Scriptures.

Campbell impressed his personality upon the Hymnody as upon everything else connected with the Disciples. He objected not only to the doctrines of current hymn books, but to the fact that they were doctrinal. They are, he said, "in general a collection of everything preached in the range of the system of the people who adopt them." "They are our creed in metre": yet "in common life men are not disposed to sing their opinions," but "love-songs, the praises of heroes, and the triumphs of wars." "Christians are the same men sanctified: let the love of God, the praises of the character and achievements of the Captain of their salvation, animate their Hymns."[20]

There was much truth in this judgment of the current misuse of Hymnody. And yet men, natural or regenerate, do like songs that express their convictions. Campbell himself could not carry out his principle. The Baptismal Hymn, "O Lord, and will thy pardoning love embrace a wretch so vile," certainly embodies his view of the connection of baptism with the remission of sins, and that beginning "Reform and be immersed" seems to express an

[20]Introduction to his *Psalms, Hymns and Spiritual Songs.*

opinion upon the mode of baptism.[21] After all, Campbell's view involved practically nothing more than discrimination in using the hymns of other Churches; and in May, 1828, he printed a small book of only 125 hymns preceded and followed by brief treatises on Psalmody and Prayer. Only five of the hymns were original, and they were unimportant.[22]

Stone and John T. Johnson had also made a hymn book, which some preferred to Campbell's, and he, in order to avoid rivalry and to supply more hymns, proposed "to make of the twain one new hymn-book."[23] It appeared as *Psalms, Hymns, and Spiritual Songs, original*[24] *and selected. Compiled by A. Campbell, W. Scott, B. W. Stone, and J. T. Johnson. Bethany, Va., 1834.* This attained a seventh edition by 1841, and in 1851 was enlarged, the words, *With numerous additions and emendations. Adapted to personal, family, and church worship. By Alexander Campbell. First edition,* being added to the title. The hymn book appearing in New York in the same year as *Sacred Poetry, selected and amended, by Dr. S. E. Shepard, by resolution of the New York State Convention of the Disciples of Christ* was a bright and independent selection.

In 1864 the Hymnody passed from Campbell's control into that of the American Christian Missionary Society, who made a fresh survey of outside hymn books, and conformed to the fashion of the time in a huge collection of 1320 hymns,—*The Christian Hymn Book: a compilation of Psalms, Hymns and Spiritual Songs, original and*

---

[21]Spiritual Songs, Nos. 96, 97; *Ps. Hys. & Sp. Songs,* rev. ed., 1851.

[22]For their first lines see R. Richardson, *Memoirs of Alexander Campbell,* vol. ii, ed. 1890, p. 658, note. These hymns remained in the hymn book as long as Campbell kept control of it.

[23]Campbell in *The Millennial Harbinger* for May, 1834, p. 239.

[24]The original material is perhaps larger than can be traced, but found no permanent acceptance. Stone was one of the hymn writers of the Kentucky Revival. For his hymns see J. Rogers, *The Biography of Eld. Barton Warren Stone,* 5th ed., Cincinnati, 1847, pp. 313 ff.

selected. By A. Campbell and others. Revised and enlarged by a committee. Cincinnati: H. S. Bosworth, publisher. 1866. Tunes were provided in *The Christian Hymnal* (Cincinnati, 1871). *The new Christian Hymn and Tune Book (Cincinnati,* 1882 and 1887) is a collection of hymns and "Gospel Songs" without distinction. The original material of 1866 is small. It would be interesting to accept the fact that the committee could find 1320 hymns in current books where Campbell in 1828 found only 125 as evidence that the churches had come to accept his canons of Praise. But in fact the better part of the additions of 1866 is from XVIIIth century writers.

III

MAKING ITS WAY INTO CONGREGATIONAL AND PRESBYTERIAN CHURCHES

1. THE ERA OF REVIVAL (1790-1832): "VILLAGE HYMNS"

The religious apathy that bound New England after the Revolution was indifferent to any enlargement of the church Hymnody and averse to any heightening of its emotional atmosphere. It had taken the fervor of the Great Awakening to turn the churches from Metrical Psalmody to Watts, and it was in the renewed warmth of revival that the Evangelical Hymnody began to prove acceptable. About 1790 a movement made itself felt that, without the leadership of a Whitefield or the questionable measures of the earlier revival, spread into a Lesser Awakening.

In the revival services Watts' *Psalms and Hymns* had to be depended on because most available. *Olney Hymns* itself was reprinted in New York as early as 1787, and again in 1790 (Hodge, Allen and Campbell), in Philadelphia in 1792 (William Young), and often thereafter. It is not likely that it was much used as a hymn book, though doubtless some of the hymns of the Evangelical Revival were introduced by lining them out from this and other collections.

A "very great demand" arose for hymns of the newer type, and "several booksellers" consulted the Hartford pastors "for advice, which of the many selections of hymns extant it would be most advisable to reprint."[25] They reported in favor of a new hymn book, adapted to local conditions, and were persuaded to undertake it. None was more active in the revival than Nathan Strong, the sturdy pastor of the First Church, and with the assistance of Abel Flint, pastor of the Second Church, and of Joseph Steward, one of his own deacons, he prepared *The Hartford Selection of Hymns, from the most approved authors. To which are added a number never before published* (Hartford: John Babcock, 1799). Most of its 378 hymns were from *Olney Hymns,* Doddridge, and Rippon's *Selection,* with some originals, of which "Swell the anthem, raise the song" is remembered. By prearrangement Jonathan Benjamin issued an accompanying book of tunes (*Harmonia Coelestis,* Northampton, Sept. 1799) mostly in the florid manner of Madan's *Lock Collection,* and leaving the compiler's promise to provide for all "the particular metres" unfulfilled.

The Hartford Selection brought into the churches something of the atmosphere of the Olney Revival, and was so warmly welcomed as to reach an eighth edition in 1821. In 1833 a competent witness wrote :—

"It has been printed in greater numbers, has been diffused more extensively, and has imparted more alarm to the sinner, and more consolation to the saint, than any other compilation of religious odes in this country, during a period of nearly thirty years." [26]

But it did not much affect the supremacy of Watts in the church services of established parishes. There is no evidence that either of the Hartford compilers and pastors

[25]Preface to *The Hartford Selection,* 1799.
[26]Rev. Luther Hart in *Christian Spectator,* Sept., 1833, pp. 344, 345.

introduced it into his own church.[27]   It was rather the
precursor of the Evangelistic Hymn Book; used in the revival services then so general, in the conference meetings
of older parishes and in the new congregations which the
Connecticut Association was forming in the new settlements. *The Hartford Selection* remains one of the landmarks of New England Hymnody,—the first on the Calvinistic side to get beyond the all-sufficiency of Watts, the
earliest of a series of hymn books born of the revival spirit
and without ecclesiastical sanction that first paralleled the
authorized Hymnody in Congregational and Presbyterian
churches and then contributed more or less to modify and
enrich it.

The relations of Connecticut Congregationalism with
Presbyterianism were so close as narrowly to escape coales-
cence. No doubt the missionaries of both used *The Hartford Selection* in their joint labors in the new settlements,
and an actual junction of the authorized Psalmody of the
two bodies was effected by their common adoption of
President Dwight's rescension of Watts' Psalms of 1801.[28]
He knew what was expected of him, and in his appended
hymns kept mainly within the school of Watts, taking only
two of *Olney Hymns,* and one of Charles Wesley which
he attributed to "Rippon."

Eighteen years later Dr. Worcester's *Select Hymns*[29]
began to supplement Watts in Congregational churches of
the Massachusetts type, and were to prove a rival of the
authorized *Psalms and Hymns* in the Presbyterian Church.
He went further afield for his hymns than Dr. Dwight,
though with an astounding ignorance of geography,[30] and

[27]The First Church adopted "Dwight's Watts" very soon after the
publication of *The Hartford Selection.* G. L. Walker, *History of the
First Church in Hartford,* Hartford, 1884, pp. 349, 394.

[28]See chap. iv, part IV, sect. I, 1.   [29]*Ibid.*

[30]He ascribed "Jesus, Lover of my soul" to Cowper; "Guide me,
O Thou Great Jehovah" to Robinson; "Blow ye the trumpet, blow"
to Toplady; "Angels, roll the rock away" to Gibbons; "All hail the
power of Jesus' Name" to Duncan.

his eclectic selection brought a number of the Evangelical Hymns into church use.

When Asahel Nettleton began his evangelistic labors in New England and New York he used Watts' *Psalms and Hymns,* and took special pleasure in hearing "the friends of the Redeemer express their unqualified attachment" to them.[31] But he soon felt their deficiencies and became aware that the element in Congregational and Presbyterian churches that was willing to cooperate with him was precisely that which had grown dissatisfied with Watts and wanted a change. In 1820, when the General Association of Connecticut appointed a committee to devise measures of promoting religion, "the first item proposed was a New Selection of Hymns." From within the bounds of Albany Presbytery, and "very extensively in the West and South," the call for such a work was "imperious and pressing."[32]

Both the Association and the Assembly put the matter off. At length, when partially laid aside by illness, Nettleton prepared and published in 1824 *Village Hymns for social worship. Selected and original. Designed as a Supplement to the Psalms and Hymns of Dr. Watts. By Asahel Nettleton* (New York). It contained 600 Hymns. Nettleton was indebted to Strong's *Hartford Selection,*[33] Worcester's *Select Hymns,*[34] and to *Hymns for the Monthly Concert,* printed in 1823 by Leonard Bacon, while a student at Andover, where the foreign missionary movement had just begun. Bacon's little book and Nettleton's "missionary" section mark the beginning of American Missionary Hymnody.[35] Of the Watts school Miss Steele had the largest representation in 32 hymns; but Newton was the favorite,

[31]Preface to *Village Hymns.*   [32]*Ibid.*

[33]It is by Nettleton's ascriptions of authorship that 7 of Strong's hymns and 4 of Steward's, taken from *The Hartford Selection,* are now identified.

[34]Worcester's blundering ascriptions are repeated in *Village Hymns.*

[35]"From Greenland's icy mountains" is included. It had appeared in 1823 in the reprinted *Christian Observer,* and in *The Missionary Herald.*

and the selections from *Olney Hymns* constitute one eighth of the *Village Hymns*. There were also nearly a score from the Wesleys. The change from Watts had been so long deferred in America that Nettleton was able to include some writers of the modern school, notably Montgomery. He sought too to bring forward American writers. Of Abby B. Hyde's nine contributions, "Dear Saviour, if these lambs should stray" is best remembered; of Phoebe Brown's four, "I love to steal awhile away" became a great favorite. Of that indefatigable hymn writer, William B. Tappan, Nettleton inserted " 'Tis midnight, and on Olive's brow," but somehow missed "There is an hour of peaceful rest," printed in 1818, and destined to become equally popular.

Nettleton knew a good hymn when he saw it, and produced the brightest evangelical hymn book yet made in America. Revival hymns he eschewed as at best ephemeral and "unfit for the ordinary purposes of devotion—as prescriptions, salutary in sickness, are laid aside on the restoration of health."[36] In the way of tunes he printed before each hymn the names of one or more that were suitable, and followed Nathan Strong's lead in providing a tune book (*Zion's Harp*) with settings of the hymns in "particular metres."

The soil was prepared for the new planting, and seven editions of *Village Hymns* sprang up within three years. Its variety and vivacity were a revelation to many accustomed to more didactic strains and gave it a long popularity. It served as a source book to numerous compilers, who thus spread its hymns even more widely.

Nettleton lived to oppose the "new measures" and "New School Theology" which Finney introduced in 1826 into the revival in the Presbytery of Oneida, New York. But with Finney's first coming to New York city, his supporter Joshua Leavitt, late a Connecticut pastor, published on March 6, 1830, the first number of a weekly, *The Evangelist,* "to promote revivals of religion." In the number for

[36]Preface.

October 2 he began to print specimen hymns and tunes of a revival hymn book to be issued in monthly parts. The first six parts appeared in April, 1831, as *The Christian Lyre. By Joshua Leavitt. Vol. I. New York: published by Jonathan Leavitt:* vol. II followed in October; and before the end of the year a *Supplement,* containing "more than one hundred Psalm tunes, such as are most used in churches of all denominations." In the six months between the appearing of the first and second volumes, nine editions of the first, of 2,000 copies each, had been sold,[37] and of the whole, bound up together in 24mo, the eighteenth edition appeared in 1833; the twenty-sixth in 1842.

"Every person conversant with revivals must have observed," Leavitt said, "that wherever meetings for prayer and conference assume a special interest, there is a desire to use hymns and music of a different character from those ordinarily heard in church."[38] He thought Nettleton had supplied "in a good degree" the church need, and he aimed to supply the revival need with somewhat lighter and more songlike hymns with rippling rhythms and sometimes "chorusses." But the tunes which carried them were designedly the feature of *The Christian Lyre,* printed as they were in the book itself on the page opposite the words of corresponding hymns.

By this time there had arisen a movement to reform Church Music, of whose leaders Lowell Mason had Congregationalist, and Thomas Hastings Presbyterian, affiliations. They claimed not unnaturally that the neglected condition of Congregational Song in the churches was due to the ignorance and indifference of Christian people.[39]

[37]Note prefixed to the *Supplement.*   [38]Preface.

[39]"Go where we may into the place of worship . . . when the singing commences . . . the congregation are either on the one hand gazing at the select performers to admire the music, or on the other expressing their dissatisfaction by general symptoms of restlessness. . . . We observe everywhere the universal appearance of restlessness or relaxation." Thos. Hastings in *Biblical Repertory,* July, 1829, pp. 414, 415.

They set themselves the task of reforming it by lectures and writings, by establishing singing schools for the young, and singing classes for congregations, and by training church choirs to be leaders of congregational singing. For their use Hastings began in 1816 and Mason in 1822 the publication of tune books, lengthening out with their lives into a very extended series. Many of the tunes were their own composition, Mason especially gauging and providing for the average capacity and feeling with amazing fertility and success. The tunes of these men were simple but correct, and the cardinal principle of their voluminous addresses, their teaching and composition, was devoutness, to which all else was subordinated. Their work had already begun to tell upon the spirit and practice of congregational singing, and their characteristic type of hymn tune was becoming familiar and appreciated.[40]

Leavitt was not the equal of these men in musical knowledge,[41] nor one with them in method. He aimed at hearty revival singing and the gathering of a brighter sort of tunes than those in the oblong tune books of the Hastings and Mason school. To secure swinging melodies he drew freely upon the popular songs of the past and present and secured new tunes more or less of kin. The result was, on a smaller scale, very much like that of the more recent enterprise of Moody and Sankey. A fresh impulse was given to singing both within and without the Church, and the new hymns and tunes threatened to make their way into the stated church services. Criticism and protest followed, and it seemed to many that Leavitt had debased the coin of the Kingdom. The church press[42] and church authorities

[40]For a bibliography of Mason to 1854 see *The American Journal of Education*, Sept., 1857, p. 148: for a study of the careers of both see F. L. Ritter, *Music in America*, New York, ed. 1895, pp. 165-181.

[41]He had to defend himself against the charge of ignorance of the rudiments of musical grammar (*The Evangelist* for Sept. 3, 1830) and to correct often the two-part music of early editions of his *Lyre*.

[42]The *Christian Spectator* welcomed the *Lyre*, especially commending its employment of secular melodies (vol. iii, 1831, pp. 664-672).

were divided in opinion, and no interference followed
except from such action as was taken by parochial authority.
And some of Leavitt's tunes came in course of time to be
generally regarded as not incompatible with devoutness.

To Hastings and Mason it seemed that Leavitt and such
as he were threatening to undo all their work. "In these
enlightened days of reform" the public is called upon "to
recognize in the current love songs, the vulgar melodies of
the street, of the midnight reveller, of the circus and the
ballroom, the very strains which of all others, we are told,
are the best adapted to call forth pure and holy emotions,
in special seasons of revival!"[43] Mason had just published
for use in church service a full collection of psalms and
hymns as *Church Psalmody* (Boston and Philadelphia,
1831),[44] which was meeting with success. And now with
Hastings he began the publication in twelve numbers, of a
social hymn book, with the tunes printed in Leavitt's manner, that should offset the evil influences of *The Christian
Lyre*. It appeared complete as *Spiritual Songs for social
worship: adapted to the use of families and private circles
in seasons of revival, to missionary meetings, to the
monthly concert, and to other occasions of special interest.
Words and music arranged by Thomas Hastings, of Utica,
and Lowell Mason, of Boston* (Utica, 1832).

This little book will always have a place in American
Hymnody, if only for its originals, which included Ray
Palmer's "My faith looks up to Thee," Samuel F. Smith's
"The morning light is breaking," and very many of Hastings, including "Gently, Lord, O gently lead us," "Hail
to the brightness of Zion's glad morning," "How calm
and beautiful the morn," and "Return, O wand'rer, to thy
home."[45] But the book was also immediately successful.

[43]Preface to *Spiritual Songs.*
[44]*Manual of Christian Psalmody* (Boston and Philadelphia, 1832)
is a variant of this book for Baptist use.
[45]Some of these are in the ed. of 1833. Hastings became one of the
most voluminous American hymn writers. Many of his 600 hymns are
in his *Devotional Hymns and religious Poems* (N. Y., 1850).

Its fresh Hymnody, its simple melodies, and the spirituality of its atmosphere, fitted it to meet what its editors regarded as an emergency, and its success helped to maintain a devout tone in the less formal exercises of worship.

All of the hymn books just considered were private enterprises and without ecclesiastical sanction. But Congregational churches by their constitution, and Presbyterian churches by declaration of the Assembly of 1806,[46] were quite free to introduce them not only into the prayer meeting but into the church service. Many did so for the sake of their warmer hymns or appealing tunes, only to find the little books quite inadequate to meet the varied demands of church use. Such use had however made the newer Hymnody familiar in many congregations and increased the demand for a corresponding enrichment of the authorized Hymnody.

2. THE ERA OF COMPROMISE (1828-1857): "PSALMS AND HYMNS"

(1) PRESBYTERIAN PSALMS AND HYMNS (1831)

The Presbyterian Church had authorized nothing since the allowance of Watts' *Hymns* and Dwight's rescension of his Imitations, with its appendage of hymns, in 1802. Mindful of the Psalmody Controversy and aware of conflicting opinions within its borders, it had never ventured to make a praise book of its own. But in 1819 a proposal to do so reached the Assembly.[47] The Assembly of the year following decided that it might proceed "without offending any of our churches," and appointed a committee to prepare a compilation of Psalms and "a copious collection of hymns and spiritual songs from various authors, giving the preference to those now authorized [i. e. Watts' Hymns] so far as good taste, sound sense, and enlightened piety admit."[48] After years of wrestling with the delicacies

[46]*Minutes of General Assembly, 1789-1820*, Phila., n. d., p. 360.
[47]*Ibid.*, p. 716.   [48]*Ibid.*, p. 740.

of the situation, its report and papers were put into the hands of a committee for revision and publication;[49] Dr. Archibald Alexander being the working member of both committees.

Its book was printed at Princeton by William M'Hart in two parts; the first in 1828 as *Psalms adapted to the public worship of the Christian Church,* the second in 1829 as *Hymns adapted to the public worship of the Christian Church,*[50] bound up in mottled sheep, lettered "Psalms and Hymns," and presented to the Assembly of 1829, who declined it as it stood,[51] recommitting it for "some necessary improvements and corrections."[52]

These being made the book was accepted in 1830,[53] though not without opposition, and published as *Psalms and Hymns adapted to public worship, and approved by the General Assembly of the Presbyterian Church in the United States of America. Philadelphia: published for the General Assembly, by Solomon Allen. 1831.* The 490 Hymns of 1829 have become 531, with some altered texts; otherwise the books are the same. Dr. Alexander's preface of 1829 reveals his guiding principles: 1st, the unsurpassed excellence of Watts' Hymns, and the predilection for them of the majority of serious worshippers; 2nd, a sharp discrimination between hymns that are or are not suitable for public worship.

The collection is of the "Watts' and select" type, opening with a solid body of 199 of his hymns that make two fifths of the whole. In the remainder some seventy authors can be traced, including 12 by Charles Wesley and 27 from *Olney Hymns,* but the school and manner and monotonous

[49]*Minutes, 1821-1837,* Phila., n. d., p. 237.

[50]It would be interesting to know Dr. Alexander's reason for thus avoiding the denominational name.

[51]The Assembly of 1831 was puzzled what to do about and with this repudiated Princeton edition (*Minutes,* p. 306). Some copies were long used in a Philadelphia colored congregation.

[52]*Minutes,* p. 272.

[53]*Ibid.,* p. 306.

metres of Watts so predominate as to produce an atmosphere even then old-fashioned. Dr. Alexander had taken pains to gather a large collection of hymns, and those excluded by his canons of church worship he proceeded to publish as *A Selection of Hymns, adapted to the devotions of the closet, the family, and the social circle* . . . *monthly concerts of prayer for the success of missions and Sunday schools; and other special occasions* (New York: Jonathan Leavitt, 1831), of which three editions were called for.

It would have been better if the process had been reversed: if "the majority of serious worshippers" had been left to the enjoyment of Watts' Hymns without unwelcome omissions, and Dr. Alexander's brighter and more varied selection had been authorized for use by those in full sympathy with the newer Hymnody. As it was the *Psalms and Hymns* of 1831 satisfied neither element in the church; and never came into anything like general use.[54]   It was the only hymn book made by the undivided Church, and after the split of 1837 commended itself to neither "school."[55]

(2) OLD SCHOOL PSALMS AND HYMNS (1843)

The initial Old School Assembly in 1838 took steps for its revision, laboriously accomplished by a committee whose proposed book aroused in the Assembly of 1842 "a most

[54] The reports of the Publishing Agent, so far as given, show an edition of 24,000 in 1831, one of some 8000 in 1832, one of some 4500 in 1835, and one of 5000 in 1837. *Minutes of Gen. Ass.*, v. d. The communicants in 1831 were 182,017.

[55] "The want of some improvement in the existing Psalmody, and particularly of an enlarged and arranged collection of Hymns . . . has for a considerable time been felt and acknowledged." Preface to *Psalms and Hymns*, 1843. This "felt want," as expressed by numerous correspondents of *The Presbyterian*, was quaintly regarded (outside) as an argument for the exclusive use of Psalms in two articles on "Psalmody of the Presbyterian Church" in *The Religious Monitor* for April and May, 1840.

violent though happily a very limited opposition."[56]   The
book was sent back for some amendment and then publication, appearing as *Psalms and Hymns adapted to social,
private, and public worship in the Presbyterian Church in
the United States of America.   Approved and authorized
by the General Assembly.   Philadelphia: Presbyterian
Board of Publication. 1843.*   Of the 531 hymns of 1831,
419 were retained, and 261 were added, a total of 680.   It
served the Old School body, not wholly to its advantage,
for some twenty-five years; provided with tunes in Hastings' *The Presbyterian Psalmodist* (1852), supplemented
by *The Presbyterian Social Psalmodist* (1857) for the
lecture room, *Hymns for Youth* (1848) and *New Hymns
for Youth* (1855) for the Sunday school.   The circulation
of the *Psalms and Hymns* of 1843 during the period of
its use reached the amazing total of 888,650 copies[57] in a
denomination having only 159,137 communicants at the
date of its publication.

(3)   NEW SCHOOL PSALMS AND HYMNS (1843)

The New School Presbyterians naturally included the
sympathizers with the "new measures" and "new theology"
of the Oneida Revival of 1826.   They were as a body of
more independent spirit than the Old School, and more
jealous of a centralized church control.   In New York
State and the Northwestern states fully one half of their
congregations had declined the authorized *Psalms and
Hymns,* and were, before the division, using Worcester's
Watts' and select, Church Psalmody, or one of the hymn
books born of the revival spirit.[58]   One of the leaders both

[56] "The New Hymn Book" in *Spirit of the XIX. Century* for Dec.,
1842. The heated proceedings may be followed in the *Minutes* and in
an account in *The Presbyterian* for June 4, 1842. For a precise
"Documentary History" of the revision see *Spirit of XIX. Century*
for Nov. 1843. The satisfaction that psalm singers took in the debate
is frankly expressed in *The true Psalmody,* Phila., 1859, pp. 157, 158.

[57] Ms. records of The Board of Publication.

[58] *Cf.* an undated pamphlet, *Review of a pamphlet entitled "The
Church Psalmist,"* p. 5.

of the Revival and the new denomination, Dr. Beman of Troy, had already published *Sacred Lyrics: or select Hymns, particularly adapted to revivals of religion, and intended as a Supplement to Watts. By Nathan S. S. Beman. Troy: N. Tuttle, printer, 225 River-street, 1832:* and he proceeded to publish a much larger collection for church use as *Sacred Lyrics, or Psalms and Hymns adapted to public worship. Selected by Nathan S. S. Beman. Troy, N. Y.: published by A. Kidder, 1841.*

The General Assembly of 1840 had authorized an *ad interim* committee to procure "an edition of Psalms and Hymns" for general use without expense to the Assembly.[59] They, under arrangement with Dr. Beman and his publisher, adopted his *Sacred Lyrics* with some required changes, and published it as *Church Psalmist; or Psalms and Hymns, for the public, social, and private use of evangelical Christians. New York: Mark H. Newman, 199 Broadway. 1843.*[60] It was accepted and recommended to the churches without opposition.[61] Beman's book had originally been prepared as a competitor of Worcester's *Watts' and select,* aiming to omit the more didactic parts of Watts and to improve the lyrical standard of hymns.

A more formidable rival appeared from the hands of a group of clergymen who in connection with a Philadelphia publisher, had taken up the hymn book question independently. They first published for use in "evening meetings" *Parish Hymns for public, social, and private worship* (Philadelphia: Perkins & Purves, 1843); and then an extensive collection for church use, *Parish Psalmody. A Collection of Psalms and Hymns for public worship* (Philadelphia: Perkins and Purves, 1844). This contained "Dr. Watts's versification of the Psalms of David, entire," 200

---

[59] *Minutes* (of the New School Branch), *1838-1858,* reprinted Phila., 1894, pp. 99, 104.
[60] Beman also issued the Hymns separately, as *Social Psalmist* (N. Y., Mark H. Newman, 1843).
[61] *Ibid.,* pp. 128, 129.

of his hymns and nearly 500 other hymns. It appealed to those who resented Dr. Beman's treatment of Watts and resented yet more his undoubted lobbying in the interests of a book which was his copyright property. Both books were edited by Seth Collins Brace, just licensed by Wilmington Presbytery, later a Congregationalist.[62] He wrote hymns for it and secured original contributions from Mrs. Lydia H. Sigourney, Ray Palmer and Dr. George W. Bethune.

An open war followed the appearance of *Parish Psalmody*. Fourteen Philadelphia churches, and many beyond, adopted it, numerous Presbyteries and two Synods commended it, and an array of pastoral recommendations was obtained.[63] Dr. Beman appeared before the Assembly of 1846 in the interests of uniformity of Praise, and secured a renewed recommendation of the *Church Psalmist*.[64] In the ensuing pamphlet controversy the publishers of *Parish Psalmody* had the best of it, but in the end Dr. Beman prevailed. In 1857 the Publication Committee purchased the book outright, and the large Supplement of "such hymns as may be necessary to make the work complete" then arranged for seems to have been intended to conciliate the opponents of the *Church Psalmist*.[65]

Thenceforward the *Church Psalmist* was more generally regarded as the official praise book of the New School body, and a selection of its hymns for prayer meetings was published in 1865 as *Social Hymn and Tune Book for the lecture room* &c. Even so uniformity was not secured. A special report by Dr. Beman to the Assembly of 1863 regretfully announced that some fifteen hymn books beside his own were "in use in our churches."[66]

[62]S. W. Duffield, *English Hymns: their authors and history,* 2nd ed., Funk and Wagnalls, 1886, p. 359.

[63]See the *Review of a pamphlet,* pp. 44-58.

[64]*Minutes, 1838-1858,* p. 154. For the debate see *Review of a pamphlet,* pp. 14, 15.

[65]*Minutes,* p. 580.

[66]*Special Report,* Phila. [1863], p. 14.

(4) Presbyterian Hymnody in the '40s

A modern hymnologist has somewhat misapprehended the actual conditions of Presbyterian Hymnody in this period, in saying,—

"The Presbyterian body has always included a large proportion of the intelligence, culture and learning in these United States; and yet it long sat contented under the weight of those marvels of decorous dullness, the 'Psalms and Hymns' of 1843, and the 'Church Psalmist' of 1847 (*sic.*). Short of vulgarity and eccentricity, it would not be easy to find two more painful compilations; but they have been superseded only within the last twenty years or so." [67]

This criticism fails to take any account of the independence of New School churches and their use of other books. But doubtless these two and *Parish Psalmody* represent the general state of Presbyterian Hymnody in the '40s. The waves of revival that had quickened congregational singing had spent their force; the little hymn books of the revival time had lived their day; and there was a tendency to fall back upon "Watts' and select." [68]   But even so the three books represent not what the people cared to sing, but what their pastors thought good for them.

It was the clergy who made and used these ponderous compilations of *Psalms and Hymns*.   The books were ponderous because the leaders of the Church were still under the weight of the Metrical Psalmody tradition, [69]

[67] Rev. Fred. M. Bird in *The Churchman*, August 3, 1889.

[68] *Cf.* M. J. Hickok, pastor of Washington St. Church, Rochester, in *Review of a pamphlet* (p. 57) :—"We had tried several experiments. . . . The *Village Hymns*, linked with so many pleasant memories to all the natives of New England, were found to be so far behind the age, that their sweet savor of revivals, and early Christian experience, could not redeem them from neglect. We obtained the *Sacred Songs*, but a short experience convinced us that they were *far too limited in their range, for all* the purposes of devotion." He proceeds to narrate his adoption of *Parish Hymns* and his hope of introducing the larger *Parish Psalmody*.

[69] "This General Assembly . . . totally disapprove of those books of Psalmody which, in their arrangement, blot out the distinction between those songs of devotion which are God-inspired and those which are man-inspired." N. S. Assembly, 1863: *Minutes* (of the N. S. branch), vol. ii, Philadelphia, 1894, p. 234.

and the older generation wished to retain a large body of Watts' Hymns, while joining the younger in demanding an ample representation of the newer Hymnody. The books were didactic because the concern of the clergy was mainly for the doctrinal aspects of hymns,[70] and practically all the clergy used them to enforce the points of their sermons;[71] and being thus didactic were dull but not so dull as Mr. Bird thinks; brightened rather with many choice hymns of the Evangelical Revival and of later time, which the Church still likes to sing.

It would, however, be more true to say that "the Presbyterian body" sat unconcerned than that it "sat contented" under these ponderous books. With the hymn books not only dull but misapprehended and misused in the pulpit, and the constantly changing tune books confined entirely to the choir loft, the congregations had fallen into the habit of leaving the choir to do all the singing.[72] And the predominant movement for the "improvement of Psalmody" was that for supplanting the simple melodies of the Lowell Mason school by sacred quartets in that parlor-music type

[70]This appears in the discussions of the time. In *Review of a pamphlet,* for instance, the *Church Psalmist* is charged with suppressing "native depravity" (p. 27) and with a scarcity of allusions to the "eternity of punishment" (pp. 29, 30). Among the grounds for recommending *Parish Psalmody,* one synod, three presbyteries, two pastoral associations and twelve divines specify its inclusion of the Confession of Faith and Catechism (pp. 44 ff.).

[71] "It is now a rare thing, in some of our congregations, to be invited to unite in a single Psalm or hymn that is distinctively one of praise. If the preacher design to discourse to us upon some point of doctrinal theology, or to present us with some peculiar phase of religious experience, or to exhort the impenitent . . . he seeks in all his psalmody to enforce his teachings." Henry Darling, "Worship as an Element of Sanctuary Service," Pres. Quar. Rev., April, 1862, and separately, p. 20.

[72]A writer on "Church Music" in *The Princeton Review* for Jan. 1843 (the year of the Old School Assembly's *Psalms and Hymns*), describes congregational singing as neither general nor devout in churches having a precentor (p. 89), and as "how often" non-existent in churches having a choir (p. 91).

of choir tunes for which Henry W. Greatorex was sponsor.

If the authorized Presbyterian Hymnody thus looked backward in its devotion to metrical Psalmody and to Watts, both the Old School and New School collections nevertheless marked an advance in the appropriation of the newer Hymnody. Dr. Beman certainly would have been chagrined to foresee his *Church Psalmist* coupled with the Old School *Psalms and Hymns* of 1843, under a common charge of "decorous dulness." In intention, to say the least, he belonged with the literary movement already begun elsewhere, and aimed to get away from the didactic type of hymn and to cement an alliance between Lyrical Poetry and Presbyterian Hymnody.

(5) Congregationalist Psalms and Hymns (1836-1845)

It is quite certain that the Congregationalist Hymnody of the time was not in advance of the Presbyterian, and that it was of no greater interest to the people. At the close of the extended tour of the churches made by the British deputies, Dr. Reed reported that

"The singing generally, and universally with the Congregationalists, is not congregational. It is a performance entrusted to a band of singers, more or less skilful. . . . You have the sense of being a spectator and auditor; not of a participant; and this is destructive of the spirit of devotion." [73]

In the way of hymn books some churches adopted Hastings and Patton's *The Christian Psalmist* (New York, 1836), which appears on the title page as another "Watts' and select." More were using Mason and Greene's *Church Psalmody,* a compilation of no less than 454 psalms and

[73]A. Reed and J. Matheson, *A narrative of the visit to the American churches by the deputation from the Congregational Union of England and Wales,* New York, 1835, vol. ii, pp. 82, 83. As to the continuance of the same conditions through the '40s, see F. A. Adams, "Congregational Singing," in *The New Englander,* February, 1849.

731 hymns, of which 421 are from Watts. Mason's book was approved by the Pastoral Association of Massachusetts[74] for its rich additions to Hymnody, but its professed disregard of the authors' texts, its excisions and alterations in the supposed interests of music, should have put it beyond the bounds of their tolerance. The great dependence was on the cumbrous Worcester's *Watts' and select,* which, said Charles Beecher, even as late as 1863, "still weighs down the psalmody of some antediluvian districts like a nightmare."[75]

In Connecticut the proposal of 1820 for a new hymn book was not taken up. In 1833 Dr. Bacon issued *Additional Hymns* to be bound up with "Dwight's Watts" still in general use; and eventually Dwight was superseded by *Psalms and Hymns, for Christian use and worship; prepared and set forth by the General Association of Connecticut. New Haven: Durrie and Peck. 1845.* This book was among the largest; containing 1203 numbers. The hymns, numbering 705, were also set forth separately as *Chapel Hymns.* They are in the main the standard Evangelical Hymns, with a preponderance of Watts, whose contributions constitute five-twelfths of the whole. But some seventy hymns were taken from English collections new in this country, and for it Leonard Bacon recast his "O God, beneath Thy guiding hand," and wrote four other hymns.[76] The new hymn book had thus a progressive as well as a conservative side. It fitly closed the compromise period of "Psalms and Hymns," and carried the Connecticut churches up to the time when the tunes were put into the hands of the people, and real progress in congregational singing was thus made possible.

[74] See *New England Puritan,* Nov. 18, 1841.
[75] *Autobiography of Lyman Beecher,* New York, ed. 1865, vol. ii, p. 150.
[76] Dr. Bacon was chairman of the committee on the new hymn book. While it was preparing the Revs. Horace Hooker and Oliver E. Daggett gave their whole time to its editing. Daggett has an account of "The New Hymn Book" in *The New Englander* for July, 1846.

IV

HYMN SINGING IN THE PROTESTANT EPIS-
COPAL CHURCH

1. The Beginning of Hymn Singing (1786)

The Church of England congregations in the American
colonies imported their prayer books, and sang the metrical
psalms bound in at the end, whether Sternhold and Hopkins'
Old Version or Tate and Brady's *New Version.* In some
parishes no doubt before the Revolution an occasional hymn
was given out from the *Supplement to the New Version*
or some other source.

The first step toward forming these congregations into
a Protestant Episcopal Church was taken in 1784. In
September of the following year a convention representing
seven states met in Christ Church, Philadelphia, and applied
themselves to making necessary changes in the Prayer Book
and proposing improvements of the service and statements
of doctrine.[77]   The embodiment of these alterations was
left to Drs. William White, afterward bishop, William
Smith and C. H. Wharton;[78] who issued *The Book of
Common Prayer . . . as revised and proposed to the use
of the Protestant Episcopal Church at a convention of the
said Church . . .* (Philadelphia: Hall and Sellers, 1786).

The preface to this "Proposed Book" cites both as a
warrant and platform certain proposals for revision in
William and Mary's time (1689) that included the addition
of hymns and anthems from the Prophets and the New
Testament to the metrical psalms, the better to provide
for the heads and occasions of Christian worship.[79]   In
accord with which, the preface goes on to say:—

"A *selection* is made of the . . . *singing* Psalms . . . and a *collec-*

[77]*Cf.* William White, *Memoirs of the Protestant Episcopal Church,*
2nd ed., New York, 1836, pp. 21-23.

[78]Wm. Stevens Perry, *Journals of the General Conventions,* Clare-
mont, N. H., 1874, vol. i, p. 28.

[79]Preface, pp. [7, 8].

tion of hymns are added, upon those *evangelical* subjects and other heads of christian worship, to which the psalms of *David* are less adapted, or do not generally extend." [80]

The selection thus offered in lieu of the complete Psalter is numbered I-LXXXIV, arranged in groups under general heads; and followed by a group of fifty-one hymns, introduced by this rubric:—

"¶HYMNS suited to the Feasts and Fasts of the CHURCH, and other Occasions of public Worship; to be used at the discretion of the Minister."

These proposals invite attention; for, while the Proposed Book never was ratified, its provision for Congregational Praise passed substantially into the church constitution and has determined its practice till the present day. The proposals had really no precedent in those of 1689, which contemplated nothing more than the addition of other Bible Songs to the Psalms. And they had no precedent in the contemporaneous movements to introduce hymns into the Church of England. The English movements were private enterprises; for even the singing of metrical psalms had never secured ecclesiastical recognition as a part of the Prayer Book system of worship. The American proposals gave the singing of psalms and hymns the status of a church ordinance; and in the Proposed Book as printed they appear as an integral part of the book itself, followed by the rubric, "End of the Prayer Book."[81]

Of these related proposals the more significant is that for singing hymns. It brought about what Bishop White

[80]*Ibid.,* p. [13].

[81]Dr. Smith wrote Dr. White (30 Jan. 1786), basing the Committee's right to introduce hymns on the ground of their being only a "Supplement," and that neither Psalms nor Supplement "are more than an Exercise of our best Discretion in the Work committed to us, and not an essential Part of our reformed Liturgy." (*Journals,* vol. iii, p. 155). Dr. White replied (Feb. 1): "In ye old Book [the Psalms] were no Part of ye common Prayer, but were only used by ye Royal Permission; with us, as I conceive, they are to be part of ye Liturgy" (p. 157). In this judgment (which he afterward reversed) he seems to include the hymns.

called "a most remarkable change," by which the psalm singing Church of his youth became the hymn singing Church of his maturity.[82] In some other communions such a change was regarded as revolutionary and accomplished with distress. And it is interesting to inquire how it happened without any disturbance.

The explanation lies in the fact that the change was effected not in open convention nor in committee-room, but through correspondence between two men; one of whom, William Smith, was determined to introduce hymn singing into the new Church.

In reading the passages dealing with this matter in the Proposed Book's preface, as already quoted, we seem to be listening to the united voice of the delegates from seven States proposing an innovation. In reality the preface was not prepared in convention, but by Dr. Smith himself.[83] The suggestion that hymns be added to the psalms does not appear to have been proposed, much less debated, in the Convention of 1785, whose only action in the premises was that the Committee to prepare the book

"Be authorized to publish, with the Book of Common Prayer, such of the reading and singing Psalms, and such a Kalendar of proper lessons for the different Sundays and Holy-days throughout the year, as they may think proper." [84]

But within a few days after adjournment Dr. Smith proposes to his colleague Dr. White that there be added to the metrical psalms "some of *Watts'* best Psalms, and Hymns for the Festivals and other Occasions," expressing a hope that "some may be offered by Members of our own Church in America, who are distinguished for their Poetical Talents."[85] It was Dr. Smith who selected all the hymns, forwarding them to Dr. White, with the plea that "multitudes of our most serious and religious members" would favor their introduction, and adding with Scottish prudence

[82]See his note NN in *Memoirs* already referred to.
[83]*Journals,* vol. iii, p. 148, and see p. 200.   [84]*Ibid.,* vol. i, p. 28.
[85]Letter of "October, 1785"; *Journals,* vol. iii, p. 127.

that they would help to sell the forthcoming book. He assured Dr. White that all the hymns, except a few from Watts, had "long been in Use in the Church" in the *Supplement to Tate and Brady* or collections of religious societies; and as for Watts' "you know Dr. Johnson gives them a high name."[86]

Dr. White's share in the project went no further than a verbal criticism and a final approval of the hymns laid before him. He did indeed, with the support of Francis Hopkinson, then widely regarded as a specialist in Psalmody, venture an objection against including certain extracts from metrical psalms among the hymns. Dr. Smith replied:

"I pay great Regard to the Judgment of Mr. Hopkinson," but "some Dependence on my own Judgment also, and should be happy if you and the other Gentlemen could agree to have the Specimen of Hymns offered to the public with as few deviations as possible from the Plan which upon great Deliberation I have submitted to you, and Dr. Wharton, if he can be consulted."[87]

"I give up," Dr. White said, "my sentiment respecting ye hymnifying ye Psalms."[88] The introduction of hymns did not in fact personally appeal to him. He had accepted Dr. Smith's representations that the churches demanded and should have some hymns, though aware that the committee were "extending their powers pretty far."[89] But personally he was a confirmed psalm singer, and gained the repute of never, unless at Christmas, having given out a hymn at Christ Church to the end of his life.[90] His real concern in 1786 as in 1826 was to keep down the number of authorized hymns to the lowest point practicable.[91]

[86]Jan. 23, 1786, *Ibid.*, vol. iii, pp. 151-153. [87]*Ibid.*, p. 164.
[88]*Ibid.*, p. 167. [89]*Memoirs of the P. E. Church*, p. 108.
[90]*Cf.* H. W. Smith, *Life and Correspondence of the Rev. William Smith, D.D.*, Phila., 1880, vol. ii, p. 221, note. This is not inconsistent with his fondness for certain hymns as sacred poetry, and his wish to have them read in his last hours. See J. H. Ward, *Life and Times of Bishop White*, N. Y., 1892, pp. 171, 172.
[91]See his *Memoirs of the P. E. Church*, p. 257, and the document at p. 384.

Dr. Smith himself had no love for the "Methodists" in the Church of England who were introducing evangelical hymn books into extra-parochial services. But he had watched the spread of Wesleyan Methodism in Maryland, and wrote Dr. White that "the Methodists captivate many by their attention to Church Music, and by their Hymns and Doxologies, which when rationally and devoutly introduced are sublime Parts of public and private worship."[92] His own collection, though larger than at first intended,[93] is hardly more than a supplement to the Psalter, such as the more progressive psalm singers in the Church of England favored. Indeed the *Supplement to the New Version* furnished 7 of the 51 hymns, and the *Hymns, Anthems and Tunes used at the Magdalen Chapel*[94] furnished no less than 14, if we include its 4 by Addison, which Dr. Smith already knew in *The Spectator*.[95] But Watts, with 12 numbers, had the largest representation of any single author.[96] The only American contributions were psalms adapted to July 4th and "the first Thursday of November" by Francis Hopkinson,[97] who also arranged the "half-sheet" of engraved tunes appended at a cost alarming to Dr. White.[98] The Hymns of 1786 represent no dogmatic basis, but simply a desire to cover New Testament occasions with New Testament hymns.

The Proposed Book made few friends and had a very limited use.[99] Its failure being assured, the main duty of

[92]*Journals,* vol. iii, p. 151.   [93]*Ibid.,* p. 151.

[94]From this source "Hark, my gay friend, that solemn toll" was chosen, and Bishop Ken's three hymns were left.

[95]*Journals,* vol. iii, p. 152.

[96]Dr. Smith's remark that "even some of Watts's are not new in *our* Church," creates the impression that some of the parishes had employed his *Psalms and Hymns* before the Revolution.

[97]*Journals,* vol. iii, pp. 167, 177.   [98]*Ibid.,* p. 162.

[99]Dr. Smith speaks of the pleasure his Maryland congregations took in the Good Friday and Easter Hymns, but especially in two Communion Hymns as adding "a Solemnity which they confess'd they had not experienc'd before." "Have you yet introduced them in this way?" he asks Dr. White. *Journals,* i, 194.

the Convention of 1789, now sitting as two houses, was to prepare and adopt a prayer book. The new book was ratified in October 16th of that year, appearing as *The Book of Common Prayer . . . according to the use of the Protestant Episcopal Church in the United States of America* (Philadelphia: Hall and Sellers, 1790).

The Bishops took the initiative in "the form and manner of setting forth the Psalms in metre,"[100] and raised no question as to the inclusion of some hymns. They appeared in the Prayer Book of 1790 with a separate title-page, as *The whole Book of Psalms, in metre; with Hymns, suited to the feasts and fasts of the Church, and other occasions of public worship* (Philadelphia: Hall and Sellers). This title is meant to emphasize the return to a complete Psalter.[101] Such return was contrary to Bishop White's taste. He favored discrimination in using the Psalms in Christian worship,[102] but had become convinced that no selection could satisfy everybody.[103]

But in dealing with Dr. Smith's "Supplement of Hymns" he found his opportunity. The House of Bishops in 1789 was only Seabury and himself, and by dropping the "hymnified Psalms" he had objected to in 1786, by curtailing the provision for feasts and fasts, and by omitting "Hark! my gay friend," he reduced the hymns from the 51 of the Proposed Book to the 27 of 1790. The hymns were still of Dr. Smith's selection, and indeed suffered little from curtailment by the bishop.

The ratification of this book set the Church's seal upon Dr. Smith's original proposal of hymn singing as a church ordinance. These 27 hymns are "set forth, and allowed to be sung in all congregations . . . before and after Morning and Evening Prayer; and also before and after Sermons,

---

[100]*Journals,* vol. i, p. 119. See p. 111.
[101]The title is misleading. *The whole Booke of Psalmes collected into English meetre* had been the title of the *Old Version* since 1562, but the Psalter here set forth was the *New Version* of Tate and Brady.
[102]*Memoirs of P. E. Church,* p. 108.   [103]*Ibid.,* pp. 384, 385.

at the discretion of the Minister."[104]   This assumed the
Convention's prerogative of selecting specific Psalm versions
and hymns for use, and seemed to carry the implication that
parishes were to be confined to them. And such has been
the more general interpretation of the situation till now.[105]
The attitude thus assumed was in sharp contrast to what
Bishop White called the "unbounded license" that grew
up under the peculiar tenure of Psalmody in the Church of
England; a freedom that entailed some disadvantages but
proved a golden opportunity for the development of English Hymnody.

The separate title page to the Psalms and Hymns in 1790
was presumably to distinguish them from the Prayer Book
proper, though the colophon, "End of the Prayer Book,"
still followed the Hymns. In 1791 this became simply
"The End"; and the distinction between Prayer Book and
Psalms, &c. bound in was settled by Convention in 1820.[106]
This distinction was practically important, because it left
the Hymnody open to improvement, without arousing the
strong feelings involved in Prayer Book revision.

2. THE EVANGELICAL PERIOD (1789-1858)

To those wishing to use hymns the diminutive allowance
of 1789 was no more than a thin wedge inserted in a
fissure of the ancient Psalmody, and pressure began at once
with a view of widening the aperture. The vestry of Trinity
Church, Boston, impatient of the contrast of the Church's
provision with the rich abundance of Jeremy Belknap's
Sacred Poetry used by their neighbors, decided not to wait
upon the General Convention for relief, and issued on their
own account *Hymns selected from the most approved*

[104]Certificate on *verso* of title page, 1790. Bishop White's hand
appears in the accompanying provision that the minister shall control
the tunes and suppress "all light and unseemly music." *Cf.* his
Thoughts on the singing of Psalms and Anthems, 1808.

[105]Such authority has been questioned by S. D. McConnell, *History of
the American Episcopal Church,* Phila., ed. 1897, pp. 271, 272.

[106]*Journals,* vol. i, pp. 557, 558: White, *Memoirs,* p. 45.

authors, for the use of Trinity Church, Boston (Boston, 1808).[107] It had 152 hymns, the first 27 being those of 1789. Its devotion to Anne Steele, evidenced by the inclusion of 57 of her hymns, has already been noted. With these may be grouped 23 of Watts and 10 of Doddridge as representing the Evangelical side of Hymnody. In contrast are 18 from recent collections of English Arians, and 3 of the Swedenborgian Joseph Proud. This motley complexion of the book is no more than a reflection of Belknap's, from whose collection the hymns were taken.[108]

The Maryland Convention proceeded in a more orderly way by instructing its deputies to the General Convention of 1808 "to enforce the necessity of adopting an additional number of hymns."[109] Thirty additional hymns were allowed, but with the rider of an annexed rubric requiring that a portion of the Psalms in metre "be sung at every celebration of divine service."[110] Of the new hymns, 25 out of 30 came from English Independent sources. The whole collection of 57 hymns thus allowed included 14 by Watts, 9 by Doddridge, 10 by Steele, 2 by Charles Wesley and 1 by Beddome, and must be regarded as bearing the clear marks of the Evangelical Hymnody.

It was indeed in Maryland and Virginia that the influence of the Evangelical Revival had first made itself felt in the Episcopal Church; and through the first third of the XIXth century there was an ever-enlarging body of clergy holding the evangelical theology and putting the emphasis on personal experience.[111] The new views and feelings,

---

[107] "The necessity of a larger collection was generally felt, and at length the vestry authorized the present publication." Preface, p. 4.

[108] "In this selection, we are chiefly indebted to Dr. Belknap, whose book unquestionably contains the best specimens of sacred poetry extant." Preface, p. 4.

[109] *Journals*, vol. i, p. 341.

[110] The rubric, as printed below the Hymns, made psalm singing compulsory not at every service, but whenever hymns are sung at any service.

[111] *Cf.* Wm. Stevens Perry, *The History of the American Episcopal Church*, Boston, 1885, vol. ii, pp. 192, 193.

here as at Olney long before, expressed themselves in parochial prayer meetings. And here as everywhere the evangelical fervor called for new hymns. This need was largely met by the extended circulation of a book prepared by an Evangelical leader, J. P. K. Henshaw, for a women's prayer-circle in his Brooklyn parish of St. Ann's, and published as *A Selection of Hymns, for the use of social religious meetings, and for private devotions* (Brooklyn, 1817).[112] Its tone is that of the Evangelical Revival: it contains more than fifty *Olney Hymns*, many of the standard hymns of Christian experience, and a few American revival hymns "with chorus."

Henshaw's ample provision for prayer meetings did nothing to satisfy the wide-spread desire[113] for an enlarged Hymnody for the Sunday services. The relief of the situation became the personal concern of a remarkable man, William A. Muhlenberg, then a rector at Lancaster. He began with *A Plea for Christian Hymns*, addressed to a friend in the General Convention of 1821.[114] No result following, he prepared his own collection of psalms and hymns, and published it as *Church Poetry: being portions of the Psalms in verse, and Hymns suited to the festivals and fasts, and various occasions of the Church. Selected and arranged from various authors. By Wm. Augustus*

---

[112] 2nd ed., 1820; 4th, 1824; 5th, 1832; afterward, without date. Wm. Croswell of Boston, attending a General Convention at Philadelphia in Sept., 1838, writes from the "conference rooms" of St. Andrew's Church: "The place in which I write is a queer one. On the desks and seats about me, the principal book is 'Henshaw's Collection of Revival Hymns,' while the Prayer Books are very scarce. There is one on the desk, the only one, I believe, in the room. 'Jesus I know, and Paul I know, but who' is Henshaw, that his *Collections* should supersede the Collects?" *Memoir of the late William Croswell, D.D. By his Father:* New York, 1853, p. 214.

[113] Bird Wilson, *Memoir of William White, D.D.*, Philadelphia, 1839, p. 142.

[114] Anne Ayres, *The Life and Work of Wm. Augustus Muhlenberg*, New York, 1880, p. 62. The paper is reprinted in *Evangelical Catholic Papers, second series*, St. Johnland, 1877, pp. 11-36.

Muhlenberg, associate rector of St. James's Church, Lancaster. Philadelphia: published by S. Potter and Co. 1823. The book ranges with the contemporaneous series of "Psalms and Hymns" appearing on the Evangelical side of the Church of England, and is especially indebted to the 1819 edition of Cotterill's *Selection*,[115] whose freedom in altering texts Muhlenberg admired and extended.

Muhlenberg at once put his *Church Poetry* into use in his own congregation; a course in which he was followed by a number of rectors in various places.[116] Within six months of its publication the General Convention of 1823 appointed a committee on the enlargement of the Psalms and Hymns, of which Dr. Muhlenberg was a member.[117] The committee was presumably ill-prepared for its task, which was wholly neglected[118] until in the summer of 1826 Dr. Muhlenberg, with the assistance of Dr. H. U. Onderdonk of Brooklyn, prepared and put through a collection of hymns,[119] which was approved by the General Convention in November of that year[120]

The new hymns and those already in use were amalgamated and published as *Hymns of the Protestant Episcopal Church, in the United States of America. Set forth in General Convention of said Church, in the years of our Lord, 1789, 1808, and 1826. Philadelphia: published by S. F. Bradford. 1827.*[121] This collection of 212 hymns

[115]See chap. vii, part IV, section 4.

[116]Ayres, *Life*, &c., p. 63.

[117]*Journals*, vol. ii, pp. 19, 69.

[118]Bishop White's disapproval of enlargement, expressed in his *Thoughts on the proposal of alterations in the Book of Psalms in metre, and in the Hymns, now before a committee of the General Convention: by a member of the committee* (see his *Memoirs*, &c., pp. 384-387), no doubt created a serious embarrassment.

[119]For Dr. Muhlenberg's own account of its preparation, see Ayres' *Life*, &c., pp. 84-86.

[120]*Journals*, vol. ii, pp. 174, 191.

[121]His 16mo ed. of that year, with the Committee's certificate dated April 10, 1827, is "the standard edition" ordered by General Convention: his 8vo ed. of that year is dated May 5th.

was an excellent one for its time. To say that English XVIIIth century Dissent furnished a majority of the hymns, with Watts, Doddridge, Steele and Charles Wesley leading, is merely to say that it bore the marks of its time. Numerous other writers, older and newer, were also represented. The tone of the book was decidedly evangelical, and quite colorless in ecclesiastical and sacramental directions. A recent historian, writing of "The Catholic Renaissance," is surely mistaken in saying that its continued use infused "a more distinctive churchly sentiment among the people."[122] What the book did was to meet in considerable measure the demand of those who had wanted more hymns and to extend the practice of hymn singing in parochial worship. In other communions also the book was favorably regarded, and "Episc. Coll." became a familiar ascription indicating the source of hymns in their hymn books.

The permanent distinction of the *Hymns* of 1827 is its contribution to English Hymnody. It brought to the fore no less than five American Episcopal hymn writers whose hymns have survived. Dr. Onderdonk contributed nine, all of which came into use, and one of which ("The Spirit in our hearts") is widely accepted. Dr. Muhlenberg contributed five, of which "Saviour, who Thy flock art feeding" is possibly our best Baptismal Hymn; "Shout the glad tidings" a favorite Christmas Hymn; "I would not live always" a classic of evangelical "otherworldliness"; and "Like Noah's weary dove" is only now passing out of use. From George W. Doane's *Songs by the way* the compilers chose two, "Thou art the way" and "Softly now the light of day," passing over his renderings of Latin church hymns. They included also J. Wallis Eastburn's "O Holy, Holy, Holy Lord," which had been in Henshaw's book, and Francis S. Key's "Lord, with glowing heart I'd praise Thee," which had been in Muhlenberg's.

The improvement of the metrical psalms (a return to the selective principle of 1786 being now desired) remained

[122] S. J. McConnell, *op. cit.*, p. 327.

in the hands of the committee, and was finally accomplished by a joint commission of the General Convention of 1832.[123] The first copies of their work appeared in 1833 as *Psalms, in metre, selected from the Psalms of David*. With some fourteen exceptions, the selections were all from Tate and Brady's *New Version*. As bound up with the Prayer Book these Psalms and the Hymns of 1827 together took the title of *Selections from the Psalms of David in metre, with Hymns, suited to the feasts and fasts of the Church, and other occasions of public worship*.[124] This continued in use without change or addition until 1866, so that the *Hymns* of 1827 remained as the only authorized Hymnody of the Episcopal Church for forty years.

It cannot however be said that either wing of the Church remained satisfied for so long with the official provision of hymns. With the development of a high church party came the desire for a more liturgical and sacramental Hymnody. But just now we are more concerned with the low churchmen who carried on the traditions of the Evangelical Party, craved a fuller use of the Evangelical Hymnody, and followed the example set by Henshaw. Both Stephen H. and his son Dudley A., Tyng published collections of "Additional Hymns" for use at lectures and prayer meetings. The son's collection, bound up with "The Prayer Book Collection" and *Chants and Tunes for the Book of Common Prayer*, appeared as *The Lecture-Room Hymn-Book* (Philadelphia, 1855), and had some circulation. Even more aggressive was Dr. C. W. Andrews, whose "Additional Selection," bound up with the *Hymns* of 1827, first appeared in 1843. It was based very largely upon the English collections of Simeon, Baptist W. Noel and the elder Bickersteth; but Watts, Charles Wesley and *Olney Hymns* were the principal sources. From this grew Andrews' larger collection, *Hymns and devotional Poetry*, published by the Society for the Promotion of Evangelical

[123]*Journals*, vol. ii, pp. 408, 437.
[124]Commonly referred to as "The Prayer Book Collection."

Knowledge in 1857, often reissued and later revised. As bound up with prayers, prose Psalms and the *Hymns* of 1827, it became *Service Book . . . for use in prayer meetings, and on other informal occasions* (Philadelphia, 1858) ; and so suggests a certain rivalry with Tyng's *Lecture-Room Hymn-Book* published at the same place three years earlier.

In these privately issued books the Evangelical Hymnody found opportunity for a quite unfettered presentation. Apart from their interest as ministering to and embodying a past phase of church life, they exercised some permanent influence in securing for the Evangelical Hymnody a suitable representation in the future hymn books of the Episcopal Church.

V

ENGLISH HYMNS IN THE REFORMED DUTCH CHURCH (1767-1868)

The Reformed Protestant Dutch churches in the colonies continued too long for their own good to conduct their services in the language of the fatherland. But in New York English preaching was decided upon in 1762.[125] Two years later an English psalm book was planned,[126] and Francis Hopkinson was engaged to prepare it.[127] This he did by adapting the *New Version* of Tate and Brady to the metres of the accustomed melodies of the Dutch Psalter. The English service book appeared as *The Psalms of David, with the Ten Commandments, Creed, Lord's Prayer, &c. in metre. Also the Catechism, Confession of Faith, Liturgy, &c. translated from the Dutch. For the use of the Reformed Protestant Dutch Church of the City of New York* (New York: James Parker, 1767). The Dutch rule of Psalmody was a strict one. Nothing could be sung in church until authorized, and nothing was authorized but

---

[125]*Ecclesiastical Records: State of New York,* vol. vi, Albany, 1905, p. 3819.
[126]*Ibid.,* p. 3872.   [127]*Ibid.,* p. 3931.

versions of the "Psalms of David; the ten commandments; the Lord's prayer; the 12 articles of the Christian faith; the *songs* of Mary, Zachariah, and Simeon versified. . . . All others are prohibited, and where any have been already introduced, they shall be discontinued as soon as possible."[128] To this rule of the Synod of Dort the contents of the New York psalm book were conformed without question, and the rule was formally recognized and ratified at the first General Meeting of the churches in October, 1771.[129]

The new psalm book did not long satisfy the English-speaking congregations, presumably on account of the peculiar metres and the melodies adapted to them, and also from a restlessness under confinement to strict Psalmody. After the Revolutionary War the General Meeting became the General Synod,[130] succeeding to the authority of the Synod of Dort, and in 1787 it directed that a new psalm book be prepared "out of other collections of English Psalms in repute and received in the Reformed churches."[131] The peculiar phrasing was very likely intended to include *The Psalms of David imitated* of Dr. Watts, which were winning repute in neighboring churches but were questionable from the point of view of a strict Psalmody. They must have had many admirers in the extending English-speaking congregations, but the Reformed Dutch Church as a whole never yielded to the spell of Watts' *Psalms and Hymns* which for so long dominated the Service of Praise in other denominations.

The proposal that the Church should abandon its historic position and adopt hymn singing does not seem to have

[128] "Rules of Church Government established in the National Synod, held in Dordrecht, in the years 1618 and 1619," art. lxix, as translated in *The Constitution of The Reformed Dutch Church in the U. S. A.,* New York, 1793, p. 289.

[129] *Ecclesiastical Records,* vol. vi, p. 4224.

[130] *Acts and Proceedings of the General Synod,* vol. i, New York, 1859, p. 128.

[131] *Ibid.,* p. 167.

come from the committee that had the new psalm book in charge but from the pastors. It took the form of instructions to that committee, made "upon mature deliberation" by the General Synod of 1788:—

"5. And since it is regarded necessary that some well-composed spiritual hymns be connected as a supplement with this new Psalm-Book, it is ordained that the committee also have a care over this matter, and print such hymns in connection with the Psalms." [132]

"This new Psalm-Book" appeared in the following year as *The Psalms of David, with Hymns and Spiritual Songs. Also the Catechism, Confession of Faith, and Liturgy, of the Reformed Church in the Netherlands. For the use of the Reformed Dutch Church in North-America. New-York: printed by Hodge, Allen and Campbell, and sold at their respective book-stores.* M. DCC. LXXXIX.

The hymns are numbered as an even hundred; in reality 135. They were selected by Dr. John H. Livingston[133] from the whole breadth of the Evangelical Hymnody and beyond,[134] in view of the needs of the Church. Their classification reveals the special uses for which hymns had been desired. No less than 84 (numbered as "Hymn 1 to 52" with their alternates) are "suited to the Heidelbergh Catechism," for consecutive singing on the afternoon of each Sunday through the year in connection with the exposition of the Catechism.[135] "Hymn 53 to 73, are adapted to the Holy Ordinance of the Lord's Supper." "Hymn 74, to the end, are on Miscellaneous Subjects," mostly occasional, and including "Christmas," "Resurrection," "Ascension" and "Whitsunday."[136]

The Synod of 1790 perceived "with much satisfaction

[132] *Acts and Proceedings,* vol. i, p. 182.
[133] See "Explanatory Articles," No. lxv, *Constitution,* ed. N. Y., 1793, p. 348.
[134] One was taken from the Moraviah Hymn Book of 1754.
[135] See *Acts and Proceedings,* vol. i, pp. 80, 176.
[136] For the Church's qualified recognition of "Holy days" see "Explanatory Articles," No. lxvii, and D. D. Demarest, *The Reformed Church in America,* 4th ed., N. Y., 1889, pp. 166-168.

that the English Psalms, together with the selection of Hymns formerly approved by Synodical decrees, have been happily committed to the press, and are printed and already in use in many congregations." The Synod went on to inform the churches naively enough "that, according to the intention of the Synod of Dordrecht, hymns which have been approved by a Synod should not be excluded from the churches."[137] This deliverance was intended to soothe the consciences of any who had supposed that the Synod of Dort aimed to use Synodical control for the conservation of a purely Scriptural Psalmody, or perhaps to serve notice on a psalm-loving minority that the resistance to hymn singing then disturbing the Presbyterian Church would find no countenance in the Reformed Dutch.

The use of the Hymns of 1789 naturally created a desire for more, and by request of the Synod of 1812[138] Dr. Livingston expanded the collection to 273 hymns on the same lines and with the same grouping. The new book appeared in 1814 both at New York and New Brunswick as *The Psalms and Hymns, with the Catechism, Confession of Faith, and Liturgy of the Reformed Dutch Church in North America. Selected at the request of the General Synod. By John H. Livingston, D.D., S.T.P.* Adopting this book Synod regarded it as one of the "Standards of the Church"; and in 1815 proceeded to deal with a printer who ventured upon some "improvements" of the text of certain hymns.[139]

This book became the basis of the denominational Hymnody, standing alone till 1831, intact till 1847; and, with its contents distributed and rearranged, retained in use till 1869. It became "Book I" of the enlargement of 1831 when Dr. Thomas De Witt's committee added 172 hymns. They were first printed as *Additional Hymns, adopted by the General Synod . . . June 1831, and authorized to be used in the churches under their care. Phila-*

[137]*Acts and Proceedings,* vol. i, p. 212.
[138]*Ibid.,* vol. i, p. 424.   [139]*Acts and Proceedings* of 1815, p. 37.

delphia: published by G. W. Mentz & Son, 1831; and thereafter they became "Book II" of the authorized *Psalms and Hymns.* This supplement introduced to the Church many of the now classical hymns of the XVIIIth century Revival, such as "Jesus, Lover of my soul," "Rock of Ages," and "Guide me, O Thou Great Jehovah"; some recent hymns, such as Heber's "Brightest and best" and "From Greenland's icy mountains"; but "I would not live alway" was the only one of the novelties in the Protestant Episcopal collection of 1827 that was utilized.

The *Sabbath-school and Social Hymn Book of the Reformed Dutch Church,* approved in 1843, was made to cover prayer meetings, in view of information that unauthorized hymn books were being introduced into the lecture-room "in many parts of the Church,"[140] but had been designed "to increase the attention of our young people to sacred music."[141]   In the parochial school system the Dutch had attempted to establish in this country, the leader of the church Psalmody was also the schoolmaster.   But no attempt was made to introduce music study, and generation after generation grew up with little ability to participate in Church Song.[142]   The decadence of congregational singing and the apathy of the people were before the Synod in 1836[143] and 1837,[144] and that of 1840, which recommended "the introduction of music in our district schools" and urged upon the classes "attention to sacred music."[145]

The Synod of 1845 was more concerned with the literary side of Hymnody in the church service and as an instrument of Christian education in the home, and put the improvement of the hymn book into the hands of a committee.[146] Their 341 *Additional Hymns . . . adopted . . . June, 1846* appeared at Philadelphia, 1847; and, rearranged with

---

[140]*Acts and Proceedings,* vol. vi, p. 164.   [141]*Ibid.,* vol. iv, p. 533.

[142]*Cf.* Demarest, *op. cit.,* pp. 161, 162; John Bodine Thompson, in *The Christian Intelligencer,* July 11, 1906.

[143]*Acts and Proceedings,* vol. iv, p. 533.   [144]*Ibid.,* vol. v, p. 89.

[145]*Ibid.,* vol. v, p. 421.   [146]*Ibid.,* vol. vi, p. 478.

the hymns already authorized, and accompanied by the metrical psalms, standards and liturgy, as *The Psalms and Hymns, . . . of the Reformed Protestant Dutch Church in North America. Authorized by the General Synod to be used in the churches under their care* (1847).

The *Additional Hymns* were still predominantly of the Evangelical school, but later writers were by no means neglected; and more varieties of metre were sought, in deference to the statement of Thomas Hastings that "they were needed by city choirs."[147] Many pastors had a different feeling toward the strange metres and no welcome for some of the new hymns. The Classis of Bergen and the North Classis of Long Island complained of "ninety preaching hymns," "praise to dead saints" (e. g. "Sister, thou wast mild and lovely"), "heretical expressions," "bad taste," "nonsense," "a lack of devotion" in some hymns, and too many "peculiar metres."[148] They and other malcontents were appeased by some slight changes and by permission to continue in using the earlier Hymn Book.[149]

There was no further change in the authorized Hymnody for more than twenty years. The collection of 1847, with its 324 "Psalms" and 788 "Hymns," was indeed more than ample. The distinction between psalm and hymn thus preserved was largely formal, many of its psalms being free hymns and some of its hymns being Psalm versions; and two successive Hymnody committees favored a rearrangement in one series.

The contribution of the denomination to hymn writing during all this period was small. It is likely that some of the didactic hymns of the 1789 book were prepared for it. In the *Psalms and Hymns* of 1847 two hymns by George W. Bethune are included:—"O for the happy hour," and the translated "It is not death to die." But this was a

---

[147]*Ibid.*, vol. vii, p. 204.

[148]For an interesting review of these charges by a committee of Synod, see *Acts and Proceedings*, vol. vii, pp. 200-205.

[149]*Ibid.*, vol. vii, p. 281.

small representation alongside of the thirty-five there printed from the Mss. of the Presbyterian Thomas Hastings.[150] The really outstanding names are those of the successive compilers, each of whom made a practically unhampered selection of hymns,—Dr. John H. Livingston, Dr. Thomas De Witt, and Chancellor Isaac Ferris; notably Dr. Livingston, from whose honored hand the Church took its Hymnody in 1789 and 1813, and whose compilation remained intact till 1847. He was thanked for his great service in 1813, and it was ordered that his name appear on the title-page of the hymn book,[151] where it remained till 1847. Some of the editions had also a copper-plate portrait of him for frontispiece.

The Reformed Dutch hymn books before 1847 had a denominational distinctiveness in their didacticism, their exposition of the Heidelberg Catechism and their limited recognition of the church year. But the really disinctive feature of the denominational Hymnody was the continued insistence upon the principle of church control of the Praise, by which congregations were restricted to the use of selections made by church authority. This principle of church control was an inheritance from the Synod of Dort, but was exercised in this country not in the interest of a Scriptural Psalmody but with a view to "the preservation of a sound theology."[152]

VI

ENGLISH HYMNS IN THE GERMAN REFORMED CHURCH (1800-1858)

With the dawn of the XIXth century the introduction of English into the worship of German Reformed churches became at once a necessity and an occasion of bitter strife.[153]

[150]Ibid., vol. vii, p. 93.
[151]Ibid., Synod of 1813, p. 17.   [152]Cf. Ibid., vol. vii, p. 94.
[153]See J. H. Dubbs, The Reformed Church in Pennsylvania, Lancaster, 1902, pp. 270 ff.

From that date the process of Anglicizing the Church went steadily forward. The Reformed Dutch hymn book was generally introduced into the early English-speaking congregations,[154] but the *Psalms and Hymns* of Watts were also resorted to.[155] The use of hymns involved no change in denominational principle or practice. The Reformed immigrants brought with them hymn books used at home, and the American Synod had already printed a German hymn book of its own.[156]

In view of the increase in the use of English the Synod adopted in 1830 a collection made by the Classis of Maryland: *Psalms and Hymns, for the use of the German Reformed Church, in the United States of America. Published by the Synod of said Church.* The Psalm versions numbered 150 precisely: the hymns, 422, increased in 1834 by an appendix to 520.

It was no doubt natural that a generation disposed to disparage the ways of the fathers, and attaining release from them with difficulty, should turn its back upon the riches of the German Hymnody, and wish for a book like those its American neighbors were using. And such was the *Psalms and Hymns* of 1830. The Psalm versions were largely those of Watts, and the Evangelical Hymnody of the XVIIIth century furnished the majority of the hymns, though a number of later writers were represented. There was a great preponderance of the long, common and short metres, but the book as a whole is brighter than the contemporaneous Presbyterian *Psalms and Hymns.*

This first English hymn book of the denomination was also the only one in the period preceding the Liturgical Con-

---

[154]Dubbs, *Historic Manual of the Reformed Church in the United States,* Lancaster, 1885, p. 356.

[155]The writer's copy of Woodward's Philadelphia ed. of 1817, containing "Barlow's Watts" and the Hymns, was "Bought for the German Reformed Church at Harrisburg, and placed in the pulpit . . . on the 20th December, 1820."

[156]*Das neue und verbesserte Gesangbuch,* Philadelphia, Steiner u. Kämmerer, 1797: 2nd ed., 1799.

troversy. Its use indeed extended further, a 66th edition appearing in 1872. Through all these years the *Psalms and Hymns* was printed without tunes and without any indication of the authorship of the hymns. One other English book from within the denomination before the controversy was *The Saints' Harp: a Collection of Hymns and Spiritual Songs, adapted to prayer and social meetings, and seasons of revival. Selected and arranged by Rev. J. F. Berg* (Philadelphia, 1839: 2nd ed., 1843). It contains some good hymns and many revival songs of a surprisingly low order; also five originals by Dr. Berg, all but one of which picture the wrath to come. It was no doubt prepared for those "protracted meetings" that characterized Dr. Berg's pastorate in the old Race Street Church in Philadelphia.[157]

VII

ENGLISH HYMNS IN THE LUTHERAN CHURCH
(1756-1859)

The differing tongues of early Lutheran immigrants presented a bar to a common Lutheran worship; and the process of Anglicizing that worship encountered not only the difficulties of a new language but was hindered by the jealousies it awakened.[158]

In New York Muhlenberg tried to meet the situation by preaching in Dutch in the morning, in German in the afternoon, and in English in the evening. The book from which he lined out the hymns at the English services was a copy of *Psalmodia Germanica,* a collection of rather crude versions of German hymns, mostly by John Christian Jacobi, Keeper of the Royal German Chapel at St. James' Palace,

---

[157]D. Van Horne, *A History of the Reformed Church in Philadelphia,* Phila., 1876, p. 79.

[158]*Cf.* Henry E. Jacobs, *A History of the Evangelical Lutheran Church in the United States* (Am. Church Hist. series), N. Y., 1893, p. 251.

London (first published in 1722; a second part in 1725: the two united in 1732).

When it was clear that English services were to be continued, a reprint of the edition of 1732 was made, appearing as *Psalmodia Germanica: or, The German Psalmody. Translated from the High Dutch. Together with their proper tunes, and thorough bass. The third edition, corrected and very much enlarged. London, printed: New York, re-printed, and sold by H. Gaine, at the Bible & Crown, in Queen-Street, 1756:* with *A Supplement to German Psalmody: done into English* . . . as a second title.[159] This was the first English hymn book of American Lutheranism. It was used at the English services of the (Dutch) Trinity Church, at Hackensack, and probably in other churches along the Hudson.[160] It included many of the best Lutheran hymns; and, had the English versions been of better quality, might have afforded a nucleus for the development here of a characteristic Lutheran Hymnody.

In 1784 the scholarly Dr. Kunze became pastor of the united Christ Church and Trinity in New York, and was deeply concerned with the development of an English-speaking Lutheranism. He published *A Hymn and Prayer-Book: for the use of such Lutheran Churches as use the English Language. Collected by John C. Kunze, D.D. Senior of the Lutheran Clergy in the State of New York* (New York: Hurtin and Commardinger, 1795). This interesting book is of even date with Jeremy Belknap's Boston *Sacred Poetry,* but is not to be judged by the same standard. Kunze had first of all to provide a body of hymns from the German that could be sung to the original melodies. The two available sources he commanded were Gaine's reprint of *Psalmodia Germanica*[161] and the English

[159]There is a facsimile of the title-page of this rare book in *The Journals of Hugh Gaine,* N. Y., 1902, vol. i, p. 95. [160]Jacobs, p. 339.
[161] "With which many serious English persons have been greatly delighted." Kunze's preface.

Moravian *Collection* of 1789, which he regarded as "an excellent collection." From these he took in about equal number some 150 hymns. He had then to choose the most desirable English hymns, of whose sources he knew little, and whose language he imperfectly comprehended. Of these he included about 70, with Watts in the lead, followed by Charles Wesley, Newton and other evangelical hymn writers, with two by Bishop Ken and one by Erskine.[162] To an appendix he relegated six hymns of his own, five by his assistant, George Strebeck, and four by J. F. Ernst, a pastor in the Albany region: of these some are translations from the German, and the others sound as if they were. The Lutheran and Moravian, Wesleyan and Evangelical, strains thus mingle in this pioneer hymn book; but on the whole the Moravian seems to preponderate.

Kunze was thus the first hymn book editor, and he and his associates the first hymn writers, of English-speaking Lutheranism in America. His book contributed little in the way of materials toward a Lutheran Hymnody; and yet he indicated, and according to his opportunities followed out, the three lines on which such Hymnody must develop :— the Englishing of the best Lutheran hymns, the selection of the most available English hymns, and the writing of hymns by American Lutherans.

The first English-speaking congregation was Zion's, New York; formed in 1796 out of Dr. Kunze's German Church,[163] and Strebeck became its pastor. Alleging "the unsuitableness of the metres of our English Lutheran Hymn Book, published in 1795" and the request of his own congregation,[164] he prepared for it *A Collection of evangelical Hymns, made from different authors and collections, for the English Lutheran Church, in New York: by George Strebeck* (New York: John Tiebout, 1797). Like Kunze he gave prominence to the church year, but

[162]From F. M. Bird's analysis of the book in "Lutheran Hymnology," *The Evangelical Quarterly Review*, January, 1865.

[163]Jacobs, *op. cit.*, p. 319.   [164]Preface.

retained only 48 of Kunze's hymns; and of them only 10 are from the German, 3 of John Wesley's translations being added. Two-thirds of Kunze's book was of German origin, of Strebeck's only one twenty-third. Of the remaining 256 hymns, one half represents Watts and his school, one-fifth Charles Wesley, one-eighth *Olney Hymns*.[165] The editor apologized for so many hymns from un-Lutheran sources, but within a few years carried the bulk of his congregation over to the Protestant Episcopal Church.

When Ralph Williston became Strebeck's successor at Zion in 1805, the vestry and trustees requested him to make a new hymn book, as not a copy of the earlier book was to be had, and its "obvious deficiency" made reprinting inexpedient.[166] "The Evangelical Lutheran Ministry" of New York State had made a resolution, of some years standing, "that a new edition of the English Lutheran Hymn-book should be procured," [167] and either joined in Williston's work of compilation, or else accepted it when complete. The new book appeared as *A choice Selection of evangelical Hymns, from various authors: for the use of the English Evangelical Lutheran Church in New York. By Ralph Williston* (New York: J. C. Totten, 1806). Among the Passion Hymns are seven transferred from Dr. Kunze's book, but Watts and Charles Wesley contribute nearly three-fourths of the whole. The rest are from the school of Watts and other Evangelical writers. Notwithstanding Dr. Kunze's certificate that none of its hymns are "dissonant to our doctrine," neither its arrangements nor contents suggests Lutheranism. It was in fact a good evangelical collection and was used widely within the New York Ministerium, and was introduced into the new English-speaking St. John's Church of Philadelphia.[168]

Williston, who had been a Methodist, proceeded to ad-

---

[165]*Cf.* Bird, *ut supra.*   [166] "Advertisement" prefixed.
[167]Certificate, signed "John C. Kunze."
[168]Jacobs, *op. cit.,* p. 341.

minister a great blow to English-speaking Lutheranism by
seceding to the Protestant Episcopal Church. He carried
his congregation with him, and the only English Lutheran
church in New York was reincorporated as "Zion Protestant Episcopal Church" in 1810.[169]

There was thus no occasion to reprint Williston's book,
nor did it continue to recommend itself to the Synod of
New York.[170] The Synod was entering a period generally
characterized as "rationalistic," under the leadership of Dr.
Frederick H. Quitman of Rhinebeck. In 1813 the Synod,
meeting in his church, ordered the preparation of a new
hymn book; which appeared as *A Collection of Hymns,
and a Liturgy, for the use of Evangelical Lutheran
Churches: published by order of the Evangelical Lutheran
Synod of the State of New York* (New York and Philadelphia, 1814).

It accommodated itself to the tendencies of the time
and place by avoiding the types of experience developed in
the Methodist and Evangelical Revival, and reverting to
the school of Watts, including Thomas Scott and others
more or less Arian, yet not rejecting the warmth of Anne
Steele, who has some 70 hymns. It dropped out Williston's section on "The Trinity," qualified the Passion
Hymns, and like current New England books, emphasized
natural religion. But from its point of view the selection
was good and conveniently arranged. Its tone was deepened and enriched, and many of its omissions supplied,
by the *Additional Hymns* published in 1834. Thus
strengthened, the *Collection* of 1814 retained for many
years its hold upon English-speaking churches not only
within but beyond the Synod of New York. As late as
1865 Mr. Bird reports it as still used in New York city,

---

[169] J. G. Wilson, *The Centennial History of the Diocese of New
York,* New York, 1886, p. 248.

[170] In its preface of 1814, Synod lumps the previous hymn books
as the attempts of individuals, which "evidently admit of great
improvement."

Albany, Easton, Reading, in half a dozen country churches in New York and New Jersey, and perhaps a few in Pennsylvania.[171]

Different from anything that had preceded it, and much more churchly, was a hymn book prepared by Paul Henkel, pastor at New Market, Virginia, and missionary at large; one of a family noted for the aggressiveness of its conservatism:—*Church Hymn Book, consisting of newly composed Hymns, with an addition of Hymns and Psalms, from other authors, carefully adapted for the use of public worship, and many other occasions. By Paul Henkel, Minister of the Gospel. First edition. New Market: Shenandoah County (Virginia.), printed in Solomon Henkel's Printing Office, 1816.* It has 347 Hymns, followed by a complete metrical Psalter from Watts and others. The first part is a "Hymnal Companion to the Liturgy," with "Hymns adapted to the Gospel and Epistle throughout the ecclesiastical year" and to the various occasions and offices of the church; followed by more general hymns. Unfortunately a large part of the contents was from Henkel's own pen, and is nothing more than didactic prose broken up into short phrases that serve as lines of verse.

But it was the Henkels and their sympathizers who broke away from the Synod of North Carolina, and formed in 1820 the new Synod of Tennessee. By its direction a revised and enlarged edition of Henkel's book was prepared by his son Ambrose. Over three hundred of Henkel's hymns are retained in the now official book, and eleven are by members of his family. The bulk of the remainder is from Watts and his school, Charles Wesley, and the writers of the Evangelical Revival, with Watts predominant. A third edition, with trifling changes, appeared in 1850, and a fourth, with additions, in 1857. But it is probable that the use of the book was confined within the limits of the Synod, and that on Lutheran Hymnody in general it exerted no appreciable influence.

[171]*Ut supra,* p. 38.

The General Synod, convened at Frederick, Maryland, in 1821, represented the first effort to give a central government and direction to the forces of Lutheranism in America; and was to become an active agency in the Anglicizing of Lutheran churches. It was really the creation of the Ministerium of Pennsylvania, under a resolution adopted in 1818. But the Ministerium had elected to remain a German-speaking body, and had no English hymn book of its own. In the English-speaking congregations allowed (not without protest) within its bounds, the New York *Collection* was used.[172] But the New York Synod had not come into the General Synod, and moreover the experience of the congregations using their *Collection* had proved it to be in some respects inadequate.[173] There was thus an opportunity for something in the way of a common hymn book, and for the forward step in Hymnody which the situation and the needs of the churches plainly called for.

The project of a new hymn book was referred in 1825 to a committee, with Dr. S. S. Schmucker as chairman. Three years later it appeared as *Hymns, selected and original, for public and private worship. Published by the General Synod of the Ev. Lutheran Church. First edition. Published, Gettysburg, Pa. Stereotyped by L. Johnson, Phila., 1828.* The title was misleading, the original material being trifling both in extent and importance,[174] and was so inept as to suggest that the compilers were unaware of, or unequal to, their unusual opportunity. Such as it was, the title remained affixed to the authorized Hymnody of the General Synod for more than forty years.

The contents of the book hardly fulfil even the measure

[172]E. T. Horn "Chronological Summary of the Acts of the Synod of Pennsylvania," 1878, p. 19—.

[173]The official preface of General Synod's hymn book of 1828 describes it as "a most excellent work," but lacking sufficient variety, and omitting many of the choicest English hymns.

[174]Two hymns by Dr. Schmucker himself constitute the only material identified as original in the 1828 edition.

of promise held forth in the title. It was plainly purposed to embody the full scope of evangelical theology and every phase of evangelical experience in these 759 hymns, songs and exhortations. At the time the wave of rationalism was being succeeded by a wave of revivalism, and revival methods were replacing catechetical. The book is in full sympathy with the new methods, appropriating many rude revival songs. The textual treatment of the standard hymns is often distressing, and as containing the authorized Hymnody of a historic Church, with its inherited standards of doctrine and churchmanship the *Hymns* of 1828 seems singularly unworthy.

In 1841 a supplement of 199 hymns was added, and the book reached its 56th edition by 1849. In the year following appeared a new edition, prepared by a representative committee headed by Dr. William M. Reynolds, containing some 800 selections from the old edition, and 200 that were new. It had thirty hymns from the German;[175] but at that date the committee were largely dependent on Henry Mills' somewhat prosy *Horae Germanicae* or their own powers of translation. In the remainder, Watts and his followers, Wesley and the hymn writers of the Revival, are represented in about the proportions of the New York Collection. Of late writers, there are nine by the English Heber and seven by the American Samuel F. Smith.[176] The number of revival songs is much reduced; and in all respects the revision benefited Lutheran Hymnody.

But in Lutheran as in other Churches congregational hymn singing was suffering from the encroachments of the choir. In adopting the hymns of their neighbors, they necessarily gave over the use of the German chorals, and were dependent upon their neighbors for suitable tunes also. Some of the tunes thus appropriated were "worn out worldly tunes," caught up from social life or from their use in revivals. Even more menacing was the unfailing

[175]There is a list in the "large edition" of 1852.
[176]*Cf.* Bird in *Evangelical Quarterly Review,* April, 1865, p. 219.

succession of American tune books, which appealed to the choirs by their novelty, and kept them supplied with tunes which the people did not know; resulting in "the present neglect or discontinuance of congregational singing." [177] By way of remedy, Drs. Seiss, McCron and Passavant offered to the General Synod an edition of *Hymns selected and original* which they had revised and for the first time set to music. Failing the acceptance of Synod, it appeared on their own responsibility as *The Evangelical Psalmist: a collection of Tunes and Hymns for use in congregational and social worship. Philadelphia: Lindsay and Blakiston, 1859.* In this sincere effort to better Lutheran Praise, the selection and arrangement of hymns was improved, the texts less so. The musical features were at least above the average level of the time, and mainly for their sake the book found some congregational use.

Within the limits of the General Synod, there were also the beginnings of a Lutheran Sunday school Hymnody. The elder Dr. Krauth printed at Philadelphia in 1838 his *Hymns, selected and arranged for Sunday schools, of the Evangelical Lutheran Church, and adapted to Sunday schools in general;* and in 1843 Dr. Passavant printed at Baltimore his *Hymns, selected and original, for Sunday schools, of the Evangelical Lutheran Church.* They contained little specially appealing to childhood.

The General Synod never at any time included all the synods or a majority of Lutherans, but, in the absence of any English hymn book put forth by the Pennsylvania Ministerium, its *Hymns selected and original* came the nearest to being the common hymn book of English-speaking Lutherans. It came into use in probably not less than four-fifths of their congregations.[178] Its successive editions mark the progress of the Anglicizing process, and cover a period in which the ways of surrounding denominations

[177]Report on Congregational Singing to Ministerium of N. Y., Sept. 8, 1857, p. 7.
[178]Bird, *ut supra*, p. 223.

prevailed over Lutheran traditions. The Hymnody itself is not Lutheran, but is drawn from outside; it may rather be described as well within the lines of the Evangelical Hymnody, though somewhat heightened in color through revivalistic influences.

The foresight of the prevalence of English in the General Synod had kept the Synod of Ohio, organized in 1818 on missionary ground, from joining in its formation.[179] But provision was early made for English services, at which the General Synod's *Hymns* was used.[180] The Joint Synod of Ohio and other States was formed in 1833, and kept its independence in the interests of strictly confessional Lutheranism. It is therefore not surprising that Synod discovered "the strange bias of many hymns in the book [of General Synod]." This, and the difficulty and expense of obtaining books from the East[181] led to the publication of *A Collection of Hymns and Prayers for public and private worship. Published by order of the Evangelical Lutheran Joint Synod of Ohio. Zanesville, printed at the Lutheran Standard office, 1845.* Its compilers were required to make the General Synod's book, as already considerably in use, their basis, and they added some hymns from the New York *Collection* and the Episcopal "Prayer Book Collection." A very churchly collection could not have been made from these sources, but a much better collection than these 453 hymns could readily have been made. To avoid the "bias" of the old book, such hymns as "Jesus, Lover of my soul," "Rock of Ages," "Love Divine, all loves excelling," and "When I survey the wondrous cross," were passed by. The new book belongs to the school of Watts. He and Doddridge and Steele furnish more than half the hymns, while Wesley and the writers of the Revival have less than forty.

The book did not satisfy the churches, and after various

---

[179] Jacobs, *op. cit.,* p. 359.
[180] Ohio Synod's preface, 1845.
[181] *Ibid.*

resolutions in the several districts, the Joint Synod published *Collection of Hymns for public and private worship. Published by order of the Evangelical Lutheran Joint Synod of Ohio. Columbus* (n. d., 2nd ed., 1855; 3rd ed., 1858; 4th ed., 1863). It was a sincere and not ineffective effort to make a Lutheran hymn book. The compilers had been instructed "to adapt the hymn book to the ecclesiastical year," [182] but found "our English hymnology rather barren," and were able to provide only for the greater feasts and fasts. The collection includes 51 versions of German hymns, and brings forward as translators and hymn writers Dr. Matthias Loy (nine versions, 7 originals), Prof. L. Heyl (7 versions, 1 original), J. H. Good (4 versions), Dr. William M. Reynolds (2 new versions, with 3 taken from General Synod's book).

This later edition of the Ohio book marks the transition from the earlier period of Lutheran Hymnody, when it was satisfied merely to appropriate the current Evangelical Hymnody, to the later period when the Hymnody was made to embody Lutheran traditions and ideals.

VIII

DIVERSE CURRENTS OF HYMNODY

Even in colonial times some trends of theological thought began to manifest a departure from the old orthodoxy. And to these were added by importation from abroad various exotic growths of religious opinion and practice which found here more or less congenial soil and developed into independent sects openly antagonistic of the faith and church order of the denominations already established in America.

Among the earliest and most interesting of the new movements was the Unitarian revolt whose early dealings with the accepted Hymnody we have already traced in connec-

[182] Preface.

tion with the New England Congregationalism from which it proceeded. With some other aspects of the Hymnody of theological revolt we have now to concern ourselves.

1. EARLY UNIVERSALIST HYMNS (1776-1849)

Expelled from Whitefield's meeting, and coming to America in 1770 as an avowed disciple of James Relly, John Murray became the founder of American Universalism. As part of a propaganda of the new faith he secured 223 subscribers to a reprint of the Rellys' *Christian Hymns, Poems and Spiritual Songs, sacred to the praise of God our Saviour* (London, 1770),[183] from the press of Isaac Collins at Burlington, N. J., in 1776. Among the subscribers were 38 persons in the First Parish of Gloucester, Mass., where Murray had preached, who soon formed the First Independent Church of Christ, introduced the Relly book, and continued to use it until 1808.[184] It thus became the first hymn book of American Universalism. A historian of the denomination says that from the hymn books then in general use "it was difficult for Universalists to select any that did not decidedly antagonize their belief." [185] A much greater difficulty must have been found in making use of the Relly book with its irregular metres, especially in a church where the singing was accompanied by a crank organ having in its barrel only ten psalm tunes.[186]

A second reprint of the Relly book appeared at Portsmouth, N. H., in 1782, for Noah Parker, a convert of Murray's who preached to a congregation gathered in that town.[187] Appended were five "Hymns, by J. [ohn] M. [urray]." They have little originality but are smooth in rhythm, and show that Murray understood the Congregational Hymn much better than did the Rellys.

---

[183] See chap. vii, part III.

[184] Richard Eddy, *Universalism in Gloucester, Mass.,* Gloucester, 1892, pp. 21, 48, and appx. E.

[185] R. Eddy in "American Church History Series," vol. x, p. 473.

[186] *Universalism in Gloucester,* p. 21. [187] *Ibid.,* appx. E, p. 129.

Mention has already been made of an independent movement disrupting the First Baptist Church of Philadelphia, where Elhanan Winchester had preached "an universal restoration," and of the two collections of hymns made for his expelled followers who organized in 1781 as "The Society of Universal Baptists." [188]   Winchester's theology was very different from Murray's, and his hymn books much nearer the evangelical type than the Rellyan book; and he brought large accessions to the Universalist ranks, especially from Baptist congregations.[189]

The need of establishing a common basis and some sort of organization among the congregations brought about the Philadelphia Convention of 1790, which at its 1791 session perfected arrangements for a common hymn book. But correspondence with the Boston church revealed in the matter of Church Song also divergence of opinion. The Philadelphians were preparing a metrical exposition of Universalism: the Bostonians demanded a book of praise. Agreement proving unattainable, each party to the controversy proceeded to publish its own book. The Convention hymn book appeared as *Evangelical Psalms, Hymns and Spiritual Songs, selected from various authors, and*

[188]Chap. iv, part IV, section III, 2, (1).

[189]D. Benedict, *A general History of the Baptist Denomination*, Boston, 1813, vol. i, p. 275. In England also, where he spent more than six years (1787-1794), Winchester preached Restorationism and published hymns and hymn books. In 1794 appeared *The Universalist's Hymn Book; containing I. Original Hymns . . . by Elhanan Winchester. II. An Appendix, consisting of a small but choice Collection of Hymns, from several authors, particularly designed for the use of those congregations who believe in the Millenium, and the Universal Restoration* (London: printed for the author). In 1797 (the year of his death on April 18 at Hartford) appeared in London *The Psalms of David, versified from a new translation, and adapted to Christian worship. Particularly intended for the use of such Christians as believe in the universal and unbounded love of God, manifested unto all his fallen creatures by Christ Jesus. To which is added A Collection of Hymns by various authors* (London: printed for the author). This is generally attributed to Winchester and was evidently connected with the chapel where he preached.

*published by a committee of the Convention of the Churches,
believing in the restitution of all-men, met in Philadelphia,
May 25, 1791* (Philadelphia, T. Dobson, 1792). There
are 192 hymns arranged in groups under the name of the
author or source, and 114 are from Universalist sources:
38 of them from the Relly book, with the 5 added by
Murray. There are 35 by Silas Ballou, an argumentative
rhymer of Vermont who had printed his *New Hymns on
various subjects* in 1785 (Worcester: 2nd ed., Newbury,
1797): and 15 from Winchester's *Choice Collection* of
1784, many of which are however Evangelical standards
One of the compilers, Artis Seagrave of New Jersey, contributed 21 original hymns which are much better than
Ballou's. The remainder of the book consists of groups
from Watts, Hart, Rippon's *Selection,* J. Barclay and Ralph
Erskine.

The Boston book appeared in the same year, as *Psalms,
Hymns, and Spiritual Songs: selected and original.
Designed for the use of the Church Universal, in public
and private devotion* (Boston, 1792). The originals were
52 hymns of moderate merit contributed by the principal
editor, the Rev. George Richards,[190] whose preface is still
suggestive. Richards' "name and fame" as a "forgotten
poet of American freedom and harmonious elegist of
General Washington" was revived by Edward Everett
Hale,[191] but his personality and his hymn book are more
interesting than his hymns. Declining to set forth "the
attributes and perfections of Deity," he started at Creation
and followed the progressive revelation of salvation. Beginning with a purpose of revising and enlarging the Relly
book, hitherto used in the Boston church, he surveyed the
whole field of the Evangelical Hymnody, and ended by

[190]They were omitted from a 2nd ed. of the Boston book as copyrighted property, and restored as an appendix to the third ed. (Boston,
1808) by Richards' permission.
[191]In *Old and New* for February, 1872, and see Eddy, *Universalism
in America,* vol. i, pp. 291, ff.

accepting Rippon's "beautiful collection" as the model hymn book.

The Boston book was followed by two others made for local use and flavored with the Rellyan theology. One was made by Edward Mitchell[192] and printed in 1796 for the New York congregation; the other, for the Gloucester church, appeared at Boston in 1808.[193] In the same year appeared a book designed for more general circulation:— *Hymns composed by different authors, by order of the General Convention of Universalists of the New England States and others. Adapted to public and private devotion* (Walpole, 1808). The Convention had designed a collection:[194] what its committee produced and published was a body of crude originals by the chairman, Hosea Ballou, Abner Kneeland, and Edward Turner.[195] The book found, nevertheless, some acceptance, and reached a second edition (Charlestown, 1810) : at least one of the hymns remaining till now in Universalist use.

All three of these authors tried their hands again. Kneeland put his name to *The Philadelphia Hymn Book* (Philadelphia, 1819), which was merely a reissue of Eddowes and Taylor's Arian *Sacred Poetry,* with an appendix in which the three figure largely. In 1821 Ballou and Turner brought out *The Universalists' Hymn Book* (Boston: 2nd ed., 1824), in which much of the inferior materials they had contributed to their former book gave way to standard hymns.

Christian Hymns adapted to the worship of God our Saviour (Boston, 1823) was made for the society in Bulfinch Street. It drew from Arian, Evangelical, Swedenborgian and Universalist sources, but failed to classify the hymns. Such an inconvenience in this and other books is given as one of the reasons for publishing *The new Hymn*

---

[192]*Ibid.,* p. 468.
[193]See an account of it in *Universalism in Gloucester,* pp. 204 f.
[194]See the preface.
[195]*Cf.* Eddy, in "American Church History Series," pp. 476 f.

Book designed for Universalist Societies by Sebastian and Russell Streeter (Boston, 1829), which reached a 35th edition in 1845. Also widely used was *A Collection of Psalms and Hymns for the use of Universalist Societies and families. By Hosea Ballou, 2nd* (Boston, 1837: 14th ed., 1843); and the two books were not unlike in seeking a somewhat more critical principle in the selection of their hymns.

From a number of unimportant books Abel C. Thomas' *Hymns of Zion with appropriate music* (Philadelphia, 1839) may be selected as the first within the denomination to provide tunes for the hymns. But his special mission was to correct "the prosaic and inelegant style" of "Watts, Rippon, the Wesleys, and other devout men." Adin Ballou's *The Hopedale Collection of Hymns and Songs, for the use of practical Christians* (Hopedale, Mass., 1849) sounded a new note in his call for social reform, offering sections of hymns upon anti-slavery, non-resistance, a new social state, and like themes.

It thus appears that the first seventy-five years of American Universalism were prolific in the production of hymn books, and of hymn writing also, since almost all of the editors offered original hymns. The multiplicity of the books is explained by the growth of the denomination and the inconvenience of using books compiled from a different point of view. The hymn writing is partly explained by the desire to give expression to new found convictions, partly, it must be confessed, by a lack of culture that failed to perceive the want of poetic feeling or expression in what was offered, and made hymn writing very easy. All of this writing failed to produce a single classic of Universal Salvation, or much that even Universalism has cared to preserve. To the Churches outside it has not contributed a single hymn, or in any way affected the course of English Hymnody; a fact the more notable in view of a somewhat widespread sympathy outside with "Universal" tenets or hopes.

2. SWEDENBORGIAN HYMNODY (1792-1830)

The doctrines of Swedenborg were preached in this country as early as 1784, and in 1792 a society of his followers organized at Baltimore. For its use at once appeared a neat reprint of the third edition of the New Jerusalem Church Liturgy, printed at London, 1790, by Robert Hindmarsh, including a reprint of the Hymns by Joseph Proud, first appearing at London in 1790 as *Hymns and Spiritual Songs for the use of the Lord's New Church.* Its title was *The Liturgy of the New Church, signified by the New Jerusalem in the Revelation. . . . Also Hymns and Spiritual Songs, by the Rev. Mr. Joseph Proud, Minister of the New Church. The fourth edition* (Baltimore: Samuel and John Adams, 1792); and the hymns number 304. The American branch of the New Church was thus at once put into possession of a sufficient body of hymns, brimfull of its peculiar doctrines and written much in the Doddridge manner.

By 1817 there were societies enough to justify a convention, which met at Philadelphia. Five years later appeared *Hymns for the use of the New Church, signified by the New Jerusalem in the Apocalypse. Published for the use of the New Church, by T. S. Manning, printer, Philadelphia, 1822–66.* The 285 hymns, separately paged, were bound in with *The Liturgy,* bearing the same imprint. They constitute a fresh selection, with less of Proud than would be expected; his hymns having perhaps proved too didactic and monotonous. By that date several English New Church collections were available as sources, and a large use was also made of hymns familiar in other Churches. The 292 hymns making a part of *The Order of Worship, for the use of the Second New Jerusalem Church of Philadelphia* (Philadelphia, 1830) were substantially the same selection, with modifications.

"The New Church" thus began its career in this country with an unusual equipment in the way of a Hymnody strictly denominational, but none the less with a decided disposition to retain or to adapt much of the standard Hymnody of "the Old Church." The doctrine of the unity of the Godhead in Jesus left available a considerable body of the Evangelical Hymnody celebrating Christ's divinity; and the New Church was still ready to sing "Blest be the tie that binds" and "Let party names no more." [196]

3. "SHAKER MUSIC" (1774-1893)

Mother Ann Lee came to America in 1774 with the revelation of the Kingdom and way of life she had received during her English imprisonment, and established a celibate community at Watervliet, N. Y. In this and the communities later formed, the inspirational gifts of the early Church were renewed, as manifested by "involuntary operations of singing and dancing"; and the devoted "were filled with melodious and heavenly songs, especially while under the operation of dancing." [197] There was no printed hymn book for common use till 1812-13, when 140 hymns composed in the various communities were gathered up in *Millenial Praises, containing a Collection of Gospel Hymns, in four parts; adapted to the day of Christ's second appearing. Composed for the use of his people. Hancock, printed by Josiah Tallcott, junior, 1813.* The hymns are set forth not as inspirational, but as the fruit of "the labors of Believers" "in this line." They are argumentative, descriptive, homiletical, doctrinal, but practically never worshipful with a direct address to God; filled on the one hand with Scripture history and terminology, and on the other with references to Mother Ann:—"So says our blessed mother"; "our Mother paved the way"; "The Son of Man, Who was revealed in Mother Ann"; (reminiscently) "As Mother Ann did say." The doctrine is aggressively Shaker, and like almost all sectarian Hymnody the hymns have no literary merit.

[196]Collection of 1822, Nos. 213, 214.
[197]*A summary view of the Millenial Church,* Albany, 1823, p. 80.

The Canterbury community published in 1847 *A Collection of Millenial Hymns, adapted to the present order of the Church,* and in 1852 *A sacred repository of Hymns and Anthems,* accompanied by original melodies. By this time the store of Shaker anthems and hymns had become "a multiplicity." These selections show more metrical facility and an uninterrupted praise of "The Queen of fair Zion." In the West, especially, Richard McNemar has been regarded as the poet of Shakerism, the father of its songs and journalism.[198] He gathered in 1833, under the pseudonym of Philos Harmoniae, *A Selection of Hymns and Poems; for the use of believers* (Watervliet, O.), including many of his own.

There was some elementary, "but little scientific, musical education" in the communities, and the composers, like the writers "chiefly relied upon the teachings of the Spirit." [199] *Shaker Music. Inspirational Hymns and melodies illustrative of the resurrection life and testimony of the Shakers* (Albany, 1875: rev. ed. New York, Pond & Co., 1884) and *Original Shaker Music. Published by the North family of Mt. Lebanon* (Pond, 1893), are for the benefit of the outside world, and reveal the inspirational music as not greatly differing from the middle-century Bradbury type of Sunday school songs.

4. ADVENTIST HYMNS (1843-1887)

It was not till the second quarter of the century that William Miller went from town to town with his interpretation of Prophecy and his charts, and raised the "Midnight Cry" of the end of the world in 1843. The alarm-call sounded by him and his band of preachers, and circulated in lurid tracts, propagated a revival of the fanatical sort, whose converts up to the expected day of Christ's coming

[198]See J. P. MacLean, *The Life of Richard McNemar* (Franklin, O.) ; and, for Shaker hymn books, his *A Bibliography of Shaker Literature,* Columbus, 1905.

[199]Preface to *Shaker Music,* 1884.

have been estimated at over 50,000.[200] The atmosphere of the tent meetings was intensely emotional, and the excitement found expression in what has been called a "barbaric ecstacy" of song, quite beyond the control of the more sober leaders. The hymns or "spirituals" are preserved in a little pamphlet of 36 pages: *Hymns, designed for the use of the Second Advent Band. "In eighteen hundred forty-three, Will be the year of Jubilee." Published by N. Stevens and H. B. Skinner, 1843.* The opening hymn begins (omitting the repeats) :—

> "You will see your Lord a coming
> To the old church yards,
> With a band of music,
> Sounding it through the air."

It was the great favorite, sung to "The Old Granite State," [201] and is typical of the whole collection.

When the tense expectancy of the last-day meetings remained unrewarded, and 1843 had passed, Miller organized his followers, at Albany in 1845, as "Adventists," with a chastened faith in the imminent and literal Second Coming. With renewed hope came growth that still continues, and with new prophets came disintegration, until now the original "Millerism" is represented by six distinct sects of Adventists.

The EVANGELICAL ADVENTISTS, with the American Millenial Association, represent the original body; and their Hymnody became the care of J. V. Himes, one of Miller's early disciples. His earlier book, *Millenial Harp: for meetings on the Second Coming of Christ,* appeared in three parts, and complete in 1846 (Boston) : and, as modified in the light of use, reappeared as *The Advent Harp; designed for believers in the speedy coming of Christ* (Boston: J. V. Himes, 1849). It is of odd construction, consisting of a church hymnal of 310 numbers, followed by 259

[200]Jane M. Parker, in *The Review and Expositor* (Louisville), January, 1911, p. 51.
[201]*Ibid.*, p. 53.

pages of Advent and other songs, unnumbered, that are set to music. The authors of the Advent songs are unnamed, but they are less crude than at first, and it is notable that many express no more than the conventional longing for heaven. *The Harp: compiled by John Pearson, jr.* (Boston: J. V. Himes, 1856)[202] is even more of the church hymnal type, with the usual provision for subjects and occasions, though an unusual emphasis on "Messiah's triumph and reign." Its ample provision of 1164 hymns would suggest to the uninitiated the expectation of a long wait.

The ADVENT CHRISTIANS organized in 1861 with the doctrine of conditional immortality and the practice of immersion in their principles. *The Jubilee Harp* (Boston: Advent Christian Pub. Soc., 1867) shows a preference for hymns and music of the lighter type, including "You will see your Lord a coming." *The New Jubilee Harp* of 1881 is largely of the "Gospel Hymns" type. It is interesting to note that a supplement became expedient to meet the demand for more "of the hymns of the fathers"; which phrase seems to include familiar church hymns as well as early Advent songs. The *Hymns of the Morning* (Concord, N. H., 1872), compiled by Charles C. Barker of West Meriden, was in the nature of a small alternate to *The Jubilee Harp,* and pointed an unintended contrast by its large use of the Advent hymns of Horatius Bonar. It was enlarged as *Hymns of the Advent* (Springfield, 1881).

Hymns and Tunes for those who keep the commandments of God and the faith of Jesus (Battle Creek, Michigan, 1876) represents the organized SEVENTH-DAY ADVENTISTS, obeying the commandment to keep that day holy. It has a sober standard of hymns and tunes, with which most of the Advent hymns, not unduly numerous, comply. *The Seventh-day Adventist Hymn and Tune Book: published by the General Conference* (Washington, 1887) is a com-

[202]First published anonymously: reprinted by the American Millenial Association (n. d.) with trifling changes, and attributed to Pearson.

promise between a church hymnal and a gospel song book; "some old melodies of which were favorites in the great Advent movement of 1840-44" giving interest to the latter department.

The three remaining sects of Adventists are very small. It will be sufficient to mention as recent rather than eminent *The Christian Hymnal* (Plymouth, Ind. 1887), edited by James W. Wilson for *The Churches of God in Christ Jesus,* better known as "Age-to-come Adventists." A candid review of Adventist Hymnody compels the conviction that both the original "Midnight Cry," the later "Waiting Church" and "the new Dawn," which are its special themes, have found far more adequate treatment elsewhere.

5. MORMON HYMNS (1830-1891)

The Mormon movement was practically contemporaneous with Millerism, and was also prolific in hymns. In July of the same year in which the *Book of Mormon* was published (1830) came a "revelation through Joseph the Seer" to Emma Smith:—"It shall be given thee also to make a selection of sacred hymns, as it shall be given thee, which is pleasing unto me, to be had in my church; for my soul delighteth in the song of the heart, yea, the song of the righteous is a prayer unto me." [203] This revelation and inspirational hymn writing was at one with the visions, ministries of angels, tongues, healings, miracles, which supported the unique claim of Mormonism to supernatural origin. Several early hymn books followed: *A Collection of sacred Hymns* (New York, 1838), and one at Nauvoo (then the principal seat) in 1841; *A Collection of sacred Hymns adapted to the faith and views of the Church of Jesus Christ of Latter-day Saints. Compiled by John Hardy* (Boston: Dow and Jackson's press, 1843; reprinted, Voree, 1849); *A Collection of sacred Hymns for the*

---

[203] *The doctrine and covenants . . . given to Joseph Smith, jun., the Prophet,* ed. Salt Lake City, 1883, p. 136.

Church of Jesus Christ of Latter-day Saints. By Sidney Rigdon (Pittsburgh, 1845) and one with similar title by Charles A. Adams (Bellows Falls, 1845).

The principal interest attaches to a collection made for the important English mission which became so great a feeder to the denomination in America, with a preface signed by Brigham Young, Parley P. Pratt, and John Taylor (Manchester, 1840; 8th ed., Liverpool, 1849; 11th, Liverpool, 1856; 13th, Liverpool, 1869). It was printed in Utah for the first time as *Sacred Hymns and Spiritual Songs, for the use of the Church of Jesus Christ of Latter-day Saints. Fourteenth edition* (Salt Lake City: George Q. Cannon, 1871; 20th ed., with additions, 1891).

The Mormon hymn book is an exception to the rule of dulness governing sectarian Hymnody. Its interest is not in the familiar hymns of worship (*e. g.* "Sweet is the work, my God, my King") or of experience (*e. g.* "God moves in a mysterious way"), though these take a new color from their surroundings. The interest of the Mormon Hymnody is its intense sectariansm. The Mormon history reads like a romance rather than a reality; and the hymn book presents almost every phase and important event of that history as imbedded in contemporaneous hymns or songs that are at worst human documents and that often rise to the level of effective song. We thus have:—

> "The Spirit of God like a fire is burning!
> The latter-day glory begins to come forth;" [204]

one of the hymns with which the first Mormon elders accompanied their preaching from town to town, and which cast something like a spell upon emotional hearers:

> "Adieu to the city where long I have wandered
> To tell them of judgments and warn them to flee;"

Elder P. P. Pratt's lamentation over New York in 1838, on

[204] No. 244 (ed. 1891, W. W. Phelps); and *cf.* T. B. H. Stenhouse, *The Rocky Mountain Saints,* New York, 1873, pp. 1, 2.

leaving it to its prophesied ruin: the song of Exodus,—

> "The shepherds have lifted their sweet warning voice,
> And called us to flee to the land of God's choice:" [205]

and those of the march; such as

> "We'll find the place which God for us prepared,
> Far away in the West:" [206]

the elegy of the murdered prophet,—

> "He's free! he's free! the Prophet's free:" [207]

the visions of Zion among its hills, beneath the flag of its temporal sovereignty,—

> "O Saints, have ye seen o'er yon mountain's proud height,
> The day-star of promise so brilliantly beaming!
> Its rays shall illumine the world with its light,
> And the ensign of Zion, exultingly streaming:" [208]

and last the appealing song of the Church at home,—

> "In thy mountain retreat, God will strengthen thy feet;
> On the necks of thy foes thou shalt tread;
> And their silver and gold, as the Prophets foretold,
> Shall be brought to adorn thy fair head.
> O Zion! dear Zion! home of the free,
> Soon thy towers shall shine with a splendor divine,
> And eternal thy glory shall be." [209]

Many of the songs that enlivened the Mormon pilgrimage are naturally omitted from their book of worship, and of the hymns of Mormon doctrine the most peculiar has been dropped from later editions:—

> "The God that others worship is not the God for me;
> He has no parts nor body, and cannot hear or see; . . ."
> (2) "A Church without a Prophet is not the Church for me."
> (5) "The Heaven of sectarians is not the heaven for me." [210]

The Hymnody of Zion has played a great part in the

---

[205] Hymn 305 (W. Ross).

[206] Hymn 47, stanza 3 (W. Clayton).

[207] Hymn 290, stanza 4 (J. Taylor).

[208] Hymn 58 (P. P. Pratt).

[209] Hymn 316, stanza 3 (C. W. Penrose) sung to "Lily Dale." "No words can express the electrifying influence of this song upon a Mormon audience." Stenhouse, *op. cit.*, p. 374.

[210] No. 297 (Anon.) of the edition of 1871.

upbuilding of Mormonism, as by its virility and contagious enthusiasm it was well fitted to do. It appropriates the whole history of Israel and in enshrining historical occasion resembles the Old Testament Psalter. It has been naturally a Hymnody apart from that of the historic Church, from which it has borrowed to some extent, and from which it does not differ so far as the manner of using hymns in worship is concerned.

CHAPTER IX

THE HYMNODY OF THE ROMANTIC MOVEMENT

I

THE LITERARY HYMN

The early years of the XIXth century saw that revival of Romanticism which gave new life and wealth, new themes and methods, to English Poetry. Hymnody at its worst lies within the realm of verse, and is likely to reflect the poetic ideals and lyrical manner of its time. But English Hymnody caught from the Romantic Movement much more than a reflection or even an enrichment: it took an impulse and direction that permanently modified it and will in the judgment of some eventually transform it.

If Shelley's unmoral attitude of artistic elevation had been the standpoint of the new movement, it might doubtless have come and gone with no perceptible influence on Hymnody. The actual conditions were such as to induce *The Eclectic Review* to say that "either poetry is growing more religious, or religion more poetical." [1] Among the leaders Coleridge had his "Religious Musings" and "Hymn before Sunrise," Wordsworth his *Ecclesiastical Sonnets,* Scott his "Hymn of Rebecca" and *Dies Irae,* Moore his *Sacred Songs,* and even Byron his *Hebrew Melodies.* And from the lesser poets and the general chorus came a copious outpouring of sacred song. As early as 1799 Thomas Gisborne published his *Poems sacred and moral,* appending his hymns in 1803. Joseph Dacre Carlyle's *Poems* appeared in 1805, and Sir

[1] For October, 1825.

435

Robert Grant printed the first of his hymns in *The Christian Observer* in 1806. Ann and Jane Taylor published *Hymns for the Nursery* in 1806, and *Hymns for Infant Minds* in 1809. In 1807 Southey edited the *Remains* of Henry Kirke White. In 1809 Reginald Heber printed his *Palestine,* and between 1811 and 1816 many of his hymns. Mrs. Hemans began her essentially religious verse in the volume of 1812, and James Edmeston in *The Search* (1817) and *Sacred Lyrics* (1820) began his voluminous hymn writing. James Montgomery published his *Songs of Zion* in 1822, and *The Christian Psalmist* in 1825; John Bowring his *Matins and Vespers* in 1823, and his *Hymns* in 1825; Thomas Grenfield his *The Omnipresence of God* in 1824; Bernard Barton his *Devotional Verses,* and Caroline Bowles Southey her *Solitary Hours,* in 1826.

Then came the remarkable year 1827, in which appeared John Keble's *The Christian Year,* Robert Pollok's *The Course of Time,* James Montgomery's *The Christian Poet,* the posthumous *Hymns* of Bishop Heber with those of Henry Hart Milman, and *The Union Collection of Hymns and sacred Odes* edited by John Curtis.

Of the leaders of the Romantic Movement whom we have named all but Shelley have been given some place in the hymn books, though, except for Moore, their voluntary contribution to Hymnody was small. Coleridge wrote a carol, a hymn for Christ's Hospital and two or three more.[2] Wordsworth wrote "The Labourer's Noon-day Hymn" ("Up to the throne of God is borne"), and was much gratified to learn of its use in a village school.[3] Some of Byron's *Hebrew Melodies* were so closely akin to hymns as to draw from friends a laughing comparison with Sternhold and Hopkins.[4]

---

[2] His "Child's Evening Prayer" is in Dr. James Martineau's hymn books.

[3] Wordsworth, *Poetical Works,* Globe ed., 1888, p. 731, note.

[4] Moore's *Works of Lord Byron,* 1832, vol. iii, p. 190. Three of the *Melodies* have found place in hymn books.

However casual the hymn writing of these greater poets, the influence of their example in allying poetry with the themes of religion took shape in a deliberate effort of many lesser poets and verse makers to put poetic feeling and literary art at the service of Hymnody. In the series of their publications already noted, and thenceforward, we have a new school of hymn writers, consisting of poets who do not hesitate to work in the hymnic form, and of hymn writers who aim to produce hymns that shall make the impression of poetry. And we have a new type of hymn,— the Poetic Hymn one is tempted to call it; but in view of variance in the quality and degree of inspiration and of the uncertain criteria of poetry, safety lies in regarding it as the Literary Hymn. The Literary Hymn may be described as one in which heightened feeling seeks to confine an impression of some reality of religion within the limits of the hymn form. The Poetic Hymn is simply the Literary Hymn at its highest, in which the spirit of pure devotion, apart from didactic or utilitarian ends, reveals the essential poetry of our infinite relationships. There was thus within the limits and under the inspiration of the Romantic Movement in English Poetry a distinctive Literary Movement in English Hymnody.

II

REGINALD HEBER'S ROMANTIC HYMNAL
(1827)

The hymns of Reginald Heber, if not actually the very earliest, were the first to reveal the full scope of the new departure; and in inaugurating and giving direction to the new movement he was unquestionably the leader.

Heber's correspondence shows him in 1809 purposing to introduce hymn singing at Hodnet as a novelty calculated to increase the attendance at the parish church, and inquiring as to the purchase of a supply of *Olney Hymns,* for some of which he expresses great admiration.[5]   He speaks of them as Cowper's, and it seems improbable that his admiration covered many of Newton's.

In *The Christian Observer* for October, 1811, Heber, over the initials "D. R.," published four original hymns as specimens of a proposed series to be sung between the Nicene Creed and sermon on the Sundays and principal holy days of the year; the themes of the hymns to be more or less connected with the epistle and gospel for the day.   In a prefatory note he calls attention to the fulsome, indecorous or erotic language found in "popular collections of sacred poetry," and claims for his own hymns no more than their freedom from such profanities, except that in alluding to them he calls them "poems."   He printed additional hymns in subsequent numbers of *The Christian Observer* down to May, 1812, and a few more in January, 1816.

The hymns thus appearing represented Heber's personal contribution to a hymn book he had projected on distinctly literary lines; a hymn book that should be in reality "a collection of sacred poetry."   From the work of earlier hymn writers he made selections from Drummond, Ken, Dryden, Addison, Pope, Cowper, and also (unrecognized by himself) from Watts and Charles Wesley.   But he proposed that his book should represent the great lyrical development of the contemporary school of Romantic poets.   To the picturesque and ringing melodies of Scott, Byron, Moore and Campbell, he conceived his own hymns.   And he eagerly sought the co-operation of Scott, Southey, Milman and others of his literary friends;[6] though securing actual contributions from Milman alone.[7]

Rumors, more or less vague, of this projected hymnal of the poets, spread not only in England but, through the Epis-

[5] *Life of Reginald Heber,* by his Widow; ed. New York, 1830, vol. i, p. 334.

[6] *Life,* ii, 26, 30, 57.

[7] It needs to be recalled that Milman was one of the most popular of the Romantic poets, receiving five hundred pounds each for his three religious dramas.

copal periodicals, in America. Muhlenberg in the preface
of his *Church Poetry*, 1823, doubts if the project will ever
be realized, and from his evangelical standpoint heartily
disapproves of it. The harps of Southey, Scott and Moore,
he says, "have not been tuned to the songs of Zion."

For this Romantic hymnal Heber sought the imprimatur
of the Bishop of London and the Archbishop of Canterbury.
To that end he entered in 1820 into correspondence with the
Bishop of London,[8] to whom he submitted the manuscript in
its incomplete state. He secured the Bishop's sympathy and
admiration, but also his judgment that the time was not ripe
for an authorized hymnal.[9] This manuscript Heber took
with him to India, purposing its immediate publication for
use there; an act from which his sudden end debarred him.
In the year after his death the book was published at London by his widow as *Hymns, written and adapted to the
weekly church service of the year. By the Right Rev.
Reginald Heber, D.D., late Lord Bishop of Calcutta.
London: John Murray, Albemarle-street. MDCCCXXVII;*
with a permitted dedication to the Archbishop of Canterbury. Murray brought it out not in the form of a hymn
book but as a wide-margined octavo with uncut edges, bound
in gray boards, uniform with his presentation of the new
poems of Byron and others on his list. It was reprinted in
India and at New York;[10] and many times at London, both
sumptuously and in more compact form for use in parochial
worship.

The book contained 57[11] hymns by Heber, and 12 by
Milman. It became and has remained self evident that
Hymnody had a great accession in the work of Heber and
Milman. It is claimed for Heber, what could be claimed
for no other considerable English hymn writer, that every
hymn he wrote is to-day in common use.[12]

---

[8] *Ibid.*, ii, 21-29.   [9] *Ibid.*, ii, 28.
[10] G. & C. Carvill, 108 Broadway, 1827.
[11] One was added in the edition of 1828.
[12] *Cf.* W. G. Horder, *The Hymn Lover*, London, n. d., p. 145.

Upon the development of the English Hymn itself Heber's influence was quite as marked. His book offered a new standard of Hymnody; that of a pure but carefully restrained devotion accommodated to the church year, and expressed in flowing rhythms with poetic grace and ornament. The novelty of the proposal is best apprehended by taking a retrospective view of the development of the English Hymn.

Dr. Johnson in his *Life of Waller* had divorced religion and poetry, on the ground that the intercourse of the soul with God was in a realm above and beyond poetry, and an attempt to give it poetical expression necessarily failed. Pious verse might be useful to assist the memory, but there was no religious poetry. With differing views, but practically on these lines, Dr. Watts laid out the model of the modern English Hymn. He aimed at casting the ordinary speech of plain people into metrical form to assist their devotions. He wrote pious verses, and when he rose to poetry it was unconsciously. And he transmitted to a school of writers, and established throughout Dissent, an ideal of Hymnody that shrank from free rhythm and poetic elevation. Charles Wesley set aside the Watts model and also the ordinary bonds of spiritual restraint, and poured out from a surcharged heart his inmost thoughts and feelings in a voice naturally musical. His rapid, impulsive work greatly modified the ideal of the Hymn in tone and form, and in contents. But his work was spontaneous, and its motive was not literary, and at the time perhaps only his brother realized that at certain moments it attained the spirit and vesture of poetry. The Evangelicals made use of both the dissenting and the Methodist models, inclining on the whole to Dr. Johnson's ideal of pious verse that would be useful. Of their movement indeed nothing could be less characteristic than any effort to balance or to reconcile the claims of religion and of culture. Cowper was their only poet, and his hymns were simply the natural and sincere expression of very deep religious feeling. Of the Evangelical hymn

writers contemporaneous with Heber, the most outstanding
and voluminous was Thomas Kelly, whose earnest evangelical preaching was repressed by the Archbishop of
Dublin, and who became a dissenter. He began to publish
his hymns in *A Collection of Psalms and Hymns extracted
from various authors, by Thomas Kelly* (Dublin, 1802).
This was followed by *Hymns on various passages of Scripture* (Dublin, 1804-1812) and *Hymns by Thomas Kelly*
(1815-1853). Moderate and fluent, sometimes attaining
excellence and utility, one is hardly conscious of any direct
influence upon Kelly of the great contemporaneous outburst
of English poetry. As a whole he cultivated rather the
commonplace, and over the area of his 765 hymns he beat
it out to palpable thinness.

But with James Montgomery there is a change. He may
be accounted as a minor member of the current Romantic
school, and even in that great day he created and retained
a provincial dissenting public for his musical verse. In the
preface to his *Christian Psalmist* (Glasgow, 1825), he com-
bats Johnson's theory of sacred poetry and Watts' theory of
the Hymn, and criticizes the "negligence, feebleness, and
prosing" [13] of current Hymnody. But he is able to gather
461 hymns, apart from his own, as up to his standard. And
the collection as a whole shows the actual standard to be that
of a refined edification. This indeed was the line of Montgomery's excellent work for Hymnody. He helped to
refine the taste of the dissenting churches especially; at the
same time keeping the Hymn close to Scripture and true to
the ends of edification. Montgomery himself wrote hymns
worthy of a place in the poetical anthology, but he did not
make an anthology of his hymn book. [14]

Heber's *Hymns* appeared two years later than Mont-

[13] p. xxii.
[14] Of Montgomery's 400 hymns one quarter have been in common
use. Of the Hymn type the best are perhaps "Angels from the realms
of glory," "Hail to the Lord's Anointed" and "Go to dark Gethsemane":
of the Devotional Poetry type, "For ever with the Lord" has been most
loved, and "Prayer is the soul's sincere desire" most used.

gomery's *Christian Psalmist,* but both his hymn writing
and his project for reforming Hymnody antedated Montgomery's. In any case he was the first to propose making
the current taste in poetry the touchstone of English hymns.
His poetic standard was new—that of the Romanticists, and
he applied it with a frankness and consistency of which
Montgomery would not have dreamed. He was thus the
founder of a movement to subject English Hymnody to
the literary motive.

Heber's and Milman's own work illustrates both the
strength and the limitations of the new movement. It attains instant success in such a hymn of adoration of the
Triune God as "Holy! Holy! Holy! Lord God Almighty!"
upon a height where the poet's is the only human voice one
cares to hear. It succeeds almost as well in the descriptive
hymn, celebrating the events chronicled in the Christian
Year. But in the hymn of spiritual experience the literary
motive seems to invite inquiry whether its intrusion has
lowered the spiritual temperature, and whether its welcome
involves any sacrifice of spiritual reality or depth. It is
of course an open question whether or not these hymns
trenched upon the domain of Devotional Poetry as distinct
from Hymnody proper. But on the whole they appear to
have justified themselves. And the acceptance of them by
the Church established a new type of hymn, with the spirit
and expression of lyrical poetry, a conscious literary motive,
and an untrammelled metrical development. One of Heber's
hymns, "The Son of God goes forth to war," seems to
reflect the whole course of the development of the English
Hymn. Its lyric virility is in such contrast to the plodding
strains that preceded it, the first impression it created so
novel, until, this wearing off, it became a standard hymn
in all the Churches, only to be questioned at last by a new
spirit uprisen in the Churches, and recast by Samuel Longfellow in his "God's trumpet wakes the slumbering world":
and who shall say whether in the course of the XXth
century, the recast may not shelve the original?

III

THE LITERARY MOVEMENT IN ENGLAND

We have now to trace the hindrances and progress of the Literary Movement thus inaugurated.

I. In the Church of England

1. It is Overshadowed by the Liturgical Movement

The immediate influence of Heber's *Hymns* did not so much affect the standard as the status of the Hymn. It marked the turning of the tide of hymn singing in the Church of England. Heber's accomplishments and position and death had made his a great name. He was a Tory and a churchman of opposite tendencies to those of the Evangelicals. Moreover his hymns were beautiful and also made the fullest recognition of the holy days of the liturgical year. All this went far to recommend hymn singing to the circles in which Heber had moved. His influence was very great in removing from that ordinance the reproach of dissent and even the flavor of Evangelicalism.[15]

The vogue of Heber's *Hymns* as a hymnal was very limited. His ambitious scheme of furnishing an "authorized hymnal" had failed, and was not to be revived. Its inexpediency was admitted by Milman himself in *The Quarterly Review*,[16] and in 1837 he published his own *A Selection of Psalms and Hymns adapted to the use of the Church of St. Margaret, Westminster,* of which he was rector. And certainly Heber's collection was unfitted for any such position as was hoped for: the lack of available tunes was decisive in itself.

And it had no successor of its own type. Heber's influence operated as leaven gradually permeating the body of Hymnody, but it was not able to establish his ideal of a

[15]*Cf.* a paper, "Hymns for Public Worship" (by Jno. Mason Neale) in *The Christian Remembrancer* for January, 1843, p. 46.

[16]For July, 1828.

Romantic Hymnal. The hymn book making of the succeeding years took another turn under an influence stronger
even than Heber's. For the eventful year 1827 had seen
the publication not only of his *Hymns,* but of Keble's *The
Christian Year,* foreshadowing the rise of the Oxford
Movement and of a corresponding Liturgical school of
Hymnody. The two books stand together at the beginning
of a new period in English Hymnody, and mark the two
lines of its development in the XIXth century as Literary
and Liturgical. But the two lines are not parallels that
never approach. Heber, in accommodating Hymnody to
the Prayer Book and in suggesting a reversion to Latin
Hymns,[17] was something of an influence toward a Liturgical
Hymnody, and Keble was certainly an influence in raising
the literary standard of Hymnody.

Nor did Heber's ignoring of any distinction between the
Metrical Psalm and the Hymn affect the addiction to psalm
singing in the Church; and the compromise period of *Psalms
and Hymns* went on for many years. His influence told,
however, in favor of a more "poetical" Psalter. Miss
Harriet Auber in her *The Spirit of the Psalms* (London:
Cadell, 1829) tried to put "elegance" and "poetic language"
into a new version of selected Psalms, accompanied by
original[18] and select hymns of literary quality. John Keble
followed somewhat regretfully in his *The Psalter or Psalms
of David; in English verse; by a member of the University
of Oxford* (Oxford, 1839). Henry Francis Lyte of Brix-
ton, a minor poet in two senses, contributed both to Literary
Hymnody and to an improved Psalmody in his *Poems
chiefly religious* (London, 1833), and *The Spirit of the
Psalms* (1834).[19] But the progress of the Oxford Move-

---

[17]His *Hymns* included three of the versions of Latin hymns sometimes attributed to William Drummond.

[18]Her "Our blest Redeemer, ere He breathed" appeared in this
volume.

[19]His "Abide with me; fast falls the eventide" appeared in his
Remains (London, 1850).

ment so absorbed men's minds and so turned their thoughts from the Psalter to the Prayer Book as to quench their desire for an improved Psalmody in the new stream of a Liturgical Hymnody.[20]   Henry Latham's elaborate *Anthologia Davidica* (London: Rivington, 1846) was confessedly an attempt to revivify a lapsed ideal.

The Literary Hymn became also a matter of comparative unconcern at a time when the hymn books were thus made the special embodiment of the sacramental theology and church principles of the Oxford party, and of differing or opposing views in the other parties into which the Church was dividing.   To the extreme high church party the Literary Hymn as exemplified in Heber's collection was as much an offence as the Evangelical Hymn itself.   To one of its leaders, John Mason Neale in 1843, it seemed "wonderful both that [Heber] should have *made* such a collection, and that it should have taken such hold, even for a time, on the public mind."[21]   He found the metres fantastical, the poetic merit slight, the tone more fitted to the drawing-room than the church.

The Literary Hymn found its opportunity for church use in an occasional parish collection, and a wider opportunity in the Public School hymn books which make something like a separate department of Church of England Hymnody.[22]   They began with *Psalms and Hymns for the use of Rugby School Chapel* in Arnold's time, followed in 1855 by (Dean) Vaughan's *Hymns for the Chapel of Harrow School,* by *Psalms and Hymns for use in the Chapel of Marlborough College* (1856), for Repton (1859), Wellington (1860), Clifton (1863), Sherburne (1867), Uppingham (1874) and Rossall (1880).   The books vary in churchliness from the simplicity of Rugby's to the Breviary-like collection of Dr. (Archbishop) Benson

[20]*Cf.* preface to *Anthologia Davidica,* p. 2.

[21]*Christian Remembrancer,* Jan., 1843, p. 46.

[22]For bibliography and descriptions see Julian, *Dict. of Hymnology,* pp. 936 ff.

for Wellington; and in the case of the older schools the early books are only the first of a series changing with the times. But naturally there is none which does not suggest literary culture and does not contain hymns chosen for their literary beauty; the Marlborough series being quite conspicuous in these respects.

2. A LATER LITERARY SCHOOL (1862-1899)

It was a fondness for hymns as "a copious and interesting branch of popular literature" that led Roundell Palmer, later Lord Selborne, to compile his famous *The Book of Praise from the best English hymn writers* (Macmillan, 1862). The then novel work upon the text and history of the hymns done for this book by Daniel Sedgwick gave it an interest and importance to which the editor's selection of materials perhaps hardly entitled it. But it served for a generation or two as the popular presentation of English Hymns as "mere literature," and afforded Matthew Arnold a handy butt for his gift of teasing. From this book John Hullah arranged *A Hymnal, chiefly from "The Book of Praise"* (Macmillan, 1868) and by him set to music. This must no doubt be regarded as a literary Hymn Book, the first since Heber's, and like it in ineffectiveness for church use. The voluminous *Hymnologia Christiana* (London, 1863) was also especially hospitable to the Literary Hymn, and if still ineffective served many compilers as a convenient source book. Some 200 contributions of the editor, Benjamin Hall Kennedy, entitle him to a minor place among hymn writers.

A better writer, Godfrey Thring, a rector in Somerset, began to publish hymns in 1866, and in looking over the field reached the conclusion that "nearly all the hymnals which have obtained any large circulation have chiefly owed that circulation to the fact of their having been put forward by avowed representatives, or those who were supposed to be representatives, of different parties in the Church." [23]

[23] Preface of 1880.

As a protest "against this system of party hymn-books" which inevitably deprived congregations of the use of some of the best hymns, he conceived and published *A Church of England Hymn Book adapted to the daily services of the Church throughout the year* (London: Skeffington, 1880).

This was not a literary hymn book as opposed to a liturgical one, but rather a liturgical hymn book with full provision for every occasion and kind of worship and with a literary standard higher than any hymn book of its time. It was a revelation of what skill and judgment and good taste could do for the improvement of Hymnody when not perverted by the spirit of party.[24] And yet the doctrinal attitude of Thring's book could not have been unacceptable to those using *Hymns ancient and modern* with a literary standard so much lower, and it is to be regretted that the vogue of the latter prevented Thring's collection from becoming the Church of England Hymn Book in reality.

As a hymn writer Thring belongs to the Literary school as contrasted with the subjective and didactic method of the Evangelicals, the close adherence to Scripture in so many earlier writers and in Bishop Wordsworth among his contemporaries, and the tendency toward liturgical verse in the Liturgical school. "From the Eastern mountains" represents his lyrical facility; "Saviour, blessed Saviour" his hopeful spirit; "Jesus came, the heavens adoring" his strength; and "The radiant morn hath passed away" his tenderness.

Most of the contemporary hymn writers in the Church of England belong on the liturgical side, through their connection with the Oxford Movement. On the literary side Dean Stanley was the most conspicuous. His hymns originally appeared in *Macmillan's Magazine*. All of them (13) were gathered in *The Westminster Abbey Hymn Book* (London, 1883) which was a tribute to his memory. But

[24]For a glimpse of the book in its making see H. Housman, *John Ellerton*, S. P. C. K., 1896, pp. 92-97.

in truth they added little to his literary reputation or to the store of available hymns.

Of the hymnals that followed it the 1889 edition of *Hymns ancient and modern* aimed once more at a liturgical rather than a literary standard, while the 1890 edition of Bishop Bickersteth's *The Hymnal Companion* might almost be called a "literary hymnal." These will be noticed in another connection. It remains to notice an unique episode with which the literary history of Church of England Hymnody in the XIXth century closes.

Dr. Robert Bridges, a poet of repute and later the Laureate, interested himself in Congregational Song and took charge of that of the village of Yattendon. For its use he prepared and published sumptuously *The Yattendon Hymnal* (Clarendon Press, 1899), containing 100 hymns set to music of a very high order for 4-part unaccompanied singing, of which 44 were of his own workmanship as author or translator. Its way was prepared in a paper on "Some principles of Hymn-singing," [25] and the hymns were published separately as *Hymns from the Yattendon Hymnal, by Robert Bridges, with notice of the tunes for which they were written* (Oxford: Daniel Press, 1899). The special purpose of this interesting experiment was to revive certain church melodies, notably those of *The Genevan Psalter,* and to provide hymns worthy of them. The results cannot as yet be judged. Thirteen of Bridges' hymns and versions were included in *The English Hymnal;* two of which at least, "The King, O God, his heart to Thee upraiseth" and "The duteous day now closeth," have attracted attention to their signal beauty. One of its editors, the Rev. Percy Dearmer,[26] regards Bridges' hymns as "the advance-guard of a movement which will lead the Englishman of the future to read hymn books for the poetry that is in them." But the decision in such a matter lies with the

[25] In *The Journal of Theological Studies,* October, 1899, and separately, Oxford, 1901.
[26] In the London *Daily Mail.*

people, who have not hitherto responded heartily to the elevated appeal of Bridges' verse.

II. James Martineau Provides Unitarians with a "Poetry of Pure Devotion" (1840)

A movement to improve the literary materials of worship was congenial to the Unitarian mind, and the appropriation of the new hymns began in John Hamilton Thom's *A Selection of Hymns for Christian worship* (Liverpool, 1836), supplementing an earlier one made by Roscoe for the Renshaw Street congregation. In this he made large use not only of Montgomery, Heber and Milman, but also of Keble's *Christian Year*. But the new Hymnody reached the body of the people very largely through the filter of one brilliant and devout mind, that of James Martineau. With his profound interest in Hymnody and his ever growing influence it may be said that from 1840 to the end of the century Unitarian Praise was in the main moulded by his hand.

He first felt his way, while a pastor in Dublin, with *A Collection of Hymns for Christian worship* (1831) compiled for his own people from inadequate materials. But in *Hymns for the Christian Church and Home. Collected and edited by James Martineau. Printed for the editor; and sold by John Green, 121, Newgate Street, London, 1840*, he deliberately aimed at a Poetic hymnal. A remarkable preface discloses his point of view :—

"Worship is an attitude our nature assumes, not *for a purpose* [i. e. of being efficacious with God or beneficial to man], but *from an emotion*. From this natural view of worship springs sacred poetry. Every spontaneous utterance of a deep devotion is poetry in its essence, and has only to fall into lyrical form to be a Hymn. No expression of thought or feeling that has an ulterior purpose (i. e. instruction, exposition, impression) can have the spirit of poetry ; but always misses the true lyrical character and furnishes only rhymed theology, versified precepts or biblical descriptions, capable of being sung but merely hiding their didactic spirit under the borrowed style of poetry."

Watts would have felt concerned to know that the application of this poetic touchstone left him at the head of English Hymnody, with Doddridge and Montgomery closely following. Of the Romantic poets Martineau passed over Byron and Moore and included Wordsworth (2), Coleridge (1), Scott (2), Campbell (1), Montgomery (56), Hemans (11), Heber (29), Milman (10), Keble (6), H. K. White (6) and Bowring (5). The inherent interest of such an anthology by Martineau was greatly impaired by his conviction that the "dogmatic theology" of Christian poetry was an accident and not an essential of its excellence and by his alterations of text "to give theologically a translation but in respect to piety and poetry the precise originals of the several authors."

For three years the book sold so slowly as to entail a loss,[27] but gradually it superseded all earlier collections. The hymn books of subsequent years were for local use. J. H. Thom would not allow his *Hymns, Chants and Anthems* (Liverpool, 1858) to be advertised, lest it seem to compete with Dr. Martineau's.[28] The most interesting of the local books was William J. Fox's *Hymns and Anthems* (London, 1841) to which Sarah F. Adams contributed "Nearer, my God, to Thee" and other hymns, and which enrolled Chaucer, Shakespeare, Shelley and Browning among its contributors.[29]

After the third of a century had passed Dr. Martineau perceived a great change in the spirit and complexion of broad church piety. It was "disposed to loosen itself even from sacred history" and to walk with God "in a present that is divine." He thought that the critical studies had killed the appeal of older hymns dealing with Scripture incident, and that the new generation demanded "the poetry of the inner life," identifying "Christianity with the reli-

[27]J. Drummond, *Life and Letters of James Martineau,* New York, 1902, vol. i, p. 112.
[28]His letter in *The Spectator* for Jan. 23, 1902.
[29]For this curious book see R. Garnett, *The Life of W. J. Fox,* London, 1910, pp. 218 ff.

gion of Christ in its pure and personal essence." [30]   To
meet the change he published *Hymns of Praise and Prayer.
Collected and edited by James Martineau, LL.D.* (Long-
mans, 1874). It had 417 hymns from the earlier collection
and 380 added. Not Watts but Montgomery stands first
with 67 hymns, Charles Wesley following with 58, Watts
with 49. The new Anglican and American Unitarian
sources are alike drawn upon, and the old freedom of
alteration abides "for grave reasons of religious veracity."

Martineau had once more interpreted correctly the spirit
of Unitarian piety and acceptably provided for Unitarian
devotion in a new generation. A musical edition of the
new book appeared in 1876, and it continued in very general
use until the XXth century. This hymnal of "the inner
life" largely disassociated from Scripture records presents
a striking and intended contrast to the contemporaneous
Anglican hymn books devoted more and more to the celebration of the historic events of the gospel, the persons of
the saints and the ordinances of the church.

III. The Baptists Cling to a Homiletical Hymnody
(1827-1879)

It is a forgotten fact that in the very year of publication
of Heber's *Hymns* John Curtis, a Baptist layman of Bristol,
brought out *The Union Collection of Hymns and sacred
Odes, additional to the Psalms and Hymns of Dr. Watts*
(London, 1827), aiming especially to refute Dr. Johnson's
dictum that "contemplative piety could not be poetical."
Curtis made use of Coleridge, Scott, Byron and Moore,
among the Romantic poets, and Heber, Milman, Montgomery, Bowring, and many more of the new Literary
school of hymn writers. But the book was large and venturous, the selection perhaps not very judicious, and not
calculated to further those homiletical uses of Hymnody
which still dominated Baptist ideals and practice.

[30]Preface of Dec. 1, 1873.

The Particular Baptist *A new Selection of Hymns* (London, 1828), which in the revision of 1838 became *A Selection of Hymns for the use of Baptist congregations,* and circulated to the extent of a million copies, was a Supplement to Watts of the older evangelical type. The same is true of *The General Baptist Hymn Book* (1830), but in their *The new Hymn Book* (1851), more use was made of the later hymns.

The modern period of Baptist Hymnody begins with the Particular Baptist *Psalms and Hymns . . . prepared for the use of the Baptist Denomination* (London, 1858), and its supplements, and *The* (General) *Baptist Hymnal* of 1879. The compilers of *Psalms and Hymns* had the assistance of George Rawson, a Congregationalist layman of fine poetical feeling, and to it he contributed many of his own hymns.[31] Both books aimed to elevate the literary standard, and made large use of the new hymn writers, both of the Literary and Liturgical schools. Mr. Spurgeon's *Our own Hymn Book* (1866), made for his Tabernacle but used also in congregations presided over by his former students, deserves mention for the breadth of his studies and his care for the texts of the hymns. Its didactic motive contrasts strongly with Dr. Martineau's concern for spontaneity in worship.

The trustees of *Psalms and Hymns* and those of *The Baptist Hymnal* took part in preparing *The Baptist Church Hymnal: Hymns, Chants, Anthems, with music* (London: Psalms and Hymns Trust, 1900). In this very modern production the hymns, embedded in a wealth of tunes and followed by chants and anthems occupying one half of the volume, seem relatively inconspicuous; and the impression produced upon the eye is so liturgical that one feels a certain surprise that the choice and arrangement of the hymns was not made for liturgical ends. But the selection is a catholic one, and, while freely employing the Anglican Hymnody, seeking the best from all sources.

[31] Notably "By Christ redeemed, in Christ restored."

IV. The Enrichment of Congregationalist Hymnody

1. The Ministers of Leeds Break the Watts Tradition (1853)

The movement to elevate the literary standard of Congregationalist Hymnody began with Josiah Conder's *The Congregationalist Hymn Book* of 1836.[32] His book was designed to supplement Watts, and as an editor and hymn writer he may be said to have occupied common ground with his friend Montgomery. His 56 hymns contributed to this collection, with others appearing elsewhere, show an understanding of the Hymn derived from his study of Watts, a devout spirit, metrical variety and good literary expression; and a considerable use is still made of a few of them.[33]

Conder made some use of Heber's hymns, but he felt more at home with Montgomery's. The quality of elegance and the alleged defect of that quality in Heber's hymns caused many then and since to look askance at them. To dissenters trained in the school of Watts, and to the Evangelical with sober standards of edification, they seemed to violate the canons of spiritual simplicity. This feeling is expressed by Josiah Miller in his *Singers and Songs of the Church*:—their "rhetorical flow and an elevation of manner and imagery . . . threaten to take them out of the class of hymns, and rob them of the pious moderation we ordinarily expect to meet with in such productions." [34]

Of the books immediately following Conder's, Dr. John Campbell's *The Comprehensive Hymn Book* (London, 1841) and Andrew Reed's *The Hymn Book* (London, 1842), reverted to the old lines. Some of Reed's plain hymns are still remembered. John Leifchild's *Original*

---

[32]Chap. iii, pt. III, section I, 1.

[33] "The Lord is King! Lift up thy voice," and "How shall I follow Him I serve" are of his best: "Bread of Heaven, on Thee I feed" is perhaps most familiar.

[34]2nd edition, London, 1869, p. 379.

Hymns (London, 1842) attempted to elevate devotional poetry with a fresh collection of hymns contributed to it or hitherto unused. But the opening line, "O Thou, uncaused, unseen, immense," was already somewhat discouraging.

Eleven years later appeared *Psalms, Hymns, and passages of Scripture for Christian worship. London, Partridge and Oakey, 1853.* Prepared by the Congregational ministers of Leeds, and known as "The Leeds Hymn Book," it drew freely from the old treasury of Latin Hymnody, the German hymns and the new Church of England writers both of the literary and liturgical types. It marks the real transition of Congregationalist Hymnody from the type and tone given it by Watts into the more catholic-hearted and yet more selective spirit of modern Hymnody. So great was its influence that it became in 1859 the basis of *The new Congregational Hymn Book,* officially published by the Congregational Union; and it may thus be said to have determined the line of development of the authorized Hymnody of its denomination.

2. The Rivulet Controversy (1856)

Among recent writers omitted from the Congregational Union's new hymn book was one whose hymns had lately given that body much disquietude. Partly with a view to occasional use by his congregation in Grafton Street,[35] London, Thomas Toke Lynch published in November, 1855, *The Rivulet: a contribution to sacred song* (London: R. Theobald).[36] It was welcomed by *The Eclectic Review,* but in *The Morning Advertiser* for January 7, 1856, James Grant averred that "nearly the whole might have been written by a Deist" and that it contained "not one particle of vital religion or evangelical piety" although written by a

---

[35]T. T. Lynch, "Review of the Rivulet Controversy" in *The Monthly Christian Spectator,* Nov., 1856, p. 701.

[36]2nd ed., 1856; 3rd, enlarged, 1868; 5th ed., 1883.

professed minister of the gospel.[37]   In a later issue *The Eclectic Review* was called upon to retract its "incriminated notice of the book."   Instead of which that periodical printed in its March number a protest by fifteen Congregational ministers[38] expressing their "utter hatred" of the method and manner of the attack upon Lynch and his book. With this fuel added to the fire the flame became a conflagration.   Dr. John Campbell, editor of the Congregational Union's magazines, diligently fanned the flames, charging Lynch with contradicting the word of God, defaming the character of His Son, and giving the lie to the teachings of His Spirit.[39]   Lynch responded in *The Ethics of Quotation and Songs controversial: by Silent Long,* and several of the fifteen protesters took a hand in the pamphlet war. The controversy thus grew into the bitterest theological strife within the memory of men then living.   And it remained open until time settled it in Lynch's favor, leaving, in the meanwhile, him and his hymns under a cloud of suspicion in the eyes of thousands who had read the charges but not the hymns.

Lynch's hymns were novel then and inimitable now in their curious combination of subtlety and simplicity, their fresh feeling, their original expression, and their deep experience.   They founded no school, but stand alone, at the dividing line between Hymnody and devotional verse. Thomas Binney, their original defender, took pains to say that they were not adapted to congregational use.[40]   Of many of the finest of them the saying remains true.   But some gradually found their way into hymn books, and the number in actual use to-day is larger than ever before, and

[37]The *Advertiser* articles were reprinted as *The Controversy on important theological questions,* London, 1856.

[38]Reprinted in *"What's it all about?" or both sides of the "Rivulet" Controversy,* London, 1856, p. 5.

[39]*Nonconformist Theology, by John Campbell, D.D.,* London, 1856 (reprinted from *The British Banner*).

[40]Letter *To the Members of the Congregational Union,* London [May, 1856], p. 18.

the favor with which they are regarded more general.[41] "The Rivulet Controversy" is thus at last decided.

3. The Advance toward Heber's Ideal: Loss and Gain (1859-1887)

The Congregational Union's first hymnal was published in 1859, to be followed by a successor in 1887. Between these two dates the independent work of three men deserves notice.

Dr. Henry Allon had a share in the first book, and published *Supplemental Hymns* in 1868 (enlarged, 1875), *Children's Worship* in 1878, and the elaborate *The Congregational Psalmist Hymnal* in 1886. *The Congregational Psalmist* itself, first appearing in 1858, was a tune book of a high order with scholarly annotations, and with his valuable Exeter Hall lectures and his collections of chants, anthems and children's music, indicates the special line in which he did much to elevate Congregational Song. The service of praise at his Union Chapel, Islington, became a model and an incentive even beyond the bounds of Nonconformity.[42]

The incursion of "Dale of Birmingham" into hymn book making was a protest against "the sensuous sentimentalism which had been encouraged by some recent Hymn-writers."[43] He called his collection of 1260 hymns *The English Hymn Book* (London, 1874) as seeking the "manly simplicity" of the national type of faith and feeling and avoiding whatever in ancient or German or English Hymnody seemed "foreign and unfriendly" to healthy English tradition and habits.

[41]The most familiar, "Gracious Spirit, dwell with me," is perhaps least characteristic. Others are "O where is He that trod the sea," "Dismiss me not Thy service, Lord," and "Christ in His word draws near." The statement of Lynch's biographer in *The Dictionary of National Biography* that none of his hymns is popular in the churches is contrary to observed facts.

[42]See "Union Chapel, Islington," in J. S. Curwen, *Studies in Worship Music,* 3rd ed., London, n. d., pp. 365-375.

[43]Preface.

The motive explains unwelcome omissions and needless changes, and Dr. Dale's preoccupations explain the careless texts and the lack of finish and of grace. Its inclusion of 39 hymns from *The Golden Chain of Praise* (1869) by Thomas Hornblower Gill, whom Dale regarded as the best of living hymn writers,[44] called attention to hymns largely unknown. They have distinction and originality; a thoughtfulness demanding close reading, and a quaintness tending toward mannerism.[45] Their unfettered spirit and lack of churchliness limits their use in one direction, their delicacy and avoidance of commonplace in another.

Unlike Dale's, the work of W. Garrett Horder has been that of a life-long student of Hymnology and one who welcomes the emotional side of Hymnody. In Horder's editorial work the Literary Movement comes to its fullest expression since Heber. "Pious moderation," he wrote in 1889, "has been the curse of hymnody." [46] "The time is fast coming," he said in May, 1902, "when no hymn will be included in our best collections which is not in greater or less degree the result of the vision and faculty divine." "To hasten that has been one of the dreams and purposes of my life." [47] His work began with *The Book of Praise for Children* (London: Lewis, 1875), patterned outwardly upon Roundell Palmer's *Book of Praise*. It was followed by *Congregational Hymns* (London: Elliot Stock, 1884); to which there was in 1894 a supplement of *Hymns. Supplemental to existing collections;* and in 1905 appeared a revised edition as *Worship Song with accompanying tunes* (London: Novello). *The Hymn Lover. An account of the rise and growth of English Hymnody* (London: Curwen, 1889) may be regarded as a historical companion to

[44] A. W. W. Dale, *Life of R. W. Dale,* London, 1898, p. 223.
[45] "Dear Lord and Master mine" early became a favorite. "O mean may seem this house of clay," and "Our God, our God, Thou shinest here," are also in wide use.
[46] *The Hymn Lover,* p. 145.
[47] The Carew Lecture at Hartford in *Hartford Seminary Record,* August, 1902, p. 292.

the hymn book. *The Treasury of American sacred Song* (Oxford Press, 1896) does for American verse what Palgrave had done for the English.

When *Congregational Hymns* appeared, Frederic M. Bird said in *The Independent* that "Dissent never had such a hymnal as this before"; and we may include both establishments in the remark. So much of its materials was very recent that it could not have been compiled much earlier than it was. And its editor was equally modern in his indifference to tradition while yet unaffected by the liturgical tendencies of his time; and thus free to embody his ideals with no limitations other than those suggested by pastoral experience. From his point of view his hymn book may fairly be regarded as the fullest and best yet made.

Regarding this collection as substantially the embodiment of the aims of the Literary Movement up to the limits of the present resources of Hymnody, we are in a position to consider that movement in its tendencies and results.

It became inevitable when once the Churches accepted such hymns as Heber's "Holy! Holy! Holy!" or even his "Brightest and best of the sons of the morning." Such acceptance at once sets up a standard of inevitable comparison; and with the dissemination of culture this literary standard operated by way of the exclusion of materials no longer regarded as up to the mark. It happens that the greater part of the material thus winnowed by criticism is the hymns contributed by the Evangelical school; and thus the literary standard combines with a changing doctrinal emphasis to make the share of the old Evangelical Hymnody a diminishing proportion. In the case of the Congregational Churches, for instance, Mr. Horder's book completes a transformation of their Hymnody. It had consisted at first of Watts' Psalms and Hymns alone, and then as supplemented by hymns of kindred writers and those of the Evangelical Revival. In *Congregational Hymns* the contributions of Watts are 26 in a total of 841, and the other writers of the old school are treated proportionably.

Here then is the price to be paid for a Literary Hymnody: one that will be variously appraised. Turning to the gains, we perceive much that has both strength and beauty, and deserves a universal welcome. But in much else we hear the brooding note of culture and encounter a spiritual "delicacy" that raises the question whether these refined meditations have the virility of the old hymns to quicken and maintain a robust and effective faith. This question yet remains to be answered in a generation that has been nourished and inspired by a Poetic Hymnody.

Horder's book found a warm welcome and attained wide use, but did not become the authorized hymnal of the denomination. The Congregational Union had already, in 1883, determined to make "such further provision for the service of praise as the new life and methods of the day required," and committed to the competent hands of George S. Barrett the preparation of a new hymnal on the lines of the "Leeds Hymn Book" of 1853 and *The new Congregational Hymn Book* of 1859, to which there had been a *Supplement* as late as 1874. The *Congregational Church Hymnal* (London: Congregational Union, 1887) aimed to distinguish sharply hymns from sacred poems, to preserve as much as was practicable of the hymns associated with the history and life of Congregationalism, to draw freely from the Hymnody of all sections of the Church, to conserve the original texts of the hymns, and to set them to the best available tunes under the editing of Dr. E. J. Hopkins. Less traditional than Dr. Allon's hymnal, more theologically explicit and less poetic than Mr. Horder's, it filled out the prospectus with skill and care, and put the authorized Hymnody of Congregationalism fully abreast with that of other Churches both from a literary and musical standpoint.

The Hymnody of Scottish Congregationalism is unimportant. Dr. W. Lindsay Alexander's *Selection* of 1849 continued to be reprinted till quite recent years. The Evangelical Union, formed by the Morisons, published their *Hymn Book* in 1856, and a better one in 1878 as *The*

Evangelical Union Hymnal. John Hunter's "liberal" *Hymns of Faith and Life* (Glasgow, 1889) will be noticed in another connection. *The Scottish Congregational Hymnal* (Edinburgh: Congregational Union, 1903) is a composite book, partly reprinted from *The Evangelical Union Hymnal,* and filled out from current English Congregational hymn books.

IV

THE LITERARY MOVEMENT IN AMERICA

I. "Songs of the Liberal Faith"

1. A Notable Series of Hymn Books (1830-1864)

In America as in England the Unitarians felt most free to appropriate anything that seemed good, from whatever source and however novel. It is hence not surprising that a body including the best blood and highest culture of Massachussets shared in the Literary Movement, and succeeded in imparting to its hymn books a freshness of interest in great contrast to those of orthodox Churches.

Of the hymn books of the '30s the first was Samuel Willard's *Sacred Poetry and Music reconciled; or a Collection of Hymns, original and compiled* (Boston: L. C. Bowles, 1830), in which everything was subordinated to the theory that religious impression required "an invariable coincidence between the poetic and the musical emphasis." [48] To most people it seemed that the game of trimming the hymns to fit the theory was not worth the candle, and the adoption of Willard's book was trifling.

Whether we regard the predilection for Watts as lingering in the free air of Unitarianism with something of the force of tradition, or whether we think with Willard that the love of the old hymns was deliberately revived,[49] the

---

[48]For his theory see the review of his earlier *Regular Hymns* (1823) in *The Christian Examiner,* May, 1824, p. 224.

[49]*The Christian Examiner,* July, 1845, p. 114.

fact remains that both the other hymn books of the '30s were confessedly based upon "the writings of Watts and Doddridge." The popular book of the period was *A Collection of Psalms and Hymns for Christian worship* (Boston: Carter and Hendee, 1830) by F. W. P. Greenwood of King's Chapel, which in five years reached a sixteenth edition, and (with R. C. Waterston's supplement of 1845)[50] rounded out a fiftieth. Greenwood made much use of Montgomery's *Christian Psalmist* and Miss Auber's *Spirit of the Psalms,* and some of Bowring and Heber, and he may be said to have introduced Charles Wesley to the Unitarians. His book had thus freshness as well as familiarity, and its conveniently arranged 560 hymns were a pleasing contrast to the cumbersome "Watts' and select" or "Psalms and Hymns" of other denominations. *The Springfield Collection of Hymns for sacred worship. By William B. O. Peabody* (Springfield: Samuel Bowles, 1835) was more pronounced in its attachment to the old hymns, notably Doddridge's, and followed Greenwood's lead in using the Wesleyan Hymns. He exceeded Greenwood in the freedom of alterations and rearrangements he made in the texts to an extent that evoked criticism even among Unitarians.[51]

Somewhat aside from the succession of church hymn books stand two that have a significance of their own. *The Sunday school Hymn Book* (Boston, 1833: 4th ed., 1835; followed by *The Sunday school Hymn and Service Book,* 1844), was the work of a pioneer among Unitarians, Lewis G. Pray. *The Chapel Hymn Book* (Boston, 1836; 4th ed., 1842) was compiled principally by Charles F. Barnard, who had consecrated his life to help the neglected children of the poor of Boston. Avoiding hymns professedly written for children, he aimed at a simplicity of thought and expression that would find acceptance in mission chapels as well as in Sunday schools.

The Christian Psalter: a Collection of Psalms and Hymns

---

[50]It was at that time used by 50 congregations (preface).

[51]See notice in *The Christian Examiner,* Sept., 1835, p. 133.

for social and private worship (Boston, 1841) was made
by William P. Lunt for the First Church of Quincy, which
had just celebrated its 200th anniversary. Not unfittingly
the hymn book seeks the older type of Hymnody and avoids
the new; but if old-fashioned it was excellent and serviceable. An interesting feature was 22 pieces from a complete
metrical Psalter and other manuscript devotional poetry
which Mr. Lunt's parishioner, ex-President John Quincy
Adams, put into his hands for such use as he cared to make
of them.[52]

Many of the most accomplished men in the denomination
were turning their minds to Hymnody as writers or editors
or both, and from their hands proceeded in the ensuing
years a series of hymn books whose literary interest was
very notable. Dr. James Flint of Salem, in *A Collection
of Hymns, for the Christian Church and Home* (Boston,
1843),[53] was largely guided in his choice of the older hymns
by the wish of his congregation to retain as many as practicable from the collection of his predecessor, Dr. Bentley.
But he sought also hymns new or unknown in America,
though failing to acknowledge his indebtedness to James
Martineau's collection, from which he borrowed his title
and much of his materials. Chandler Robbins' *The Social
Hymn Book* (Boston, 1843) was avowedly based upon
Watts and Doddridge, but made much use of the Breviary
Hymns and other unfamiliar sources. Prepared for the
vestry and smaller congregations it abounded with devotional feeling and added an appendix of 21 tunes as a novel
feature. Another small collection, *The Disciples' Hymn
Book* (Boston, 1844) of James Freeman Clarke, greatly
endeared itself to those associated with the new Church of
the Disciples,[54] and indeed appealed to all lovers of sacred

[52]W. P. Lunt, *At the interment of John Quincy Adams,* Boston,
1848, p. 60. "He who had occupied the throne of the people was, like
the Hebrew monarch, also a Psalmist in our Israel." *Ibid.,* p. 41.

[53]It had an extensive notice in *The Monthly Miscellany* (1843;
reprinted separately) and in *The Christian Examiner,* July, 1843.

[54]See an editorial in the *Boston Transcript,* August 26, 1911.

poetry. It had the distinction of introducing "Nearer, my God, to Thee" into the United States.

Many who wished something more "modern" than Greenwood's *Collection* found these books too individual and also inadequate to the full round of church occasions. This led to the preparation of *Christian Hymns for public and private worship. A Collection compiled by a committee of the Cheshire Pastoral Association* (Boston, 1846), which was edited by Abiel A. Livermore. It had more than 900 hymns, including many by American Unitarian writers, and sought a greater metrical variety, apparently to please the choirs. It afforded another proof that while many people prefer a small hymn book, the preachers demand a full one; and it attained a wide use that called for no less than sixty editions.

George W. Briggs of Plymouth, like Martineau, cared only for the Hymnody of the inner life, and in his *Hymns for public worship* (Boston, 1845) sought "to bring together the most fervent expressions of a profound spiritual life." [55] He therefore drew more largely than was usual upon the Wesleyan Hymns, and hymns unknown to the other collections. Dr. George E. Ellis' *A Collection of Psalms and Hymns for the Sanctuary* (Boston, 1845), was made to take the place of *The Springfield Collection*, already out of print, in the Harvard Church. On that and Greenwood's it was based in the main, though drawing from a wide range of sources. The "Psalms" were in prose arranged for antiphonal use: the hymns as a whole more didactic than in other books of the series now under consideration.

A Book of Hymns for public and private devotion. Cambridge: Metcalf and Company, printers to the University, 1846 was prepared by Samuel Longfellow and Samuel Johnson, while fellow-students at Harvard Divinity School, and is a landmark in Unitarian Hymnody. The book grew out of an offer to provide a new hymn book for a young

[55]See preface.

pastor who found even the recent ones too antiquated.[56]
The radical tendencies in theology of the editors were perhaps suggested rather than embodied. In the large number
of hymns relating to Christ He was still called Lord and
Saviour, and his miracles were emphasized, but the immediate relation of the worshipper to the indwelling Spirit
and the humanitarian aspect of religion were given new
prominence.[57] The literary motive was predominant, and
all available sources of poetical devotion were industriously
studied. Its advance in a poetical direction has been somewhat overestimated to the disparagement of its predecessors,
but it was quite marked. Newman's "Lead, kindly Light"
was found without name in a newspaper, and printed "Send
kindly light" as it there appeared. Not only English poets
but Longfellow, Whittier, Lowell, Jones Very, Theodore
Parker, Mrs. Stowe, and others at home were drawn upon;
and the contributions of the editors themselves were notable.
A breezy freshness and literary charm pervaded the book,
and gave it distinction and importance even in a remarkable series of hymn books.

The book was at once severely handled and warmly
welcomed. It was first adopted by Edward Everett Hale's
new Church of the Unity at Worcester and then by Theodore Parker's Music Hall congregation;[58] though it seldom
replaced the accepted hymn books. It took two years to
exhaust the first edition, at the end of which time it was
revised and reprinted. The editors themselves soon out-
grew its theology, but it left a mark in Hymnody and contributed to its permanent resources.

Hymns of the Sanctuary (Boston, 1849) was prepared
by Cyrus A. Bartol and others as a new edition of the West
Church Collection, and was not unlike Dr. Ellis' hymn book

[56]Saml. Longfellow in *Lectures, Essays, and Sermons*, by *Samuel
Johnson*, Boston, 1883, p. 30.

[57]*Ibid.*, p. 31; and *cf.* Joseph May, *Samuel Longfellow*, Boston, 1894,
p. 51.

[58]Joseph May, *op. cit.*, p. 52.

of 1845. There seemed books enough. But interest was aroused by the announcement that Frederic H. Hedge and Frederic Dan Huntington were collaborating in preparing a new one. It appeared in handsome form as *Hymns for the Church of Christ* (Boston, 1853; 8th 1000, 1861), and reasonably fulfilled all expectations; being hailed by *The Christian Examiner* as "by much the best book of hymns yet published." The sweep of its catholic spirit included Breviary Hymns and Toplady's "Rock of Ages" unaltered on the one hand and the ethical verse of Emerson and W. J. Fox on the other. It was pervaded by a lofty and tender spirit of devotion, and maintained a literary standard of strength and beauty. Convenient for use, and outwardly comely, it perhaps reached the high-water mark of a full-tided time. Dr. Hedge's mind was breaking away from conventional Christianity, while Dr. (afterwards Bishop) Huntington's was turning toward catholic tradition, and before leaving Unitarianism he wrote the "Preface to the *Lyra Catholica*" in Caroline Whitmarsh's *Hymns of the Ages* (Boston, 1858); a volume regarded, not without reason, by some of the reviews as an exotic in the Cambridge atmosphere.

The only other book of note in the '50s was Chandler Robbins' *Hymn Book for Christian worship* (Boston, 1854), an enlargement and freshening of his earlier *The Social Hymn Book,* with Watts, Doddridge and Montgomery still in the lead. Dr. Samuel Osgood, a New Englander in New York, gathered a choice collection of 159 hymns, that was both literary and liturgical, into his *Christian Worship* (New York, 1862); a service book in which his preference of the Prayer Book system of worship was already revealed.

Dr. Osgood's book indicated an individual reversion to the faith and forms of historic Christianity. An opposite tendency in New England Unitarianism found two years later a full expression in *Hymns of the Spirit* (Boston: Ticknor and Fields, 1864), the second book of Samuel

Longfellow and Samuel Johnson, which they prepared while in Europe together to take the place of *A Book of Hymns*.[59] Both men had adopted the view-point of universal religion of which Christianity was at best only an illustration, passing from Unitarianism into pure theism. In their new book they aimed to exclude all hymns "which attributed a peculiar quality and special authority to Christianity, and recognized a supernatural element in the personality of Jesus." [60] Longfellow dropped out even the hymn "Christ to the young man said," written for his ordination by his brother, because "he would not by that one name disturb the simplicity of his faith in the one Source of the soul's higher life." This scheme of a theistic hymn book involved among other things a great literary loss, both in the sacrifice of many of the most beautiful hymns of the earlier book, and in the tinkering of the materials included. This was partly compensated for by the new hymns contributed by the editors. For the loss in circulation involved in the changed doctrinal standard the editors were doubtless prepared.

Comparing this series of hymn books with those in contemporary use by other denominations, it is obvious that New England Unitarians led the advance in elevating the literary standard of American Hymnody; an office for which their culture and free spirit naturally fitted them. The books had a common origin in the desire to furnish a devotional manual expressive of the liberal faith, but their motive was cultural or literary rather than liturgical. There was no doubt a liturgical movement in Unitarianism, for which the modified *Book of Common Prayer* in use in King's Chapel afforded an always available though artificial precedent. Clarke's, Hedge's, Robbins' and Osgood's hymn books were accompanied by service books, and Longfellow published *Vespers* in 1859. The Unitarians led also in appropriating the old Latin hymns: in 1843 Flint intro-

[59]*Lectures* &c. by *Samuel Johnson*, pp. 61, 62.
[60]May, *Samuel Longfellow*, p. 214.

duced four of Chandler's versions of Breviary Hymns and Robbins twenty of Bishop Mant's. But the spirit of liturgics is traditional and the spirit of Unitarianism is free, and where Unitarians developed real liturgical feeling, as in the cases of Huntington and Osgood, they passed over into Episcopacy. To the rest the ancient prayers and hymns were simply literary material to be used so far as attractive or altered to suit.

Indeed it is this freedom of adaptation that occasioned the great drawback to an appreciation of a series of hymn books otherwise so interesting. Unitarians had always claimed the right to adapt Watts' Psalms and Hymns to their own views on the ground that if Watts had lived he would have done so himself. But they proceeded to exercise the same privilege in the case of all hymn writers whose doctrinal views or religious experience differed from their own. In the series of books before us this has become so much a matter of course that only rarely is any note made of the alterations; the author's name being freely signed to what he did not write nor perhaps believe. And yet none was ever quicker than Samuel Johnson to feel the offensiveness of such a course as applied to his own hymns. He prided himself on having "written calmly to the Reverend Dr." who in "a Presbyterian Hymn-book" altered "Father" into "Saviour" in his "Father, in Thy mysterious presence kneeling." [61] It is possibly a surprise that several of these editors should have retained hymns addressed to the Saviour, including "Jesus, Lover of my soul," and their omission would under the circumstances occasion no criticism. But the alteration of Charles Wesley's hymn in the books of Lunt and Bartol and the Cheshire Association into "Father, Refuge of my soul" is an offence against literature itself.[62]

[61]*Lectures* &c. *by Samuel Johnson,* p. 133.
[62]Throughout this period *The Christian Examiner* repeatedly protested against the prevailing practice. For its views see "Alterations of Hymns," May, 1862, p. 352.

2. UNITARIAN HYMNODY (1830-1864)

The period of Unitarianism covered by these hymn books —between the '30s and the Civil War—was precisely the era of religious debate between the historical and the new conceptions of Christianity rather than a time of what is regarded as religious revival. And it is somewhat remarkable that it should have been characterized by a spirit of devotion expressed in a great outpouring of hymns, such as we ordinarily associate with a revival era.

If this was due in part to the influence of Channing, his spirit at all events found its personal expression in sermons and not in hymns. But Henry Ware jr. made his *Christian Disciple* a vehicle of Hymnody, printing his own "Lift your glad voices in triumph on high" as early as 1819. Hymns by Andrews Norton, William H. Furness and others followed, and in 1827 Sarah E. Miles' "Thou, who didst stoop below."

Of the hymn book editors themselves, Willard, Flint, W. B. O. Peabody, Pray, Lunt, Hedge, Huntington, Clarke, Waterston, Robbins, A. A. Livermore, Bartol, Samuel Longfellow, and Johnson, were also writers of hymns. Others among the clergy were Samuel Gilman, N. L. Frothingham, William Newell, Stephen G. Bulfinch, Theodore Parker, Edmund H. Sears, Samuel D. Robbins, Frederic A. Whitney, Thomas Hill, William R. Alger, and O. B. Frothingham. Among the laymen were Thomas Gray jr., William H. Burleigh, and Samuel B. Sumner. Of women writers were Eliza Lee Follen, Sarah W. Livermore, Caroline Gilman, Louisa G. Hall, A. R. St. John, Mary W. Hale, Caroline A. Mason, and Margaret Fuller. Among Unitarian poets and men of letters who also wrote hymns were Bryant, Emerson, H. W. Longfellow, O. W. Holmes, Lowell, Jones Very, Higginson, Charles Sprague, John Pierpont, Charles T. Brooks, and James T. Fields.

All of these writers have contributed hymns that are or have been in actual use in Unitarian worship. Of those who have enriched the Hymnody of the Church at large, two names stand apart. Of Dr. Holmes' hymns, "Lord of all being, throned afar" and "O Love Divine, that stooped to share" are classics of devotion. And the hymns of Samuel Longfellow, however radical his theology, seem to gain with every year a larger appreciation and a wider use, due simply to their spiritual beauty and ardor.

In reviewing the body of this new Unitarian Hymnody its extent is in itself impressive as revealing so widely-felt an impulse to give devotional expression to the Unitarian faith. Representing in the main the work of men and women who were prose writers or preachers rather than poets, the elevation of manner and the choiceness of literary expression in the hymns are notable, and show a high common level of culture and literary ability; though here as everywhere the divine fire is confined to the chosen few. In content the hymns are no doubt colored and limited by the theology of their writers, but are devotional rather than dogmatic: when the polemical tone is heard, it is in the later theistic rather than in the earlier Unitarian writers. We may safely accept from their anthologist his characterization of these "Songs of the liberal faith":[63]

"They reveal, as a class, a strong faith and tender trust in God as the Father; a fine appreciation and love of all that is grand and beautiful in Nature; a deep conviction that a divine hand is in all things, and is guiding all things on to a glorious issue and end; a profound and earnest reverence for Christ, as the Way, the Truth, and the Life, and a heartfelt recognition of his Cross as the emblem and pledge of victory; a genuine 'enthusiasm for humanity' and a sense of the supreme value of a good life, and a large and genial sympathy and fellowship with all true and faithful souls in every sect or communion."

The marked contrast of these hymns with the Evangelical Hymnody is in the type and tone of spiritual experience they embody, the substitution of a certain spiritual complacency for the earlier sense of sin, dependence on the

[63]Alfred P. Putnam, *Singers and Songs of the liberal faith*, Boston, 1875, p. ix. It contains full selections of the hymns and verse of American Unitarians, with biographical sketches.

Redeemer and craving for deliverance. George W. Briggs' resort to "the Wesleyan hymns, and others of a kindred character" for "the most fervent expressions of a profound spiritual life" has been referred to. One recalls also how the heart of Dr. Holmes, Unitarian and poet, turned in his old age to the Evangelical Hymnody, perceiving in it "the old ring of Saintliness" and the virility he could not find in the modern hymns. "When I turn to the hymn book, and when one strikes my eye, I cover the name at the bottom and guess. It is," he said, "almost invariably either Watts or Wesley; after them there are very few which are good for much." [64] To others it will be just as obvious that the doctrine and experience of the Evangelical Hymnody are outworn, and it will be conceded by all that they are not "Romantic."

3. MODERN TENDENCIES (1861-1894)

From so much zeal in bettering Unitarian Hymnody the natural · inference would be that Congregational Song thrived during the period just covered. In fact there was little congregational singing of any sort, and in the more cultured congregations none at all. The hymns were announced and often read by the minister, and were sung by the choir; the part of the people being as passively receptive in praise as during the sermon. One of the planks in Freeman Clarke's platform for the Church of the Disciples in 1841 was "Congregational Worship":—"By congregational worship I mean that to some extent the congregation should join in the hymns and prayers." [65] The proposal was then regarded as a novelty. [66] "We have sought," say the committee of the Cheshire Association, three years later, "to give a lyrical character, and thus adapt it [*Christian Hymns*] to the choir as well as the pulpit." [67]

[64] Annie Fields, *Authors and Friends,* Boston, 1896, pp. 152, 153.
[65] *James Freeman Clarke: Autobiography* &c., Boston, 1892, p. 158.
[66] *Ibid.*, p. 145.
[67] Preface to *Christian Hymns,* 1844.

The tunes were neither in the hands nor mouths of the people. The tune "Merton" which, with "Federal Street" by the same composer, survives as a memorial of the time, is said by Henry K. Oliver's biographer to have been written out in the choir loft during a service in the North Church, Salem, to fit the hymn appointed to be sung after the sermon, and to have been rendered by the choir from the manuscript.[68]

The introduction of hymnals provided with tunes in other denominations, and their success in increasing the interest of public worship, led to a desire for a Unitarian hymn and tune book.[69] Samuel Longfellow had published *A Book of Hymns and Tunes* (Boston, 1860) for "the children of the New Chapel," Brooklyn, but with some hope that it might encourage congregational singing; and the demand for a church collection with tunes became so urgent that the American Unitarian Association took the matter in hand, and issued *Hymn and Tune Book for the Church and the Home* (Boston, 1868). The collection, edited by Leonard J. Livermore, marked no advance over its predecessors but its tunes were well up to the average level and gave it a great advantage. It was not only the one available hymnal with music, but the first in the nature of an authorized denominational hymnal. Its adoption and use by the churches was very wide, and it helped to establish congregational singing. *The Hymn, Tune and Service Book for Sunday schools* (Unit. Assn., 1869) followed, and the church collection was carefully revised in 1883.

These books represented the more conservative side of Unitarianism, as did Rufus Ellis' *Hymns for the Christian Church, for the use of the First Church of Christ in Boston* (1869), which really belongs to the earlier series as being a revision of Lunt's *Christian Psalter* and also without tunes. In 1890 two hymn books appeared which sought to

[68] John Wright Buckham in *The New England Magazine,* December, 1896, p. 389.
[69] Preface to *Hymn and Tune Book,* 1868.

appropriate the newer Anglican tunes and much of the
wealth of the Oxford school of hymn writers :—*Hymnal:
amore Dei: compiled by Mrs. Theodore C. Williams* (Boston, 1890), and *Hymns of the Church Universal. Compiled
by the Rev. Henry Wilder Foote* (Boston, 1890). The
latter, a posthumous publication, was not unworthy of its
title, and represented the spirit of fellowship with all
Christians which Mr. Foote had cultivated at King's Chapel.
Mrs. Williams' collection was revised in 1897, and Mr.
Foote's was substantially adopted by the American Unitarian Association, reappearing as *Hymns for Church and
Home. With tunes* (Boston, 1895).

In the thirty years' dissension between the "Christian"
and the "free" elements of Unitarianism following the
organization of the National Conference in 1864, the radical
side developed its own school of hymn writers and embodied its views and practices in its own hymn books. The
hymn writing is much more important than the hymn books.
John W. Chadwick, of Brooklyn, who has been called poet
laureate of the liberal faith, wrote his best-known hymn,
"Eternal Ruler of the ceaseless round," for his own graduation at Harvard Divinity School in 1864. His later hymns
and verses are gathered in *A Book of Poems* (1876), *In
Nazareth Town* (1883), and *Later Poems* (1905). Less
known are the hymns of Minot J. Savage, contributed, to
the number of 43, to *Sacred Songs for public worship. A
Hymn and Tune Book. Edited by M. J. Savage and
Howard M. Dow* (Boston, 1883).

In 1880 Frederick L. Hosmer, William C. Gannett, and
J. Vilas Blake cooperated in editing *Unity Hymns and
Carols* in which both theology and liturgics were frankly
uprooted from a Christian basis and replanted under freer
skies. In 1885 Hosmer and Gannett again cooperated in
a book of devotional verse, *The Thought of God in Hymns
and Poems* (Boston: Little, Brown & Co.), followed by a
second series (Boston: 1894). The beauty and devoutness
of their work at once commended it to all religious minds,

and it has already become a source book for editors of all religious persuasions. These volumes contain the most important original contribution to "liberal" Hymnody since the books of Longfellow and Johnson. And it is somewhat noteworthy that four hymn writers so widely acceptable should have viewed Christianity from the same angle of incidence.

II. The Enrichment of Congregationalist and Presbyterian Hymnody is Left to Private Enterprise

1. Henry Ward Beecher Leads the Movement for Congregational Singing (1851)

When Henry Ward Beecher came to the new Plymouth Church, Brooklyn, in 1847, the conditions of Congregationalist and Presbyterian Church Song were those already described as of the middle century:[70]—the "Psalms and Hymns" in the hands of the congregation were not very appealing and were without music, and the singing was almost wholly in the hands of the choir.

There was no doubt much dissatisfaction with the prevailing method and some preparation for its betterment; but if the spirit of change was in the air, the determination of the new pastor to have congregational singing was still regarded as "one of Mr. Beecher's oddities."[71]   He induced Darius E. Jones, then conductor of music in Plymouth Church, to prepare a congregational hymn and tune book, and the firm of Mason (sons of Lowell Mason) to undertake the publication under a sufficient guaranty.[72] It appeared as *Temple Melodies: a Collection of about two hundred popular tunes, adapted to nearly five hundred favorite Hymns, selected with special reference to public,*

[70]Chap. viii, part III, section 2, (4), (5).

[71]Lyman Abbott, *Henry Ward Beecher,* Boston, 1903, p. 88.

[72]See Beecher's account of its publication and his share in it in W. C. Beecher and S. Scoville, *Biography of Henry Ward Beecher,* New York, 1888, pp. 363, 364.

social, and private worship. By Darius E. Jones (New York, 1851). Several clergymen assisted in selecting the hymns; three, including George Duffield jr., contributed originals: Mr. Beecher's organist, John Zundel, helping with the music.

Its success was great enough to please its editor,[73] but Beecher was not satisfied with the new book, and began to prepare a larger collection, with the aid of his brother Charles and Zundel in the musical department.[74] No publisher could be persuaded to undertake the risk, and it was printed with funds privately furnished[75] as *Plymouth Collection of Hymns and Tunes; for the use of Christian congregations* (New York: A. S. Barnes & Co., 1855),[76] The tunes, whether familiar or new, were such as appealed to the feelings. While not a musician, Beecher loved simple music, and regarded himself "as a pioneer" [77] in the great cause of congregational singing; and with this book in the people's hands he wrought great things at Plymouth Church. The hearty singing of the vast congregation became almost as much of an attraction as his preaching.[78] Its fame spread far and wide, encouraged countless congregations to emulate it, and carried the *Collection* itself into Baptist and Presbyterian, as well as Congregational churches.

2. THE ENRICHMENT OF HYMNODY FOR HOMILETICAL ENDS (1855-1858)

Mr. Beecher gathered his materials from hymn books of all denominations without special knowledge of source or text. The number of hymns (1374) is sufficient evidence that the ruling motive was not literary. The poets

[73]Preface to his later collection on the same lines, *Songs for the new life* (Chicago, 1869).
[74]Preface to *Plymouth Collection.*
[75]Beecher and Scoville, *op. cit.,* p. 364.
[76]Also without music as *Plymouth Collection of Hymns,* 1855.
[77]Preface, p. viii.
[78]*Cf.* N. L. Thompson, *The History of Plymouth Church,* N. Y., 1873, p. 133.

and literary hymn writers were made use of, just as were many older writers far from being literary, whenever Beecher thought they had "power to excite pious emotions," and were thus "useful." [79]   Still less was the motive liturgical.   The use made of Latin hymns was not from the feeling that they were churchly, but in the "joy" of discovery that some "Roman Catholic Hymns" were "truly evangelical."   The tone of the *Collection* itself is decidedly evangelical, with Watts and Wesley in the lead; the use made of the New England Unitarian Hymnody being slight.

The interests of the new singing in connection with a constructive theology and a point of view perhaps more intellectual and less emotional than Beecher's, led to an elaborate undertaking on the part of two Andover professors, Edwards A. Park and Austin Phelps.   They published *The Sabbath Hymn Book: for the service of song in the House of the Lord* (New York: Mason Bros., 1858), and, with Lowell Mason's help, *The Sabbath Hymn and Tune Book* (New York, 1859) revised as *The new Sabbath Hymn Book* (1866).   As compared with Beecher's *The Sabbath Hymn Book* is best described as a work of scholarship.   Its editors explored the sources of Hymnody, did not hesitate to apply literary criteria, and treated their materials with a scholar's precision.   Their aims and methods, then so novel, were expounded and vindicated in three papers in *Bibliotheca Sacra;* afterward gathered up and enlarged in *Hymns and Choirs: or, the matter and the manner of the service of song in the House of the Lord* (Andover, 1860); the first and still the only American treatise on Hymnology.   They believed that much of the Hymnody of Watts and his school was outgrown to an extent that made the current "Watts' and select" ideal regressive; that both hymn writing and "hymnologic taste" had been greatly elevated by the Romantic Movement; and that it was the Church's duty to welcome "new songs" of a higher lyric strain.[80]   They brought many of these to

[79]Preface, p. iv.   [80]*Hymns and Choirs,* p. 55.

the attention of the churches, and called to their aid several living writers, of whom the most notable were Horatius Bonar of Scotland and the American Congregationalist, Ray Palmer. Palmer, who seems to have been silent since the day of *Parish Hymns* (1843) contributed a series of hymns that established his reputation and have kept *The Sabbath Hymn Book* in permanent remembrance. Among them were, "O Bread to pilgrims given," "Jesus, Thou Joy of loving hearts," "Come, Holy Ghost, in love," "Jesus, these eyes have never seen," and "O Christ, our King, Creator, Lord."

The "Andover book" received almost unqualified praise from many eminent clergymen and such periodicals as *The New York Observer, The Congregationalist, The American Theological Review* (August, 1859), and *The Congregational Quarterly* (January, 1859), and it was adopted and used in many congregations. But it had rivalry in Elias Nason's *The Congregational Hymn Book* (Boston, 1857) and *The new Congregational Hymn and Tune Book* (Boston, 1859), both books of taste and careful editing; and their publisher retorted to the notices of the Andover book in *The Sabbath Hymn Book reviewed* (Boston: Jewett & Co., 1858). There was other opposition also; as in *The merits of the "Sabbath Hymn Book," and of the means which are employed to introduce it into the churches. By a clergyman of Massachusettts* (Boston: Crocker & Brewster, 1859). *The Methodist Quarterly Review* (January, 1861) objected to its Calvinism, and (not unjustly) to many of its textual alterations.

These two books mark the transition from the hesitations and limitations of the compromise era of "Psalms and Hymns" to the free and catholic-hearted use of available resources that characterizes modern Hymnody.

And yet, notwithstanding the progressive features of the two books, their type was still homiletical rather than liturgical in either a larger or narrower sense. *Plymouth Collection* contained 1374 hymns, and upon adopting it in 1856

Miami Conference added 90: the Andover book 1290. We ask the meaning of these vast collections that render any real familiarity with the hymns a hopeless task, and whether the people really demanded them. We find the answer in the index of texts in *The Sabbath Hymn Book* covering twenty-two large 8vo columns in fine print, and followed by an "Analytical Index of Subjects" covering 32½ columns. Only a trained theologian could have made this analysis, and by such only could it be used. It was the minister and not the people who wanted this analysis for homiletical purposes, this great array of corresponding hymns. In both books, that is to say, the motive of sermon illustration and enforcement still conditioned Congregational Praise.

3. THE NEW TYPE OF CHURCH HYMNAL (1855)

The *Plymouth Collection* of 1855 marks also the transition from a Hymnody rendered by the choir to congregational singing, and from the older type of hymn book to the church hymnal of today. Beecher's perception of the necessity of putting the music as well as the words of the hymns into the hands of the people who were to be encouraged to sing came of course from his observation of the success of such books as *The Christian Lyre* and Hastings and Mason's *Spiritual Songs*. But the application of the principle to the church hymn book was a novelty, and the doubtful result of the enterprise appears from Beecher's inability to find a publisher willing to assume the risk. It is worthy of remembrance however that Leonard W. Bacon, then pastor of St. Peter's Church in the Presbytery of Rochester, published as of even date with *Plymouth Collection,* a similar but smaller aid to congregational singing, as *Church Music; with selections . . . from the Psalms and Hymns of the Presbyterian Church. Adopted and recommended by St. Peter's Church, Rochester* (Rochester, 1855). In this he was followed by Dr. Nathaniel C. Burt in *A*

Pastor's Selection of Hymns and Tunes (Philadelphia, 1859).

The bringing of the tunes into the church hymnal greatly advanced congregational singing. Nevertheless *Plymouth Collection* set a bad model, which the Andover editors copied, and which has been perpetuated in many subsequent hymnals. A tune was printed across the top of an octavo page, and the space beneath (divided into two columns) and even an opposite page was filled with hymns to be sung to it. It was seldom that all the hymns were adapted to the tune, and the method led also to the inclusion of surplus material as "filler," or to the mutilation of good hymns for lack of available space to print them in full. So poor and mechanical an expedient was suggested no doubt by the impracticability of printing its own tune to each of so great an array of hymns.

4. DR. ROBINSON'S POPULAR HYMNALS (1862-1875)

In the ensuing years the provision of hymn books for such Congregational and Presbyterian churches as did not retain older books fell to a surprising extent into the hands of one man, Dr. Charles S. Robinson, a Presbyterian pastor, who made hymn book compilation what must be called a business. Between 1862 and 1892 he published not less than fifteen, including Sunday school books and abridgments for chapel use. He aimed at edification, and sought popularity, but with a gradually advancing literary and musical standard.

The earliest of the series was *Songs of the Church: or, Hymns and Tunes for Christian worship* (New York: Barnes and Burr, 1862). It offered a compromise between choir music and congregational singing, with 859 hymns "for the congregation" printed under tunes in the *Plymouth Collection* manner, and 334 "for the choir" without tunes. The hymns, often shortened to fit the page, were largely of the older Evangelical type. The selection of hymns and the general tone were much modernized in Robinson's second book, *Songs for the Sanctuary* (New York: Barnes, 1865), and the unset choir hymns were now distributed in groups through the book. It met an extraordinary success; more than 200,000 copies coming into use within seven years in nearly 2000 congregations, and the book was kept in print until the end of the century. Much of the popularity of these collections was due to their musical editor, Joseph P. Holbrook, a tune writer in the parlor music style, and his use of the popular melodies of Mason and Hastings, Bradbury and Root, Greatorex and Kingsley. Holbrook furnished settings for the choir hymns in *Songs for the Sanctuary* in his *Quartet and chorus Choir* (New York, 1871), and sought more recognition than had been given him in a hymnal of his own, *Worship in Song* (New York, 1880); a book that found no welcome.

Dr. Robinson's third book, *Psalms and Hymns and Spiritual Songs. A manual of worship for the Church of Christ* (New York: Barnes, 1875) was arranged throughout for congregational use, and had more of the new hymns. It became the official praise book of the Southern branch of the Presbyterian Church; and the anticipation of such adoption no doubt explains Dr. Robinson's belated reversion to the "Psalms and Hymns" model.

This adaptation to the usage of the Southerners is an index also to the method of his work and to the secret of his success in such leadership in Hymnody as must be accorded to him. He originated nothing. His books were modelled upon those of Beecher and the Andover professors. In freshness and freedom of selection his first book was a step backward; and he was a timid follower of their zeal to establish congregational singing. He shared with them the prevailing homiletical conception of Hymnody but guarded the advance of the literary motive, lest it disturb sacred associations. In some things he was more judicious than they, especially in consulting and meeting the general taste. He aimed to please the choirs by giving them a recognized choir hymn to set at will and to render; to please the ministers by giving them immense collections (1193, 1342, 1294) from which to choose sermon illustrations; and to please the people by giving them tunes they loved to sing in church and at home. Perhaps this atmosphere of good will and general interest in Hymnody was a result as happy and as important as any could have been; coupled as it was with a gradual improvement in the choice of hymns and, more slowly, in the religious quality of the music.[81]

Dr. Robinson found his opportunity in the remissness of the church authorities in meeting the needs of the time. Incidentally his labors proved very profitable to him and his publishers and unhappily proved a great stimulus to the commercial side of hymn book making. And a commercialized Hymnody is not a pleasant object of contemplation to any one who cares for the sanctities or the best interests of public worship. We may defer the consideration of Dr. Robinson's later work, which came under the influence of Anglican ideals in Hymnody and church music emanating from the Oxford Movement.

III. OTHER DENOMINATIONS FOLLOW THE UNITARIAN LEAD

1. "THE CHRISTIAN HYMN BOOK" (1863)

No denomination profited more from the Unitarian movement for the improvement of Hymnody than the sect of Christians, whose revival origin and somewhat illiterate hymns have been referred to. With a view to superseding various books and "pamphlets" in use the Book Association had published *Hymns and spiritual songs—original and selected—for the use of Christians. By D. Millard and J. Badger* (Union Mills, N. Y., 1831; 8th ed., 1840); made

---

[81] For a somewhat differing estimate of Dr. Robinson's place and work in Hymnody see Jas. H. Ross in *The Homiletic Review*, April, 1899.

up of selections from Watts, and hymns of a very mixed character. But in 1863 appeared *The Christian Hymn Book, for the Sanctuary and Home* (Boston: Crosby and Nichols, 1863), edited by T. C. Moulton, E. Edmunds and W. Hathaway. This marked a change indeed. It was worthy in make-up and method and contents to be one of the current Unitarian series of hymn books on which it was modelled; and was indeed regarded by *The Christian Examiner* as "unsurpassed by any collection that has been published." [82]

2. THE NEW UNIVERSALIST HYMNODY (1846-1895)

The same influences affected Universalist Hymnody, both in manner and contents. *Hymns for Christian Devotion; especially adapted to the Universalist denomination. By J. G. Adams and E. H. Chapin* (Boston, 1846) announced itself[83] as representing "a liberal and progressive Christianity" and as profiting by the sheets of "the new Cambridge Unitarian Hymn Book." Its more cultured tone proved not unwelcome, and it reached a 17th edition as early as 1853, and was republished in 1871 by the denominational Publishing House (Boston). Mr. Adams followed it up independently with *The Gospel Psalmist; a collection of Hymns and tunes* (Boston, 1861); interesting as the first attempt to provide the music for congregational singing, "coming into practice in other Christian churches"[84] *Vestry Harmonies* (Boston: Universalist Publ. House, 1868) was a third compilation of Mr. Adams, and smaller. In taking up *Hymns for the Church and the Home: with a selection of Psalms. Portland Collection* (Boston: Universalist Publ. House, 1865), one gets the impression that the publishers have put the denominational imprint upon some one of the current Unitarian hymn books. The impression is strengthened by the combination of a service

[82] July, 1863.
[83] Preface.
[84] Preface.

book with the hymns in *A Book of Prayer for the Church and the Home* (n. d.) in the manner of several Unitarian editors. But the *Portland Collection* was a new compilation by Dr. E. C. Bolles and Israel Washburn jr. The book was without music, but the movement to introduce congregational singing encouraged the publishers to issue a musical edition, with the addition of some 200 hymns, necessary "to make each page complete," as *Church Harmonies: a collection of Hymns and tunes for the use of congregations* (Boston: Universalist Publ. House, 1873).

With *Church Harmonies new and old* (Boston: Universalist Publ. House, 1895), the denomination secured a hymnal of the modern type. Its hymns and music are edited with some care, and it preserves a certain distinctiveness and regard for denominational traditions in a decade when most church hymnals sought catholicity.

Of the Universalist hymn writers of this later period John G. Adams and Edwin H. Chapin are known within the denomination, and Adams' "Heaven is here: its hymns of gladness" was in *The Plymouth Hymnal,* though altered and patriotically ascribed to President John Quincy Adams. The Cary sisters are better known poets of Universalist faith. Phœbe's tender "One sweetly solemn thought" is in wide use,. but has suffered much from the editorial pruning knife. Alice's "Earth, with its dark and dreadful ills," "O day to sweet religious thought," and "To Him who is the Life of life," are included in Horder's *Worship Song.*

V

THE OFFSET: THE "GOSPEL HYMN"
(1851 to date)

The Literary Hymn has as its offset the "Gospel Hymn." The movement to elevate the literary and musical tone of church worship leaves indifferent a large class both in and beyond the Church whose taste is for light music and

emotional verse. It thus invites, and, in the opinion of many
earnest Christian workers, justifies a counter-movement to
reach that element upon the plane of their own taste and
accomplishment. Hence the Evangelistic Hymn, the Camp
Meeting and Revival Song, and in our own day the Gospel
Hymn.

The modern Evangelistic Movement and its Hymnody
centres in the interdenominational Young Men's Christian
Association, organized at London in 1844, and at Montreal
and Boston in 1851. The rendering of familiar church
hymns by male voices in a then strange atmosphere of
"Union" was the first novelty of its Hymnody. In the
revival of 1858 the great agency was the "Union Prayer
Meeting" in large cities, and the prayer meeting developed
spontaneity and brevity in the use of hymns. *Union Prayer
Meeting Hymns* (S. S. Union, 1858) were mainly the
familiar hymns of the Church. During the ensuing years
of Civil War the Association followed the young men to
field and camp and hospital, under the name of The Christian Commission. Several societies cooperated in supplying little hymn books for the field, which became a striking
feature of army work.[85] *The Soldiers' Hymn Book*
(Y. M. C. A.) reached a circulation of over 100,000 copies:
that of *The Hymns and Tunes for the Army and Navy*
(Am. Tract Soc.) was even larger; and *The Soldiers'
Pocket Book* (Presbyterian Bd. of Publ.) was a favorite of
the camps. These, as also the hymn books for the Southern
army, were mainly confined to hymns already familiar in
church or school at home.

But in its city work after the war the Association was
soon committed to the Evangelistic or Revival type of
Hymnody. *The Young Men's Christian Association Hymn
and Tune Book* (Boston, 1867: Philadelphia, 1872), made

[85]See Jas. H. Ross, *Hymns and Singers of the Y. M. C. A.*, Boston:
The Pilgrim Press, 1901; chap. iv, "The Hymns of the Soldiers;" also
"Hawkeye's" letter from the field in *The* (Philadelphia) *Presbyterian*,
Nov. 1, 1862.

by Secretary L. P. Rowland, is not very different from the earlier "social" and "revival" hymn books, but enriched by newer melodies of Bradbury and others. *The North-Western Hymn Book,* compiled by Dwight L. Moody, then the leader of the Chicago Association, is of similar type, with a larger use of the stirring Sunday school songs of the Hull and Bradbury school. Indeed the long series of Sunday school song books of George F. Root, William B. Bradbury, Asa Hull, Horace Waters, Silas J. Vail, Robert Lowry, William G. Fischer and others, beginning in the late forties and extending forward unbrokenly, demand recognition for the part played by their fresh songs and contagious melodies in developing a taste in the young for the lighter type of religious song. They prepared the way; and as the Sunday school work mingled with that of the Association, and of the Christian Commission during the war, to go forward in a broadening stream of evangelistic effort, these Sunday school books furnished the evangelists with the earliest examples of what are now known as Gospel Hymns. Among them were Bradbury's settings of "Sweet hour of prayer," "Lord, I hear of showers of blessing," and "He leadeth me"; Fischer's of "I love to tell the story"; Lowry's "Shall we gather at the river," and O'Kane's "O think of a home over there"; each exhibiting the now familiar marks of the Gospel Hymn, even the inevitable refrain.

More specifically the prominence of the Gospel Hymn in modern evangelism grew out of the "Praise services" organized as early as 1851[86] by Eben Tourjée, who became President of the Boston Y. M. C. A. in 1871, and the singing of H. Thane Miller and W. H. Doane at the Association conventions; the "Services of Song" given by Philip Phillips at Sunday school conventions and Christian Commission meetings and indeed around the globe, and in association with the Sunday school and evangelistic campaign of

[86]Elias Nason, *Lives of Moody and Sankey,* etc., Boston, 1877, p. 297.

John H. Vincent and Dwight L. Moody in the West;[87] and the work of Philip P. Bliss in connection with Moody's missionary labors in Chicago. Phillips regarded himself as the pioneer in introducing "the sacred solo into religious meetings, as defined worship" [88] and his association with Moody as "doubtless the precedent which was followed by the gospel partnership of Moody and Sankey." [89]

At the Indianapolis Y. M. C. A. convention of 1870 Moody first met Ira D. Sankey, and claimed him as a helper in the Chicago work.[90] In 1872 they started together for the first evangelistic campaign in Great Britain. The extreme unpreparedness of England for Sankey's gospel songs and methods, so much emphasized by his biographers, was perhaps characteristic of conventional church circles rather than of the public he sought to reach. Richard Weaver had introduced solo-singing at his meetings; *The Revival Hymn Book* (Morgan and Chase, 1858) had proved immensely popular in connection with them, and was followed by the serial *Heart Melodies* and by *Hymns of Grace and Glory*.[91] William Booth began his tent meetings at Whitechapel in 1865, from which arose The Christian Mission, to become in turn the Salvation Army; and in the late '60s published *The Christian Mission Hymn Book,* the predecessor of *The Salvation Soldier's Hymn Book*. It contained gospel songs in abundance, including many of the new American Sunday school songs. Moreover Philip Phillips was just completing his second British campaign, and had made his method of "singing the gospel" widely familiar. His *The American sacred Songster* had been published by the British Sunday school Union

[87]Philip Phillips, *Song Pilgrimage around the world,* Chicago, 1880. p. 64.

[88]*Song Pilgrimage,* p. 63.

[89]*Ibid.,* p. 64.

[90]Wm. R. Moody, *The Life of Dwight L. Moody,* Chicago, 1900, p. 125.

[91]Geo. E. Morgan, *R. C. Morgan, his life and times,* New York, n. d., pp. 58, 174; and for Weaver and his songs, pp. 118, 122.

and attained a circulation claimed as over one million one
hundred thousand copies.[92] In Scotland and Ireland Sankey's sacred songs and ways were more novel, and under
his hands the American melodeon did much to break down
the Presbyterian prejudice against "organs." [93]

One of Philip Phillips' song books, *Hallowed Songs,*
was adopted by Moody and Sankey for their meetings, and
Sankey made use of various songs he had brought from
Chicago. Copies of these were so often asked for that an
effort was made to have them appended to *Hallowed
Songs.*[94] On its publisher's refusal Morgan and Scott
printed them in a 16-page pamphlet, lettered *Sacred Songs
and Solos,*[95] and sold for sixpence. This was the nucleus
of the "Moody and Sankey Hymn Book," but in England
it kept its original name, and has since grown by gradual
accretions to a volume of 1200 pieces. The evangelists,
it is pleasant to record, refused the royalties, amounting
by the end of their tour to £7000.[96]

At home, P. P. Bliss had followed Sankey's lead, and
associated himself for evangelistic work with D. W.
Whittle, preparing for their use a small collection of *Gospel
Songs* (Cincinnati, 1874). In this were no less than fifty-
two tunes of his own composition, in many cases set to
words also written by him. The hymns were striking and
sometimes dramatic: the tunes were hardly original, being
full of old and familiar ideas and phrases, but were of a
vivacious sort sure to become popular when they found their
opportunity. Upon Moody's return it was decided to unite
the *Sacred Songs and Solos* used abroad with materials
furnished by Bliss' book, and the joint collection was published as *Gospel Hymns and sacred Songs. By P. P. Bliss*

[92]*Song Pilgrimage,* p. 62.
[93]J. S. Curwen, *Studies in worship music,* 2nd series, London, n. d.,
p. 40.
[94]Moody, *op. cit.,* p. 170.
[95]Without date, but first advertised in *The Christian* for Sept. 18,
1873. Moody, p. 171.
[96]Moody, *op. cit.,* p. 172.

and Ira D. Sankey, as used by them in gospel meetings
(Biglow and Main and John Church and Co., 1875).

The book was introduced at the great Moody meetings in
the Brooklyn Rink and the old Pennsylvania Railroad depot
in Philadelphia and at other cities with a somewhat overwhelming effect, and was circulated in immense quantities
throughout the country. The Gospel Hymns may be said
to have carried the more emotional and less cultivated
element of religious people off its feet, and to have furnished for a time the familiar songs of vast numbers
hitherto unacquainted with hymns and unused to public
worship. The new melodies penetrated even the music
halls and were whistled by the man on the street. Some of
the new hymns became household words; notably "Ho!
my comrades, see the signal," "Let the lower lights be
burning," "Light in the darkness, sailor," and "Almost
persuaded now to believe," by Bliss; "Safe in the arms of
Jesus" and "Rescue the perishing" by "Fanny Crosby";
"I love to tell the story" and "Tell me the old, old story"
by Miss Hankey; and "I need Thee every hour" by Annie
S. Hawks.

Bliss and Sankey became the heads of an evangelistic
school of hymn and tune writers (the hymns and tunes
being hardly separable); and as Moody's work continued,
they with James McGranahan, George C. Stebbins, D. C.
Towner and others, met the demand for new songs with
fresh contributions. *Gospel Hymns and sacred Songs* was
followed in 1876 by *Gospel Hymns, No. 2,* and in 1878 by
No. 3; the series ending with *No. 6* in 1891,[97] succeeded by
similar collections with other names but under the same
auspices. The later books naturally lacked the fresh interest of the first, and encountered also very many rivals
which the early success had developed.

It ought now to be evident that while the Gospel Hymn
is inevitably associated with the names of Moody and

[97] For annotations on the hymns, see Ira D. Sankey, *Sankey's Story
of the Gospel Hymns,* Philadelphia, 1906.

Sankey, their part was to bring an older movement to the culmination of a great popular success rather than to inaugurate a movement that was novel. Nor did the songs they brought forward with so much effect constitute either in words or music a type of hymn distinctively new or even clearly marked off from its predecessors. And yet their popular success was certainly distinctive, and presents a new phase of hymn singing as notable in its way as the XVIIIth century outburst of Methodist Song; and it remains to be accounted for.

It came largely from the fresh appeal to the emotions which this group of tune writers was able to infuse into its compositions. In the original *Gospel Hymns and sacred Songs* this appeal was shared in to a large extent by the hymns written or chosen to carry the tunes. But there is suggestiveness in Sankey's confession that he found it "much more difficult" to get suitable words than tunes;[98] and as the series proceeds, a rereading of the hymns becomes on the whole a dull exercise, the proportion that quickens feeling or tickles the sense of rhythm becoming comparatively small. The tunes also become more mechanical, no doubt; but the early melodies that lived are of the sort that appeal to the average emotional nature through the senses. They are "easy," and "catchy" and sentimental, swaying with soft or martial rhythm and culminating in the taking "refrain"; calling for no musical knowledge to understand and no skill to render them; inevitably popular with the unfailing appeal of clear melody.

Even so the popular appeal of these Gospel Hymns cannot be disassociated from the persons and occasion that first brought them into general notice any more than the Methodist fervor of song can be separated from Wesley and the Revival. They were first heard in the sweet tones of a magnetic singer in the intense atmosphere created by Moody's preaching, and first sung in unison with a great throng of deeply moved people. Something of the spiritual

[98] J. S. Curwen, *Worship Music,* 2nd series, p. 39.

impression they made was reflected from the simple and sincere personalities of the evangelists. They were plain men employing the arguments and illustrations, the music and verse, that appealed to themselves in the conviction that such preaching and song was best adapted to appeal to their hearers.

Why then (so the argument runs) since the great majority of people who come under revival influences, whether of Moody or his successors, are likewise plain and uncultivated, is not the Gospel Hymn best adapted to the ends of evangelistic work? And if happily these people are brought into the worshipping congregation, why should they be asked to forego the sentimental verse and popular melody that appeal to them in favor of a more literary Hymnody and more artistic music? That there is some force in the argument is beyond doubting. Many hearts have been quickened through these hymns that seem to the critical crude in sentiment and unrefined in expression. And the editor of one of the choicest of modern musical hymnals has admitted that through the compositions of the "Gospel Hymns" school "music has become the expression of the spiritual life for thousands who before were without a voice in public worship, and, as suppressed feeling easily dies, were often without any share in public worship." [99] But there is truth also in the limitation of Prof. Pratt:—

"The defenders of this popular hymnody . . . very often very gravely underestimate the capacity of the popular mind to rise above vulgar embodiments of truth and to shake itself free from perverted sentimentality, and they constantly mistake the zest of animal enjoyment in a rub-a-dub rhythm or the shout of childish pleasure in a 'catchy' refrain for real religious enthusiasm." [100]

On the whole it is quite consistent with a faith in the pure motives of the inspirers of Gospel Hymns and a recognition of the good they have done to believe that

[99] Lyman Abbott, "Historical Introduction" to *The Plymouth Hymnal*, New York, 1894, p. xii.
[100] Waldo S. Pratt, *Musical Ministries in the Church*, Revell Co., 1901, p. 62.

Wesley's elevated standard of Revival Hymnody is more devout and hence more prudent, and that his conjunction of the educational process with revival enthusiasm is the more complete and satisfying system.

It was the lack of any educational ideal or development in the "Gospel Hymns" school of Hymnody that has caused its rapid deterioration. Countless imitators of *Gospel Hymns* were raised up, without the inspiration and sometimes without the unmixed motives of the leaders. Every new evangelist following Moody's methods must have his Sankey and his own hymn book. Moreover the immense pecuniary success of the *Gospel Hymns* series (in which Moody and Sankey took no share for personal use) offered great temptations to publishers and writers, and the making of such books soon became a trade. They deteriorated partly because the standard of popular music and verse descended to the rag-time level, and partly because it is simpler to deal with the great public on its own plane, or a little below it, than to attempt to uplift it.

The diminished usefulness of Gospel Hymns became so obvious that a movement to return to a more sober Hymnody began in the same Young Men's Christian Association that had led the way in introducing them. Under the inspiration of Charles Cuthbert Hall appeared the excellent *Praise Songs* (New York, 1897) for Y. M. C. A. use. It was followed in 1898 by *Church Hymns and Gospel Songs* (Biglow and Main Co.), in which Sankey, McGranahan and Stebbins themselves restored the standard hymns to their rightful precedence. It was again Cuthbert Hall who arranged the *Hymnal for the Jubilee Convention of Young Men's Christian Associations* (1901), made up almost exclusively of the choicest hymns and tunes of *The Hymnal* (1895) of the Presbyterian Church.

As to the effect of the Gospel Hymn movement upon church Hymnody, it threatened at first to be very serious. In the Methodist Episcopal Church it almost uprooted the established Hymnody, and made the task of those who would conserve the old standard of worship very difficult for a time. In many other denominations the Gospel Hymns took possession of the Sunday schools, Christian Endeavor societies and devotional services, and encouraged a generation to grow up largely without the help and inspiration of great hymns. To many of these the tone of Church Praise seems still to lack the "go" and vivacity to which they had grown accustomed; and Gospel Hymns, old or new, keep knocking at the church gates for admission. The time has come when it is perceived that all songs called Gospel Hymns are not a homogenous mass, and that they should be judged like other hymns upon their individual merit. And as affecting the standard of that judgment it cannot count for nothing that a generation of active Christians has been accustomed to associate these sentimental verses and contagious melodies with the offices of religion.

One influence of the Moody and Sankey movement on Church Song, already very marked, is the new recognition or at least tolerance of an Evangelistic Hymnody given by all denominations. Either as a department of "mission services" in the church hymnal or as an authorized "mission hymnal," the needs of evangelistic work are being met. In these, it seems likely that some of the Gospel Hymns may find some permanence. The recent *The English Hymnal* (Oxford, 1906) contains for instance no less than five hymns[101] with their original settings from the first number of *Gospel Hymns and sacred Songs.*

Many have prophesied that the older type of evangelism and Evangelistic Hymnody has largely fulfilled its mission and lost its attraction; and is to undergo a change of method and spirit. And it is possible that the phenomenal XXth century evangelistic campaign of William A. Sunday has surprised a church whose mind was strongly turned away from the emotional side of religious experience toward

---

[101] "Ho! my comrades," "I hear Thy welcome voice," "Safe in the arms of Jesus," "Tell me the old, old story," and "There were ninety and nine."

social and ethical aspects of religion. With attractive power quite equal to Moody's, though with some devices Moody would have declined, Sunday has gained a wide hearing for Whitefield's gospel of the XVIIIth century Great Awakening, even repeating Gilbert Tennent's fierce indictment of the churches. But to a less degree than either Whitefield or Moody he has evoked or depended upon the fervor of popular song. He has not found, and perhaps not sought, a Sankey; and *Great Revival Hymns No. 2* (Chicago, 1910) is both in its contents and its appeal a contrast indeed to *Gospel Hymns and sacred Songs.* The great success of the Sunday movement opens anew the question of the future of the older type of evangelism and Evangelistic Song, which, as we shall show, is now confronted by a new "Social Gospel" and a somewhat aggressive activity in the development of a popular "Social Hymnody."

CHAPTER X
THE HYMNODY OF THE OXFORD REVIVAL

I

IT DOMINATES THE CHURCH OF ENGLAND

1. The Movement to Restore the "Primitive" Church Hymnody (1833)

Keble's *The Christian Year* appeared in the same year as Heber's *Hymns,* and like them had been long delayed. The book was not a hymnal, by intention or in effect. The meditative verse lends itself reluctantly to hymnic use, and the familiar Morning and Evening Hymns[1] extracted from the opening pieces have been taken at the cost of marring the beauty of those poems. It had little direct influence upon Hymnody except as it elevated the standard of sacred verse. Its influence lay in the glamour of poetry it threw upon the feasts and fasts of the liturgical year, its call upon the imagination to prepare the way for the Oxford Movement. Of this Movement Keble was the undoubted founder, and his Assize Sermon of 14th July, 1833, was ever regarded by Newman as its actual start. And this Movement was destined to exert a most direct and pronounced influence upon the Hymnody of the Church of England first of all, and ultimately upon that of all English-speaking Churches.

The Prayer Book with its elements of compromise between Catholic and Reformed types of churchmanship, was to give opportunity for the movement and to prove the center of its operations.

[1] "New every morning is the love" and "Sun of my soul, Thou Saviour dear."

The task of demonstrating the essential catholicity of the Prayer Book was undertaken by William Palmer of Magdalen. His *Origines Liturgicae, or Antiquities of the English Ritual,* published in 1832, was an essential factor of the preparations for the Movement. Now, in the Prayer Book the daily order for Morning and Evening Prayer replaces the Divine Office for the observance of the daily Hours of Prayer in the old system. But Morning and Evening Prayer are so trifling in the extent of their contents against the vast bulk of the Divine Office as gathered in the four volumes of the Breviary, that it suited Palmer's thesis to show how complicated and cumbrous the Office had become, and that before the Reformation various expedients of abridgment were resorted to; thus indicating the prudence of the Reformers in reducing the Hours of Prayer to two, and dropping the great mass of appointed materials.[2] Among the materials missing from Morning and Evening Prayer were the metrical hymns that made a stated part of the Office. Hence it suited Palmer's purpose to slight the hymn-singing feature of the Breviary, and by citing in a foot-note decrees of certain Councils prohibiting it, to leave the impression that hymn singing was not Catholic in the "semper" and "ubique" sense.[3]

If this position had been maintained by the other Oxford leaders, the subsequent fortune of the English Hymn would have been different from what we know. Some of them undertook the study of the Breviary in a different spirit, as expressed by Newman in the title of his 75th number of the famous *Tracts for the Times,* "On the Roman Breviary as embodying the substance of the devotional services of the Church Catholic." Newman's thesis was that the Breviary was an inestimable treasure of devotion, of which the Roman Church had defrauded the Church at large, by retaining the ancient Latin form, and that the Church of England should reappropriate what it had lost by mere

[2]Vol. i, "Antiquities" etc., chap. i, pt. i, "Hours of Prayer."
[3]Ed. 4, 1845, vol. i, p. 224 and note.

inadvertence.[4]   To this end he appended 123 pages of selections from the Breviary translated by him, including in their proper places versions of ten of the Office Hymns rendered into his limpid verse.

As early as 1829 Bishop Lloyd's divinity lectures at Oxford upon the sources of the Prayer Book had directed attention to the breviaries, and the contents of a copy of the *Paris Breviary* brought over by Sir John Prevost took Keble and Isaac Williams "much by surprise." [5]   Charmed by the beauty of its hymns, Williams at once began to translate them, and in 1833 to publish his versions in *The British Magazine.*   In 1839 he gathered them into a volume, *Hymns translated from the Parisian Breviary* (London, Rivington).   But Williams dreaded the use of unauthorized hymns in the Church services, and originally chose "unrhythmical harsh meters to prevent this." [6]   This course he subsequently modified, and, in the preface of 1839, expressed the opinion that Cranmer had omitted the Breviary hymns from the Prayer Book because of the lack of competent translators, but that they were more congenial to the spirit of the book than the modern hymns so often introduced in connection with it.   Newman, on the other hand, thought the hymns had been "discarded because of associations with which they were then viewed, and of the interpolations by which they were disfigured, but that, when purified from these, they at once commended themselves to the thoughtful mind who would repair the breaches of the Reformation.[7]   The average opinion of the time is illustrated in John Chandler, fellow of Corpus Christi and curate· of Witley, who had become a seeker for things primitive.   He had not been aware that there were any good ancient hymns extant, and regarded those contained in what he calls "Popish missals" as "barbarous in their latinity as defective in their doc-

---

[4]*Tract No. 75*, pp. 1, 2.

[5]*Autobiography of Isaac Williams, B.D.*, 2nd ed. London, 1892, pp. 36, 37.

[6]*Ibid., p.* 37, note.   [7]Preface to *Hymni Ecclesiae*, 1838.

trine." [8] To the English hymns in current use he objected likewise, not only as unauthorized, but because "many are from sources to which our Primitive Apostolic Church would not choose to be indebted." [9] His attention was caught by Williams' versions of the Parisian hymns, appearing in *The British Magazine*. He purchased a copy of the *Paris Breviary* and of Casander's *Hymni Sacri* of 1556, and set to work upon the translation of the hymns. In 1837 he published *The Hymns of the primitive Church, now first collected, translated and arranged, by the Rev. J. Chandler*. The work was hasty, and the versions far from reproducing the originals. But it was opportune, and the hymns were rhythmical; and Chandler's book played a considerable part in the revival of Latin hymns.

In the same year, an Irish bishop, Richard Mant, published his *Ancient Hymns, from the Roman Breviary, for domestic use*, with a preface commending the hymns and other parts of the Breviary as an acceptable manual of private devotion. In 1838 Newman followed with his *Hymni Ecclesiae*, being two volumes of the texts of Latin hymns, the first from the *Paris Breviary*, the other from the *Roman Breviary* and other sources.

The prominence of the *Paris Breviary* and the Breviary of Urban VIII in this movement to restore things primitive is curious enough. The hymnal of the *Paris Breviary* from which Williams worked, and in which Chandler found *The Hymns of the primitive Church*, was substantially the work of a group of French poets writing to the order of the Archbishop of Paris; and whose work appeared in 1736, with the intention of supplanting the ancient hymns by these on modern lines. And the Breviary Hymns of Bishop Mant were from the Renaissance hymnal which Urban VIII introduced into the *Roman Breviary* of 1632, to satisfy the pseudo-classical taste of his time. One gets the impression that among this first group of restorers Newman alone knew

[8]Preface to *Hymns of the primitive Church*, 1837, p. viii.
[9]*Ibid.*, p. iv.

what he was about. To the others, in the elation of discovery, everything Latin was assumed to be primitive, and
to men educated in the classical atmosphere of Oxford the
language of the later hymnals, in its approach to classical
models, appealed more than the early hymns could have
done, even had they known them.[10] They were working
with no adequate knowledge of their materials; but their
work, however amusingly ineffective for the specific purpose they had at heart, proved effective enough in the
general interests of Hymnody.

2. THE RESULT: THE LITURGICAL HYMN

And what their work did for Hymnody may be summed
up under three heads:—

(1) *It put hymn singing in the Church of England upon
an entirely different status.* Just as psalm singing had
come into the Church with the taint of Geneva on it, a
practice to be tolerated at best and kept apart from the
authorized Prayer Book system, but had in course of time
been taken up by the churchly party itself as a venerable
institution to be protected and conserved against encroachment; so it was now to be with hymn singing. The Hymn
was the badge of dissent, and had obtruded itself into the
Church under the impulse of revival enthusiasm outside.
It was the particular encroachment that threatened the
integrity of the Metrical Psalmody which the high church
party would protect. It was a lawless novelty of the
Evangelicals, but perhaps under all the circumstances, to
be tolerated and made the best of. But unexpectedly these
new researches into things primitive revealed the Hymn
as distinctly one of them, a constituent part of the Daily
Office and even of the Mass, embedded in their structure,
sung everywhere from most ancient days at their rendering.
Hymn singing instead of being Evangelical was revealed as
Catholic. The logic of the situation was inevitable, and

---

[10]*Cf.* Jno. M. Neale's article in *The Christian Remembrancer,* 1850,
hereafter referred to.

hence all this zeal to provide versions of the historic hymns, and the present agreement of Catholic and Evangelical in accepting the status of hymn singing in the Church of England.

(2) *It revealed the Latin hymns to the Church and acclimated them.* The rich sources of Church Song thus opened up had remained till then practically unexplored; and it was a great enrichment of English Hymnody that the Ambrosian Hymnody embodied in the Breviary and laid aside at the Reformation, together with the later accretions of church hymns, whether Roman or Gallican, should once more be restored to English use. This enrichment and restoration has in the course of time become so much an accepted thing that we hardly appreciate the changed point of view involved. But it is doubtful if anything short of Tractarian principles, or any urgency less than the Oxford upheaval, would have had the force to overcome the deep prejudices and deliberate ignorance that had kept the old church hymns outside the pale of Protestant sympathy.

(3) *It affected the motive and content of the English Hymn itself; establishing* (rather than introducing) *a distinct type—the Liturgical Hymn.*

The Evangelical Hymn is inevitably the voice of the believer; the Liturgical Hymn is the voice of the worshipping church. The Evangelical Hymn deals primarily with inward experience; the Liturgical Hymn, even though expressive of common experience, relates it objectively to the hour of worship, the church season or occasion, the ordinance and sacrament. The Evangelical Hymn is free; the Liturgical Hymn, in theory at least, is the metrical element of a closely articulated liturgical order, having its fixed place which determines its contents. Bishop Heber's mind and hand were turned toward this ideal, and served as a preparation for its fulfillment at the hands of the Oxford Reformers and their disciples. Newman's *Tract No. 75* exemplified the Liturgical Hymn *in situ.* And the early group of books of hymns,—Williams', Chandler's, Mant's,

—were all liturgical. With an appearance of being accommodated to the familiar Prayer Book, they were in reality articulated by the far more complicated framework of the Breviary, and brought with them something of its doctrine and terminology. Each day of the week has its special hymns, and Chandler provides for the daily nocturns, matins and even song. There are hymns for the Sundays and familiar fasts and feasts not only, but for their vigils and octaves, for a line of saints' days, and for the commemoration of the Blessed Virgin Mary, the holy martyrs, bishops, presbyters, virgins, etc.

The Liturgical Hymn was thus one of the earliest products of the Movement, and came into life full fledged. This happened naturally from the amount of attention given the Breviary. And the Breviary furnished precisely that portion of the ancient system of devotion which could be incorporated into the English with the least degree of friction, because it was adapted for private recitation, and was so used in the Roman Church. It is true that *Tract No. 75* brought upon Newman "a great deal of censure"[11] Even Keble and Williams were frightened on learning that two of Newman's pupils were on the point of publishing a complete English translation of the *Roman Breviary,* with the hymns translated by Newman, who yielded to their remonstrances with some heat.[12] But no one could interfere with Newman's daily recitation of the Breviary Offices, and in this practice he was soon followed by Pusey.[13] Daily public service in the church had been established by Thomas Keble at Bisley since 1827, later at Oxford by Newman and Williams,[14] and also in London at the Margaret Chapel, the chosen place at which Tractarian principles were to be applied to public worship. It was not possible to substitute

---

[11]*Letter to the Bishop of Oxford,* Oxford 1841, p. 9.
[12]Williams, *Autobiography,* p. 103.
[13]H. P. Liddon, *Life of Edward B. Pusey,* 2nd ed., London 1893, vol. ii, pp. 145, 146.
[14]Williams, pp. 75 ff.

the Breviary Offices for Morning and Evening Prayer at such services. But Hymnody was as free for Tractarians as for Evangelicals. And the use of the Breviary Hymns afforded the most available means of recognizing any desired number of holy days, and of imparting a Tractarian atmosphere to the whole service.

3. EARLY TRACTARIAN HYMNALS: JOHN MASON NEALE
(1836-1858)

There was therefore a need of new hymn books. The first of note after the beginning of the movement was the *Psalms and Hymns adapted to the services of the Church of England,* published in 1836 by W. J. Hall of Tottenham. This has generally been regarded as high church, for no reason apparent other than the mitre embossed upon the cover, or its arrangement of the hymns under the Sundays of the church year, after the model of Heber. It won the approval of the Bishop of London, and a circulation of 4,000,000 copies is claimed for it.[15] It represented the Oxford leaders in no way, and was unacceptable to them.[16]

A small collection printed by J. Holt Simpson in 1837, *Psalms and Hymns, original and selected,* included some translations of Mant, Chandler and Williams. More significant was *A Selection of Psalms, to which are added Hymns chiefly ancient,* published the same year by Dodsworth, the incumbent of Margaret Chapel. Several of Chandler's versions are in *Hymns selected for the parish of Sandbach* by J. Latham in 1841; and in 1842 Chandler himself revised and arranged his translations in hymnal form, as *The Hymns of the Church, mostly primitive, collected, translated and arranged for public use* (London, Parker). In 1849 appeared *Introits and Hymns for Margaret Chapel* (enlarged ed. 1852); and two books of 1850, Henry Stretton's *Church Hymns,* and Joseph Oldknow's *Hymns for*

---

[15]*Cf.* Julian, *Dictionary of Hymnology,* p. 336.
[16]Jno. M. Neale in *The Christian Remembrancer,* (1850), calls it "one of the worst."

the services of the Church, are largely made up of the translations of the Oxford group. An anonymous London *Hymn Book for the use of churches and chapels* introduced some of the versions of Edward Caswall. His *Lyra Catholica,* appearing in 1849, contained versions of all the hymns in the Roman Breviary and Missal. Caswall was among the earliest Oxford Tractarians to pass over (in the succeeding year) to Rome. But his translations found general favor, and were reprinted in New York in 1851.

This early group of Tractarian hymnals evinces the disposition of a widening circle to follow the Oxford leaders in their search for the old paths. They accepted the materials furnished by the Oxford translators, and employed it with little knowledge or discrimination. The books might serve to experiment with in local use, but no one of them commended itself to Tractarians generally, or was worthy to become the nucleus of an "Anglo-Catholic Hymnal."

These facts were set forth in an article on "English Hymnology, its History and Prospects," contributed by John Mason Neale to *The Christian Remembrancer* in 1850. This pungent paper reviewed the current Evangelical Hymnody in a very contemptuous spirit, but dealt just as freely with the Oxford translators:—Their zeal for the newly discovered primitive Hymnody had carried them off their feet, and in choosing the *Paris Breviary,* they had mistaken the new paths for the old; their work was careless and inadequate, and its metres badly chosen; as embodied in the new hymn books, it was unworthy of acceptance by the Church. At the time, Neale's proposals for the ideal hymnal did not go beyond a better selection and better translation of the Breviary Hymns, with some 12 or 15 of the best English hymns added, the whole to be revised by competent scholars.

No man in England had an equal right with Neale to say these things. And this paper may be said to mark the point of contact of his gifts and scholarship with the actual Hymnody of the Church. He was among the earliest Cambridge disciples of the Tractarian Movement, already spending the long vacations in researches in ecclesiastical archaeology.[17] He made himself a master of post-classic Latin, and began to prepare for a history of the mediaeval Latin poets.[18] These neglected authors he loved for their own sake, accounting Adam of St. Victor the greatest Latin poet of all ages.[19]

Neale pursued his hymnological studies with life-long ardor, and with results that put the study of mediaeval Hymnody upon a new basis for English-speaking people. His study of "The Ecclesiastical Latin Poetry of the Middle Ages" contributed to *Encyclopaedia Metropolitana*,[20] laid out the field. By patient researches among the manuscript sources on the continent, he "brought to light a multitude of hymns unknown before." [21] In his treatise on Sequences,[22] he for the first time revealed the actual essence and structure of these most characteristic hymns of the Middle Ages. And by his translations he added a great wealth of mediaeval Hymnody to the actual resources of English-speaking Churches. Of these versions the earliest were gathered in 1851 as *Mediaeval Hymns and Sequences;* ninety-four appeared in the *Hymnal noted* in 1852-54. The *Rhythm of Bernard* followed in 1858, and *Hymns chiefly mediaeval in* 1865. After Neale's death a few more of his translations appeared in *S. Margaret's Hymnal* (privately printed, 1875).

These translations have been challenged by Roman Catholics, on the one hand, as wanting in fidelity to the whole doctrinal contents of the originals, and on the other by Protestants as importing too much of the Roman atmosphere into the Church of England. On the whole it may be

[17]E. A. Towle, *John Mason Neale*, London, 1906, p. 35.
[18]*Ibid.*, p. 31.
[19]Preface to his *Mediaeval Hymns*, 2nd ed., p. ix.
[20]Vol. 25.
[21]Printed in *The Ecclesiologist*, of which he was joint editor.
[22]Originally attached to his *Mediaeval Hymns*, and enlarged for Daniel's *Thesaurus Hymnologicus.*

said of Neale's method of translation that his aim was practical and his ameliorations or omissions were generally those suggested by prudence or good taste, with a view to the admission of the hymns to the Church of England. A literal fidelity would have gratified a few scholars. As it was, these strong and beautiful versions just filled the needs of contemporary and later Tractarians, and many of them passed the bounds not only of party but of the Church of England, and gave a new color to Protestant Hymnody. The atmosphere of the time was favorable to the dissemination of the monastic conceptions of religion. Evangelicalism itself was more other-worldly than now. And Dr. Neale was able to say that his "Jerusalem the golden" was the most popular hymn of the Church.

This practical aim of Dr. Neale rapidly developed into nothing short of a proposal that the Church of England should forego the use of English Protestant hymns altogether in favor of English versions of the pre-Reformation hymns. He had been careful to preserve the original metres and rhythm of these hymns in his own work, and now took the position that if they were to be sung at all, they lost greatly by being separated from their original melodies. He argued, moreover, that the Gregorian music had not only the claim of a remote antiquity, reaching back in some part to the usage of the first temple, but that it was the only music that had any imprimatur of the Church acting in its corporate capacity.[23]

This proposal Neale embodied in a hymn book, under the sanction and with the co-operation of the Ecclesiological Society, and the musical editorship of Thomas Helmore. The first part of the *Hymnal noted* appeared in 1852, containing 46 hymns, mostly from the Sarum office books, set to their plain-song melodies; the second part in 1854, with 59 hymns from various ancient sources: the work in final form with accompanying harmonies in 1858; 94 of the 105 hymns being Neale's own work.

[23]Preface to *Hymnal noted,* ed. 1858.

In this hymnal the seekers for the ancient paths had
reached their goal. But their position was inevitably lonely.
The average organist and singer could not even decipher
the strange Gregorian notation. The general absence of
definite rhythm and clear melody and the accumulation of
unessential notes in the festal tunes, put the congregational
performance of this ancient music among things least
likely of attainment. The number of cathedral and parochial authorities prepared to return to the hymns and tunes
of the Sarum office books was inconsiderable.

We feel, in looking back, that proposals so revolutionary
and so impracticable might not only have failed to accomplish their purpose, but might have caused also a reaction
in which the whole subject of a liturgical Hymnody should
have sunk out of the hearing of English-speaking Churches.
But such was not the case. The *Hymnal noted* had but a
trifling adoption.[24] It met with ridicule and contempt in
certain quarters. But it was also a full realization of Tractarian dreams of a "Catholic" Hymnal.

Neale's proposals remain in the mind of the more consistent Anglicans as an ideal that has never been foregone.
There has never ceased to be a party to keep before the
Church the paramount claims of the ancient hymns set to
the ancient tunes. The place of the hymns is now secure
enough. The opportunity of the Gregorian music is equally
free. Quite beyond the bounds of Tractarianism, the historic sense is gratified by the use of historic hymns set to
their proper tunes. But it still remains to the advocates
of Gregorian music to convince the English peoples that it
contributes, as a whole, either to their edification or their
pleasure. It is, however, to be noted that each of the three
latest Church of England hymnals in wide use makes provision for singing a number of the more liturgical hymns

[24] It became best known through its long use at St. Alban's, Holborn,
where it furnished words and melodies for the "Office Hymns," which
were supplemented by hearty congregational song provided for in a
series of supplements and the very modern "St. Alban's Tune Book."

to their plain-song melodies.   Such unanimity is interesting:
its effects remain to be seen.

In other directions also Dr. Neale's work for Hymnody
was of note; in his zeal for a better Children's Hymnody,
and his carols and original hymns.   Especially he was a
pioneer in the re-discovery of the hymns of the Greek
Church.   His researches in this overlooked and not super-
ficially attractive field were pioneer work.   His translations
and transfusions published as *Hymns of the Eastern
Church,* first appearing in 1862, again enlarged the resources of the Church.   Dr. Neale has performed the *a
priori* impossible feat of making a few of the Greek hymns
a part of the standard Hymnody of English-speaking
Churches, even though by methods of free dealing and
adjustment.   In the way thus opened, a small school of
hymn translators has followed.   In the *People's Hymnal* of
Dr. Littledale (1867), no less than 28 Greek Church hymns
appear as candidates for actual use.   With such recognition
of a new field, Allen William Chatfield published in 1876
his *Songs and Hymns of earliest Greek Christian Poets,*
and, among others, Robert Maude Moorsom followed in
1901 with his *Renderings of Church Hymns from Eastern
and Western Office Books.*   The most diligent, and not the
least successful, present worker in this great field is a Scottish Presbyterian, Dr. John Brownlie of Port Patrick.   In
Hymns of the Greek Church (1900), *Hymns of the Holy
Eastern Church* (1902), *Hymns from the Greek Office
Books* (1904), and the other volumes of his extending
series he has dealt in varying fashion with a large body of
suggestive material.   And some of his renderings of Greek
Church hymns have been given place in recent Church of
England hymnals.

Greek Hymnody has a special interest to that party in
the English Church which turns toward the Eastern
Church rather than to Protestants for any immediate realization of church unity.   But the barriers separating the
Eastern and Western mind and taste are conspicuous in

Hymnody. And the translating of a Greek hymn for English use is really a process of filtering it through an English mind.[25]

4. The Emergence of "Hymns Ancient and Modern" (1861)

The decade following the publication of Neale's *Hymnal noted* was one of marked activity in Church of England Hymnody. Almost every school and tendency expressed itself in a hymn book, but as a whole the trend was in favor of the high church party, and ended in their ascendency.

A Selection of Psalms and Hymns arranged for the public services of the Church of England, by Charles Kemble of Bath (London, 1853) is one of a number that proceeded in the old-fashioned ways, as though nothing had happened. It found extensive use, and was modernized in 1873, but was regarded by the Oxford party as unchurchly.[26]

The Evangelical succession had been duly maintained by such earlier books as Josiah Pratt's popular "Collection" of 1829, and especially Edward Bickersteth's *Christian Psalmody* (1833: revised, 1841), the representative hymn book of those putting the emphasis on Christian experience. It was carried forward in Edward H. Bickersteth's *Psalms and Hymns, based on the Christian Psalmody* of his father (1858), which in turn was enlarged to become the best known Evangelical hymn book of our own time.

And in the same way a little collection of *Hymns* published in 1852 by the Society for the Promotion of Christian Knowledge, was to develop by successive revisions (1855, 1863, 1869) into the *Church Hymns* of 1871, which gained much vogue in the musical edition of Sir Arthur Sullivan (1874), and which in its last revision continues to be the only formidable rival of *Hymns ancient and modern,*

[25]*Cf.* Moorsom, *op. cit.,* p. xx.

[26]*Cf.* W. H. B. Proby, *Annals of the "Low-Church" Party,* London, 1888, vol. ii, pp. 505-508.

representing a lower type of sacramental doctrine and a less self-assertive churchmanship.

The Psalms and Hymns for public and private worship (1855) of Edward Walker of Cheltenham, whose reprintings extended into the '80s, filled an unique function in introducing to the knowledge and use of the Church a large number of hymns by a group of men who had recently assumed the distinctive name of Plymouth Brethren. The peculiarities of their faith were already embodied in a series of hymn books:—*Hymns for the use of the Church of Christ,* by R. C. Chapman (1837), *A Selection of Hymns by Sir Edward Denny* (1839), J. N. Wigram's *Hymns for the poor of the flock* (1838) and J. G. Deck's *Psalms and Hymns and Spiritual Songs* (1842). To these all four of the editors, with J. N. Darby the founder of the sect, contributed original hymns, of which other worldliness and the all-sufficiency of the Lamb of God are the special themes. Walker, who was Deek's brother-in-law, printed over thirty of his hymns, one the well-known "O Lamb of God, still keep me," and twenty of Sir Edward Denny's, including "What grace, O Lord, and beauty shone" and "Light of the lonely pilgrim's heart."

The interest in German Hymnody had been quickened by the good work done in Frances E. Cox's *Sacred Hymns from the German* (1841) and Henry J. Buckoll's *Hymns translated from the German* (1842). This found expression in the *Psalms and Hymns, partly original, partly selected* (Cambridge, 1851) of Arthur T. Russell, in which the German hymns played a very large part, the Latin a very small one; the very arrangement of the hymns being based on old Lutheran hymn books. In 1854 appeared Richard Massie's *Martin Luther's Spiritual Songs,* and the first of four parts (1854-1862) of *Hymns from the Land of Luther* by Jane Borthwick and her sister Sarah Findlater. In 1855 and 1858 Catherine Winkworth published the first and second series of her *Lyra Germanica,* and was to follow them in 1863 with *The Chorale Book for England.*

The work of this group of translators, and notably of Miss Winkworth, has secured a firm place in English hymn books for a number of German hymns.

German hymns and chorals had a part in the *Church Psalter and Hymn Book* of William Mercer of Sheffield (1854). Much interest in its preparation was taken by James Montgomery, in his last years an attendant of Mercer's church. This was the most successful of all the books of the decade, from the standpoint of actual use; partly because it contained the prose Psalter set for chanting and the tunes of the hymns edited by Sir John Goss. It was used in St. Paul's Cathedral until 1871, ten years after the publication of *Hymns ancient and modern*.[27] This book represents one of the characteristic movements of the decade; a desire to get the Hymnody back into the people's hands and make it congregational. This grew partly out of observation of the hearty congregational song of dissenting churches; that of Dr. Allon's in London attracting wide attention. It was favored also by the disposition to open the naves of cathedrals for popular services, a project effected at St. Paul's in 1858.[28] The success of congregational singing of the better type required a return to the Reformation practice of including the tunes, as well as words, in the people's hymn books. This seems to have been first done in W. J. Blew's *Church Hymn and Tune Book* of 1852. But his book was impracticable. In Mercer's book of 1854 it was done effectively, and though not immediately followed, it set the permanent standard, and marks the transition to the modern type of Church of England hymnal. Godfrey Thring's *Church of England Hymn Book* of 1880 was the last one of any note to appear without music, although word editions of the others are generally furnished.

The extreme devotion to the Latin Church Hymnody exemplified in Dr. Neale, was also embodied during the decade by William J. Blew in his *Church Hymn and Tune Book*

[27]Bumpus, *English Cathedral Music*, London, n. d., vol. ii, p. 513.
[28]Bumpus, ut supra.

(1852) just referred to. He thus greatly enriched the store of versions of Latin hymns without appreciably affecting the actual situation.

The key to the actual future of the Church Hymnody was held by a group of men of Tractarian beliefs and practices, who shared Neale's and Blew's sense of the unique position of the hymns of the ancient and undivided Church, but who at the same time realized that many modern hymns, including some by dissenters, were dear to the people and spiritually effective; and that a selection could be made of such as might be used without any real violation of liturgical propriety.

In such a spirit G. Cosby White published in 1852 his *Hymns and Introits,* F. H. Murray in the same year *A Hymnal for use in the English Church* (Mozley), as also Cooke and Denton their *Church Hymnal* (London: J. Whitaker). They were followed by Keble's and Earl Nelson's *Salisbury Hymn Book* of 1857. These were all men in thorough sympathy with the development of church ideals and practices that had now proceeded for a generation, and most anxious for the adequate expression of these ideals' in a popular Church Hymnody, for which the materials were now at hand in abundant measure. But while at one in opinion and judgment, they were in fact competitors for the adoption of their several books. Each book prevented the success of the other in their own circle, and no one could force its way into the majority of parishes, which adhered to books representing a lower type of churchmanship.

The way out was found by the Rev. Francis H. Murray, a Kentish rector. Through the Rev. Sir Henry Williams Baker, he secured an agreement with the proprietors of competing hymn books that he and they should withdraw their respective books, and join in the preparation of a common collection of "Hymns ancient and modern"; and through advertising in *The Guardian,* he secured the promise of 200 clergymen to co-operate. The Committee began work in 1859; and in 1861 issued *Hymns ancient and modern for use in the services of the Church: with accompanying tunes compiled and arranged by William Henry Monk* (London: Novello and Co.), containing 273 hymns, with accompanying tunes, with provision for days of the week, feasts, fasts and services of the Prayer Book, occasions and saints days, including the Annunciation and Purification of "the Blessed Virgin Mary," and a group of 67 "General Hymns." There were 132 versions of Latin hymns, mostly altered, 10 of German hymns, 12 original hymns, and 119 English hymns already in use.[29]

The success of this book has had no parallel, except in the case of Dr. Watts and of the Wesleyan Hymnody. Like these earlier instances its influence went far beyond the sphere of Hymnody. It became an effective means, in the hands of the people who used it, for spreading broadcast not only high church views and practices but the high church atmosphere. But in Hymnody its part in establishing, as it did, the type and tone of the representative Church of England Hymnody, and its influence on the Hymnody of other denominations, entitle its publication to rank as one of the great events in the history of the Hymnody of the English-speaking Churches.

In its immediate reception hostility of course mingled with appreciation,[30] and there are reminiscences of serious disturbances ensuing upon attempts to introduce it. But there must have been a large body of clergy already prepared to welcome it; for in the first three years its sales reached 350,000. Then came the Appendix of 1868, the revised edition of 1875, the complete edition of 1889, and the recent revision of 1904. An official inquiry, made about 1895, showed that in 13,639 churches no less than 10,340 used *Hymns ancient and modern*. At the same date the

---

[29]For the full history and contents of *Hymns ancient and modern,* see the "Historical Edition" (London, 1909).

[30]*E. g.* Edw. Harper's *Strictures on Hymns ancient and modern and on the Appendix to that work* (London, n. d., 3 editions) aimed to disclose its "treason to the Church of England."

book was used in 28 cathedrals, almost universally in the Scottish Episcopal churches, and universally throughout the Army and Navy. These facts prepare us to accept the statement that its circulation by the end of 1912 reached the amazing total of more than 60,000,000 copies. The further growth of this circulation has been affected, temporarily at least, by a refusal of the churches to accept the last revision, on the ground mainly of omissions or alterations of familiar hymns and tunes and a superfluity of chorals and plain song.[31]

If we seek the cause of this success, it appears that it was partly predetermined. The ideal of a "Catholic" worship involved a liturgical Hymnody. This had been already provided by many books. But it involved also the ideal of uniformity, and in its interests a number of the accustomed books had been withdrawn, and those using them committed to the new book. And the book itself answered the demands of the moderate High Churchmen: viz., that the daily and Sunday and sacramental and saints' day services should be covered by the appropriate ancient hymns, and that a body of modern hymns should be provided for general use. And with the principle of growth recognized by successive revisions, the book continued to satisfy them. The opposition made to the book brought it to the universal attention of the laity, to many of whom the ideal of ancient hymns was thus first practically presented, and they in increasing numbers responded to it.

It is true that *Hymns ancient and modern* never became the hymnal of the entire Church of England. But it laid down the lines of Hymnody for the whole Church, on which even the hymnals of the Evangelical party have been content to advance. Of these the most distinguished by far is *The Hymnal Companion to the Book of Common Prayer*

---

[31]To meet the flood of objections the compilers issued a defence, *The new Edition of Hymns ancient and modern: a survey of the reviews;* printed separately the tunes omitted from the new edition, and reprinted the old edition for those preferring it.

(1870) edited by Bishop Bickersteth, on the plan of seeking the hymns approved by most general use, to take the place of his *Psalms and Hymns* of 1858. Its form and method and its tunes, to say the least, especially in the revisions of 1876 and 1890, owe much to *Hymns ancient and modern*. Somewhat akin is the only important collection of the Church of Ireland, *The Church Hymnal* of 1864, enlarged and authorized in 1873 and supplemented in 1891. Notable for its hymns and music, the work of Major G. A. Crawford for its indexes of writers and composers was the best of the kind that had been done.

In the Church of England in Canada *Hymns ancient and modern* found a constantly growing acceptance. *A Church Hymn Book published under the sanction of the Lord Bishop of Toronto* (Toronto, 1862; 3rd ed., 1863) and *Church Hymnal. Compiled and arranged by a committee appointed by the Bishop of Montreal* (Montreal, 1875), were of a lower sacramental tone, and with other books found considerable use; but by the end of the XIXth century *Hymns ancient and modern* was reported as in use by some seventy-five per cent of the parishes.[32] It may be added here, for the sake of completing the record, that the vogue of the English book has been brought to an end by the desire of the Canadian Church for consolidation and autonomy. The Synod of 1908 adopted and authorized a hymnal prepared by its committee of 1905; published as *The Book of Common Praise being the Hymn Book of the Church of England in Canada . . . The music edited by Sir George C. Martin* (Oxford: the University Press, 1909); and put its parishes in possession of a book hardly excelled in the care of its preparation and its fitness for service.[33]

[32] Canadian Correspondence in *The Churchman* (N. Y.) for October 10, 1908.

[33] The prefatory matter contains a full account of its genesis. A special interest of the book is its principle of "inclusiveness" of varying party views. See also the excellent *Annotated Edition* (Frowde, 1909) by James Edmund Jones, a leader in the movement for a Canadian Church Hymnal.

Within Church limits the hymn book remaining most independent of Oxford influences, carrying forward the traditions of Madan and Toplady, was Charles B. Snepp's *Songs of Grace and Glory* (London: Hunt and Co., 1872). The hymns were in three divisions,—The Trinity, the Book and Church of God, and Man; and the type of theology is that embodied in Miss Havergal's well known hymns, most of which are in it. Musically the book stood for the ideals of her father's *Old Church Psalmody* (1847), from which she prepared *Havergal's Psalmody and Century of Chants* (London, 1871) as a companion to *Songs of Grace and Glory*. *The Royal Hymnal* (London: Marlborough, n. d.) represents the party who carried their protest against *Hymns ancient and modern* and all it represents to the point of dissent, and is the authorized hymnal of the Reformed Episcopal Church. It is of the "favorite Hymn" order, professing to be gathered by plebiscite of those concerned. Its difference from the Anglican books was intensified by the refusal of their proprietors to allow the insertion of their copyrighted material.

It was open to any one in the Church of England to supply any deficiencies of *Hymns ancient and modern,* and its various editions were followed by a line of "supplements," "appendixes," and "supplemental tune books" for parochial use, as well as by numerous independent collections, of which *The Parish Hymn Book* (1863), Alford's *Year of Praise* (1867), *The Temple Church Hymn Book* (1867), Earl Nelson's *Sarum Hymnal* (1868), *The Anglican Hymn Book* (1868), Monsell's *The Parish Hymnal* (1873), *Common Praise* (1879), *The Office Hymn Book* (1889), Darling's *Hymns for the Church of England* (1889), and some others are remembered, if at all, for the sake of their contribution of some hymn or tune to the common stock.

Hymns ancient and modern became also something like a point of departure in constructing hymn books for the more extreme high church and ritualistic parties, with constantly advancing standards of doctrine and ceremonial. *The People's Hymnal* (1867) was prepared by Dr. R. F. Littledale and J. E. Vaux to furnish high sacramental hymns and to give emotional hymns combined with the more sober ancient ones for singing by the people. Dr. Neale's coadjutor, Benjamin Webb, with Canon W. Cooke, brought out *The Hymnary: a book of Church Song* (1870, 1872); the most complete manual of High Anglican Hymnody, in its provision for hour and day, times, seasons and occasions, with a view to daily "celebrations." There is great use of Latin hymns, much new material and alteration of the old, and an ecclesiastical if not monastic atmosphere remote from actual life. Its musical editor, Sir Joseph Barnby, gave it such importance as a source-book of tunes, that it is generally known as "Barnby's Hymnary." Of the hymn books providing for a worship centering in the Real Presence upon the altar *The Eucharistic Hymnal* (1877) has the most original material; but far the most elaborate is *The Altar Hymnal* (1884) prepared mainly by Miss Claudia F. Hernaman, a hymn writer and editor of several children's hymnals. It contains full materials for the choral celebration of the mass according to the "Sarum Use," with the hymns "proper of season" and "common."

5. THE ANGLICAN HYMNODY AND CHURCH MUSIC

Verse writing was as characteristic of the Tractarian propaganda as it had been of the Wesleyan, and the talent for it much more widely diffused. Keble's *The Christian Year* ushered in the Movement, and the series of poems, contributed to *The British Magazine* by Newman, Keble, Froude and others, and reprinted as *Lyra Apostolica* (1833) was contemporaneous with *Tracts for the times*. Bishop Mant's *Holydays of the Church* (1828-31) was even earlier, and Isaac Williams published *The Cathedral* in 1838, *The Baptistery* in 1842 and *The Altar* in 1847. In 1846 Keble followed up *The Christian Year* with *Lyra Innocentium*.

The motive of this earlier verse writing was not to

enrich worship, but with a view of "recalling or recommending . . . important Christian truths . . . in a way to be
forgotten." [34] And so long as the Latin hymns kept their
glamor, original hymn writing was held subsidiary to the
work of translating them. Nevertheless the new enthusiasm and ideals of worship called for new and appropriate
hymns, and the editors of hymn books and others set themselves at an early date to meet the demand. The hymns of
Joseph Anstice were published posthumously in 1836,
Bishop Mant's in 1837, the first of J. S. B. Monsell's many
volumes in 1837, Williams' *Hymns on the Catechism* in
1842, William J. Blew's in his hymn book of 1852, and
Henry Collins' *Hymns for Missions* in 1854.

The Oxford hymn writing thus (naturally) preceded
the publication of *Hymns ancient and modern,* and it would
be unjust to claim that the successive editions of that book
became the medium for the publication of Anglican hymns
in the way the *Gospel Magazine* had served for the publication of the early Evangelical hymns. It did not become
even an anthology of the new Hymnody. It is true none
the less that every important name among Anglican hymn
writers is represented in one or other edition of *Hymns
ancient and modern,*[35] that it was the means of introducing
these men to the church at large, and that it still affords
the most convenient approach to a numbering of the new
Anglican school of hymn writers.

The largest contributor to the first edition of *Hymns
ancient and modern* (1861) was its editor, Sir Henry Williams Baker, but his "The King of Love my Shepherd is"
did not appear till 1868. Of the Oxford school (apart
from translations) Keble had eight pieces, Neale four,
Henry Collins two ("Jesu, meek and lowly" and "Jesu,
my Lord, my God, my All"), Joseph Anstice two (including "O Lord, how happy should we be"), Emma Toke

[34] Preface to *Lyra Apostolica.*
[35] William J. Blew, R. R. Chope, and Greville Phillimore are possible
exceptions.

two ("Glory to Thee, O Lord" and "Thou hast gone up
on high"); and the following one each:—Cecil F. Alexander ("The roseate hues of early dawn"), R. M. Benson,
Edward Churton, W. Chatterton Dix ("As with gladness
men of old"), Henry Downton, John H. Gurney ("Lord,
as to Thy dear cross we flee), W. Walsham How, Bishop
Mant, J. E. Millard, Edward Osler, George R. Prynne,
William J. Irons, G. H. Smyttan, William Whiting ("Eternal Father, strong to save"), Gilbert Rorison, W. B.
Heathcote and Thomas Whytehead.

Of this group Keble is generally regarded as the founder
of Anglican Hymnody, and Neale is important even apart
from his translations; Mrs. Alexander attained something
like fame as a writer for children; Chatterton Dix reached
high distinction, as did Bishop How both as writer and co-
editor of the S. P. C. K. hymnals; and most of the others
wrote hymns still in use.

The new contributors to the 1868 Appendix were Sabine
Baring Gould ("Now the day is over") whose picturesque
"Onward, Christian soldiers" was also included; Henry
Twells ("At even, ere the sun was set"), Lawrence Tuttiett
("O quickly come, dread Judge of all"), Mrs. Eliza S.
Alderson, J. J. Daniel, William Bright, and V. S. C. Coles.
Of Anglican writers whom it brought into wider use were
Christopher Wordsworth ("O day of rest and gladness"),
whose *The Holy Year* (1862), only a year later than
Hymns ancient and modern, has an important place, not as
a hymn book and not only for its original hymns, but for
the influence of its preface, insisting on the conformity of
hymns to Scripture, and urging that liturgical restraint
should exclude the "I" hymns in favor of the "we" of a
corporate body; Samuel J. Stone ("The Church's one
Foundation," a masterpiece of didactic Hymnody, and
"Weary of earth and laden with my sin," transcending
"liturgical" limits); E. H. Plumptre ("O Light, whose
beams illumine all," and "Thine arm, O Lord, in days of
old"); John Ellerton ("Saviour, again to Thy dear Name

we raise" and "This is the day of light"), more intimately
associated with the S. P. C. K. *Church Hymns,* and possibly
the best of the Liturgical hymn writers;[36] Godfrey Thring
("Saviour, blessed Saviour," "Fierce raged the tempest o'er
the deep," "The radiant morn hath passed away"), Mary
F. Maude ("Thine for ever, God of love"), and Lewis
Hensley ("Thy kingdom come, O God"). The inclusion
of Newman's "Lead, kindly Light" set to music by Dr.
Dykes, was an event in itself.

Of the writers of hymns added in the 1875 edition of
Hymns ancient and modern, William D. Maclagan ("Lord,
when Thy Kingdom comes, remember me") is best known;
but the hymns most widely copied are J. E. Bode's "O Jesu,
I have promised," Caroline M. Noel's "At the Name of
Jesus," I. Gregory Smith's "By Jesus' grave on either
hand," George S. Hodge's "Hosanna we sing, like the
children dear," Archer T. Gurney's "Christ is risen; Christ
is risen," and W. St. H. Bourne's "The sower went forth
sowing." A group of men better known as translators
were represented by original hymns,—John Chandler, J. W.
Hewett, A. W. Chatfield, Gerard Moultrie, James R. Woodford, and D. T. Morgan. A department of Metrical
Litanies by R. F. Littledale, Thomas B. Pollock, and the
editors, was added in this edition. It gave currency to a
type of hymn, then comparatively new, which best fulfills
the definition of a hymn as Liturgical Verse, and has resulted in the general acceptance of the new type.

The "Supplemental Hymns" of 1889 gave recognition as
hymn writers to Archbishop Benson, Dean Hole, John
Julian, F. W. Farrar, F. T. Palgrave and the picturesque
R. S. Hawker; and for the first time included hymns by
the veterans, J. S. B. Monsell ("Fight the good fight")
and Edward Harland. It gave status to Dorothy Blom-
field's Wedding Hymn, "O perfect Love, all human thought
transcending," and confirmed that of E. A. Dayman's "The

[36]For Ellerton's hymns and the history of *Church Hymns,* see H.
Housman, *John Ellerton,* S. P. C. K., 1896.

Lord be with us when we sail," and Francis Potts' "Angel-voices, ever singing." Of the contributors or newer hymn writers Arthur J. Mason and Claudia F. Hernaman belong with the extreme school of Anglicanism; Jackson Mason shows most vigor as a translator; while W. H. Turton's "Thou, Who at Thy first Eucharist didst pray" has become a favorite hymn of sacramental unity.

It is only by such particularizing that one gains any real sense of the extent and importance of the contribution of the Oxford school to English Hymnody, and of the elements it has infused into the English Hymn; and incidentally of the quite unparalleled part which *Hymns ancient and modern* has played in the development of modern Hymnody. In appraising this influence we must add also its share in acclimating the Latin, Greek and German hymns and in making accessible the work of the group of men who, like Newman, left the English Church for the Roman, such as F. W. Faber, Edward Caswall, E. Oakeley, Henry Collins and M. Brydges.

To the Hymnody of Christian Experience as carried forward by the Evangelical school within the Church of England during the period under review *Hymns ancient and modern* was inevitably less hospitable; although its inclusions of Charlotte Elliott, Dean Alford, Bishop Bickersteth and Miss Havergal, gave to the great body of the Church its only knowledge of their hymns.

These four are the outstanding names of the Evangelical school. Henry Alford published hymns in *The Christian Observer* as early as 1830; printed "In token that thou shalt not fear" in *The British Magazine* in 1832; his Harvest Hymn, "Come, ye thankful people, come" in his *Psalms and Hymns* (1844) for Wymeswold; and many more in his *The Year of Praise* (1867) for Canterbury Cathedral. Though not sacramentarian, his views and hymns were distinctively liturgical. Hugh Stowell of Manchester contributed many hymns to his *Selection of Psalms and Hymns* (1831) in its numerous editions, and his son, Canon

Thomas A. Stowell, carried forward both the *Selection* and the hymn writing. Charlotte Elliott printed hymns in *The Invalid's Hymn Book,* in her brother's somewhat important *Psalms and Hymns for public, private and social worship* (1835) and in later volumes of her own work. She was the typical Evangelical, with the devoutness and plaintive note of Anne Steele and a better style. Her ministry in the sick room is beyond estimate: her best known hymns are the three in *Hymns ancient and modern*:—"Just as I am," "My God and Father, while I stray," "Christian, seek not yet repose." Julia Ann Marshall's (who married H. V. Elliott) *Poems on sacred subjects* (1832) is remembered by her "Great Creator, who this day." Miss Anna L. Waring's *Hymns and Meditations* (1854, 1863) share the method and beauty of Miss Elliott's work.

Bishop John Charles Ryle became the leader of the Evangelicals, though his *Spiritual Songs* (11th ed. 1860), *The additional Hymn Book* (1875), and *Hymns for the Church on Earth* (1860), had only a minor importance in its song. But the great task of furnishing an adequate hymn book fell to Bishop Bickersteth. His *Hymnal Companion,* already referred to, practically superseded all other Evangelical books and by 1893 was used in 1478 churches.[37] His hymns of sentiment are represented by "Peace, perfect peace," and "Till He come! O let the word." To this time belongs Frances Ridley Havergal, the most voluminous, most diffuse and best loved of the Evangelical school, whose hymns were gathered into volumes ranging from 1869 to 1883. Her "I gave My life for thee," "Take my life, and let it be" and "Lord, speak to me that I may speak," reveal her supreme devotion to the spiritual life; "Golden harps are sounding" is her nearest approach to the Liturgical Hymn.

William Pennefather furnished *Hymns original and selected, by W. P.* (1872) for his Mildmay Conference,

[37] G. R. Balleine, *A History of the Evangelical Party,* London, 1908, p. 282.

and quite a Keswick school of hymn writers is represented in J. Mountain's *Hymns of Consecration and Faith* (n. d. c. 1876); many of them followers of Miss Havergal or of the "Gospel Song" model. Some of the hymns of Bishop H. C. G. Moule, included in his prose books of devotion, are also favorites of the Keswick Convention. The hymns of Charles D. Bell, often of considerable beauty, have not gone much beyond his *Appendix to Walker's Psalms and Hymns* (1873) and that to the *Hymnal Companion* (1884), his *Hymns for the Church and Chamber* (1882), and his comely *Church of England Hymnal* (1895). The hymns of W. M. H. Aitken are mainly connected with the recent evangelistic movement in the Church of England and found in the mission hymn books.[38] It may be that in course of time they will be regarded as indicating a development of Church of England Hymnody as notable as that effected by the Anglicans.

The Anglican Hymnody as presented in *Hymns ancient and modern* could not have won the acceptance it did apart from the music with which it was associated; for a hymn has no mission until an acceptable musical setting is found. This finds illustration in Newman's "Lead, kindly Light," which was written in 1833, but whose popularity began only when Dykes' "Lux Benigna" was set to it in the Appendix of 1868; a fact of which the Cardinal was well aware.[39]

In the years preceding *Hymns ancient and modern* much had been done for Congregational Song. Henry Parr in his *Church of England Psalmody* (1847) investigated and recovered the older English psalm tunes, and W. H. Havergal in his *Old Church Psalmody* (1847) and Dr. Maurice in his *Choral Harmony* (1854) introduced many of the German chorals. The "Society for promoting Church Music" dealt especially with the choir parts of the service,

[38]For these see his article in Julian's *Dictionary*, 2nd suppl., p. 1672.
[39]J. T. Fowler, *Life and Letters of John Bacchus Dykes,* London, 1897, p. 104.

with some interest in the movement to set plain song melodies to Latin hymns which culminated in Helmore's *Accompanying Harmonies to the Hymnal noted* (1852-58). But
its periodical, *The Parish Choir,* held aloof from congregational hymn singing, because of the conflicting opinions
involved and its own question of the legality of the practice.[40]   Eventually it fell in with the current movement
and published a collection of hymn and psalm tunes.

The older leaders, Goss, Elvey, S. S. Wesley and others,
based their own composition upon the solid psalm tunes,
but a newer type of hymn tune, based on the secular part-
song of the period, came to the fore in thirteen tunes contributed to John Grey's *Hymnal* (1857) by John B. Dykes,
precentor of Durham cathedral.   Hearing of the proposed
Hymns ancient and modern, Dykes sent seven tunes including "Horbury," "Melita" and "Hollingside," which
were accepted by its musical editor, William H. Monk;[41]
and from first to last fifty-five of his tunes were included
in the book.[42]   These tunes, with Monk's own rich contributions and those of Elvey, Gauntlett, Redhead, Reinagle
and others, with Monk's choice and arrangement of ancient
melodies and psalm tunes, crystallized the musical tendencies
of the time into a definite form of Anglican hymn tune,
with restrained melodies and close harmonies wonderfully
adapted to liturgical worship, and yet appealing to the taste
of the people.   These tunes constituted the immediate appeal
of the book not only within but beyond the bounds of the
Church.   Into the choir lofts of a great many dissenting
churches it was introduced simply as a tunebook, from
which to render their own hymns, but in many homes the
hymns to which they were set also became familiar.   The
hymns as well as the tunes of the Anglican school soon
began to find their way into the books of the dissenting
Churches and the Church of Scotland. And, largely through

[40]*The Parish Choir,* Oct. 1847, p. 21.
[41]Fowler, p. 71.
[42]*Ibid.,* p. 321.

the medium of *Hymns ancient and modern,* the Oxford
Movement has become one of the marked factors in giving
its present form and manner and contents to the Hymnody
and the hymn books of these Churches, and of those across
the sea.

II

OXFORD INFLUENCES ON THE HYMNODY OF ENGLISH DISSENT

1. LITURGICAL IDEALS IN CONGREGATIONALIST AND BAPTIST WORSHIP (1861-1900)

Even from the musical side it would be difficult to
measure with actual precision the influence of the Oxford
Movement upon the dissenting Churches of England. We
must remember that *Hymns ancient and modern* itself was
to some extent a product of the middle century movement
to improve church music in which dissent had a considerable part. The lectures of John Hullah, and the great
Psalmody classes of the Rev. J. J. Waite, were to a large
extent among Nonconformists, and Dr. Allon led in an
actual demonstration of the possibilities of Congregational
Song at his Union Chapel. Dr. Gauntlett made himself a
connecting link between the Church and dissent, editing the
second part of Waite's *The Hallelujah* (1849), leading the
worship at Union Chapel, and editing Dr. Allon's *The
Congregational Psalmist* (1858), of which over 50,000
copies were circulated.[43] The movement moreover had
the announced purpose of giving not only more simplicity
but also an ecclesiastical tone to the music.[44] But when,
with *Hymns ancient and modern,* the movement developed
into an Anglican school and crystallized into a distinctive
Anglican type of hymn tune, it speedily became recognized
by dissent as well as in the Church as the prevailing school

[43]Preface of 1867.
[44]Preface to *The Hallelujah* (1849), p. iv.

of church music. The evidence of this is not merely the appropriation by dissenting Churches of the Anglican tunes but their putting their successive hymn books into the hands of the Anglican leaders for musical editing. For this purpose Dr. Allon had the services of Dr. Gauntlett, and, for his last revision of *The Congregational Psalmist Hymnal*, of Monk himself. The Presbyterians chose Dr. Rimbault to edit their hymn book of 1866. And when the Wesleyan Methodists issued the *New Supplement* to Wesley's *Collection*, they turned over its musical editing to Dr. Gauntlett, then to George Cooper, and, at his death, to Dr. Hopkins; notwithstanding the distinctiveness of their own musical traditions and their wish that the best of these should be preserved.

In most of the denominations the introduction of the Anglican chant, set to prose Psalms and the Prayer Book canticles, followed that of the hymn tunes; also the choir-anthem, and in many churches anthems rendered by a trained congregation. As illustrating the development we may take the later authorized praise books of two denominations, already referred to, *The Congregational Church Hymnal* (1888) and *The Baptist Church Hymnal* (1900). They are very complete and in construction identical, each in three sections. Section 1 is a rich collection of hymns set to an even larger collection of tunes in which the Anglican standard prevails. Section 2 is the "Litanies and Chants," a collection of metrical litanies and pointed Psalms, Scriptures, "ancient Hymns of the Church" etc. The Baptist is the fuller, with eight settings of the Sanctus, five of Kyrie, Baptismal and offertory sentences and Amens, with special provision for Christmas, Good Friday, Easter and Whitsuntide. The 3rd section of each book is a large selection of anthems and of the Prayer Book canticles set anthem-wise.

Comparing these authorized praise books with Dr. Watts' "System of Praise" that once sufficed in both denominations, it would be idle to pretend that no change has come

over the ideals and practice of Nonconformist worship, or
to raise any question as to the influences that have brought
it about. It was, more than anything else, the Anglican
Music that brought into and diffused through these Churches
a liturgical atmosphere in which the old simplicities with-
ered, and from the little collections of verses which were
the praise books of an earlier time developed and sustained
these stately structures, in which indeed the music so dominates as almost to obscure the words. There is special
significance also in the fact that neither denomination had
further need to call upon Anglican musicians, but from the
generation now grown up within its own ranks each was
able to produce musicians fully capable of giving an Anglican setting to its worship.

Turning now to the influence of the Oxford Hymnody,
on its literary side, upon Nonconformist ideals and practice,
it could not be claimed that it spread its high sacramentarian doctrine or that it supplanted the more subjective
Hymnody of dissent by the Liturgical Hymn. But it did
nevertheless recommend the observance of first the feasts
and more gradually the fasts of the Christian Year. And
in doing so it infused more of the festal tone into the
Lord's Supper, which had become in reality the Nonconformist Good Friday and the special occasion for the
Passion Hymn. The Oxford Hymnody was a Liturgical
Hymnody that centred at the altar as distinctively as Nonconformist Hymnody was an Evangelical Hymnody that
centred in the personal experience of salvation. And the
surprise in the case is not that Nonconformity should have
found a new ground for dissent in the sacramentarian
teachings of the Oxford Hymns, but that it should have
been open-hearted enough to perceive much that was good
and elevating in the new Hymnody and to utilize it freely
for its own ends. In this way Nonconformist Hymnody
was immensely enriched, and though not transformed was
happily broadened out on the distinctively worshipful side
of Church Song.

Dr. Allon's *Supplemental Hymns for public worship* (1868), published a year later than *The People's Hymnal,* has for its preface an *apologia* which may serve as a permanent record of the appreciative but strictly discriminating spirit in which Nonconformity began its appropriation of the new Hymnody of the Oxford Revival as a desirable "supplement" to its own:—

"The remarkable development of Hymnology during the last few years—in the Romish and Anglican Churches especially, in which hitherto it has been neglected and disparaged—has produced innumerable writers of hymns, of various degrees of excellence. It is in these churches chiefly, strange to say, that both the poetry and the music of our church-song are just now threatened with a corruption as meretricious as that which, in former times, was charged upon Puritans and Methodists. But just as the latter could also boast great singers like Dr. Watts and Charles Wesley, with whose hymns no book of church-song could now dispense; so modern Romanists and Anglicans have contributed very beautiful and very precious additions to the worship of the church: first, by fine translations of old Church Hymns; and next, by original compositions of great fervour and excellence. Many of these have so rapidly and so deservedly become popular, that it is very generally felt to be desirable that they should be available for use in churches. . . . From the unhappy polemics that now array churches in hostile parties, and that are specially associated with rival Hymnals, the Free Churches of Great Britain are happily exempt; no suspicion of sinister proclivities attaches itself to them, because they use hymns derived from Romish or Anglican sources. They are able, therefore, to introduce into their worship whatever, either in words or in music, may contribute to their devoutness and joy. . . . The Sacramentarian developments of late years have supplied a great number of tender and devout Hymns for the Lord's Table, where, if anywhere, sanctified affection demands free expression. Of these I have freely availed myself; avoiding, I hope, every taint of the fatal heresy for which, chiefly, at the Reformation, English Christians forsook the Church of Rome."

2. THE PRESBYTERIANS ENRICH ANGLICAN MUSIC (1866)

Inquiry as to the materials of Praise began in the Synod of 1841,[45] but throughout the Church there was much prejudice against hymns,[46] and nothing was accomplished

[45] *Acts and proceedings of the Synod,* 1841, p. 20.
[46] See "Psalms and Hymns" in *The English Presbyterian Messenger,* Feb. 1849.

till the authorization in 1856[47] and publication in 1857 of a
small collection of *Paraphrases and Hymns* to supplement
the Scottish *Psalms of David in metre*. It was one of
those meagre and timid collections with which each of the
Presbyterian Churches in Great Britain began its tentative
hymn singing, and it satisfied nobody. Introduced by the
session of Regent Square Church, the opposition was so
loud that a count of heads became expedient,[48] and then a
course of lectures by the pastor, Dr. James Hamilton, to
justify the session. Dr. Hamilton became the great champion of hymns, publishing his Regent Square lectures as
The Psalter and Hymn Book (London: Nisbet, 1865), and
the leader of the hymn lovers in their dissatisfaction with
the collection of 1857. When the demand for an enlarged
Hymnody grew widespread, but Synodical action remained
hesitant, he formed with others a voluntary company[49]
(with the tacit consent of a majority of the members of
Synod), who prepared and presented in 1866 a collection
of psalms and hymns which the Synod looked into and
authorized[50] for publication and use as *Psalms and Hymns
for divine worship. London, James Nisbet and Co., 21
Berner's street, W. 1866*. The psalms were the Scottish
Version unaltered; the hymns numbered 521.

Dr. Hamilton had hopes that English Presbyterianism
might prove a refuge for the Protestant element in the
Church of England,[51] and his book made no concessions
to the principles or methods of the Oxford party. By
including 43 of the old Paraphrases, some 40 alternate
Psalm versions and 50 of the hymns of Horatius Bonar, he
even imparted something of a Presbyterian flavor to the
Hymnody. But he did not hesitate to use Anglican hymns
or tunes he regarded as suiting his purpose, and from his

[47]*Acts and proceedings,* 1856, pp. 166, 167, 169.
[48]W. Arnot, *Life of James Hamilton,* London, 1870, pp. 573, 574.
[49]*Life,* p. 570.
[50]*Acts and proceedings,* 1866, pp. 143, 163.
[51]*Life,* pp. 195-197.

standpoint of an evangelical theology and a warm devotion his collection was excellent. The proportion of its contents still in active use is great, but the surpassing merit of the book is in the tunes to which the hymns were set by Dr. Rimbault. In its gatherings from English and German sources, its originals and harmonizations, *Psalms and Hymns* was a good second to *Hymns ancient and modern*. Among the tunes it has contributed to common worship are "Regent Square," "Lancashire," "Intercession," "Crucifier," "Rutherford," "Heathlands," "Everton," "Bentley," Smart's "London" and "St. Leonard," and Dykes' "Faith"; to say nothing of its arrangements and harmonizations. Its wide influence upon its successors in the choice and settings of hymns has been little understood; partly perhaps because in the succeeding hymnal of its own Church, it was not acknowledged as the source even of the tunes with which it had enriched all Churches.

In 1876 The Presbyterian Church in England united with congregations of the United Presbyterian Church of Scotland to form "The Presbyterian Church of England." The United Presbyterian section kept on using the then recent *The Presbyterian Hymnal* of their mother Church, while *Psalms and Hymns* kept its place in the English section, and was also widely used in Presbyterian churches through the British colonies.[52] In the interests of uniformity, rather than from any pressing need, the Synod of 1881 appointed a committee to prepare a new church hymnal, with the Rev. W. Rigby Murray of Manchester in the chair which the late Dr. Hamilton had filled so well.

The new book appeared, apart from the Psalms, as *Church Praise: with tunes* (London: Nisbet, 1882). The number of hymns is substantially unchanged, but they are better arranged, and much new material is introduced to replace hymns that had gone out of vogue. A large selection of hymns for the young is a new feature, and these with some Gospel Hymns modify the musical standard;

[52]W. Rigby Murray in Julian's *Dictionary*, p. 908.

which otherwise is well maintained, and more distinctively Anglican; the number of tunes from *Hymns ancient and modern* being 55 as against 5 in *Psalms and Hymns*. An appendix of ancient hymns and canticles, sanctuses and anthems, also testifies to Anglican influences. In 1870 the Church had at last withdrawn its former rulings against instrumental music, and took henceforth a somewhat leading place in cultivating Congregational Song. *The Bible Psalter: being the Authorized Version of the Psalms pointed for chanting, by Sir Herbert Oakeley* (London: Nisbet, n. d.) suggests surely the natural way of restoring the Psalter to its place of honor in Presbyterian worship. It seems regrettable that the situation should have been complicated by issuing *The Revised Psalter* (1886) as an attempt to adapt the Revised Version to chanting. In a XXth century revision of *Church Praise* (London: Nisbet, 1907) some selected metrical psalms were appended; indicating not so much a reversion to that form of praise as its disuse to a degree making it hardly worth while to carry a separate Psalter to church.

3. CATHOLIC APOSTOLIC HYMNODY (1864)

Dr. Hamilton was the successor of Edward Irving at Regent Square. Otherwise the connection of the Church formed by Irving's followers with Presbyterianism seems slight. The Catholic Apostolic Church drew its liturgical ideals from the same fountains as the Oxford Reformers, and its elaborate ritual reproduces more closely than theirs the liturgy of the Latin Church. Of this hymns were regarded perhaps rather in the light of an appendage than as a constituent part. But in 1864 the Church was provided with an authorized collection, *Hymns for the use of the churches* (London: Strangeways and Walden), containing 205 hymns, enlarged to 320 in 1871. The hymns are largely Anglican and Roman, with some from the German, and a few of Dr. Bonar's. Of its original contributors, the compiler, Mr. E. W. Eddis, alone allows his name to be known. His version from the Greek, "O brightness of the Immortal Father's face" has found a place in numerous collections, and others by him are of decided merit.[53] In the Catholic Apostolic liturgy the Liturgical Movement may perhaps be regarded as reaching its fullest development, but in respect of Hymnody the honors remain with the Anglican *Altar Hymnal* as most definitely embodying the conception of a Liturgical Hymn Book.

4. SWEDENBORGIAN HYMNODY (1790-1880)

The New Church had no authorized hymn book till the appearance of *Hymns for the use of the New Church signified by the New Jerusalem in the Revelation. Compiled by order of the General Conference. London: T. Goyder and H. C. Hodson, 1824.* It was intended as a hand book of the new faith, and was largely conditioned by the didactic motive. Natural prominence was given to hymns of New Church writers; of whom Joseph Proud had published *Hymns and Spiritual Songs for the use of the Lord's New Church* (London, 1790); Manoah Sibly his *Hymns and Spiritual Songs* in 1802; and F. M. Hodson his *Original Hymns* in 1819. The 600 hymns were chosen or altered to put the emphasis on the doctrine that Christ is the only object of faith and worship.

The Church was liturgical, in the sense of favoring formal as against free worship, and the *Hymns* came to be bound up with *The Morning and Evening Services as contained in the "Liturgy";* but the liturgy was largely independent of the *Book of Common Prayer.*

A not very successful effort to introduce versions of Latin and German hymns occasioned the *Supplement of Hymns for the New Church. Compiled by order of the General Conference. London: James Speirs, 1872.* And in 1880 this gave way to a new hymn book, with the same

---

[53]For the music at the Gordon Square Church, see J. Spencer Curwen, *Studies in Worship Music,* 1st series, 3rd ed., n. d., p. 397.

title as that of 1824 (London: James Speirs), not greatly differing in type or method; but availing itself "of such outbirths of Sacred Song as the New Age, the Second Advent of our Lord Jesus Christ, has produced in the English language." The book is interesting and worthy, and less Anglican in manner than many of its contemporaries. Of later New Church writers represented, William Mason, who published *Hymns of Spiritual Experience* in 1840, is most conspicuous; and over all is the trail of the editorial blue pencil, altering alike the hymns whether of the old Church or the New.

III

OXFORD INFLUENCES IN SCOTLAND AND IRELAND: PRESBYTERIAN HYMN SINGING

When we recall that in 1839 John Keble introduced his metrical version of the Psalms with the remark that psalm singing had prevailed so long and so universally in the Church of England "that there is small hope at present of changing it," [54] it is not surprising that Scotland proved tenacious of a practice based on conscientious scruples as well as upon national tradition.

1. THE CHANGES IN UNITED PRESBYTERIAN HYMNODY (1848-1877)

The United Presbyterian Church was made up of the elements most favorable to hymn singing. We have noted the adoption of a little selection of *Sacred Songs and Hymns* by the Synod of Relief as early as 1794. It was forty-six years later when another member of the Scottish secession, the United Secession Church, began to consider a selection of paraphrases and hymns for its congregations, and had actually printed it[55] when negotiations began for

[54]Keble's preface, p. viii.
[55]See C. G. McCrie, *The Public Worship of Presbyterian Scotland*, Edinburgh, 1892, p. 333.

union with the Relief Synod. Within five days of that union's consummation the United Presbyterian Church appointed a committee on Psalmody, who recommended that a book of hymns be prepared, published a draft in 1848, and in 1851 another which was authorized and published as *Hymn Book of the United Presbyterian Church* (Edinburgh: Oliphant, 1851). So little was the Church then moved by liturgical considerations that the 460 hymns were arranged in the order of the Scripture passages on which they were based.

The book as a whole was not popular, and was superseded by *The Presbyterian Hymnal with accompanying tunes* (Edinburgh, 1877) which had been authorized in 1876. In this the Anglican influences were most marked. The book opens with Heber's "Holy! holy! holy!" and in the list of acknowledgments the first is to Mrs. Alexander, the second to the editor of *Hymns ancient and modern*. The hymns are reduced to 366, making its homiletical employment impracticable; the prose *Te Deum and Gloria in Excelsis*, with Scripture passages pointed for chanting, are included; full use is made of Neale's and other versions from the Greek and Latin; Dr. Hamilton Macgill furnishes additional versions, and Dr. Wm. B. Robertson a new translation of *Dies Irae;* and Dr. Henry Smart is put in charge of the music. So great is the change of atmosphere that one would assume that the hymn books of 1851 and 1877 were representative of different denominations.

2. THE HYMNODY OF THE KIRK FALLS INTO THE HANDS
   OF THE LITURGICAL PARTY (1845-1885)

In the Established Church nothing had been done since the sufferance of *Translations and Paraphrases*. But there was always unrest, and one of the periodic movements "to enlarge the Psalmody" began in the General Assembly with the appointment of a committee on Psalmody in 1845, one on Paraphrases in 1847, and an overture referred to them jointly in 1852 concerning "an authorized collection of sacred hymns." Their *Hymns connected with passages of Sacred Scripture, collected by a committee of the General Assembly, and prepared for presentation on Friday, May 26, 1854,* and a succeeding committee's *Hymns connected with passages of Sacred Scripture, and adapted for public worship. Selected by a committee of the General Assembly of the Church of Scotland from a collection made by a former committee. May 1855,* were small (the latter containing only 25) and ineffective. Then in 1860 another committee presented a collection of 85 hymns, printed as *Hymns collected by the committee of the General Assembly on Psalmody for presentation in May 1860: David Arnot, D.D., convener* (Edinburgh: Paton and Ritchie, 1860). Revised and enlarged to 97 numbers by still another committee, this became *Hymns for public worship collected by the committee of the General Assembly on Psalmody. For presentation in May 1861. David Arnot, D.D., convener.* In expressly allowing this selection to be printed, the Assembly may be held as now authorizing for the first time (1861) the use of hymns in the Church of Scotland, but from the selection itself it withheld its sanction,[56] and the book was adopted in very few congregations.[57] It was subjected to a revision and republished in 1864, but even so with no more authority from the Assembly than is implied in permission to publish it. Poor as it was in selection and arrangement, and garbled as were its texts, it was quite largely adopted by congregations who wished to sing hymns, and had to accept what was offered.[58]

The importance of the movement brought to this stage of forwardness does not lie in the hymn book which embodies it, but in what that hymn book represents,—the authorized singing of hymns in the worship of the Church of Scotland. The hymn book survived but a few years, but the new status of the Hymn proved permanent. The

[56]McCrie, p. 332.
[57]*Cf.* A. K. H. Boyd in *Blackwood's Magazine,* May, 1889, p. 660.
[58]Dr. Sprott in McCrie, p. 332, note 38.

moving causes behind this change are not readily got at. The movement was not liturgical. Dr. Lee, the leader in liturgical "innovations," and who actually violated all Scottish precedent by introducing a harmonium into Greyfriars, fought and virtually won the battle for instrumental music, but was indifferent to metrical hymns. He thought the hymns of Scripture in prose furnished adequate materials for praise, and that the really excellent modern hymns did not number a score.[59] To some extent the old desire for evangelical songs may have been behind the movement, though the psalm singers denied it, and claimed it to be brought about to gratify the taste of "individuals and small parties," "chiefly enthusiastic lovers of music."[60] And no doubt the Romantic Movement and the improved standard of taste it disseminated is partly responsible for the distaste of a new generation for the old Psalmody and its preference for hymns; though Sir Walter himself was a confessed admirer of "Rous' Version."

It is to be understood that the movement was to enlarge the Psalmody and not to discard it, and that the hymn book proposed was a supplement to, and not a substitute for, the old psalm book. Even so, to those who cherished their recollections of the severe simplicities and spiritual fervor of the earlier Psalmody, it seemed to threaten the spirituality of Scottish worship and aroused resentment and opposition. Thus the movement toward hymns encountered bitter enemies, and had also some cold friends among the committee-men charged with its interests. The lack of system and of quality, the incessant tinkering of texts, in the collections laid before the Assembly by successive committees is perhaps explained by a ruling idea on their part of compiling a group of paraphrases and hymns to take the place of the XVIIIth century *Translations and Paraphrases*

[59]Robert Lee, *The Reform of The Church of Scotland*, Edinburgh, 1864, chap. x, "Psalms and Hymns."

[60]Jas. Gibson, *The public worship of God: Hymns and hymn books*, London, 1869, p. 97.

rather than to prepare what we call a hymnal. Otherwise the contrast betwen the Scottish *Hymns for public worship* of 1861 and the English *Hymns ancient and modern* of the same year would be difficult to account for.

In the meantime a considerable number of the Scottish clergy had come under the influences of the Oxford Revival. A group of them banded themselves together in 1865 as "The Church Service Society," [61] to study the liturgies ancient and modern, and to prepare forms of worship;[62] and into the hands of these men the interests of the Hymnody of the Church of Scotland fell at once, and, in spite of much misunderstanding and criticism, remained there with very remarkable results.

The first step toward a better Hymnody was an overture to the Assembly of 1866 which Dr. A. K. H. Boyd put through his Presbytery of St. Andrews, asking for a new committee to prepare a new hymnal "on principles exactly contradictory of those on which its little predecessor had been put together," viz.: that only hymns already accepted by Christian people for their excellence be admitted, and that they be printed (when possible) just as their authors wrote them.[63] The overture was approved by an overwhelming majority of the Assembly, and the committee appointed, but with the convener of the old committee still in the chair of the new. After he had refused during a year to call the committee together, Dr. Boyd was appointed in his stead, and the work went forward with a dominant purpose that had to yield something to conflicting views in a very large committee.[64] After presenting drafts in 1868,

[61]There is a good account of this society in McCrie, pp. 341-349.

[62]See its *Euchologion: or Book of Prayers; being forms of worship issued by The Church Service Society;* 1st ed., Edinburgh, 1867; 7th ed., 1896.

[63] "A. K. H. B." in Blackwood for May 1889; "The new Hymnology of the Scottish Kirk." This vivid article best preserves the acrimonious atmosphere in which the liturgical party wrought a great change in the Church of Scotland, and gives full particulars of the compilation of *The Scottish Hymnal.*

[64] "A. K. H. B." *ut supra.*

1869 and 1870, they were authorized to revise and publish the later one. It appeared in September, 1870, as *The Scottish Hymnal: Hymns for public worship selected by a committee of the General Assembly of the Church of Scotland. Published for use in churches by authority of the General Assembly* (Edinburgh: Blackwood, 1870); and in 1872 with tunes, under the editorship of W. H. Monk who incorporated many of his arrangements and copyright tunes from *Hymns ancient and modern.* Its 200 hymns were mainly the selection of Dr. Rankin of Muthill, who also devised the title, as felicitous for the hymnal of a national church as that of *Hymns ancient and modern* was for a partisan hymnal. Of the two books *The Scottish Hymnal* was the better both in its literary standard and the purity of its texts; freed as it was from the necessity of providing liturgical verse accommodated to numerous saints' days and like occasions. Including as it did the most appealing of the hymns of the new Literary and Liturgical schools, it is indeed difficult to see how its selection could have been much bettered within its limits.

The Scottish Hymnal settled the character and type of the Hymnody of the Church of Scotland. Some years' use of it disclosed the need of enlargement, and an Appendix of 1884 prepared by the same committee, increased the number of hymns to 358, with a supplement of 86 Children's Hymns. With the new hymns incorporated in their proper places, and the whole provided with tunes under the editorship of Albert Lister Peace of Glasgow Cathedral, *The Scottish Hymnal* took its final form in 1885. The face of the new Scottish Hymnody thus presented is undoubtedly a glowing one. To some it suggested no more than a light reflected from an alien movement in another denomination and another country than Scotland: to others it seemed to spring from a new catholicity in the heart of Presbyterianism itself, a recognition and a sharing of what was best in the experiences of its fellow-Christians.

3. THE FREE CHURCH REMODELS ITS HYMN BOOK (1882)

The Free Church, which went out at the Disruption of 1843, continued the use of metrical psalms without question until 1866, when its Assembly, in response to several overtures, appointed a committee to inquire in what way the Psalmody could be enlarged without disturbing the peace of the Church.[65] Nothing more was then contemplated than a revision of the old *Translations and Paraphrases,* and the addition of some hymns;[66] but with the developed conscientiousness characterizing the Free Church, and in view of the scruples of many against uninspired hymns, the committee divided itself into three sections, to study the usage of "The Reformed Church of Scoland," the primitive rule and practice, and the doctrinal teaching of the old Paraphrases. The committee reported in 1869 that they found no Scripture principle, primitive use or Scottish law conflicting with the use of hymns, and in 1870 presented a draft of selections from *Translations and Paraphrases* and additional hymns. After some delay and revision this was approved and allowed for public use in 1872, amid much opposition and by a vote of 152 against 61.[67] It appeared in 1873 as *Psalm-Versions, Paraphrases, and Hymns* (Edinburgh, 1873), and was provided with tunes in *The Scottish Psalmody* of the same year. Its 123 hymns included 40 of the old Paraphrases, and are more important as committing the Free Church to hymn singing than as a hymn book.

An inevitable movement to enlarge the Hymnody began almost at once, and resulted in *The Free Church Hymn Book with tunes. Published by authority of the General Assembly of the Free Church of Scotland* (Paisley 1882), a collection of 387 hymns and 30 Scriptural anthems, set to music under the editorship of the eminent Anglican musician, Edward J. Hopkins. In size and motive and manner

[65]*Proceedings and debates,* Free Church, 1866, pp. 247, 268.
[66]See Report of Committee in *The Evangelical Witness,* Octo. 1, 1869.
[67]*Proceedings and debates,* Free Church, 1872, p. 327.

it is of the same type as *The Scottish Hymnal,* but suffers in the comparison in lacking the distinguished format of that book, and by an arrangement of its hymns by their metres and not their subjects. It has more Scottish hymns, including 20 of the Paraphrases, and a larger representation of recent authors outside the Anglican school. It is remarkable that a Church that only a few years earlier was debating the lawfulness of hymn singing should be thus provided with so excellent a hymnal of the latest fashion: a result largely due to the broadmindedness and culture of Alexander B. Bruce, convener of the committee compiling it, and to the hymnological knowledge of James Bonar of Greenock.[68] The committee proceeded to set music to the metrical Psalter, the Paraphrases and some of the prose Psalms under Dr. Hopkins' supervision, as *The Scottish Psalter* (1883); and to issue a hymnal for the young of striking beauty and merit, under the musical editorship of Sir Joseph Barnby, as *The Home and School Hymnal* (Edinburgh: University Press, 1893). The Free Church provision for Praise became thus very complete.

4. SCOTTISH HYMN WRITING

Of the hymn writers put forward or represented in these hymn books, the ministry of the United Presbyterian Church furnished three: George Jacque and William Bruce contributed to *The Presbyterian Hymnal* of 1876 hymns still in use, and Hamilton M. Macgill was the first Scottish minister to bring the hymns of the Latin Church before the Presbyterian Churches.

Of the Church of Scotland, Robert Murray McCheyne's "When this passing world is done," William Robertson's "A little child the Saviour came," Principal Shairp's "Twixt gleams of joy and clouds of doubt," and Norman Macleod's "Courage, brother! do not stumble," are all in use beyond the bounds of Scotland. John R. Macduff's once

---

[68]His valuable indexes and annotations are in the larger edition without music.

popular *The Gates of Praise* (1875) is now remembered by "Christ is coming! let creation." And George Matheson wrote, among others, one of the most popular of modern hymns, in "O Love that wilt not let me go," so happily wedded to music in *The Scottish Hymnal*.

The Free Church numbered among its ministers the most eminent Scottish hymn writer, Horatius Bonar, a pastor at Kelso, later at Edinburgh, for a while regarded as the peer of Watts and Charles Wesley. Of his ten tracts or volumes of hymns (1843-1881) seven were published before his Church authorized hymn singing, and his hymns were sung in almost every communion but his own. Spontaneous, careless, and sometimes ringing the changes fatiguingly, they are warmly evangelical, often poetical, and always sympathetic. God's love in Christ, the rest of faith and beauty of holiness, the helpfulness of sacraments, the hope of the Second Coming irradiating the pathos of life, were Dr. Bonar's special themes. And while he may not have created a new type of English hymn, he had a distinctive style, a childlike simplicity and straightforwardness, a cheerful note with a plaintive undertone; and he impressed his striking personality upon the English Hymn. The appeal of his hymns to his own generation was so widespread and pronounced as almost to create a cult. Fully a hundred of his hymns have been in actual church use, many of which are gradually passing out of sight. Eighteen are in the Scottish *The Church Hymnary* of 1898, and of these such hymns as "I heard the voice of Jesus say," "Thy way, not mine, O Lord," "A few more years shall roll," "When the weary, seeking rest," and "Here, O my Lord, I see Thee face to face," are both characteristic and enduring.[69] After Bonar, James Drummond Burns, who had a charge in the Presbyterian Church of England, is the best known Free Church hymn writer, and his "Hushed was the evening hymn" and "Still with Thee, O my God" are in wide

[69]For a sufficient presentation of the hymns, see *Hymns by Horatius Bonar*, Henry Frowde, 1904.

use. Dr. Bonar has a place among students and translators of Latin hymns, and the sisters, Mrs. Sarah Findlater and Jane L. Borthwick, by their *Hymns from the Land of Luther. By H. L. L.* (1854-1862) won a high place in the useful band of translators from the German. Miss Borthwick has also three original hymns in *The Church Hymnary* (1898). Mrs. Anne Ross Cousins' *Immanuel's Land* (1876) contributes "The sands of time are sinking," "O Christ, what burdens bowed Thy Head," and "To Thee and to Thy Christ, O God."

5. Unauthorized Hymn Singing by Irish Presbyterians (1830-1894)

During all these years of change in Scotland the Irish Presbyterian Church had never authorized the use of hymns in worship, or of anything beyond "Rous' version." The subject was often debated with Irish warmth in Presbyteries and Assembly. In 1880 the Assembly published *A revised edition of the Scottish Metrical Version of the Psalms,* and so far submitted to the prevailing influences as to call upon a Dublin adherent of the Anglican school, Sir R. P. Stewart, to edit its music, adding some new Psalm versions in metres adapted to tunes from *Hymns ancient and modern* and kindred sources.

It seems, however, to have been admitted even by the advocates of exclusive Psalmody that "congregations can use any hymns they please . . . without being called to account," [70] though "without sanction." Advantage was taken of this liberty in some congregations at an early date. A collection of 220 *Hymns adapted to public worship: intended as a supplement to the Psalmody of the Church of Scotland* ("as used by most of the Presbyterian congregations in Ulster") appeared at Dublin in 1830. Into other congregations hymns came more insidiously by way of the Sunday school. "The toleration of hymns in the Sabbath

[70] Professor Dick, *The Hymnary Discussions in the General Assembly,* Belfast, 1899, p. 14.

Schools," says Professor Dick, "has greatly promoted the
movement for corrupting Divine worship." [71]   But during
the last quarter of the century "a tremendous change" came
over the opinions of the great body of Irish Presbyterians,[72]
and their demand for an authorized Hymnody became
somewhat urgent.   The contents of W. Fleming Stevenson's *Hymns for Church and Home* (London, 1873) serve
to show how much the Anglican Hymnody and the impulse it gave to hymn singing were behind this change.   It
showed too that Irish Presbyterians had at hand an excellent hymnologist and capable editor.   Even more Anglican,
and more choice also, was *Book of Common Song: being
a supplement to the Psalter in the worship of the Church*
(Marcus Ward, 1890) edited by Rev. Andrew Charles
Murphy of Belfast on the theory "that there are not more
than three hundred hymns of adequate merit in the language." [73]   But the General Assembly neither gave its sanction to Hymnody nor undertook the preparation of a hymnal
until 1895, when it appointed a committee to select materials; a project which was merged in a larger one for a
common Presbyterian Hymnal.

6.   The Movement for a Common Hymnal Yields
        to Oxford Influences (1870-1898)

Each of the Churches had dealt with the problem of
hymn singing as it arose and in a different way, and a
separate hymn book for each denomination had been a
practical necessity.   But there was in reality no denominational Hymnody, and except in a certain approach of *The
Scottish Hymnal* to the doctrine as well as the method and
manner of the Oxford Hymnody, no marked difference
between the books.   There seemed no necessity that the
unfortunate divisions of Presbyterianism should be em-

---

[71]*The Hymnary Discussions*, p. 22.

[72]*Ibid.*, p. 19.

[73]Unlike many who hold this theory, Dr. Murphy included only one
hymn of his own composition.

bodied in books of praise, and a desire arose for a hymn book which all branches of Presbyterianism might use in common.

In this movement the United Presbyterian Church led the way. When in 1870 its Synod began the preparation of *The Presbyterian Hymnal,* it resolved to approach the other Churches with a view to common action. But the Established Church was well advanced in the preparation of *The Scottish Hymnal,* and the Free could not then see its way beyond a very small selection of hymns as its first step.[74] Resolving to revise its hymnal in 1891, the United Presbyterian Church again approached the others, and this time successfully. A joint committee of the three Churches was appointed, and proceeded to the point of printing a "Draft Hymnal," revised and reissued in 1895 and again in 1896.[75]

At this point the Church of Scotland, at the instigation of what many regarded as the Ultra-Anglican party, administered a shock by withdrawing (May, 1896) from the whole project. Elsewhere interest in the project had widened and crystallized into a definite proposal[76] of a common hymnal for all the Presbyterian Churches of the British Empire. In 1895 the Presbyterian Church in Ireland, and also the Presbyterian Church of Canada, which had printed a draft hymnal of its own, sent representatives to the Joint Hymnal Committee with a view of cooperation.

The draft of 1896 was adopted by the United and Free Churches and that of Ireland, under some protest, inasmuch as numerous hymns had been inserted to gratify the dominant party in the Established Church, which some in the other Churches regarded as "Romanizing." It was contended that the situation was changed by the withdrawal

---

[74] John Brownlie, *The Hymns and Hymn writers of The Church Hymnary,* Henry Frowde, n. d., p. 4.

[75] *Draft Hymnal prepared by Joint Committee of Church of Scotland, Free Church and United Presbyterian Church. Edinburgh: printed for the committee, 1896* (598 Hymns).

[76] Agreed upon by the British delegates to the Council of the Presbyterian Alliance at Toronto, 1892. Brownlie, p. 6.

of the Church of Scotland, and that the book did not represent the consenting Churches.[77] But the body of Scottish Churchmen were also dissatisfied with the situation, and under pressure from the Presbyteries, and after some concessions were made in the draft hymnal,[78] it was also adopted by the Assembly of the Church of Scotland in 1897.

The new hymnal, one of the comeliest ever made, appeared as *The Church Hymnary, authorized for use in public worship by The Church of Scotland, The Free Church of Scotland, The United Presbyterian Church, The Presbyterian Church of Ireland. The music edited by Sir John Stainer* (Henry Frowde, 1898). Of its 625 hymns, 172 had been in the books of all three Scottish Churches, 128 in two, 119 in *The Scottish Hymnal* alone, 33 in *The Free Church Hymn Book* alone, 46 in *The Presbyterian Hymnal* alone, and 127 were in none of them.[79] The influences that were behind *The Scottish Hymnal* thus predominated in making the new *Hymnary*, affecting the Hymnody of all the Churches. At the same time all hymns were included which in the judgment of all the representatives of any one denomination had become standards in that Church.[80] The music of the book followed frankly the ideals of Monk in *Hymns ancient and modern. The Church Hymnary* in its choice of hymns, its texts, and its music,[81] to which its form and typography must be added, is of a very high order, and must always remain a distinguished representative of modern Church Praise. But apart from the Oxford

[77]*Cf.* G. T. Niven, "The Remnant of the Joint-Hymnal Committee" in *United Presbyterian Magazine,* August 1896.

[78]For outside views of the situation, see *United Pres. Magazine,* Nov. 1896, and January 1897; and *The Presbyterian and Reformed Review,* Octo. 1896 (Scottish correspondence).

[79]Brownlie, p. 7, note.

[80]The first chapter of Brownlie's book is the best account of the making of *The Church Hymnary,* and the fourteenth is a full sketch of its musical editing.

[81]Its tunes are studied historically in Wm. Cowan and Jas. Love, *The Music of The Church Hymnary and The Psalter in metre, its sources and composers,* Henry Frowde, 1901.

Revival it could not have been made, and if so could not have been accepted by Scottish and Irish Presbyterianism.

So far as the Presbyterian Church of England and the Presbyterian Church in Canada are concerned, the movement for unity failed. The former is dealt with elsewhere. The *Hymnal* of the latter, adopted in 1880, was replaced by *The Presbyterian Book of Praise: approved and commended by the General Assembly of the Presbyterian Church in Canada, with tunes. Part i, Selections from the Psalter; Part ii, The Hymnal, revised and enlarged. Oxford: printed at the University Press, 1897.* This book also is greatly enriched by the Anglican Hymnody and church music, but is more eclectic than the Scottish book. It shows more affiliation with the less severe standards prevalent in the United States and was under the necessity of providing for a great home mission work. It had the felicity of bringing forward a hymn writer of Canadian Presbyterianism, Dr. Robert Murray of Halifax; whose Home Mission Hymn, "From ocean unto ocean," has already proved its usefulness.

III

OXFORD INFLUENCES ON AMERICAN HYMNODY

We have now to consider the effects of the Oxford Movement on the Hymnody of the American Churches.

1. THE APPEAL OF THE LATIN HYMN (1840-1861)

An interest in Latin hymns was awakened here almost as soon as in England. In 1840 Dr. Henry Mills of Auburn published *The Hymn of Hildebert and the Ode of Xavier, with English versions.* Bishop Williams followed in 1845 with *Ancient Hymns of Holy Church,* and Dr. Coles in 1847 with his versions of *Dies Irae.* The body of the Breviary and Missal Hymns were made accessible to the American public in *Lyra Catholica* (New York: Dunigan, 1851), and again in the Boston *Hymns of the Ages* (1858) which F. D. Huntington introduced. How the Unitarians led in the introduction of these versions into their hymn books we have already seen.[82] Among Congregationalists, Henry Ward Beecher used *Lyra Catholica* as one of the sources of his *Plymouth Collection* of 1855, and the Andover faculty secured further versions of Latin hymns from Dr. Ray Palmer for their *Sabbath Hymn Book* of 1858. Among Presbyterians Dr. Willis Lord had included numerous versions in his *Hymns of Worship* (Philadelphia, 1858), one of many protests against the authorized Hymnody of his Church. W. C. Dana of Charleston, in his *A Collection of Hymns* (New York, 1859), referred to the ancient hymns therein represented as more attractive to some minds than the modern. And in 1861 Dr. Henry A. Boardman made a special point of including versions of Greek and Latin hymns in his *Selection of Hymns designed as a Supplement to the Psalms and Hymns of the Presbyterian Church* (Philadelphia). These books were not official, but the personality of their editors being what it was, we may say that the status of the Latin hymn was thus early secured in the Congregational and Presbyterian Churches just as effectively and far more peaceably than it had been in the Church of England.

2. Hymns Ancient and Modern in the Protestant Episcopal Church (1859-1892)

The influence of the Oxford Movement in its wider sense was naturally first felt here by the Episcopal Church. Some preparation for it had been laid by the high church party under Bishop Hobart. In 1834 George W. Doane edited the first American reprint of Keble's *Christian Year;* and the amusingly elementary character of his notes implies that he regarded the main area of Episcopalian territory as virgin

[82]See chap. ix, part iv, I.

ground to be cleared for the Oxford plow. He and Croswell and Coxe in their hymns and poems carried forward Keble's work on his own lines. Historical, doctrinal, devotional, polemical, writers completed the preparation. And in a few years the Oxford influence set in like a strong tide that carried the Episcopal Church from its former moorings to the position it occupies today.

These changes became most visible in that Church's worship;—in the conversion of the table into an altar at the east end of a gothic choir, in the change of gown into surplice with what it typified, and generally in the multiplication of services and their reorganization with more complicated ritual.

Such changes even in their earlier stages clearly called for a Hymnody more germane to the new ideals than the *Hymns* of 1827, and the *Select metrical Psalms* of 1832. But owing to the conflict of parties no authorized hymnal was practicable, and presumably private hymnals such as the Oxford Movement multiplied in England, would not have been allowed for use in church services in any diocese. From 1832 to 1858 the hymnal activity was confined to the "Selections" of the Evangelicals designed for the prayer-meeting and "lecture room." In 1859 appeared the only private hymnal of liturgical type, *Sacred Hymns; chiefly from ancient sources. Arranged according to the seasons of the Church. By Frederick Wilson, Rector of S. James the Less* (Philadelphia: Burns and Sieg). Wilson had come from an English parish, and his book consisted mainly of translations from Chandler and others of the Oxford group. Whether he was permitted to use it has not appeared.

The *Hymns for Church and Home,* compiled by Bishop Burgess, Dr. Muhlenberg, Dr. Coxe, Dr. Howe and Prof. Wharton, in 1860, seems to have been intended to call the attention of Convention to the enlarged resources of Hymnody. It had 28 versions of Latin hymns, and 19 of German, but the larger part was from the XVIIIth century

Evangelical school. This book stimulated the already wide-spread desire for an improved Hymnody. Some relief was afforded by the appearance of *Hymns ancient and modern,* which was welcomed by high churchmen, reprinted[83] and licensed for use in several dioceses; and, more generally, by 65 "additional" hymns licensed by the House of Bishops in 1865. It was only then that hymns now so familiar as "Sun of my soul," "Abide with me" and "Jerusalem the golden," were introduced to Episcopal churches. A closer conformity to the spirit and letter of *Hymns ancient and modern* characterized Dr. Batterson's *Church Hymnal* (Philadelphia, 1869); and from the same source the tunes as well as the hymns were freely drawn upon by two men who were beginning their important work for congregational praise in the Episcopal Church;—Charles L. Hutchins in his *The Church Hymnal* (Buffalo, 1870) and J. Ireland Tucker in his *The Parish Hymnal* (New York) of the same year.

But the general desire was for uniformity, and in 1872 the General Convention issued *Hymnal: according to the use of the Protestant Episcopal Church in the United States of America. Printed under the authority of the General Convention. MDCCCLXXII.*[84] It may be regarded as a compromise between Metrical Psalmody, the Liturgical and the Evangelical Hymnodies. Tate and Brady's *New Version* was the largest contributor, 60 of their versions appearing as hymns. Watts, Wesley, Montgomery, Neale, Doddridge, Steele, Newton, and Heber, followed in the order named. There are 37 hymns from the Latin; and almost every type and school has some represen-

[83]By C. T. Adams, Philada., 1866, with recommendation by Bishops Williams, Atkinson, Potter and Quintard; by Lippincott, Phila., with the 1868 Appendix; by Pott and Amery, New York, with the Appendix and L. C. Biggs's Supplement.

[84]This was the "Standard." The *Hymnal* was first printed in 1871 (Lippincott) as part of a report to the General Convention. For an annotated edition, see Chas. L. Hutchins, *Annotations on the Hymnal,* Hartford, 1872.

tation in this eclectic book, whose character was unchanged in the revision of 1874. The adoption of this book was reluctant in many advanced parishes that had been using *Hymns ancient and modern;* but in spite of local conservatisms it served the Church till the appearance of *The Hymnal revised and enlarged as adopted by the General Convention of The Protestant Episcopal Church in the United States of America in the year of our Lord 1892: being the preliminary report of the Committee on the Hymnal appointed by the General Convention of 1886, modified* (Oxford: University Press).

The new *Hymnal* conforms more to the *Hymns ancient and modern* pattern, and has no marked features of its own. The selection of the hymns was somewhat suggested by compromise between various parties and schools in the Church, none of which it appeared to satisfy. The editing of the book reflected no lustre on those concerned in it and needless mutilations of the hymns gave offence to many. Published without tunes *The Hymnal* has gained much distinction and exercised a very great influence on American church music by the numerous musical settings given to it by private enterprise. That of Dr. C. L. Hutchins (1894) led in popularity; that of J. Ireland Tucker and William W. Rousseau (1894) closely followed it. That of A. H. Messiter (1893) embodied the boy-choir traditions of Trinity, New York. That of James H. Darlington (1897) sought simple congregational tunes. That of Dr. Horatio Parker (1903) aimed to avoid the sentimental or part-song type of tune which some of the earlier settings had much fostered, and which he believed had hindered the improvement of congregational singing. It is unquestionably true that while these musical editions had gathered about the hymns a great variety of the better types of church tunes, they showed nevertheless too much tendency to cater to the choir rather than the people, and failed to effect all the improvement in congregational singing that seemed practicable. It is however to be remembered that the Episcopal

Church has delayed behind all others in putting the music into the pews.

THE REFORMED EPISCOPAL CHURCH separated from the Protestant Episcopal in 1873 in protest against Tractarianism, and organized on the basis of the "Proposed Book" of 1785.[85] It had at first (230) *Hymns recommended* [by BishopCummins] *for use in the Reformed Episcopal Church* (Philadelphia, 1874), selected from those in general use. Its *Hymnal Companion to the Prayer Book, with accompanying tunes* (Philadelphia, 1885) was more like the *Hymnal* then used in the Episcopal Church than any other, and its Communion Hymns were not any more colorless doctrinally. This book served until extensively revised and republished with the same title in 1907.

3. THE LITURGICAL CONTROVERSY IN THE GERMAN REFORMED CHURCH (1857)

Under the influence of American surroundings, notably of revivalism, the German Reformed Church had quite departed from such liturgical constitution as it originally had, when John W. Nevin caught unexpectedly from a casual reading of a volume of the *Oxford Tracts* "his first glimpse of what the church spirit really meant." [86] He proceeded forthwith to those studies which made him the founder of a "Mercersburg school" of theology, and the leader of a movement that began with the proposal to reinstate *The old Palatinate Liturgy,* but soon changed into a proposed reconstruction of the Church on a "primitive" basis, and her equipment with a liturgy that should be "in the fullest sense of the word an altar service," [87] "and not simply a pulpit liturgy"; "churchly, sacramental, and in proper measure also priestly." [88] As a result of this movement *A Liturgy:*

---

[85]Chap. viii, sect. iv, 1.

[86]Theo. Appel, *The Life and Work of John Williamson Nevin,* Philadelphia, 1889, p. 88.

[87]J. W. Nevin, *The Liturgical Question,* Philadelphia, 1862, p. 28.

[88]*Ibid.,* p. 38.

or order of Christian worship (Philadelphia: Lindsay and Blakiston, 1857) was tentatively allowed, in which the order of worship revolves with the Christian Year around "the mystical presence of Christ in the Holy Eucharist," [89] and every office and act turns toward the altar.[90] Beside the ancient hymns and canticles *in situ,* provision is made for singing hymns "in the usual manner," and *A Selection of Hymns* (104) *for public and private worship* is appended, though remote indeed from both the scheme and sources of the worship. There are but two hymns for the Lord's Supper, none from the Hymnody of the Latin Church, and no recognition of the church year. Watts and the Evangelical school prevail.

The revision of this Liturgy, after some years' use, published in 1867 as *An order of worship for the Reformed Church* (Philadelphia), developed the full heat of a liturgical controversy, with the low church West allying itself with the non-liturgical minority in the East, to resist ritualism. If the denomination was to be saved at all, it could only be by toleration; and the East was allowed the use of the *Order of worship,* while the West was permitted to make a low church one of its own. The *Hymns for the Reformed Church in the United States* (Philadelphia: Publication Board, 1874) was a Hymnal Companion to the Order of Worship, often bound up with it. It is a very choice liturgical hymn book, with hymns provided for the Sundays and other days of the church year. By contrast with it *The Reformed Church Hymnal: with tunes* (Cleveland, 1878), made to accompany the Western *Order of Service,* suffers greatly. It is given over unduly to the Mason and Kingsley school of music, and its miscellaneous hymns are mutilated to fit the space left beneath the tunes. The peace movement that began in 1878 effected a liturgical compromise, as expressed in *The Directory of worship* of 1884. A church hymnal followed, by direction of Synod

[89]*Ibid.,* p. 23.
[90]*Ibid.,* p. 24.

in 1887 as *The Hymnal of the Reformed Church in the United States* (Cleveland: Publishing House, 1890). The book is liturgical in so far that the bulk of its 793 hymns are grouped under the seasons of the church year; but the hymns are of every sort, and much of the music is of the Sunday school type represented by Bradbury. Those of liturgical tastes had, however, the *Hymns* of 1874 as a permanent possession.

4. The new Reformed Dutch Hymnody (1868-1891)

Modern influences were brought to play upon the Hymnody of the Reformed Dutch Church in a way quite peculiar. The congregations were restive under *Psalms and Hymns,* and were prevented by church law from adopting private collections. At the Synod of 1868 no less than four manuscript hymn books were laid on its table by as many clergymen who had compiled them and who requested their authorization. Under this stimulus a "Committee on Hymnology" was appointed[91] who prepared *Hymns of the Church: with tunes* (New York: Barnes, 1869) and the smaller *Hymns of Prayer and Praise* (Barnes, 1871) for devotional services. The committee, Dr. John B. Thompson, A. G. Vermilye and A. R. Thompson, made a collection in which the modern types of hymns were well represented with selections of prose Psalms for chanting. The musical editor, U. C. Burnap, made what would now be regarded as a very moderate use of the Anglican church music, but it was too far advanced for a very backward Church, and suffered the ignominy of a revision,—"putting in Lowell Mason where I had Dykes."[92] A smaller book, compiled by the chairman of the committee, *Christian Praise* (New York: Huntington 1870), though not designed for use in the Dutch Church, was authorized in 1879.

Mr. Edwin A. Bedell, an Albany organist, submitted to

[91]*Cf.* Jno. B. Thompson, "Hymns of the Church" in *The Christian Intelligencer* for July 25, 1906.

[92]Letter of U. C. Burnap to the present writer.

the Synod a manuscript collection of hymns and tunes of his own compilation. It was a preacher's hymn book of some 1400 hymns, but after some 600 hymns had been excised by a committee of Synod and some 200 added, it was endorsed by the Synod of 1890, though left in the hands of compiler and publisher to their private profit. It appeared as *The Church Hymnary, a collection of Hymns and tunes for public worship. Compiled by Edwin A. Bedell* (New York: Merrill, 1891). The book was thoroughly modern, including for example 35 hymns of John Mason Neale, 49 tunes by Dykes and 40 by Barnby, and it won a wide acceptance in and beyond the bounds of the Dutch Church. Its very size and scope appealed still to preachers; its wealth of new music to both choir and people; it was a skilfully made collection in spite of its overcrowded page; and it had at first no competitor on a similar scale and of equal quality. However undesirable the Synodical endorsement of a private commercial enterprise may have been, the Church had thus a more modern book than it could possibly have made, and the book gained a circulation and influence outside from which an official publication and imprint would have barred it.

5. Hymns Ancient and Modern in the Presbyterian Church (1866-1895)

In the authorized Hymnody of the Presbyterian Church modern influences became manifest in the ill-fated (Old School) *Hymnal of the Presbyterian Church. Ordered by the General Assembly* (Philadelphia: Board of Publication, 1866). It is a hymn book as against *Psalms and Hymns*. Prose Psalms are set to chants, and the creed and Lord's Prayer are given for recitation. Its 576 hymns were a great contrast to the 1290 of the Andover book, too great for the ministry to welcome then, and the Assembly ordered a supplement. It ordered also an index of texts, but the book could not be used homiletically with good effect. The very arrangement of the hymns in 5 groups, General Praise,

Church Seasons, Christian Life, Occasional and Miscellaneous, implies a different intention. The use of the new liturgical Hymnody in this book is very small, but there are a very few hymns from the Latin. This was the first of the authorized Presbyterian hymnals to introduce the tunes. But the musical setting was unsatisfactory to a degree that prevented the literary contents from receiving any fair test in actual use.

After the Reunion in 1870 the Assembly appointed a committee who prepared *The Presbyterian Hymnal. Philadelphia: Presbyterian Board of Publication* [1874]. It bore many marks of haste, and is largely the work of Dr. J. T. Duryea, to whom resort was had by a committee unable to agree as to what was wanted. The classification of the hymns, opening with "The Call to Praise" and "The Response," "The Call to Prayer" and "The Response," and proceeding through the articles of the Apostles Creed to "Hymns of Occasion," makes evident that the book was planned as a manual of worship rather than of doctrine or homiletics. Dr. Duryea made a use of the Latin hymns hardly if at all less than that of the Episcopal *Hymnal* of 1872-74; even going so far as to use Caswall's version (with omission of one verse) of the Breviary hymn to "The Sacred Heart of Jesus." [93] But the special medium through which the Oxford influences affected that Hymnal was *Hymns ancient and modern,* many copies of which had been brought here by Presbyterian tourists abroad, and which was familiar already in many cultivated homes. From this book numerous hymns, both those from the Latin and English, were extracted: among the latter, such as "Abide with me," "Jerusalem the golden," "Brief life is here our portion," "The Church's one Foundation" and "Saviour, again to Thy dear Name we raise." Hardly inferior to these hymns in the influence they have exerted on Presbyterian Hymnody were the then altogether novel tunes of the Anglican school taken from *Hymns ancient*

[93]*Hymnal* of 1874; no. 240.

and modern, such as "Innocents," "St. Alban," "Horbury," "St. Fulbert," "Hursley," "St. Peter," "Hollingside," and "Eventide." The older English tunes in the *Hymnal* of 1874 were in most cases the arrangements of them made by Monk to suit the ecclesiastical tone of *Hymns ancient and modern.* It may be said in brief that through the *Hymnal* of 1874 *Hymns ancient and modern* greatly enriched and considerably modified Presbyterian Hymnody, and that as regards the hymn tunes its influence has been hardly short of revolutionary.

The Hymnal was not without its rivals. One of the committee, Dr. James O. Murray, had joined with his elder, Winthrop S. Gilman, in compiling *The Sacrifice of Praise* (New York: Scribner, 1869: revised ed. 1870: musical ed., 1872), a collection of 616 hymns marked by culture and charm. It was made for the Brick Church of New York, but deservedly won favor in other congregations. Dr. Edwin F. Hatfield retired from the committee to prepare *The Church Hymn Book, with tunes* (New York: Ivison, 1872); and Drs. R. D. Hitchcock, Zachary Eddy and Philip Schaff entered the lists with *Hymns and Songs of Praise* (New York: Randolph, 1874). These were huge collections of 1416 and 1464 Hymns respectively, made possible only by grouping from two to four under each tune. In making so elaborate an appeal to the homiletical instinct both books looked backward, and were soon left behind in spite of a pamphlet war conducted in their interests. But they were edited with a care and hymnological knowledge not displayed in *The Hymnal;* and Drs. Hatfield and Schaff were the earliest hymnologists, in any real sense, of the Presbyterian Church.[94]

Dr. Robinson, who had made hymn books for so many

---

[94]Hatfield's *The Poets of the Church* (New York, 1884) showed real research. Schaff's German hymn books, his papers on Latin Hymns (see *Literature and Poetry,* N. Y., 1890), his *Christ in Song* (New York, 1870) and *A Library of Religious Poetry* (with A. Gilman, New York, 1881), are all highly esteemed.

of the churches, naturally expected to edit that for the reunited Church. Failing to come to agreement with the Hymnal Committee, he published his own *Psalms and Hymns and Spiritual Songs* (New York, 1875) already noticed, with its appeal both to psalm singers and the lovers of the new Hymnody. This he followed in 1878 by *A Selection of Spiritual Songs with music for the church and the choir* (New York) in which he compromised between "two diverging drifts of sentiment," [95] the old love for melody and refrain and a newer taste for the Anglican and German choral type. His later books, *Laudes* Domini* (1885) and *The new Laudes Domini* (1892) are much more pronouncedly under the influence of the Anglican school of Hymnody and church music, and did much to extend the popularity of both in Presbyterian and Congregational churches.

The Hymnal of 1874 had survived its earlier rivals, and reached a circulation of half a million copies.[96] But it was originally a carelessly made and inadequate collection, although the best the Church had made and authorized. It was allowed to linger much too long, until its continued use became a strain on denominational loyalty and a detriment to Congregational Song. Every pastor was being pressed by agents of hymn book publishers, and the number of churches which turned from the Assembly's authorization to the market to find their praise books was increasing with every year.

To regain the position thus sacrificed was impossible. To regain at least something of it, the only course left open was to prepare an authorized hymnal that might make its way by the force mainly of its superiority to those in the market, coupled with whatever sanction still remained in the recommendation of the Assembly.

In this task the Board of Publication took the initiative under authority to revise the church hymnal committed to

[95] Preface.
[96] Ms. records of Board of Publication.

it in 1888;[97] and in 1893 sought and obtained the approval
of the Assembly for the work of preparation already
begun.[98] The whole field of Hymnody was freshly studied
with the resources of the new Hymnology; the hymns were
chosen in the interests of devotion as distinguished from
homiletics, and their text was determined with a scrupu-
lousness that had been more common in literature than in
Hymnody. In setting the hymns a large use was made of
the Anglican music, and of the American composers developed in connection with the musical editions of the
Protestant Episcopal *Hymnal* of 1892.

The new book appeared as *The Hymnal published by
authority of the General Assembly of the Presbyterian
Church in the United States of America. The Presbyterian Board of Publication and Sabbath-school Work,
Philadelphia, 1895.* It sought to bring forward a backward
Church to the van of progressive Church Song, and to prepare a church book unexcelled for utility, beauty and
editorial carefulness. It proved at once a menace to private
publishing interests. The publisher of Dr. Robinson's
series planned *In Excelsis* (New York, 1897) as an open
competitor on a lavish scale, with a close imitation in
method, arrangement, and outward form. But against all
commercial enterprise *The Hymnal* established a new standard of Church Praise and reestablished a measure of church
uniformity; having been adopted, up to the time of its
revision in 1911, by 1880 congregations, with a circulation
of 322,000 copies. The denominational equipment for the
service of song was rounded out by the publication, under
the same editorial auspices, of *The Chapel Hymnal* (1898)
and *The School Hymnal* (1899).

THE PRESBYTERIAN CHURCH IN THE UNITED STATES
(Southern) has responded more guardedly to modern influences. Its *Psalms and Hymns,* authorized in 1866, were
ameliorated by the allowance of Robinson's *Psalms and*

[97] *Minutes of General Assembly,* 1888, pp. 71, 72.
[98] *Minutes,* 1893.

Hymns and Spiritual Songs, and, later, R. P. Kerr's *Hymns of the Ages* (New York, 1891). Under pressure from the Presbyteries the Assembly of 1898 authorized the preparation of *The new Psalms and Hymns published by authority of the General Assembly of the Presbyterian Church in the United States, A. D. 1901. Richmond, Va., Presbyterian Committee of Publication.* Prepared for a body tenacious of old usages and strongly evangelical, the new hymn book (Psalms and Hymns in name only) includes a large appropriation of the newer types of hymns and tunes under a careful editorship, especially of the music.

THE CUMBERLAND PRESBYTERIAN CHURCH was less conscious of the Oxford influences. Its own *Psalms and Hymns* of 1845 and a collection prepared by A. J. Baird and authorized in 1875,[99] were supplemented by the use of revival hymn books; and in 1889 the Assembly adopted a member of Dr. Robinson's "Spiritual Song Series" (*Spiritual Songs for Church and Choir*), republishing it as *The Cumberland Presbyterian Hymnal* (Nashville, n. d.). Seventeen years later that body and the Presbyterian Church in the United States of America became one.

But the Oxford influences on Presbyterian Hymnody did not reach their maximum in the authorized Hymnody, but in *The Evangelical Hymnal* of Charles Cuthbert Hall (New York: Barnes, 1880). He found his motive in a critical judgment of hymns, a pronounced churchliness, and a reverence that was more an essence than a grace; and he found his musical inspiration in Joseph Barnby's setting of the advanced Anglican *Hymnary.* His close addiction to Anglican models did not appeal to very many in his own denomination. *The Churchman*[100] on the contrary regarded it as "the richest collection for church worship within reach," and as "far surpassing" the Episcopal *Hymnal.* Dr. Leonard W. Bacon's *The Church Book* (New York:

[99]See B. W. McDonnold, *History of the Cumberland Presbyterian Church,* 4th ed., Nashville, 1899, p. 597.
[100]October 8, 1884.

Appleton, 1883,) is more independent. It reverts to the "Psalms and Hymns" model: its hymns nevertheless being chosen and arranged in the interests of worship as distinguished from homiletics. Dr. M. W. Stryker's *Church Song for the uses of the House of God* (Biglow and Main), 1889) stands alone in its addiction to German chorals, and with his other books reveals him as one of the most copious Presbyterian hymn writers. Of others brought forward in modern Presbyterian hymn books, the names of Aaron R. Wolfe, Robinson P. Dunn, Hervey D. Ganse, and Mrs. Prentiss, have attained a moderate recognition.

6. A New Type of Congregationalist Hymnal (1887-1893)

In intended contrast to the voluminous collections of Dr. Robinson so widely used came the first of a series of hymn books by Charles H. Richards, *Christian Praise* (later *Songs of Christian Praise,* New York, 1880), and the Oberlin *The Manual of Praise* (Oberlin, 1880; followed by *The new Manual of Praise,* 1901). The books represented a conviction that a smaller collection fulfilled the needs of worship, but were dominated neither by the literary nor liturgical motive. They sought rather the average taste and attainment. The musical standard of the Oberlin book was that of Mason and Bradbury: Dr. Richards' maintained a survival of the "parlor music" era mingling with the Anglican tunes.

From experiments made at Providence in the introduction of the Anglican tunes and a more severe standard in the choice of hymns grew up *Hymns of the Faith with Psalms* (Boston: Houghton, Mifflin and Co., 1887) edited by George Harris, W. J. Tucker and E. K. Glezen. Its form and open typography, its prose Psalter set to Anglican chants, its "more discriminating judgment of the vast number of hymns found in former collections," its arrangement of the hymns under the articles of the Apostles' Creed, and its Anglican music, infused for the first time the appeal of culture permeated by churchliness into the note of Congregationalist Praise in America. If adaptive rather than originative, *Hymns of the Faith* led the way in the movement to improve Church Song in a denomination that had somehow failed to maintain the highest standard of outward reverence in worship or to develop the amenities of sanctified culture.

As beautiful in its way, and even more frank in its recognition of the "far superior" spiritual quality of the new Anglican music, was the last important Congregationalist hymnal of the century, *The Plymouth Hymnal, edited by Lyman Abbott* (New York: the Outlook Co., 1893), so named as in proud succession to Mr. Beecher's *Plymouth Collection*. Although rich in liturgical materials and suggestion, the book gives an impression of a literary rather than a liturgical motive. It aims to embody the changes of doctrine and emphasis that have passed over Puritan theology and into Christian experience, and to stimulate the new aggressive mood of the Christian life. It may be that these novelties hindered the immediate circulation of a book whose editing and format were fitted to be a model. None the less it was in accord with the tendency of the time. And something of its spirit and even of its manner passed into *The Pilgrim Hymnal,* which may be held to represent the advanced Hymnody of XXth century Congregationalism.

7. THE BAPTISTS MAINTAIN THE HOMILETICAL TYPE TILL THE CENTURY'S END

American Baptists as a body represent the type of mind and experience least open to such influences as emanated from Oxford and most independent of liturgical considerations. *The Baptist Hymn and Tune Book* (Philadelphia: Publication Society, 1871) is a very voluminous evangelical hymn book, and would have been substantially the same if

Hymns ancient and modern had not yet appeared: it was indeed very recent. The same thing is true of *The Baptist Praise Book: for congregational singing* (Barnes and Co., 1872), edited by a company of divines, headed by Richard Fuller. The one with 975, the other with 1311, hymns, are eclectic rather than discriminating, and doubtless homiletic rather than liturgical.

The second hymnal of the American Baptist Publication Society was *The Baptist Hymnal* (Philadelphia: 1883). Beyond a reduction of the number of hymns from the 975 of the *The Baptist Hymn Book* to 703, it represents less of an effort to improve the standard of Hymnody than a wish to gratify all parties. If the new Anglican Hymnody is represented, so is "Fanny Crosby" by 17 hymns. If Dykes has 19 tunes and Barnby 8, Lowell Mason has 76 and W. H. Doane (one of the editors) no less than 35. The hymnal followed the pattern set by Dr. Robinson's earlier books, but with a literary and devotional standard made more "popular" by its large use of "Gospel Hymns."

Dr. E. H. Johnson shared in the compilation of *The Baptist Hymnal,* but could not have controlled it. He became in time the responsible editor of the Publication Society's third book, with the fancy name of *Sursum Corda* (Philadelphia, 1898). He was now certainly an advocate of the best types of modern hymns, as against Gospel Songs and much of the older Evangelical Hymnody, and an enthusiast for the superiority of Anglican church music. For his 856 hymns he provided and printed on greatly overcrowded pages no less than 1346 tunes, that every hymn might have a setting of the Anglican standard. *Sursum Corda* did not gain the popularity and use of its predecessor. A good purpose, carefully carried out with infinite pains, no doubt overreached itself. It is indeed easier to plan, within the walls of a Seminary, the elevation of the literary and musical standards of a Church's devotion, than to change the habits and tastes of a great body of people who do not share the Seminary advantages.

8. The Lutherans Develop a Churchly Hymnody
(1863-1899)

The many years' conflict which weakened and divided
American Lutheranism was in substance the variance between high church and low church ideals. Augsburg
Lutheranism had much in common with Anglicanism; and
in the Lutheran as in the Episcopal Church the controversy
was inevitably liturgical. The General Council was formed,
after the disintegrations of the Civil War period, of the
conservative and strict churchly elements. One of its constituent bodies, the Ministerium of Pennsylvania, had already entered upon the work of liturgical reconstruction
on historic lines; having in 1863 appointed a committee to
prepare a Church Book, "with an ample Selection of Hymns,
with special reference to the doctrine and usages of our
Church." [101] The Hymn section appeared tentatively as
Hymns for the use of the Evangelical Lutheran Church
(Philadelphia, 1865), and was the work of B. M.
Schmucker and Frederic M. Bird; the latter the most diligent and capable of a small group of Americans who had
undertaken the systematic study of Hymnology. The English *Church Book* appeared at Philadelphia in 1868, containing 588 hymns; being at once a liturgy and a hymnal;
and again in 1872, *with music arranged for the use of
congregations, by Harriet Reynolds Krauth.* The hymnal
is at once Lutheran and catholic. German Hymnody is
represented by 167 translations, the Greek by 11, the Latin
by 42. The remainder is an admirable representation of all
periods of English Hymnody, including the Anglican, but
with the foremost place given to Watts and Charles Wesley.
There was at the time no American hymnal so fully representative of the development of Hymnody, so discriminating
in selection, so scholarly in treatment. In Miss Krauth's
musical setting the German choral is fittingly preeminent,

[101]Preface to *Hymns* of 1865. See also A. Spaeth, "Liturgical Development of the Ministerium," *Lutheran Church Review,* Jan. 1898,
p. 116.

supplemented by the English tunes most in accord with its spirit; and the concessions to popular demand are comparatively slight. English-speaking Lutheranism had at last expressed itself in a hymnal worthy of its own traditions,[102] and on a plane where no other American denomination could hope to meet it. Beside this Lutheran hymnal of 1868 the Protestant Episcopal *Hymnal* of 1872 seems like an amateur performance, and its musical settings of even date with Miss Krauth's like an appeal to popular taste. A supplement of 62 hymns, bringing the whole number to 650, was added in the 1891 adaptation of the *Church Book* to the new "Common Service."

After the Civil War the Synod of the Confederate States remained apart under a new name, and printed its own liturgy as *The Book of Worship. Published by order of the Evangelical Lutheran General Synod in North America* (Columbia, S. C., 1867). The 465 hymns of this book have little or nothing to distinguish them from the hymn books of surrounding Evangelical denominations. The diminished General Synod also revised its Hymnody on the basis of the *Hymns, selected and original* of 1852 as *Book of Worship, published by the General Synod of the Lutheran Church in the United States* (Philadelphia: Board of Publication, 1871). This was simply a hymn book, preceded by an order of worship covering some eight pages, and followed by doctrinal and governmental standards. The hymns, both by omissions and additions, show growth in discrimination, but none toward churchliness.

The General Synod was nevertheless stirred by the revival of church life and desire for Lutheran unity that was in the air, and joined with the Southern Synod and General Council in the preparation of *The Common Service for the use of Evangelical Lutheran congregations* (1888) on the basis of the "common consent of the pure Lutheran liturgies of the XVIth century." For binding up with *The Common*

[102]For a review of the hymns and music of the *Church Book*, see "The Service of Song" in *The Penn Monthly*, Dec. 1872.

Service as its own *Book of Worship,* two committees of the General Synod of 1893 prepared *Hymns and Tunes* (1899). It is a modern collection, still strong in the XVIIIth century Evangelical Hymnody, and with more of the Anglican than the Lutheran hymns. In the tunes the Lowell Mason and parlor music type, as well as the Anglican, are largely represented; the German chorals more sparingly. The church year is much more liberally provided for, and the sacramental tone is somewhat higher.

The largest of Lutheran bodies in America is the Synodical Conference organized in 1872 on the strictest Lutheran basis, and dominated by the powerful Synod of Missouri. Originally almost exclusively German, when a beginning was made in establishing English services, a little book of *Hymns of the Evangelical Lutheran Church* (St. Louis, 1886) served; its 33 hymns being all translations from the German. In 1889 followed *Evangelical Lutheran Hymn-Book. By authority of the Evangelical Lutheran Synod of Missouri and other States* (Baltimore); enlarged and bound up with *The Common Service* in 1893. This is the most distinctively Lutheran of all the hymn books; no less than 209 of its 450 hymns being translations of German Lutheran hymns in metres permitting the use of the associated chorals. With the adoption of *The Common Service* by the Missouri Synod, the project of uniting English-speaking Lutheranism in a common liturgical worship was achieved, leaving the further project of a common hymnal for fulfilment in the XXth century.

The course of Lutheran Hymnody, as we have followed it, makes plain why that Church has done so little in the way of acclimating the old Lutheran hymns and chorals in other denominations. The English-speaking congregations wished to use the hymns of their American neighbors, and even in adopting for church use the versions of German hymns by Miss Winkworth, Mills, Massie and others, they have been followers rather than leaders. American Lutheranism presents a curious case of an immigrant Church merging its inheritance and traditions in its new surroundings until spurred by the pressure of new immigrations to recover what it had lost. And it may be that the real Lutheran influence on American Hymnody lies in the future.

9. ANGLICAN HYMNODY ACCOMMODATED TO THE "NEW CHURCH" (1863-1911)

The influence of Anglican ideals upon the New Church in America showed itself in the Rev. Frank Sewall's *The Christian Hymnal* (Philadelphia: Lippincott, 1867), especially as bound up with his *Book of holy Offices* as *A Prayer-Book and Hymnal for the use of the New Church* (1867). Its very large use of *Hymns ancient and modern* was notable at that date, as was its addiction to versions of German hymns with their chorals. Sewall was also a member of the committee compiling *The Book of Worship: prepared for the use of the New Church, by order of the General Convention* (New York, 1876), including chants, anthems and 153 hymns with tunes. In this the liturgy was much more independent of the *Book of Common Prayer,* and the Latin and German hymns were less conspicuous; but even so there were more hymns from *Hymns ancient and modern* than from the *Hymns* of the English New Church Conference. The collection was rather meagre, and some congregations had recourse to the English hymn book.

Sewall was the leading spirit in the preparation of a new collection, *The Magnificat: compiled for the use of the New Church by a committee of the General Convention* (New York, 1893). His tastes and preferences as exhibited in *The Christian Hymnal,* and his method of providing a New Church Hymnody by using that of the "old" Church, with necessary modifications of text, largely dominated *The Magnificat.* Sewall was chairman, once more, of the committee that prepared the "revised and enlarged" edition of 1911 (New York: Board of Publn.), deserving to be called a new book, yet retaining many characteristics of *The Christian Hymnal* of 1867. The New

Church presents the interesting case of a man fitting himself for leadership in the Church Song of his denomination, pursuing high ideals musical, literary and liturgical, and finding his leadership accepted through half a century. An advancing ideal has also distinguished the Sunday school Hymnody of the New Church, from the simplicities of Sewall's *The Welcome* (Philada., 1879) through *The Hosanna* (New York, 1878) and *The new Hosanna* (New York, 1902).

An examination of New Church hymn books makes it evident that the contributions from within are inadequate to its needs. No doubt its method of adapting hymns from without to its own ends by eliminating "every expression of false doctrine" [103] is, as in the case of the Unitarians, trying to those who care for the integrity of these hymns.

[103]Preface of 1911.

CHAPTER XI

TWENTIETH CENTURY HYMNODY

I

THE INFLUENCES THAT HAVE MOULDED IT

We have now studied the development in form and substance of the English Hymn as it took the place of the Metrical Psalm in the Congregational Song of English-speaking Protestantism, and have traced up to the XXth century the growth and upbuilding of the general body of this Church Hymnody. It remains only to consider our present-day Hymnody, as representing the latest stage of this development.

It will be remembered that Church Hymnody had begun to take shape before the end of the XVIIth century, but that the *Hymns* of Dr. Watts, in the first decade of the XVIIIth, did so much to establish its form, and contributed so much to its substance, as to make it the main basis of our modern Church Hymnody. The seed Watts planted sprang up and was cultivated by many hands; and upon the new growth the powerful influences of the Great Revival began to play before the middle of the XVIIIth century, imparting new color and variant forms to the original stock. The Hymnody of the Calvinistic side of the Revival and an infusion, at first small but ever growing, of the Hymnody of its Methodist side, coalesced with the hymns of Watts and his school to constitute a general body of Church Hymnody,— that already designated as the XVIIIth century Evangelical Hymnody.

The Hymnody was not originally conceived of as superseding the body of metrical psalms then in use but as supplementing it. It arose out of the conviction that the songs of the Christian Church should embody not only the prophecy of the Gospel in David but also its fulfilment in Christ, and it was hence *evangelical in motive*. It was to bear something of the same relation to the New Testament the Psalmody had borne to the Old, and was hence still *Scriptural in method*. It was to correspond with the doctrines of salvation preached from the pulpits, and was hence *theological in substance and form*. The metrical psalms still remained to meet in large measure the needs of devotion, and hence the more *special function* of the Hymnody was *homiletical*.

Upon this earlier Hymnody, as thus conceived and expressed, there have played through some two centuries all those forces and influences that on the one hand give continuity to Christianity and on the other tend to modify Christian thought and life, church worship and activities. And so when we turn to the Church Hymnody of the present day, and compare it with the earlier Hymnody, we see that it still stands on the basis laid for it in the XVIIIth century, and that a considerable though steadily diminishing nucleus of XVIIIth century hymns testifies to the continuity of its development. We see also on the other hand that in every one of the respects just mentioned—motive, method, substance, form, function—our Church Hymnody has been modified by the forces and influences that have played upon it.

These influences, as we have studied them, have shown themselves to fall mainly under four types,—revival, literary, liturgical, and doctrinal; and all four types of influences, though in themselves more or less modified by present day conditions and tendencies, continue to operate in the XXth century, conducing still further to revise and modify the Hymnody, and giving to XXth century Hymnody some features that are distinguishable even from the later XIXth century Hymnody.

II

HOW FAR AFFECTED BY MODERN EVANGELISM

The Revival Influence was the first to affect the Hymnody, and has affected it in the same way from the XVIIIth century Revival to the latest evangelism. The Methodist Movement modified the ideal of the Hymn, and created the Evangelistic Hymn, and each succeeding revival movement has turned from the established Church Hymnody and created an independent body of Spiritual Song with a fresher warmth and an immediate appeal to popular taste. And then out of each successive contribution of revival song a proportion, larger or smaller, has ultimately found its way into the permanent Hymnody of the Church. Both of these processes—the creation and the winnowing—have been already traced up to the present time.

In recent years two facts have militated against the admission of current evangelistic songs into the Church Hymnody. One is the inferior quality of the songs in themselves, giving them if any the most ephemeral popularity: the other the strictness with which any such as attain popularity are guarded as copyright property. Indeed it is only now, as the copyrights on the "Moody and Sankey songs" are beginning to expire, that some few of the best of them appear in one or another hymnal intended for church use.

III

ITS MORE EXACTING LITERARY STANDARD

The Literary Movement was at heart a protest against the theological conception of the Hymn and the didacticism of the earlier hymns. But it was inevitable that the influences of literary culture should play upon the Hymnody, just as they had done upon the earlier Psalmody, that they should raise a literary standard, and by winnowing and adding, should develop a body of more poetic hymns.

In recent years the literary tests applied to XVIIIth century hymns have tended to grow more exacting,[1] and many once familiar are passing out of use for no reason other than their unsatisfying craftmanship. In filling the gap thus created by the exclusion of older material the literary motive effected long ago an improved expression of the recognized hymn form; it now tends greatly to widen the definition of the Hymn itself by annexing to the domain of Hymnody numerous religious lyrics heretofore not regarded as within the definition of liturgical poetry. Instances of this are to be found in the ballad-like "O little town of Bethlehem" of Bishop Brooks, and in the intense and generally subjective lyrics of Miss Rossetti. It has already become somewhat difficult to define the distinction between the Hymn and the religious lyric. *The* (American) *Methodist Hymnal* of 1905 has gone out of its way to secure Dr. Holland's "There's a star in the sky," and Lanier's "Into the woods my Master went," and other current lyrics. And to the Presbyterians belongs the distinction of introducing into the hymn book Tennyson's "Sunset and evening star," whose immediate acceptance by all the Churches is itself significant.

In the Anglican Church the growth of the literary motive is still somewhat impeded by the liturgical. The new edition of *Hymns ancient and modern* (1904) is still heavily weighted with the dull and lifeless verse provided to cover saints' days and other times and seasons. Its great rival, *Church Hymns* (new edition, 1903) has more literary brightness and much more scrupulous concern for the authors' text. But in 1906 appeared a fresh collection, at once an extreme Anglican and a literary hymn book,— *The English Hymnal with tunes* (Oxford: the University Press, 1906). It aimed to present "the best hymns in the English language," and gave many new versions of ancient and foreign hymns. Free use is made of Robert Bridges'

[1]For a vigorous protest see Thos. Wright, *Augustus M. Toplady,* London, 1911, preface.

Yattendon Hymnal; and of the six compilers no less than
four (W. J. Birkbeck, Athelstan Riley, T. A. Lacey, and
Percy Dearmer) prove to be translators with the literary
touch.   Among XXth century men of letters who appear in
it as hymn writers are Laurence Housman, Arthur C. Benson, Gilbert K. Chesterton ("O God of earth and altar"),
and Rudyard Kipling, whose "God of our fathers, known
of old" has attained considerable vogue as a hymn.   With
these may be grouped Canon Scott Holland ("Judge eternal,
throned in splendor") and Arthur C. Ainger, whose "God
is working His purpose out" bids fair to attain a great
success.

The English Hymnal is notable for its charming format,
the width and freedom of its range, the unconventional use
of carol and traditional as well as plain song melodies, and its
exceptional scholarship.   Handicapped by extreme doctrine,
it has created none the less a decided impression of novel
charm, and can hardly fail to have a permanent influence
on Anglican Hymnody.   *The Oxford Hymn Book.   Oxford: at the Clarendon Press, 1908,* characterized by *The
Spectator* as "a very noteworthy collection of noble
hymns," [2] may be regarded as a protest in some sort against
certain tendencies of the literary movement;—aiming at
"simplicity, directness and genuineness of religious feeling,"
and the avoidance "of cheap sentiment, of conventional and
rhetorical form, and of weak and honeyed phrase." [3]

There can be no doubt that the literary level of recent
hymn books as a whole has been greatly raised, and it can
hardly be said that the devotional level has suffered from
that cause.   The contempt and disregard of Hymnody by
literary critics has so far yielded that the appearance of a
three-column review of *The English Hymnal* in the principal literary organ of England[4] does not now occasion
any surprise.

[2] For November 21, 1908.
[3] Preface, p. vi.
[4] *The Athenaeum* for September 29, 1906.

IV

ITS REVERSION TO A MOTIVE MORE STRICTLY DEVOTIONAL

The Liturgical Movement, to some extent from the beginning, and in later years very markedly, has shown itself as divisive rather than unifying in its effects upon Church Hymnody. The various forces that are always working to revise and modify that Hymnody have in these latter days come under subjection to what seems the irresistible religious trend of our times, that of unification: the inherited area of Hymnody characteristic of each denomination consequently tending to shrink, and the body of hymns which all alike sing in common tending to enlarge. Until now the hymns of the English-speaking Churches present a striking testimony to the spiritual unity of these Churches. To this the Hymnody of the advanced Anglican school, whether we choose to regard it as Catholic or sectarian, continues to present itself as the most conspicuous exception. G. R. Woodward's *Songs of Syon* (1904) was compiled only "for the faithful" as distinguished from "the enquirers after truth." George H. Palmer's *The Hymner, containing translations from the Sarum Breviary, together with sundry sequences and processions* (Plainsong Society, 1904), and *The new Office Hymn Book* of J. F. W. Bullock and C. J. Ridsdale, appearing in complete form in 1908, represent a party and not a church. *The English Hymnal,* whose literary distinction has been noticed claims that "it is not a party book,"[5] but it did provide for the extreme party metrical prayers for the dead, and hymns invoking the intercession of the Virgin Mary[6] and sundry saints; so that

[5] Preface, p. iii.

[6]   "For the faithful gone before us
        May the holy Virgin pray." Hy. 218, stanza 6.

    "Jesu's tender Mother,
        Make thy supplication
    Unto him who chose thee
        At his Incarnation." Hy. 213, stanza 4.

it was prohibited or pronounced against by several bishops and both archbishops.[7] In settlement of the issue raised, an abridged edition appeared in March, 1907, omitting five[8] and amending four hymns.[9] This settlement was hailed by Canon Scott Holland as "A truce of God," [10] but it was the opinion of others[11] that if the excision had extended to some score of hymns *The English Hymnal,* with "its irresistible merits" and "its profoundly interesting music," [12] would have broken the supremacy of *Hymns ancient and modern,* already weakened by the peculiarities of the edition of 1904.

If, however, the extreme developments of the Liturgical Movement are still divisive, marking a widening breach between Anglicanism and Protestantism, this is far from being true of the Liturgical Movement as a whole. We have seen how the party of the Oxford Movement took the leadership in Hymnody out of the hands of the Evangelicals within the Church of England, and the surprising degree to which not only that Church but the non-episcopal Churches outside were won over to the Oxford ideals and methods of Church Song.

To appreciate the full effects of this Oxford leadership upon the actual Hymnody and hymn singing of to-day we must recur once more to the original motive in introducing the Hymn into church worship;—the evangelical motive of securing a Church Song on all fours with the gospel preached: the Psalms remaining to respond to the needs of devotion, the Hymns added to respond to the truths preached. No doubt this evangelical motive moved the

[7]See *The Churchman,* July 7, Nov. 3, 24, Dec. 8, 22, 1906; January 26, 1907.

[8]Nos. 185, 195, 208, 213, 350.   [9]Nos. 184, 200, 218, 253.

[10]In *The Christian Commonwealth* (see *The Churchman,* Jan. 26, 1907.

[11]*Cf.* Canon Julian in his *Dict. of Hymnology,* p. 1633.

[12]Scott Holland, *ut supra.* "It would have been an unspeakable disaster if we had not been free to put it to full use. Now—all is possible."

hearts of preacher and people alike, but the preachers' craving for hymns adapted to their sermons was obviously the efficient cause of their introduction. Keach, Watts, Doddridge, Stennett, Newton, wrote their hymns under the glow of sermon composition, and often with the intention of employing them to impress its teachings. This homiletical conception and use of hymns became a part of the Evangelical inheritance, and so predominated in practice that the more purely devotional Psalmody fell into disuse.

Through the first half of the XIXth century and beyond the hymn books of the denominations suggestively described as "non-liturgical," bear witness to the prevailing homiletical motive, in the didactic character of the hymns, their multiplication to cover the largest possible number of texts and themes, the manner of their arrangement, and the textual and analytical indexes at the end. And we have seen how fully the practice of Hymnody corresponded. It was the minister's rather than the people's ordinance, a Hymnody of expression on his part, of impression on theirs. He selected the hymns not for their intrinsic values, but because of their adaptation to his sermon theme; he read them through as poetical illustrations of his theme, though often calling for abridgment in the singing; and then they were given to the people who had no musical notes before them, and who in all the denominations evinced a very moderate desire to sing, or interest in the materials set before them.

Meantime a knowledge of Oxford ideals was being diffused; arousing a new interest in the history of the ancient and medieval Church, its prayers and hymns, and in the Common Prayer Book. The theory of worship was freshly studied and question raised whether the hearing of sermons fulfilled it: What were the right relations and proportions of homily, praise and prayer? Was not Praise worth while for its own sake; and were not its interests suffering by its being made an appendage to the sermon? Was not the ancient ideal of a Hymnody that circled with the church

year, or even the Reformation ideal of a Psalmody sung
through in course, more comely and more edifying than the
Evangelical ideal of a Hymnody appropriated by the pulpit
to furnish enforcement or illustraion of its themes?

Gradually the influence of the Oxford Movement became
apparent in many directions; in the church architecture,
decorations and fittings; in a slow but steady transition of
the conception and practice of worship from the homiletical
ideal to the liturgical; most obviously in the general recognition and hearty observance of the greater festivals of
the Christian Year.

This influence, it should be observed, has been liturgical
rather than doctrinal. None of the non-episcopal Churches
has revised its doctrine of church and sacrament under
pressure from Oxford, but all of them have modified their
worship. And the change that has passed over the face of
the Hymnody of these Churches, so far as the Oxford influences have been concerned in that change, is one corresponding to the change in public worship itself. It is more
than any change of form or method; it is a change in spirit,
a modification of the original motive underlying hymn
singing. As we have followed the Liturgical Movement it
has been striking enough no doubt to see the Latin Hymn
lose its taint in Churches which had accounted it "Roman
Catholic," to see the didactic hymn and the "preaching
hymn" give way to new hymns from Anglican sources, to
see the Hymnody of the times and seasons of the Christian
Year established in Churches that once studiously ignored
festival and fast, to see the Anglican type of hymn tune
displacing the parlor-music type:—but the change brought
about in Hymnody by the Liturgical Movement is more
than the sum of all these specific changes. The very base
of the ordinance of Hymnody has been shifted from the
homiletical foundation on which the Evangelicals established
it, and restored to the more devotional foundation on which
the old Psalmody rested. And the changes in the Hymnody
are a part of the process of its reconstruction as an inde-

pendent ordinance of Christian worship expressing the devotions of God's people.

Surveying the results of this process as embodied in the
recent hymnals of "non-liturgical" Churches, one gets the
impression that the books are less didactic and more devotional than ever before, and that possibly the reconstruction
has gone as far in a liturgical direction as may be practicable or prudent. In present-day hymnals of denominations maintaining a modern standard of culture, no great
difference in structure or method can be observed between
the moderate Anglican and the non-episcopal. Each is
readily divisible into two sections. The first covers times
and seasons, including all the great facts and doctrines of
the Christian Year and occasions of worship. The second
(called "General" in Anglican books and in others by some
other name) gathers up the hymns of wider application and
especially of Christian experience. In the Anglican books
there is much provision for saints' days and other occasions
not celebrated in non-episcopal Churches; in the books of
the latter there is generally a fuller recognition of Christian
experience: and these differences substantially measure such
contrast as still exists between them. It is doubtless true
that in many pulpits the practice of handling the hymnal
as though a cyclopedia of homiletical illustrations still survives, but the modern hymnal is as ill-adapted to serve that
end as the practice itself is unacceptable to modern feeling
and taste.

V

ITS THEOLOGY

1. Changing Religious Thought Makes This a Period of Revision

The Church Hymnody as a whole has been the expression
of an evangelical theology and an evangelical experience.
Beginning with Watts it recorded the Calvinistic faith, not
polemically, but because it was the faith of him who wrote

and those who were to be induced to sing. The opposition Hymnody of Wesley's revolt against Calvinism, aggressively polemical or definitely Arminian, remained always a thing apart, and tended rather to impart to the main stream of Hymnody, through the Evangelical Revival, a more definitely Calvinistic tone. The evangelical side of the Wesleyan Hymnody fell in gradually with the main stream, and perceptibly deepened it in Christian experience, and widened it with evangelistic purpose and expression. The subsequent Unitarian Movement left the bounds of the historic Churches, and left their Hymnody unaffected doctrinally. The Oxford Movement was primarily in the domain of ecclesiology, exalting the doctrine of church and sacraments. Its primary effect on the general Hymnody was liturgical rather than doctrinal, but it operated also through its disregard of the older dogma, and more by putting the corporate Church in the place the individual saint and sinner had occupied in the older hymns of experience.

On the whole the present day Hymnody of the main body of English-speaking Churches may be claimed as consistent with an evangelical system of doctrine and with evangelical convictions and experience.

It has now, however, become evident to all observers that recent movements and tendencies of theological thought, at first operating on the outside of, or at the left of, the field of Christian thought, are now brought to bear upon its centre and right; and that even the Churches of the evangelical faith are included in a process of change which in the hope of many involves no more than doctrinal adjustment but which in the opinion of others must lead to theological reconstruction. It would be idle to pretend that changed conceptions of God and His immanence in creation, modified views of the Scriptures and novel methods of exegesis, the partial disintegration of Calvinism in denominations where it long prevailed, the rediscussion of the great doctrines of redemption, the new adjustments of temporal and eternal relations, the growth of a Christian agnosticism, and hesitation in dogmatic statement or even denial of the validity of dogma;—it would be idle to pretend that these things are working no changes in the Hymnody of the Churches they affect.

The connection between Christian thought and feeling and Christian Hymnody is inevitably close. Nothing is more futile than a congregational song that does not express the living faith of the congregation and its warmth of feeling. And with the ever present fluctuation of thought and feeling a discreet pastor is always revising the Hymnody through his selection of the hymns given out for the actual use of his congregation. A change in Christian thought and feeling affects the Hymnody in two ways. 1st, it applies a fresh test to familiar hymns, and tends to the disuse of such of them as have lost their power of appeal. 2nd, it creates a new body of hymns, and even tunes, infused with fresh feeling and responsive to current conceptions of Christian truth.[13] This explains in part why in these times of change the various denominations feel the need of revising their church hymnals at shorter intervals. It explains also why numerous leaders of recent religious thought have anticipated the authorized revision of their denominational hymnal by publishing independent hymnals

[13] "Every one at all familiar with the history of religious experience is aware how sensitive popular song has been as an index of popular feeling. Nowhere is the power of psychologic suggestion upon the masses more evident than in the domain of song. Hardly does a revolutionary religious idea, struck from the brains of a few leading thinkers and reformers, effect a lodgment in the hearts of any considerable section of the common people, than it is immediately projected in hymns and melodies. It is not too much to say that no idea has a real vital energizing power that does not so manifest itself. So far as it is no mere scholastic formula, but possesses the power to kindle an active life in the soul, it will quickly clothe itself in figurative speech and musical cadence, and in many cases it will filter itself through this medium until all that is crude, formal, and speculative is drained away, and what is essential and fruitful is retained as a permanent spiritual possession." Edw. Dickinson, "The Lesson of the New Hymnals," in *The Bibliotheca Sacra,* July 1900, p. 571.

of their own, either to meet a need they recognized or as an effective method of propaganda.

At the present time this revision of the Church Hymnody is proceeding simultaneously in so many denominations and with so much activity and zeal as to suggest a gentle upheaval and the beginning of a new epoch. In England within the opening years of the XXth century their Church hymnals have been revised by the Anglicans (unofficially), the Presbyterians, and the various Methodist Churches: in Canada by the Anglicans; in the United States by the Presbyterians, the two Methodist Episcopal bodies, the Wesleyan Methodists, the Methodist Protestants, the Congregationalists (by their Publication Society), the German Baptists, the Reformed Episcopalians and the Swedenborgians. To these we may add the Christian Scientists, in view of the novelty of their doctrinal views embodied in *Christian Science Hymnal* (Boston: rev. ed. 1898) at the century's end. At the moment of writing revisions of the denominational hymn books are in progress in England by the Congregationalists and Moravians: in Canada by the Presbyterians and Methodists: in the United States by the various Lutheran Churches in a concerted movement for a common hymnal, the Episcopalians, the German and the Dutch Reformed Churches. Apart from these bodies the current hymnodic activity and spirit of change (not necessarily of doctrinal change) is illustrated in the increasing use of vernacular hymns by the Roman Catholic Church, not only in families and schools but in parochial services other than the Mass; and also in the introduction of hymn-singing into Quaker meetings both in America and England. *The Golden Hymn Book. Compiled by M. Catharine Albright* (London: Frowde, 1903) is a book of considerable charm as well as significance. *The Friends' Hymnal . . . for the public worship of the Society* (New York: Funk and Wagnalls, 1906: rev. ed. 1908), an authorized book and fully equipped with music, will grieve some who have cultivated the silences of the old meetings.

In view of the spirit of revision so active in denominations having an authorized Hymnody, and of the increasing excellence of their hymnals, both the significance and opportunity of the hymnals still issuing independently are considerably lessened. In stimulating and in a measure guiding the improvement of church hymnals, as they have undoubtedly done, these personal and unauthorized collections have served a public function now largely fulfilled. In churches without an authorized Hymnody, such as the Church of England and American Congregationalism, they necessarily still hold the field.

2. THE NEW THEOLOGY DEMANDS A NEW HYMNODY

It is on the left wing of Christianity that the new movements of religious thought have had the freest sweep. We have already noted the passing of the old Unitarianism into a free and "universal" religion, and how as early as 1864 in America Longfellow and Johnson in their *Hymns of the Spirit* and in 1873 in England James Martineau in his *Hymns of Praise and Prayer* provided the new faith with a Hymnody that confessedly transcended the limits of historical Christianity.

The most recent authorized hymnal of a denomination, now debating the retention of the Unitarian name, is *The new Hymn and Tune Book* (Boston: American Unitarian Association, 1914); prepared by a committee of the Association; "offered to all who love perfect liberty in pure religion." It may be regarded as a revision of *The Hymn and Tune Book* of 1877, of whose 885 hymns only 242 are retained, "owing to the great changes in religious thought." [14] In its provision for the greater days of the Christian Year, and its section on "The Ministry and example of Jesus," it follows Martineau rather than Longfellow: in its aspirations for public service and social righteousness it is richer than either. Of its "authors" Frederick L. Hosmer leads with 34 hymns, closely followed by Samuel

[14]Preface.

Longfellow with 27. Whittier has 18 and T. H. Gill 11. Much of their work is universally acceptable; and to the compilers of this book one ventures to apply the avowal of Martineau's preface: "For myself, both conviction and feeling keep me close to the poetry and piety of Christendom." [15]

Within the area of a more evangelical Congregationalism the relations of Hymnody to dogmatic theology had been fought over and virtually settled in the controversy over Thomas Toke Lynch's *The Rivulet* (1855).[16] His opponents claimed that every hymn should be a statement of definite doctrine, and accused his hymns with being full of "negative theology": a charge which Lynch paraphrased (and disposed of) in his well-known lines beginning,—

> "When sugar in the lump I see,
> I know that it is there,
> Melt it, and then I soon suspect
> A negative affair."[17]

But in 1889 John Hunter, of Trinity Congregational Church, Glasgow, a devoted follower of Maurice, in his *Hymns of Faith and Life* (Glasgow, Maclehose) undertook to embody "the modern spirit" not "negatively" but positively. Dogmatic statements of older doctrines, such as the line of Heber's hymn, "God in Three Persons, blessed Trinity," were scrupulously eschewed in favor of expressions of "the largest and simplest aspects of Christian faith and life." "The divineness of the present life" was set against the unreality of the evangelical "otherworldliness," and "the larger hope" against the orthodox eschatology. Hunter's book had a very limited congregational use, but in many ways it prefigured and even influenced the trend of present-day Hymnody. The work of Garrett Horder, already noticed in connection with the Literary Movement, must be regarded as following in the same lines as Hunter's,

[15] Preface to *Hymns of Praise and Prayer,* p. xi.
[16] See chap. ix, part III, section iv, 2.
[17] *Songs controversial* (1856), no. viii.

notably in its eager repudiation of the dogmatic spirit and its frank adhesion to the modern spirit in faith and life.[18]

In America at the end of the XIXth century not only the authorized hymnals of the Evangelical Churches but the books of private enterprise gaining any extensive use within their bounds were carefully conformed to the strictest standards of orthodoxy. This is true, for example, of Bedell's *Church Hymnary* (1891), Robinson's *The new Laudes Domini* (1892), *The Coronation Hymnal* (1894), *In Excelsis* (1897) and Johnson's *Sursum Corda* (1898). Lyman Abbott's *The Plymouth Hymnal* (1893) is an exception not as aiming to exclude evangelical or even Calvinistic hymns, but rather in not seeking "to conform to any school of thought" and in seeking to represent "all phases of Christian experience." Even so his book neither found nor made for itself a wide place.

The new tendencies in Hymnody found for the first time a full presentation under "orthodox" denominational auspices in *The Pilgrim Hymnal*. *The Pilgrim Press: New York, Boston, Chicago* [1904]: the "product of a systematic undertaking" on the part of the Congregational Sunday-school and Publishing Society which had already issued *Pilgrim Songs for Sunday schools,* "to provide a uniform series of hymnals for the churches of our order." It purports to represent the desires of a large number of people, ascertained by "a questionnaire, submitted to some 200 representative men of our churches in all parts of the country," [19] a considerable number of whom served as an "advisory cabinet" to Charles L. Noyes, the editor, and Dr. Washington Gladden, the associate editor; the latter of whom merged in this the plans for a hymnal projected by himself.[20]

The Pilgrim Hymnal obviously responds to an undoubted

---

[18] "The theologian's success is the hymnist's failure." Horder, "The Theology of our Hymns" in *The Outlook* for Sept. 11, 1897.

[19] "Editorial Notes," p. 570.   [20]*Ibid.,* p. 571.

demand for a new Hymnody that shall in doctrinal expression and emphasis correspond with what is called the New Theology and in vigor and tone help to inspire the new-found readiness for active service. It thus becomes an important and representative document for studying the trend of the new Hymnody. Its criteria seem to be:—

1. *Modernity.* "There is a vigorous effort to omit whatever uses the terminology of the past, in favor of that which is deemed more in harmony with the present." [21]

2. *An emphasis on God's immanence,* so that in hymns of adoration He shall appear less as the throned majestic Personage, apart from the world, of the older hymns, and more as a Spirit of Power and Love resident in the world and operating within the hearts of all men.

3. *An indefiniteness as to the nature and person and work of Christ,* that shall at least avoid the dogmatic certainties of the older theology. Thus the section on God includes the Maker, the Living and Indwelling God, and the Holy Spirit; "The Lord Jesus Christ," a second section. There is no doubt a diminution, but no apparent avoidance, of the hymns that contemplate Christ as working out the atonement for sin.

4. *A non-ecclesiastical tone.* In emphasis and feeling the Kingdom takes the place the Church held in Anglican and even Evangelical books. As against any trend toward sacramentalism involved in the Liturgical Movement, *The Pilgrim Hymnal* marks a reaction. Perhaps in no modern church hymnal outside of Unitarianism is the sacramental tone so low as in its meagre provision for the Communion. Liturgically also there is no advance. The Christian Year is ignored. Such liturgical suggestiveness as the book presents is mainly in the appended materials; and, even so, from the Psalter as it was arranged either for chanting or responsive reading in *Hymns of the Faith* (1887) to these miscellaneous responsive Scripture Readings arranged by "topics" there is a long descent from liturgical propriety.

[21] *Hartford Seminary Record,* Nov. 1904, p. 64.

5. *A modified conception of the Christian life,* with the emphasis on activity as against inward experience. In the section on "The Christian Life" "Following Christ" takes the place of "Repentance" and "Faith" in the evangelical books. There is a large disuse of the Evangelical Hymnody, notably of the XVIIIth century, in favor of newer hymns representing more liberal conceptions of Christianity. Of its 547 hymns 115 are ascribed to Unitarians.[22] Samuel Longfellow has 20 as against 13 of Watts: Hosmer has 12 as against 11 of Charles Wesley or 4 of John Newton.

6. *A new sense of the inherent importance* of the present life, with an avoidance of the hymns that emphasize its probationary relations to the future life. There is less no doubt of the other world than in most evangelical books, but an enlarged area of the earthly life is brought within the motives that inspire Christian song.

7. We come now to the most characteristic and novel feature of the new Hymnody, as embodied in *The Pilgrim Hymnal,—its pronounced humanitarianism.* Coordinate with its emphasis on God in every-day life, on the Kingdom as against the earlier emphasis upon the Church, on practical effort as against inward experience, on the present life as our appointed sphere of operation, comes its insistent call not for mere adoration or contemplation, still less for introspection, but for service of a broad humanitarian type as against technical "church-work." The old conception of a banded brotherhood pursuing a narrow way to heaven widens into a human brotherhood with a living Christ at its head, and of all who serve their fellows as of his company. And we thus have a new Hymnody of Social Service. It is so far at one with the songs of "Ethical Culture" that Felix Adler's "Sing we of the Golden City,

[22]In view of past controversy in New England, this proportion inevitably attracted notice. It was explained by Dr. Gladden as due to the fact that the largest number of the best hymns within the past twenty-five years have been written by Unitarians (*The Congregationalist* for July 30, 1904, p. 147). It may be added that among the 115 are a considerable number in wide acceptance.

Pictured in the legends old," [23] becomes a church hymn; and with the evolutionary anticipations of a new humanity as to adopt John Addington Symonds' "These things shall be,—a loftier race." [24]   In the amelioration of social conditions it sees fulfilled the prophesied coming of Christ: and hence in *The Pilgrim Hymnal* there is an entire omission of the department of the Second Advent of Christ and the Last Judgment.

It has thus perhaps become evident that *The Pilgrim Hymnal* embodies a Hymnody in several respects new, whose doctrinal contents and leanings do not, by intention, conform at all points with the earlier Evangelical Hymnody. The doubtless disappointing reception of the book proved indeed that its changes went considerably beyond the bounds of any general demand in American Congregationalism. It never won the status of a denominational hymnal to which its publication by the Pilgrim Press presumptively entitled it, but continued to represent the considerable group of ministers and churches which had cooperated in its production. Among more recent Congregationalist hymnals *Hymns of the Church new and old* (New York: Barnes, 1912), edited by W. V. W. Davis and Raymond Calkins, and *Songs of the Christian Life* (New York: Merrill, 1913), edited by Charles H. Richards, may perhaps be regarded as applying the retort courteous to *The Pilgrim Hymnal*. After some years' use *The Pilgrim Hymnal* was revised and reissued under its original title in 1913. The new edition omits some hymns of the New England theistic school, provides some more suitable hymns for the Communion, and restores some standard hymns.

But the larger significance of the new edition is in the particular lines of its enrichment, answering the latest demands of the churches and made possible by the latest hymn writing:—"to respond to the yearning of the life and faith of to-day for more hymns to express communion with God

[23]*The Pilgrim Hymnal*, No. 401.
[24]*Ibid.*, No. 403.

in his nearness and living presence, fellowship with Christ, enthusiasm for humanity, the passion for service, and consecration to the Kingdom of God on earth." [25]   On these lines *The Pilgrim Hymnal* of 1913 was quite as much a follower as a leader; for they indicate the definite lines on which the revision and enrichment of Church Hymnody is just now proceeding in, one may say, all denominations. It was, for instance, with an eye on the market that the publishing house which had chosen the high-sounding name of *In Excelsis* for its recent hymnal, called its new one *Hymns of Worship and Service* (New York: The Century Co., 1905).   It was from one of the best ordered parishes of the Presbyterian Church, once widely served by Dr. Robinson's *Hymns of the Church* and *Songs for the Sanctuary,* that proceeded Dr. Coffin's *Hymns of the Kingdom of God* (New York: Barnes, 1910).   Indeed the passage quoted from *The Pilgrim Hymnal* of 1913 might almost have been taken from the preface of the revised hymnal of that still conservative denomination,—*The Hymnal published in 1895 and revised in 1911 by authority of the General Assembly of The Presbyterian Church in the United States of America* (Philadelphia: Presbn. Bd. of Publn., 1911); which announces a purpose "to bring the book abreast of the latest developments of hymnody, and of the present state of Christian thought and feeling; especially to meet the demand for the recognition of God's nearness to every-day living, the coming of the Kingdom in the sphere of common life, the spirit of brotherhood and of manly and resolute Christian life and service, social betterment, and evangelistic work."

VI

THE HYMNODY OF SOCIAL DEMOCRACY

One remembers indeed that Congregational Song was itself the sign and expression of a new democracy of reli-

[25]Preface, p. [iii].

gion, when the Reformation took Church Song out of the hands of the hierarchy and put it into the hands of the people. And he begins to perceive that the influence so powerfully operative in Congregational Song to-day is not so much a new theology rewriting church symbols of doctrine as a growth in the spirit of social democracy deeply affecting the working faith of the plain people who do the singing if they do not make the symbols. We perceive its revolutionary side in the songs of voluntary societies for ethical culture that replace the church and ignore the supernatural; its still militant side in "the hymns of the liberal faith" that herald a religion freed from all authority and yet calling itself Christian: and we perceive the shadow which that militancy casts even on evangelical churches in their hesitancy to sing any longer hymns of humble adoration to the enthroned and omnipotent Jehovah of the Psalms. But we perceive also the pacific side of the democratic spirit in new hymns that sing of God's concern for common life and common people, songs of brotherhood and social redemption, and of the homely coming of that Kingdom, which no doubt we shall soon be trained to regard as "The republic of God."

This infusion of the democratic spirit into Congregational Song appears to be the special contribution of the XXth century to English Hymnody. The old hymn, "When I can read my Title clear," represents the old Evangelical Hymnody (no doubt at its extreme) in its individualism, its otherworldliness, its introspection. The new hymn, "Where cross the crowded ways of life," represents the new "Hymnody of Social Service" in its socialism, its this-worldliness, its concern for those who are not in church. It is true that social service is not a novelty in church ideals, and that older hymns of social service were not wanting. "Charity hymns" were among the earliest sung in the Church of England. The anti-slavery agitation, the temperance movement, the peace movement, and others, all produced church hymns. But it is substantially true that "this propaganda of beneficence, this constant attention to the moral and physical improvement of persons who have been neglected, is quite recent as a leading feature of religion." [26]   And how recent the Hymnody of Social Service is in any practicable sense is best known to him who has searched XVIIIth and XIXth century hymn books for examples.   It is only now in the making and as existent is in a state undeniably crude.

We see it in the making, as it were, in the "Social Hymn Number" (January 3, 1914) of *The Survey,* the organ of allied social workers.   Here, after elaborate preparations, with a hymn-editor and twelve referees representing most types of religion and ethics, were gathered "One hundred hymns of brotherhood and social aspiration."   The first object was to find "hymns that could be sung by all people in all places, whether in churches, in halls, in schools, in the open": "which Jew and Gentile, Protestant and Catholic might sing with equal fervor."   On this account partly, and also to avoid gloominess, "no hymns of atonement, sin and sacrifice" were included.   Professor Simon N. Patten, in his paper on hymn writing, would go farther, and avoid in the new Hymnody the very imagery and "expressions of war, depravity, and woe, upon which the emotional value of earlier hymns depends" and aim at "the socialization of language itself." [27]

The *Survey* hymns have since been reprinted as *Social Hymns of Brotherhood and Aspiration.   Collected by Mabel Hay Barrows Mussey.   New York: the A. S. Barnes Co., 1914,* in a form at once suggesting the evangelistic song book, but with a gospel in marked contrast with that of evangelism.   It deals not with the individual but with humanity in the mass, not with spiritual experience but with "social living," not with the salvation of the soul, but with the uplift of society.   The hymns are grouped under the categories of "Aspiration and Faith," "Liberty and Justice," "Peace," "Labor and Conflict," "Brotherhood,"

[26][Edmund Gosse] *Father and Son,* New York, 1907, p. 334.
[27]*Ibid.,* p. 408.

and "Patriotism." They include a number already in church use, notably the newer hymns of the Kingdom, but of the Church as an appointed agent of social regeneration there is no recognition, and apart from the aspiration for a "new city" on earth, no vision of the life beyond.

In the new Social Hymnody as here presented one feels that there is not necessarily any antagonism to the Christian Church or to Christian Doctrine, but rather a sense of their irrelevancy in view of an absorbing aim in whose promotion it is necessary to find common ground on which men of good will may meet to labor and to sing. And this feature of the Social Hymnody is no doubt worthy of keeping in mind by the Church itself which is now so obviously engaged in revising her own Hymnody in the light of the new ideals of social democracy.

It has already been suggested that the XXth century Church is deeply moved by the spirit of the new philanthropy and even disposed to modify her ideals in accord with the new humanitarianism. She is inclined for the present at least in the interests of "service" to subordinate that concern for spiritual experience and for eternal life which entered into the warp and woof of the Evangelical Hymnody, and even that spirit of adoration which is the heart of the Liturgical Hymnody. The significance of such a title as that of the recent *Hymns of Worship and Service* is in its definite proposal of praise and service as the two coordinate themes of Church Song. More striking still is the pamphlet of hymns and prayers of a social bearing, issued by the Social Service Commission of the Episcopal diocese of Massachusetts, in its recognition of social service as the particular form of service to which the Church is at present called and its determination to relate the social service movement to the Church's devotional life. And now from another source comes the suggestion, not that the Church should make its own Social Hymnody but that *The Survey*'s collection of *Social Hymns of Brotherhood and Aspiration* "might well be in the pews of any church whose people believe in the social gospel, as a supplementary hymn book." [28]

The situation is thus obviously one in which the best interests of Church Hymnody demand some consideration. There will be few indeed to deplore the Church's new concern for social life. And if any is disposed to maintain that the Church Hymn is not the proper vehicle of the new emotions and aspirations his thesis must be regarded as merely academic. The ideal of the Hymn, which Augustine once defined acceptably to the Church as "Praise of God in song," [29] has been strained and even stretched, with the progress of Christian centuries, to cover many religious activities other than praise. Doubtless it can be further stretched to cover the special activities of the new social awakening. It is rather the perpetual surprise of our historic Hymnody that it should have proceeded so far with so little sense of human fellowship, so little concern for the inequalities and burdens of the society in which the Church was set. So devout and mystical a soul as George Matheson, author of one of the most cherished hymns of a deep inward experience,[30] has expressed a thought common to many in saying of our hymns generally:—

"To my mind they have one great defect; they lack humanitarianism. There is any amount of doctrine in the Trinity, Baptism, Atonement, or the Christian life as such, but what of the secular life—the infirmary, the hospital, the home of refuge? . . . I don't think our hymns will ever be what they ought to be, until we get them inspired by a sense of the enthusiasm of, and for, humanity. It is rather a theological point, perhaps, but the hymnists speak of the surrender to Christ. They forget that Christ is not simply an individual. He is Head of a body, the body of humanity; and it no longer expresses the idea correctly to join yourself to Christ only, you must give yourself to the whole brotherhood of man to fulfil the idea." [31]

And now that the need thus disclosed is in the way of

[28] *The Christian Work and Evangelist* for July 18, 1914.
[29] Ennar. in Ps. cxliii.
[30] "O Love that wilt not let me go."
[31] D. Macmillan, *The Life of George Matheson*, New York, 1907, p. 185.

being provided for, there would seem to be two features of the situation worthy of attention by those concerned for the best interests of Church Hymnody.

First: The Church should make her own "supplementary hymn book." The "theological point" made by Dr. Matheson may or may not define accurately the ground of the Church's participation in the social awakening. The real point is that the Church believes in her own call to lend a hand, finds her own motives in Christ, and has her own social gospel. She remembers also that those who are bringing about "social living" are well on the way to individual dying, and that the hope of heaven is an encouragement while making progress toward the happier world we shall not live to see. The Church should not be expected to renounce these great inspirations while joining hands with all who would do good. And at a time when very many regard a Social Hymnody ignoring the Church and Christian doctrine as prophetic, it becomes the Church to embody her own faith in social songs.

Second: Even granting that "worship and service" are to be the two coordinate themes of XXth century Church Hymnody, it need not follow that the element of praise is to lose its primacy. It should rather follow that the note of praise shall pervade the Hymnody of Service. If the relations of God and man are what the Church has hitherto believed them to be, she must continue to stand on her old foundation as fundamentally a worshipping Church, with her activities conditioned by her devotional life.

In every vital movement we may expect and allow for a certain exaggeration and loss of the sense of proportion. The Evangelical Revival overemphasized the Hymn of Experience and even encouraged a Hymnody of egotism. Evangelistic fervor has in many times and places cast a shadow of unreality and aloofness over the sober Church Hymnody, and temporarily supplanted the church hymnal by the revival song book. And something of the kind may be anticipated in connection with the social awakening.

We shall soon perhaps have *Hymns of Service and Worship*, with a change only in the order of precedence ("To do Thy will is more than praise"); then *Hymns of Service* ("Thy sacramental liturgies the joy of doing good"); and then *Hymns of Social Service* as the Church's hymn book ("To worship rightly is to love each other").

In all these successive movements of religious life, in the social awakening as much as in the Evangelical Revival, and through all these varying phases of Church Song, we may contentedly read the unfolding purpose of that Sovereign Love which broods over church and world. And we can perceive that a change of emphasis as regards phases of truth contributes to the fulfilment of that purpose. One might even encourage the XXth century Church to sing those things it believes most vividly and feels most deeply, confident that in any case the permanent foundation of Church Song ("Praise God from whom all blessings flow") is unshaken.

INDEX

A

Abbott, Lyman, 473, 489, 558
Abingdon Presbytery, 189
Abridgment of Dr. Watts's Psalms and Hymns, 133
Abridgment of Mr. Baxter's History, 83
Accompanying harmonies to Hymnal noted, 521
Actes of the Apostles (Tye), 55
Acts and Proceedings (Gen. Synod, Ref. Dutch), 403, 404, 405, 406, 407, 408 (Engl. Presbyn. Synod), 525, 526
Acts of General Assembly (Ch. of Scot.), 57, 59, 148
Adam of St. Victor, 502
Adams, F. A., 388
Adams, John, 184
Adams, J. G., 481, 482
Adams, John Quincy, 462, 482
Adams, Sarah F. 450
Adamson, John, 57
Addison, Joseph, 210, 211
Additional Hymn Book (Ryle), 519
Additional Hymns (Lutheran, 1834), 414 (Refd. Dutch) 1831, 405; 1847, 406 (Tyng), 401
Additional Psalmody, 159
Additional Selection (Andrews), 401
Address at 200th Anniversary, 1st Bapt. Ch., Boston, 204
Advent Christians, 430
Advent Harp, 429
Adventists, 1843–1887, 428
Advice to a young clergyman, 222
Adgate, Andrew, 192, 193
Adler, Felix, 582
African Meth. Episc. Church, 306
African Meth. Episc. Zion Church, 307
African Methodist Hymn and Tune Book, 307
Age to come Adventists, 431
Ainger, A. C., 569
Ainsworth, Henry, 101
Aitken, W. M. H., 520
Albright, Jacob, 314
Albright, M. C., 577
Alderson, Eliza S., 516
Alexander, Archibald, 381, 382
Alexander, Cecil F., 516, 531
Alexander, W. Lindsay, 157, 459
Alford, Henry, 513, 518
Alger, William R., 468
Alison, Francis, 188
Allen, James, 323, 325, 326
Alline, Henry, 366, 367
Allison, Burgis, 200
Allon, Henry, 456, 459, 508, 522, 525
Altar, the (Williams), 514
Altar Hymnal, 514, 529
Alteration of Hymns, see Hymn "Tinkering"
Ambrosian hymns, 39, 205, 498
American Bibliography (Evans), 162, 199, 271, 338, 359
American Christian Missionary Society, 371
American Church History series, 327, 410, 421, 424
American Journal of Education, 378
American Millenial Association, 429, 430
American Presbyterianism (Briggs), 179

American Revisions of Watts' Psalms, 166, 194
American Theological Review, 476
Amis, Lewis R., 312
Amsterdam, 101
Ancient Hymns of Holy Church, 543
Anderson, C., 146
Anderson, J. S., 146
Andover Seminary, 475, 476
Andrews, C. W., 401
Anglican Hymn Book, 513
Anglican hymns and church music, see England, Church of
Anglican Hymnology, 25
Anglo-Catholic ideal, see Hymnal
Annals of English Presbytery, 130
Annals of Low-church Party, 506
Annals of Scottish Printing, 33
Annals of Unitarian Pulpit, 177
Annotations on the Hymnal (Hutchins), 546
Annual Report, Am. Hist. Assn., 326
Annus Sanctus, 44
Anstice, Joseph, 515
Anthems, 43, 183, 243, 523
Anti-Burghers, 154
Anti-effort Baptists, 203
Antrim, Jacob, 312
Anxious bench, 293
Anthologia Davidica, 445
Apology (Barclay), 95
Apology for Printers, 162
Apostles' Creed, 27, 29, 30, 34, 77
Appel, Theo., 548
Appendix (Boston), 173
(Cecil), 352
(Venn), 352
Appendix from the Olney Hymns, 201
Appendix to Hymns ancient and modern, 510, 516, 520
Appendix to Hymnal Companion (Bell), 520
Appendix to Tate and Brady (Boston), 173
Appendix to Walker's Psalms and Hymns, 520
Apple-tree hymn, 202
Arber, Edward, 92
Archibald, Robert, 189
Arian movement in England, 130; in New England, 172
Arminian Theology: Wesleyan, 232, 358; General Baptist, 91; American Baptist, 198, 362
Arminian Magazine, 235, 236
Arnold, John, 346
Arnold, Matthew, 446
Arnold, Thomas, 445
Arnot, David, 532
Arnot, William, 526
Arrangement of Watts with Selection, 204
Art of Singing (Law), 193
Asbury, Francis, 281, 283, 289
Ash and Evans' *Collection*, 144, 259
Aspland, Robert, 135
Asplund, John, 200
Associate Presbytery: N. Y., 180; N. C., 190
At the interment of John Quincy Adams, 462
Athanasian Creed, 28, 36
Athenaeum, 318, 569
Athenian Oracle, 221
Auber, Harriet, 444
Augsburg, 560

591